A HISTORY OF
MODERN PSYCHOLOGY
IN CONTEXT

A HISTORY OF MODERN PSYCHOLOGY IN CONTEXT

Wade E. Pickren

and

Alexandra Rutherford

WILEY

A JOHN WILEY & SONS, INC., PUBLICATION

Published by John Wiley & Sons, Inc., Hoboken, New Jersey.
Published simultaneously in Canada.

Library of Congress Cataloging-in-Publication Data:
Pickren, Wade E.
  A history of modern psychology in context / by Wade E. Pickren & Alexandra Rutherford.
      p. cm.
  Includes bibliographical references and index.
  ISBN 978-0-470-27609-9
1. Psychology—History. I.   Rutherford, Alexandra, 1971-.   II. Title.
  BF81.P48 2010
  150.9—dc22

                                                                2009031711

Printed in the United States of America

10 9 8 7 6 5 4 3 2 1

To Emily and Graham, your idealism
and love of living are always an inspiration to us.

BRIEF CONTENTS

CONTENTS

PREFACE AND ACKNOWLEDGMENTS

We are very pleased that you are reading this book. For the two of us, the task of writing it was a positive challenge. When we agreed to co-author the text, we did so with the understanding that we wanted to write an inclusive history of psychology, not simply another textbook that would tell yet another version of the same familiar story. For us, inclusivity means that we pay attention to the ways that culture, race, ethnicity, and gender have contributed to the making of psychology's history. We are committed as well to a narrative approach that situates psychology within its larger social, political, and economic contexts that have played out around the globe in different ways over the last 150 years. Our objective is to present psychology as a socially embedded science and profession.

While there is much in our text that will be familiar to those who teach the course in colleges and universities, there is also a great deal of material that is unique. For example, we pay greater attention to the development of psychology in non-Western and even non-Northern hemisphere countries. The study of the growth of psychology in multiple cultural and national contexts is one of the most exciting developments occurring today, and we hope we have begun to place this growth in a historical context. Still, we are sensitized to the reality that much of our book still places American psychology at the center of the story. We have tried, however, to write self-consciously and reflexively, acknowledging wherever possible our standpoint as North American historians of psychology trained in a fairly Eurocentric tradition. We look forward to feedback and comments from our readers on how to improve our narrative for our second edition.

For each of our chapters, we have included a focus story about a person or event that highlights some aspect of the chapter. These are written in an informal style that we hope will be easily accessible and interesting. We have also included a glossary of key terms presented alphabetically at the end of the book. These terms are bolded the first time they appear in each chapter. Each chapter also has a timeline that will help guide students through the events that are discussed in that chapter. Although the overall flow of the book does move from psychology's early origins to the present day, we do not take a strictly chronological approach in the progression of the chapters. There is significant overlap in terms of time periods covered from chapter to chapter, and since many psychologists made substantive contributions across different areas, some of the same people reappear across chapters. Students, for example, will find Kurt Lewin and Frederic Bartlett in more than one chapter. We hope the timelines help in keeping you organized as you move through the material.

We discovered rather quickly that writing a textbook is the best way to find out how much we don't yet know! This has made us very appreciative of the rich and ever-expanding body of scholarship on the history of psychology and the human sciences. We are very fortunate to be writing at a time when the quality and quantity of historical scholarship in our field is extremely strong. We are in the debt of our colleagues around the world, both past and present, who have shared so much of their expertise with us over the years.

We especially thank the reviewers of our text. Their comments were insightful, helpful, and saved us from some egregious errors. The second author would especially like to thank Janice Yoder for her careful reading of the entire manuscript, but particularly Chapter 11. Her comments made it a stronger contribution. The errors and weaknesses that remain are entirely ours, of course. We are also deeply thankful to our editor at John Wiley & Sons, Patricia Rossi. She and her skillful staff have prompted and prodded us when necessary and given us room and time when we needed it most.

We would like to acknowledge the expert assistance of three of our former students in the history of psychology, Axelle Karera, Sara Crann, and Meghan George. They helped us prepare the bells and whistles that accompany the text. Thanks as well to Aidin Keikhaee for his assistance with the PowerPoint slides. Many thanks to Lizette Royer at the Archives of the History of American Psychology (AHAP) for her help with many of the photos that grace these pages. AHAP is an incredibly important resource for historians of psychology and depends on the support of all of us who want to see the record of psychology's past preserved and made accessible to students and scholars alike.

We hope that instructors and students will experience some of the pleasure that we did while writing the book. And, more importantly, we hope that students will gain an even deeper understanding of psychology as they come to understand its history.

Finally, we would like to thank our family and friends for being patient with us as we have put in the hours necessary to produce this volume. Benny was especially forgiving when walks, ball-time, and dinner were delayed because we were still sitting in front of the computer.

Wade Pickren and
Alexandra Rutherford

INTRODUCTION

Historians decide what is significant, and they do this by locating an event or action, and its causes, in a narrative or story. Which story the historian chooses . . . depends on the historian's purposes.

—Roger Smith, *Being Human*, 2007

No historical study, whether of psychology or of something else, ever consists simply as a jumble of unrelated facts. Some thematic unity always ties the facts together.

—Kurt Danziger, "Universalism and Indigenization in the History of Modern Psychology," 2006

The story of the history of psychology can be told in many ways, from many vantage points, and for many purposes. The pool of facts about the history of psychology is practically, if not theoretically, infinite. How are we to make sense of them, to tie them together, to make a story? One frequently invoked, and useful, strategy is to recount this story through the lives and careers of the people who made important contributions to the field. Biography, especially well-crafted biography, makes for interesting reading and has the potential to reveal much, not only about its subjects but also about the times in which they lived and the influences upon their thought. But a dilemma soon presents itself. How does the historian decide who is, or was, important enough to be included? That is, who should be at the center of the story, who should be at the periphery, and who should be left out entirely? These thorny historiographic issues have, until fairly recently, been ignored by those who write history from the center, including ourselves.

Another strategy, again commonly employed by textbook writers, is to present the history of psychology as a story of the important schools of thought that have characterized the field, such as behaviorism, humanistic psychology, and psychoanalysis. This approach has the advantage of organizing psychological knowledge neatly, but the implicit assumption is that any way of thinking about psychology outside the discipline, or any way of thinking about psychology that did not achieve the status of a school, was relatively unimportant. Disciplinary achievements and successes are at the center, while nondisciplinary, nonscientific, everyday psychology, or smaller, more critical movements within the field, exist only at the periphery of the story, if they are mentioned

at all. Social, cultural, and political factors that may have affected the schools of thought and their influence tend to be minimized.

So how have we decided to tie the jumbled facts of the history of psychology together in the story we tell in the upcoming pages? What is our story's purpose? The goal of this text is to present a version of the history of psychology that resists the traditional storylines of great achievements by eminent people or schools of thought that rise and fall in the wake of scientific progress and that instead attempts to reveal the complex trajectory of psychology as a socially embedded set of theories and practices that both reify and reflect the contexts from which they arise and to which they return. Although

American and western European psychology has often been portrayed as a universal form of psychology, and is typically at the center of the story, we attempt to show how this psychology is as socially embedded as any other. Although the United States and Europe are often at the center of our account, we attempt to make them self-consciously so, rather than assuming that this form of psychology is *the* psychology, or even that within this context psychologists adhere to one way of organizing and interpreting reality. As later chapters explicitly show, even within American psychology challenges from feminists and psychologists of color have disrupted the notion of a one-size-fits-all psychology.

We also attempt to complicate the notion of *who* is at the center and *who* is at the periphery of the history of psychology by bringing in actors and events that, through identity, geography, orientation, or some other reason, have heretofore been marginalized in historical accounts. Although we are somewhat inconsistent in our attempts, at least the attempt is made.

With these ideas as starting points, we would now like to entice you with some reasons we—and others—feel that the history of psychology, in all of its guises, is an interesting and important subject in its own right.

WHY HISTORY? WHY HISTORY OF PSYCHOLOGY?

Psychologists claim as their subject matter some of the most intimate and personal aspects of human experience. For many students, this is what makes psychology so fascinating. Stated most broadly, psychology is the scientific study of being human. While we each have access to our private experience, psychologists approach and study this experience more systematically and scientifically than we are able to do on our own, as individuals. What assumptions have psychologists made about the nature of this experience, and how best to arrive at knowledge about it, in order to wrestle so intimate a

subject matter into a form that is appropriate for scientific study? How have they made "being human" observable, quantifiable, manipulable, and reducible to a manageable form? How have their vantage points and positions influenced this process?

As you will discover in the following pages, there have been, and continue to be, many responses to the challenge of how to make the study of being human scientific. Agreement has never been total, consensus has never been reached, and local norms, as well as practical and professional considerations, have often played important roles in how psychology is practiced. In our view, this state of affairs, in combination with the unique intimacy of psychology's subject matter, renders it one of the most intriguing and exciting of the human sciences. It invites, and indeed demands, historical scrutiny.

As historians of psychology, we hope to convince you that historical knowledge of the way these decisions have been made, and their impact on the scientific knowledge about human nature that psychologists generate, offers a compelling form of insight into being human that can influence your study of contemporary psychology in important ways. As Roger Smith, a historian of the human sciences, has pointed out, *historical* knowledge is foundational to being able to understand ourselves as humans. History provides an approach that allows us to examine "what people have said and believed about being human" (Smith, 2007, p. 3). These discourses and beliefs have had, and continue to have, real consequences for how people view and conduct themselves and the forms that social systems take. The *history* of psychology allows us to see what role psychological knowledge has played in what people say and believe about being human and what impact these beliefs have had on what people actually do. We hope your knowledge of this history will make you a more discerning consumer *and* producer of psychological knowledge.

With this goal in mind, several conceptual distinctions and historiographic issues have heavily influenced our thinking and writing about the history of psychology, and Psychology. Henceforth, we try to employ the useful distinction between "little p" psychology and "big P" Psychology as we write about the history of both and the ways in which they have interacted. **"Big P" Psychology** refers to the formal, institutionalized, discipline of Psychology that includes academic departments, journals, organizations, and other trappings of professionalization. **"Little p" psychology** refers to psychological subject matter itself and includes the everyday psychology that has always existed as people make sense of their lives. Taken at face value, this is a straightforward distinction (note, however, that when we are actually referring to *both* Psychology *and* psychology, we will by default use small "p" psychology instead of repeating both). Things become more complicated when we consider that Psychology has been actively involved in creating its own subject matter, has often changed the subject matter that it has taken up in complex ways, and has arguably created constructs that would (probably) never have existed without it. Psychology's subject matter (psychology) is thus a moving target, which, some argue, is best understood in terms of the historical processes that shape its emergence and development.

For example, the intelligence quotient (IQ) is a product of American and European Psychology that was devised in response to a particular set of historically-contingent intra- and extra-disciplinary demands, whereas "intelligence" (or whatever word you would like to use to characterize intelligence since time immemorial) is a psychological term, not necessarily a Psychological term. To complicate things further, a form of everyday psychology has always existed that people have used to give meaning to, guide, and shape their lives. Before Psychology, this everyday psychology took many forms and has existed in many places. With the advent of Psychology in western Europe and North America in the late 1800s, a set of interesting processes unfolded in which the knowledge generated by this new discipline has had to find its own place alongside,

or in combination with, preexisting psychological knowledge and practice. In some parts of the world, like the United States, this process has been unfolding for more than 100 years. In other parts of the world, where scientific Psychology has not been as influential, this process is at a different point and may be unfolding as we speak.

Three additional, related concepts have guided our selection of, and orientation to, the topics that you will read about in the following chapters. They are important and interesting concepts in their own right, and knowing about them will help you think more deeply about the intriguing complexity of psychology, its centers, and its peripheries. They are reflexivity, social constructionism, and indigenization.

Reflexivity

Many historians and theoreticians of psychology have noted that psychologists produce knowledge about humans that has the potential to change how humans actually think about themselves. Although knowledge about geology does not change the essential nature of rocks or minerals, knowledge about psychology can change humans. We are both the agents and the objects of scientific study in psychology and are thus active generators and recipients of that knowledge. We attempt to highlight some implications of the subject–object or reflexivity conundrum as they have influenced the development of psychological theory and practice throughout our account.

Although what we offered in the preceding paragraph is a fairly succinct description of reflexivity, it can take various forms and operate in different ways. To elaborate, we define **reflexivity** as the fundamental conflation of the agent and the object of study in psychology so that (1) the knowledge produced by agents and the characteristics of these agents themselves influence how objects respond in the very course of their being studied and (2) the knowledge produced by psychology applies as much to the agents of production as to the objects they are attempting to explain. Put more simply, the "objects" of psychological study—usually humans—are not passive; instead, they actively interpret their worlds, experiences, and interactions in ways that cannot be factored out of their performance as research participants, either in isolation or across time. In addition, since psychologists are also humans, any theory of human behavior that they generate presumably applies equally well to them as to the people they study, and their theories may unwittingly reflect their experiences, biases, and beliefs about being human. Despite psychologists' consistent attempts to do so, it remains difficult to disentangle the subject from the object.

Jill Morawski, a historian and theoretician of psychology, has described reflexivity in action by examining several examples in the history of psychology where "psychologists themselves engaged reflexivity in critical analysis of experimentation" (2005, p. 78). In one of her examples she shows how African American psychologist and educator Horace Mann Bond called into question the supposedly neutral and objective status of White intelligence testers vis-à-vis their Black test-takers. By adhering carefully to the established rules of the experimental game, as he characterized it, Bond showed that results on intelligence tests changed dramatically when a Black tester versus a White tester administered the tests to Black test-takers. He thus "outed" the White experimenter, challenging the belief that the experimenter was a purely neutral, unbiased feature of the objective, experimental situation whose race, class, gender, and general position in society would remain invisible to those subjected to the tests. The "rules of the game," Bond pointed out, did not allow for the possibility that the test-takers might have certain reactions to the test-givers or that the test-givers might have any biases or social expectations that could intrude into the experimental situation.

What Morawski's analysis demonstrates is not that reflexivity renders experimentation impossible in psychology but that an understanding of its effects is sometimes required to make our interpretations of psychological data more meaningful. Furthermore, historical reflection upon, and analysis of, these issues can facilitate more careful and discerning use of scientific tools and practices in the present.

Social Constructionism

As several other textbook authors have done before us, we consistently address how social, political, and cultural factors have both shaped and been shaped by the development of a modern scientific discipline whose adherents claim an expert, scientific knowledge of their subject matter. Scholarship by historians of psychology over the last couple of decades has become increasingly informed by the perspective that Psychology and psychologists are embedded in a matrix comprising a host of extradisciplinary and extrascientific factors that indelibly shape how Psychology is defined and practiced, the form and content of the knowledge it creates, and how this knowledge is received. This is a view known as **social constructionism**. To the extent that we are able, we attempt to ground our presentation of the history of psychology in a social constructionist position.

A good example of a social constructionist approach is the work of the historian of psychology Kurt Danziger. He has written historical accounts of the origins and development of psychological research practices in Germany, France, and the United States. He has shown how different models of how to conduct research arose in different contexts and, further, how the particular forms that these research practices took influenced the type of psychological knowledge that was generated. For example, early in Psychology's history, the psychological experiment was structured in at least two different but coexisting ways. In the Leipzig model, developed in Germany by Wilhelm Wundt and his students, an experimenter would typically work with a small handful of subjects and would often be a subject in his own research. The other subjects were often the experimenter's coresearchers and colleagues. Unlike today, where the researcher is usually in a position of authority over the participant in terms of expert knowledge of psychology, the rules of scientific method, and the setup and purpose of the experiment itself, in the Leipzig model the roles of experimenter and "experimented upon" were often interchangeable; the experimenter did not have higher status than the subject. The goal was to investigate the structure of the normal human mind, and it was assumed that participating in the experiment would not interfere with the act of theoretical conceptualization. Danziger has also noted how the social structure of this model, where members of a research laboratory collaborated and experimented upon one another under the direction of their supervisor (as was the case with Wundt and his students) was a natural extension of the preexisting social structure of the German university system where the new Psychology was just developing.

In France, however, at the same time as the Leipzig model was emerging, a different approach appeared. The Paris model, as Danziger has called it, was influenced by the medical context in which investigations of experimental hypnosis were being undertaken. In hospitals and clinics, numerous hysterics and somnambulists provided a captive population upon which expert researchers could try their experimental manipulations and place their subjects in hypnotized states in an effort to uncover the origins of their symptoms. In this model, the experimental roles were quite rigidly defined, with the experimenter clearly in a position of authority over the subject and the subject clearly the recipient of some intervention or manipulation by the experimenter. This was a direct extension of the preexisting doctor–patient relationship. In this model, the object of interest was not the normally functioning, but the abnormally functioning human mind.

Danziger also explores how aspects of the Paris and Leipzig models, along with developments in statistical, correlational methods that had their origins in England, combined to produce an early model of psychological research in the United States that was best represented by G. Stanley Hall's research laboratory at Clark University. With these three examples, Danziger makes the point that a historical analysis of the structure of the psychological experiment *itself* reminds us that there has never been such a thing as *the* psychological experiment, or only one way of doing research. Furthermore, the models that have been used are intimately connected to, and in many cases were derived from, preexisting patterns of social relationships circumscribed by place and culture. When we survey contemporary psychology, we see an array of research practices. A historical, social constructionist sensibility may help us understand why certain types of research practices dominate in certain times and places while others flourish or fade when these contexts change.

Indigenization

Although Psychology as a scientific discipline and human service profession has been developed and professionalized most extensively in Europe and North America, we attempt to move beyond an exclusive focus on the development of North American and European psychology to explore the development of psychologies in other indigenous contexts, especially from the mid-20th century onward. Although we have, partly because of our own location, training, and expertise, taken western psychology as our center, we move between this center and other emerging centers to explore the forms that psychology is taking in many contexts. There has been a growing recognition among both psychologists and historians of psychology that the development of psychology in North America and western Europe, although the dominant form for many decades, is giving way to alternative forms of psychology informed by the local contexts and regions in which they develop. The process whereby a local culture or region develops its own form of psychology, either by developing it from within that culture or by importing aspects of psychologies developed elsewhere and combining them with local concepts, is called **indigenization**. Although the content and methods of North American Psychology have been spread throughout the world, they are as much an indigenous form of psychology as any other. How American Psychology has developed its theories, methods, and structures is intimately tied to many aspects of American culture and the values that have been dominant in that culture. These include the importance of individuality and autonomy, a belief in progress and self-improvement, and a faith in science and technology to solve human problems.

Because of this indigeneity, American psychology often does not travel well or has limited relevance when exported to radically different societies and cultures where different values predominate. How this disjuncture interacts with the evolution of local theory and praxis is a process that is unfolding as we write, and you read, this book. Centers and peripheries are in constant flux. For example, Indian psychologist Girishwar Misra has written how the exported Western psychology that was dominant in Indian universities, especially during British colonial rule, is now giving way to a form of psychology that draws increasingly upon India's own religious and spiritual traditions. This has led to a reformulation of constructs such as leadership, self, personality, morality, achievement, and therapy, among others, so that they are closer representations of the realities of people in India.

OTHER ASPECTS OF OUR STORY

From the outset, we should highlight several other aspects of our account of the history of psychology. Until fairly recently, most historians of psychology have tended to tell a story that has foregrounded the history of scientific psychology, focusing largely on important theoretical developments, schools of thought, and classic experiments. These features have formed the core, or center, of their accounts, as we noted earlier. By contrast, the simultaneous development of applied and practical psychology has been situated at the periphery. A few historians have begun to change this state of affairs, and we attempted to weave their scholarship into our account. In our story, we pay almost as much attention to practice and application as to theory. Well before there was a scientific discipline called Psychology, people used knowledge about themselves, others, and their world to try and change or improve their lives. When scientific psychology arrived on the scene, new applications, such as testing and psychotherapy, were developed. These practices either displaced or competed with existing practices, and these processes have, in some cases, been quite interesting. As one historian of psychology has noted, "the history of psychology as a science and that of the psychological profession are inseparable" (Ash, 2003, p. 252).

Practice and application also offer an easily identifiable point of contact between the scientific discipline of Psychology and its consumers. When scientific psychological knowledge comes into direct contact with the public, the public responds to it in various ways. Sometimes it is openly resisted, but more often it is modified to fit personal experiences and existing discourses, and sometimes psychological insights are incorporated seamlessly into how we view ourselves and our relationships. In every case, Psychology as a modern scientific discipline produces knowledge that changes the individuals, societies, and cultures in which it is embedded, and these changes then feed back into psychological theory and practice.

Finally, we extend our historical coverage through the science wars and postmodern critiques of the latter half of the 20th century to explore their implications for Psychology, and psychology, and its centers and peripheries. Common to most of these critiques was the attempt to destabilize the rational, individual, and autonomous self that was the centerpiece of modernity and to substitute a relational and socially and communally forged self. The belief that science proceeds progressively and linearly toward an ever-increasing approximation of an underlying, universal truth was also challenged by postmodern critics. In its place emerged a view that the conduct of science, as much as any other social practice, is subject to the influence of local norms, cultural values, and even interpersonal and political processes.

By bringing you through this period of challenge, we show you how these critiques have changed psychology, its subject matter and methods, and even whose science and whose knowledge counts in the field. Women, ethnic minority psychologists, and others from traditionally marginalized groups used this period of critique as a platform to demand the overthrow of Psychology's traditional power structures and to supplant the hegemony of White, largely masculine, Eurocentric theory with a more pluralistic and inclusive approach. By presenting our historical account this way, we explore the questions of who was at the center and who was at the periphery, why, and to what effect.

Along with the challenge of the traditional, linear view of scientific progress came revisions to the rules that had governed how to write the *history* of science, including psychology. In her classic article on the subject, titled "The New History of Psychology" (1989), Laurel Furumoto brought these historiographic considerations to the attention of psychologists and called upon historians of psychology to develop new methods and adopt new assumptions about how to write their histories. Although histories of psychology had begun to appear early in the discipline's development, most of these histories were written about the great men and ideas of psychology and were often celebratory or ceremonial in nature. They often told the story of psychology through the lens of the present, seeing as important only the scientific advances that had led incrementally toward the presumably superior state of contemporary knowledge and leaving out the stories of those who did not fit

into this progress narrative. They often invoked **origin myths** in the process, retrospectively selecting great thinkers and classic experiments to buttress the legitimacy of present views and to impart a sense of continuity and tradition about the development of psychology.

Furumoto proposed a new, more critical approach that would be contextual, inclusive, and historicist. Instead of presenting psychology as the creation of great men working in relative isolation, psychology would be presented as a communal, socially constructed endeavor heavily influenced by time, place, and culture, involving a diversity of constituents. This history would be reconstructed—not through the lens of the present but within the context of its own time, with an appreciation of the different values and states of knowledge that would have been dominant at those times. She noted that practitioners of the new, **critical history** would use archival and primary documents to avoid repeating anecdotes and myths that had a tendency to pass from one textbook generation to the next. To as great an extent as possible, we attempt to use the historiographic approach of the new, critical history in the following account. As we noted at the beginning of this introduction, we conceptualize the history of psychology as a dynamic and continuous negotiation among many participants involving the question of who is professionally sanctioned to inhabit and define a sharply contested—and never precisely delimited—scientific and practical space. We hope to produce a narrative that reflects this conceptualization, although we cannot hope to do justice to every aspect of this or all of its participants.

Clearly, the story of how Psychology has refashioned subjective experience as an object of scientific study is filled with intrigue, fraught with tension, and fully relevant to your study of psychology in its contemporary form. We hope that we have at least begun to convince you that history and psychology are complementary—if not mutually dependent—approaches to understanding the complex, ever-changing phenomenon of being human.

ORGANIZATIONAL OVERVIEW

This text begins, unlike some other texts that start much earlier, with the organization of psychology into a self-consciously scientific discipline in the mid- to late 1800s, that is, with the advent of disciplinary or "big P" Psychology in Europe and America. Inevitably, however, a host of predisciplinary developments influenced the rise of the new field and made its emergence possible. We therefore take a couple of steps back to examine several of these in the first two chapters and attempt to bring some developments, especially those pertaining to predisciplinary *practices*, in from the periphery. We then use the third chapter to discuss the decisive role that debates over subject matter and methods played in defining early American and European psychology. We emphasize the role of cultural and institutional contexts in the development of the new Psychology in Germany, the United States, Britain, and France. In Chapter 4 we proceed to examine American psychology's indigenization, pulling in several more strands that influenced the development of psychology in this specific context. In Chapter 5 we turn to psychology's interface with medicine in Europe and the United States, exploring especially the influences of Jean-Martin Charcot and Sigmund Freud. In Chapter 6 we remain in the Western world, examining the influence of World War I on American psychology, and examining the emergence of many forms of psychological testing as a response to social demands and to further psychologists' professional aims. In this first section, our organization is more thematic than chronological, and you will find some overlap among the chapters, both in terms of people and time periods covered.

The next five chapters proceed more or less chronologically, using the two world wars as crucially important professional and developmental milestones for Psychology around the world. Chapters 7 and 8 cover psychology in the interwar period in the contexts of the United States and Europe, respectively. Nowhere, perhaps, was the Second World War more important in establishing the status and international influence of Psychology than in the United States. This increase in influence and prestige, especially after World War II, had many effects on the field, which we discuss in Chapter 9. This increase in influence, however, came with a price. For various reasons, American psychology in the post–World War II period became perceived as a tool of the state and a defender of the status quo, which was seen as increasingly unjust and oppressive, both at home and around the world. Challenges to the status quo, not only in the United States but also as part of a global, anti-colonial, liberation struggle, ensued. We recount the effects of this period of challenge on the theoretical, institutional, and practical developments in psychology in Chapters 10, 11, and 12. In our last chapter, we return to internal, scientific developments and outline the rise of cognitive psychology, highlighting its embeddedness in the interdisciplinary matrix of the cognitive sciences that have retrieved consciousness as the orienting point of their studies. In our conclusion, we complete the trajectory of our narrative by hypothesizing how the historical account that we have provided will continue, develop, and shift as Psychology—and psychology—moves steadily into the 21st century and unfolds in distinctive ways around the world.

BIBLIOGRAPHIC ESSAY

For his extended discussion of the role of historical knowledge in self-understanding and its relationship to the human sciences, we have used Roger Smith's book *Being Human: Historical Knowledge and the Creation of Human Nature* (2007). Smith offers a more focused account of how the history of psychology fits into the history of self-understanding, and the historiographic issues involved (including the role of reflexivity), in his article "The Big Picture: Writing Psychology into the History of the Human Sciences" (1998). Another useful article about the nature and scope of the history of psychology, including a discussion of many important historiographical issues, is his "Does the History of Psychology Have a Subject?" (1988). For additional material on reflexivity, including several historical examples in which psychologists themselves have used reflexivity to analyze psychological practices, see Jill Morawski's article "Reflexivity and the Psychologist" (2005). In his classic essay "Social Psychology as History," Kenneth Gergen (1973) suggests that social psychological knowledge is historically contingent and therefore constantly in flux. He also comments on the impact of knowledge about social behavior on the behavior itself (an early remark on the conundrum of reflexivity).

For a discussion of general historiographic issues, including the distinction between psychology and Psychology, reflexivity, and social constructionism, see the introductory chapter of Graham Richards's incisive text *Putting Psychology in Its Place: A Critical, Historical Overview* (2002). An important and groundbreaking work on social constructionism and its implications for writing the history of psychology is Kurt Danziger's *Constructing the Subject: Historical Origins of Psychological Research* (1990a). For an earlier, and shorter, articulation of part of this book, see Danziger's "The Origins of the Psychological Experiment as a Social Institution" (1985). For a general overview of indigenization and its implications for a modern history of psychology, including the inspiration for our use of the center-and-periphery metaphor, see his chapter "Universalism and Indigenization in the History of Modern Psychology" (Danziger, 2006). For an overview of the issues involved in transporting Western psychology to other contexts and the process of indigenization, see "Psychological Science in Cultural Context" (Gergen, Gulerce, Lock, & Misra, 1996).

Laurel Furumoto's overview of the new history of psychology can be found in her 1989 chapter "The New History of Psychology." Mitchell Ash's approach to the history of psychology in his "Psychology" chapter in the seventh volume of *The Cambridge History of Science* (2003), *The Modern Social Sciences*, is one we have attempted to emulate throughout this book.

A HISTORY OF MODERN PSYCHOLOGY IN CONTEXT

Chapter 1
TIMELINE 1220–1920
(In 25-year increments)

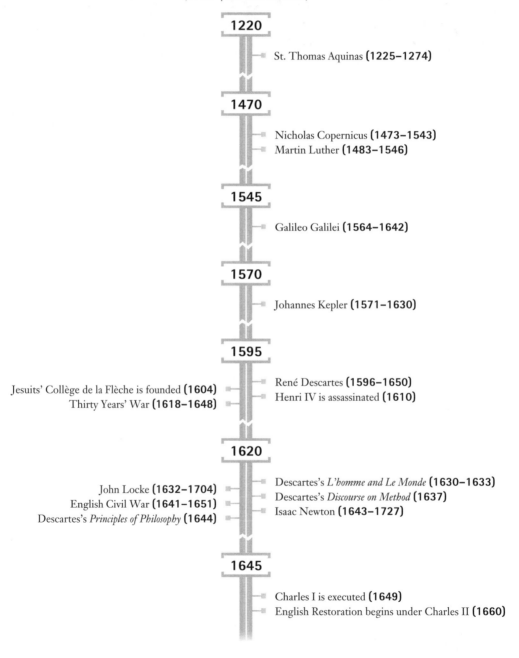

1220

St. Thomas Aquinas **(1225–1274)**

1470

Nicholas Copernicus **(1473–1543)**
Martin Luther **(1483–1546)**

1545

Galileo Galilei **(1564–1642)**

1570

Johannes Kepler **(1571–1630)**

1595

Jesuits' Collège de la Flèche is founded **(1604)**   René Descartes **(1596–1650)**
Thirty Years' War **(1618–1648)**   Henri IV is assassinated **(1610)**

1620

John Locke **(1632–1704)**   Descartes's *L'homme and Le Monde* **(1630–1633)**
English Civil War **(1641–1651)**   Descartes's *Discourse on Method* **(1637)**
Descartes's *Principles of Philosophy* **(1644)**   Isaac Newton **(1643–1727)**

1645

Charles I is executed **(1649)**
English Restoration begins under Charles II **(1660)**

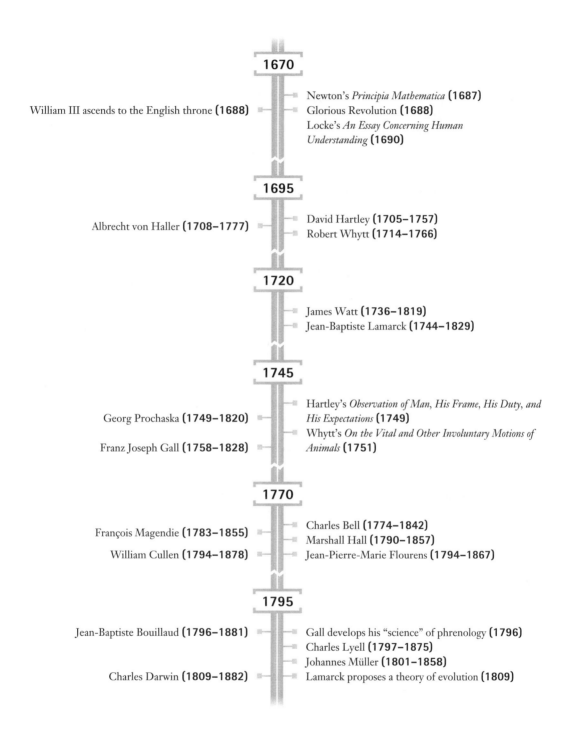

1670

Newton's *Principia Mathematica* **(1687)**
William III ascends to the English throne **(1688)**
Glorious Revolution **(1688)**
Locke's *An Essay Concerning Human Understanding* **(1690)**

1695

Albrecht von Haller **(1708–1777)**
David Hartley **(1705–1757)**
Robert Whytt **(1714–1766)**

1720

James Watt **(1736–1819)**
Jean-Baptiste Lamarck **(1744–1829)**

1745

Hartley's *Observation of Man, His Frame, His Duty, and His Expectations* **(1749)**
Georg Prochaska **(1749–1820)**
Whytt's *On the Vital and Other Involuntary Motions of Animals* **(1751)**
Franz Joseph Gall **(1758–1828)**

1770

François Magendie **(1783–1855)**
Charles Bell **(1774–1842)**
Marshall Hall **(1790–1857)**
William Cullen **(1794–1878)**
Jean-Pierre-Marie Flourens **(1794–1867)**

1795

Jean-Baptiste Bouillaud **(1796–1881)**
Gall develops his "science" of phrenology **(1796)**
Charles Lyell **(1797–1875)**
Johannes Müller **(1801–1858)**
Charles Darwin **(1809–1882)**
Lamarck proposes a theory of evolution **(1809)**

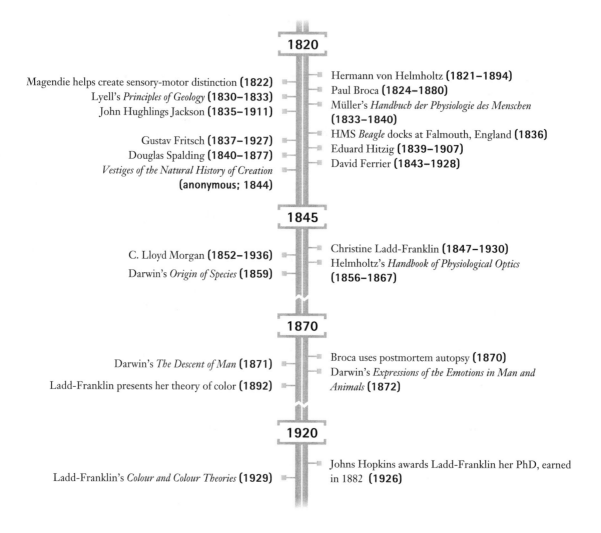

1820

Magendie helps create sensory-motor distinction **(1822)**
Lyell's *Principles of Geology* **(1830–1833)**
John Hughlings Jackson **(1835–1911)**

Gustav Fritsch **(1837–1927)**
Douglas Spalding **(1840–1877)**
Vestiges of the Natural History of Creation
(anonymous; 1844)

Hermann von Helmholtz **(1821–1894)**
Paul Broca **(1824–1880)**
Müller's *Handbuch der Physiologie des Menschen*
(1833–1840)
HMS *Beagle* docks at Falmouth, England **(1836)**
Eduard Hitzig **(1839–1907)**
David Ferrier **(1843–1928)**

1845

C. Lloyd Morgan **(1852–1936)**
Darwin's *Origin of Species* **(1859)**

Christine Ladd-Franklin **(1847–1930)**
Helmholtz's *Handbook of Physiological Optics*
(1856–1867)

1870

Darwin's *The Descent of Man* **(1871)**
Ladd-Franklin presents her theory of color **(1892)**

Broca uses postmortem autopsy **(1870)**
Darwin's *Expressions of the Emotions in Man and
Animals* **(1872)**

1920

Ladd-Franklin's *Colour and Colour Theories* **(1929)**

Johns Hopkins awards Ladd-Franklin her PhD, earned
in 1882 **(1926)**

ORIGINS OF A SCIENCE OF MIND

Since it is the understanding that sets man above the rest of sensible beings, and gives him all the advantage and dominion which he has over them; it is certainly a subject, even for its nobleness, worth our labour to inquire into.

—John Locke, *An Essay Concerning Human Understanding*, 1690

INTRODUCTION

The discipline of Psychology, the history of which we explore in the following pages, did not exist before the mid- to late 19th century. Thus, to begin our history, we have to understand the intellectual and practical developments that made the emergence of such a field possible. As we discuss in this and the next chapter, at least four strands of thought and practice were important for the emergence of Psychology by the end of the 19th century: philosophy, physiology, evolution by natural selection, and creation of a psychological sensibility through everyday practices. Taken together, these four strands made possible both the science and the profession of Psychology, which Graham Richards has termed "big P" Psychology to differentiate the discipline from its subject matter, "little p" psychology (Richards, 2002). The latter includes the everyday psychology that people have used, and continue to use, to make sense of their lives.

The last strand, the creation of a psychological sensibility, is explained and elaborated in the next chapter. In this chapter, we unravel the first three strands by introducing you to basic ideas from the work of philosophers René Descartes and John Locke, the development of an experimental approach to understanding the relation between mind or brain and behavior in 19th-century physiology, and Charles Darwin's work on evolution and how it included humans within the domain of natural laws.

We take as our point of departure the early modern period, that is, from the 17th century on, as the appropriate time to begin our analyses of the events that made possible the relatively recent emergence of Psychology. In terms of place, we begin with events and people in England and western Europe. This is not to claim that people in no other place or time wrote or thought psychologically about life; as we argue in later chapters, a background of thought relevant to psychology in other cultures came to the fore nearer our own time. Rather, our aim is both pragmatic and historiographical. We are pragmatic because space is limited. Our historiographic rationale is that we think a sound argument can be made that the psychological sensibility characterizing our own time is of relatively recent origin, dating from changes in human experience and human society that were first directly noticeable in the early modern period in England and Europe, and then exacerbated by rapid social changes brought on by such macroscale events as the Industrial Revolution and the spread of Protestant religious beliefs and practices.

Lastly, we think it is useful to consider events and contributions to the development of a psychological sensibility from both elites—that is, those of the upper classes who had access to resources, education, and the power to disseminate their views—and everyday people. It is more usual in a textbook to consider only the contributions of elites, typically philosophers or "men of science"; this chapter focuses on such contributions. The next chapter examines changes in everyday life that many people encountered and incorporated to make meaning in their lives. If, as we suggested in the introduction of this book, Psychology emerged from ways of living, then it follows that we should ask questions about when and how changes in everyday life occurred. While a full set of answers is not possible, since no complete record exists of how people lived and acted in earlier periods, we can provide at least a partial description and analysis based on extant records and writing. While we have an extensive record of philosophical thought from the early modern era, which we draw on in this chapter, in the next chapter we use what is available in the historical record to suggest how nonelites contributed to the emergence of practices that are also part of the lineage that led to the emergence of Psychology.

PHILOSOPHY: DESCARTES AND LOCKE AS EXEMPLARS

The gradual emergence of thought about man in naturalistic terms occurred, paradoxically, in the context of faith, both Protestant and Catholic. Religion and conflicts about correct beliefs and the proper conduct of daily life provided a background for this thinking that held both promise and threat. Nations went to war, and humans lost their livelihoods and often their lives over these matters. Both Descartes and Locke were profoundly affected by this context of religious and political strife, and each attempted to find ways to restore certainty of knowledge and order in civil society. Importantly, their thought also contributed to the eventual emergence of Psychology.

If any one word could characterize the 17th century in England and Europe, it might well be "uncertainty." The modern nation-state was emerging, and war among nations was endemic. Civil strife that led to civil war in England brought horrors nearly unimaginable that left

their marks for generations afterward. The English civil war was directly related to religious beliefs and practices, but religion was also an important factor in changes elsewhere in Europe as the new orientation to personal faith and religious practice introduced by Martin Luther (1483–1546) in the 16th century spread unevenly across the continent. Families, as well as nations, were often divided over questions of faith, whether to follow the traditions of the Roman Catholic Church or one of the new Protestant faiths. When these faiths were linked to the power of the state, many people were persecuted and killed for their beliefs and many fled to other countries. So, on both the national and the personal levels, it was a time of uncertainty as the fabric of life was rewoven in a period of intense social upheaval.

Although no one event sparked the changes in the structure of life and thought in Europe, the assassination of the king of France, Henri IV (Henry of Navarre), in 1610, was crucial in that it made salient the need to find a new foundation for civil society. Henri IV was tolerant of religious diversity and provided guarantees for the civil rights of religious minorities, who were primarily Protestant. Powerful Catholics feared that he secretly planned to weaken Catholicism, and they arranged to have him killed. His assassination was a rejection of religious tolerance. Given the tensions between faiths across Europe and the high political stakes involved, Henri's assassination was taken as evidence that only force could resolve religious disputes. In 1618, the Thirty Years' War began that involved most states of Europe and led to widespread devastation and a marked reduction in population. Among the elites, those with time to reflect and write, a pressing concern became how we can find certainty for knowledge and living that religion seemingly failed to provide.

Not only was there religious conflict, but the challenges to orthodox understanding of the natural world by Nicholas Copernicus (1473–1543), Galileo Galilei (1564–1642), and Johannes Kepler (1571–1630) seemed to shake the foundations of knowledge laid down by Aristotle and his 13th-century Christian interpreter, St. Thomas Aquinas (1225–1274). The calls by Sir Francis Bacon around the beginning of the 17th century for a science based on observation of the world and the collection of those observations into a coherent framework through inductive reasoning was also a challenge to orthodox thinkers. This context for the new philosophies placed the study of man within a naturalistic framework. While several philosophers were prominent, we have chosen two, Descartes and Locke, as our exemplars of the new natural philosophy. What linked these two preeminent thinkers was their quest to find a certainty that could underpin civil life.

René Descartes (1596–1650)

Descartes was 22 years old when the Thirty Years' War began. Descartes's mother died when he was young. He lived with his grandparents and his two older siblings because his father, a lawyer, worked some distance away. A precocious child, at age 8 he was placed in the Collège at La Flèche, a Jesuit school. When he graduated at age 16, he had probably received as excellent an education as was available at the time. He was schooled in the Aristotelian beliefs, for example, about the organic soul and the intellective soul. Only humans were blessed with the latter and its chief characteristic, reason.

Two cautions are needed as we proceed. First, Descartes was not a psychologist, nor was he a protopsychologist. He was a philosopher concerned with placing knowledge on a sure foundation and from that foundation constructing knowledge about how the Creation worked, including the human brain and body. Descartes's worry about the certainty of knowledge was with him even as he finished school. What compounded this worry was the state of his world as a young man. As the long period of conflict that became the Thirty Years' War continued,

Descartes, along with other thoughtful people, perceived that the underpinnings of society were inadequate to support an enduring civil society. This, combined with the disputatiousness and inconclusive arguments of the leading philosophers and theologians of the day, led Descartes to seek a way to have certain knowledge.

His search led him to the method of doubt. Descartes decided to accept only those things that were so clear and distinct to him that there could be no possibility of doubt. As he later wrote, "Immediately I noticed that while I was trying thus to think everything false, it was necessary that I, who was thinking this, was something" (cited in R. Smith, 1997, p. 129). This led him to the famous phrase, *cogito ergo sum*, "I am thinking, therefore I exist." For Descartes, the rational soul, the I, was central. From that point, then, an argument was made for the existence of God and God's perfection as expressed in natural law. These indubitable facts, Descartes argued, were the foundation stones that made certainty of knowledge possible.

Second, Descartes was very much a person of his culture, time, and place. That is, he was a Catholic who sought avidly to keep his work within the bounds of orthodox belief. His adherence to Catholicism can be seen in his insistence that the mind is immaterial and the province of God. This meant that the soul (mind) is entirely distinct from the body. The soul is the seat of reason and directly amenable to divine influence; it cannot be reduced to materiality or explained in terms of mechanics. However, the implication of this is that all that is not soul can be examined in terms of mechanics and is amenable to explanations based in natural law. Descartes proposed that many functions previously considered to be mental and immaterial should be considered properties of the body. These included memory, perception, imagination, dreaming, and feelings; all of these were properties of the body and so could potentially be understood in naturalistic terms. This is the basis of what came to be referred to as the mind–body split or **mind–body dualism**.

To explain these functions, Descartes relied on an understanding of mechanics derived partly from then-recent discoveries in medicine—William Harvey's (1578–1657) articulation of the heart as a pump for the blood—and from the artists and craftsmen of his time who had refined automata. Automata are self-moving mechanical objects, such as robots. Evidence shows that automata date from early in Chinese history, but they had been refined and made newly popular in the 16th and 17th centuries. The word "automaton" was coined in the early 17th century. Some automata that Descartes would have been familiar with included dolls that seemed to play musical instruments or enact a play. He also knew the royal gardens at St. Germain-en-Laye, outside Paris. There, using hydraulic pressure activated when visitors stepped on hidden plates, statues would move seemingly on their own. Descartes used the principle of this mechanical movement as a generative metaphor for understanding the functions of the body, including memory and other properties of the nervous system. He supposed that the cavities in the brain, the ventricles, were filled with animal spirits, which could flow through (hollow) nerves to effect bodily movement, just as the water filled the pipes at St. Germain and caused the statues to move.

FIGURE 1.1 René Descartes

Still, the question remained as to how the body and soul interact. Descartes proposed the pineal gland in the center of the brain. The pineal gland, Descartes supposed, could both receive impressions of the body via the animal spirits and transmit motions to the body. This had the effect of reserving the soul as the seat of reason and the special province of divine influence. This approach fit with both the teachings of the Catholic Church and the new mechanical philosophy.

What is important about Descartes for the later development of both a psychological sensibility and the discipline of Psychology is that his work was critical for the transition to understanding humans in terms of natural law from the older conceptions that placed man at the apex of creation, a "little lower than the angels," as the biblical psalmist had it. That is, his work was critical for a new articulation of man that placed his attributes firmly in the natural world, with what was increasingly referred to as human nature. His writings became a point of departure for many later writers who responded to his work, not always sympathetically. What emerged from his contributions was a legacy that led toward an understanding of man as fully part of nature.

John Locke (1632–1704)

How do we gain knowledge? For Locke, this was a fundamental question to which the answer was human experience. In proposing that human knowledge comes through sense experience, Locke laid the foundation for both empirical philosophy and, much later, the human sciences, including Psychology. As with Descartes, however, Locke was not a protopsychologist, nor did he seek to establish a discipline of Psychology. Locke was concerned with finding a basis for civil society that would diminish the likelihood of incessant conflict and loss of human life. For Locke, the way to do so was through helping people form clear and distinct ideas, free of the excesses of political and religious enthusiasms.

Locke's desire to find a new, less conflictual basis for human society is understandable given the political and religious context of his life.

When Locke was only 10 years old, the first English Civil War began, with the usual horrors that such wars bring. For the next 19 years, until the restoration of the monarchy in 1661, the British Isles were in near-constant conflict—political, military, or both. Religious differences were the contextual surround for the war, but political machinations between the king and Parliament were central. When King Charles I was captured and then beheaded, it marked perhaps the passing of an age in which it was thought that the monarch was God's representative on earth. The viciousness on both sides of the war must have brought great distress to Locke. When Charles II was crowned and the monarchy restored in 1661, Locke was still a young man, making his primary living as a tutor and adviser to the Earl of Shaftesbury. Locke was engaged with the politics of his age and was drawn into the political intrigues of the time. For a period in the 1680s, Locke had to leave England and live in Holland. He was there when the Glorious Revolution occurred, which deposed King James, brought William and Mary to the throne of England, and led to the establishment of a constitutional monarchy with enhanced power for the English Parliament.

Given these events, we can understand why Locke became so committed to finding a new basis for society. His ideas developed from the 1660s to the publication of his major work, *An Essay Concerning Human Understanding*, in 1690. The *Essay* is remarkable in many ways, but especially noteworthy is Locke's use of mind rather than soul. In doing so, he deliberately changed the terms of the debate about human knowledge. Descartes had reserved reason as an attribute of the soul, thus always leaving a space for the operation of divine influence, especially in regard to innate ideas given by God. Locke rejected the notion of innate ideas, such as God, although he did argue that humans have an innate power to reflect on their experiences. Instead of

FIGURE 1.2   John Locke

innate ideas, Locke argued that all ideas come through experience. That is, at birth our minds are a *tabula rasa* (blank slate) on which sensory experiences are inscribed. The contents of the mind are those ideas that come from experiences.

Knowledge, then, is a matter of the mind gathering experiences, or ideas, from the material world. Locke proposed a way in which we could understand how ideas could move from simple to complex through association. In doing so, Locke seemed to offer a model of mental life that corresponded to Sir Isaac Newton's model of the mechanical basis of the physical world. Newton's *Principia Mathematica* was published in 1687, 3 years before Locke's *Essay*, and in some ways Locke's work echoes that of Newton. Just as Newton had proposed a model of how complex substances are due to the combination of less complex materials, so Locke's model suggested that complex ideas form from combinations of simple ideas, a position that became known as **associationism**. As he wrote, "As simple ideas are observed to exist in several combinations united together, so the mind has a power to consider several of them united together as one idea; and that not only as they are united in external objects, but as itself has joined them together. Ideas thus made up of several simple ones put together, I call complex; such as are beauty, gratitude, a man, an army, the universe" (Locke, 1690, p. 159). Why is this so important for us today? First, Locke, like Newton, made human experience central to knowledge. This led to subsequent emphases by philosophers on what was later called epistemology, the study of the way we know. And it placed a premium on **empiricism**, that is, knowledge gained through the senses, which came to characterize British philosophy and led to later developments that were crucial for a discipline of Psychology.

Beyond this, Locke's work made individual experience gained in the material world highly important. In the political and religious context of his time, this generated great debate, with some even labeling Locke an atheist. But the practical result was the privileging of the empirical world, thus strengthening arguments for natural religion and for a society predicated upon human experience. It is this emphasis on human experience that is arguably Locke's greatest contribution and one that had the greatest import for later developments in political and scientific, including psychological, realms.

The Legacy of Descartes and Locke for Psychology

The time from the publication of Locke's *An Essay Concerning Human Understanding* in 1690 to the early years of the 19th century is often called the "long" 18th century. Some scholars and texts have referred to it as the Age of Enlightenment or Age of Reason. Many people contributed to the debates about intellectual and practical issues that were conducted among educated people and were central to changes in governance and the way humans in Europe related to one another. The legacy of Descartes and Locke found in these contributions and debates is that now such issues about man are framed as part of nature and that the right way to understand and discuss them is in terms of human nature. This is not to say that religious beliefs and creeds played no part in these discussions. Especially in the case of

Descartes, the relationship of this new thinking to religious belief was much pondered. The outcome, however, was that man was increasingly seen as part of nature and was to be understood in terms of the natural world.

PHYSIOLOGY AND MEDICINE: THE SEARCH FOR MATERIAL EXPLANATIONS OF HUMAN NATURE

While philosophers and educated people engaged with notions of man as part of nature, efforts were also made to systematically explore what this would mean in terms of the functions of the human body, including the brain. The term "experiment" or "experimental" came into vogue to express this systematic exploration. By the end of the 19th century, the experiment became the method of discerning truth and the laboratory became the place where truth, through experimentation, was discovered. In terms of the human nervous system, this was a long and circuitous route with many points of contention and debate. The legacy of Descartes to this debate was that the higher mental powers—rationality, purposiveness, and so on—remained the province of divine influence. So while the functions of the body, including the "lower" centers of the brain and the nervous system, could be understood in naturalistic or mechanical terms, the higher powers, including the cerebrum, were off limits. The effort to extend naturalistic explanation to the higher mental powers—indeed, to equate the brain and the mind—became a major debate in the 19th century. Perhaps not surprisingly, medicine was an arena where this work first occurred.

Medicine and Naturalistic Explanation

Harvey had described the circulation of the blood in 1628, demonstrating empirically that circulation of the blood is due to the action of the heart, thus potentially understandable in naturalistic terms. After Locke, in the 18th century, physicians began to describe the actions of the mind in physiological terms, thus opening the door to experimentation as a way to potentially demonstrate this. The British physician David Hartley in his *Observations on Man, His Frame, His Duty, and His Expectations* (1749), employed Newton's suggestion that vibrations in nervous tissue could be responsible for some visual effects to develop a physiology of the nervous system predicated on association of ideas that could account for relations between mind and body. However, it should be noted that Hartley's aim was religious, to inspire his fellow man to pursue God's design for humans.

The experimentation and writing of the 18th-century British physicians Robert Whytt (1714–1766) and William Cullen (1794–1878) both facilitated the public's understanding that mind and brain were intimately connected and offered a way to elide the old mind–body dualism that bedeviled research on mental processes. Whytt suggested in his 1751 book *On the Vital and Other Involuntary Motions of Animals* that an organism's response to stimuli involved the action of volition, a function of the higher mental powers, but this volitional response was not necessarily conscious. Whytt called this the principle of sentience, whose main function was the preservation of life and the unity of the organism. Before Whytt, only two kinds of action were thought possible: voluntary (rational) and physical (mechanical). Whytt's work proposed a third action, the action of stimuli on the organism. Thus, stimulated motion was best viewed as occurring on a continuum between voluntary and automatic, rather than as in absolute categories of free will or mechanism, and depended on the conditions necessary for preservation. The result of this stimulated motion was always to preserve the organism; thus, self-regulation was the effect. This implied the importance of function and offered an alternative to Cartesian dualism in understanding the relation of mind and body.

Why was this important for the later development of psychology? Whytt argued that the effect of a stimulus did not depend on whether it was a physical or mental event. The importance of the stimulus lay in its function. A mental event could function as a stimulus, just as a physical event could. This implied that the mind was intimately involved in bodily actions, not categorically separate as Cartesian dualism suggested. If mental and physical events were functionally equivalent, then perhaps psychological topics could be investigated without being bound by the old categories of Cartesian dualism. This, in fact, is what began to occur.

Cullen, who succeeded Whytt at the University of Edinburgh, advanced Whytt's work with an even greater emphasis on function and the role of stimulated motion as a self-regulatory principle. Cullen replaced Whytt's principle of sentience with the concept of energy as the vital principle. Energy was quantifiable, and the measure of excitation in the organism was possible. Gustav Theodor Fechner (1801–1887), who is discussed in Chapter 3, drew upon this work for his later development of psychophysiology. The impact of the work of Whytt and Cullen has not often been noted in histories of psychology because of their affiliation with medicine, but their work was crucial in that they provided a language and a group of principles that placed the role of the nervous system front and center in understanding how the mind and body are related.

Relatedly, the work of Whytt and Cullen was part of a broader movement in the late 18th and early 19th centuries toward emphasizing the importance of understanding the relation between the organism and the environment in terms of self-regulation. The latter principle came to the fore by the end of the 18th century in several fields, the political economy of Adam Smith (1723–1790) being a prime example with its invisible hand as the regulator of the market (see Chapter 2). Here, again, we see the relation between technology and science in terms of guiding or generative metaphors. In the 17th century, we saw how Descartes drew upon the popular technology behind automata to explain how the body works. In the 18th century, the idea of a governor or self-regulator as found in the new steam engines of James Watt was employed to explain how the organism engaged in self-regulation via feedback loops between mental–physical events and their stimulation of the organism.

In Europe in this period, several physicians investigated the relationships among mind, brain, and body. Perhaps most notable was Albrecht von Haller, whose experiment-based theories suggested a way for the mind to act on the body through the nervous system. By the end of the 18th century, the Austrian physician and anatomist Franz Joseph Gall (1758–1828) had begun to argue that the brain was the organ of mind and that its faculties were empirically demonstrable. Gall was a major figure in what became a nearly century-long debate over the extent to which mental abilities, or the functions of the brain and nervous system, could be understood in naturalistic terms. An implication of this was the question of whether a soul or some higher power was needed to account for the most complex mental abilities, including the will. Some investigators sought to avoid the theological debate by contending that mechanical processes only extended as far as the subcortex. The cortex was reserved for the divine influence of some higher natural law. Gall's work called that contention into question.

Gall was born in Germany and settled in Vienna, where he received his medical degree. In Vienna he made his first scientific contributions when he demonstrated that two types of substance were found in the brain: gray matter (the cell bodies of nerve cells) and white matter (subcortical brain areas containing nerve cell axons). He also showed that the two hemispheres of the brain were connected by commissures. However, what Gall became known for was his organology, later renamed **phrenology** by some of his followers. **Organology** was Gall's method of discerning mental abilities by reading the bumps on

FIGURE 1.3 Franz Joseph Gall

someone's skull. Gall said that these ideas began when he was a schoolboy and noticed that some of his classmates who performed better on memory tasks than he did had bulging eyes. In his adult career, Gall further developed this schoolboy insight.

The brain, Gall argued, was composed of distinct parts, each of which had a function. Furthermore, the size of each of these parts, as observable through the examination of the skull, reflected the strength of the assigned function. Gall was not the first person to suggest that mental abilities or functions might occur at specific locales (the idea can be found in ancient medical texts), but his contention that the brain was the organ of mind and its workings could be understood entirely by empirical means did create controversy. First, it circumvented the duality of mind and body proposed by Descartes. Gall argued that all mental functions, including the higher powers reserved by Descartes as the province of divine influence, could be understood as the workings of the brain. In that sense, Gall was engaging in a philosophical argument, one that had important implications for future research. How was knowledge organized? Was it just a collection of sense impressions? Gall argued that there had to be a physical, innate foundation for organizing the knowledge that came to us through our senses. Unlike the followers of Descartes, Gall's point was that there was no division of mind and body and no need to reserve higher mental functions for the providence of God.

Second, the search for a materialist basis for mind proved extremely important, although controversial. Perhaps the controversy helped make it important. Gall insisted that an empirical approach to the question of brain function was crucial. While Descartes had split the mind and body and set the terms for discussion of mental faculties, his approach was philosophical. As we have seen in the cases of Whytt and Cullen, investigators were increasingly seeking to account for mental abilities in terms of bodily processes. These investigators were relying on empirical rather than purely rational or philosophical methods. Their efforts were strongly resisted by some who felt they needed to allow for higher processes in terms of mental faculties that were uniquely human, for example, the will and the intellect.

But the movement begun by Descartes and Locke to study man as part of nature, to find natural laws to account for human mind and behavior, had already reset the agenda or the terms for what counted as fact. By the end of the 19th century, the investigation of the nervous system—of mind and brain—was firmly on the empirical and experimental basis on which Gall had insisted. Even those who sought to retain Descartes's division of mind and body were constrained to provide evidence gathered empirically and experimentally.

Jean-Pierre-Marie Flourens (1794–1867), a physiologist and member of the French medical and scientific establishment, was firmly committed to the Cartesian position that reserved the mind's higher faculties as the province of divine influence. He reacted strongly to what he perceived as Gall's materialist arguments. Flourens sought to discredit Gall and his followers by showing experimentally that no division of cerebral function existed. Using birds and a few mammalian species, Flourens systematically

FIGURE 1.4 Jean-Pierre-Marie Flourens

removed or ablated parts of the brain and then observed what happened when the animal recovered. He found no specific losses of function but rather general losses across several functions. He argued that this preserved the unity of the soul. What some critics, including Gall, pointed out was that Flourens had not been discriminate enough in carefully removing portions of the brain but had cut across several possibly distinct areas. Nevertheless, Flourens carried the day, at least among the medical and scientific establishment, because of the prestige of his social position, the compatibility of his findings with the established medical and philosophical views, and the usefulness of his results in discrediting the basis of what was now being called phrenology, which had become part of a social movement perceived as radical and antiestablishment (more on this in Chapter 2). Finally, and perhaps most importantly, Flourens's use of the experimental method fit with what was becoming the scientific norm for establishing fact—man could be understood in naturalistic terms as long as the investigation was experimental and laboratory based.

Flourens's championship of the unity of soul and mind and discounting of the localization of brain functions was the received view in French medicine and physiology for many years. There were dissenters such as the respected physiologist Jean-Baptiste Bouillaud (1796–1881), who collected more than 100 clinical cases that he suggested supported **localization of function.**

Bouillaud argued especially that language must be localized somewhere in the frontal lobes of the brain. It was the work of Paul Broca (1824–1880), however, that firmly established localization of articulate language through the case of Monsieur Leborgne, who had lost his ability to speak. Before the case of LeBorgne, Broca had already established himself as a respected scientist. Like many other scientists of his day, he was influenced by scientists elsewhere in Europe, principally Germany, who were arguing that it was necessary to break phenomena down to their most essential elements to study them. Broca thought that perhaps the best way to understand the complexity of the nervous system was to look at the building blocks of mental activity; localization of function potentially offered a way to do this. Recent mapping of the surface of the cerebrum showed its diversity of form, and Broca argued that a law of physiology was that structure or form and function were related. Thus, different parts of the cortex may have different functions. When LeBorgne died, six days after coming under Broca's care, an autopsy revealed damage to the rear portion of the left frontal lobe. Other cases soon were found where damage to the same area, second or third frontal convolution of the frontal lobe, was found with attendant loss of speech. While these findings did not settle the debate conclusively, they did sway medical and scientific opinion toward an acceptance of some sort of localization of function.

After Broca's work became widely known, other investigators began providing support for localization of cerebral function, thus extending naturalistic explanations to the highest levels of the nervous system. In Germany, two physicians, anatomist Gustav Fritsch (1837–1927) and psychiatrist Eduard Hitzig (1839–1907), used recent improvements in the control of electricity to stimulate what is now called the motor cortex of a dog. They found five sites that, when electrically stimulated, resulted in distinctive movements—on the opposite side of the body. Flourens had argued that the cortex had nothing to do with movement or motor control. Fritsch and Hitzig understood their work as directly contributing support to cerebral localization. Perhaps paradoxically to 21st-century students, Fritsch and Hitzig were, like Flourens, committed to a Cartesian model of divine influence on higher centers of the brain and so restricted their conclusions on localization of motor control to motor centers and reserved other parts of the cortex for the higher mental powers.

David Ferrier (1843–1928) had no such compunctions. Ferrier, later knighted, built on the work of Gall and John Hughlings Jackson, a fellow neurologist, to demonstrate experimentally the wide extent of cerebral localization. Where Fritsch and Hitzig had found five areas of motor control, Ferrier found 15. His experimental animals included fish, birds, amphibians, monkeys, and chimpanzees. Ferrier quite self-consciously referred to his work as "scientific phrenology." The title of his book summarizing his work on localization was *The Functions of the Brain*, and he dedicated it to Gall. Gall had predicted 50 years earlier, in his book *On the Functions of the Brain*, that someone would scientifically validate his insights in the next 50 years! Together with work in sensory–motor physiology, covered in the next section, this work on localization of function helped make a science of Psychology possible.

Research in the Physiology of the Nervous System

The discovery of the distinction between sensory and motor nerves, made independently by Charles Bell (1774–1842) in 1811 and François Magendie (1783–1855) in 1822, helped create the conditions for the exploration of the psychological implications of nervous system functions. Both Bell and Magendie pointed out that each type of sensory nerve was specific to a sensory modality—vision, hearing, touch, and so on. This became in the hands of Johannes Müller the doctrine of specific nerve energies, discussed later. Two research streams were linked to this conceptualization. One was the concept of cerebral localization, already discussed. The other was work on the nervous system that led from the concept of specific nerve energies to a mechanistic model of human nervous system function. Both streams were part of the extension of a naturalistic model to encompass all of human nature. The concept of reflexes or reflex action was part of both streams. The discovery of specific sensory and motor nerves helped refine the previously ill-defined concept of reflex actions.

The concept of reflexes was not new to the 19th century. Whytt had employed the concept in his work on stimulated movement. The work of Whytt and his successor, Cullen, as noted, was critical in making it possible to link psychological questions to physiological methods. The Moravian-born physiologist Georg Prochaska employed the concept of reflexive action as part of his *vis nervosa* and *sensorium commune*. The former referred to the latent energy of the nerves that found expression in reflexes. *Sensorium commune* encompassed the medulla, basal ganglia, and spinal cord. Its role was to link sensory input to motor responses, without reliance on consciousness. These earlier uses of the reflex concept were typically not precise or precisely linked to physiological processes. But with the articulation of the sensory–motor distinction, the English physiologist Marshall Hall offered a specific connection between local nerve action and behavior. Hall's use of the reflex concept meant that behavior could be described in terms of nerve action, that consciousness does not have to be involved in behavior. This challenged the mentalistic conceptions of human behavior. If the brain and soul are equivalent, and the soul directs human behavior, then neurophysiology or experimentation is unnecessary. If, however, at least some aspects of human behavior are based in stimuli and responses at the physiological level, then experimental approaches to understanding human behavior are needed. Hall's proposal of reflex action and behavior was, at first, accepted only as accurate for the lower nerve centers. By the end of the 19th century, reflex action was extended to the highest centers of the brain, as the work of Fritsch and Hitzig and that of Ferrier showed.

The Mechanization of the Brain

Johannes Müller (1801–1858) is often referred to as the person who made physiology a truly scientific field. His work occurred when German universities were expecting from professors original research by scholars devoted to specific topics. His handbook of physiology, published in several volumes from 1833 to 1840, fostered a critical, experimental approach to investigations of bodily processes that became the norm for other scientists. Müller extended the Bell-Magendie sensory–motor distinction with his **doctrine of specific nerve energies**. Each sensory modality, Müller argued, is specialized to respond in ways that are unique to it. So, visual nerves when stimulated give visual sensations. For example, pressing on the eye gives a visual sensation, just as looking at an object does. The doctrine also suggests that what determines our sensory experiences are not the objects-out-there in the physical world; rather, it is the structure and function of our nervous systems that determines what we sense. In this work and in his handbook, Müller promoted the importance of laboratory-based experimental work. In doing so, Müller

FIGURE 1.5 Johannes Müller

opened a line of research in physiology that led directly to Hermann von Helmholtz and Wilhelm Wundt and helped make a physiologically based Psychology possible.

Helmholtz (1821–1894), perhaps the greatest scientist of the 19th century, made contributions that changed physics, physiology, optics, audition, and psychology. While a student with Müller, Helmholtz joined with several fellow students—Emil du Bois-Reymond (1818–1896), Rudolf Virchow (1821–1902), and Ernst Brücke (1819–1892)—in committing himself to scientific explanations that relied only on physical and chemical explanations for all phenomena. Their work over the next half century made Germany the center of first-rank scientific work in several fields. The application of their mechanistic approach by others was also vital for helping transform Germany into an industrial and military powerhouse by the end of the century. It was also the background for the later development of Gestalt and holistic theories, especially after the defeat of Germany in World War I.

The contributions of Helmholtz to psychological topics included the measurement of the nerve impulse, previously thought to occur instantaneously. This indicated the possibility of measuring aspects of mental activity, using what was soon called the reaction time method. Helmholtz also showed that the **law of conservation of energy** applied to living organisms, including humans, as well as to the inorganic world. Using frogs as his experimental animal, Helmholtz showed that the energy and heat expended by a frog were equal to the calories available in the food the frog consumed. He went on to further work with these principles and eventually formulated the law of the conservation of energy: Energy cannot be created or destroyed; it can only be transformed from one kind to another. What this suggested was that machines, including the human machine, are devices for transforming energy from one kind to another kind. His work on optics led to a crucial distinction between sensation and perception. **Sensations** are, Helmholtz argued, merely the

FIGURE 1.6 Hermann von Helmoltz
Courtesy of the authors.

raw data that comes through our senses. These data are made meaningful by perception. In this account, **perception** is a psychological process that depends on the brain, prior learning, and our experiences.

In other psychologically related work, Helmholtz argued for a trichromatic theory of color vision. Like the earlier work of the English scientist Thomas Young, Helmholtz suggested that color vision resulted from the stimulation of specific receptors in the retina. It is a trichromatic theory because there are three primary receptor types—one each for red, green, and blue-violet. Other colors result from stimulation of more than one receptor; white results if all three receptor types are stimulated. One of American psychology's first-generation woman psychologists, Christine Ladd-Franklin (1847–1930), traveled to Germany to work in Helmholtz's laboratory and subsequently published her own theory of color vision that was long regarded as the best available account of both the physical processes and the psychological experience of color perception. In 1892, she presented aspects of her theory to the International Congress of Psychology in London. Helmholtz was in attendance and received her paper extremely favorably. In 1929, her book *Colour and Colour Theories*, which reprinted over 37 years of her work on

color vision, was published. One reviewer for the *Saturday Review of Literature* characterized Ladd-Franklin's work as an account of the "evolution of the color sense from its beginnings to man" and proclaimed that "in the field of color and color theories she has no peer" (Helson, July 20, 1929). While not all aspects of Helmholtz's and Ladd-Franklin's theories have held up, both theories were, in their own time, considered quite successful in accounting for color vision.

Sidebar 1.1   Focus on *Christine Ladd-Franklin*

Christine Ladd was born in Windsor, Connecticut, on December 1, 1847, to a well-established New England family. When Vassar College, America's first college for women, was established in 1865, Ladd was ecstatic. After a vigorous campaign to convince her father and aunt (her mother had died when she was 12 years old) to let her attend the college, she was admitted to the second entering class in 1866. While at Vassar, her main academic interests were science and mathematics. She was particularly influenced by the prominent astronomer Maria Mitchell who was on faculty there. She graduated in 1869 and spent the next decade teaching science and math in secondary schools throughout the Northeast. She quickly came to abhor teaching, however, and she continued to study mathematics, occasionally publishing articles in the *Educational Times*.

In 1878, on the strength of her articles and her Vassar degree, she applied to Johns Hopkins University to pursue graduate studies in mathematics even though the university did not admit women. Her credentials were sufficient to convince the board of trustees to let her enroll as a special student. While at Johns Hopkins, she published several articles in the *American Journal of Mathematics*. Under the influence of the work of Charles Peirce, who acted as her dissertation adviser, she also became increasingly interested in symbolic logic. She turned her attention specifically to a long-standing problem in symbolic logic called the transformation of the syllogism. Her solution of this problem led prominent philosopher Josiah Royce of Harvard University to remark, "It is rather remarkable that the

(Continued)

FIGURE 1.7   Christine Ladd-Franklin
Courtesy of Rare Book and Manuscript Library, Columbia University, New York.

crowning activity in a field worked over since the days of Aristotle should be the achievement of an American woman" (as cited in Burr, June 24, 1922).

While at Johns Hopkins, Ladd also met and married Fabian Franklin, one of her graduate instructors in mathematics. In 1886 she conducted an investigation of a mathematical question concerning binocular vision, thus initiating her unfolding research on color vision. In 1891–1892, during her husband's sabbatical year in Europe, Ladd-Franklin studied in the Göttingen laboratory of George Elias Müller and then with Helmholtz in Berlin. In 1892, she delivered a paper outlining her own theory of color vision at the International Congress of Psychology in London. She spent much of the rest of her career elaborating upon and defending this theory.

Although Ladd-Franklin had completed all requirements for her doctorate in mathematics and logic in 1882, and had earned fellowships throughout her graduate training, she was not awarded the degree until 1926 on the 50th anniversary of Johns Hopkins. Although almost 80 years old, she attended the ceremony to receive her degree. Despite her impressive accomplishments, she never held a formal, full-time academic position. Determined to change the academic situation for other women, she was instrumental in establishing research fellowships for women and campaigned tirelessly for women's equal participation in academic life. For more on her efforts to fight sex discrimination in Psychology, see Chapter 11.

Like Müller before him, Helmholtz's theory placed importance on what happens within the human brain and nervous system rather than on the "real" physical properties of light waves. Again, this is part of the move toward placing all of nature, including humans in all their complex functions, within a framework of nature governed by definable natural laws. In Chapter 3, we show how the work in the physiological tradition of Müller and Helmholtz was directly linked to the emergence of Wundt's physiological psychology. Later in the book, we return to some issues raised by cortical localization when we explore the rise of neuroscience. Now, we turn to the work of Darwin to examine how it finally established human nature as just that, part of nature and thus subject to lawful relationships like the rest of nature.

DARWIN, NATURAL SELECTION, AND THE LAWS OF NATURE

Charles Darwin (1809–1882), naturalist, was a careful observer and thinker who was both a person of his time and a person whose ideas transformed the course of history. His work affected many intellectual and scientific fields, including Psychology. At least four key contributions came to the development of Psychology from the work of Darwin. Perhaps most importantly, Darwin provided convincing evidence, both theoretical and practical, that humans are part of nature, subject to the same natural laws as all other creatures. Second, Darwin's approach called attention to the importance of considering the function of attributes and behaviors, thus making even more salient the role of functional explanations begun by earlier scientists like Whytt and Gall. Third, the scope and approach of Darwin's work created a space for the study of man in comparison with other animals (what became the field of comparative psychology) and the necessity of understanding the development of humans (what became the field of developmental psychology). Fourth, the emphasis on the role of natural selection of human variability facilitated thinking about individual differences, which became especially important in the development of American Psychology and helped create applications of differential psychology to vastly diverse populations: students, criminals, the mentally disordered, and so on.

Darwin was born in the small village of Shrewsbury west of Birmingham, England, the son of a well-to-do physician, Robert Darwin, and his wife, Susannah. Darwin was of an impressive lineage. His father, Robert, was the son of Erasmus Darwin, a well-known physician of the late 18th century and author of a poetic treatise on evolution, *Zoonomia* (1794–1796). His mother was the daughter of Josiah Wedgwood, the founder of Wedgwood china. Charles Darwin married his cousin, Emma Wedgwood, in 1839.

By all accounts, Darwin was an indifferent student at the local Shrewsbury school, although he did have an insatiable appetite for nature—often going off on long hikes to collect worms, bugs, and other creatures. His father sent him to Edinburgh, Scotland, to be trained as a physician. Darwin had no stomach for the brutalities of surgery, and the medical training did not take. At last, he was sent to Christ College, Cambridge University, to become an Anglican clergyman. This seemed to suit Darwin fine, as he could easily envision himself as a country parson with plenty of free time to pursue his naturalist research.

While Darwin was not a great classroom student, his formal education was useful. He was an avid learner of those things that appealed to his interests in natural history both at Edinburgh and at Cambridge. For example, at Edinburgh, Darwin studied homologies, similarities due to a common descent, in marine animals with Robert E. Grant (1793–1874), who also espoused a theory of evolution proposed by Jean-Baptiste Lamarck (1744–1829). At Cambridge, where classwork was not necessarily the main engine of instruction and learning, Darwin came under the tutelage of John S. Henslow (1796–1861), professor of botany, and Adam Sedgwick (1785–1873), professor of geology. Both of these men, like the other professors at Cambridge, were Anglican priests. Neither of them believed in evolution,

but both were excellent instructors, not only formally but also in the many excursions and walks that Darwin participated in with them. In the summer of 1831, before he was to take Holy Orders, Darwin accompanied Sedgwick on a geological mapping tour of Wales. This experience and the close bond he had with both men were critically important in helping him move on to the next phase of his education and launch his professional life, as the onboard gentleman of science for the voyage of the HMS *Beagle*.

Journey to the Galapagos

In September 1831, Darwin interviewed with Captain Robert FitzRoy of the *Beagle* for the position of gentleman companion to the captain for a voyage to South America. The *Beagle* was commissioned to map the coasts of South America, and a 2-year voyage was planned. Instead, the voyage lasted nearly 5 years and became a trip around the world. Darwin, as the naturalist on board, busied himself collecting specimens and making careful geological observations throughout the trip. He sent home, via other returning ships, more than 2,000 specimens, including the fossils of previously unknown species. He filled a large scientific diary with thousands of geological and zoological data. While on the trip, Darwin sent back to his mentors in England numerous letters filled with his observations. Material excerpted from these letters was circulated in scientific circles and made Darwin a celebrated figure in British science even before he returned.

When Darwin set out on the voyage, he was a believer in what is called the **argument from design**. This was the view that all species had been designed by a Divine Creator for their specific place in nature. Darwin had also been exposed to theories of evolution, especially that of Lamarck, as noted earlier. Lamarck proposed a theory of evolution in 1809 that began with the spontaneous generation of living matter from nonliving matter. Since then, Lamarck suggested, there has been a steady progression from simple forms of life to ever greater complexity. One mechanism for this progression, Lamarck posited, was the **inheritance of acquired characteristics**. This mechanism meant that changes in the adult organism can be passed on directly to the offspring. The well-worn example is the neck of a giraffe. According to the doctrine of inheritance of acquired characteristics, giraffes stretching their necks to reach higher leaves resulted in an increasingly elongated neck over many generations.

The implications of Lamarck's theory were quite unsettling to many people, especially those intensely vested in and privileged by the status quo. It suggested that life was not due to divine intervention and that human beings were just animals, although perhaps more developed than other animals. Lamarck's theory had a note of progress in it, that life and society were better characterized by change than by a static model. In the 1820s and 1830s in Britain, Lamarck's ideas were taken up by reformers, some of whom were radical. Many of the scientific elite, including Darwin's Cambridge instructors and his peers when he returned from his voyage, perceived these reformers as a threat to civil society and actively worked to discredit them. An extremely popular book in the 1840s, *Vestiges of the Natural History of Creation*, published anonymously, created a sensation with its claims of a naturalistic origin of life. Although technically not a natural history of evolution but instead a tract espousing a progressivist notion that change was necessary to have a society with greater equality of opportunity, the book did put the word "evolution" in the mouths and on the minds of much of the rapidly expanding reading public. It was also roundly condemned by all whom Darwin held in highest esteem. So, when he was developing his theory after the voyage, this was the context for his work.

No one event or observation on the voyage of the *Beagle* catapulted Darwin toward his eventual theory. Rather, and this was consistent with his character, it was the accumulation of many observations and the careful pondering of what they meant that led him to slowly develop his theory over several years. However, the geological observations he made in South America, where it was clear that what had once been ocean floor or beach was now thousands of feet above sea level, and the myriad life forms on the Galapagos Islands were among the most important experiences he had. The former suggested that the earth had changed over a long period. This position was called the **uniformitarian hypothesis**, and it fit with the ideas of Charles Lyell, a geologist whose book, *Principles of Geology*, Darwin carried with him on the voyage. The uniformitarian hypothesis suggested that the physical geology of the earth was formed as a result of long, gradual processes. It contrasted with the notion that geological forms were the result of sudden, catastrophic changes, usually the result of divine intervention or handiwork—as in the biblical flood. Thus, the earth was much older than the literal reading

FIGURE 1.8 Charles Darwin

of the Bible would suggest and allowed enough time for the gradual change in organisms that could possibly result in new species.

The visit to the Galapagos Islands eventually provided Darwin with the material that he would use to articulate species change. The Galapagos are a series of small volcanic islands about 600 miles west of Ecuador on the equator. Darwin collected a large variety of species there and noticed the distribution of similar species, especially birds, across the islands. At the time, he did not see that many of the birds were of the same family. After his return to England, ornithologist John Gould pointed out that many of the birds were finches, each uniquely adapted to their island environments. When Darwin returned to England and began to develop his ideas about species change, the geographical distribution of the finches would become important for the development of his theory.

The *Beagle* docked at Falmouth, England, on October 2, 1836, nearly five years after it left Plymouth Sound. By the time it landed, Darwin's name was well known in British naturalist circles. His father arranged investments for him so that he could devote himself to a life of science. He soon launched a careful consideration of all data he had gathered and was puzzling over what it meant. We know from his notebooks—Darwin kept careful records of his observations and thoughts, which has proven a real boon for historians of science—that the question of species change emerged early in his puzzling.

Continuity: Humans and Natural Law

Darwin's theory of evolution by natural selection made humans subject to the same natural laws as other animals. This principle of the continuity of life was one of the most controversial aspects of Darwin's work, one he did not stress in the *Origin of Species* (1859). Yet, by insisting on continuity, Darwin helped make it possible to think of universal laws underlying behavior. If evolution occurs through a natural selection of variations that help an organism adapt to its environment,

then an important question becomes, What is the function of the characteristic under study, whether it be an elongated bird beak or human consciousness? How does the characteristic help the organism adapt and survive? We have seen that the question of function had become a topic of investigation in the research Whytt, Cullen, Prochaska, and others. Darwin made the question of function central to an evolutionary perspective. When the field of Psychology emerged some years after Darwin's work, questions of adaptation and function and of their derivative, learning, became central, especially in the utilitarian American context.

The possibility of using animals to understand human behavior emerged from Darwin's work and became the field of comparative psychology. Darwin himself explored this area in two books written later in life, *The Descent of Man* (1871), and *Expressions of the Emotions in Man and Animals* (1872). George Romanes, a protégé of Darwin's, extended the application of Darwin's evolutionary framework in an investigation of animal mental ability. While his writing about animals was fascinating, it suffered from a reliance on anecdotes about the supposedly amazing abilities or mental feats of various animals. It should be kept in mind that there was (and is) a long, time-honored tradition in Britain of anthropomorphizing animals (anthropomorphism is attributing human characteristics to animals). Others who followed, however, made the comparative method more rigorous, including C. Lloyd Morgan and Douglas Spalding. We explore these developments in later chapters, especially how studying animal behavior came to be used as a model for understanding how humans learn and adapt.

Darwin's theory also provided an impetus to the study of children as a way of understanding evolution. Darwin kept a diary of the development of his first son, William, and later published an article based on it, "Biographical Sketch of an Infant" (1877). Infants and young children, some thought, allowed us to see what humans were like earlier in the evolutionary process. A more extreme version of this idea, although not espoused by Darwin, is captured in the phrase "ontogeny recapitulates phylogeny." That is, the development of a human, beginning with conception, displays all stages of human evolution. The study of children's lives and how such studies help us understand human behavior was an important aspect of the early years of the development of Psychology in North America and in Europe.

Finally, the notion that variability provides the material with which natural selection works gave rise in psychology to the idea of individual differences. Darwin's cousin, Francis Galton (1822–1911), was captivated by the possibility of understanding human differences within an evolutionary framework. We explore Galton's

work in a later chapter, especially in relation to the development of methods in psychology. Again, the development of Psychology in America facilitated a differential approach, and the idea of understanding different capacities (e.g., intellectual or academic) or different propensities (e.g., criminality and creativity) seemed important in managing a rapidly changing society. The idea of learning and adaptation that was inherent in Darwin's theory lent itself to a focus on applied problems, both in research and in practice. So, especially in America, psychological expertise was viewed as having application to the diverse questions of how to improve schools and the performance of children in those schools, how to understand worker performance, and dozens of other applied questions.

SUMMARY

In this chapter, we sketched a history of some principal sources of a science of mind. These sources included philosophical debates, empirical and experimental work in medicine and physiology, and the naturalist work and evolutionary theory of Darwin. We hope we have indicated how deeply these sources were linked to one another. That is, work in physiology and medicine drew upon philosophical debates about the nature of being human and questions of epistemology, and philosophers were keenly interested in developments in science, often seeking to use research results in support of their own theories. Darwin was an inheritor of much prior work that had placed questions about humans in a framework of naturalism. In turn, he interpreted the data drawn from his naturalistic observations as showing that man was a creature subject to natural law like all other animals. His work, like that of others before him, helped place great emphasis on function. When the new Psychology developed a few years later, questions about the function of behavior and the mind

became crucial in the new science, especially in the United States. It would be going too far to say that by the end of the 19th century there was a consensus about human nature. What we can confidently say is that for most educated people in the Western world at the end of this era, humans were understood to be part of nature and, thus, subject to the laws of nature. By this time, the discipline of Psychology had begun (see Chapter 3), and many of these new psychologists saw their work as explaining just what these laws were in regard to human thinking and behavior.

Lastly, we also sought to indicate in this chapter just how deeply embedded these origins of a science of mind were in the social and cultural context of their times. War, political struggle, economics, religion, and technological changes were all critical parts of the cultural matrix from which modern science, including Psychology, emerged. In the next chapter, we turn to the practices of everyday life in this period to examine the emergence of the Western notion of the self. This was the necessary counterpart to the developments outlined in this chapter in that the formation of an everyday psychology was needed for the psychological sensibility upon which disciplinary Psychology could rely for its subject matter.

BIBLIOGRAPHIC ESSAY

A key text that has both inspired us and guided our thinking about the history of psychology in context, not only for this chapter but for all of our writing for this text, is Roger Smith's *Norton History of the Human Sciences* (1997). His 2007 volume, *Being Human*, has been equally helpful to us in how to think through the implications of historical narratives about human nature. Although idiosyncratic, Graham Richards's *Mental Machinery* (1992) is an immensely useful book for the philosophical background of this chapter. We also used his *Putting Psychology in its Place* (2002) for the contrast between "Big P Psychology" and "little p psychology." As part of our general overview, we also found useful several chapters in *The Cambridge History of Science* volume *The Modern Social Sciences*, edited by Theodore Porter and Dorothy Ross. For the early modern period and the roles of war, civil and religious strife, and philosophical problems engendered by the emerging nation-states, Stephen Toulmin's *Cosmopolis* (1990) has been influential. Our understanding of key events in the emergence of modern science owes a great deal to the work of Stephen Shapin, especially, *Leviathan and the Air-Pump* (1985), *A Social History of Truth* (1994), and *The Scientific Revolution* (1996), although any fault of interpretation is entirely ours. Roy Porter's *Flesh in the Age of Reason* (2003) helped us understand debates about body and mind in the 17th- and 18th-century contexts.

For work in physiology and medicine, we found many helpful articles and books, chief among them were Anne Harrington's *Medicine, Mind and the Double Brain* (1987), Kurt Danziger's article "Origins of the Schema of Stimulated Motion" (1983), and Roger Smith's article "The Background of Physiological Psychology in Natural Philosophy" (1973). John van Wyhe's 2002 article on Gall helped us locate Gall's work in the context of medical debates about the functions of the brain. The philosophical and social implications of the localization of function debate have been superbly articulated by Robert Young's *Mind, Brain, and Adaptation in the 19th Century* (1991). *Origins of Neuroscience* (1994) by Stanley Finger is a useful encyclopedic approach to most of the major, and many of the minor, figures and events in the prehistory of the neurosciences.

For information on Ladd-Franklin's fascinating life and career, we recommend two publications by historian of psychology Laurel Furumoto: "Joining Separate Spheres" (1992), and "Christine Ladd-Franklin's Color Theory" (1994).

There is such a vast literature on Darwin that it is hard to know where to start or stop. Peter Bowler's short biographical study (1990) was helpful. *Darwin and the Emergence of Evolutionary Theories of Mind and Behavior* by Robert Richards (1987) and *From Darwin to Behaviourism* by Robert Boakes (1984) were both helpful and are drawn on again for later chapters.

Chapter 2
TIMELINE 1390–1860
(In 25-year increments)

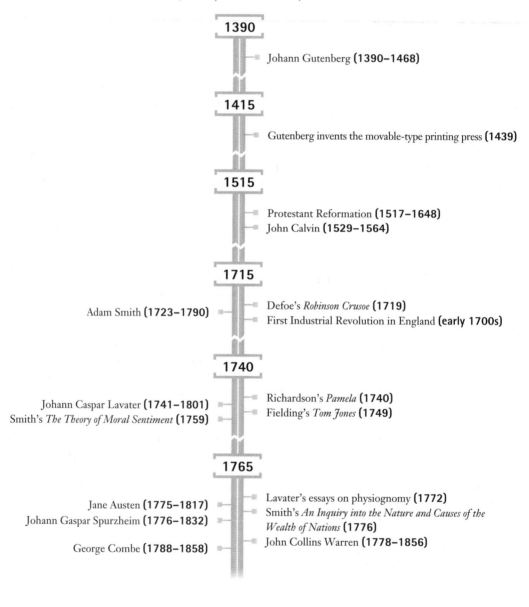

1390

Johann Gutenberg **(1390–1468)**

1415

Gutenberg invents the movable-type printing press **(1439)**

1515

Protestant Reformation **(1517–1648)**
John Calvin **(1529–1564)**

1715

Adam Smith **(1723–1790)**

Defoe's *Robinson Crusoe* **(1719)**
First Industrial Revolution in England **(early 1700s)**

1740

Johann Caspar Lavater **(1741–1801)**
Smith's *The Theory of Moral Sentiment* **(1759)**

Richardson's *Pamela* **(1740)**
Fielding's *Tom Jones* **(1749)**

1765

Jane Austen **(1775–1817)**
Johann Gaspar Spurzheim **(1776–1832)**

George Combe **(1788–1858)**

Lavater's essays on physiognomy **(1772)**
Smith's *An Inquiry into the Nature and Causes of the Wealth of Nations* **(1776)**
John Collins Warren **(1778–1856)**

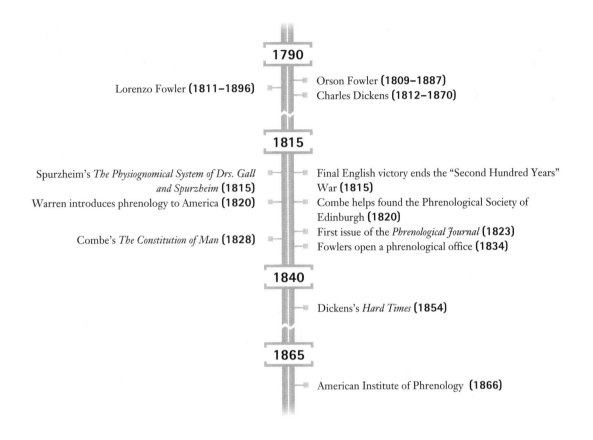

1790

Lorenzo Fowler **(1811–1896)**

Orson Fowler **(1809–1887)**
Charles Dickens **(1812–1870)**

1815

Spurzheim's *The Physiognomical System of Drs. Gall and Spurzheim* **(1815)**
Warren introduces phrenology to America **(1820)**

Combe's *The Constitution of Man* **(1828)**

Final English victory ends the "Second Hundred Years" War **(1815)**
Combe helps found the Phrenological Society of Edinburgh **(1820)**
First issue of the *Phrenological Journal* **(1823)**
Fowlers open a phrenological office **(1834)**

1840

Dickens's *Hard Times* **(1854)**

1865

American Institute of Phrenology **(1866)**

EVERYDAY LIFE AND PSYCHOLOGICAL PRACTICES

The question why men's behavior and emotions change is really the same as the question why their forms of life change.

—Norbert Elias, *The Civilizing Process: The History of Manners,* 1978

INTRODUCTION

In the previous chapter, we outlined several strands of thought that contributed to the emergence of a science of Psychology in the late 1800s, including philosophical debates (Descartes and Locke), empirical and experimental work in medicine (Whytt, Cullen, Flourens, and Broca) and physiology (Müller and Helmholtz), and evolutionary theory (Lamarck and Darwin). Soon after Psychology became established as a scientific field, the new psychologists began to envision how to make practical use of their new science. Among the first products of this impulse were mental tests, which we discuss in the next chapter. However, before these formal practices there existed a range of *everyday* practices that people used to make sense of their lives and give order and meaning to their social, family, and even business relationships. We define **psychological practices** broadly to mean the use of psychological knowledge in making sense of oneself and the world, as well as the practical strategies of self- and social management that arise out of this knowledge. These practices included a range of activities, from writing in a diary to engaging in the marketplace.

Psychological practices owed their possibility not only to the changing philosophical and medical discourses of the 18th and 19th centuries but perhaps more importantly to the emergence of a sense of self, comprising a sense of individuality and interiority, that is a taken-for-granted aspect of life in the 21st century. In this chapter, the origins of a sense of self or subjectivity are explored. The creation and shaping of subjectivity occurred on the level of everyday lived experience and was the crucial counterpart to the changes in philosophical discourse and physiological research that made a scientific discipline of Psychology possible.

So far, we have only written about the ideas of those whom it is fair to call the elites of their day—philosophers, physicians, and clerics.

These people were fortunate to have the time to reflect on the conditions around them, the literacy skills to write about their reflections, and often the political connections to have their voices heard. It may well be that one reason for the continuing influence of these writers is the privileged positions that many of them held. Yet, the origins of both everyday psychology and disciplinary Psychology also owe a great deal to the development of new ways of thinking about the person and new practices among nonelites, that is, everyday people who were challenged to order their lives in periods of major social change.

In this chapter, we offer an account of these practices that emerged in the 17th to 19th centuries. We seek to show how such practices fostered a new sense of self and gave rise to the subjectivity that we now take for granted but upon which rested the foundation and possibility of both a science and a profession of disciplinary Psychology. At the end of the 19th century, scientific psychologists emerged as a new cadre of experts who claimed as their object of study this very sense of self and the interior processes implicated in it. They were not without competitors, however, and to this day psychologists vie with other groups for their cultural authority as experts on human subjectivity. The rendering of subjectivity into an object of scientific study was one strategy psychologists employed to strengthen their cultural authority, as well as understand their subject matter in new ways. Our point in this chapter is that the emergence of scientific psychology depended, in part, on the very existence of a certain kind of subjectivity that was itself forged from both elite and everyday practices.

We begin with the role of new technologies and indicate how such technologies facilitated changes in people's sense of themselves. The growth of Protestant religion in this period was one of the keys to people focusing more on their interior life, and we examine the technologies that emerged to support devotion and piety, as well as self-perception and expression more generally. Many of these technologies, such as devotional aids known as **conduct books** and diaries, were linked to increased literacy and facilitated an increased emphasis on self-control. In this period, too, the role of the individual in everyday life came to hold a greater fascination and interest for many people. While no one factor accounts for this, contributing factors included the emergence of commercial society, the growth of print-based popular culture, and changes in the family. Specific technologies that mark this period include the diary as a record of one's own life; the practice of letter writing to explore and express intimate experiences; the rise of the novel as an account, a narrative, of possible lives; and the invention and commercial distribution of the perfected mirror.

After examining these technologies, we turn to the macrosocial changes that gave rise to and accompanied the Industrial Revolution. As many scholars have pointed out, the Industrial Revolution remade home and work life, and it created hierarchical relations among strangers in an atmosphere of competition and struggle for advancement. Nonelites, far from being overwhelmed, demonstrated great ingenuity in creating new resources, in some cases reinventing older cultural resources to survive, and in the process creating a new middle class and new order in Western capitalist societies. Prominent among the strategies deployed were physiognomy and phrenology, practices one scholar has characterized as "reading the signs of the body" (Samuel, 1991, p. 88). We show how these practices were inextricably woven into daily and commercial life and were crucial for creating the everyday psychology, or everyday subjectivity, upon which disciplinary Psychology so successfully drew for its own authority.

The philosopher Charles Taylor asked some years ago, "What brought the modern identity about?" (1989, p. 202). Taylor then noted that this was one of the most difficult questions for historians and philosophers to answer! Clearly, we are not able to answer this question fully in one chapter. Instead, we provide an overview that will help you understand the broad outlines and a few particular points of how our modern sense of identity or self emerged, especially as they ultimately relate to the practices of Psychology.

NEW TECHNOLOGIES

Technologies of Devotion and Piety

Profound religious changes in western Europe and the British Isles during the 16th and 17th centuries contributed to a new sense of self, which was partly tied to how one viewed one's relationship with God. When, in 1517, Martin Luther (1483–1546) nailed his *Ninety-Five Theses* to the church door in Wittenberg, Germany, thus challenging many common practices of the Roman Catholic Church, he initiated what became known as the **Protestant Reformation**. Leaders of the Reformation such as Luther, Ulrich Zwingli, and John Calvin propagated a Christian faith that asserted that salvation would come by faith alone and that believers were responsible for their own relationship with God, unmediated by priests or the institutional church. This direct relationship, then, demanded that Protestant Christians pay careful attention to their inner life and devote themselves to spiritual practices (Watkins, 1972).

For our purposes, three important consequences arose from these changes. First, the emphasis on a personal, private relationship with God and its maintenance, helped facilitate a sense of inwardness, of the need to pay attention to one's interior life, and thus increased a sense of subjectivity. Second, the practices of everyday life attained a new importance, as one's faith was seen as much in conduct of business and management of the tasks of daily living as in church attendance. Third, technologies were developed to help Christians maintain their personal relationship with the divine. These technologies included spiritual conduct books and the personal diary. We use the word "technologies" to indicate that these devices or instruments assisted in achieving some end. Another technology, the movable-type printing press, invented by Johann Gutenberg in 1439, was crucial to all of the preceding events.

As literacy grew in Europe and England in the 17th and 18th centuries, conduct books became popular as aids to devotion. Today, for many Christians, the equivalent is the daily devotional book; for many others, the equivalent can be found among the vast self-help literature. Believers were encouraged to reflect on their own spiritual state through the maxims found in the book, which were also meant to assist people in self-improvement in their walk with God. Self-control—of thoughts, sinful impulses, and so on—was the intended outcome. To understand why this was important, we can compare this with the conception of faith in the Roman Catholic

tradition as it was then practiced. Salvation, in the Catholic faith, was mediated by the church, thus the individual identity was submerged in the collective identity of church membership. This was, in part, why the threat of excommunication from the church was so feared. In Protestantism, however, each person was an individual with agency, that is, able to act in such a way as to affect personal destiny. Again, this placed a new premium on the matters of everyday life. We return to this issue when we discuss the emergence of capitalist, commercial society.

The new focus on the inward life and its sense of agency in all matters of conduct, both everyday and spiritual, found further expression in the diary. A diary is a personal record of an individual life. Again, the possibility and popularity of the diary reflects the rise in literacy in Europe. In 17th-century England, in particular, diaries became a popular way of privately recording thoughts, actions, and aspirations. Christians were encouraged to keep a diary to assist the development of self-reflection and, ultimately, to facilitate self-control.

Technologies of Self-Perception and Self-Expression

On a practical level, the modern glass mirror was an important new technology that literally allowed people to see themselves in a new way. Humans have used reflective devices for much of human history, with evidence of polished bronze and copper mirrors dating to nearly 3000 BC in Egypt. However, until the technology of the modern mirror was perfected in Venice in the early 16th century, what people saw in mirrors was a distortion of their appearance. The perfected mirror can be viewed as a technology to enable individuals to see themselves more clearly and thus to literally self-perceive, that is, to come closer to seeing themselves as others saw them. This facilitated a heightened sense of self.

In terms of technologies of self-expression, letter writing as a form of personal expression, rather than a means of formal or business communication, emerged strongly in the 18th and 19th centuries. During this period, literacy rose and more people were migrating, so families were geographically dispersed, sometimes separated by oceans. The efficiency of postal systems also improved. Thus, although humans have written letters as a method of communication for hundreds, if not thousands, of years, in the 18th and 19th centuries, an epistolary genre arose in Europe and North America that treated letters as vehicles through which personal experiences and sentiments could be expressed to others. As one historian has noted, "Around the middle of the 18th century, the reading public in England and America began to embrace new cultural ideals of letter writing. These new ideals revolved around what was called the 'familiar letter,' a mode of letter writing devoted to the expression of affection and duty among kin, family, and friends" (Dierks, 2000, p. 31). Thus, letters became a medium through which individuality could be asserted, and they were increasingly personalized and private.

In the first half of the 18th century, the novel appeared as a new form of literary art in England. This paralleled the emergence of the professional writer in English society. We can see this not only in the novel but also in the dramatic rise in popularity of magazines and newspapers. The novel, however, was unique. Daniel Defoe (*Robinson Crusoe,* 1719), Samuel Richardson (*Pamela,* 1740), and Henry Fielding (*Tom Jones,* 1749) were among the first novelists. The novel both reflected and shaped this new subjectivity. In these new literary forms, the characters had everyday names, not allegorical ones as in, for example, John Bunyan's *Pilgrim's Progress* (published in two parts in 1678 and 1684), whose characters have names like Christian and Evangelist. The subject matter of these novels was everyday life, the twists and turns of everyday people in recognizable situations. The thoughts and emotions of the characters were placed in the foreground in such a way that readers could identify with them; that

is, they could recognize their own thoughts and emotions in the characters they read about. The net result was greater attention to the ordinary, the mundane, and the subjective.

PSYCHOLOGICAL CONSEQUENCES OF COMMERCIAL SOCIETY

Around the same time that Protestant religious practices, such as the conduct book, and new literary forms, like the novel, were helping turn individuals' focus inward, people became aware that a new type of society was emerging. People in North American and Europe were beginning to refer to and experience what they termed **commercial society**. To what does the term refer? Different scholars have used the term in various ways, but when it was first used, it generally referred to an understanding that people and their relationships were defined by what they bought, sold, or produced, including their labor, capital (financial resources), and land, or even by what they owned or rented. When this sense emerged, it was thought to be a new type of society.

Why is this relevant to the development of the private self, of interiority or subjectivity? How, in other words, did the advent of commercial society foster a new sense of individuality? Broadly speaking, commercial society and its new demands helped shape a sense of the private self by creating a sense of obligation, promise, or contract among people—including strangers—by encouraging a self-auditing or monitoring of behavior. In addition, it was part of the new attention and emphasis placed on everyday matters. Because commercial society placed new demands on people's lives and had such powerful implications for traditional human relations, including religious obligations and how nations governed their citizens, it became a focus for many thinkers and writers, including the Edinburgh philosopher and educator Adam Smith (1723–1790). Perhaps best known for his two books, *An Inquiry into the Nature and Causes of the*

FIGURE 2.1 Adam Smith
Courtesy of the authors.

Wealth of Nations published in 1776 and *The Theory of Moral Sentiment*, first published 1759 but revised many times, Smith articulated the moral implications of this new kind of society, with its emphasis on the individual and one's own labor.

In commercial society, a person's work, or labor, was a key aspect of self-definition. As Smith argued in *Wealth of Nations*, labor was so important because it had replaced agriculture as the source of a nation's wealth. In earlier periods, individuals owed their labor and its productions to the landowner or feudal lord. Now people were increasingly likely to "own" their own labor and be able to exchange it for goods produced by some other person. Society, then, was made up of individuals who were motivated to look after their own material interests. Two things are worth noting here. One is the emphasis on material conditions, that is, the way people actually lived and worked. Second, this change suggests that a possible outcome could be disorder and unchecked greed and selfishness. Why was this not always the inevitable outcome?

Some scholars have pointed out that capitalism, or commercial society, actually encouraged a greater sense of social obligation. In a capitalist mode, individuals in the marketplace have to consider the consequences of their actions. So, if a promise is made to deliver goods or to receive them at a certain price, then failure to do so could jeopardize future relations, not only with the other party but also by reputation with future potential partners. Conscience, therefore, enters into a primary place in human relations. Conscience is both a moral and a psychological characteristic or function. That is, having a conscience or acting conscientiously is likely to increase one's sense of subjectivity.

Part of this argument, then, is the implication of discipline and order rather than disorder and chaos. For our purposes, the key point is that the marketplace, which was and is the focal institution of commercial society, heightened an awareness of self-regulation. Smith famously used the phrase **invisible hand** to point out that when every person seeks personal interests, the net result is that the interests of all are served. Smith's famous phrase has been cited to support various economic philosophies, many of which have been characterized by greed and corporate rapaciousness. However, careful reading of his work and an understanding of his era indicates that Smith was greatly concerned about the moral implications of commercial society.

For Smith, the market encouraged self-control or self-regulation because humans need functioning relationships with other people. This is what Smith called **moral sentiment**. Yes, Smith argued, we act for our own interests, but in doing so we are mindful of the regard of others. It is this, Smith said, that makes society possible. Self-command or self-regulation is crucial to the moral functioning of society, and the invisible hand uses this to meld interests. Thus, the emergence of the market with its demands for self-accounting was critical in reinforcing emergent self-regulation. We want to emphasize that this process was chronologically uneven across England, Europe, and North America, with such processes occurring most broadly first in England. Concurrent with these and the developments discussed earlier were changes in family life and work relations. We turn to these sites next.

CHANGES IN FAMILY LIFE

Historians of the family have documented notable changes in family life in England and western Europe around the beginning of the 18th century. The primary change involved a trend toward greater intimacy and affection within families and a movement toward a greater child orientation within the family. These changes were unevenly distributed across social classes and certainly were more noticeable first among the urban upper and professional classes and then in the urban middle class. The term "nuclear family" is often used to indicate a family unit consisting primarily of parents and children, with close ties to grandparents and, sometimes, to aunts, uncles, and first cousins. Extensive evidence shows variations on the nuclear family existed well before 1700, but at that point, at least among many urban families, the smaller, nuclear family became the primary unit. These

families were marked by an emphasis on intimacy and affection. Privacy also became the norm, as the influence of the outside world waned. That is, the opinions of those outside the family came to have less influence on what happened within the family.

What contributed to these changes and what followed from them? Certainly, the developments we have been describing were all part of the evolution of family life. The influence of Protestantism on the individual's sense of responsibility toward God was crucial. This, we have seen, influenced the turn toward private, personal life. The introspection of conduct books and diary writing, the fascination with the imagined lives of the new literary form, the novel, and the focus on the everyday formed the background for changes in families, at least among urbanites of a certain class.

Another change was a new emphasis that marriage should be based on affection. This is not to say that before this time marriages were loveless or without affection, but marriage for romantic love was the exception rather than the norm in all social classes. Issues of property, inheritance, and admission to a guild for tradesmen were all part of the marriage contract. Parents, extended family, and even fellow villagers or townspeople all played a role in mate selection and how family life was conducted. During the 18th century, this changed for many people. The autonomy and individualism that was becoming a more common aspect of life facilitated a change toward marriage being a choice, something one entered into voluntarily and with a person of one's own choosing. Affection and love became more important as the basis for the marriage, rather than the wishes of the family. The role of the parents, relatives, and townspeople became less important as autonomy and individual choice became more important.

The corollary to this was an increased emphasis on privacy. Students today would be shocked if they could see a typical household of the 1500s. There was little or no privacy. Most people lived in small houses, often one to three rooms in size, and many people other than the nuclear family lived there as well. Apprentices, boarders, other people's children, relatives, orphans, and others could all be found in a household. Perhaps it is worth noting the use of the term "household," rather than "home." Home has a more sentimental meaning to us today, but it was common for many people in the past to live in a household, that is, with other, often unrelated, people. In such a household, then, there would have been a great deal of influence from neighbors. Indeed, historians of the family have often noted that court records of earlier periods are filled with charges brought against neighbors for various complaints—ranging from adultery, to spouse abuse, to failure to provide food to strangers—all brought on the basis of what the neighbor observed or heard from one of the occupants of the household.

This began to change by the 1700s, as family life became more private. The household became more like the home of today, with only family members living in it. This meant less intrusion by the neighbors and by relatives. Over time, even the design of houses changed so that rooms had specific purposes—parlors, bedrooms, and so on—that were meant to give family members greater privacy even within the family. Again, the spread of these practices occurred unevenly across Europe and North America over the succeeding centuries. Indeed, some of the earlier forms of family life are still extant.

In this more private family life, secluded from relatives and neighbors, affection and intimacy between spouses and with children became the norm. This required a high level of personal commitment and attention that presupposed individuality and autonomy. The family consisted of individuals who chose to be together and who based their togetherness on mutual affection. This affection was then extended to their children, who became more central to family life. This is not to say that before the 1700s married people did not love each other or their children; rather, such affectional bonds took on new importance in the definition of

family life. The affection and the sentiment that flowed from it came to be seen as crucial to what made life enjoyable and significant. Although this began among the wealthier strata of society, such as entrepreneurs and successful merchants, it soon spread to the middle classes and beyond. Consequently, the family came to be seen as a loving, caring social unit, separate from the rest of the world. It was made up of autonomous, self-regulated individuals who chose to form family bonds and who then socialized their children to be self-regulated individuals.

These changes all played out over time, and their chronology was shaped by place and social class. But they were well under way by the time of the great transformation of work and family life known as the first Industrial Revolution. The impact of industrial capitalism and efforts to manage the self in its wake are our last topics in this chapter.

READING THE SIGNS OF THE BODY IN THE ERA OF INDUSTRIAL CAPITALISM

All of the developments described so far point toward an understanding of how our modern sense of the self emerged. Subjectivity, the sense of an inward private life, and what we now think of as the sensibility of an everyday psychology, grew from a range of practices and changes in social structures. Protestant beliefs and religious practices were instrumental in these changes and had the consequence of creating self-regulating individuals, mindful of their behavior across the range of everyday actions. But other, perhaps unanticipated, consequences occurred as the new emphasis on the mundane prepared the way for the novel, for self-expression through diaries and letters, and for participation in the marketplace. The demands of the latter for looking after one's own interests in a dynamic setting facilitated the development of self-auditing and self-regulation, as the philosopher Smith articulated. As we have seen, family life also began to change in this period, with a new emphasis on intimacy and affection and with attendant demands for privacy for the family and within the family. All these changes were well under way by the mid-1700s, when the first Industrial Revolution in England created the greatest dynamic of change yet known in the modern Western world. In this context of rapid social change, self-regulation of individual behavior became paramount as individuals sought to secure their place and advancement in the intensely competitive world of industrial capitalism. It is not coincidental that out of this era the modern social sciences emerged as the foundation sciences for understanding and managing individuals in complex societies. The first sciences to promise such self- and social management were physiognomy and phrenology.

In this section, we offer a brief outline of the Industrial Revolution, covering what it was and what its consequences were for social order, and then we turn to an account of the sciences of the body, physiognomy and phrenology, that dominated popular culture among the industrial working and middle classes. With their development and popularity came an implicit message of social and individual improvement and reform.

The First Industrial Revolution

The beginnings of industrial capitalism can be traced back to the late Middle Ages and early modern period in places like Venice and Genoa in Italy, Hamburg in Germany, and Amsterdam in the Netherlands. However far back one traces its beginnings, it is clear that England in the mid-18th century became the primary location for the first large-scale, rapid industrialization of society. Once begun, industrialization spread unevenly across Europe, with some countries not really becoming industrialized until the 20th century. So, our focus is on England with the caveat that we cannot easily generalize to other European states.

Over the course of approximately a century and a half, from 1700 to 1860, England changed from being primarily an agricultural and cottage-industry state to the world's first industrialized country. Economic historians have pointed out that this rapid change was possible because of the improvements in agricultural productivity, which, by the beginning of the period, provided an adequate food supply for the population. By this time, as well, a large pool of skilled and professional labor could be drawn upon for the emergent industries. The British Isles were also rich in coal; thus, an energy source was close at hand to literally fuel industrialization. In terms of international relations, England's navy, both military and commercial, made it the dominant country in world trade and provided a critical part of the foundation for the industrializing process by facilitating a supply of raw materials and the export of finished goods.

The British economy experienced unprecedented rates of growth from 1760 to about 1860. In the second quarter of the 19th century alone (1826–1850), income grew more than five times as fast it had in the first half of the 18th century (1701–1750). One scholar predicted that if the rate of income growth from 1826 to 1850 had been maintained, income would have doubled every 28 years (O'Brien & Quinault, 1993). This was remarkable, especially compared to the 120 years required to double income before the Industrial Revolution. Certainly, the citizens of Britain in this period noticed the changes around them and found them remarkable. So did other European countries. By the early 1800s, and particularly after the final English victory over France in 1815, other countries were openly worried about Britain's commercial and military power. For many, the choice was clear: They had to find a way to emulate the events in Britain.

What social changes followed in the wake of rapid industrialization? Again, we want to be careful not to make statements that are too broad. Industrialization of the workforce was uneven across England, Scotland, and Wales. Some places, in fact, have remained the bucolic pastoral backwaters so beloved of viewers of such American television programming as *Masterpiece Theatre*. Where industrialization did occur, changes appeared in nearly every facet of British life, from home to the market, in social relations among and within classes, and in how people understood themselves. People in such commercial and industrial settings began to view themselves as living in an increasingly competitive world. That world was progressively an urban one, as people moved from villages and towns to cities to take advantage of the new factory jobs becoming available. In general, the rate of urbanization increased dramatically with industrialization and has remained a continuing trend ever since in all parts of the world.

With urbanization, the number of cities experiencing rapid growth grew significantly. Before industrialization, about 75 percent of the English population lived in rural areas or villages. By 1850, Britain was the first country in the world where more than half the population lived in urban areas. Not only did London grow in population, but regional industrial centers such as Liverpool, Birmingham, and Manchester became large cities in their own right. Manchester, probably the most important industrial city of the 19th century, numbered more than 350,000 people in 1850. So, by the mid-19th century, millions of Britons—men, women, and children—lived in crowded, often unsanitary, dirty cities and often worked long hours in unsafe conditions. The horrors of such places are well captured in the novels of writers like Charles Dickens (1812–1870), whose fictional Coketown in *Hard Times* (1854) has become the dominant image of the negative social impact of industrialized life in England. Of course, for many people advantages resulted from industrialization. The standard of living, measured in economic terms such as wages and opportunity to buy goods, increased for many people. At the upper end of the economic scale, industrial capitalism increased the wealth of many entrepreneurs and investors. Finally, as noted, the workforce did not all move to large

factories. Quite a few industries continued on a relatively small scale, with many "factories" employing fewer than 20 employees. Still, there were significant losses: Many women who had been employed in weaving as part of England's vast cottage textile industry (work sites were typically in a home, where women gathered to weave cloth) lost their livelihoods.

How is this important for the emergent social sciences, particularly Psychology? In an increasingly urbanized society, where conditions of employment depended on competition among workers and advancement became based on meritocracy rather than family lineage, the need to make sense of one's life and to understand where one stood vis-à-vis other workers became critically important. Two sciences, if we take the word "science" in its meaning at the time as systematic knowledge, came to be employed in this new world: physiognomy and phrenology.

Reading the Signs of the Body

Physiognomy and phrenology shared some characteristics. Both were based on the assumption of a link between the physical body, or some part of it, and internal qualities or abilities. There is a long history of humans across time and across cultures "reading" the physical body as a signpost toward understanding behavior and predicting possible outcomes. Palmistry, numerology, and the practice of examining stools are all ancient practices, employed for thousands of years to understand and predict human behavior. In the Western world, as the power of exact sciences grew to explain ever more natural phenomena, the reliance on these earlier systems declined, at least to some degree, among the formally educated citizenry. However, for those without access to education and formal learning, the body remained a resource for understanding self and others. This was the case in the Industrial Revolution as modes of life changed from rural–small town to urban and from farm labor or small-shop employment to factory life.

Physiognomy

Physiognomy was an ancient system of understanding human character that was revived and popularized in the late 18th century by a Swiss pastor, Johann Caspar Lavater (1741–1801). Briefly, in the hands of Lavater, physiognomy was a system of knowledge about human nature that claimed a direct link between the physical, outward appearance of a person and one's inward nature or character. Lavater insisted that physiognomy was a science because it was based on careful observation (i.e., it was empirical) that made it possible to offer laws of behavior and relationships. While anyone could make such observations, Lavater insisted that only the trained person could fully and accurately describe human character based on physiognomy. His science, Lavater claimed, promised to explicate individual differences and help individuals understand their own nature and feelings, as well as those of others. Thus, it held the promise of facilitating self- and social management. Because its target was the inner life of the person, physiognomy played an important role in forming a psychological sensibility in modern Western society. That is, it was part of the everyday or practical psychology that arose in Western societies in the 18th and 19th centuries and that made the eventual discipline of Psychology possible.

The philosopher Immanuel Kant (1724–1804, see Chapter 3), embraced physiognomy as a part of the kind of psychology he thought possible, even though he argued that psychology could never be an exact science in the manner of mathematics. In fact, Lavater's ideas were taken up as part of the general debate about education in German-speaking states in the first half of the 19th century. This debate was part of the argument for the development of an empirical psychology that would serve the interests of education and was advanced by such educational philosophers as Johann Friedrich Herbart (1776–1841).

Apart from such high-minded applications, physiognomy became extremely popular among nonelites. It gave everyday people a psychological language and rubric with which to understand themselves and their neighbors: their feelings, their similarities, and their differences. Lavater published his physiognomic system in four well-illustrated volumes (1775–1778). These volumes remained in print for over a century and were translated into French, Italian, Dutch and English. Many of these translations went into multiple editions, 20 in English alone. Despite Lavater's insistence that a person needed training to become an expert, people in everyday life could look at the illustrations and believe they saw themselves or their loved ones and neighbors in a light that explained previously hidden characteristics. This, perhaps, helps account for the great popularity of the system and the volumes. Novelists of the time incorporated physiognomy as a shorthand for explaining their characters; the novels of Jane Austen (1775–1817), for example, are full of physiognomic references.

By the beginning of the 19th century, physiognomy was part of the cultural and popular scene, providing an interpretive framework for self-understanding in a dynamic, changing social context. Before long, phrenology had usurped its role and incorporated many of its insights into a new system. In the minds of many people, the two were not differentiated.

Phrenology

The 19th-century phrenologists claimed physiognomy was more akin to folk wisdom than

FIGURE 2.2 Johann Caspar Lavater

science and so argued that their science provided a sounder basis for understanding the relationship between human character or abilities and the human body. What was the basis for **phrenology** as a systematic (scientific) explanation for human behavior or functioning? To understand it, we must review the contributions of Franz Joseph Gall (1758–1828) that we articulated in Chapter 1.

You may recall that Gall argued that human mental abilities are tied to the brain as the organ of the mind and that these abilities are innate. His point at the time, the late 18th and early 19th centuries, was that a Cartesian split between mind and body was unnecessary. Since the brain, Gall argued, is the organ of the mind, then the higher mental functions need not be separated into a category reserved for divine influence. As we noted then, Gall's work was highly controversial, as it challenged long-held notions about the mind and how it could best be understood. Gall was decidedly in the natural law camp, that is, that man's mental functions operated according to lawful processes and that these processes could be discovered through empirical investigation. In the world of physiology and medicine, Gall's theories and descriptions prompted a century's worth of empirical and experimental research that culminated in a general consensus among scientists that the human central nervous system and its actions could be understood by naturalistic means.

However, there was another side to Gall's work: the impact and appeal his ideas had to the general public, who sought practical knowledge about themselves, their abilities, and their bodies. Gall was a master self-promoter who reached out to these people through public lectures and publications in Vienna, Paris, and many of the other cities of Europe. He called his approach the science of **organology**.

The basic tenets of Gall's system were as follows. The brain was composed of many parts, and each of these parts had a distinctive function. The strength of these abilities or functions was reflected in the size of the part of the brain where they were located. Because the skull hardens over the brain in early childhood, the shape of the skull reflects the underlying organization of mental abilities, their strengths, and their weaknesses. Such abilities can be ascertained through empirical examination. Gall originally proposed 27 brain areas or organs covering a range of abilities or propensities, from acquisitiveness to the talent for architecture.

Gall, although eager to make his knowledge available to the public, was not primarily concerned with popularizing his work. He saw it foremost as a scientific system. However, his colleague and assistant Johann Gaspar Spurzheim (1776–1832) saw in the public's response to Gall's organology an opportunity to advance his own career. Gall and Spurzheim parted company in 1813, with Spurzheim developing organology into a more elaborate and practical system that he began to call phrenology. Oddly, however, his first publication on the subject was titled *The Physiognomical System of Drs. Gall and Spurzheim* (1815). Spurzheim went on to become a popular lecturer and writer and was just completing a set of lectures in Boston in 1832 when he died. On one of his lecture tours to Scotland, Spurzheim met a young Edinburgh lawyer named George Combe (1788–1858). Combe, after first being doubtful of the claims of phrenology, was won over and embarked on his own career as an advocate for the new science. Combe wrote several treatises on phrenology, especially in relation to his commitment to education reform. His volume summarizing his views, *The Constitution of Man* (1828), became one of the best sellers in Victorian Britain. Along with his brother, Andrew Combe, he helped make phrenology a social force of considerable significance in the first half of the 19th century in Britain.

A simple recounting of some of the key figures in the early history of psychology does not give an accurate picture of the immense popularity of phrenology. In 1820, George Combe helped found the Phrenological Society of Edinburgh, which three years later began publishing the

FIGURE 2.3 George Combe

Phrenological Journal. Within a short time, phrenological societies had been established in 29 other cities. Most of them published a newspaper or some other form of public communication and held open meetings for their members and the public. Phrenology's successful appeal across the public spectrum was widely remarked upon at the time. To what did it owe its appeal, especially to the working and middle classes?

We noted earlier that industrialization in Britain had brought about new work and social relations. This was especially true in the new factory towns and cities. The mechanization of the workplace created new specific roles where tasks were well defined and performance was closely measured. The **division of labor**, which Smith had made much of as the necessary arrangement to maximize human productivity and so increase wealth, was also hierarchically arranged so that different status levels had attendant differences in pay levels. A person could work up such a system to become a supervisor or manager of others and thus increase status and pay. This made the workplace a site for competition among workers. Thus, a person's ability to perform a role well had important implications for future work roles and advancement. Workers were often pitted against one another in intensely competitive conditions. Phrenology offered an insight into how to use this competition to advantage by suggesting that mental abilities are, like physical ones, divisible. That is, the phrenological system posited a division of mental labor that mirrored the division of physical labor in industry. In the competitive atmosphere of the factory, an understanding of one's own abilities and propensities could help one advance at work. Perhaps more importantly, understanding how to read the signs of the body could help workers assess their competitors and, thus, potentially gain an advantage over them.

Being aware of one's strengths and weaknesses did not mean that they were fixed and unchangeable. This was an aspect of phrenology that helped give it such wide appeal. In the hands of Combe and others, phrenology became part of the reform efforts in British education. Not only could phrenology provide the initial assessment of abilities, but as it was developed a secondary body of knowledge emerged in how to use phrenological readings to provide advice and guidance for self-improvement. This principle was extended from the workplace to the schoolyard.

Phrenologists argued that understanding the division of mentality, couched in the language of distinct abilities or faculties, could also help in the care and education of children. Since abilities were malleable in relation to one another and the environment, it made sense to reform education so as to give greater attention to instruction that would encourage the further development of positive propensities and lessen the impact of those considered negative.

It was these developments that gave phrenology such a broad appeal across several classes of British society, especially those who stood to gain some social or economic advantage from self-understanding and self-improvement. But phrenology's appeal was not limited to the British Isles. It had its adherents across much of Europe. And nowhere did it have as enduring an appeal as in the new country across the Atlantic Ocean, the United States.

Phrenology in the United States

Phrenology came to America for the first time in 1820, with a lecture to the Massachusetts Medical Society by John Collins Warren. It received its critical impetus for growth in America from the first and last visit by Spurzheim to Boston in 1832. Spurzheim's lectures on phrenology were so popular that he felt compelled to repeat them. Unfortunately, he became ill and died suddenly just as he was completing a lecture series in nearby Cambridge, Massachusetts.

Phrenology found fertile soil in America and persisted in its popular appeal for the next century. In its success we can see groundwork for the emergence of a psychology of individual differences and the provision, for a fee, of psychological services. Phrenology in America was of the practical variety. Whatever its theoretical merits or its place in arguments about the material basis of human functioning, in the United States its success was linked directly to its application to problems of daily living and adjustment in a dynamic society. America was (and is) a pragmatic society; Americans were interested in what works, what helps, and what is practical. Phrenology was just such a practical science. Not long after Spurzheim's death in Boston, an enterprising family, the Fowlers, developed a successful business providing phrenological consultations in several major cities of the United States. These fee-based consultations offered an analysis of the person's abilities, strengths, and weaknesses, as well as guidance for self-improvement. For upwardly mobile clients, or for those who desired to be upwardly mobile, this service was part of the American ethos of self-improvement.

As historian of psychology Michael Sokal has shown, the popularity of phrenology in America was to be found outside the main cities in small towns and the countryside. Itinerant phrenologists, some of whom were self-trained, staked out territories that they then toured, offering counseling and guidance to the citizens. The standard mode of operation in these settings was for the phrenologist to offer a series of free or low-cost lectures in a public building. In these lectures, the virtues of the science were touted and many examples of its usefulness given. Once interest had been stirred, the phrenologist would offer private readings, for a fee, to those who could afford it. Sokal has documented the three main domains in which phrenologists offered professional advice: vocational guidance, family or marital counseling, and child rearing. Careful readings of the skull, documented in annotated charts prepared especially for such sessions, formed the basis for the practical advice then offered. If a client was strong in one area and weak in a complementary one, instructions were given as to how to balance the propensities. Marital advice was given based on a couple's complementary and antagonistic faculties. Child-rearing advice often centered on how to encourage the development of the child's natural propensities as indicated by the phrenological reading. It was this kind of practical advice that Americans were seeking and that helped give phrenology such a durable appeal, an appeal that lasted much longer than it did in Britain or other parts of Europe.

Sidebar 2.1 Focus on the *Fowler Brothers*

A pair of enterprising brothers was particularly successful in capitalizing on the popular appeal of phrenology in America. The Fowler brothers, Orson (1809–1887) and Lorenzo (1811–1896), along with their brother-in-law Samuel Wells, opened phrenological clinics in New York, Boston, and Philadelphia in the 1830s. The purpose of the clinics was to give phrenological examinations or readings, often in response to specific requests from clients. For example, parents might want insight into their children's behavior problems, or engaged couples might want to assess their compatibility. Traveling phrenologists also toured the country, announcing their circuit in advance of their arrival and renting space to deliver readings to eager customers.

The Fowler brothers franchised their business by training phrenologists and selling phrenological supplies. These supplies would have included phrenological busts for display and teaching, calipers for taking head measurements, display charts for the offices, and manuals to sell to customers. More than just entrepreneurs, however, the Fowlers were concerned with the professional side of their practice as well. They started the *American Phrenological Journal* in 1838, which remained in existence for more than 70 years. They also founded a group called The Phrenological Cabinet which, in 1866, became the American Institute of Phrenology.

The immense appeal of phrenology, as we have shown, reflected a widespread interest in self-improvement and the cultural authority of a "science" of self-improvement. The public accepted and believed that personality and character could be studied scientifically and objectively and that with appropriate training they could also be modified. The Fowlers and other trained phrenologists provided individualized self-help manuals and eventually published a range of what we would now consider self-help books. Titles included *Phrenology and Physiology Explained and Applied to Education and Self-Improvement, Phrenological Self-Instructor,* and *How to Read Character: A New Illustrated Handbook of Phrenology and Physiognomy,* which was published by Wells in 1879. At one point there were even plans for a phrenological vending machine that would provide character analysis through a self-administered test on a coin-operated machine.

Despite the enormous popular appeal of phrenology and the efforts of the Fowlers to establish its professional legitimacy, it consistently received criticism in terms of its scientific validity. Some historians have argued that the Fowler brothers ignored this criticism and were unconcerned with phrenology's scientific status. But a look at the contents of their journal reveals that many articles specifically attested to the scientific validity of the practice—thus indicating that this was a concern for them. It has been argued that the popularity of phrenological readings declined by the early 20th century not because of its lack of scientific validity—which had always been in question—but because different sets of tools were being developed by different sets of practitioners that came to supplant phrenology. These

(Continued)

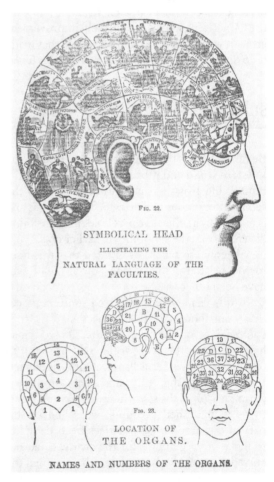

FIGURE 2.4 A phrenological diagram from *How to Read Character: A New Illustrated Handbook of Phrenology and Physiognomy* (New York: Fowler & Wells Co., 1896)

practitioners included applied psychologists who were developing mental tests (see Chapter 6). However, the British Phrenological Society was not disbanded until 1967, and Lorenzo Fowler's daughter Jessie Fowler continued to practice until her death in 1932. One moral of the story is that the popular appeal of psychological practices does not always vary in direct proportion to the extent that they are viewed as scientifically credible.

Phrenology was important in America for the later development of a psychology grounded in individual differences. Its fee-for-service basis helped prepare Americans for a practical and professional Psychology. It appealed, too, because it was a practical science that fit well with the American self-help and self-improvement ethic; it was a science of human nature that made it possible for everyone to help themselves. It was optimistic, which also fit with the American belief that change is always possible. Lastly, but certainly not least importantly, it was not intellectual; one did not need much of an education to understand its results. Thus, it was available to the "common man." One writer has called it the first real psychology of modern life (Bakan, 1966b).

SUMMARY

Beginning from the early modern period in the Western world and proceeding to our own time, remarkable growth occurred in the sense of the self as autonomous and private. This self was and is marked by a subjective psychological sensibility different from the sensibility of earlier eras. It has now become so taken for granted that it is hard for people today to imagine how it could ever have been otherwise.

In this chapter, we indicated some practices that contributed to this subjectivity, or psychologizing, of the interior life. As you may have noticed, this is a topic that is hard to pin down, as the term "subjectivity" indicates. Unlike the writings of philosophers or the experiments of scientists, which have come down to us in published accounts, we relied in this part of our account on practices from daily life to make our arguments for the changes that occurred. Such evidence is more nebulous than the well-reasoned arguments of John Locke or the careful experiments of Hermann von Helmholtz. But the results are just as substantial in their impact on human behavior and relationships. What we can say with confidence is that the sense of personal identity has undergone a remarkable change in Western society over the last 400 years. Every facet of life, from religion to the marketplace, both contributed to this change and, of course, reflected it in an endless feedback loop.

Everyday people, typically without the resources of the elites discussed in the previous chapter, found ways to adapt to their changing worlds. This is not to portray these processes of change as anything less than wrenching; for significant numbers of individuals, they were traumatic, as large-scale change often is. We who live today in the Western world owe our sense of ourselves, as selves, to what has gone before. It is our predecessors' adaptation over the last several centuries that created our current conditions of life and made the discipline of Psychology possible. Without a sense of self, a science of the self could never have emerged.

BIBLIOGRAPHIC ESSAY

The published resources that we used for this chapter were wide ranging. Again, Roger Smith's *Norton History of the Human Sciences* was indispensable as a conceptual guide. Two books on the self were crucial: Charles Taylor's magisterial *Sources of the Self* (1989) and Jerrold Seigel's *The Idea of the Self* (2005). Each of these authors synthesized material from many other authors, as well as contributing their own brilliant interpretations.

Max Weber's classic, *The Protestant Ethic and the Spirit of Capitalism*, written in 1904 and 1905 and published in English in 1930, remains one of the most insightful works on the role of religion in the formation of modernity. *The Rise of the Novel* by Ian Watt (1957) offers a cogent argument about the links between the novel and the social and religious contexts of the 18th century. For this chapter as well, Roy Porter's *The Creation of the Modern World* (2000) was a useful resource for understanding popular culture of the 18th century.

Seigel's chapter on Smith (2005) was insightful and helped us understand Smith's keen psychological insights as he wrote about the marketplace. Thomas Haskell's near-legendary article on capitalism and the humanitarian impulse, "Capitalism and the Origins of the Humanitarian Sensibility" (1985) fostered our understanding of the links between the demands of the market and the need for self-regulation. David Ormrod's *The Rise of Commercial Empires* (2003) made clear the role of international trade and the importance of Britain's naval power to the growth of industrial capitalism. The edited volume *The Industrial Revolution and British Society* (O'Brien and Quinault, 1993) has several insightful chapters about the economic impact of industrialization.

Phillipe Ariès's much-debated and criticized volume, *Centuries of Childhood* (1962), nevertheless proved of great help in understanding changes in family life. But the classic volume that we found indispensable was the work by Lawrence Stone, *The Family, Sex, and Marriage in England, 1500–1800* (1977).

We owe a large debt to the scholarship of others on physiognomy and phrenology. Roger Cooter's *The Cultural Meaning of Popular Science* (1984) has become the standard work on the political meanings of phrenology and is a quite useful reference for other resources. Michael Sokal's "Practical Phrenology as Psychological Counseling in the 19th-Century United States" (2001) was extremely useful, as was David Bakan's earlier article, "The Influence of Phrenology on American Psychology" (1966b). Madeline Stern's *Heads and Headlines* (1971) gives more detail about the enterprising Fowler family and phrenology in the American context. Jan Goldstein's brief but insightful section on phrenology as part of her contribution to the recent *Cambridge History of Science* volume *The Modern Social Sciences* (2003), "Bringing the Psyche into Scientific Focus," helped us put phrenology into perspective as a 19th-century psychology. Likewise, Katherine Arens's *Structures of Knowing* (1989) helped place both phrenology and physiognomy in their respective lights. Lastly, Alan Collins's article "The Enduring Appeal of Physiognomy" (1999) has continued to be a resource for our thinking about psychological understanding among everyday people.

Chapter 3
TIMELINE 1700–1920
(In 25-year increments)

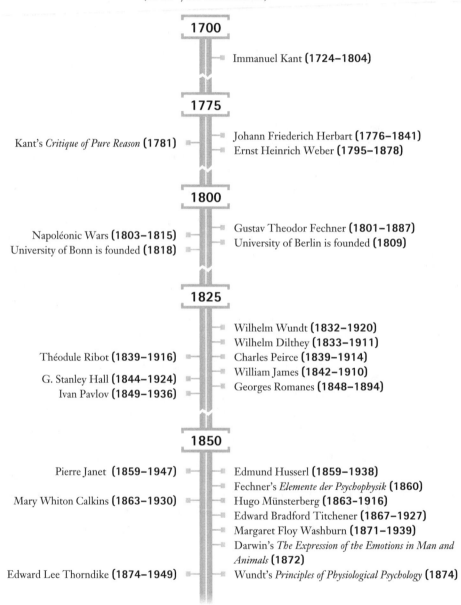

1700

Immanuel Kant **(1724–1804)**

1775

Kant's *Critique of Pure Reason* **(1781)**

Johann Friederich Herbart **(1776–1841)**
Ernst Heinrich Weber **(1795–1878)**

1800

Napoléonic Wars **(1803–1815)**
University of Bonn is founded **(1818)**

Gustav Theodor Fechner **(1801–1887)**
University of Berlin is founded **(1809)**

1825

Théodule Ribot **(1839–1916)**

G. Stanley Hall **(1844–1924)**
Ivan Pavlov **(1849–1936)**

Wilhelm Wundt **(1832–1920)**
Wilhelm Dilthey **(1833–1911)**
Charles Peirce **(1839–1914)**
William James **(1842–1910)**
Georges Romanes **(1848–1894)**

1850

Pierre Janet **(1859–1947)**

Mary Whiton Calkins **(1863–1930)**

Edward Lee Thorndike **(1874–1949)**

Edmund Husserl **(1859–1938)**
Fechner's *Elemente der Psychophysik* **(1860)**
Hugo Münsterberg **(1863–1916)**
Edward Bradford Titchener **(1867–1927)**
Margaret Floy Washburn **(1871–1939)**
Darwin's *The Expression of the Emotions in Man and Animals* **(1872)**
Wundt's *Principles of Physiological Psychology* **(1874)**

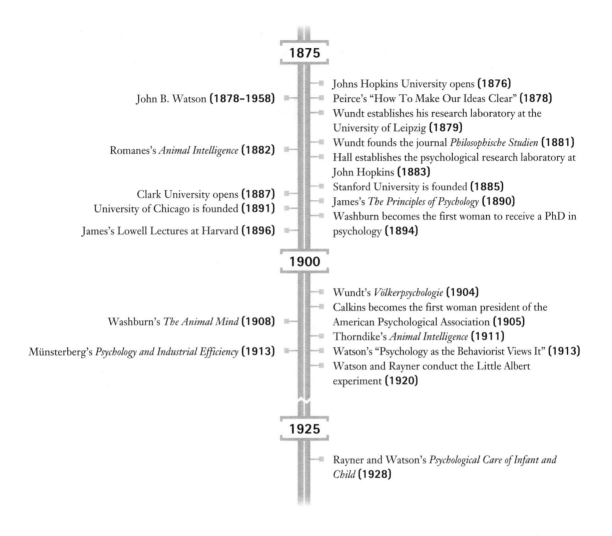

1875

John B. Watson **(1878–1958)**

Romanes's *Animal Intelligence* **(1882)**

Clark University opens **(1887)**
University of Chicago is founded **(1891)**

James's Lowell Lectures at Harvard **(1896)**

Johns Hopkins University opens **(1876)**
Peirce's "How To Make Our Ideas Clear" **(1878)**
Wundt establishes his research laboratory at the
University of Leipzig **(1879)**
Wundt founds the journal *Philosophische Studien* **(1881)**
Hall establishes the psychological research laboratory at
John Hopkins **(1883)**
Stanford University is founded **(1885)**
James's *The Principles of Psychology* **(1890)**
Washburn becomes the first woman to receive a PhD in
psychology **(1894)**

1900

Washburn's *The Animal Mind* **(1908)**

Münsterberg's *Psychology and Industrial Efficiency* **(1913)**

Wundt's *Völkerpsychologie* **(1904)**
Calkins becomes the first woman president of the
American Psychological Association **(1905)**
Thorndike's *Animal Intelligence* **(1911)**
Watson's "Psychology as the Behaviorist Views It" **(1913)**
Watson and Rayner conduct the Little Albert
experiment **(1920)**

1925

Rayner and Watson's *Psychological Care of Infant and
Child* **(1928)**

SUBJECT MATTER, METHODS, AND THE MAKING OF A NEW SCIENCE

Psychology is to be treated as a natural science in this book. This requires a word of commentary.

—William James, *Psychology: Briefer Course,* 1892

INTRODUCTION

Two of Psychology's biggest challenges in the process of becoming an authoritative science in the late 19th century were (1) to delineate and define its subject matter and (2) to develop an appropriate method for the systematic study of this subject matter. For the new psychologists, one solution lay in treating Psychology as a natural science. This meant developing a rigorous method that would establish a clear break with mental philosophy (a topic we cover in the next chapter), despite overlap in the subject matter of interest to both psychologists and philosophers, such as the will, consciousness, habits, and other processes of the mind. A rigorous method would determine whether Psychology could become equivalent in scientific legitimacy to its natural science counterparts such as physics and chemistry. Underlying the search for this method was the very question of whether the study of what was called the mind, the soul, and later, conscious experience and mental processes could ever be conducted scientifically, a question we introduced in Chapter 1. Several major philosophers had argued that this kind of subject matter could *not* be subjected to rigorous scientific analysis. Their arguments were based on specific beliefs about the nature of science and the nature of mind. In the first part of this chapter, we review several of these arguments and the work that subsequently challenged these beliefs. Interestingly, it may have been those who argued *against* the possibility of a scientific psychology who actually hastened its eventual emergence by catalyzing the work that made the new science possible.

We can safely point out, without giving away the end of the story, that by the late 1800s enough researchers believed they had demonstrated that psychological subject matter could be approached scientifically for it to become a science. Germany is often identified as the birthplace of the new science, and indeed, scholars working at German universities in the mid- to late 1800s contributed much of the work that we retrospectively identify as important for the emergence of scientific psychology. We examine some contextual factors that influenced why scientific psychology emerged in such a specific time and place, thus grounding this part of our analysis in the social constructionist view we outlined in the introduction to the text.

Importantly, these new scientists of the mind settled on a method. Experimental introspection, as originally developed in Wilhelm Wundt's psychological laboratory in Leipzig, Germany, emerged as the method of choice in the first 30 or so years of the new Psychology. In the second part of this chapter, we explore the promise and problems of introspection in both German and American contexts and examine the role of this method in the debate over Psychology's identity as a science. Although introspection was the wedge that opened the door for the science of Psychology, introspective methods were not to become lasting features of Psychology's methodological arsenal in the United States.

American psychology's gradual deemphasis of experimental introspection in favor of comparative and observational approaches was tied to several factors, which we explore in the third part of the chapter. This shift was accompanied by a distinct change in the subject matter of psychology away from consciousness and toward observable behavior. This was not a universal phenomenon, and we touch briefly on other traditions that developed in France and Germany, engaging with both the centers and the peripheries of the new Psychology. We then outline the emergence of behaviorism that took American psychology by storm in the 1910s, 1920s, and 1930s. In the backdrop of all of these developments, from the late 1800s on, was a growing emphasis on precise control, measurement, and standardization as the ideals for scientific psychology in the United States. Combined with statistical and individual difference approaches, and embedded in the progressivist values of early 20th-century American culture, we show how Psychology embraced a technoscientific attitude that served both its scientific and its practical aims. This form of Psychology, stressing the function and practical value of psychological knowledge, was exemplified by functionalism, a fully indigenous form of American psychology. We end by discussing some early functionalists and their contributions, and we elaborate more fully on this topic in Chapter 4.

CAN PSYCHOLOGY BE A SCIENCE?

Although we now take the existence of the *science* of Psychology for granted, the possibility of its existence was not always so certain. Psychologist William James alluded to this uncertainty in the quote we chose to begin this chapter, stating that

psychology, as a natural science, "requires a word of commentary" (1892, p. 1). Many scholars in the 18th and 19th centuries, in fact, felt that the subject matter of psychology—the mind, or soul—was impervious to objective, scientific study.

In the first chapter, we discussed how French philosopher and mathematician René Descartes (1596–1650) conceived of the mind (or soul) as qualitatively distinct from the body. To summarize, although the body, like other aspects of the physical world, consisted of matter extended in space, the mind was immaterial. Descartes felt that the key to knowing the mind was rational reflection and that the mind was not amenable to objective investigation. Descartes proposed that the body without the soul would be a mechanical automaton and the mind without the body would be conscious but would contain only innate ideas. The body, through the experience of the senses and the material world, he argued, contributes to the contents of the mind. According to Descartes, these interactions of mind and body occurred in a specific part of the brain, the pineal gland. His position became known as interactive dualism. As we noted in Chapter 1, Descartes's position was influential in resituating human nature as part of the natural rather than the divine order, without succumbing to a completely mechanistic or materialistic model of the mind that would have been a serious break from his religious tradition.

KANT'S CHALLENGE

German philosopher Immanuel Kant (1724–1804) argued that there were serious impediments to a natural science of the mind, but despite this position his ideas actually propelled the emergence of scientific psychology. They did so by challenging subsequent philosophers and scientists to test and refute his contentions

FIGURE 3.1 Immanuel Kant on a German stamp

and by providing a rationale for a new object of study. Kant proposed that there are two separate domains of reality, one inside the human mind and one external to it. The external world consists of objects in a pure state that have an existence independent of human experience. Kant called this the **noumenal world**. He believed that this noumenal world can never be known directly because our experience of it is always and inescapably mediated through the activity of our mind and of our senses. We can perceive it, but our perception is never a pure representation of the essence of the object because we filter it through our own mental and sensory apparatus. When the noumenal world encounters the human mind, it becomes transformed into the inner or **phenomenal world**. Thus, humans never directly experience the pure reality of things in themselves but, rather, experience a series of appearances (phenomena) that are created by an actively perceiving mind as it encounters the noumenal world.

Why would this be an important idea for psychology? The implication of Kant's position is that the mind is active, rather than passive, and that these activities of the mind might become important processes to study. His ideas *suggested* that the role of the mind in structuring our experience could be an important topic to investigate in and of itself. Kant believed that in transforming the noumenal world the mind uses certain rules. For example, the mind always locates phenomena in time and space. Kant called these two dimensions "intuitions." Furthermore, he suggested that the mind has 12 categories according to which it automatically organizes phenomena. Included in these categories is the concept of causality. As humans, we always experience the world as oriented in time and space and as operating according to causal laws. This is not, Kant argued, because the world is fundamentally organized that way, but is instead because the mind is set up to structure its experience of the world in that way.

Kant's legacy for psychology is twofold: Although he made a claim for the importance of the mind's organizing properties, thus creating a role for psychology in terms of studying these properties and the experiences they create, Kant also insisted that mental phenomena, the mind or soul, could not be studied in the same way the natural sciences studied their subject matter. Kant based his reasoning on the fact that it is impossible to have any *a priori* knowledge of the human mind; it is impossible to know the nature of mind or "I" because one has to first experience one's own mind and use this experience as the basis of all knowledge, which is an empirical process. There can thus be no pure, rational knowledge of the soul (rational psychology), and psychology can at best be an empirical science (empirical psychology). However, Kant also argued that psychology could not even be an empirical science because mental phenomena have no physical existence and are therefore not open to observation or experimental manipulation. Any attempt to observe mental phenomena would, in the act of observing them, change the phenomena themselves. This was a critique of introspection that others shared and to which we later return. The impossibility of internal observation was an irresolvable dilemma, in Kant's thinking. Finally, he also argued that mental processes, since they exist only in time but have no spatial dimension, cannot be reduced to mathematics. Mathematics was the hallmark of pure science and the basis for the statement of *a priori* relationships that are required in natural science proper.

Therefore, Kant felt that psychology must always remain a historical, philosophical, and descriptive, rather than truly scientific, discipline. He advocated a form of anthropological investigation based on the external observation of interactions among people as the basis for an empirical psychology. As historian of psychology David Leary has pointed out, "Kant's heritage to psychology was a challenge" (1978, p. 116). Subsequent generations of thinkers would take Kant's prescriptions for natural science, i.e., that it be mathematical and experimental, and his exhortation that psychology could never measure up to these ideals, to show that they could indeed bring mental processes under the control of experiment and formulate mathematical laws to predict psychological phenomena, namely, sensation. Three figures who took up Kant's challenge of making psychology mathematical were Johann Friederich Herbart, a philosopher; Ernst Heinrich Weber, a physiologist; and Gustav Theodor Fechner, a physicist. All were influential in creating **psychophysics**, a branch of study involving the physical measurement and quantification of psychological phenomena.

PSYCHOPHYSICS AND THE POSSIBILITY OF A NEW SCIENCE

Johann Friedrich Herbart (1776–1841) was an admirer of Kant's philosophical system but took

as his task the extension of this system. Specifically, Herbart took seriously Kant's contention that psychology needed to be mathematical to be a true science. Drawing on an idea he had encountered in Kant's writings, he proposed that numbers could be assigned to psychological experiences of different intensities (he called them "presentations"). Furthermore, he argued that these intensities could be distinguished from one another as more intense or less intense and that the degrees of intensity would vary over time. Herbart suggested that for each increase in the intensity of one presentation a corresponding decrease in the intensity of another presentation would ensue, such that one could explain psychological dynamics by means of an equilibrium model consisting of exact mathematical equations. Herbart faced a problem with his mathematical system, however. Although he could arbitrarily assign numbers to presentations of different intensities, he had no way of relating them to an objective standard. As a philosopher, Herbart was dealing in the realm of the abstract rather than in the realm of experience, and his mathematical formulations were thus deemed insufficiently empirical. He also stopped short of proclaiming that psychology could be experimental. Because of the fluidity and constant flux of mental life, he did not see how any part of it could be isolated and stabilized for experimental investigation. Although **atomism**, an approach that involved breaking down subject matter into its smallest elements for study, was beginning to take hold in the physical and life sciences (e.g., by 1860, the atomic theory was generally accepted as a physical reality in chemistry), Herbart stopped short of embracing this model for psychology. Importantly, however, he had shown a *role* for mathematics in the description of psychological phenomena.

The role of mathematics in psychology was refined by the work of physiologist Ernst Heinrich Weber (1795–1878). Weber conducted experiments on his own sense of touch, finding that when he stimulated the tip of his forefinger or his lips with two compass points placed at varying distances from each other he could not reliably distinguish between the two points when they were less than 1/20 of an inch apart. He then tested people's ability to distinguish accurately between weights of similar appearance but different mass. For example, when he asked participants to judge whether a second weight was lighter or heavier than a standard weight, he found that the ability to make an accurate distinction relied on the relative rather than the absolute differences in the weights. That is, heavier standard weights required that the second, compared weight be heavier by a proportion of the original, not by an absolute amount, to make an accurate sensory discrimination. Most notably, these proportions appeared to be constant and reliable and could be calculated for each sensory experience (e.g., the brightness of a light, the loudness of a sound, and the length of a line). Weber calculated the proportions and established what he called the **just-noticeable difference**, or jnd, for each sensory discrimination. For example, the jnd for weight discrimination was always an amount equal to 1/30th of the heavier of the weights being compared.

Weber's work intrigued Gustav Fechner (1801–1887), who was struggling with a way to empirically demonstrate a lawful relationship between the physical and the psychological worlds. Fechner had been trained as a physician but subsequently became self-educated in physics and mathematics by translating textbooks. He made some notable contributions to the former field and then occupied the chair in physics at Leipzig University, stepping down in 1840 due to poor health. From then on, he set about elaborating his philosophy. Fechner was quite interested in life after death and the problem of man's relationship to and place in nature. He conceived of man and nature as a unity but diverged from some of his contemporaries by insisting that all forms of life, from plants to humans, have some form of consciousness. Of central concern to Fechner

FIGURE 3.2   Gustav Theodor Fechner

was the relationship of the physical world (the physic) with the psychological (the psyche). His experimental approach to this problem came to be known as psychophysics.

Although the relationship between the physical and the psychological worlds seems like a large topic, Fechner addressed it by narrowing his focus of investigation to the level of sensation, a psychological experience with a physical referent. The experimental investigation of sensation had been addressed by both physicists and physiologists since the beginning of their disciplines and philosophers had identified sensation as the vehicle through which to examine the mind–body problem, so it was a natural choice for Fechner. Building on his colleague Weber's work on the jnd, Fechner reasoned that if the jnd was a constant fraction for each of the senses, then it could stand as a theoretical unit of measurement representing the subjectively experienced intensity of a stimulus. If one took the smallest or lowest intensity of a stimulus that could be perceived as the zero point on a scale of psychological intensities and then plotted successive jnds as a function of the increase in actual physical intensities needed to produce them, what resulted was a psychophysical curve that showed remarkable regularity across sensory experiences. The function that described the curve was a logarithmic function that could be expressed in a concise mathematical equation, which Fechner called Weber's law, but eventually came to be known as Fechner's law. To generate the experimental data for this work, Fechner actually lifted his arms with a weight in each hand more than 67,000 times. He carefully recorded whether he could tell a difference between the lighter and the heavier weights and then calculated the physical difference that corresponded to the subjectively perceived difference. For his painstaking work, what Fechner discovered was no less than a mathematical law allowing him to both describe and predict the relationship between the physical world and our subjective experience of that world. This proved to Fechner that man and nature are in harmony, part of a unity.

Fechner formulated his law in 1850 but spent 10 years refining it and expanding on its implications. In 1860 he published *Elemente der Psychophysik*, where he put forth his work publicly for the first time. As historian of psychology Gail Hornstein (1988) has pointed out, what was interesting about the reception of Fechner's law, and psychophysical investigations more generally, was that despite serious and persistent theoretical and philosophical arguments about the very possibility of psychophysics, including a heated debate over whether a stimulus and the sensation of a stimulus could ever be meaningfully distinguished, these criticisms did nothing to slow the rate of development of the field and its methods. Furthermore, these theoretical debates have shown up infrequently in historical accounts of the importance of psychophysics and quantification in the making of the new Psychology. Hornstein has pointed out that despite these substantive critiques, psychophysics offered a compelling, reliable, and publicly verifiable demonstration that quantification had a place in psychology, and it offered a clear set of methodological procedures. For a science struggling to gain its autonomy, this latter feature was especially attractive. Thus, despite the theoretical problems with psychophysics, it offered procedures that were inexpensive, provided clear results, could be taught easily to research

assistants, and appeared scientifically respectable. As she noted, "in the face of these practical benefits, the theoretical debates surrounding the meaning of the data could well have appeared to be of little relevance to individual researchers" (Hornstein, 1988, p. 8). This early disjuncture between theory and method, Hornstein argued, laid the foundation for the later view that methods are theoretically neutral tools that carry with them no implications regarding the nature of the subject matter they are used to investigate.

With the rise of psychophysics, combined with other developments recounted in Chapter 1, it was a short step to the establishment of the first psychological laboratory and the formalization of the new science. Before turning to this important event and the work of the figure credited with founding scientific psychology, Wilhelm Wundt, however, let us revisit an idea from the introduction and consider the following question: If context is important in understanding the emergence of psychological knowledge and practice, what contextual factors influenced the origins of the new Psychology? Many of the figures we have talked about—Hermann von Helmholtz, Kant, Herbart, Weber, and Fechner, for example—were all working in a collection of German states that would become the German Empire in 1871 (preceded by the German Confederation). Was there something about the context in which these men worked that facilitated the rise of experimental psychology?

THE GERMAN INTELLECTUAL TRADITION

One answer can be found in the structure of the German university system and the educational philosophy it reflected that became dominant in the 19th century. Until this time, and indeed since the Middle Ages, German universities were organized into four schools or faculties, three of which provided training for professional vocations. These professional faculties were law, theology, and medicine. The fourth faculty was the artistic or philosophical faculty, which, instead of providing training for a profession, served the other three faculties by giving courses that were required background for these vocations. The philosophical–artistic faculty had comparably lower status, and graduates received the title of magister rather than doctorate, which was reserved for lawyers, theologians, and physicians. This system was changed in the early 19th century as a result of rather extensive Prussian educational reforms. Schools and universities previously influenced by the church were instead run by the state, and the monarchy took an active interest in supporting scholarship and the university system. In 1809, King Frederick William III helped found the University of Berlin. In 1818 he also founded the University of Bonn. In a country politically beleaguered by the war with Napoleon of France (1803–1815), education and educational reform were seen as paths to national recovery.

The new system was modern, secular, and a clear break from the medieval university. Instead of law, theology, and medicine, the new universities emphasized the pursuit of higher learning rather than training for professional or civil service careers. As a result, the previously low-status Philosophical faculty took on new importance. The latest discoveries and theories in geography, politics, mathematics, and the natural sciences were also accorded new importance. The middle class used higher education and scholarship to attain improved social positions, and education was accessible to all who passed their secondary school examinations. Although modern and secular, the universities took as their goal the creation of true scholars. As one writer put it, "the most unusual figure on the European social scene during the 18th century was the German scholar, the man of pure learning" (Ringer, 1969, p. 8). German professors commanded great respect in society.

Two characteristics of German universities in this period, beginning in the early 18th century, contributed significantly to the creation of men of pure learning: **Lehrfreiheit**, the freedom to teach, and **Lernfreiheit**, the freedom to learn. The principle of freedom to teach meant that German professors were free to lecture on any topics they chose, to present them in any way they chose, and to express any views about them, without any interference or direction from university officials or others. This intellectual freedom and independence of thought was a highly prized feature not only of the universities but also of German national life. Professors often met with small groups of students in seminars instead of lecturing didactically, and these interactions with one's professors were highly valued. Students took a comprehensive examination at the end of their university career, rather than tests at the end of each semester. The emphasis, therefore, was not on details of lectures but on synthesis, analysis, and breadth of knowledge.

Students, for their part, were allowed to choose their course of study, including what they learned, how often they attended classes, and with whom they studied. Students could move freely among universities to gain access to a range of educational opportunities, especially to learn from the best professors in their fields of interest. Freedom of learning, combined with the prizing of the pure scholar, encouraged most students to study a range of subjects and to sample freely across disciplines. Many psychologists benefited from this freedom. For instance, Wundt studied physiology at the University of Tübingen, then studied medicine at Heidelberg (where he was also Helmholtz's research assistant), and took time out to study with Johannes Müller (1801–1858) at the University of Berlin.

It is relatively easy to imagine how this kind of educational system could give rise to numerous significant scholars, as was the case in 18th- and 19th-century Germany. However, the question remains as to why so many of these scholars contributed to the rise of the new Psychology. In addition to Lehrfreiheit and Lernfreiheit, the

German concept of **Wissenschaft** contributed to this development. For Germans, science was not determined by its subject matter. It was a way of looking at things, or Wissenschaften. Thus, any topic could be treated scientifically or approached in a scientific manner. In contrast, science in Britain and France was largely equated with physics and chemistry. In the broad and encompassing German view, all manner of topics could be investigated with a scientific attitude, including the human mind. Note that the notion of Wissenschaft is conceptually distinct from the debates over whether the study of the mind or soul could become an exact science using mathematics and experimentation. Relevant here is the distinction between *Naturwissenschaften* (loosely translated as "natural sciences") and *Geisteswissenschaften* (loosely translated as "human sciences") that has more to do with what *kind* of science can be conducted on what *kind* of subject matter. This distinction did become important somewhat later in Wundt's work, and we return to it shortly.

Thus, the new science of Psychology that arose in Germany at the end of the 19th century can be seen as a product of this unique milieu or, in part, socially constructed. Woven from the multidisciplinary strands of physiology, medicine, physics, mathematics, and philosophy and bound with a broad scientific sensibility that facilitated the systematic investigation of a range of phenomena, German experimental psychology can be seen as a product of the Lehrfreiheit, Lernfreiheit, and Wissenschaft traditions.

At least one other contextual feature distinguished the professionalization of experimental psychology in Germany from its soon-to-be-developed American counterpart. By the end of the 19th century, the German university system was characterized by a highly respected philosophical tradition and emphasized independent research. Because of this, experimental psychologists had little reason to break away from the highly regarded philosophy, and they felt they could flourish under its expansive umbrella. By 1910, although the study of psychology was expanding, there were still only four academic positions in psychology, independent of philosophy, in the whole university system.

In the United States, however, the concept of a research university that was nonsectarian was relatively new, and the university system was expanding as population growth increased. Johns Hopkins University in Baltimore, Maryland, which opened in 1876, was among the first of these new research universities. Initially, it was devoted solely to graduate education. Soon after its founding, Stanford University, Clark University, and the University of Chicago were established. Colleges with strong undergraduate curricula, some of which had previously used "university" in their title, such as Harvard, Princeton, and Yale, established programs of graduate education and research. The rhetoric of the new universities was decidedly scientistic to distinguish them from the religious colleges whose mission was to teach students moral philosophy, religious devotion, and discipline. Research, especially scientific research, would be the hallmark of this new education and necessitated a distancing from the religious and philosophical traditions of yesteryear. Thus, the new Psychology in the United States developed in tandem with these changes in the expanding university system and quickly set as its task the incorporation of scientific ideals and a divorce from philosophy and religion, both institutionally and intellectually.

WILHELM WUNDT AND THE NEW PSYCHOLOGY

Born near Mannheim, Germany, Wilhelm Wundt (1832–1920) was a product of the open German intellectual tradition we just discussed. Wundt's grandfather had been a professor of history at the University of Heidelberg, and two

FIGURE 3.3 Wilhelm Wundt

of Wundt's uncles were physicians and professors of physiology. Although a relatively undistinguished secondary school student, Wundt eventually hit his academic stride at the University of Tübingen, where he studied medicine and conducted experimental research.

Wundt soon discovered that he preferred research and publishing to clinical work, and after receiving his degree in medicine at Tübingen, he became accredited by the University of Heidelberg as a lecturer. Soon thereafter, Helmholtz (1821–1894) was recruited to come to Heidelberg and set up an Institute of Physiology. Wundt became his research assistant and proceeded, independently, to conduct studies of vision and the perception of space, although these topics were of interest to both men. During his tenure as Helmholtz's assistant, Wundt also conducted a study that built on his knowledge of his supervisor's work on the speed of the nervous impulse but extended it to a process of the central, rather than peripheral, nervous system. For this study, Wundt built an apparatus he called the thought meter.

The purpose of the thought meter was to test the assumption that when we are exposed to two different sensory stimuli at the same time—in the case of the thought meter, seeing a pendulum pass a specified point on its trajectory and hearing a bell chime at the same instant—we are consciously aware of them at the same time. Wundt built an apparatus that delivered these two events simultaneously and then attempted to report the exact point of the pendulum swing at precisely the instant he heard the bell chime.

When he attempted to do this, he found that in his judgments he reliably placed the pendulum at a point just beyond the point it actually was when the bell rang, even though he felt he was experiencing them simultaneously. He interpreted this lag (usually between 1/8th and 1/10th of a second) as the time it took to experience each sensation in consciousness, even though they had occurred at the same time.

Wundt quickly realized that his measurement of an act of conscious experience placed him in the tradition of Fechner and Helmholtz and again challenged the Kantian assumption that the mind could not be subjected to quantification and experimentation. Recognizing that by now a small tradition of similar work had arisen, Wundt wrote a text called *Principles of Physiological Psychology*, published in 1874. In this book, he set forth a new domain of science that would bring together physiology and psychology, combining the methods of experimental physiology with psychological introspection to study the processes of sensation and voluntary movement. Wundt thus proposed and outlined a new field he called experimental psychology. In 1879, he also established a research laboratory at his new home university, the University of Leipzig, where Fechner and Weber were still working. Students could come to the laboratory to be trained in the new science, and many did. Two years later, Leipzig designated Wundt's laboratory and program the Institut für Experimentelle Psychologie, and increased his research space. The method of study developed by Wundt, and used in his laboratory, came to be known as **experimental introspection**.

Experimental introspection was distinguished from existing forms of philosophical, or armchair, introspection by the introduction of laboratory apparatus that would standardize and mechanize presentations of stimuli upon which subjects would report. Wundt saw the drawbacks to the form of introspection that involved instructing subjects to perform fairly complex cognitive tasks, such as adding a column of numbers, and then asking them to produce an introspective report outlining exactly what went through their mind in the process of adding. Wundt felt that this kind of self-observation was not useful in a scientific psychology because it conflated the act of perceiving with the act of observing by demanding the simultaneous perception, observation, and reporting of internal events. Wundt's solution was to manipulate the conditions of internal perception so that they approximated the conditions of external perception as closely as possible through the use of experimental apparatus and by limiting introspection to the study of basic mental processes. For example, in the case of the thought-meter experiment, repeated experimental presentations of the pendulum and the chime could easily be generated so that subjects could make repeated observations of their own perceptions almost automatically, with limited need for a memory of the event and a short interval between the experimental presentation and the report. The goal was to enable subjects to be as passive, automatic, and accurate reporters of their own internal perceptions as possible—literally, to separate the subject from the object. Wundt called this method "experimental introspection."

As historian of psychology Deborah Coon has remarked (1993), Wundt intended experimental introspection to be analogous to the observation of the natural sciences. The introduction of experimental apparatus that could provide automatic, repeated, and standardized presentations of stimuli was fully in line not only with these scientific ideals but with technological ones as well. As Germany and the United States experienced the rapid and large-scale changes wrought by industrialization, including an emphasis on standardization and mechanization, a technoscientific ideal of science itself arose and affected the new Psychology.

Wundt was also an important professionalizer of the new field of experimental psychology. He not only set up a laboratory and wrote a textbook but also published a journal, *Philosophische Studien*, or *Philosophical Studies*, which was devoted to the new science. Wundt attracted numerous students, among them several Americans who were drawn to the new science and the freedom to learn offered by the German university system. James, an important figure for the founding of Psychology in the United States, came to Germany in 1867, some years before Wundt established his laboratory and became widely known. A medical student recovering from physical and mental strain by convalescing in Europe, James heard that Helmholtz and Wundt were conducting experiments on the physiology of the senses and thought he might learn something from them. Although he was not able to meet with them in person, he read their work and was considerably influenced by it. Later, G. Stanley Hall (1844–1924), one of James's students, was one of the first Americans to study in Wundt's laboratory. Hall returned to the United States to establish the first formal laboratory for psychological research at Johns Hopkins in 1883.

Students in Wundt's laboratory typically undertook investigations in one of three areas: psychophysics, studies of the time sense, and mental chronometry. Reaction-time studies were common, and elaborate devices were invented to measure and record reaction times and present standardized stimuli. Another American student, James McKeen Cattell (1860–1944), was particularly taken with the reaction-time experiment. He conducted his PhD studies in Germany and was then invited to take a position at Cambridge University in England, largely on the strength of his firsthand experience of the Leipzig laboratory. Although he only stayed for a couple of years before returning to the United States, he did set up a small laboratory there. After his return to America, Cattell devised a series of mental tests, including measures of reaction time that could be used to generate data about the distribution of individual differences. These tests bore the mark of both his Leipzig and his Cambridge experiences (see Chapter 6).

Thus, Wundt was clearly a key figure in establishing the science of psychology and its institutional presence. An important caveat to this characterization is necessary, however. According to Wundt, experimental introspection was useful for the study of basic mental processes such as sensation and perception but could tell us little about complex processes such as thought and language. Thus, although Wundt has rightfully been called the founder of experimental psychology, he also saw the limits of experimentation and placed a large and important segment of psychology firmly in the Geisteswissenschaften (human science or cultural science) rather than Naturwissenschaften (natural science) tradition. In his massive multivolume *Völkerpsychologie* published in 1904, he expounded on this part of his psychology, in which he discussed language, myth, custom, and social behavior and the historical and comparative methods that are needed to study them.

Clearly, Wundt's legacy is complex. To reiterate, although Wundt is considered by many to be the founder of scientific Psychology, he nonetheless felt that a large and important part of psychology could not be studied with methods of natural science. In addition, far from being hegemonic in its own time, Wundt's experimental psychology occupied one place at a large table of alternative systems, many of which, if even mentioned, have been relegated to the periphery of historical accounts. Other German scholars formulated their own versions of psychological study that were viable institutional and intellectual alternatives to Wundt's system. For example, in the 1870s, Rudolph Hermann Lotze (1817–1881), Franz Brentano (1838–1917), Carl Stumpf (1848–1936), and others developed systematic psychologies that presented different views on the subject matter and methods of psychology. Perhaps most significant was the human scientific critique of experimental psychology formulated by Wilhelm Dilthey (1833–1911). Dilthey's human scientific psychology took as its subject matter experience in its totality. Appropriate methods included description and analysis, with the goal of understanding. For Dilthey, the mind was the medium through which meaning

FIGURE 3.4 Wilhelm Dilthey

was formed; thus, the content, rather than the structure, of the mind was of most interest to him.

Despite the appearance of linear progress toward the crowning achievement of a fully scientized study of the mind, buttressed by all the appropriate trappings of professionalization, the story of Psychology's inception was far from that simple. Just a few decades after Wundt's achievements, considerable controversy arose in Germany over the status of experimental psychology. For example, in 1912, Edmund Husserl (1859–1938), a phenomenological philosopher, launched an organized attack against experimental psychology. He and more than 100 of his colleagues signed a petition to block the hiring of any experimental psychologists. Although unsuccessful, events such as these challenge the notion of a unified and universally accepted German discipline of Psychology.

PSYCHOLOGY IN BRITAIN AND FRANCE

Although Germany was a central site for the formation of the new Psychology, developments were also unfolding in nearby France and Britain. Developments in each of these countries were complex amalgams of imported ideas and local philosophical, intellectual, and institutional traditions. In France, Théodule Ribot (1839–1916) is traditionally named as the founder of scientific Psychology. To distance himself from the dominant position of Auguste Comte, the prominent French philosopher who argued that psychology could never be a positive science, he drew on English philosophies of evolutionism and **associationism**. The latter posited that the complex contents of consciousness were built from elementary sensations through several laws of association, such as contiguity, contrast, and cause and effect. Ribot also incorporated the idea, found in the work of renowned French physiologist Claude Bernard, that normal and pathological states or experiences fall along a continuum. For Ribot, then, the normal human mind could be understood by investigating malfunction. He thus formulated the pathological method, a method that was to influence the course of the new Psychology in France. One of Ribot's students, Pierre Janet (1859–1947), would become a prime exemplar of this approach. We discussed the French clinical tradition and the Paris model briefly in the introduction, and return to it in more depth in Chapter 5.

In England, one of the major developments that would affect not only the course of British psychology but also the course of psychology in the United States was Francis Galton's (1822–1911) work on statistical research practices. Unlike the German or French traditions, which focused on understanding the processes of the individual human mind (normal or abnormal), the Galtonian approach focused on the distribution of psychological characteristics in large numbers of individuals in a population. Combined with hereditarian theories of the origins of both physical and mental characteristics, and the influence of Darwinian evolutionary theory, Galton used this information to promote a eugenicist program to ensure the continued status of an educated elite (of which he was a member) in the face of a democratizing society. Galton's brand of eugenics, termed **positive eugenics** because it encourages the interbreeding

of eminent individuals to improve the quality of the genetic stock, can be contrasted with **negative eugenics**, which some psychologists also advocated. Negative eugenics involves restricting the ability of so-called unfit individuals to procreate, often through sex segregation or enforced sterilization. We return to Galton and his important, although controversial, role in psychology in Chapter 6.

THE NEW PSYCHOLOGY IN AMERICA

If, in the traditional account, the new Psychology can be said to have arisen in Germany in the late 1800s, it can also be said that despite its European origins it proliferated most rapidly in another context entirely: the relatively young and rapidly industrializing United States of America. One of the key figures in the development of scientific psychology in America was William James. Like Wundt, James was an important professionalizer of the new Psychology. After his visit to Heidelberg, he returned to the United States in 1868 and was offered a lectureship in physiology at Harvard. He set up a collection of experimental apparatus in a room at the university as early as 1875, although it was too informal to be called a laboratory. He taught the first American university courses in the new scientific Psychology, and he wrote an influential text, *The Principles of Psychology*, that was published in 1890 after 12 years of work. But like his German counterpart Wundt, James had some distinct reservations about the scientific standing of psychology and struggled to find a method that would both be rigorous and produce meaningful data about mental life.

William James and a Science of Psychology

William James (1842–1910) had an eclectic education. Born the eldest of five children into

FIGURE 3.5 William James

an affluent and cosmopolitan family, James spent much of his young life traveling and he received his education from private tutors and private schools from one continent to another. His home life was intellectually stimulating, and his younger brother, Henry James Jr., became a famous novelist. William James was artistically inclined, but family pressure to take up a more respectable vocation led him to the study of chemistry at Harvard. He soon switched to physiology but then took up medicine when a change in the family fortune indicated that he might need to earn a living.

Soon after his switch to medicine, he began to experience physical health problems that, some have suggested, had psychological roots. James convinced his father that a trip to Germany would help with both his physical and his emotional recovery. As we mentioned, while there he read about the interesting work in experimental physiology by Helmholtz and others and became intrigued with the notion of **mechanism**, the position that all natural phenomena can be explained in terms of the causal interactions among material particles, without any reference to an external, supernatural force or agency. He was also exposed to some of the work of the young Wundt and vowed to learn more about the possibility of a scientific psychology that could connect physical changes in the nervous system with the experience of consciousness.

One aspect of the mechanistic philosophy and its application to psychology that he encountered

in Germany particularly troubled James, however. Specifically, James saw that mechanism held within it a deterministic element. If conscious experience were to be studied mechanistically, did that mean that there was no room for free will in the description and explanation of mental life? James was disposed to believe in free will because it accorded with his religious and spiritual beliefs, but he felt that free will was fundamentally incompatible with the methods and aims of a science of psychology. If there were no natural laws, regularities, or environmental determinants of mental life, why apply science to studying it?

Eventually, James resolved this personal and philosophical dilemma by adopting a belief in free will for his private life while adopting a deterministic model for scientific psychology. Each belief, he reasoned, would be functional in its own domain. This was a pragmatic decision, and it invoked the function the belief would serve in each area. In his personal life, believing in free will was consistent with his personal values. In his professional life, a belief in determinism allowed him to develop his ideas about a science of psychology.

The Principles of Psychology

In his work *The Principles of Psychology*, written between 1878 and 1890, James grappled further with the status of Psychology as a natural science. In a chapter called "The Methods and Snares of Psychology," James laid out what he saw as the subject matter and methods of Psychology, conceived as a natural science. In terms of subject matter, James described psychology as the "science of mental life," consisting of the description and explanation of states of consciousness, including sensations, desires, emotions, cognitions, reasonings, decisions, and volitions. He stated that the object of scientific enquiry in Psychology was to be "the mind of distinct individuals inhabiting definite portions of a real space and a real time" (James, 1890, p. 183) to distinguish it from metaphysics. Scientific psychology involved the study of conscious processes and mental activity, conceptualized as objects in a world of other objects. Therefore, James concluded, psychology should leave the metaphysical question of how we can report on the mind to the philosophers and take it as a given that we have the ability to study conscious processes objectively.

To put Psychology on the same footing as other sciences and to distinguish it from philosophy, James pointed out that all natural sciences assume a world of matter that exists independently of the human mind. Chemists and botanists, he argued, do not trouble themselves with how the mind comes to know what it knows or whether anything exists beyond what we actually experience. And so, James concluded, neither should psychologists. To acknowledge this as an important difference between psychology and philosophy, he argued, was to take a significant step toward establishing Psychology as an independent discipline and closer to the status of a natural science like chemistry or botany.

In terms of method, James privileged introspection but differed considerably from Wundt on the nature of introspection and the procedures to be followed. In fact, James outlined three methods for Psychology: introspection, experimentation, and comparison. James defined introspection, quite differently from Wundt, as "the looking into our own minds and reporting what we there discover" (James, 1890, p. 185). What we will discover, he asserted, are states of consciousness. James regarded this fact, that we all have states of consciousness and can observe them, as the most fundamental of all postulates of psychology.

James equated experimentation with the experimental introspection that was being conducted in Germany and was highly skeptical of what he sarcastically termed the "prism, pendulum, and chronograph-philosophers" of the Wundtian tradition (James, 1890, p. 193). James critiqued the forms of experimental introspection that were being developed in Germany partly because he objected to what he perceived as a

kind of dissection and reduction of mental life to discrete and meaningless units such as reaction times and jnds. By contrast, James theorized that consciousness and thinking had a stream-like, dynamic quality that could not be captured by an atomistic, reductionistic approach. Thus, the form of introspection that he advocated was closer to the tradition of philosophical introspection against which Wundt had developed his experimental methods, even though James was still arguing for a form of scientific psychology. Due to the broad conception of German science as Wissenschaft, Wundt could deal with the limitations of experimental introspection by confining this method to the study of sensation and perception while arguing that the rest of psychology could be approached in the human scientific tradition of Geisteswissenschaften. James, without this broad conception of science, clung to an older form of introspection so as to preserve what he saw as the complex, holistic, and dynamic nature of psychology's subject matter. It was, however, hard to have things both ways, and James, as we show later, eventually retreated from psychology and turned to his interests in philosophy and spiritualism.

But before he withdrew from psychology, James formulated a position on the goal or objective of the new science that came to be quite influential. It was a position known as **functionalism**. According to James, the point of a scientific psychology was to uncover the functions of the mind, not its contents or its structure. This reflected an orientation that was prevalent in American society at the end of the 19th century and influenced by Darwinian evolutionary theory—the position that understanding should be based on an analysis of function rather than structure and that to know what something does is to understand what it is. Just as Charles Darwin (1809–1882) had emphasized that the evolution of physical characteristics could be understood by looking at the functions they served in giving the organism reproductive advantages, in psychology functionalism was used to understand how the mind and its contents had evolved by looking at the functions of different thoughts and beliefs, functions that were objectively observable in terms of actions.

As early as 1871 James had been influenced by a philosophy proposed by another Harvard-educated Bostonian, Charles Peirce (1839–1914), with whom he interacted in a gathering called the "Metaphysical Club." Peirce's philosophy, called **pragmatism**, was the position that scientific ideas and knowledge can never be certain and therefore should be judged according to the work they do in the world, or according to their degree of practical effectiveness. Under the influence of the theory of evolution by natural selection, pragmatists proposed that beliefs, too, were acted upon by a process of natural selection, with the most adaptive beliefs persisting and the least adaptive beliefs fading away. While Peirce was refining these ideas to publish a paper called "How To Make Our Ideas Clear" in 1878, James was working on his own version of pragmatism. This position meshed nicely with James's aforementioned personal convictions, and he expanded on the philosophical implications of this approach, applying it to religious, ethical, and emotional, as well as scientific, ideas.

During the years following James's publication of *The Principles of Psychology*, he devoted most of his time to philosophy, concluding that psychology was a "nasty little subject. . . . All one cares to know lies outside"(James, 1920, p. 2). Frustrated by the limitations and uncertainties of the subject he had so carefully laid out, he turned to philosophy and spiritualism for his intellectual sustenance. He was a founder and active member of the American Society for Psychical Research and contributed regularly to its publications. His interest in psychical phenomena seemed to peak in the late 1890s during his involvement with the prominent Boston medium Leonora Piper, whom Hall, along with his colleague and former student, was trying to scientifically discredit. In fall 1896, James conducted a series of lectures at Harvard called the Lowell Lectures on Exceptional Mental States. In these lectures, he presented eight topics, many of which are familiar to

students today: dreams and hypnotism, automatism, hysteria, multiple personality, demoniacal possession, witchcraft, degeneration, and genius. Fourteen years later, in 1910, James died in Cambridge. His *New York Times* obituary summed up the eclecticism of his accomplishments and interests: "William James Dies; Great Psychologist, brother of novelist, and foremost American philosopher was 68 years old. Long Harvard professor, virtual founder of modern American psychology, and exponent of pragmatism, dabbled in spooks" (*New York Times*, August 27, 1910, p. 7).

THE DEMISE OF INTROSPECTION IN AMERICAN PSYCHOLOGY

Up to this point, we have been considering how psychology achieved scientific and institutional status at the end of the 19th century. We surveyed the contexts in which this process occurred, but we foregrounded work in philosophy, physiology, and psychophysics in Germany, which is often regarded as the birthplace of the discipline. As we mentioned earlier, many American students went to Germany to study the new Psychology. However, even those Americans who felt that they were importing Wundt's methods often gave them their own idiosyncratic twist. Edward Bradford Titchener (1867–1927), for example, is often credited with bringing Wundt's psychology and methods to the United States, but Titchener distorted Wundtian introspection and ignored the half of Wundt's scientific psychology that belonged to Völkerpsychologie, often extending introspection to processes that Wundt felt were outside the realm of this kind of investigation.

Historian of psychology Michael Sokal (2006), reflecting on the rapidly divergent character of American psychology despite the preponderance of American students who made the trek to Germany, concluded that the Americans did so less to learn about psychological ideas and more to acquire the prestige of a European degree, to gain professional credentials, and to receive practical instruction in the use of instruments. They returned to a country in the throes of what historians have termed the Progressive Era, demarcated roughly as the period between 1890 and 1920. In the face of rapid industrialization, urbanization, increasing specialization in the professions, and expansion of higher education, Americans were looking for solutions to many practical and social problems and saw science and technology as the means to achieve and enact these solutions. We have already seen, in an earlier period, how quickly and powerfully phrenology took hold in the United States as a scientifically derived system of self-improvement. Scientific psychologists were working within the same ethos that prized practical knowledge. The psychology that they encountered in Germany had to be adapted to this context to earn its place not only at the academic table but also in the eyes of the public.

We have seen how James, in his adherence to pragmatism and belief in the functional objectives of scientific psychology, had already begun to shape the character of the new science in the United States. Fairly rapidly, however, even the psychology that James envisioned underwent some rather dramatic changes to bring it more in line with the technoscientific ideal we have just described. In this section we trace several developments that contributed to the rise of behaviorism in the early 1910s.

From the time of the publication of James's *The Principles of Psychology* in 1890 to the appearance of John B. Watson's behaviorist manifesto, *Psychology as the Behaviorist Views It* in 1913—a span of less than 25 years, the new Psychology underwent a profound reconceptualization that brought it more fully in line with the progressivist values of social order, control, and management. Significant components of this reconceptualization were the rejection of introspection and the study of consciousness by many psychologists and the introduction of a new kind of subject matter for Psychology: behavior. To understand how this

transition occurred, we need to look at several developments.

Thorndike, the Animal Mind, and Animal Behavior

In the first chapter we introduced the idea that Darwinian evolutionary theory paved the way for psychologists to study the animal mind, not only for clues to human functioning but also for its own sake. In 1872, Darwin published what could arguably be considered the first work of modern comparative psychology, *The Expression of the Emotions in Man and Animals*.

Darwin had a friend and colleague named George Romanes (1848–1894) who carried on this work and published a book in 1882 called *Animal Intelligence*. Romanes, like many other animal psychologists of his time, used the **anecdotal method**, combined with the method of inference, to study his subjects. That is, he would collect descriptions or vignettes of animal behavior from many sources and then sort through them to come up with reliable inferences about the functioning of the animal mind. Although this work does not appear scientific by today's standards, it marked a slight divergence from introspectionist approaches. Only animal *behavior* was observable, even though Romanes then extrapolated to the realm of the mind. In 1908, Margaret Floy Washburn (1871–1939), the first woman to be awarded a PhD in psychology at Cornell University (although she was not the first woman to *earn* a PhD, see Chapter 1), wrote an influential textbook, *The Animal Mind: A Text-book of Comparative Psychology*, which mainly covered sensory function and learning. It was to be the standard textbook in the field for 25 years.

By the early 1900s, the anecdotal method began to evoke derision among more experimentally minded American psychologists. One of the first comparative psychologists who turned from the anecdotal to the experimental method was Edward Lee Thorndike (1874–1949). As an undergraduate student, Thorndike read James's

FIGURE 3.6   Margaret Floy Washburn
Courtesy of the Archives of the History of American Psychology, University of Akron, Akron, OH.

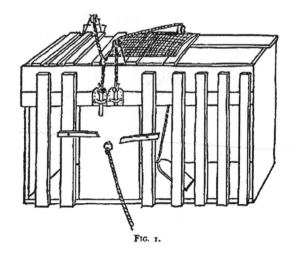

Fig. 1.

FIGURE 3.7   A typical Thorndike puzzle box

The Principles of Psychology. In 1896, when he went to Harvard for graduate study, he signed up for courses with James and eventually majored in psychology. Thorndike took up the study of learning in animals, even though Harvard had no tradition of animal psychology, and he quickly ran into the problem of where to house the chicks he was using for his research. Eventually, James came to the rescue and let Thorndike set up his chick experiments in the basement of his own house. Thorndike's research focused on instinctive reactions on the pecking behavior of chicks. Before he could complete his dissertation, due to dwindling institutional and intellectual support at Harvard, Thorndike moved to Columbia University to study with Cattell. Here he finished his dissertation study and published it in 1898 in a work called

"Animal Intelligence: An Experimental Study of the Associative Processes in Animals." Results from these famous puzzle-box experiments with cats, dogs, and chicks led Thorndike to conclude that animals learn solely by trial and error and by reward and punishment. When an animal is placed in an enclosed box, it displays various random behaviors. If an animal accidentally makes a response that opens a door so that it can escape and receive food, the next time the animal is in the box, it takes less time to emit this same response. Finally, the animal makes the response immediately upon being placed in the box. From these observations, Thorndike concluded that animals do not learn by observation, imitation, or reasoning but purely by association. Furthermore, the animal was not associating the idea or mental image of being in the box with the idea or mental image of the escape response; rather, what was being associated was a stimulus (being in a certain position in the box) and a response (pushing the pedal). In 1911, in his book *Animal Intelligence*, Thorndike forcefully suggested that we study animal behavior, not consciousness, and that this method be extended to humans.

Thorndike's work was criticized by other comparative psychologists who were fans of the anecdotal method and who felt that the laboratory method placed such overwhelmingly artificial constraints on an animal's behavior that no conclusions could be reached about its actual behavior in natural settings. Wesley Mills (1847–1915), the founder of the Association for the Study of Comparative Psychology, wrote that Thorndike "placed cats in boxes only 20 × 15 × 12 inches and then expected them to act naturally. As well enclose a living man in a coffin, lower him, against his will, into the earth, and attempt to deduce normal psychology from his behavior" (Mills, 1899, p. 266). Nonetheless, the laboratory method took hold, as did the focus on behavior rather than the animal mind that had characterized earlier work.

Pavlov, Animal Learning, and the Environment

The work of Russian physiologist Ivan Pavlov (1849–1936) was influential in dismantling introspection in the American context partly because of its thoroughly objective, mechanistic, and materialistic orientation. Pavlov was influenced by the founder of modern Russian physiology, Ivan Sechenov (1829–1905). Sechenov had studied with Helmholtz and believed that psychology could only become scientific if it were to embrace the objective methods of physiology and ignore consciousness. Pavlov also embraced objective methods and avoided references to the mind. Through his work on the classical conditioning of reflexes in dogs, Pavlov demonstrated how the environment, or external stimuli, could come to control behavior, and he rejected "mind" as the cause of behavior. He was able to show, under carefully controlled laboratory conditions, how the manipulation of environmental variables, such as ringing a bell when dogs salivated to meat powder, could produce learning. After several pairings of bell ringing and food presentation, dogs would salivate to the bell alone, without the presentation of food. Pavlov thus dispensed with mentalistic explanations and focused on how

FIGURE 3.8 One of Pavlov's dogs

associations could be built up in consciousness. His view of thinking was atomistic and reflexive; that is, he believed that thinking consisted of elementary associations and the formation of chains of associations that could be traced to external conditions. His work influenced behaviorist Watson, to whom we shall turn shortly, as well as radical behaviorist Burrhus Frederic Skinner (1904–1990), who was just beginning his study of psychology when he encountered Watson and Pavlov.

Perry and Changing Beliefs About the Nature of Consciousness

During the period under discussion, major developments also occurred in philosophical debates about the nature and functions of consciousness. Many of these debates centered on whether we have to rely on introspection to uncover consciousness and whether consciousness is a private experience or has certain shared properties. American neorealist philosopher Ralph Barton Perry (1876–1957), a student and eventual biographer of James, argued that although asking someone to introspect is certainly one way of entering consciousness, theoretically, the contents of consciousness to which a person is attending could be determined if observers were present at the time when the contents were originally laid down. That is, since the contents of consciousness are produced through experience, if someone is there to witness that experience, theoretically, they would know the contents of your mind. Thus, Perry argued that the mind is not necessarily private. Even the conscious experience of one's own internal sensations, such as headaches and stomach pains, is presumably shared by others and not unique. Although one does not have direct access to another's subjective experience, presumably we have analogous experiences.

Perry concluded that mentalistic psychology is misguided because consciousness is not private, known only to oneself, and shared only through introspection. Rather, consciousness is a collection of sensations derived from the external world or our own bodies. Therefore, although introspection is certainly one method, since mind is always on view as behavior, psychology can become a purely behavioral enterprise. As we saw earlier, this conclusion was also being reached in animal psychology, where the study of animal mind through introspection was functionally impossible. It was in this intellectual milieu that Watson developed his career as a psychologist.

Watson and the Rise of Behaviorism

Watson (1878–1958) arrived at the University of Chicago in 1900 with $50 in his pocket. Fresh from Furman University in Greenville, South Carolina, where he had excelled in philosophy and psychology, an energetic Watson quickly formalized his plan of study: He would major in experimental psychology with James Angell (1869–1949), a Chicago functionalist, and Henry Donaldson (1857–1938), a neurologist who had developed the popular Wistar strain of laboratory rats. He would do minors in philosophy and neurology.

Watson was at once put off by introspectionist psychology. This was partly due to his aversion to interacting with human subjects and partly due to

his own inability to perform under the conditions of introspection. When asked to introspect, he felt uncomfortable and unnatural, and he referred to the methods as mental gymnastics resulting in scientific inadequacy. Thus, he chose animals as his experimental subjects and completed his dissertation by correlating the growth and differentiation of the central nervous system with the complexity of behavior in the white rat. The work was titled "Animal Education: The Psychical Development of the White Rat."

In 1904, Watson continued his work as an assistant to Angell, studying the sensations of maze-running rats, but he was growing frustrated with the lack of institutional support (in terms of funding and space) that he was receiving at Chicago. In fall 1907, psychologist James Mark Baldwin (1861–1934) at Johns Hopkins offered Watson a full professorship, and Watson gratefully accepted. (He had received only an instructorship at Chicago during this time.) Watson completed a great deal of important comparative work in the years immediately following his move to Baltimore and before emerging as the putative "father of behaviorism." This included careful and physically demanding fieldwork on the behavior of noddy and sooty terns in the Dry Tortugas. It was a busy time for Watson.

Within weeks of his arrival at Johns Hopkins, Watson witnessed a fateful turn of events. A police raid on a Baltimore brothel uncovered the private activities of his senior colleague Baldwin, who was forced to resign from the university. In the process, he handed over the editorship of the journal *Psychological Review* to his junior colleague. Watson also became the director of the psychological laboratory at Johns Hopkins, all at the age of 30. Over the next six years, in this position of relative authority, Watson would develop the ideas that ultimately appeared in his 1913 paper, "Psychology as the Behaviorist Views It." Although it is tempting to characterize

Watson as the founder of behaviorism, this paper must be seen as the product not of Watson's independent thought but of the confluence of trends we have just outlined. It was a particularly polemical summary of a body of extant behaviorally oriented thinking that was percolating in many places at this time. Although Watson's ideas were not necessarily original, he did emerge as a prominent systematizer and popularizer of the behaviorist position.

In 1913, after giving a talk on the subject at Columbia University in New York City, Watson published "Psychology as the Behaviorist Views It" in his journal, the *Psychological Review*. The major line of argument in Watson's paper was as follows:

1. Human psychology has failed to live up to its natural science aspirations and has failed to address problems that vitally concern human interest.

2. The failure to replicate findings using the introspective method is a serious and irresolvable flaw in psychology's claims to have scientific method.

3. Consequently, one must dispense with consciousness and the introspective method if psychology is to achieve a scientific status and if it is to yield useful, practical findings.

4. The behavior of animals and man can be investigated without appeal to consciousness and must be viewed as being equally essential to a general understanding of behavior.

Watson used this argument to set forth a revised conceptualization of psychology, which came to be known as **behaviorism**. He argued that psychology "as the behaviorist views it" is a "purely objective experimental branch of natural science. Its theoretical goal is the prediction and control of behavior. Introspection forms no essential part of its methods.... The behaviorist... recognizes no dividing line between man and brute. The behavior of man, with all of its refinement and complexity, forms only a part of the behaviorist's total scheme of investigation" (Watson, 1913, p. 158).

Behaviorism: Influential but Contested

Although many accounts of the history of American psychology have been seduced by a traditional storyline that presents Watson's exposition of behaviorism as a sweeping reform, clearly there were both antecedents of his pronouncements and opposition to them. In the latter category was Mary Whiton Calkins's (1863–1930) response to Watson's polemic in a *Psychological Bulletin* article published later in 1913. Her reactions summed up those of many of her colleagues. She was opposed to the wholesale elimination of introspection as a psychological method and remained certain that some psychological processes could be studied only by introspection. She pointed out that introspection is itself a method for studying behavior, especially complex behavior such as that of imagining, judging, and reasoning. However, she was sympathetic to Watson's observation that psychology had become too far removed from the problems of everyday life and criticized Titchener's structuralism in this regard. She suggested that psychologists could continue to use introspection as a method for studying consciousness but urged that this be the study of the conscious self in relation to its environment. Calkins, herself an eminent Harvard-trained psychologist and philosopher, was working on an influential theory of the self and had served as president of the American Psychological Association in 1905. In 1918, she served as president of the American Philosophical Association.

Sidebar 3.1 Focus on *Mary Whiton Calkins*

Mary Whiton Calkins (1863–1930) earned her PhD at Harvard under the tutelage of such eminent figures as philosopher Josiah Royce, William James, and Hugo Münsterberg, all of whom enthusiastically endorsed her work. Despite completing all requirements for the doctoral degree, and being proclaimed by Münsterberg to be the strongest student in his laboratory since he had arrived at Harvard, in 1895 Calkins was refused her PhD by the Harvard Corporation (which continues to refuse to grant the degree posthumously) on the grounds that Harvard did not accept women. Thus, although Calkins is now recognized as one of the most important first-generation American psychologists—she established one of the first psychological laboratories in the country at Wellesley College, published four books and more than 100 papers in psychology and philosophy, and was ranked 12th in a list of the 50 most eminent psychologists in the United States in 1903—she was never awarded the doctorate she had earned.

Calkins's dissertation research was an experimental study of the association of ideas in which she initiated the paired-associates technique of studying memory. She then spent a large part of her career developing a system of scientific self psychology

FIGURE 3.9 Mary Whiton Calkins
Courtesy of the Archives of the History of American Psychology, University of Akron, Akron, OH.

to which she was ardently committed. Calkins based her system upon the conviction that the foundational unit of study for psychology should be the conscious self. On the one hand, she felt that although introspection could be used to scientifically study the self, most introspective studies of abstracted mental states or processes tended to be *impersonalistic,* that is, devoid of any relationship to the self. She characterized this as atomistic or idea-psychology. On the other hand, she described her brand of introspective psychology as *personalistic.* She defined personalistic introspective psychology as the study of conscious, functioning, experiencing selves that exist in relationship to others. For example, in her seminal 1900 paper entitled "Psychology as Science of Selves" in which she introduced her system, she described perception as a consciousness of sharing the experience of several other selves. She did not see the self as metaphysical but argued for its legitimacy, and indeed primacy, as a scientific object in psychology; she also argued for the social nature of the self. In her autobiography, published in 1930, the year of her death, she attributed her conception of the self as social to the influence of Royce and James. She also wrote, "For with each year I live, with each book I read, with each observation I initiate or confirm, I am more deeply convinced that psychology should be conceived as the science of the self, or person, as related to its environment, physical and social" (pp. 42–43).

In an extended discussion of the question, "Was there a behaviorist revolution in psychology in 1913?" historian of psychology Franz Samelson (1981) concluded that there is little evidence that Watson's paper was the cataclysmic event for psychology that many histories have portrayed it to be, and that Watson perhaps wanted it to be. Echoing Calkins, but 8 years later, Robert Sessions Woodworth (1869–1962) wrote the following in his 1921 textbook, *Psychology: A Study of Mental Life*:

> What the behaviorists have accomplished is the definitive overthrow of the doctrine ... that introspection is the only real method of observation in psychology; and this is no mean achievement. But we should be going too far if we followed the behaviorists to the extent of seeking to exclude introspection altogether, and on principle. There is no sense in such negative principles. Let us accumulate psychological facts by any method that will give the facts. (p. 13)

When viewed as a more gradual and never monolithic process, it is nonetheless true that American psychology became, over the next several decades, less reliant on introspective methods and more decidedly behavioral. For a significant period, behaviorism *was* American psychology in a way that introspectionist psychology could never have been. Why?

BEHAVIORISM AND AMERICAN LIFE

We stressed in Chapter 2 how Psychology and its products, both theoretical and practical, emerge from ways of living and in turn affect how people make sense of and act upon the world. Behaviorism was in a very real sense both a creation of and a contributor to a way of living in early 20th-century America guided by the progressivist ideals of practicality, order, and control. As psychologist David Bakan noted, behaviorism was both a school of thought within

Psychology and a "cultural expression" (1966a, p. 8). The late 19th and early 20th centuries were marked by intense industrialization and urbanization in the United States. Large-scale migration occurred to urban centers from rural areas, and immigration increased. The migration to cities was fueled by the need for a larger urban workforce and the mechanization of farming, and it produced a radical shift in the social fabric of American life. Whereas in the 1870s small-town life had been the norm in the United States, by the early 1900s people increasingly exchanged the agrarian rhythms and face-to-face contact of the small town for the comparatively chaotic and anonymous experience of the large city. Whereas small towns had been relatively homogeneous in terms of religion, ethnicity, and values, with the church and town hall as stable centers of religious and civic life, urban centers were heterogeneous, less centralized, and seemingly disorganized. This disorganization increased as the population influx stressed municipal services such as water, sewers, and transportation. Immigration to the United States, especially to cities, from southern and eastern Europe created large cultural gaps and, at times, intergroup conflicts that seemed threatening and dangerous.

Adding to this picture of rapid change was increased specialization in the professions and formalization of new professional and social roles. The psychologist, one of these new professionals, emerged as a scientific expert who could offer advice on ways to restore order, balance, and civility in everyday life. Psychologists were aware of this cultural opening, and many did not hesitate to step into it. Mental testing, some suggested, could be used to help quantify ability and sort children into appropriate groups in an expanding educational system called upon to serve an increasingly diverse student body. Industrial psychology emerged as an applied science to help organize the workplace, to make it more efficient, and to make workers more productive. The application of scientific principles to human behavior was key. In 1913, the same

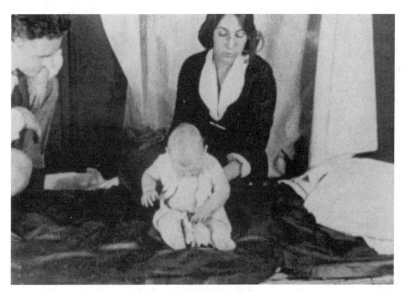

FIGURE 3.10   John Watson and Rosalie Rayner conditioning Little Albert
Courtesy of the Archives of the History of American Psychology, University of Akron, Akron, OH.

year as Watson's behaviorist manifesto, Harvard's Hugo Münsterberg (1863–1916; recruited by James in 1892 to take over the psychological laboratory there) published *Psychology and Industrial Efficiency*. In this book he argued that matching the right worker to the right job was essential to maximize workplace efficiency and that psychology had the assessment tools to scientifically determine this match. He called this the psychotechnical method.

Thus, when Watson asserted in his book *Psychology from the Standpoint of a Behaviorist*, published in 1919, that "Every human individual needs the data and laws of behaviorism for organizing his own daily life and conduct" (1919/1924, pp. 8–9), he was appealing directly to a social and personal desire for increased mastery and control and a belief in the value of science to deliver them. He was even quite specific about the need for behaviorism in the face of the challenges of urban life, writing in the preface to the book, "If we are ever to learn to live together in the close relationships demanded by modern social and industrial life, we shall have to . . . enter upon a study of modern psychology. . . . One of the most recent and practical of [the] new viewpoints in psychology is that of the behaviorists" (p. xi). In a society that appeared uncontrollable and unpredictable, these were soothing words indeed.

Watson, himself a farm boy from South Carolina, was forced to leave academia soon after his book was published. His departure was precipitated by a scandal involving his affair with his research assistant, Rosalie Rayner. Watson and Rayner had just conducted their famous Little Albert experiment, in which they produced a fear of a white rat in a young infant by pairing the presentation of the rat (and other furry items) with a loud sound. Watson had a theory that humans are born with only three basic emotions, fear, rage, and love, and all other emotions are built from these three. He also stated that innate fear in infants would only be expressed in response to loud noises or a sudden loss of support. He used the innate fear of loud noises to condition Albert's fear of a white rat, using this as support for his theory that all such fears are built through conditioning.

Despite Watson's scholarly and professional reputation, his affair with Rayner and his unwillingness to publicly recant his behavior proved too much for conservative Baltimore society and ultimately for Johns Hopkins administrators. He was asked to leave the university. Despite this turn of events, Watson leveraged his scientific credentials, theoretical outlook, and considerable personal charisma into a successful career in advertising with the J. Walter Thompson Advertising Agency in New York. He married Rayner in 1920, and they had two sons. In 1928, they published *Psychological Care of Infant and Child*, outlining their behaviorist advice for child rearing. Just seven years later, at the age of 35, Rosalie Rayner Watson died of dysentery. Years later, as adults, the Watsons' two sons each sought psychoanalytic help for personal and emotional problems. Psychoanalytic ideas were popular in American culture through this period, while behaviorist ideas were coming to dominate academic psychology departments.

SUMMARY

In this chapter, we have shown how psychologists forged psychology's identity as a natural science by developing methods that allowed them to treat consciousness like any other scientific object: as an observable, measurable, and even quantifiable phenomenon. While Germany can be seen as the birthplace of modern laboratory psychology due to Wundt's work and widespread influence, we have discussed the limitations that Wundt saw in treating more complex mental functions experimentally. In addition to the complexity of his own views on the topic, we showed how Wundt's system was certainly not the only one proposed at the time. Alternative systems, such as Dilthey's hermeneutic, human science approach, have exerted some influence in psychology to this day. We also discussed aspects of the German university system, and distinctive features of the German intellectual and cultural tradition, that contributed to the rise of the new Psychology in this time and place. We then briefly touched on some early work in psychology in Britain and France and turned to developments in the American context.

In the United States, as the 19th century gave way to the 20th, introspective methods were deemed to be of little use in developing a practical psychology and were increasingly under attack for not being rigorously scientific. Although many American psychologists were trained in Wundt's Leipzig laboratory, when they returned to their home country they met different institutional, intellectual, and cultural terrain. By 1913, Watson could confidently assert to his American colleagues that psychology should abandon introspection and become the study of behavior. Behaviorism offered a more authoritatively scientific and, perhaps more importantly, an eminently practical form of psychology. Although behaviorism had some impact on psychology in other parts of the world, it had its greatest influence in the United States, where it fit particularly well with the Progressive Era emphasis on using science and the scientific method to solve the practical problems of society.

BIBLIOGRAPHIC ESSAY

For a useful overview of many developments discussed in this chapter, consult Alfred Fuchs and Katharine Milar's "Psychology as a Science" (2003) in the Wiley *Handbook of Psychology*'s first volume, *History of Psychology*. For an account that offers comparative analyses of the new Psychology in England, France, Germany, and the United States, see Mitchell Ash's "Psychology" chapter (2003) in the seventh volume of *The Cambridge History of Science, The Modern Social Sciences*.

For material on various figures and their work, including Herbart, Kant, Fechner, Wundt, and James, we owe a great debt to Ray Fancher's (1996) sparkling text *Pioneers of Psychology* (3rd edition). For material on the German philosophers Herbart, Kant, and Dilthey, as well as background information on empirical and rational psychology, we consulted *The Critique of Psychology* by Thomas Teo (2005). For more details on Kant and Herbart, we found David Leary's article "The Philosophical Development of the Conception of Psychology in Germany, 1780–1850" (1978) very useful. We also consulted parts of Kant's *Critique of Pure Reason* (1781/1998).

The contributions of Herbart, Fechner, and Wundt to the quantification of psychology are ably discussed in M. L. Zupan's article "The Conceptual Development of Quantification in Experimental Psychology" (1976). Further discussion of the roles of psychophysics and mental testing in the rise of quantification, including our brief note about the reception of Fechner's law, is found in Gail Hornstein's chapter "Quantifying Psychological Phenomena" (1988). For our coverage of Wundt, especially the distinction between self-observation and internal perception, we relied on Kurt Danziger's article "The History of Introspection Reconsidered" (1980), as well as Chapter 3 in his book *Constructing the Subject*, titled "Divergence of Investigative Practices: The Repudiation of Wundt" (1990b).

The section on the 19th-century German university system is drawn from three sources: the prehistory offered in Fritz Ringer's (1969) book *The Decline of the German Mandarins;* an article by Velma Dobson and Darryl Bruce titled "The German University and the Development of Experimental Psychology" (1972); and an article by Horst Gundlach, "Psychology As Science and as Discipline" (2006), which also offers an interesting discussion of the existence of a discipline of psychology starting with Christian Wolff (1679–1754) at the University of Halle. For our brief comparative look at French psychology and the work of Ribot, we used Jacqueline Carroy and Régine Plas's "The Beginnings of Psychology in France" (2006).

We consulted several primary sources for our coverage of American psychology. William James's classic two-volume *The Principles of Psychology* (1890), John B. Watson's *Psychology from the Standpoint of a Behaviorist* (1919/1924), and Hugo Münsterberg's *Psychology and Industrial Efficiency* (1913) are all extremely accessible to the contemporary reader and provide interesting glimpses into psychology at the turn of the last century. A good overview of this period of development is Michael Sokal's "The Origins of the New Psychology in the United States" (2006). An extremely rich analysis of American psychology up to the emergence of behaviorism is John O'Donnell's *The Origins of Behaviorism*. In the section on the abandonment of introspection and the turn to behavior, we relied heavily on Thomas Leahey's organization and discussion of the rise of behaviorism in his text *A History of Psychology* (1997). For information on Thorndike and others who studied animal behavior in the late 1800s and early 1900s, Donald Dewsbury's *Comparative Psychology in the Twentieth Century* is a useful volume. Deborah Coon's article "Standardizing the Subject" (1993) helped contextualize experimental introspection as part of a larger movement toward standardization and automation in American society. For more information on the reception and influence of Watson's behaviorism, see Franz Samelson's "Struggle for Scientific Authority" (1981). David Bakan's article "Behaviorism and American Urbanization" (1966a) provided much of the material for the section on behaviorism and American life; it also offers more interesting details on Watson's personal background and how it may have affected his thinking. For a good full-length biography of Watson, see Kerry Buckley's *Mechanical Man* (1989).

Several excellent primary and secondary sources on the life and work of Mary Whiton Calkins are available. Her own autobiographical statement is published in the Carl Murchison series *A History of Psychology in Autobiography* (Calkins, 1930). Historian of psychology Laurel Furumoto is an authority on Calkins. We would recommend her 1979 article for a good overview of Calkins's life and career. For an assessment of the motivations underlying Calkins's adherence to self-psychology, including a short but interesting discussion of her writings on ethics, see Phyllis Wentworth's article "The Moral of Her Story" (1999).

Finally, for a social–economic–political history of the Progressive Era, with an emphasis on the effects of urbanization, industrialization, and immigration on restructuring the American experience, we used Robert H. Wiebe's (1967) *The Search for Social Order, 1877–1920*.

Chapter 4
TIMELINE 1560–1920
(In 25-year increments)

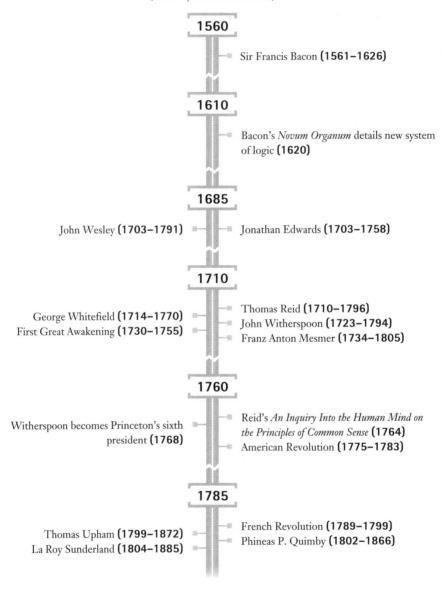

1560

Sir Francis Bacon **(1561–1626)**

1610

Bacon's *Novum Organum* details new system of logic **(1620)**

1685

John Wesley **(1703–1791)**   Jonathan Edwards **(1703–1758)**

1710

George Whitefield **(1714–1770)**   Thomas Reid **(1710–1796)**
First Great Awakening **(1730–1755)**   John Witherspoon **(1723–1794)**
Franz Anton Mesmer **(1734–1805)**

1760

Witherspoon becomes Princeton's sixth president **(1768)**   Reid's *An Inquiry Into the Human Mind on the Principles of Common Sense* **(1764)**
American Revolution **(1775–1783)**

1785

Thomas Upham **(1799–1872)**   French Revolution **(1789–1799)**
La Roy Sunderland **(1804–1885)**   Phineas P. Quimby **(1802–1866)**

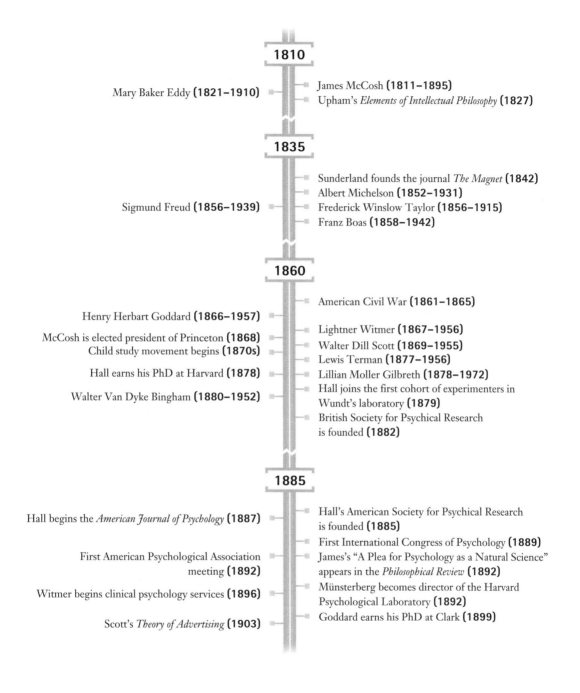

1810

Mary Baker Eddy **(1821–1910)**

James McCosh **(1811–1895)**
Upham's *Elements of Intellectual Philosophy* **(1827)**

1835

Sunderland founds the journal *The Magnet* **(1842)**
Albert Michelson **(1852–1931)**
Sigmund Freud **(1856–1939)**
Frederick Winslow Taylor **(1856–1915)**
Franz Boas **(1858–1942)**

1860

American Civil War **(1861–1865)**

Henry Herbart Goddard **(1866–1957)**
McCosh is elected president of Princeton **(1868)**
Child study movement begins **(1870s)**

Lightner Witmer **(1867–1956)**
Walter Dill Scott **(1869–1955)**
Lewis Terman **(1877–1956)**
Lillian Moller Gilbreth **(1878–1972)**
Hall joins the first cohort of experimenters in Wundt's laboratory **(1879)**
British Society for Psychical Research is founded **(1882)**

Hall earns his PhD at Harvard **(1878)**

Walter Van Dyke Bingham **(1880–1952)**

1885

Hall begins the *American Journal of Psychology* **(1887)**

Hall's American Society for Psychical Research is founded **(1885)**
First International Congress of Psychology **(1889)**
James's "A Plea for Psychology as a Natural Science" appears in the *Philosophical Review* **(1892)**
Münsterberg becomes director of the Harvard Psychological Laboratory **(1892)**
Goddard earns his PhD at Clark **(1899)**

First American Psychological Association meeting **(1892)**

Witmer begins clinical psychology services **(1896)**

Scott's *Theory of Advertising* **(1903)**

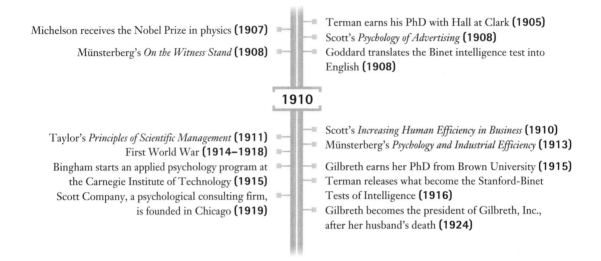

Michelson receives the Nobel Prize in physics **(1907)**

Terman earns his PhD with Hall at Clark **(1905)**

Scott's *Psychology of Advertising* **(1908)**

Münsterberg's *On the Witness Stand* **(1908)**

Goddard translates the Binet intelligence test into English **(1908)**

1910

Taylor's *Principles of Scientific Management* **(1911)**
First World War **(1914–1918)**
Bingham starts an applied psychology program at the Carnegie Institute of Technology **(1915)**
Scott Company, a psychological consulting firm, is founded in Chicago **(1919)**

Scott's *Increasing Human Efficiency in Business* **(1910)**
Münsterberg's *Psychology and Industrial Efficiency* **(1913)**
Gilbreth earns her PhD from Brown University **(1915)**
Terman releases what become the Stanford-Binet Tests of Intelligence **(1916)**
Gilbreth becomes the president of Gilbreth, Inc., after her husband's death **(1924)**

FROM PERIPHERY TO CENTER: CREATING AN AMERICAN PSYCHOLOGY

Religion in the shape of mind-cure gives to some of us serenity, moral poise, and happiness, and prevents certain forms of disease as well as science does.

—William James, *The Varieties of Religious Experience,* 1902

INTRODUCTION

In our last chapter, we discussed the beginnings of disciplinary Psychology and showed how it owed its emergence to particular contexts of time and place. As we noted, the time and place that became one of the first centers of the new Psychology was the laboratory of Wilhelm Wundt (1832–1920) in the late 19th century in Germany. Students from many countries came to Germany to study with Wundt and others of the first-generation German psychologists. Especially noteworthy was the number of students, 16, from the United States who earned their doctoral degrees in Leipzig. Although the new psychological science gradually found a permanent place in Germany, its growth in the United States was nothing short of phenomenal after its introduction in the late 19th century. In fact, while Psychology in the United States began as peripheral both to American science and to American life, its indigenization was rapid and so complete that by the mid- to late 20th century American psychology was dominant within the science of Psychology and had utterly penetrated American social and cultural life.

How did this new science that emerged in a specific European context become transformed when it was exported to the United States? We began answering this question in the previous chapter by looking at the contributions of William James (1842–1910) and John B. Watson (1878–1958). Here, we take a step back to examine the distinctive American context that facilitated the work of James, Watson, and their colleagues in the new discipline. Our argument is essentially that developments in religion, education, and everyday life converged to create a cultural opening that facilitated receptivity to the new science and profession and shaped the contours of a distinctly American psychology. This approach also allows us to illustrate how the establishment of the center and periphery of a science is a negotiated and often conflictual process.

In this chapter, we first discuss the events and trends in American life, beginning in the first half of the 19th century, that helped create this cultural receptivity. In American colleges, the dominant approach to explaining human thought and behavior was a mental and moral philosophy grounded in Scottish common sense realism. This, as historians have shown, was an important and necessary precursor to disciplinary Psychology. We then turn to other events in the same period but outside the universities and colleges, where another movement was taking place that created America's first psychology. This movement involved religion, phrenology, mesmerism, and eventually, spiritualism and New Thought. Each of these helped create a psychological sensibility, or everyday psychology, among Americans.

These antecedent events and movements were crucial in preparing the American public for the introduction of what came to be called the new Psychology. Once introduced, this new Psychology underwent a remarkable naturalization or, more accurately, indigenization. Recall that in the introduction to this text we defined indigenization as the process whereby a local culture or region develops its own form of psychology, either by developing it from within that culture or by importing aspects of psychologies developed elsewhere and combining them with local concepts. The Indian social psychologist Durganand Sinha (1998) referred to these processes, respectively, as endogenous and exogenous indigenization. We examine his work later in the book when we recount the history of psychology in India. It may seem more natural to students in North America to think of the development of psychology in India in terms of indigenization than it is to refer to American psychology as having been indigenized. Yet that is what happened in North America, and in this chapter we explain how this process unfolded.

Part of this indigenization process was the conflicted encounter between the proponents of the emergent everyday psychology—mind science, New Thought, spiritualism—and the new, graduate-trained psychologists who viewed themselves as scientists. Once the new scientific Psychology was on the scene, the older mind science and spiritualistic approaches were its competitors for professional and scientific credibility. We explain how and why it was necessary for the new, scientifically trained psychologists to distinguish themselves and their field from these other approaches. These psychologists argued that their academic credentials and professional expertise made their science superior to those of their competitors.

In the first half of the chapter, we explore how a unique psychological sensibility emerged in 19th-century American life. This sensibility was forged as Americans sought to understand and use the new sciences of phrenology and mesmerism. It is worth noting that both phrenology and mesmerism were imported from Europe and underwent an indigenization in the United States that reshaped them to fit American life. In the second half of the century, spiritualism and New Thought built on the earlier sciences in ways that many Americans found attractive.

In the second half of the chapter, we examine the growth of the new Psychology, imported from Germany and transformed by its practitioners to better fit the American context. In doing so, these new psychologists fought to make a place for themselves among the new intellectual elite. We discuss how the growth of this new Psychology was rooted in the pragmatic approach that came to be called functionalism. As functionalism became the dominant school of thought, application was not far behind. To illustrate this, we examine the application of psychology to education and business (we discuss psychology and mental health in the next chapter). In applying their expertise, psychologists made the claim that their knowledge and methods led to more successful applications to problems of American society than either the earlier mental philosophy or the mind sciences of phrenology, mesmerism, New Thought, or spiritualism.

If we are able to take a long-range view of these events, it will help us see how indigenization is a process, sometimes a conflict-ridden process, that melds different cultural traditions, bringing about something new as a result. Many students are familiar with the old adage about America as a melting pot, where people from diverse cultures and countries all blend together in a new American identity. While scholarship has shown that this is *not* what happens with people, perhaps it may be applicable to psychology. With regard to psychology, in the United States, this process involved a key issue that remains with us today, an issue concerning what constitutes the intellectual and practical center of the discipline and what constitutes the periphery. We hope that by the end of the chapter you will better understand that these are human processes, full of negotiation and competition, rather than inevitable outcomes dictated by some unseen hand of progress.

AMERICAN MENTAL AND MORAL PHILOSOPHY

The story of psychology in America that we began in the last chapter relies heavily on the standard storyline that experimental psychology was born in the Leipzig laboratory of Wilhelm Wundt and was brought to the United States by a bevy of enthusiastic American students who traveled to Germany to study the new science. As the standard story goes, after bringing back what they learned in Leipzig to their native land, they combined it with the can-do, practical, functionally oriented ethos of the American context, importing some aspects of Galtonian individual-difference approaches along the way. What this account fails to elaborate are the preexisting strands of psychological thought and practice in the United States onto which these new psychologists superimposed their German experiences.

In terms of intellectual antecedents, several historians of psychology have shown that a firmly established tradition of American mental philosophy and moral philosophy clearly addressed psychological topics before the new psychologists declared their new science and of which they were often well aware because of their previous training. In typical historical accounts, American mental and moral philosophy has been presented (when referred to) as the old way of thinking from which the new Psychology was a radical departure and to which the new psychologists owed nothing. The rhetoric of the new psychologists was intended to promulgate the view that theirs was a revolution, rather than an evolution, in thinking. As several historians of psychology have persuasively argued, however, the actual process whereby the new Psychology indigenized to its local context was more like a changing of the guard than a palace revolution. As historian of psychology Al Fuchs has remarked, "The psychology that evolved in the United States was indebted not only to the laboratories of Europe but also to the mental philosophy that the first

generation of the new psychologists had learned from their college texts" (2000, p. 3).

This "college text" mental and moral philosophy had a history of its own. It was heavily imbued with the Scottish common sense school represented by Dugald Stewart (1753–1828), Thomas Reid (1710–1796), and Thomas Brown (1778–1820), with some influence from the associationism of John Locke. The Scottish common sense school, formed partly in reaction to the idealism of George Berkeley and the skepticism of David Hume, stated that we perceive the world directly through our senses and that this "common sense" information is the source of accurate knowledge about real things in the world. John Witherspoon (1723–1794), a minister with the Church of Scotland, has been credited with bringing Scottish common sense realism to the United States. Witherspoon was heavily influenced by the writings of Reid, especially his *An Inquiry into the Human Mind on the Principles of Common Sense* (1764). He adhered to the Scottish realist view that knowledge acquired by way of the senses is superior to knowledge based purely on reasoning. In this view, mental philosophy would be the study of the God-given faculties of the mind—namely, the understanding (knowing), the will (doing), and the affections (feeling)—through direct experience and inductive methods. Witherspoon was critical of the deistic views that had gained momentum among college students under the influence of Newton and Locke. **Deism** was the belief that although God designed the universe and set the clockwork in motion, He had no direct influence, and did not intervene, in the day-to-day affairs of humans. As a belief system, Deism derived from Enlightenment rationalism and was oriented toward the new scientific approaches to understanding nature and man's place in it. Many forward-thinking people of this era were Deist.

In the late 1700s, on the heels of the American and French revolutions, students at American colleges were displaying unprecedented levels of atheism, deism, and materialism. This was particularly worrisome, given that almost all American colleges were affiliated with one of the Protestant Christian religions. Harvard was Unitarian, Yale was Congregationalist, and Princeton (then still the College of New Jersey) was Presbyterian. Of these branches of Protestantism, Presbyterianism was the most dominant. It was through the influence of Witherspoon that the mental and moral philosophy of the Scottish enlightenment was to change the course of American philosophy and reign in some of the worrisome student revolt by providing not just intellectual guidance but moral guidance as well. **Moral philosophy** was the branch of philosophy that dealt with ethics and conduct. **Mental philosophy** dealt with the elements and processes of the mind and how they influenced action. Most mental and moral philosophers were trained as ministers. In the United States, seminary training was the sole route to graduate education until the new research universities emerged at the end of the 19th century.

Witherspoon became president of Princeton University in 1768 and used his position to spread Scottish common sense realism throughout the curriculum. As historian of psychology Rand Evans (1984) has noted, by the 1820s, Scottish philosophy was the norm in American colleges, often taught by the president of the university in the required course on mental and moral philosophy. By the time it reached the textbooks read by the future vanguard of the new Psychology, however, it had acquired a distinctly American inflection. One of the earliest—and most influential—textbooks of American mental philosophy was written by Thomas Upham (1799–1872) of Bowdoin College.

Upham received his graduate training at the Andover Theological Seminary. He wrote *Elements of Intellectual Philosophy* in 1827. This work is notable in that its table of contents appears to delineate, somewhat presciently, the subjects that would come to be of interest to the later experimental psychologists. Included are sections on sensation and perception, attention, dreaming, consciousness, association, memory, reasoning, emotions, and instincts, to take just a small sample. It is systematic and heavily inductive, reflecting the immense popularity that Baconian philosophy of science enjoyed in that period; that is, it summarized, organized, and attempted to find lawful relationships among a large body of facts. In 1832, Upham retitled his book *Elements of Mental Philosophy* to more accurately reflect the scope of topics he covered, which included not only the intellect but the sensibilities and the will as well. His complete table of contents listed 495 topics in all.

Upham's text, and indeed American mental philosophy generally, emphasized the active processes of the mind, or the mind-in-use, and had a distinctly functional character. Nonetheless, the American mental philosophy of the pre–Civil War period was still closely tied to the view that humans and the human mind were the unique creations of a Protestant God. Darwinian evolutionary theory, as well as the emerging research on physiological psychology, posed a materialistic challenge to this view. Some later Scottish realist mental philosophers in America, such as James McCosh (1811–1895), dealt with this by regarding evolution as an example of God's handiwork. McCosh was elected president of Princeton in 1868, about 100 years after Witherspoon. He was remarkably open to the new developments in psychology. Although a strong Scottish realist mental philosopher, McCosh was

FIGURE 4.1 James McCosh

interested in the new experimental psychology, especially the work in physiological psychology, and encouraged his students to further their studies of these topics. James Mark Baldwin (1861–1934) was one of his students. Baldwin recalled that, in McCosh's class on natural realism, the students read Wundt and learned about the theory of biological evolution. Princeton faculty members, at the request of McCosh, gave laboratory demonstrations in the new Psychology.

Thus, historians have argued that a more accurate story of the arrival of Wundtian experimental psychology in America would emphasize the important role played by training in the experimental method but would show that within a few short years the Wundtian focus on mind-as-contents would disappear. Instead, the strongly entrenched Scottish philosophy of mind-in-use and its emphasis on mental functions would combine with the experimental method to produce a distinctly American amalgam. The new psychologists resisted explicitly acknowledging their debt to their American mental philosophy forebears, however. This was partly due to their desire to separate their new science from both philosophy and religion. In the case of religion, they walked a fine line. University administrators and the public were reluctant to embrace a new discipline that appeared to endorse godless materialism. As we show later in this chapter, several rhetorical strategies were used by professionalizers of the new science, such as G. Stanley Hall, to convince the public that psychology and religion, or science and soul, could coexist.

FORGING A PSYCHOLOGICAL SENSIBILITY: FROM RELIGION TO PSYCHICAL RESEARCH

Outside the walls of the academy, exciting developments proved to be key elements in the creation of psychological sensibility. Religion played an important role in these events, especially what historian of religion Catherine Albanese (2007) has called the metaphysical stream of American religion. We explore this more later. First,

we need to contextualize our story with a brief overview of 19th-century American life.

At the beginning of the 19th century, the United States was largely a rural society whose population, while not entirely homogeneous, was principally of Anglo-Saxon and Northern European descent. Over the course of the century, the country became both more urbanized and industrialized. In the second half of the century, immigrants from southern and eastern Europe and China made the country more ethnically diverse, although it should be noted that these immigrants were subject to intense discrimination. Native Americans and African Americans, most of whom were brought over in the slave trade, were also an important part of the population and contributed to the events we describe in ways that historians are still seeking to understand. All of these trends reshaped American life in ways that were important to our story.

Education also underwent dramatic changes during the century. Although educational progress was slow and uneven, by midcentury the United States had the highest literacy rate in the world. This helped create a demand for printed materials of all kinds and made dissemination of new ideas easier. Americans of all classes developed an appetite for information and new knowledge, whether it was disseminated through books, newspapers, and pamphlets or via public lectures and demonstrations.

However, education for the professions and for science was decidedly mixed in the first half of the century. Until the late 19th century, one could still become a physician through an apprenticeship without any formal medical education. Scientific education and training were available only to a privileged few; until late in the century, most Americans, indeed most educated people in the Western world, understood science to be any form of systematic knowledge. It was not until 1876 that the United States had its first graduate university, when Johns Hopkins University was established in Baltimore.

A critical aspect of the events and changes we describe was the belief that every person could think and decide for themselves, whether the matter concerned religion, medicine, or any other issue. This populism grew rapidly after the American Revolution and was celebrated in the presidency of Andrew Jackson in the 1820s. Jackson was a rough-and-tumble "common man" who inspired an ethos of the self-made man and a disregard for the privileges typically accorded the elites. In this antiauthoritarian environment, the canons of traditional societies with their social hierarchies were challenged, along with the received authorities of religion, science, and the professions. Many individuals asserted their own interpretations of science and religion. In one sense, this promoted an age of exploration of new ideas about human nature. The populism exemplified by Jackson was also found in religion and among religious leaders, often leading to new religious groups and idiosyncratic interpretations. This should be kept in mind as we explore the contributions to an American psychological sensibility.

We should also note that the movements and practices we describe here held immense appeal to people in all strata of American society. Phrenology, mesmerism, spiritualism, and New Thought attracted followers from among the best-educated and from among the least-educated members of the population. Each movement developed its own literature—books, magazines, journals, pamphlets—and had its own lecture circuit. In other words, these events and movements were not on the margins, but were very much in the public spotlight. At the peak of each movement, they were very much on the minds of Americans who were hungry to know more about the phenomena they described and to receive whatever benefit they promised.

Religion and Revival

From their arrival, European settlers brought their religious views and practices with them to what became the United States. Indeed, for many

of them, freedom to practice religion was their motivation to immigrate to such a far shore. Since then, there have been periodic upswings in religious fervor that acted like a social contagion in its spread across great swaths of the country. New and renewed religious movements in the 18th century in German-speaking countries (the Pietists), England (the Methodists), and Scotland (among Congregationalists and Presbyterians) also had their counterparts in America. What historians call the First Great Awakening of the 1730s and 1740s was one such period marked by renewed religious fervor and conversion across New England. One facet of this awakening was embodied in the great American preacher of the time, Jonathan Edwards (1703–1758), who articulated a religious psychology that characterized the soul as an inseparable unity of understanding, will, and affections.

Another, more dynamic facet of the Awakening was the Methodist revivalism led in America by George Whitefield (1714–1770) and John Wesley (1703–1791). Both men preached up and down the Eastern seaboard colonies, often to open-air crowds numbering in the tens of thousands. The legacy of their work was not only many new Christian believers but also openness to deep and profound religious experiences, sometimes manifested in marked physical demonstrations, such as shouting, falling down, visions, and trance-like behaviors. As we demonstrate, this shout tradition had implications for the development of an everyday psychology in the 19th century.

In the 19th century, a new religious revival swept over the North and Midwest of America. Out of this revival, new religious and philosophical movements emerged that helped create a psychological sensibility in the United States. The religious movements included Methodism, Seventh-Day Adventism, and Mormonism. We use Methodism to illustrate the contribution to the creation of psychological understanding.

The Methodist Episcopal Church grew from the work of Wesley and his colleagues in England in the mid-18th century. By the early 19th century, it was the fastest growing denomination in the United States, doubling its membership from 1820 to 1830 to a half-million adherents. The rapid growth of Methodism reflected what historian of American religion Nathan Hatch (1989) has termed "religious populism." Methodist meetings became known for involvement of the lay members in the services, with signs of grace and conversion often being acted out physically, much as in the traditions laid down earlier. The physical demonstrations of conversion and personal transformation came to be referred to as the **shout tradition** in American revivalist religion. The emotional and psychological intensity of these experiences, while religious in character, began to be perceived by some observers and participants as analogous to other psychological phenomena, especially the recently imported mesmeric practices.

Mesmerism and Religion

In the next chapter, we explore the origins of **mesmerism** in greater detail and trace its influence into psychiatry and the psychology of mental health. Here, we will give a brief background.

Franz Anton Mesmer (1734–1805) was a Viennese physician who drew upon then current theories about the influence of various physical forces—stars, planets, magnets—to promote an understanding of health and disease based upon the balance of bodily fluids. The mesmeric state was characterized by a deep connection between the mesmerist and the subject; the connection was one of sympathy between the two. Later, this connection was thought of as the psychological characteristic of suggestibility. Once in this state, it was thought individuals could be directed to perform physical and intellectual tasks that were outside their capacity in the normal state. Often, upon being "awakened" from the mesmeric state, people could not remember what had occurred.

FIGURE 4.2   Franz Anton Mesmer

Mesmer was discredited in both Vienna and Paris, but his ideas and practices were kept alive by his followers and from the late 18th century into the 19th century were exported across Europe and England and to North America. Mesmer's most important disciple, Marquis de Puységur (1751–1825), expanded the psychological possibilities of mesmerism with his demonstration of the mesmeric trance state, which he called magnetic somnambulism. The trance state, Puységur discovered, could be induced with a series of arm movements or "magnetic passes." In England, mesmerism became part of the reform of medical education and practice and was eventually transformed into hypnosis. In both England and the United States, mesmerism was often combined with phrenology and was part of the armamentarium of itinerant healers and lecturers. This, too, is an untold part of the history of everyday psychology in America.

Mesmerism was also perceived by some ministers as a possible way to understand the workings of the human mind normally hidden from view. Historian of psychology David Schmit (2005, 2009) has begun to explain the complex relationships among mesmerism, American religion, and spiritualism, indicating that the questions raised by mesmeric and spiritualistic practices led to attempts to scientifically or systematically investigate them for their psychological meaning. Among the practitioners of mesmerism during its most popular period in the United States in the 1840s were several ministers and former ministers, including La Roy Sunderland (1804–1885). His work was critically important in articulating a psychological view of religious experience based on insights gained from mesmerism.

Sunderland was converted and called to the Methodist ministry in the early 1820s. For 10 years, he was a Methodist revivalist preacher in the shout tradition. He then worked as a reformer and advocate for abolition of slavery for several years before leaving the Methodist ministry in the early 1840s. Sunderland then focused on developing his psychological theories and practices and embraced spiritualism for a short period in the 1850s.

What is critical about Sunderland's involvement is that he sought to understand the religiously inspired phenomena in psychological terms. His periodical, *The Magnet*, was an outlet for his theorizing about the connections between the mesmeric state and the experiences of those caught up in religious ecstasies in camp meetings and revival settings. He claimed, based on his experience as a minister, that the phenomena were the same. Such naturalistic explanations placed the two states on a continuum of normality, however abnormal they may have appeared to outsiders.

In the 1840s, Sunderland, like many of his colleagues, attempted to merge mesmerism with phrenology, another recent import from Europe. We have already discussed phrenology's trajectory in the United States (see Chapter 2). As noted there, phrenology had a remarkable appeal to people in every walk of life, including those who often engaged in enthusiastic worship traditions. This phrenomesmerism did not persist, as the two approaches were based upon different premises of human functioning. By the 1850s, Sunderland had embraced spiritualism and its claim that it was possible to communicate with the spirit realm and, thus, with the dead. Although he did not remain a spiritualist, Sunderland was typical of his day among those whose interests lay in the intersection of religion and psychology.

Spiritualism

Spiritualism emerged in the mid-1800s in a time when religious enthusiasm was still pronounced and mesmerism and phrenology were accepted by a growing number of Americans. It, too, was part of the beliefs and practices that helped make Americans psychologically minded.

The link between spiritualism and mesmerism was that some practitioners, such as Sunderland, believed that the mesmeric state was like a doorway into the spirit realm, providing empirical and verifiable proof of the existence of that realm. The psychological understanding of the mesmeric state promoted by people like Sunderland and others made it appear to be a natural, rather than a supernatural, phenomenon. This naturalism of mesmerism, then, helped make communication with the spirit realm also seem natural. To many spiritualists, theirs was an experiential religion, based on a belief in the immortality of souls and an afterlife, just as in Methodism or other belief systems. Many spiritualist leaders also sought to explain their approach as scientific psychology, based on empirical evidence, and some sought the involvement of scientists in validating their claims. We discuss the role of psychologists in these matters later.

Spiritualism drew upon technological innovations, such as the wireless telegraph, to explain spiritualist phenomena. When X-rays were discovered in the 1890s, many suggested that it was only a matter of time before scientists discovered the heretofore secret energy rays that made spiritualist practices work. We should note that spiritualism enjoyed a great popularity, among all classes, especially after the American Civil War (1861–1865). So many men were killed in the war, more than 600,000, that many homes had no adolescent or adult males in residence for several postwar years. In this atmosphere, the longing to communicate with these lost loved ones helped inspire great faith in spiritualist practices. As far as much of the public was concerned in the last quarter of the 19th century, spiritualism was psychology.

New Thought

The work of Phineas P. Quimby (1802–1866) represented a bridge to new metaphysical movements that arose in the second half of the 19th century. Quimby's work led to what became known as **New Thought** and influenced Mary Baker Eddy (1821–1910), who went on to found Christian Science. Early in his career Quimby had been a clockmaker, but he became a mesmerist and healer after hearing a series of lectures on mesmerism in the late 1830s. By the 1850s, he had developed his system of thought about the influence of one mind on another to move beyond mesmerism to a practice of psychological healing. His method was one of intense empathy with the other person so that, as he said, he could then see the false belief (about disease) that was the true cause of the illness. He could then, he claimed, correct the false belief and the person experienced healing.

Quimby's influence was remarkable. In the charged atmosphere of the time, many embraced his psychology of health and disease. As mentioned, one person he had treated successfully, Mary Baker Eddy, went on to found

FIGURE 4.4 Mary Baker Eddy
Courtesy of the authors.

the Church of Christ, Scientist (Christian Science). By the mid-1890s, other followers had created a body of mental science that came to be called **New Thought**. Many of these writers, such as Warren Felt Evans (1817–1889), drew upon evidence from mesmerism, a psychological practice, to validate their claims of spiritual senses acting independently of the body. For those who embraced New Thought, mental science and healing were solidly grounded in an everyday psychology of human experience.

Psychical Phenomena

The Society for Psychical Research (SPR) was founded in England in 1882 and its American counterpart, the American Society for Psychical Research (ASPR) was formed three years later. Both societies had as their members prominent

FIGURE 4.3 Phineas Quimby

scientists, philosophers, scholars, and business-people. The purpose of the societies was to scientifically investigate psychical phenomena. The formation of these specialty organizations and their leadership by such prominent individuals is an indicator of how popular and widespread psychical phenomena were. Mesmerists, spiritualists, clairvoyants, mind readers, and mediums, not to mention astrologers, palmists, phrenologists, and faith healers, were doing steady business in most large cities and many towns, in addition to the itinerant healers and phrenologists.

The ASPR created committees to investigate many of these phenomena and their practitioners, including thought transference, hypnotism, telepathy, clairvoyance, and trance states. The psychologist William James was a prominent member of the ASPR and served as its president in 1894. James argued that since we know so little about these states, it was better to attempt to study them scientifically. If there was any validity to the phenomena, they would certainly lie within the province of psychological science.

As we detail later, James's stance was extremely problematic for many of his colleagues, who saw themselves and their new science as threatened by the public's confusion of psychical with psychological phenomena. In some ways, these psychologists were correct in identifying these other psychologies as competitors. As we have shown so far in this chapter, these practices and belief systems *were* psychologies for much of the American population. Psychologists, then, had to find ways to distance themselves from what they perceived as pseudoscience, without turning the public off to psychology. That is, they had to try to "own" psychology.

Before exploring this, it is worth pointing out that the phrenologists, mesmerists, spiritualists, and New Thought practitioners were instrumental in creating a psychological sensibility, or everyday psychology, among Americans from all walks of life. By the time the new disciplinary psychologists came on the scene, Americans had already begun to think psychologically and to be open to their own internal experiences. It was this sensibility that the new disciplinary psychologists were able to build on, yet this sensibility also made the mind sciences formidable competitors for the attention and allegiance of the American people and the resources needed to institutionalize disciplinary Psychology.

BOUNDARY WORK AND THE NEW PSYCHOLOGY: ESTABLISHING THE CENTER AND MARKING THE PERIPHERY

What strategies did the new psychologists use to own Psychology? As we alluded to earlier and in Chapter 3, one of the challenges faced by the new psychologists, as they established themselves in the United States, was to convince university administrators and colleagues that their new discipline was distinct from philosophy. This was accomplished, in part, by using the experimental methods they had learned in Germany to argue that Psychology was a *scientific* approach to studying mental processes and thus unique. They also self-consciously distanced themselves from the extant traditions of mental and moral philosophy by rhetorically declaring themselves uninfluenced by and divorced from this tradition, as we have already discussed. These strategies were successful in securing Psychology's place in the rapidly expanding university system. Psychological laboratories sprang up across the country and were quickly filled with the latest brass instruments. Psychology journals were set up, and textbooks were written. Eventually, separate departments of psychology were established. The strategies used to secure Psychology's place as institutionally and conceptually distinct from philosophy were, by and large, quite successful.

But a somewhat larger battle had to be waged and won in the struggle to own psychology. Psychologists not only had to create institutional space and legitimacy for their new discipline, they also had to secure their status as psychological experts in the eyes of the public. Specifically, the scientists of the mind needed to loosen the hold of psychical research and spiritualism on the public imagination. One way to characterize this is as a struggle over what should be the center of psychological theory and practice. At this time, early in the history of disciplinary Psychology, it was not clear that the new science of Psychology would gain dominance over the everyday psychologies represented by phrenology, spiritualism, psychic phenomena, and mental science. In addition, many Americans had learned to rely on these everyday psychologies to understand themselves and for practical advice in matters of health, business, and child rearing.

In the late 1800s, the psychological topics that most interested the American public were not reaction times and perceptual discriminations but whether or not they could communicate with the dead, whether mental telepathy was real, and whether psychics or seers could actually foretell the future. When the new psychologists began to ply their trade, they were often approached with questions on these subjects. Psychologist Hugo Münsterberg noted that when he first arrived at Harvard in 1892 rarely a week would go by in which he was not asked to comment on spiritual, mystic, or paranormal phenomena.

Given that most of the new psychologists felt their connection with spiritualism endangered their scientific credibility, one strategy would have been to denounce it altogether and distance themselves from these alternative psychologies, as they perceived them. Several of the new psychologists did make public statements condemning spiritualism and disavowing psychical research. But herein lay a problem: Psychical research was what the public wanted, and what the public was willing to support, when this support was particularly crucial for the fledgling discipline. In many cases, major bequests to fund journals and academic research were earmarked for psychical research. This dilemma demanded a creative solution. How could psychologists maintain their scientific credibility *and* capitalize on the public's enthusiasm for the study of psychic phenomena?

In some cases, terminological obfuscation provided a way to conduct *psychological* research with funds designated for *psychical* research. In other cases, psychologists attempted to assert their authority as the only experts qualified to evaluate (and, implicitly, discredit) spiritualism by using careful, systematic, scientific methods. They could thus engage with spiritualism while still asserting their scientific authority. In one famous example, G. Stanley Hall and Amy Tanner took on the case of Leonora Piper, a famous Boston medium, and attempted to show she was a fraud. They spent several sessions administering various psychological and physiological tests while she was in a trance state, but their results were equivocal. Interestingly, in their attempts to discredit Piper, they were taking on not only Piper herself but also Hall's former mentor and the most well-known psychologist in America: William James (1842–1910).

James, as we mentioned earlier, was one of the founders of the ASPR. He was interested in spiritualism and paranormal experiences and was not as quick as some of his scientifically minded colleagues to disavow the possibility of a spirit world. Indeed, James believed that proof of the existence of the afterlife might possibly create a new secular faith and the moral regeneration of society. He was quite aware, however, that the best arbiters of the evidence would be scientists, not only because of their objectivity but also because of their cultural authority. Among other founding members of the ASPR were psychologists Hall, Baldwin, Joseph Jastrow, and Christine Ladd-Franklin. Although all had dropped their affiliation by 1890, James remained involved. James's dual affiliation in the public's mind as psychologist and psychical researcher was a bête noir for his colleagues, who were desperately trying to assert the identity of the new science and combat the "malevolent ghost preventing public confidence in scientific naturalism," as historian Deborah Coon has written (1992, p. 149).

Psychologists had to do battle on another front in their campaign for the public acceptance of scientific naturalism; they also needed to reassure a pious public (including university presidents) that theirs was not a godless science. Although the Progressive Era was marked by increased faith in science and technology and several challenges to received religious views, psychologists still had to be careful to persuade the public that their discipline would not threaten the spiritual welfare or moral propriety of its followers. In writing for the popular press, psychologists such as Hall and Edward Wheeler Scripture emphasized that training in the new Psychology would instill the moral virtues of perseverance and industriousness. As Wade Pickren has written, "It can be argued that work held a meaning almost synonymous with morality in American life" (2000, p. 1023). The new psychologists were exemplars of the Protestant work ethic and promoted the character-building qualities of their endeavor. They also commented specifically on the relationship between Psychology and religion. This relationship, far from being antagonistic, they argued, was in fact harmonious. Hall suggested that the wonders exposed by the new science, such as the functions of the brain, would simply highlight the exquisite handiwork of an all-knowing Creator. Thus, harmony between the new science and the religious worldview was maintained.

Finally, we should mention that even after the first couple of decades of their new science, psychologists were called upon to continue their boundary work in the face of the popularity of psychoanalysis. We discuss this boundary work between psychologists and psychoanalysis, as well as the impact of psychoanalytic ideas on the mental health professions in America, in Chapter 5.

AMERICAN PSYCHOLOGISTS: ORGANIZATION AND APPLICATION

As we indicated earlier, American psychologists faced some difficult challenges in the first era of the new Psychology in the United States. In this section, we examine two other strategies that were used by psychologists to strengthen their identity and to stake their claims to a legitimate place in American society. These two strategies were to organize themselves as a discipline and to demonstrate their usefulness to society. Broadly conceptualized, both of these strategies now appear to have been integral to their indigenization in America. They also illustrate the relationship between everyday psychology and disciplinary Psychology.

Organizing for Science

In July 1892, G. Stanley Hall (1844–1924) met with a small group of men to discuss the possibility of organizing a psychological association. Although the details of the meeting are not known, the group elected 31 individuals, including themselves, to membership, with Hall as the first president. The first meeting of the new American Psychological Association (APA) was held in December 1892 at the University of Pennsylvania. Membership growth in the APA was modest in its first two decades. There were 31 members in 1892, 125 members in 1899, and 308 members in 1916. Nevertheless, APA played a critical role in making psychology a recognized science in this era.

The founders of the APA were a small group of White men interested in what was called the new Psychology, as we mentioned earlier. APA's founding can best be understood as part of the many changes occurring in the United States at that time. The emergence of several of what are now standard academic disciplines, such as psychology, economics, political science, biochemistry, and physiology, in the last two decades of the 19th century was part of a reorganization of American knowledge production, reflecting a division of intellectual labor similar to the division of manufactory labor. Like its fellow disciplines, the new Psychology grew and prospered as it responded to the needs of American society.

Within the modern university system that emerged after the American Civil War, the new disciplines quickly developed advanced degrees that provided credentials. These validated the discipline's members as experts in their special field. As we noted in our discussion of John B.Watson in the previous chapter, this was the era of the Progressive movement, which called for a more efficient, less corrupt, social order. The synergism of these two developments—specialized expertise and rationalized government—helped create the demand for trained personnel to fill the new professional niches created by the demands for a more efficient society. Psychology was one of the most successful of the new disciplines in making itself useful for the social management of an increasingly complex and diversified society.

Hall was one of the more colorful and controversial figures in the history of American psychology. He grew up in Massachusetts in a religious family; his mother had hopes that he would become a Christian minister. Although he did enroll in Union Theological Seminary after he graduated from Williams College in 1867, it soon became clear that ministry was not for him. Instead, after serving as a private tutor, Hall became a faculty member for two years at Antioch College in Ohio. His responsibilities at Antioch were immense: teaching four subject areas, serving as debate coach and the college librarian. In addition, Hall taught occasionally for nearby Wilberforce College, a historically Black college.

Hall, understandably, grew unhappy at Antioch and left with the idea of perhaps studying this new Psychology he was reading about. He became a student of James at Harvard and earned his doctorate with James in 1878. Hall's dissertation was on a psychological topic, although his approach was philosophical, and he was awarded what is likely the first American degree in psychology. Although James was a good adviser to Hall, the two men were only 2 years apart in age and, in time, Hall seemed to view James as more a rival than a mentor. On the matter of

FIGURE 4.5 G. Stanley Hall

psychical research discussed earlier in the chapter, for example, James advocated an open-minded stance toward psychical phenomena, while Hall took the position of dismissing it. In 1879, Hall spent the fall term in Leipzig, Germany, with Wundt and so was among the first cohort of experimenters in Wundt's pioneering laboratory.

Hall returned to the United States but without a full-time position. Over the next couple of years, he worked hard to find a faculty job and finally landed a position at the then-new Johns Hopkins in 1882. Within a couple of years he had attracted several capable graduate students and founded the first working laboratory of psychology in the United States. But Hall had already begun showing some of the characteristics that made him a controversial person. Questions arose, for example, about how he had won the Johns Hopkins faculty position, with some evidence that he had deliberately undermined the candidacy of the other suitable applicant, Charles Peirce. Then, James McKeen Cattell, perhaps his brightest student, left Johns Hopkins over a dispute with Hall about a fellowship and went on to Leipzig, where he earned his doctorate with Wundt. Some scholars have suggested that Hall was not comfortable when he had other top-level individuals in the same working environment.

In 1887, Hall, who was then still a member of the ASPR, was approached by another member who offered substantial financial support if Hall would start a journal to report on the scientific exploration of psychical phenomena. Hall agreed to do so, took the money, but began the *American Journal of Psychology*, which never reported on any scientific investigation related to psychical research. However, it was America's first scientific journal devoted to psychology and so was a crucial part of giving the new discipline a scientific identity. In the same year, a wealthy Worcester, Massachusetts, industrialist, Jonas Clark, approached Hall about helping him found a college for working-class young men. Jonas Clark left the matter in Hall's hands, with adequate funds made available, and left for Europe. Hall thus became the founding president of Clark University. He attracted a small but distinguished faculty, most of them young and several of whom went on to worldwide fame. For example, Albert Michelson (1852–1931), one of the first winners of the Nobel Prize in physics (1907) was on faculty at Clark from 1889 to 1892, and Franz Boas (1858–1942), considered by many to be the founder of modern cultural anthropology, was at Clark until 1892. Financial problems, however, resulted in many of his stellar faculty, including Michelson and Boas, leaving for employment elsewhere. From 1890 to 1920, Clark produced more doctorates in psychology than any other institution. The range of topics was eclectic, and we return to this work later in this chapter.

It was in this context that Hall led the effort that created the APA in 1892. In some ways, the founding of APA can be seen as an attempt by Hall to keep himself in the leadership of the now rapidly growing field. But many of his peers in the field were not sure he was trustworthy, and while he was respected, he never again was one of the organizational leaders of the discipline.

Making Psychology Useful

> What every educator, every jail-warden, every doctor, every clergyman, every asylum-superintendent, asks of psychology is practical rules. Such men care little or nothing about the ultimate philosophic grounds of mental phenomena, but they do care about improving the ideas, dispositions, and conduct of the particular individuals in their charge.
>
> —William James, "A Plea for Psychology as a Natural Science," 1892

James was prescient in this 1892 passage. Perhaps he simply understood the American character: that Americans are ultimately a practical or pragmatic people who want to know how something will work or how a body of knowledge will benefit them, rather than wondering about its intellectual or philosophical basis. In America, this was exemplified in the development of a functionalist psychology. **Functionalism**, as you should recall from Chapter 3, meant that the goal of psychology was to understand how the mind and its contents had evolved by looking at the functions of different thoughts and beliefs, functions that were objectively observable in terms of actions. The implications of functionalist psychology were that it held promise of usefulness.

Certainly, James has been proven correct in his assertion that Americans wanted a psychology that was useful. In this section, we give several examples of application in this first generation of organized Psychology in the United States and argue that this trend toward application was part of the indigenization process and was an example of the interdependence of everyday and disciplinary psychologies.

Engaging the Public

As James asserted, Americans wanted a useful psychology. Evidence in support of James's assertion can be found throughout American culture—literary, scientific, educational, and popular—in the era of the first generation of disciplinary Psychology. It is clear that Americans were expecting their sciences to improve their daily lives and to bring order and control to American society. University administrators wrote about the need for offering instruction that had both practical and social relevance. Psychologists, to secure the goodwill of the university presidents and administrators who held the strings to employment and research support and of the public who demanded some lasting good, promised to provide results that would meet these expectations.

Psychologists responded to social expectations with several publications. Even before the founding of organized Psychology in America, psychologists were writing for the popular press, hoping to explain their work, to differentiate their efforts from those of their competitors, and to advance their explanations of psychological functioning. Psychologists have continued to do so even up to our own time. The period from approximately 1890 until 1920 was a fruitful time for psychologists writing for a popular audience. Magazine circulation was going up, the urban population was increasing rapidly, and literacy rates were growing steadily. Psychologists such as Hall wrote about religion and psychology and others wrote about psychology and education, but many of the popular articles and books centered on the potential usefulness of psychology for the everyday person. In fields like education, industry, advertising, and personnel selection, psychologists promised the public that their science was up to the task of improving performance through understanding the psychology of the people involved. Münsterberg, at Harvard, wrote about the use of psychology in the court system, especially the usefulness of psychology in eyewitness testimony. He also published one of the first American books on psychotherapy, in 1908. But what he was mostly known for was his work on human relations and efficiency in the workplace. In popular magazine articles and books, Münsterberg sought to demonstrate the superiority of a psychologically informed science of work. We discuss

his contributions in more detail later in this chapter.

Other psychologists also wrote for the public in this era, but our point here is not to examine these popular press materials. Instead, we simply emphasize that psychologists engaged the public both in response to public pressure for utility and in an effort to gain an audience for their work.

Education: The Pay Vein That Supports the Mine

One arena that was critical for the growth of psychology in this era was education. Hall was instrumental in making education the first real application of psychology. Even before Hall became a professor at Johns Hopkins in 1882, he was involved in what was then called the child study movement. This was a movement that began in the 1870s among physicians, parents, educators, and social workers to better understand how children learn. Hall sought to make psychology part of this movement and argued that children needed to be studied scientifically to establish developmental norms and to facilitate childcare. Hall left the child study movement for a period when he went to Johns Hopkins and then on to Clark University. However, by the mid-1890s, Hall was again involved. Many of his students at Clark, although trained as psychologists, were primarily focused on some aspect of education in their research. We discuss a few of these people and their work here.

Child study is not the same as education, although the two are related. The child study movement was a precursor to the rapid growth of psychology's involvement with education. Why was there such growth?

As we noted before, the Progressive period, roughly 1890–1920, was a time of a reordering or rationalizing of many aspects of American life. Education was one area dramatically affected. Compulsory schooling, which means children have to attend school for a certain number of years or to a certain age, became the norm in this period. When combined with a high birth rate and a large influx of immigrants, the impact on school systems across North America was dramatic. Two statistics are worth noting to help us understand this impact. First, from 1890 to 1920, enrollment in schools increased by more than 1,000 percent! Second, the investment of state and federal money in education more than doubled in this period. With this growth came a need for the efficient management of students and appropriate training for teachers.

Psychologists believed they could provide a methodology and technology for both of these needs. The professional school administrator became a new member of the educational hierarchy, and educational psychologists were soon producing quantitative studies indicating the best ways to measure educational outcomes. It is worth noting that the work of psychologists in this new field, people like Edward Lee Thorndike (1874–1949), was not about the process of learning and how to improve the learning process for students. It was mostly about how to place children and how to manage the institutions in such a way that they were efficient. This was a similar approach to what was happening in industry at the same time, as we explain later. This was a growth field for psychology; by 1910, more than three-quarters of all American psychologists who were involved in applied work were occupied with educational applications.

This was when psychologists also began to develop expertise with school-related problems and helping schoolchildren. In African American communities, whose schools were segregated and poorly funded by White school boards, teachers trained at one of the historically Black colleges and universities that provided an early form of child guidance. Although graduate education for African Americans, in psychology and every other field, was rare, the interest in psychology was high (Guthrie, 1998). Wilberforce in Ohio, for example, had a 40-member Psychology Club in 1914. Since graduate education was not readily available to these students, many

graduates practiced as psychologists in their schools and communities with a bachelor's degree. When the Rockefeller Foundation began awarding fellowships to African Americans and others in the 1910s, archival records show that many of the African American recipients used their fellowships to advance their education in psychology.

At Clark University, as mentioned, many students did their dissertation research on educational topics and most of these students then went on to careers in psychology and education. Henry Herbart Goddard (1866–1957) earned his PhD with Hall at Clark in 1899. After teaching in a normal school for a few years (a normal school was a college for training teachers), he became the director of psychological research at Vineland Training School for the Feebleminded in New Jersey. It was in this context, working with children who were developmentally delayed and retarded, that Goddard brought the first test used to measure intelligence to the United States from France. Lewis Terman (1877–1956) earned his PhD with Hall at Clark in 1905. Due to health concerns, he relocated to California, where he worked at the Los Angeles Normal School (now University of California, Los Angeles) and then moved up the coast to Stanford University, where he had one of the most distinguished careers in the history of American psychology. At Stanford, he revised the Binet test that Goddard had brought back from France, which became the Stanford-Binet Tests of Intelligence. It became one of the most widely used tests in the world. Terman, like Goddard, was a key figure in the debates over intelligence and its assessment. We examine the work of both Goddard and Terman in the context of debates about intelligence and eugenics in Chapter 6.

In 1896, at the University of Pennsylvania, a young psychologist named Lightner Witmer (1867–1956), who had earned his PhD in Germany under Wundt, began offering services to help schoolchildren with learning problems. He called this approach clinical psychology. Much of the work was related to assessment of physical problems, such as hearing loss, that were interfering with the child being able to perform adequately. The new field of clinical psychology grew over the next 25 years to encompass a broader range of school and social problems. However, the term "clinical psychology" did not mean in this period what it came to mean after World War II, when it primarily referred to services such as psychological assessment of mental problems and the application of psychotherapy to those problems.

Psychologists in Industry

Education was a primary application for psychologists in the first generation of American psychology. But the growth of the applications of psychology to various industrial settings and problems was also remarkable. In one 10-year period, 1907–1916, more than 40 industry-funded applications of psychology could be found in the United States. This is remarkable given the relatively small number of psychologists.

The work of psychologists in industry was part of their involvement in social management. With other new professions they were engaged in the business of practically ordering human affairs. We give a couple of examples of this business: psychologists and advertising and psychologists and industrial efficiency.

First, however, we need to contextualize the application of psychology to industry by mentioning the work of Frederick Winslow Taylor (1856–1915). Taylor was an engineer who became convinced that business and industry could be studied scientifically and placed on a rational and orderly basis. His book, *Principles of Scientific Management* (1911), was a summation of work he had published earlier, and it created a sensation among business and industry leaders and spawned hundreds of imitators from various disciplines and professions. Taylor's work, in hindsight, can be understood as part of the Progressive movement in a society that sought greater efficiency in every domain. Psychologists

were among those professionals who saw in the popularity of Taylor's ideas an opportunity to apply their work and extend the reach of their field into new areas.

Münsterberg (1863–1916) was a German psychologist who earned his PhD with Wundt in 1885 and then earned an MD 2 years later in Heidelberg. He was recruited to become director of the Harvard Psychological Laboratory by James at the First International Congress of Psychology in Paris in 1889, a position Münsterberg took up in 1892. There, he built the laboratory into a first-rank site for experimental work. At first, he was somewhat skeptical of the possibility of applying psychology. Then, influenced by his colleagues in Germany who were beginning to apply psychology to such practical problems as improving railroad performance and safety and understanding the psychology of eyewitness testimony, he became one of foremost advocates and popularizers of applied psychology. In 1908, he recounted his involvement in what was then called the "trial of the century," the sensational case of the murder of a former governor of Idaho, allegedly by a hit man hired by the fledgling labor unions. Münsterberg took a train to the trial site, with one entire car devoted to psychological apparatus to conduct his tests. His book about the case, *On the Witness Stand*, brought him great notoriety as a psychological expert. The book

FIGURE 4.6 Hugo Münsterberg

is often noted as the first example of forensic psychology. However, Münsterberg drew upon work on the psychology of testimony done some years earlier by Alfred Binet (France) and William Stern (Germany). To further complicate matters, Münsterberg's court testimony based on his psychological investigation, which helped to convict the defendant of the murder, was later proven inaccurate. Nevertheless, the case gained great attention for psychologists and for Münsterberg as experts on a major social need.

Münsterberg also, as noted, wrote on psychotherapy, but a major contribution was his 1913 book, *Psychology and Industrial Efficiency*. Despite his skepticism about applied work after he moved to the United States, Münsterberg had developed mental tests for children in 1891 and had argued for a rigorously scientific applied psychology while he was still living in Germany. According to his biographer, Matthew Hale (1980), Münsterberg was part of a new science of work that involved physiological, psychological,

and psychiatric components. Münsterberg sought to improve the output of workers by understanding and alleviating problems like fatigue. Individual factors of each worker, he argued, such as personality, intelligence, training, attitude, and susceptibility to fatigue, affected individual output. The intent was to find ways to conform the worker to the task and thus improve the financial bottom line of industrial companies.

A different approach was taken by the psychologist Lillian Moller Gilbreth (1878–1972). Gilbreth argued that it was necessary to change the working conditions to better fit the worker. She argued that humans were not machines and that personality and motivational factors had to be taken into consideration when designing workplaces and improving output. After the death of her husband, Frank, she took over the leadership of Gilbreth, Inc., and made it a global leader in a psychologically informed approach to management.

Sidebar 4.1 Focus on *Lillian Moller Gilbreth*

Lillian Moller was raised in an independent-minded family in Oakland, California. She earned her bachelor's and master's degrees in literature at the University of California, Berkeley. At age 26, she married Frank Gilbreth, nine years her senior and already a successful consulting engineer and contractor in Boston. Lillian became the vice president of Gilbreth Consulting and was fully involved in the business. She and Frank became experts in the new field of industrial efficiency, inventing the Gilbreth clock to measure worker efficiency and pioneering the use of film to conduct motion studies in the workplace.

Although a proponent of scientific management, Lillian grew dissatisfied with the rigid focus on conforming the worker to the job, coming to believe that psychological factors were important in understanding worker efficiency. She enrolled in Brown University and earned her doctorate in applied psychology in 1915. Under her guidance, the firm had great success with both labor and management. When Frank died suddenly in 1924, Lillian became the president of Gilbreth, Inc., and continued their successful work consulting to industry and teaching motion study methods. She became a leading figure in industrial relations in the United States and the world, serving on national and international commissions devoted to topics such as reducing unemployment during the Great Depression. A postage stamp was issued in her honor by the U.S. Post Office in 1984; she is the only psychologist to ever be honored with an American stamp.

FIGURE 4.7 Lillian Moller Gilbreth

What characterized her work was a consistent concern for workers and their environments. To make the work of the homemaker easier, for example, she invented the foot-pedal trash can, which continues to be one of the most widely used models of garbage cans in the world. She also designed kitchens for people who were disabled.

Remarkably, with all the work-related achievements of her life, Gilbreth and her husband had 12 children. The Hollywood version of their family life can be seen in the movies *Cheaper by the Dozen* (1950) and *Belles on their Toes* (1952).

The applications of psychology in education and worker efficiency were notable in this period, but there were many others. For example, Walter Dill Scott (1869–1955), after earning his PhD with Wundt in 1900, supplemented his meager salary at Northwestern University with public speaking. A series of invited talks Scott gave to a group of advertising executives in Chicago helped move him to a successful career in business psychology. His books *Theory of Advertising* (1903), *Psychology of Advertising* (1908), and *Increasing Human Efficiency in Business* (1910) made him a leader in the new field. In his work on advertising, Scott argued that increasing desire among consumers rather than appealing to their reason was the key to sales. He parlayed his early success into a visiting position at a new program in applied psychology at the Carnegie Institute of Technology (now Carnegie Mellon University) in 1916 as the first "professor of applied psychology." After World War I, he founded the Scott Company in Chicago (1919), counted by many as the first psychological consulting company.

His friend and colleague at Carnegie Tech was the applied psychologist Walter Van Dyke Bingham (1880–1952). Bingham was trained as an experimental psychologist at the University of Chicago and earned his degree there in 1908. In 1915, he accepted the offer to start a new kind of psychology program in applied psychology at Carnegie Tech. Over the next 9 years, he created a division of applied psychology comprising a talented group of young psychologists, both men and women. At Carnegie Tech, these young psychologists, joined by Scott for a year in 1916, created programs tailored for the Bureau of Salesmanship Research and the School of Life Insurance Salesmanship. They received large grants from Pittsburgh corporations to improve worker productivity, increase sales, and generate new products. It was a remarkable period of the application of psychology and bridged the surge of interest in and growth of applied psychology in the 1920s and 1930s, which we detail in another chapter.

SUMMARY

In this chapter, we have traced the complex development of the new discipline of Psychology in one national and cultural context: the United States. We have shown how American life in the 19th century helped prepare the country for the rapid indigenization of disciplinary Psychology. The Americanization of psychology had both elite and nonelite origins. Revivalist religious practices—Methodism, camp meetings, the shout tradition—were important in raising questions about the psychological nature of the religious phenomena exhibited in these practices. The indigenous self-help orientation of the American people, especially in the era after the great democratization of public life following Andrew Jackson's presidency, also contributed to Psychology's origins. In the first half of the 19th century, this was especially so in the emergence and widespread popularity of phrenology and mesmerism, which were often promulgated among the same portion of the population that was receptive to revivalist religion. Through the agency of such skillful practitioners as Sunderland and Quimby, millions of Americans were sensitized to an interior psychological dimension of everyday life. Organically related to the movements stirred by phrenology and mesmerism were the development of spiritualism and New Thought in the second half of the century. Thus, by the time the new Psychology was introduced to the United States in the late 19th century, an everyday psychology was already in place.

In the second half of the chapter, we saw how American society turned to science for pragmatic solutions. This was part of what was called the Progressive Era in American politics and social life. The psychologizing of education and the study of work were part of the desire to view all life on an orderly and scientific basis. This focus was not without problems and was intensely resisted both by workers, who saw it as an extension of oppression by owners, and by old-money elites, who viewed it as a deepening of the crassness of American life. Psychologists seized the opportunities offered by education and by industry to define their science and discipline as useful and, in so doing, fostered an American psychology geared to American ideals. This, we argued, was critical for the full indigenization and naturalization of psychology in the United States. In other national and cultural contexts, both process and outcome were different, as scientists and practitioners attempted to construct a psychology that fit their own context. We explore some of those contexts in later chapters.

Finally, we again make the point that the events and outcomes we described in this chapter illustrate how the center and periphery of a science is a negotiated and competitive process. When disciplinary Psychology came to the United States, it was very much at the periphery of science when compared with the centers of Germany or France. It was also peripheral to American society and in direct competition with the everyday psychologies that had grown out of a mixture of religion and mind science practices over the course of the 19th century. It was these everyday psychologies, we have shown, that actually created a psychological sensitivity among millions of Americans. Thus, the success of disciplinary Psychology depended, somewhat paradoxically, on building on the everyday psychology of its competitors. That is, disciplinary psychologists had to employ careful rhetorical and practical strategies to attract and hold the attention and eventual support of Americans who owed their psychological awareness to other sources, while at the same time drawing clear distinctions between their new Psychology and the psychology of mental science, spiritualism, and religion. The success of disciplinary Psychologists in this process enabled American psychology, over the course of the 20th century to move not only to the center of disciplinary Psychology around the world but to the center of American social life. However, even with success, this outcome was not inevitable; one can argue, as we do in a later chapter, that psychologists have never been able to gain complete cultural and intellectual authority over the subject matter of psychology. That is, as historian Roger Smith has stated, in America "everyone became her or his own psychologist" (1997, p. 577).

In this chapter, we have sought to portray these events in such a way that it will help you, as a student, see how psychological science and its applications, like all sciences, are human processes. As such, they are subject to the compromises, conflicts, and constructions that make up human society. It is this human dimension, we believe, that both gives us cause to celebrate the knowledge produced by psychologists and cautions us to take all such knowledge as provisional and contingent on time and place. The historical perspective on these events that we have offered here may help us see more clearly that historical knowledge is crucial to understanding ourselves.

BIBLIOGRAPHIC ESSAY

For our section on mental and moral philosophy, we relied on the scholarship of Al Fuchs, whose article "Contributions of American Mental Philosophers to Psychology in the United States" (2000) gave us the context for the reception of the new Psychology in the United States. Rand Evans's seminal chapter (1984) on the influences of the Scottish philosophers in American mental philosophy was foundational for our understanding. The work of James Hoopes, especially his *Consciousness in New England* (1989), was valuable. We also drew on the scholarship of Graham Richards, "To Know Our Fellow Men To Do Them Good" (1995) for his account of the moral dimension of mental philosophy in American colleges.

An extensive literature exists on the role of religion in American life in the 19th century, and much of it touches on the connections between religion and psychological thinking. We found the following to be especially useful: *The Democratization of American Christianity* (Hatch, 1989) and *Fits, Trances, and Visions* (Taves, 1999). The recent books by Catherine Albanese, *A Republic of Mind and Spirit* (2007), and Christopher White, *Unsettled Minds* (2009), were also helpful.

The recent work of David Schmit (2005, 2009) has been of great critical help in our understanding of the complex relationships among religion, mesmerism, and spiritualism in the near-chaotic mid-19th-century America; his comments on our work were also extremely valuable. Eugene Taylor's *Shadow Culture* (1999) was helpful for understanding the links among religion, spiritual movements, and the emergence of psychology in the 19th century. The fascinating and complex intersection of mesmerism, religion, phrenology, New Thought, spiritualism, and psychology has been well documented. We also drew upon Robert Darnton's *Mesmerism and the End of the Enlightenment in France* (1968) for background on the power of mesmeric explanations and relied on Alison Winter's fine book, *Mesmerized: Powers of Mind in Victorian Britain* (1998). For the American context, Robert Fuller's *Mesmerism and the American Cure of Souls* (1982) was most helpful. We returned to it repeatedly for inspiration and correction. Sheila Quinn's recent article (2007) on the man who began the popularization of mesmerism in the United States, Charles Poyen, was quite helpful. Although it is an insider's history, with all the faults that such a status entails, Horatio Dresser's *A History of the New Thought Movement* (1919) was still useful.

The problematic relationship between these everyday psychologies and the new disciplinary Psychology is most expertly described in Deborah Coon's "Testing the Limits of Sense and Science" (1992); in addition, Wade Pickren's "A Whisper of Salvation" (2000) articulates the complex and conflicted relationship of the new psychologists with religion. We also found the aforementioned *Shadow Culture* (Taylor, 1999) and *Fits, Trances, and Visions* (Taves, 1999) helpful for this section.

We relied on standard accounts of events in the sections on organizing and applying psychology. Thus, Dorothy Ross's biography of Hall (1972) was relied on extensively. But we also drew upon the work of African American historian of psychology Robert Guthrie for his account of the use of psychology by an early cohort of African American students and professors, *Even the Rat Was White* (1998). Jackson Lears offered a stimulating account of how elites rejected the changes in American society in the decades just before and after the turn of the 19th century, *No Place of Grace* (1981). Matthew Hale's biography of Münsterberg was very helpful, as was the account of Münsterberg's work in *The Human Motor* (1990).

Chapter 5
TIMELINE 1700–1950
(In 25-year increments)

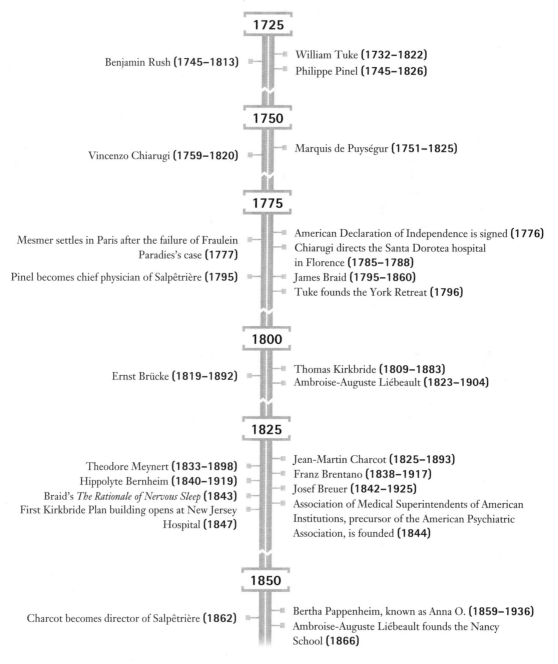

1725

Benjamin Rush (1745–1813)

William Tuke (1732–1822)
Philippe Pinel (1745–1826)

1750

Vincenzo Chiarugi (1759–1820)

Marquis de Puységur (1751–1825)

1775

Mesmer settles in Paris after the failure of Fraulein Paradies's case (1777)

Pinel becomes chief physician of Salpêtrière (1795)

American Declaration of Independence is signed (1776)
Chiarugi directs the Santa Dorotea hospital in Florence (1785–1788)
James Braid (1795–1860)
Tuke founds the York Retreat (1796)

1800

Ernst Brücke (1819–1892)

Thomas Kirkbride (1809–1883)
Ambroise-Auguste Liébeault (1823–1904)

1825

Theodore Meynert (1833–1898)
Hippolyte Bernheim (1840–1919)
Braid's *The Rationale of Nervous Sleep* (1843)
First Kirkbride Plan building opens at New Jersey Hospital (1847)

Jean-Martin Charcot (1825–1893)
Franz Brentano (1838–1917)
Josef Breuer (1842–1925)
Association of Medical Superintendents of American Institutions, precursor of the American Psychiatric Association, is founded (1844)

1850

Charcot becomes director of Salpêtrière (1862)

Bertha Pappenheim, known as Anna O. (1859–1936)
Ambroise-Auguste Liébeault founds the Nancy School (1866)

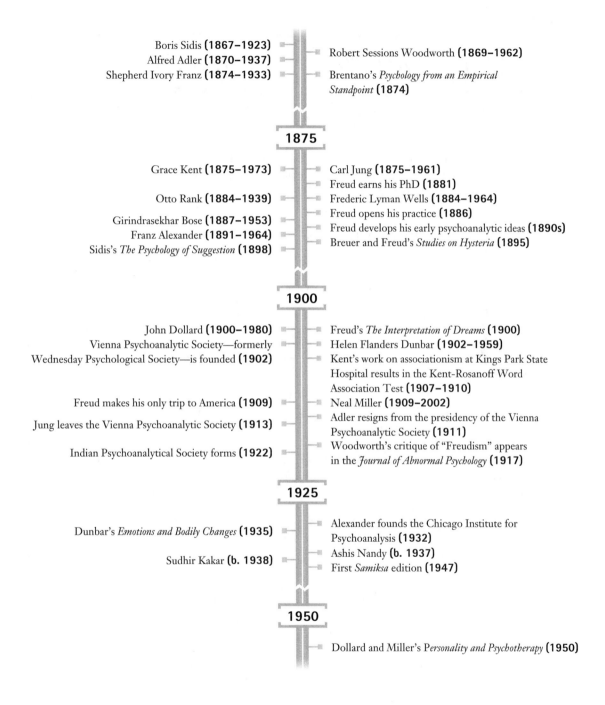

Boris Sidis **(1867–1923)**
Alfred Adler **(1870–1937)**
Shepherd Ivory Franz **(1874–1933)**

Robert Sessions Woodworth **(1869–1962)**
Brentano's *Psychology from an Empirical Standpoint* **(1874)**

1875

Grace Kent **(1875–1973)**

Otto Rank **(1884–1939)**

Girindrasekhar Bose **(1887–1953)**
Franz Alexander **(1891–1964)**
Sidis's *The Psychology of Suggestion* **(1898)**

Carl Jung **(1875–1961)**
Freud earns his PhD **(1881)**
Frederic Lyman Wells **(1884–1964)**
Freud opens his practice **(1886)**
Freud develops his early psychoanalytic ideas **(1890s)**
Breuer and Freud's *Studies on Hysteria* **(1895)**

1900

John Dollard **(1900–1980)**
Vienna Psychoanalytic Society—formerly
Wednesday Psychological Society—is founded **(1902)**

Freud makes his only trip to America **(1909)**

Jung leaves the Vienna Psychoanalytic Society **(1913)**

Indian Psychoanalytical Society forms **(1922)**

Freud's *The Interpretation of Dreams* **(1900)**
Helen Flanders Dunbar **(1902–1959)**
Kent's work on associationism at Kings Park State
Hospital results in the Kent-Rosanoff Word
Association Test **(1907–1910)**
Neal Miller **(1909–2002)**
Adler resigns from the presidency of the Vienna
Psychoanalytic Society **(1911)**
Woodworth's critique of "Freudism" appears
in the *Journal of Abnormal Psychology* **(1917)**

1925

Dunbar's *Emotions and Bodily Changes* **(1935)**

Sudhir Kakar **(b. 1938)**

Alexander founds the Chicago Institute for
Psychoanalysis **(1932)**
Ashis Nandy **(b. 1937)**
First *Samiksa* edition **(1947)**

1950

Dollard and Miller's *Personality and Psychotherapy* **(1950)**

THE PRACTICE OF PSYCHOLOGY AT THE INTERFACE WITH MEDICINE

In the history of science it has often been possible to verify that the very assertion which, at first, called forth only opposition, received recognition a little later without the necessity of bringing forward any new proofs.

—Sigmund Freud, *History of the Psychoanalytic Movement,* 1910

INTRODUCTION

In the previous chapter, we described the creation of an American psychology, beginning in the 19th century and moving forward into the first two decades of the 20th century. Its creation was the product of both an everyday psychology organically grown from the soil of phrenology, mesmerism, mind science, and mental philosophy and the importation of the new laboratory-oriented science of Psychology from Europe. To flourish in the United States, we argued, the new disciplinary Psychology had to prove its usefulness, which it did through applications in education and industry. In this chapter, we turn to another critical facet of modern Psychology: its uses in problems traditionally a part of medicine.

The 19th-century medical theories of mental function and dysfunction in Europe and the United States became foundational for the 20th-century psychological theories of mind and its disorders. This medicalization of mentality came to center on notions of disordered consciousness in the work of French physicians at the Salpêtrière Hospital in Paris, such as Jean-Martin Charcot, Pierre Janet, and their followers. In Vienna, the young neurologist, Sigmund Freud, formulated a nonmedical theory of mental order and disorder and developed clinical applications based on his theory; both theory and technique were called psychoanalysis. Freud's ideas and practices came to have worldwide influence by the time of his death in 1939. In this chapter, we use these figures and their work to offer a historical account of the development of the practice of Psychology in the delivery of mental health services. We articulate how these events were important precursors to the development of modern clinical psychology.

The background for many of these developments was the Enlightenment discourse about madness and its appropriate treatment. We begin with a brief discussion of madness in the Enlightenment and then articulate in turn two traditions of theory and treatment that developed in the 19th century, moral management and the work that followed from the techniques introduced by Franz Anton Mesmer, which were then medicalized as hypnosis. These were not the only medical theories and treatments of mental disturbance, but we use these two to show how the work of Freud both developed and became influential.

ENLIGHTENMENT AND MADNESS

In Chapter 1, we introduced the ideas of René Descartes (1596–1650) and John Locke (1632–1704) and suggested that as their ideas gained currency, the period that ensued came to be called the Age of Enlightenment or the Age of Reason. Recently, historians have demonstrated that the 18th century was more complex than such simple characterizations indicate. Nonetheless, these terms are still useful for us. This was a period when the power of human reason to understand the world and to govern human affairs was accorded the primary place in philosophy, politics, education, and many other areas of life. Man was conceptualized as a creature of reason. The gendered term is intentional; women were typically regarded as creatures of emotion rather than reason.

In this period, when men's rational powers to understand the world were accorded primary status, madness or lunacy, as it was often called, was an example of the failure of reason. The mad, in much of Europe, were usually kept at home or allowed to roam. When a mad person was institutionalized, and few such settings existed anywhere in Europe, treatments typically included bleeding, cold baths, or purging. The most commonly cited medical theory used to justify such treatments was the ancient theory of humors, first formulated by the Greek physician Hippocrates (460–370 BC). Humoral theory asserted that health was regulated by the balance of the four humors in the body: phlegm, black bile, red or yellow bile, and blood. When these humors became disregulated, emotional and behavioral disturbances would ensue. Bleeding, purging, and other techniques were meant to restore this balance and return the person to health.

During the Enlightenment, madness or lunacy was reconceptualized as a problem of loss of reason. Treatments took on a new cast as reform movements that began in the late 18th century in England and France spread to other sites, including North America. In Italy, in the 1780s, Vincenzo Chiarugi (1759–1820) instituted reforms at Santa Dorotea hospital in Florence and later at Bonifacio Hospital. He outlawed the use of chains to restrain patients and introduced more humane treatment. In France, after the Revolution of 1789, Philippe Pinel

FIGURE 5.1 Hippocrates

(1745–1826), the newly installed director of the large Paris hospital for women, the Salpêtrière, instituted changes in the care of those thought to be mad. Pinel drew upon the writings of Locke and the French philosophers Voltaire (François-Marie Arouet), Denis Diderot, Étienne Bonnot de Condillac, and others who were advocates of the values of the Enlightenment. He instituted a new regime of treatment in which many patients were released from their shackles and treated as reasonable humans, able, with help, to regain their faculties of reason. His program had remarkable success. While it is likely that many inmates had never been mad as, at this time, the poor, debtors, and others were all placed with the insane, Pinel's approach still clearly marked an improvement over the earlier treatments and was gradually adopted in other houses and hospitals that had the insane or mad in their charge.

In York, on the northeast coast of England, another remarkable experiment began in 1796, about the same time as Pinel's work in Paris. Local Quakers, concerned about the treatment of some of their members who were suffering from mental disorders, decided to open an institution especially for other Quakers. Under the leadership of a well-to-do Quaker businessman, William Tuke (1732–1822), the York Retreat

FIGURE 5.2 Philippe Pinel

was organized with the belief that mental illness was a state from which a person could recover with the right treatment. Tuke and the Quakers used the model of the God-fearing home as the setting for their treatment. The Retreat's staff employed an attitude of benevolence, personal care, and opportunities to engage in useful tasks to nurture their patients back to health.

From the beginning, the York Retreat reported great success. Many patients treated there were able to leave the retreat and return to their homes. Although it was originally designed to serve Quakers exclusively, before long non-Quakers were also admitted. It should be pointed out that the Retreat was built to house only 30 people and actually began with only about a third of that number. The small size of the patient population, as it turned out, was vital to the success of the treatment.

The success at York led to its imitation elsewhere and was a crucial part of the reforms of the treatment of the insane throughout England, especially after Tuke testified before committees of the British Parliament that were inquiring into the appalling treatment of the insane. Word of the success at York, in Florence, and at the Salpêtrière in Paris gave rise to what was called in English **moral treatment**. This was treatment based on regarding patients as inherently reasonable and providing humane care that

would help them return to their reason. Patients were expected to act reasonably and contribute their labor by completing household tasks.

In the United States, a positive response resulted from this approach. The physicians who led the efforts to treat the insane were called alienists. This word was used because it was believed that the cause of mental disorders was becoming alienated from one's reason. American physician, Benjamin Rush (1745–1813), one of the signers of the American Declaration of Independence, began using treatments inspired by Enlightenment ideas, including novel forms of restraint such as the crib, in which patients had to lie still as there was no room to move. The thought was that as patients calmed down, they would gradually be restored to their senses and their reason would return.

By the 1830s, moral treatment was the standard treatment approach in most of the asylums that had begun to be built in the countryside near many American cities. At first, the patient population was small and there were many successes. Many patients were able to return to their families. With success, however, came problems. In the 1850s, Thomas Kirkbride (1809–1883), a Quaker alienist and leader of moral treatment, developed what became known as the Kirkbride Plan for the design of mental institutions and the care of their patients. For their day, these were large institutions whose orderly design was intended to restore order in the minds of the patients housed within. Again, at first these institutions had remarkable success that continued as long as the patient population was small. However, by the last third of the 19th century, such institutions began to be overwhelmed with an increase in patient population and a decrease in support from private and public sources. Moral treatment was labor intensive; it required that staff, usually nurses and orderlies, give a great deal of time and attention to the patients. With increases in patient numbers and decreases in resources, moral treatment devolved into simple palliative care where patients were fed and perhaps allowed to walk outside once a day. So, by the end of the 19th century, except in a few private and expensive institutions, the majority of asylums had become warehouses of the insane.

With the failure of moral treatment, the alienists, who were organized as the Association of Medical Superintendents of American Institutions for the Insane (now the American Psychiatric Association), began desperately to search for other explanations and causes of mental disorders. Increasingly, they looked to etiologies rooted in the human body: Bad teeth, infections, and intestinal problems were among the explanations offered.

The discovery of germ theory in mainstream medicine in the second half of the 19th century, with its ability to explain cholera, typhoid, and other deadly diseases, placed mental medicine or psychiatry, as it was beginning to be called, even further from the medical mainstream. Although many theories of the etiology and treatment of mental disorder were proposed by alienists in this period, few had any major impact, leading historians of psychiatry to refer to this time as an era of **therapeutic nihilism**, or absence of belief in the possibility of developing effective treatment. It was in this atmosphere that psychiatrists, as they were beginning to call themselves, turned to other disciplines for help, including Psychology.

The atmosphere of therapeutic nihilism also created an opening for psychological explanations of mental disorder and a basis for treatment. This was the opening that Freud stepped into with the theory and treatment that he called psychoanalysis. To better understand Freud's emergence and impact, however, we have to trace another thread back to the late 18th century, to the work of Mesmer. We follow the development of his technique in the clinics and hospitals of England and France and examine the formulation of what was called the clinical approach to psychological disorders among French physicians and psychologists.

FROM MESMERISM TO HYPNOSIS

The modern era of psychological healing was ushered in by a most improbable figure, Franz Anton Mesmer. He was an inventive physician and eccentric thinker, whose work centered around physical healing.... It is one of the strange ironies of history that a man who made no attempt to explain the workings of the mind set in motion a series of events that revolutionized the way we view the human psyche.

—Adam Crabtree, *From Mesmer to Freud*, 1993

We introduced Franz Anton Mesmer (1734–1815) in Chapter 4. There we discussed the important conceptual contribution of his theory and practice to the emergent indigenous American psychology. Here, we explain more about him and how his ideas and practices laid the foundation for later developments in psychoanalysis. Mesmer was a Viennese physician who, during his medical studies, became convinced that just as there are tides in the ocean affected by celestial motion, so must there be tides in the human body also affected by the movement of planets and stars. He called these tides "animal magnetism" and explored how one could manipulate animal magnetism to treat illnesses. As historian of psychology Adam Crabtree points out in the preceding quote, Mesmer's work unwittingly set in motion a series of developments that led to the acceptance of the notion of a dynamic unconscious and the possibility of altered consciousness and dissociation.

Mesmer posited a healing reservoir that stored vital fluids to which patients were connected to restore their personal harmony. Mesmer believed the human body contained a magnetic force that could be manipulated with the use of animal magnetism. This animal magnetism was capable of penetrating objects and acting on them from a distance. It could cure disorders by restoring the equilibrium between the patient's magnetic levels and the levels prevalent in the environment. At first Mesmer claimed to reverse illness by having patients touch iron bars that were magnetized. He then came to believe that any object, not just iron, could be magnetized by his own magnetic force. Later Mesmer would touch the patients, believing that his own magnetic force would be transmitted into their bodies by his touch or even by his glance.

Mesmer was remarkably successful in Vienna and surrounding areas until the case of Fräulein Paradies, a 17-year-old pianist who had been blind since the age of three. After undergoing his treatment, Mesmer claimed that she could see, but only in his presence. Already the object of physicians' distrust and envy, this claim proved too much for many to believe, and Mesmer was forced to leave Vienna.

He settled in Paris in 1778 and was almost immediately successful. His patients were initially drawn from aristocratic circles, including Queen Marie Antoinette. His treatment was so popular that he decided to treat several patients at once. In a typical group treatment he filled a large tub with mesmerized water. Protruding from the tub were iron bars, bent at right angles so that the patients could easily grasp them. Beautiful music played in the background and the air was filled with the fragrance of flowers. Into this scene would step Mesmer dressed in regal robes of lilac and waving a yellow wand. This ritual was designed to induce a "crisis" in the patients. During this crisis, the patient would typically sweat, convulse, and even scream. When one patient would experience such a crisis, others would soon also experience one.

His success in Paris aroused the envy and ire of the medical establishment, which accused him of being a charlatan. In response, Mesmer challenged the French Academy of Medicine by suggesting that 20 patients be chosen, 10 be sent to him and 10 to the academy, and the results to be compared. The academy refused and the clergy accused him of being in consort with the devil. In 1784, the Society of Harmony, devoted to the promotion of animal magnetism, persuaded the king to charter a Royal Commission to study the effects of animal magnetism. The commission consisted of Benjamin Franklin, Antoine Lavoisier, and Joseph Guillotin. The commission concluded that animal magnetism did not exist and that any positive results were from imagination. Mesmer was investigated, branded a fake, and was again forced to flee. This time he fled to Switzerland. Mesmerism, however, remained popular, especially in the United States, where it was mixed with evangelical religions such as Methodism and became a part of popular psychology, as we discussed in Chapter 4.

The Society of Harmony continued to operate in France, and one of its members, Marquis de Puységur (1751–1825), became the advocate for a modified version of animal magnetism. Puységur discovered that magnetizing did not need to involve the violent crisis that Mesmer's approach necessitated. Simply placing people in a peaceful, trance-like state was enough. Although the individuals appeared to be asleep, they would still respond to commands. The condition was renamed artificial or magnetic somnambulism. Puységur found many of the phenomena we know today to be characteristic of the hypnotized state: Paralysis could be moved around the body by suggestion, laughing and crying could be produced on command, and if subjects were told that a part of their body was anesthetized, they could tolerate previously painful stimuli without distress.

Although Mesmer had become a controversial figure, interest in mesmerism and hypnotism and in their practical applications continued, as we saw in Chapter 4. John Elliotson, an English surgeon, suggested that mesmerism be used during surgery, but the medical establishment did not support the practice (although it was done). In India, the English surgeon James Esdaile performed more than 250 painless operations on Hindu convicts, but his results were dismissed because his operations had been performed on "natives" and therefore had no relevance to England. About this time, anesthetic gases were discovered and interest in the use of mesmerism in surgery faded.

Mesmerism or somnambulism was renamed hypnotism. James Braid, a Scottish surgeon (1795–1860), studied the phenomenon extensively and in 1843 published his book, *The Rationale of Nervous Sleep*, where he explained animal magnetism in terms of concentration and exhaustion and renamed it neurohypnology, which was shortened to hypnosis.

In France, a physician, Ambroise-Auguste Liébeault (1823–1904), became convinced of the value of hypnosis and began offering it as part of treatment for free (since his patients were skeptical). He gained a collaborator in Hippolyte Bernheim (1840–1919) who became a major spokesperson for the view that all humans were suggestible but some were more suggestible than others. Bernheim also found that the beliefs about health practices of highly suggestible people were important for relieving their medical symptoms. The work of Liébeault and Bernheim proved important for later conceptualizations of hypnosis and the role of suggestion. It was in Paris, however, that hypnosis found its most effective advocate in Charcot.

CHARCOT: THE NAPOLEON OF THE NEUROSES

Jean Martin Charcot (1825–1893) became the director of the Salpêtrière in 1862. Trained as a neurologist and internist, Charcot has been described as one of the best-known clinicians of the second half of the 19th century. Although he interned at the Salpêtrière, his decision to return there to start his career was somewhat unusual—the hospital was not considered a prestigious post, even though some other major figures in the history of French psychiatry

FIGURE 5.3   Jean Martin Charcot

had previously taught there. Charcot chose the Salpêtrière because he was highly interested in the "anatomical–clinical" method. In this method, the patient's body was examined at autopsy to determine the cause of death, and these pathological findings were then related back to the signs and symptoms recorded, before death, in the patient's hospital chart to establish the disease's distinctive clinical signs.

When Charcot started his career, the method had not been employed systematically in neurology. Charcot saw in the Salpêtrière's patient population the opportunity to try this method on the organic diseases of the nervous system. Since the Salpêtrière was a chronic care facility, most patients at the hospital would be there until they died, affording Charcot the opportunity to follow them to death and then perform autopsies.

To carry out his work, Charcot gradually converted the Salpêtrière into a research hospital. He then made a string of important contributions to the understanding of diseases of the nervous system, including mapping out the anatomical–clinical picture of multiple sclerosis. It was in this context that Charcot became interested in the disease known as hysteria. If he could map out other illnesses, why not one of the most mysterious?

Charcot believed that hysteria, a collection of neurological signs and symptoms that could not be traced to an organic cause, was nonetheless an inherited, functional disease of the nervous system. He spent a great deal of time and energy describing the symptoms of the disease and classifying the characteristics and stages of convulsive hysterical fits. He became a master diagnostician, able to discern in even the most innocuous symptoms—such as excessive yawning—the presence of hysteria. Charcot, with other physicians of his time, felt that the ovaries might play a significant role in the onset and cessation of hysterical fits, specifically, that irritations of the ovaries might bring on such fits and pressure applied to the ovaries could terminate them. Charcot did not consider ovarian irritation an explanation for hysteria per se; rather, he saw this susceptibility as a symptom of the disease. In many cases he was able to terminate hysterical fits by pressing on a patient's ovaries, and he often used this to dramatic effect.

Charcot was a flamboyant showman, as well as a brilliant neurologist. Physicians and researchers from many countries came to study with or observe him, including Freud. Charcot began the practice of conducting public lectures one day a week during which he would invoke and resolve hysterical fits at will in a patient heretofore unknown to him. Hypnosis became an important part of these demonstrations. Because hypnosis and hysteria could produce the same symptoms, such as paralysis, Charcot concluded that hypnotizability, although it could be used to treat hysteria, also indicated its presence. This brought him into sharp conflict with the theories of Liébeault and Bernheim, who believed that hypnotizability was simply a form of suggestibility, a trait that existed in the normal population.

Charcot became highly speculative about hysteria and hypnosis. He hypothesized that trauma caused some ideas to become dissociated from consciousness and thus isolated from the restrictions of rational thought. This is how hysterical symptoms developed, such as insensibility to pain. He then speculated that hysterical symptoms such as paralysis had a psychological rather than an organic cause. According to Charcot, the sequence of events from trauma, to pathogenic ideas (that produce physical symptoms), to the symptoms themselves could only occur in individuals who were predisposed to hysteria. Those so disposed were also capable of being hypnotized. With hypnosis, the hypnotist's suggestions created the same "annihilation of the ego" that traumatic experience did.

Charcot felt that hysteria, in theory, could occur in both women and men. He developed a theory of male hysteria that outlined identical symptoms in men. However, he remained preoccupied with the ovaries, and in practice he almost exclusively treated female patients. Hysteria and its close cousin, neurasthenia, some historians have argued, were distinctly "female maladies" in the mid- to late 19th century. In this period, various gynecological procedures were proposed and tried on female patients. Many gynecological surgeons adhered to reflex theory, in which the cause of the female patient's emotional distress was located in her reproductive system. Proponents of this theory stipulated that organs (such as the uterus) could influence other organs (such as the brain) via nervous connections and thus engaged in various "local treatments," such as repairing prolapsed uteri, removing ovaries, and even excising the clitoris in particularly troublesome cases, such as nymphomania. Gynecological surgeons were more likely than their alienist and neurologist counterparts to subscribe to this theory. Charcot, although he elaborated his own theory of hysteria that we have just outlined, also resorted to pressing on ovaries when a quick resolution to a hysterical fit was required.

By historical coincidence, Freud was studying with Charcot as Charcot was formulating his theory. We move next to Freud but need to point out that another of Charcot's colleagues at the Salpêtrière, Pierre Janet (1859–1947) developed the theory of dissociation even further and soon came to study and publish on the occurrence of multiple personalities or those with co-consciousness. It was Janet's ideas on this that had the first powerful impact on American thought, especially in the medical establishment, as well as among psychologists like William James (1842–1910). It was the French clinical tradition that initially most influenced the theory and treatment of mental disorders in the United States.

SIGMUND FREUD (1856–1939)

The Austrian neurologist Sigmund Freud borrowed from the theories of Charcot, Liébeault, and Bernheim and the French clinical tradition of which they were a part. He also drew upon writers and philosophers from his own excellent education in Vienna, although he was sometimes reluctant to acknowledge their contributions to his theoretical and clinical work. Freud borrowed from these theories and combined them with insights from philosophy and his own clinical work to forge what he termed psychoanalysis. In doing so, Freud, a figure of the Jewish Enlightenment, used reason to show the limits of reason (R. Smith, 1997). The theory and praxis he constructed over his long career were major influences on the forging of a psychological subjectivity in western Europe and North America during the 20th century. Although later theorists and practitioners often disagreed with his theory or methods, Freud had shown it was possible to offer a workable theory of treatment

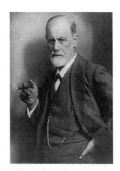

FIGURE 5.4   Sigmund Freud

predicated upon purely psychological grounds. In this section, we place the work of Freud in its historical context and show how his work came to be so influential in the development of the practice of Psychology in the delivery of mental health services. We then examine his influence in the United States, India, and Argentina.

Freud was born in what is now Pribor, a city in the eastern section of the Czech Republic. His father, Jakob, was a wool merchant, who had had two sons from a previous marriage, one of whom had his own first child just before Sigmund was born. Sigmund's mother, Amalie, was 20 years younger than her husband, and Sigmund was her firstborn; she and Jakob eventually had eight children. When Sigmund was four years old, Jakob moved his family to Vienna, Austria, a little more than 200 miles to the west. The family's migration was part of a general movement of Eastern European Jews to points further west, due primarily to centuries of persecution and pogroms in Eastern Europe. Vienna also represented greater opportunity for the children of the Freuds, as the restrictions on Jews were less onerous there than in Pribor or other Eastern Europe locations.

Sigmund Freud flourished in Vienna, showing strong academic skills and a voracious intellectual curiosity. His interests at school came to center on history and literature. During his last year of *Gymnasium*, however, he read the essay, *On Nature*, by the great German dramatist scientist, and intellectual, Johann Wolfgang von Goethe (1749–1832), and decided that science would be his endeavor at university. The options available to young Viennese Jews were limited, and Freud chose medicine at the University of Vienna.

In his early years at medical school, Freud was much impressed by the young philosopher Franz Brentano (1838–1917). Brentano, a priest at the time (although he soon left the priesthood over the issue of papal infallibility), had developed an approach that he called act psychology. His 1874 volume, *Psychology from an Empirical Standpoint*, stressed the importance of motivational factors on human action and argued that human thought and action are dynamic, that is, characterized by direction, intention, and desire. Freud took five courses with Brentano and even considered earning a philosophy degree with him after he completed medical school. Although Freud ultimately did not earn a philosophy degree, it is clear that Brentano sensitized Freud to the importance of motivation and the dynamic character of human cognition and behavior.

Freud came under the influence of the physiologist Ernst Brücke (1819–1892) in his third year of medical school. Brücke, like Hermann von Helmholtz (see Chapter 1), held that all physiological processes could be explained by ultimate reference to their physical–chemical properties; thus, no invisible, secret, or "vital" forces animated living beings. All events have causes, thus the principle of determinism in science. Once he came under the influence of Brücke, Freud set himself to become a great scientist. To work toward his goal, he spent six years working in Brücke's laboratory, doing microstudies of the nervous system of fish, among other creatures. He was able to publish in his area of research but soon came to realize that a career as a researcher would not pay the bills. He finally earned his medical degree in 1881. The

following year Freud met and fell in love with Martha Bernays. Due to bourgeois expectations that a man could not marry until he could show that he was capable of supporting his wife in the manner commensurate with her social standing (an issue that Freud complained about for the rest of his life), Freud then decided to become a clinician, specializing in patients with diseases of the nervous system. For several years he treated cases of cerebral palsy, aphasia, and other disorders of the "nerves." He brought with him, then, from his education and training, a humanist's love of learning and the ambition of a scientist to understand the underlying causes of the phenomena he investigated. Both served him well.

Freud gained clinical experience in Vienna hospitals, particularly the General Hospital, where he worked with well-known neuroanatomist Theodore Meynert (1833–1898). Meynert was intensely involved in the scientific debates about localization of brain function (see Chapter 1) and argued that memories are contained in specific brain cells that are systematically connected with one another in what he called the "ego." Under Meynert's direction, Freud became known for his acumen in diagnosing brain disorders. To further his clinical understanding, Freud sought for and won, upon Meynert's recommendation, a 6-month fellowship for the winter of 1885–1886 to study with Charcot in Paris.

Charcot by this time was perhaps the best-known neurologist in Europe. He had begun to treat hysterics with hypnosis a few years before Freud's fellowship. Hysteria as a disease category had been recognized since the ancient Greeks, who used the term to describe the complaints of women (the term derives from the Greek word for uterus). By Freud's time, it was known that both men and women could suffer from hysteria. Hysterical symptoms were characterized by a mismatch between the complaint and the known functioning of the nervous system. Thus, a patient might report being unable to move fingers, but physical examination would reveal that the nerves responsible for both sensation and movement of the hand were not damaged. The patient's symptoms followed popular conceptions of how the body or nervous system worked rather than how it actually works. Often, when the hysteric's symptoms were successfully treated, within a short time (i.e., hours or days) other symptoms would reappear in some other part of the body. Needless to say, established clinicians sought to avoid taking on such cases. Charcot, however, was determined to describe, classify, and understand hysteria, as we have discussed earlier. While Freud was in Paris, Charcot suggested that trauma may play a role in hysteria in that it could lead to ideas becoming dissociated from rationality.

Freud took these ideas and Charcot's technique of hypnosis back with him to Vienna, where he began to fashion his own theory and treatments. He was finally able to marry and settle into his clinical practice. Still, as a young Jewish clinician, Freud was not in a position to dictate his patient load. As a result, he often had to take as patients individuals who were suffering from complaints, such as hysteria, that more established clinicians sought to avoid. Like Charcot, Freud decided to understand the origin of hysteria and find successful treatments.

Hysteria, then, was Freud's testing ground for what became the theory and technique of psychoanalysis.

After Freud opened his practice in 1886, he developed, over the next 15 years, the basic theoretical framework of psychoanalysis. He traveled, for example, to Nancy, France, in 1889, where he learned from Bernheim and Liébeault that the hypnotized state did not indicate pathology; rather, hypnosis could be used to treat such disorders as hysteria. Perhaps his most important collaborator in these early years was Josef Breuer (1842–1925), a neurologist some 14 years his senior. Breuer had been a friend, a confidant, and perhaps equally important, an important source of referrals to the young doctor. He related to Freud the curious case of a young woman named Bertha Pappenheim (1859–1936) who had come to him for treatment of hysterical symptoms in December 1880. Pappenheim, better known by her case name, Anna O., was treated by Breuer for approximately 18 months for symptoms that had arisen around the illness and death of her father, to whom she had been close. Breuer discovered that if he could induce Anna O. to talk about her emotions and her father that many of her hysteric symptoms would abate. It was Anna O. who called this her "talking cure."

Sidebar 5.1 Focus on *Bertha Pappenheim*

Although Bertha Pappenheim's private pain has become immortalized through her treatment with Josef Breuer and her place in the history of psychoanalysis, historians have also discovered the story of an incredibly accomplished and socially conscious Jewish feminist who recovered from her debilitating emotional condition and went on to devote herself to organized feminism and the social welfare of women and children. As historian of psychology Meredith Kimball has noted, in the years following her treatment, Pappenheim "actively struggled to reconstruct herself and moved successfully from her world of private fantasies into a world of political and social change" (2000, p. 31).

Born into an Orthodox Jewish family in Vienna in 1859, Pappenheim received the kind of education that was typical for her gender and class at that

(*Continued*)

FIGURE 5.5
Bertha Pappenheim, or "Anna O"

time. She undertook both religious and secular training, the latter consisting of 10 years in a private Catholic school where she learned languages, music, and needlework. Her religious training was basic, with instruction in the running of an Orthodox Jewish kitchen and in Hebrew and Yiddish prayers but no formal education in Jewish laws and traditions. This more serious study was reserved for male children and men. Nonetheless, upon leaving school at age 16, she was fluent in English, French, and Italian in addition to her native German. Suffice it to note that upon graduation, Pappenheim, like young women of her social standing, was expected to adopt the role of the young woman-in-waiting, occupying herself with pleasant but unstrenuous domestic and social diversions until marriage. Later in her life, Pappenheim denounced the practice of restricting young women in this way, and she was joined by several prominent German feminists who had also experienced the intellectual stultification produced by these social norms.

In 1888, when she was well on her way to recovery from the symptoms that had brought her into Breuer's care, Pappenheim and her mother moved from Vienna to Frankfurt. There she continued her reconstruction by connecting with the city's vibrant Jewish community, which had a tradition of charity work. She went on to become a leader in this community, devoting herself to improving the lives of women and children, especially unwed mothers. In 1895, Pappenheim took a position as head of a Jewish girls' orphanage. In 1902, she founded the organization Care by Women to bring the goals of the feminist movement to Jewish social work. In 1904, she and other Jewish feminists founded the League of Jewish Women, an umbrella organization that by the 1920s had 400 affiliates and 50,000 members. She served as the president of this organization for 20 years. In 1907, she established her own institution for unmarried Jewish mothers and their children, which, by the time it was destroyed by the Nazis in 1938, had housed 1,500 people.

In this brief biographical sketch of Pappenheim and her accomplishments, we suggest that her place in the history of psychology, as Breuer's hysterical patient Anna O., has perhaps obfuscated the richer account of an extraordinary life that moved, as Kimball has put it, beyond "private pain" into "public action" (Kimball, 2000, p. 20).

In the early 1890s, Breuer and Freud collaborated on a book, *Studies on Hysteria*, published in 1895, that reported five case studies of hysteria. Freud proposed a theory of hysteria based on these cases in which he argued that hysterical symptoms begin in memories marked by such powerful emotions that they then become inaccessible to our recall. Thus, the famous statement from Breuer and Freud, that "the hysteric suffers mainly from reminiscences" can be understood (Breuer & Freud, 1895/1957, p. 7). The result is pathogenic ideas divorced from our rational state but that are full of the emotional energy from the suppressed memories that can then be converted into hysterical symptoms (note the similarity here to Helmholtz's work on the law of the conservation of energy; see Chapter 1). Hypnosis was the technique that Freud and Breuer used at this point to treat hysterical symptoms, which seemed to allow for the energy associated with the pathogenic ideas to be discharged.

However, Freud had already grown dissatisfied with hypnosis as a therapeutic tool. For one, not every patient could be hypnotized. His search for an alternative led him to develop the technique of free association. In this technique, the patient is instructed to recall as much as possible all thoughts and feelings associated with a symptom, without editing the flow of ideas. This became an important breakthrough for Freud, especially when he used the technique on himself.

In 1896, Freud's father died. Freud counted this as one of the most significant events of his life and one which led him to undertake an intense self-analysis. Free association and a new approach, dream analysis, were employed by Freud in his self-analysis to help him through the crisis brought on by his father's death. Freud analyzed his own dreams and found in them, as is often said, the royal road to the unconscious. With the use of these two techniques, he explored wishes and urges about his father that he termed the Oedipus complex, after the Greek myth of Oedipus, who killed his father and married his mother. His analysis revealed to him that he had wished for his father's removal as a child so that he, Freud, could possess his mother for his own pleasure. This later was incorporated by Freud into his theory of psychological development. His analysis of dreams led him to suggest that dreams have two levels of meaning, the manifest, which is superficial and does not contain the real psychological meaning of the dream, and the latent, which is the real meaning, dressed in symbolic form. Dreams, Freud suggested, are wish fulfillments whose latent meaning is intended to disguise their socially unacceptable nature. In this way, Freud said, dreams are like hysterical symptoms in that both represent ideas or wishes that are too dangerous to be expressed in everyday life. Freud brought together all of this material in what many scholars and historians, and even Freud himself, consider his greatest book, *The Interpretation of Dreams* (1900).

Freud continued to develop his theory, publishing many elaborations and corrections to his ideas over the next four decades, as he constantly learned from the application of his ideas in an active clinical practice. Broadly, Freud theorized about children's development, the origin

of neuroses, the role of instinctual behavior, and the emergence and use of psychological defense mechanisms. He also wrote about the role of religion, the problematic role of the civilizing process on individual personalities, and even a psychoanalytic biography of American President Woodrow Wilson.

After 1900, a small group of Jewish intellectuals began to gather around Freud and met at Freud's home every week as the Wednesday Psychological Society to discuss psychoanalysis. Some of these men, such as Otto Rank (1884–1939), Alfred Adler (1870–1937), and Wilhelm Stekel (1868–1940), went on to become leaders themselves of the psychoanalytical movement. In 1907, Carl Jung (1875–1961) and Ludwig Binswanger (1881–1966) visited from Switzerland, thus extending the geographic reach of psychoanalysis; Jung and Binswanger were also the first non-Jews to join the psychoanalytic circle. Freud's circle of influence grew but inevitably led to splits. Adler and Jung broke from the inner circle in 1911 and 1913, respectively. In 1909, Freud made his only visit to North America, where he gave a series of lectures on psychoanalysis at the celebration of the 20th anniversary of the founding of Clark University in Worcester, Massachusetts. Invited by Clark's president, G. Stanley Hall, Freud's lectures were a public triumph. Major newspapers of the day covered the visit and wrote favorably about Freud's lectures. This was crucial for the spread of Freud's ideas, or at least a version of them, in America, a topic to which we return later. While at Clark, Freud also met with American psychologists, including the ailing William James, who reportedly told Freud that the future of psychology lay with Freud's ideas. Jung accompanied him and gave a series of lectures at Clark on the word association technique.

After World War I, in which two of his sons served, Freud revised and expanded his theories to include his now-famous structural account of the psyche: id, ego, and superego. Freud continued to revise and rework his theory and its therapeutic applications until his death. Freud had resisted leaving Vienna even after the Nazis occupied the city. Finally, under threat of death and after large sums of money had been paid to the Nazis, Freud and his family moved to London in 1938. He had suffered from cancer of the jaw for many years. He died on September 23, 1939.

FREUD'S IMPACT ON PSYCHOLOGY AS A MENTAL HEALTH PROFESSION

World War I brought validation to Freud's theory of hysteria. The First World War was particularly brutal, with millions killed and much of the damage done at great distances. Men in the trenches witnessed their comrades next to them suddenly killed by a mortar lobbed into the trench, or thousands would be mowed down by machine guns when senselessly ordered to charge the enemy lines over terrain filled with mud, barbwire, and other obstacles. As a result, many soldiers during the war suffered from what came to be called **shell shock**. The symptoms displayed in shell shock resembled the symptoms of hysteria—paralyses, uncontrollable shaking, inability to speak, and many others—all without demonstrable neurological damage. Some shell-shocked soldiers were court-martialed and shot; some were forced back into battle, where they were unable to function; and many were consigned to hospitals. In England, the psychologist Charles S. Myers (1873–1946) coined the term "shell shock" to describe their condition. The anthropologist–psychologist–physician William H. R. Rivers (1864–1922) was among the first to try Freud's talk therapy with these victims. To his surprise, it seemed to work with many of them. By the end of the war in Britain, psychoanalysis had found acceptance, at least as a niche therapy.

Freud's visit to America in 1909 had been well received, as noted earlier. For some years, as historian Eugene Taylor (2000) has pointed out, there had already been an indigenous psychotherapy movement in America that was centered on Boston. William James was among the members of what Taylor calls the Boston School of Psychotherapy, along with several of the city's leading neurologists, alienists (now calling themselves psychiatrists), and a few other psychologists. While their approach was different from Freud's, there was a general willingness to provisionally accept Freud's theory and techniques.

Over the next 20 or so years, as Freud's ideas or at least a version of his ideas were circulated via newspapers and magazines, many educated Americans came to accept Freud's basic tenet that humans are often motivated by irrational or unseen forces. His ideas that dreams have meanings and that sex is a critically important motivator passed into common parlance. We revisit the popularity of Freud and at least a version of his psychoanalysis in our chapter on post–World War II psychology. Now, we turn our attention to the impact of Freud and psychoanalysis on the new field of Psychology.

Therapeutic Nihilism

Recall that the 19th-century model of mental disorders and their treatment, called moral treatment or moral management, had, by the end of the century, been generally discredited. The lack of effective treatments and the inadequacy of theory helped create an atmosphere in which psychological approaches could be tried.

In addition, alienists felt increasingly isolated in their rural asylums and left behind by advances in mainstream medicine, where the development of germ theory as a cause of disease was beginning to create modern, laboratory-based, scientific medicine. The placement of medical practice on a more scientific basis led to greater success in the treatment of some diseases and raised the status of medicine in American society. These results were reciprocal with changes in medical education, especially at new institutions like the Johns Hopkins University medical school. For alienists, these changes and reforms only highlighted the increasing distance between their specialty and mainstream medicine.

A new generation of leaders among the alienists began to change the name of their specialty to psychiatry. They sought to modernize their field by aligning themselves with some of the new medical specialties, such as pathology. It was in this spirit that some leaders of the new psychiatry invited experimental psychologists to be staff members of asylums. This was a new opportunity for psychologists, who brought their skills in mental assessments and laboratory science to research on mental disorders and their treatments.

Perhaps most importantly, the crisis in psychiatry helped create an atmosphere of receptivity to psychological theories of mental disorders and to treatments based in those theories. Thus, by the time Freud visited America in 1909, there was both a scientific and cultural opening in North America for psychological ideas and treatments.

Psychologists, Psychoanalysis, and Mental Health in America

The development of psychotherapy in the United States has a complex history. American psychotherapeutics emerged in the 1890s and the early years of the 20th century. Taylor (1999; 2000) has shown that the sources for psychotherapeutics, as it was known then, were a rich mix of ideas and practices. One source was the French clinical tradition, including Charcot and Janet and the work of Alfred Binet, Théodule Ribot, and Bernheim, among others. American sources included mental science, mind cures,

and psychical research, as we documented in Chapter 4, as well as contributions from neurology, psychiatry, and a new field pioneered by James, experimental psychopathology. Freud and psychoanalysis, introduced to America by James in the mid-1890s, also began to be influential in the first two decades of the 20th century.

The geographical center for these developments was Boston, Massachusetts. The Boston School of Psychotherapy, as it came to be called, was a group of loosely affiliated men from various professions. James, of course, was prominent. Other physicians included James Jackson Putnam, Morton Prince, Richard Cabot, and Henry Bowditch; all of these men were engaged in the private practice of psychotherapy in the Boston area, in addition to practicing their regular medical specialties. Psychologists were also involved. Boris Sidis (1867–1923), who earned his PhD under James in experimental psychopathology, wrote one of the early and most important books on abnormal states, *The Psychology of Suggestion* (1898). He then went on to earn his MD, developed a large private practice, and continued to write extensively about exceptional mental states. Louville Eugene Emerson earned his PhD at Harvard University in 1909 and then spent the rest of his career providing psychotherapy in both hospital and private practice settings. Another key figure in the Boston School was Elwood Worcester, the rector of Emmanuel Church (Episcopal). In 1906, together with his assistant, Samuel McComb and several physician members of the Boston School, Worcester began holding meetings open to anyone who wanted help with moral or psychological problems. The program was highly successful in attracting and treating many Bostonians. It became known as the Emmanuel Movement and spread to several cities across North America. It drew upon the theoretical and clinical ideas of the Boston School, as well as the older indigenous ideas of New Thought and mental therapeutics. Today it is primarily considered the forerunner of pastoral counseling, but more importantly for our chapter, the Emmanuel Movement was critical for making literate Americans aware of the new phenomenon of psychotherapy.

Thus, when Freud visited the United States in 1909, there was already an emergent body of psychological ideas and practices. A few psychologists had begun to work in medical settings, providing a small range of services. Most of these psychologists engaged in research as part of the effort by progressive psychiatrists to modernize the asylums. Some also offered psychotherapy, as we saw in the case of Sidis and Emerson. It was also in this era that a few psychologists began to offer diagnostic assessments of intelligence and psychopathology.

Psychologist Shepherd Ivory Franz (1874–1933) was among the first psychologists to work in an asylum setting. After earning his PhD at Columbia University in 1899 and then teaching in a medical school, he took a newly created position at McLean Hospital, a private asylum, from 1904 to 1907. While there, he conducted one of the first studies to demonstrate the therapeutic effect of exercise on depression. In 1907, he moved to Washington, DC, where he held a joint appointment at George Washington University and what was then called the Government Hospital for the Insane, now St. Elizabeth's Hospital.

While Franz was at the Government Hospital, the medical superintendent, William Alanson

FIGURE 5.6 Danvers State Hospital, where Grace Kent served as a psychologist

White, introduced psychoanalytic theory and treatment. One of Franz's graduate students at George Washington University, Grace Kent (1875–1973), did her doctoral work at the hospital, where she modified a word association test that had been developed by Jung to detect psychological complexes in asylum patients. The Kent-Rosanoff Test, as it came to be called because of her collaboration on the project with psychiatrist A. J. Rosanoff, was an effective, if time-consuming, tool for detecting patterns of disturbed cognition. (Kent's involvement in this work is indicative of the growing number of women in mental health work and applied psychology more generally, which became widespread after World War I; see Chapter 6). Kent spent her entire career in clinical settings. Not only was she influential through the use of her Kent-Rosanoff Test, but she also mentored several psychologists who transformed clinical psychology into its modern-day form, including David Shakow (1901–1981).

Franz's replacement at McLean was Frederic Lyman Wells (1884–1964). Wells spent his career as a psychologist working in clinical settings, first at McLean and then for many years at the Boston Psychopathic Hospital. He became one of the most important individuals in the development of what is currently termed clinical psychology. An urbane, witty, articulate man, Wells was known for his keen grasp of the experimental method in psychology and his clinical abilities with patients. Wells also came to have a deep appreciation for and understanding of psychoanalysis. During the 1910s, he wrote nearly annual reports on progress in psychoanalysis in American psychology. In his work as an author and as a clinician, Wells kept psychoanalytic ideas and practices before psychologists and was influential in the application of psychology to mental health problems. In addition, he wrote influential books on mental adjustments and mental testing that served the new field of clinical psychology.

BOUNDARIES BETWEEN PSYCHOLOGY AND MEDICINE

As psychologists developed expertise relevant to medicine and mental health, the boundaries among medicine, psychiatry, and psychology had to be negotiated. First, some physicians, psychiatrists, and psychoanalysts perceived psychologists as inadequately trained to participate in health-related work in medical settings, such as mental testing. Second, in the first two decades after Freud's 1909 visit to the United States, several of the leading scientific psychologists were keen to differentiate their field from psychoanalysis. Thirdly, however, in the 1930s and beyond, sensing a new professional opportunity, some psychologists became involved in the development of a new field of medical theory and practice that drew on psychoanalytic concepts: psychosomatic medicine. In this section, we discuss three examples of psychologists negotiating boundaries with medicine.

Mental Testing

Mental testing in medical settings became controversial in this period. The difficulty arose over who was the expert—psychiatrist or psychologist. Psychologists had established themselves as testers in most settings. However, several psychiatrists in this period saw psychological testing as a potential threat. Psychologists like Wells and Franz, while respected for their laboratory research, began to be perceived as infringing on the medical domain in their use of psychological tests. This happened as well with Robert Yerkes (1876–1956) at Boston Psychopathic Hospital. What proved to be at stake was the desire of physicians to keep psychologists from being able to work independently of their supervision. Since psychiatrists and other physicians had no training in psychological assessment, they were unable to counter the test results that psychologists proffered. This conflict was eventually resolved

in favor of psychologists, and by the 1930s, psychologists were more welcome in medical settings, where they were expected to provide a useful service to medicine through their testing regimes. However, to work in medical settings, psychologists had to define their boundaries with psychoanalysis. We discuss this boundary work in the next two sections.

Psychologists and the Question of Boundaries with Psychoanalysis

It is safe to say that most new scientific psychologists viewed psychoanalysis with some wariness and did not see its immediate relevance to their newly minted research-based discipline. However, as psychoanalysis made significant cultural incursions in the 1920s, psychologists realized that, as in the case of spiritualism, they could not afford to ignore it.

According to historian of psychology Gail Hornstein (1992), the new psychologists used several strategies to deal with this challenge to their cultural authority. Initially, psychologists appeared to react with amusement to Freud's ideas, regarding them as little more than interesting and perhaps rather mystical stories about the psyche. When Freud was invited by Hall to come to Clark University in 1909 to give a talk, it seemed as though American psychologists took a merely passing interest in his theories. However, as psychoanalysis garnered more scholarly and popular attention in the 1920s, it proved to be a threat to Psychology's status as the preeminent science of the mind. At this point, psychologists refused to accept psychoanalysis as part of their own field and retreated into scientism, claiming that psychoanalysis was unscientific and establishing ever greater distance between psychology and personal experience by inventing apparatus, designing tests, and focusing on only objective and observable aspects of the human experience. In retreating into positivism, Hornstein argues, psychologists limited the scope and the social and personal relevance of psychological science.

Another thorn in psychologists' side was psychoanalysts' insistence that only those who had themselves undergone analysis were fit to evaluate psychoanalytic theory. Thus, criticisms levied against psychoanalysis were simply disregarded if the critics themselves had not undergone analysis. To psychologists, this seemed incredibly cultish. Robert Sessions Woodworth (1869–1962) of Columbia University said that psychoanalysis was an "uncanny religion" and published an extensive critique of what he called "Freudism" in 1917 in the *Journal of Abnormal Psychology* (Woodworth, 1917, p. 175).

Nevertheless, in an attempt to understand this new phenomenon, several well-known experimental psychologists embarked on analysis themselves. One of these was Edwin G. Boring (1886–1968). He entered analysis in 1934 with Hanns Sachs and received treatment for 10 months, until he eventually ran out of money (his sessions cost $10 an hour). He concluded that his own analysis had not been a success but remained open to the possibility that his experience was anomalous.

By the early 1940s, psychoanalysis had become so popular that it threatened to eclipse scientific psychology entirely in the popular mind. In response, psychologists came up with another strategy not unlike the strategy they had used in dealing with the claims of spiritualism. They decided to use their own methods—the methods of laboratory science—to examine the claims of psychoanalysis. They decided to subject psychoanalysis to the cold, objective gaze of psychological science. In the 1950s, research on psychoanalysis by psychological scientists became somewhat of a cottage industry. Two learning theorists, John Dollard (1900–1980) and Neal Miller (1909–2002), published a book called *Personality and Psychotherapy* in 1950 in which they translated several psychoanalytic principles into learning theory terms and tested them. Other studies included experimental investigations of defense mechanisms. In this way, psychoanalytic theory was operationalized, tested in the laboratory, and brought into the psychologists' own expert sphere of science.

Hornstein makes the point that it mattered less whether the experiments proved that psychoanalytic theory was right or wrong than that psychoanalytic phenomena were being made subservient to empirical test—thus vindicating empiricism and psychological science and subjugating psychoanalysis to definitions of science articulated by psychologists. Even while some psychologists were seeking to discredit psychoanalysis, others sought to find ways to use their scientific work to explore psychoanalytic concepts in the emerging field of psychosomatic medicine.

Psychoanalysis and Psychosomatic Medicine

As a new approach to understanding illness, psychosomatic medicine emerged first in German-speaking countries during the 1920s. Its core principles were grounded in psychoanalytic theorizing, but its context of development was the movement in German-speaking countries to recapture the soul of German life. This movement emerged as resistance to the mechanistic view of life that had dominated German science since the time of Helmholtz in the second half of the 19th century (see Chapters 1 and 8). You may recall that Helmholtz and his colleagues in various sciences had argued that the workings of the universe, including human life, were reducible to their physical and chemical constituents. This mechanical view of life helped make Germany a world power in industry and military might, but many critics charged that it had destroyed the German soul (*Seele*) and diminished Germany's rich cultural and philosophical heritage. This movement of resistance had many facets, but all of them incorporated some aspect of wholeness or holism. As we discuss in Chapter 8, Gestalt theory in psychology was one facet. Psychosomatic medicine as it was formulated in Germany and Austria in the 1920 was also an expression of holism.

In the late 1920s and early 1930s, psychosomatic conceptualizations of illness and treatment spread to the United States, where a somewhat modest reorientation also occurred in the life and medical sciences toward organicist–holist concepts and away from reductionist approaches.

In North America, psychosomatic medicine became an approach marked by its interdisciplinarity. Contributions to research and practice were made by scientists and clinicians from various scientific and clinical fields, including Psychology, as they sought to understand the relationships among emotions, mental processes, and illness. These interrelationships were thought to be important factors in such diverse illnesses as coronary heart disease, colitis, peptic ulcers, and asthma. Two of the primary leaders in the growth of the new field were Helen Flanders Dunbar and Franz Alexander.

Dunbar (1902–1959) was a central figure in the promotion and establishment of psychosomatic medicine in America. She held both an MD and a PhD in philosophy, with an extensive background in religion and psychology. Dunbar traveled to Europe in 1929, where she worked with some pioneers in psychosomatic medicine. According to Dunbar, emotions played a vital role in maintaining or disrupting the person's equilibrium; thus, disease was a manifestation of disequilibrium within the person and between the person and his or her environment. Her massive survey on the relation of emotion to disease, *Emotions and Bodily Changes* (1935), served as an invaluable resource for the establishment of psychosomatic medicine by providing a bibliographical guide to potential areas of fruitful research and by explicating what had already been discovered about the relationship of mind and body in health and disease.

Alexander (1891–1964) was the other key medical theorist and researcher. A Hungarian-born psychoanalyst, Alexander headed the Chicago Institute for Psychoanalysis. What psychoanalysis offered, according to Alexander, was precision concerning the role of psychological factors in disease. He offered as an example his work on psychological contributions to peptic ulcer; the route to peptic ulcer lay in the identification of being fed with being loved, an identification that occurs in infancy. The emotional association that occurs at this time is the baseline for the connection in adulthood between unmet dependency needs and peptic ulcer. Alexander drew upon the work of physiologist Walter Cannon (1871–1945) on the effects of emotions on the body to argue that the physiological linkage occurred through the action of the sympathetic nervous system. Personality, Alexander argued, was the key to understanding health and disease.

Psychologists' contributions came from a growing number of younger researchers who had begun to develop a new approach to understanding mental disorders, usually labeled experimental psychopathology, that used animal research in the laboratory to model disease. While this could not be characterized as mainstream psychological science in the 1920s and 1930s, these young psychologists were located in mainstream universities and medical settings, so they had access to communication networks and the philanthropic foundations that supported the development of psychosomatic medicine.

A leader among these younger psychologists was Saul Rosenzweig (1907–2004), who began doing research in the early 1930s on Freud's concepts of frustration and aggression while a member of psychologist Henry Murray's (1893–1988) research group at the Harvard Psychological Clinic. Rosenzweig used the phrase "experimental psychopathology" to describe the approach. During this period, young psychologists at Yale University, Brown University, Worcester State Hospital, and other institutions delved deeply into psychoanalytic concepts as a source of hypotheses to test in the laboratory. There were studies on frustration and aggression, complementary to Rosenzweig's research; studies on hoarding; and extensive research on the experimental induction of neuroses.

As the new field began to develop, philanthropies took an interest in the work for its perceived potential to help shed light on social order. As we discuss in more detail in Chapter 7, because foundation officers were positioned in such a way that they had contact with a range of trends in medicine and related sciences, they were able to bring together investigators and practitioners who might not otherwise have connected with one another. The Josiah Macy Foundation did just this in the mid-1930s when it sponsored conferences on "Problems of Neurotic Behavior" in New York City. Physicians who were oriented to psychoanalytic and psychosomatic approaches attended, along with psychologists, internists, physiologists, and several other disciplines to formulate a systematic approach to the problems exemplified by psychosomatic medicine. The immediate result of the conferences and the collaboration was the establishment of a new journal, called *Psychosomatic Medicine*, which began publishing in 1939, with many contributions from psychologists. The field of psychosomatic medicine grew rapidly during the 1940s and was an important source of theory and research for many years. It served as the foundation for the later development of the specialty of health psychology.

PSYCHOANALYSIS OUTSIDE EUROPE AND NORTH AMERICA

In the first half of the 20th century, psychoanalysis held much popular appeal in Europe and North America, despite the resistance offered by disciplinary psychologists. Psychoanalysis also gained an audience in other countries around the world. In this section, we offer a brief account of the spread of psychoanalysis outside Europe and North America to two countries, India and Argentina. However, readers should be aware that psychoanalysis also spread to many other countries.

Psychologists, Psychoanalysis, and Mental Health in India

Psychoanalysis was pioneered in India by Girindrasekhar Bose (1887–1953), a psychiatrist and psychologist, at the University of Calcutta. Out of his work the Indian Psychoanalytical Society was formed in 1922; the society began publishing its journal, *Samiksa*, shortly after World War II.

Psychoanalysis in colonial India took on distinctive characteristics of theory and practice from traditional Freudian analysis. Bose's theorization reflected the reality of the role of Hinduism in Indian family life and customs. In extensive correspondence with Sigmund Freud and his English disciple, Ernest Jones (1879–1958), Bose articulated the importance of the mother–son relationship, arguing that in India it is more important than the father–son relationship. Freud and Jones were not sympathetic to this turn and argued that the castration anxiety generated during the Oedipal state was crucial for personality development anywhere in the world.

Bose, however, developed a psychoanalysis that reflected the different forms that Indian families take and the intense relationship between mother and son characteristic of many Hindu families. The cultural reality in India, Bose insisted, was that a child was raised in a joint family system with many parent figures present. The mother–son relationship was crucial, Bose argued, because the mother had to depend on the son for status and her life and sustenance if she outlived her husband. The closeness and dependence that grew between mother and son and was encouraged by the cultural context led to the psychological dynamic of rage by the father toward both of them: his rage about the wife's "devotion to their son, and his rage about the son's access to the female object of desire" (Hartnack, 1990, p. 940). As Bose wrote to Freud,

> I do not deny the importance of the castration threat in European cases; my argument is that the threat owes its efficiency to its connection with the wish to be female. The real struggle lies between desire to be a male and its opposite the desire to be a female. My Indian patients do not exhibit castration symptoms to such a marked degree as my European cases. The desire to be a female is more easily unearthed in Indian male patients than in European. The Oedipus mother is very often a combined parental image and this is fact of great importance. I have reason to believe that much of the motivation of maternal deity is traceable to this source. (cited in Hartnack, 1990, p. 946)

Bose nurtured the development of Indian psychoanalysis until his death; for many years, the meetings of the Psychoanalytical Society were held in his home in Calcutta. His correspondence with Western leaders was important, but Bose did not let those relationships inhibit his own theorizing and the development of a distinctive Indian psychoanalysis. Through his influence and the many people he trained, psychoanalysis remained strong in India, with such critical figures in the postwar era as Sudhir Kakar (b. 1938) and Ashis Nandy (b. 1937).

Psychoanalysis in Argentina

Psychoanalysis as a body of theory and practice eventually spread around the world. In each

place, just as we saw in India and the United States, it was modified to fit the culture and the times. After World War II, psychoanalysis diversified into many distinctive expressions. In North America and much of Europe, the two decades after the Second World War marked the pinnacle of the popularity of psychoanalysis. In most countries, psychoanalysis declined in popularity after 1965, although it has remained an important source of theory in many scholarly fields.

The one exception is Argentina; psychoanalysis has remained the dominant theoretical approach in psychology there. Psychoanalysis gained a following in Argentina in the 1920s and 1930s, when a small group of mental health professionals incorporated psychoanalytic approaches into their clinical work. On a theoretical level, serious attempts were made to integrate Marxist principles with psychoanalysis, much as had been done by such European analysts as Wilhelm Reich. However, this attempted integration failed in the later 1930s as the negative pronouncements against Freud and psychoanalysis by Josef Stalin and other Soviet thinkers turned many would-be analysts away.

In the 1940s, a new movement arose that saw psychoanalysis as a way to subvert the mainstream approach and undermine the fascist government. This was also a period when many Jewish analysts fled Germany and Austria to avoid the Nazis. Several of these émigré analysts ended up in Argentina, where they had a modest influence on the further development of psychoanalysis.

SUMMARY

Psychological thought and practices have had a place in medicine since the early modern period. As concepts of mental disorders changed with

the advent of Enlightenment ideas, the notion that madness may be due to loss of reason brought a new focus on the mind. Psychological principles were developed that could, it was hoped, bring not only explanation but also successful therapeutic interventions.

The initial success of such interventions, for example, moral management, seemed to only prepare the way for later disappointment and disillusionment with mental medicine. The sense of failure in understanding and treating mental disorders by the end of the 19th century can be characterized as therapeutic nihilism. In such an atmosphere, an opportunity arose for a new psychological approach. The theory and techniques developed by Freud were received by a significant number of the members of the mental health profession as it existed at the time.

The reception of Freud's ideas by both professionals and the public had far-reaching consequences. Freud, a figure of the Enlightenment, used reason to show that there were limits to reason, and in doing so, he highlighted the critical importance of the irrational in human motivation. His work also introduced the powerful concept of a dynamic unconscious that gives shape to everyday actions and reactions. This notion contributed substantially to the rise of a psychotherapeutic ethos that continues to this day. Rather than measure the truth claims of psychoanalysis against the metric of laboratory science, it is perhaps more important to recognize that Freud's theories gave people of the 20th century a language and a conceptual framework for understanding and describing the human condition. In this sense, Freud's work deepened the psychological sensibility of humans in ways that psychological experiments in the laboratory could never accomplish. Freud also gave the 20th century a framework for self-exploration and a language with which people could describe their inner lives. It was his work, it is fair to say, that made the 20th century, and our own time, the age of psychology.

BIBLIOGRAPHIC ESSAY

An abundance of first-rate scholarship is available for the topics covered in this chapter. Roy Porter's *Social History of Madness* (1989) gives an excellent account of madness in the Enlightenment and the failure of therapeutic regimes devoted to it. Nancy Tomes's fine volume on Thomas Kirkbride, *A Generous Confidence* (1984) offers key insights into the American use of moral treatment. *Mental Illness and American Society, 1875–1940* by Gerald Grob (1983) provides a well-researched analysis of efforts to develop a sustainable approach to caring for the seriously mental ill and why those efforts failed.

The literature on Freud is vast. Once again, Roger Smith's (1997) essay on Freud in his *Norton History of the Human Sciences* provided our point of departure. Ray Fancher's essay in the *Companion to the History of Modern Science* (1990) was most helpful. We also relied on Peter Gay's *Freud* (1988) and Nathan Hale's *Freud and the Americans* (1971). On American psychology's response to psychoanalysis, we found the thoughtful volume written by David Shakow and David Rapaport, *The Influence of Freud on American Psychology* (1964), useful. Because the relationship of psychology and psychoanalysis has often been fraught with conflict and misunderstanding, we found the work of Gail Hornstein, "The Return of the Repressed" (1992), particularly helpful.

Many fascinating scholarly accounts have described the emergence and dissemination of mesmerism. We have consulted Adam Crabtree's work, *From Mesmer to Freud* (1993), as well as Robert Darnton's *Mesmerism and the End of the Enlightenment in France* (1968) and Alan Gauld's *History of Hypnotism* (1992).

We also found Alison Winter's (1998) book on mesmerism in England helpful.

Eugene Taylor's scholarship on the religious and spiritual roots of psychological practices, such as psychotherapy, is first rate. He has published prodigiously on the topic. We found his book *Shadow Culture* (1999) and his *American Psychologist* article from September 2000 to be particularly useful for this chapter. Eric Caplan's *Mind Games* (1998) expertly details the development of the Emmanuel Movement and American responses to psychotherapy.

For an analysis of Pappenheim's journey from being Breuer's patient to Jewish feminist activist and social reformer, we drew upon Meredith Kimball's article "From Anna O. to Bertha Pappenheim" (2000).

For our section on psychosomatic medicine, we drew upon the work of Donna Haraway (1976) and the fine article by Stephen Cross and William Albury (1987). Material on psycho-analysis in India came from Christiane Hart-nack's scholarship (1990) on the development of Freudian ideas there, as well as Alan Roland's excellent volume, *In Search of the Self in India and Japan* (1991). Cecilia Taiana's work (2006) on psychology and psychoanalysis in Argentina was also helpful.

Chapter 6
TIMELINE 1820–1920
(In 25-year increments)

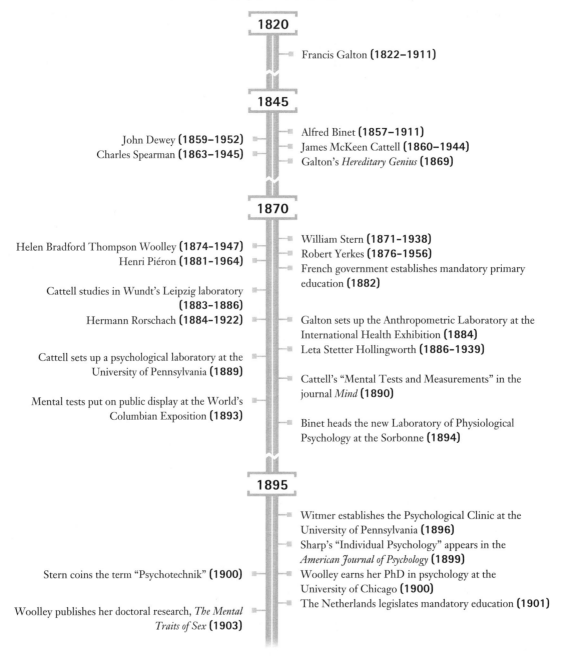

1820

Francis Galton **(1822–1911)**

1845

John Dewey **(1859–1952)**
Charles Spearman **(1863–1945)**

Alfred Binet **(1857–1911)**
James McKeen Cattell **(1860–1944)**
Galton's *Hereditary Genius* **(1869)**

1870

Helen Bradford Thompson Woolley **(1874–1947)**
Henri Piéron **(1881–1964)**

William Stern **(1871–1938)**
Robert Yerkes **(1876–1956)**
French government establishes mandatory primary education **(1882)**

Cattell studies in Wundt's Leipzig laboratory **(1883-1886)**
Hermann Rorschach **(1884–1922)**

Galton sets up the Anthropometric Laboratory at the International Health Exhibition **(1884)**
Leta Stetter Hollingworth **(1886–1939)**

Cattell sets up a psychological laboratory at the University of Pennsylvania **(1889)**

Cattell's "Mental Tests and Measurements" in the journal *Mind* **(1890)**

Mental tests put on public display at the World's Columbian Exposition **(1893)**

Binet heads the new Laboratory of Physiological Psychology at the Sorbonne **(1894)**

1895

Witmer establishes the Psychological Clinic at the University of Pennsylvania **(1896)**
Sharp's "Individual Psychology" appears in the *American Journal of Psychology* **(1899)**

Stern coins the term "Psychotechnik" **(1900)**

Woolley earns her PhD in psychology at the University of Chicago **(1900)**

Woolley publishes her doctoral research, *The Mental Traits of Sex* **(1903)**

The Netherlands legislates mandatory education **(1901)**

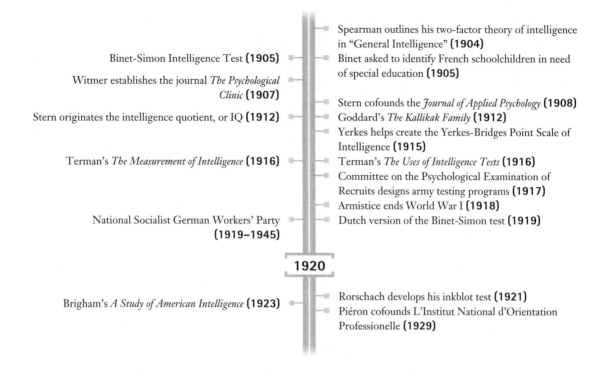

Spearman outlines his two-factor theory of intelligence in "General Intelligence" **(1904)**

Binet-Simon Intelligence Test **(1905)**

Binet asked to identify French schoolchildren in need of special education **(1905)**

Witmer establishes the journal *The Psychological Clinic* **(1907)**

Stern cofounds the *Journal of Applied Psychology* **(1908)**

Stern originates the intelligence quotient, or IQ **(1912)**

Goddard's *The Kallikak Family* **(1912)**

Yerkes helps create the Yerkes-Bridges Point Scale of Intelligence **(1915)**

Terman's *The Measurement of Intelligence* **(1916)**

Terman's *The Uses of Intelligence Tests* **(1916)**

Committee on the Psychological Examination of Recruits designs army testing programs **(1917)**

Armistice ends World War I **(1918)**

National Socialist German Workers' Party **(1919–1945)**

Dutch version of the Binet-Simon test **(1919)**

1920

Brigham's *A Study of American Intelligence* **(1923)**

Rorschach develops his inkblot test **(1921)**

Piéron cofounds L'Institut National d'Orientation Professionelle **(1929)**

PSYCHOLOGISTS AS TESTERS: APPLYING PSYCHOLOGY, ORDERING SOCIETY

All classes of intellects, the weakest as well as the strongest, will profit by the application of their talents to tasks which are consonant with their ability.

—Lewis Terman, *The Uses of Intelligence Tests*, 1916

INTRODUCTION

As we have emphasized in earlier chapters, even before there was a discipline called Psychology, people used various psychological practices to gain knowledge about themselves and organize their private and public lives. Thus, it is not surprising that scientific psychologists in the late 1800s quickly began to envision how the methods, insights, and tools of Psychology could be used for practical purposes. One of the first major contributions of Psychology to the applied realm was the development of mental tests. In 1890, the young American psychologist James McKeen Cattell published an article in the journal *Mind* called "Mental Tests and Measurements." This article probably marked the first time the term "mental test" was used in Psychology. Cattell, who had studied with both Wilhelm Wundt (1832–1920) in Germany and Francis Galton (1822–1911) in England, was quick to point out both the scientific and the practical value of mental tests:

Psychology cannot attain the certainty and exactness of the physical sciences, unless it rests on a foundation of experiment and measurement. A step in this direction could be made by applying a series of mental tests and measurements to a large number of individuals. The results would be of considerable scientific value in discovering the constancy of mental processes, their interdependence, and their variation under different circumstances. Individuals, besides, would find their tests interesting, and, perhaps, useful in regard to training, mode of life or indication of disease. The scientific and practical value of such tests would be much increased should a uniform system be adopted, so that determinations made at different times and places could be compared and combined. (Cattell, 1890, p. 373)

Cattell's statement was an important early indicator of Psychology's concern with its practical value and social utility, as well as its scientific status. This was especially true in the United States, although practical applications of psychology occurred early on in many countries where Psychology was gaining scientific status. Although concise, Cattell's statement performed significant boundary work for the new discipline (for more on boundary work, see Chapters 4 and 5). He assured his readers that Psychology was a science, like the physical sciences, because it was based on experiment and measurement. It was a useful science because these measurements could be used by individuals in their everyday lives. In addition to this usefulness for individuals, psychologists could also develop standardized procedures that would allow them to combine results collected across time and place. These aggregate descriptions of the population would increase the scientific and practical value of the

FIGURE 6.1   James McKeen Cattell
Courtesy of the Archives of the History of American Psychology, University of Akron, Akron, OH.

tests, as well as (by implication) the expert authority of the psychologist.

Cattell, like many of his colleagues, was well aware of the importance of convincing the public of Psychology's expert authority and social relevance, and he saw in mental tests a compelling vehicle to advance both of these agendas. Foremost among the advantages of mental tests was their ability to generate a precise numerical measurement of the psyche. Quantification was the sine qua non of science, and was a powerful trend in late 19th-century Psychology, as it is today. As historian of psychology Gail Hornstein has written, "After psychophysics, the line of work most important in the development of a quantitative perspective in psychology has been mental testing" (1988, p. 8). Putting numbers to otherwise ephemeral psychological qualities helped nail them down,

reify them, and make them into legitimate scientific objects.

In this chapter, we focus on several late 19th- and early 20th-century examples of applied psychology, including mental testing and its progeny the intelligence test, as well as (more briefly) early personality and personnel selection tests, to explore the origins and development of what many historians of psychology have called Psychology's social engineering, or social control, function. In their efforts to produce socially useful knowledge, psychologists in the United States and Europe found ways to apply their expertise to several problems in the service of the state. Some of these applications, such as matching army recruits with appropriate positions in the military, matching workers to the jobs in which they would be most productive, identifying "feebleminded" immigrants, or deciding which students should get special help and which were gifted, involved a "sifting and sorting" function to which psychological tests were uniquely suited. In fact, testing of many kinds (vocational, personnel selection, achievement, personality) became the mainstay of Psychology's applied endeavors until just after World War II, when testing began to share the table with other forms of applied psychology, such as psychotherapy.

In this early period, despite agendas that may now appear misguided or at times overtly racist, sexist, or both, many psychologists believed they were helping to engineer better societies, or at least maintain social order, by sorting people into categories. Helping individuals adjust to existing conditions and function better within them was their goal, rather than a radical reorientation of society itself. In the United States, the capitalist, individualist, rationalist, meritocratic, lift-yourself-up-by-your-bootstraps mentality that permeated American culture also permeated applied psychology, with few exceptions. Tellingly, historian Donald Napoli titled his book on the history of applied psychology in the United States *Architects of Adjustment* (1981) to highlight this orientation. We begin this chapter by focusing on the American context, where intelligence and ability testing achieved a measure of success unprecedented elsewhere. Later in the chapter we present some comparative, international perspectives to help unravel the ways in which testing was developed and used in contexts with different social agendas and different institutional and political structures. As the social constructionist perspective suggests, the development and use of testing was heavily influenced by contextual factors. When contexts differ, so do the concepts, tools, and practices that arise within them.

The value system that permeated American society and Psychology in the early 20th century, and contributed to the popularity of testing in this context, continues to exert its influence in the 21st century. Psychology remains tightly bound to an adjustment ethos, with few exceptions (e.g., liberation psychology and critical psychology, which we discuss in Chapters 10 and 12, respectively). It is important to understand the development of Psychology's adjustment orientation by historicizing it within the discipline's professional trajectory and the social and political demands faced by American psychologists during the last years of the 19th century and the first two decades of the 20th century.

THE ROOTS OF MENTAL TESTING IN AMERICA

To chronicle the development of mental tests in America, we need to return briefly to Germany and, indeed, to Leipzig. From fall 1883 through summer 1886, while studying in Wundt's Leipzig laboratory as a doctoral student, Cattell (1860–1944) conducted numerous reaction-time experiments that piqued his interest in the possibility of what became known as individual differences psychology. In true Leipzig style, he conducted his experiments on himself and one other student. Between himself and his colleague, he generated thousands of reaction

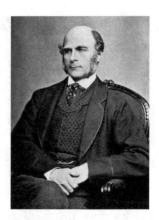

FIGURE 6.2 Francis Galton

times measured as a function of varying conditions of consciousness and awareness and affected by attention, practice, and fatigue. He noted that his times were consistently different from those of his colleague by a relatively constant ratio and suggested that the study of individual differences in reaction times might be an interesting project. Wundt, however, was not particularly interested in Cattell's proposal. The studies in Wundt's laboratory were designed to uncover the ways in which all minds were *similar* in their perceptual processes, not how individual minds *differed*. Luckily, although Wundt lacked interest in the project, Cattell had begun a correspondence with someone who was quite interested in the study of individual reaction times and in the apparatus that Cattell was using to measure them: Sir Francis Galton (1822–1911) in England.

Some years before, in 1869, Galton had published his eugenicist tract *Hereditary Genius*. In this book, he began with the observation that eminence appeared to run in families. Indeed, his own extended family was a good example of this phenomenon. Not only was the eminent Charles Darwin (see Chapter 1) a half-cousin, but Darwin's grandfather, Erasmus Darwin, had been one of the leading English intellectuals of the 18th century. In *Hereditary Genius*, Galton set out to provide systematic evidence that eminence ran in families and used this to argue that eminence must therefore have a hereditary basis. Much like adaptive *physical* characteristics were passed on through evolution by natural selection, so too, Galton reasoned, would high *mental* ability be likely to be passed on in families.

To gather the evidence to support his hypothesis, he surveyed biographical dictionaries to construct a large pool of people who were considered eminent for reasons other than pure birthright. Using the number of people in this pool, he calculated that about 1 in every 4,000 members of the population would achieve eminence. He then looked at the genealogies of the people in his pool and found that 10 percent of them had at least one close relative considered sufficiently eminent that they were included in the dictionary as well. This percentage was significantly greater than would be expected by chance alone. This, according to Galton, provided compelling evidence for the hereditary nature of eminence.

Galton overlooked the environmental factors that no doubt contributed not just to the probability of achieving eminence but also to the ability to access the education and resources required to rise to any station in life. England was organized by a rigid class system that prescribed certain roles and destinies for those born into a particular station and made others inaccessible. Regardless, Galton believed strongly in his hereditarian explanation, and he used this belief as the basis for a system of **positive eugenics** in which he advocated that eminent men and women should be encouraged to intermarry and produce offspring (see also Chapter 3).

There was one problem, however. Often eminence was not achieved or identified until late in life, long after one's years of productive childbearing were over. Galton needed a technique that would help him identify those likely to become eminent while they were still young and able to procreate. To this end, Galton developed a series of tests designed to measure the strength and size of the nervous system, variables he felt indicated general intelligence. In 1884, 15 years after writing *Hereditary Genius*, Galton set up the

Anthropometric Laboratory at the International Health Exhibition. Here, visitors were invited to pay 3 pence each to have various measurements taken, including tests of sensory acuity, dynamometric pressure (grip strength), head size, and of course, reaction times. Upon the completion of the tests, each person received an individualized report that showed where that person stood in relation to others who had taken the tests. When the exhibition closed, the laboratory was moved to London's South Kensington Museum. Eventually, Galton tested more than 9,000 people.

Cattell was familiar with Galton's work and his laboratory, so the American traveled from Germany to England, where he spent a 2-year fellowship and established a collaboration with Galton. In 1889 he returned to the United States and set up a psychological laboratory at the University of Pennsylvania. There, he continued to work in the Galtonian tradition of mental measurement by designing a series of 10 tests that he administered to college students, largely to determine the variation among individuals on performance on various tests. He also alluded to the tests possibly proving useful for a range of practical purposes. Included in Cattell's series of tests were several imported from Galton's Anthropometric Laboratory, as well as judgment of 10 seconds of time, number of letters remembered on one presentation, and reaction time to sounds. Cattell was concerned with obtaining accurate and precise measurements. Basic mental and perceptual processes, as opposed to more complex mental functions, lent themselves well to this scientific approach. In content and in form, early mental tests reflected the techniques employed in the laboratories of the new psychologists to generate information about the normal human mind.

MENTAL TESTS GO TO THE FAIR

Psychologists received one of their first opportunities to present mental tests to the public

FIGURE 6.3 Fairgrounds of the World Columbian Exposition in Chicago

on the occasion of the World's Columbian Exposition of 1893. The exposition, organized to commemorate the 400th anniversary of Christopher Columbus's voyage to the New World, was held in Chicago (one year late!) on 700 acres of reclaimed swampland on the shores of Lake Michigan. It attracted 30 million visitors and was the first time Psychology had been officially included in an international fair. For the fledgling field, this was an opportunity of unprecedented importance. As Joseph Jastrow (1863–1944), one of the psychologists involved in organizing the psychology exhibit and himself strongly interested in mental tests, proclaimed, the event was a prime opportunity to "render visible to the public" what psychologists were doing (Jastrow, 1961, p. 142). Notably, psychologists chose to showcase their new science by recreating a psychological laboratory and demonstrating mental tests.

The Columbian Exposition was the perfect venue to showcase the new, modern, scientific psychology. The Chicago fairgrounds were themselves emblematic of modernity. They had more lighting than any city in the United States at the time and were designed to promote the new urban, industrial world order best exemplified by the cities of the "new world" of America.

An examination of the content of the psychology exhibit and the psychologists' goals for their public presentation provides a glimpse into what the psychologists of the time thought was important for the public to know about their science. First, it was clear that they were concerned about the lingering association of psychology, in the public mind, with phrenology, mesmerism, hypnotism, and spiritualism, so they took pains to present psychology as a science based on replicable and systematic measurement. They made strenuous efforts to differentiate their science from the everyday psychology that then prevailed in the popular imagination. As historian Marlene Shore has noted:

> Leading American psychologists regarded the exposition as a prime opportunity to introduce their work to a wider public, hoping to gain increased professional acceptance as well as to counter continuing popular interest in superstition, mysticism, and other forms of what they considered pseudoscience. (2001, p. 63)

The actual exhibit consisted of two rooms. One room housed an impressive collection of experimental instruments and apparatus contributed by numerous universities throughout the world. On the walls were numerous charts and graphs showing research results generated by scientific psychologists. In the other room, in the spirit of Galton's Anthropometric Laboratory, fairgoers could have their "sense capacities" and "mental powers" tested for a small fee. An army of graduate student volunteers tested subjects on the various tasks. As you might imagine, the resulting data were more amusing than scientifically useful because of the noise, commotion, and time constraints that accompanied the testing in the fairground setting.

Nonetheless, the psychology exhibit was a great success and contributed positively to Psychology's ongoing professionalization efforts. Both the public and other professionals, especially educators, were particularly interested in the mental tests. The potential use of the tests in the educational system was quickly identified. Given that learning was so intimately related to the processes under study by the psychologists, such as perception, attention, and memory, it was easy to see why educators would be interested in them. It was precisely to solve educational problems that America's first psychology clinic was established.

LIGHTNER WITMER AND THE PREHISTORY OF CLINICAL PSYCHOLOGY

Lightner Witmer (1867–1956) was a graduate student of Cattell's at the University of Pennsylvania. When Cattell left Pennsylvania to take a position at Columbia University in New York in 1891, Witmer embarked on a period of study with Wundt at Leipzig, received his PhD in 1892, and then returned to Philadelphia where, as arranged previously, he took a position at the University of Pennsylvania to fill Cattell's former post. There, he was appointed lecturer in experimental psychology, but he also became involved in a series of courses for public school teachers that began in 1894. Witmer had been a school teacher himself before pursuing his doctorate in psychology. A confluence of events then led Witmer to establish the first psychological clinic at the University of Pennsylvania, and to coin the term "clinical psychology."

Witmer was approached by a teacher concerned about a 14-year-old student, Charles Gilman, who could not learn to spell. Witmer soon discovered that the child had problems with reading and language more generally and problems with his vision. After his vision problems were corrected, the child worked with Witmer for a couple of years and improved considerably in his academic performance. Cases began to pour in, and in 1896 Witmer established a clinic, assembling a clinical team consisting of physicians, social workers, and teachers, as well as psychologists. He developed an extensive assessment involving a physical examination, as well as psychological tests, and the development of some form of training or educational intervention. Witmer did not develop a systematic theory of therapy or a systematic set of interventions—instead, he pioneered a method that he called "the clinical method."

By 1907, Witmer had enlarged his clinic and established the journal, *The Psychological Clinic*. In 1908 he also established a private residential school in Wallingford, Pennsylvania. Witmer's clinic remained in operation until 1961 and eventually housed three distinct units: a speech clinic, a vocational guidance clinic, and a college-personnel clinic for problems of college-aged youth.

Although "clinical psychology" would not become formally organized as a profession until after World War II, several aspects of Witmer's work deserve mention to give some sense of his innovations. In addition to the emphasis on the in-depth assessment of the individual, which was a relatively new role for the American psychologist, Witmer viewed most problems as capable of remediation. He was an environmentalist who viewed mental retardation as just that—retardation, not a matter of innate "feeble-mindedness," as his contemporaries termed low intelligence. He often used the descriptor literally; to refer to a child as "retarded" meant that the child was being held back in school. In stark contrast to Galton, Witmer's environmentalism was scaffolded by the conviction that to ascribe a child's condition to heredity was an excuse for inaction, while to ascribe it to the environment invited remediation. He believed that with the proper training and nurturance, most children could eventually catch up to their peers.

Given that Witmer is often viewed as one of the first clinical psychologists, it is important to understand how and why he was different from the mental health professionals we think of today. Unlike the modern clinical psychologist, he did not use diagnostic labels; the point of his clinical work was to understand levels of functioning and to design educational interventions that would help children function better. Witmer

FIGURE 6.4 Lightner Witmer
Courtesy of the Archives of the History of American Psychology,
University of Akron, Akron, OH.

viewed intelligence as the ability to solve new problems and assessed it using two tests that he devised, the Witmer formboard and the Witmer cylinders. Starting around 1916, he began to use the recently revised Stanford-Binet Tests of Intelligence. Psychological assessment, largely undertaken within the educational system, was the mainstay of Witmer's work, and he can thus be viewed as a forerunner of today's school psychologists. Viewed by contemporary standards, some have argued that Sigmund Freud's (1856–1939) work was more important in the history of modern clinical psychology, given that Freud pioneered the "talking cure" or what we now call psychotherapy. Witmer was certainly aware of Freud and encouraged his students to read Freud, but the first clinical psychologists, defined as students of Witmer's, were not psychotherapists themselves.

For Witmer, the work of the clinical psychologist was largely the assessment of children and the remediation of their academic and behavioral problems. The existence of mental tests and work on intelligence testing provided the techniques that could be imported; Witmer often converted experimental apparatus into clinical apparatus. A close relationship existed at this time between the laboratory and the clinic.

Social factors also influenced the emergence of clinical psychology in close relationship to education. In the late 19th century, a large influx of immigration and increased urbanization led to a perceived crisis in public education. As ever more children of different backgrounds and levels of ability were crowding the same classrooms, both children and teachers had trouble adjusting. Psychologists were able to capitalize on this situation and present themselves as professionals who could help solve educational and academic problems by sorting children into appropriate academic levels. Educators of the time were also vying for increased professional status and felt that allying themselves with science through Psychology could be advantageous in their quest for increased stature. Clearly, institutional, professional, and social factors played large roles in defining the earliest "clinical" work that was undertaken in the United States.

SORTING THE SEXES

Although mental tests had clear practical uses, they were also research tools. As research tools, they could be used in many ways. A few early female psychologists in the United States used these tests to conduct empirical studies of sex differences, establishing an inchoate version of the field we would now call *psychology of women*. At the end of the 19th century, several beliefs about the differences between women and men were widely held in American society, and among psychologists. One view held that higher education for women would render them "functionally castrated" and that as their intellectual capacities were nurtured their reproductive capacities would diminish. Lay people and scientists alike believed that women and men differed in the very nature of their mental traits and capacities, with women and men displaying complementary, but not directly comparable, psychological and intellectual strengths. This conviction was known as the **complementarity hypothesis** and was generally used to enforce what were then considered appropriate social roles for men and women, with women excelling in the realm of the emotional, domestic, and private and men excelling in the realm of the rational, professional, and public. These beliefs persisted despite the increase in women gaining access to higher education and careers and becoming economically independent. The late 19th-century cultural discourse surrounding this "new woman," who was better educated, worldlier, and more autonomous, indicated both society's enthusiasm for, and wariness toward, changing gender ideals.

One of American psychology's "new women" was Helen Bradford Thompson Woolley (1874–1947). Born into a progressive family that strongly supported higher education for women, Woolley earned her PhD in psychology at the University of Chicago in 1900. For her doctoral research, she undertook the first large-scale experimental study of sex differences in mental traits, published in 1903 as *The Mental Traits of Sex*.

Specifically, using many of the kinds of tests formulated by Cattell, Jastrow, Galton, and others, she conducted an empirical investigation of the motor and sensory abilities, and intellectual and affective processes, of a group of 50 University of Chicago undergraduates: 25 women and 25 men. To assess motor abilities, for example, she used reaction-time tests. To test for tactile sensitivity, she employed the discrimination of weights, among other methods. Her tests of intellectual faculties included memory and association tests. Instead of reporting the group averages for men and women on each task, Woolley graphed the distributions of test results by sex

FIGURE 6.5 Helen Thompson Woolley
Courtesy of the Archives of the History of American Psychology, University of Akron, Akron, OH.

and noted that in every case the curves almost completely overlapped. In addition, while she found a few reliable average differences between the two groups (e.g., on motor ability and puzzle solving), men and women were more similar than different on most tasks. These similarities included her admittedly crude tests of emotionality, a trait believed to be highly sex typed. On tasks that did show reliable differences, Woolley cautioned strongly against hereditarian interpretations, arguing forcefully for a consideration of the ways boys and girls, men and women, were socialized differently and consistently encountered radically different environments and social expectations.

One of the students most influenced by Woolley's work was Leta Stetter Hollingworth (1886–1939). Hollingworth published numerous studies to debunk cultural stereotypes about women. For her dissertation, published in 1914 as "Functional Periodicity: An Experimental Study of the Mental and Motor Abilities of Women During Menstruation," she conducted an empirical study to test the widespread belief that women's mental and motor performance becomes impaired during menstruation. Although her work drew less directly on Cattell-like mental tests, thus reflecting some developments that had taken place in testing during the first decade of the 20th century, her work was enabled by the tradition of empirical study of individual differences in which mental tests played an important role. Based on the results of her study, she concluded, "Careful and exact measurement does not reveal a periodic mental or motor inefficiency in normal women" (Hollingworth, 1914a, p. 94).

Sidebar 6.1 Focus on *Leta Stetter Hollingworth*

Leta Stetter Hollingworth was a woman of the Nebraska prairie who made her professional mark in the faraway environs of New York City. She was born on a farm near Chadron, Nebraska, the eldest of three girls. Her childhood and adolescence were marked by both great love and great loss, as her mother died when she was 3, and after 10 years with her loving maternal grandparents, she and her sisters were reclaimed by their neglectful father and his unsympathetic wife. Leta found escape through education. She completed high school at age 15 and enrolled in the University of Nebraska. There she discovered psychology and met her fellow student and future husband, Harry Hollingworth. After their graduation, Harry was admitted to doctoral work in psychology at Columbia University with James McKeen Cattell, while Leta taught school for two years. Their plan was to be married and for Leta to enroll in graduate school as Harry was completing his studies. However, it did not quite work out as planned. After Leta moved to New York, she discovered to her dismay that as a married woman she could not teach in New York schools. Leta had long aspired to be a writer, so she attempted to sell her stories to magazines, but with no luck. Harry's salary at Barnard College was small, and the young couple was simply unable to do more than barely make financial ends meet. It appeared as though their dream of graduate education for Leta would not be fulfilled.

Fortuitously, an offer to conduct commercially-sponsored research came Harry's way. Coca-Cola had been sued by the U.S. government for adding an unhealthy ingredient to its product. The ingredient was caffeine. The trial was set for mid-1911, and early that year the Coca-Cola Company realized that it did not have any psychological research evidence concerning the cognitive or behavioral effects of its product. After a hurried search, the company contracted with Harry to do the necessary work.

FIGURE 6.6 Leta Stetter Hollingworth
Courtesy of the Archives of the History of American Psychology, University of Akron, Akron, OH.

Harry and Leta designed the study, a series of double-blind experiments in which neither the investigators nor the participants knew which participants received placebos or the active ingredients. Because Harry had to teach during the day, Leta actually led the experimental testing of participants, while Harry, Leta, and friends did the data analysis at night. The results were presented at the trial, and Harry reported that he had found no evidence of cognitive impairment as a result of the administration of Coca-Cola to the study's participants.

For the couple, the major benefit was that the payment from Coca-Cola for their services provided more than enough money for Leta Stetter Hollingworth to enroll in graduate study in psychology at Columbia's Teachers College. There, she earned her master's degree in 1913 and her PhD in 1916. After earning her master's degree, she also worked as a clinical psychologist (then primarily concerned with administering psychological tests) until 1920. She was hired in the educational psychology program at Teachers College after the completion of her doctoral degree and remained there for the rest of her career.

Hollingworth's clinical work made her aware of the challenges faced by children at both ends of the ability spectrum. Her published work on adolescence and on gifted children became standard texts in the respective fields for many years. She also was a key contributor to two special programs for exceptional children in the New York public schools. Hollingworth contributed to clinical psychology in other ways as well. She was one of the organizers of the first professional association of clinical psychologists, the American Association of Clinical Psychology, formed in 1917. And in 1918, she published the first call for a professional degree in clinical psychology, anticipating the creation of the PsyD degree by 50 years.

Hollingworth also compiled and analyzed available empirical evidence to debunk the **variability hypothesis**, a popularly held, evolutionary-inspired belief that the male of the species always demonstrates more variability than the female across both physical and psychological traits and therefore drives evolutionary progress. According to this view, men were more likely to occupy the uppermost, as well as the lowermost, ranks in the distribution of any trait. This was used to explain why men's intellectual achievements and eminence were apparently greater than those of women. In her review of the data pertaining to the variability hypothesis, Hollingworth (1914b) concluded, "The empirical data at present available on this point are inadequate and contradictory, and if they point either way, actually indicate greater female variability" (p. 529). Furthermore, she pointed out that *even if* there were greater male variability,

this fact would be impossible to interpret until women were able to participate equally with men in the fields in which eminence was possible. Hollingworth pointed out that the realms to which many women were limited (i.e., motherhood and domesticity) were not those in which eminence was ever considered or evaluated.

Thus, in the hands of some women scientists, these tests were used to empirically challenge, rather than support, commonly held and often sexist beliefs about women's inferiority. Like Woolley before her, Hollingworth emphasized the differential effects of environment, culture, and social expectations on men and women in any explanation of presumed or demonstrated sex differences.

In the period after World War I, with the rise of applied psychology and the proliferation of testing in many settings, women psychologists were increasingly funneled into applied positions. Whereas the involvement of women psychologists in the applied efforts of the war was practically nonexistent, this changed as the field continued to professionalize in the postwar years. As historian of science Margaret Rossiter noted in the first volume of her pivotal work on women scientists in America (1982), only two women, Mabel Fernald and Margaret Cobb, were listed as being involved in the World War I testing program of Robert Yerkes (1876–1956), and although they were staff psychologists at their institution, they were listed as assistants. Thus, women did not benefit professionally from connections made during the war. After the First World War, as applied work took off, a separate sphere of women's work in psychology rapidly developed. This was partly because although the number of new academic departments and positions was growing in the 1920s, so too was the number of PhD psychologists, both men and women. Men generally received first consideration for academic jobs and quickly occupied most available posts. Women were advised to use their training in clinical, vocational, or school settings and came to outnumber men in the latter. Napoli, in his history of applied psychology (1981), noted that by 1930, men made up two-thirds of the PhDs in psychology but only a small minority of the applied branch. Thus, applied psychology was clearly considered women's work, and women were remarkably resourceful in using their training in various settings, from juvenile courts to state reformatories, private schools, and child guidance clinics.

THE DEMISE OF MENTAL TESTS AND THE RISE OF THE IQ

By the early 1900s, several serious challenges to the nature and use of anthropometric testing à la Galton and Cattell had emerged. For Witmer, who was interested in the in-depth assessment of individual children, basic mental tests designed to be administered to large numbers of people for the purposes of comparison and generation

of population distributions were not that useful. Also, and more importantly, the very validity of the tests was challenged. Statistical developments in the computation of correlations allowed researchers to show that performance on mental tests was *not* predictive of academic achievement and that the mental tests themselves did not correlate meaningfully with one another and inhere around a common ability, that is, general intelligence. Ironically, it was one of Cattell's own students, Clark Wissler (1870–1947), who correlated the mental test scores with the academic grades of more than 300 Columbia University and Barnard College students (Cattell had left Pennsylvania for a professorship at Columbia in 1891), and found no relationship between results on Cattell-type mental tests and academic achievement.

The demise of mental tests in the form that Cattell and Galton had devised did not signal the demise of widespread interest in classifying and sorting mental abilities, however. In 1899, Stella Emily Sharp of Cornell University published a detailed study of various approaches to mental testing (i.e., testing sensory and motor abilities versus higher mental functions) in which she concluded that "individual psychical differences should be sought for in the complex rather than in the elementary processes of mind" (p. 390). Sharp had been influenced by an 1895 monograph on individual psychology published by two French psychologists, Alfred Binet and Victor Henri. Her statement was prescient. By 1905, a different approach to mental measurement was developed in France by Binet.

Binet (1857–1911) came from the French tradition of the in-depth assessment of individual cases. He had worked with Jean-Martin Charcot (1825–1893) at the Salpêtrière Hospital on hypnosis and hysteria (see Chapter 5), and in 1894 he headed up the newly created Laboratory of Physiological Psychology located in the Sorbonne, where he was its unpaid director for the rest of his career. He had begun to try various tests of mental ability on his daughters

FIGURE 6.7 Alfred Binet

Madeleine and Alice and found that many tests of sensory and neurological ability could not distinguish between adults and children. But certainly, he reasoned, the intelligences of adults and children were different. The tests that did differentiate between adults and children invoked more complex abilities, such as sustained attention and sophisticated use of language. He also became convinced that intelligence came in different kinds, partly through his observations of Madeleine and Alice.

From these observations and casual experiments, Binet became convinced of the following: (1) that intelligence could take many forms, (2) that individuals were unique in their kind of intelligence, and (3) that it was impossible to sum up a person's intelligence in a single number or score. Nonetheless, he also acknowledged the practical utility of being able to make comparisons among people on intelligence, a concept he defined as the practical ability to adapt to one's circumstances. And although he was convinced of the value of rich, personal case histories in revealing the uniqueness of individuals and their intelligence, he also envisioned how tests might be used as a shortcut to get at this richness in a shorter amount of time. Thus, he began collaborating with his colleague Henri on a project he called individual psychology.

Individual psychology was a research program in which Binet and Henri sought to develop a set of tests of psychological processes that could provide a complete picture of a person's abilities. But which processes were important, and how could they be measured? In collaboration with

Henri, Binet came up with 10 faculties that he felt should be assessed: memory, imagery, imagination, attention, comprehension, suggestibility, aesthetic sentiment, moral sentiment, muscular strength and willpower, and motor ability and hand–eye coordination. Binet and Henri worked on developing tests of these 10 faculties for many years but were largely unsuccessful. Scores on various tests seemed unrelated to one another, and Binet did not feel that they gave an accurate, or complete, picture of the person's abilities. Binet was then joined by a postdoctoral student named Theodore Simon who worked at a large institution for the mentally subnormal. Binet's association with Simon gave him access to a new population. Then, in 1905, Binet was presented with a practical challenge by the French government: to identify children in the French school system who were in need of special education. In 1882, the French government had passed a law that established mandatory primary education for all children aged 6–14 years. In the course of industrialization in France, higher numbers of children were already attending school, and the new law extended this trend. This meant that many children who previously would not have attended school or stayed as long were now in classes, and many were not served well when placed in classes among their higher-achieving peers.

Binet and Simon began work on this challenge by trying various tests on children already identified as developmentally delayed and those identified as normal, ages 2–12, to see which tests would differentiate the two groups. In conducting the tests, Binet had an important insight: Although both groups of children were able to pass the same kinds of tests, the normal children did so at a younger age than the subnormal children. With this insight, Binet and Simon developed a set of 30 tasks of increasing levels of difficulty, starting with simple tasks that almost all children of a certain age could pass, such as shaking hands with the tester, up to complex tasks that even the oldest children had difficulty with, such as imagining the design that would be formed if a piece of paper were folded in quarters, cut, and unfolded. Children would then progress through the tests, stopping at the point they could no longer pass them. Their achievement would be noted and compared to the age corresponding to that level. This was referred to as the child's "mental level," later referred to as "mental age." Any children who fell two years or more behind their age peers in performance were identified as subnormal.

The Binet-Simon test underwent revisions in 1908 and 1911 to extend the age range for which the test was appropriate (the 1911 test extended to adults) and to develop norms. However, Binet continued to believe that intelligence could best be conceptualized as multifaceted and malleable. He intended the test to be a time-specific snapshot of the child's current state of functioning, not a device that would be used to predict future ability or potential. Developmentally delayed children, he believed, could improve their scores and change their level of intelligence by doing various exercises he called mental orthopedics. He also believed that the tests were fallible and imprecise and that it was advisable to report scores as levels, not absolute numbers. This last intention was forever obscured when, in 1912, German psychologist William Stern originated the practice of dividing the mental age of individuals by their chronological age to obtain a precise measure of their retardation or advance. Thus, the intelligence quotient, or IQ, was born.

The ensuing development and use of the intelligence test in the American context, where it was most readily and pervasively adopted, distorted or disregarded many of Binet's original intentions. In 1908, psychologist Henry Herbart Goddard (1866–1957; see Chapter 4) traveled to Europe. Goddard had recently been appointed director of research at the Vineland Training School for the Feebleminded in Vineland, New Jersey, and was traveling to England and France to learn about the research with the feebleminded that was being conducted there. Toward the end of his trip he learned about the Binet-Simon scale. Intrigued, he returned to the United States, translated the 1908 version of the test

and tried it on the children at Vineland. He discovered that, inasmuch as ranked scores on the tests appeared to corroborate clinical opinions of residents' abilities, it did a remarkably good job of classifying the various levels of retardation.

Goddard became an enthusiastic proponent of the test and translated Binet's term *débile* into "moron," which referred to the highest grade and most common form of mental deficiency. However, he did not adopt Binet's conceptualization of intelligence as multifaceted, individual, and changeable. Goddard, like Galton, was a hereditarian and a eugenicist. He believed that, if allowed to breed, people of low intelligence would produce generations of mentally deficient offspring who would taint the "stock" of America (i.e., lower the quality of the gene pool). He also believed that feeblemindedness was directly related to various social ills, including delinquency, crime, sexual promiscuity, drunkenness, and poverty. Although he personally considered forced sterilization of the feebleminded an effective solution to the problem of degeneracy, he realized it might upset people's sensibilities. Instead, he recommended institutionalization and segregation of the sexes.

In 1912, Goddard wrote a book called *The Kallikak Family: A Study in the Heredity of Feeble-Mindedness* in which he reported the results of his study of the genealogy of the Kallikak family, conducted with his assistant Elizabeth Kite. Kallikak was a pseudonym given by Goddard to a family that had two distinct lines of descent from a common father. In one line, the father had coupled with a woman of "ill repute" and low social standing, who was presumably feebleminded. In the other line, the father had produced offspring with a respectable woman of good genetic stock. Goddard used this case study to argue that the two lines showed marked differences in ability and thus suffered markedly different fates. Around 1900, Mendelian genetics was becoming familiar to English readers. A classic paper by Gregor Johann Mendel, showing that genetic transmission could control the color of a rabbit's coat or the height of a garden pea immigrants qualified as feebleminded and suggested that unrestricted immigration could have deleterious consequences for the American stock. The practical value of intelligence testing for identifying subnormality was seductive in an era riddled with eugenicist concerns. But as long as IQ tests were used solely for the purpose of diagnosing mental deficiency, their impact, although profound, could not be widespread. For the tests to achieve cultural prominence, they would have to have value, not only at Vineland and Ellis Island but in the educational system more generally. Here, testers encountered children of normal and above-normal capacities. The range of the test needed to be extended, and the norms recalculated, on an American sample.

LEWIS TERMAN AND THE AMERICANIZATION OF INTELLIGENCE TESTING

In 1916, psychologist Lewis Terman (1877–1956) at Stanford University published a version of the Binet test that was standardized on a large sample of American schoolchildren (905, to be exact). Concerns about the cultural specificity of some items to the French context also led to changes in some of the content. Most importantly, Terman introduced the practice of multiplying the quotient of mental age over chronological age by 100 to arrive at a single number, the intelligence quotient. The IQ, Terman argued, remained fairly constant over a person's life. Although Binet would not have approved, the IQ was embraced by Terman's American peers. His revised test became known as the Stanford-Binet and proved to be a runaway success, becoming the standard test for measuring intelligence until the middle of the 20th century. In 1916, Terman also published a book called *The Measurement of Intelligence*, in which he wrote,

> Numerous studies of the age–grade progress of school children have afforded convincing

FIGURE 6.8 Henry Herbert Goddard
Courtesy of the Archives of the History of American Psychology, University of Akron, Akron, OH.

plant, led Goddard to believe that there must be a gene for feeblemindedness and that it could be passed from parents to children. In the case of the "bad" line of the Kallikak family, the bad genes from the unfortunate coupling produced a whole line of degenerates. Goddard felt that people in the highest grade of the feebleminded (i.e., morons) were a particular menace because they were not immediately identifiable by facial characteristics. They could pass as normal and were likely to procreate prolifically. He thought that a test that could identify such a menace to the American gene pool was needed, and in Goddard's view, the Binet test proved to be just such a tool.

Soon after he published the Kallikak study, Goddard became engaged in the testing of immigrants at Ellis Island. There, he concluded that a sizable proportion of Eastern European evidence of the magnitude and seriousness of the retardation problem. Statistics collected in hundreds of cities in the United States show that between a third and a half of the school children fail to progress through the grades at the expected rate; that from 10 to 15 per cent are retarded two years or more; and that from 5 to 8 per cent are retarded at least three years. More than 10 per cent of the $400,000,000 annually expended in the United States for school instruction is devoted to re-teaching children what they have already been taught but have failed to learn. (p. 3)

Terman argued that the solution to this problem was to use the tests to accurately gauge student ability and use this information to funnel students into instruction geared to their precise level. He hoped to present the IQ test as a

valid and precise sorting technology that not only would help children and students but also would save the educational system considerable money—a powerful tool indeed. Just as engineers engaged in extensive study and empirical tests of their materials before building a bridge, Terman argued, so should educational engineers "acquire a scientific knowledge of the material with which we have to deal" before building the academic infrastructure (1916, p. 5).

By this time, the assumption on the part of most American psychologists was that IQ tests were a measure of an innate, largely unchangeable and constant, individual quality and that the IQ could be used, in a meritocratic spirit, to identify children's particular abilities and prepare them for the destiny for which they were most suited. An increasingly complex society and specialized workforce demanded specialized training. It would be important, many reasoned, to identify the potential factory workers, plumbers, middle managers, and lawyers so that each could be educated according to their natural endowments and professional destinies. Fortuitously for psychologists, World War I was about to provide them with the opportunity to try just such a large-scale application.

ARMY INTELLIGENCE: WORLD WAR I PUTS PSYCHOLOGY ON THE MAP

> The story of the U.S. army's adoption of intelligence is, in part, the story ... of how notions of intelligence and its tests that had been nurtured largely away from public view came to be disseminated to the larger culture through the intersection of the practical needs of wartime, changing character of American society, and professional ambitions of psychologists.
>
> —John Carson, *The Measure of Merit*, 2007

During the 20th century, war provided many professions with unique opportunities not available during peace time. The First World War was an event of enormous professional significance for psychology. The war helped solidify

FIGURE 6.9 Lewis Terman
Courtesy of the Archives of the History of American Psychology, University of Akron, Akron, OH.

psychology's standing in the public mind, as well as in the minds of other professionals and the military. The intelligence test played an important role in this process, as did tests of occupational skill and vocational aptitudes. In this section, we describe psychologists' involvement in the war to address the following questions: How did psychologists use World War I to advance and professionalize Psychology, and how, in turn, did Psychology affect the war effort? What were the social and political factors that influenced the scientific development of psychological testing, and how did these factors determine the form and use of the IQ test in American society?

During the war, two groups of psychologists whose work had overlapped only minimally before the war came into direct contact. Under the aegis of the Psychology Committee of the National Research Council, two committees on testing were formed as the United States entered the war in spring 1917. The first group, called the Committee on the Psychological Examination of Recruits, was led by Yerkes. The committee's mandate, as they developed it, was to test the intelligence of army inductees to make recommendations for their placement within the military. The other group was led by Walter Dill Scott (1869–1955) and included Walter Van Dyke Bingham (1880–1952), Edward Lee Thorndike (1874–1949), and Louis Leon Thurstone (1887–1955), among other well-known psychologists. They formed the Committee on Classification of Personnel and served as civilian consultants to the army. Their committee was devoted to evaluating trade aptitudes among army personnel and sorting recruits into the specialized tasks for which they were best suited. Although both committees were concerned with testing, they had somewhat different experiences in the military. We turn first to Yerkes and the psychological examination of recruits.

In trying to decide how psychologists could be of most use to the military, Yerkes decided that his committee would develop proposals for the psychological testing of army inductees, whose sheer numbers posed a huge logistical problem for the army. Yerkes called upon Terman and Goddard, among others, to develop a test that would screen out mental defectives but would also help the army make basic personnel selection decisions—who should be an officer, who should be a soldier, and so on. The large numbers of recruits required that a group intelligence test be developed; the Binet test was designed for individual administration and was too cumbersome for mass testing. The tests they produced—based closely on tests that Terman brought with him from his doctoral student, Arthur Otis, were called the Army Alpha (for recruits who could speak, read, and write English) and the Army Beta (for illiterate recruits). At the height of their game, psychologists were testing 200,000 recruits a month. By the war's end, some 1.75 million men had been administered one of the two tests.

This meant that almost 2 million people were exposed to psychology and the intelligence test during the war. To be sure, this was a rather dramatic debut. However, as impressive as these numbers are, they tell only part of the story. As historian of psychology Franz Samelson (1977) has discussed, in practice the tests were beset with problems ranging from inconsistency in administration to more serious issues of validity. The conditions under which the tests were administered were less than ideal. Recruits often had to sit on the floor and might barely be able to hear the administrator's instructions. Men who had never before had to hold a pencil were asked to respond to lengthy lists of seemingly irrelevant items. Testers failed to take into account the important fact that scores on the tests were highly correlated with education and insisted on promoting the tests as measures of innate ability. One of the more alarming scientific findings that emerged from the test data, put forth by Princeton University psychologist Carl Brigham in 1923, was that the average mental age of recruits was only 13 years; 12 years was the cutoff for feeblemindedness. This was indeed shocking, and many found it hard to believe the tests were measuring intelligence accurately. Less hard to believe by the American public at the time, and less readily challenged, except by African American intellectuals such as W. E. B. DuBois and, later, African American psychologist Horace Mann Bond and others, was the finding that Black soldiers were vastly inferior to White soldiers in intelligence. Both of these findings fed into eugenicist agendas and fueled fears about degeneracy, miscegenation, and unchecked immigration.

How did the military respond to this new sorting technology? The military made little use of the mass intelligence testing, preferring to rely on its own members' professional judgment in the placement of recruits and reacting somewhat warily to the incursion of scientific researchers among their ranks. At any rate, the Armistice of 1918 made any plans to use the test findings for practical purposes obsolete, and the army dropped intelligence testing from its activities within two months of the war's end. Although the psychologists had made big promises about processing the recruits efficiently, thus saving the army thousands of dollars and considerable time, they did not have the occasion to deliver on these promises.

Another committee, the Committee on Classification of Personnel, met a somewhat different reception within the military, due in no small part to the energy and entrepreneurship of Walter Dill Scott (see also Chapter 4). Scott's committee quickly discerned that in an organization of 4 million men, the ability to assess vocational aptitudes and occupational skills swiftly and accurately, and match men up with appropriate jobs, could be an essential service. Scott had recently published work on rating scales for selecting salesmen, conducted with his colleagues at the Carnegie Institute of Technology, which consisted of group tests of intellectual ability as well as ratings of character and manner. Scott proposed a system for matching recruits to appropriate military positions and met little opposition from army brass, perhaps because of his committee's civilian status and the obvious practical utility of their task, but no doubt also due to Scott's pragmatic and

magnanimous personal style. The committee itself eventually grew to more than 175 members who oversaw the work of about 7,500 men in personnel units at army posts across the country. By the end of the war, the committee had interviewed and classified almost 3.5 million men. One-third of those classified went on to specialized duties. The committee also established a trade tests division that developed proficiency tests for 83 military jobs. In acknowledgment of these impressive accomplishments, the army awarded Scott the Distinguished Service Medal at the close of the war.

A final war development should be noted. In addition to intelligence and vocational tests, World War I also occasioned the development of the first objective paper-and-pencil tests of personality in the United States. Military officials were becoming alarmed at the number of psychiatric casualties among soldiers who were involved in trench warfare. Although some believed that this was simply a matter of normal decompensation after an extremely stressful experience, others called for a method of screening soldiers who might be predisposed to emotional breakdown in these situations. Accordingly, psychologist Robert Sessions Woodworth (1869–1962) was placed in charge of the Committee on Emotional Fitness and developed a written form of the questions routinely used by psychiatrists to assess emotional stability. Woodworth generated his test items by surveying hundreds of case reports of diagnosed neurotics to identify the emotional and personality characteristics they displayed. Based on this review, he composed hundreds of questions inquiring about symptoms and administered them to a group of normal subjects, eliminating the questions that were endorsed so often by this group that they would be of no diagnostic value. The result was the Woodworth Personal Data Sheet. Examples of items included "Do you think you have hurt yourself by going too much with women?" "Have you hurt yourself by masturbation (self-abuse)?" "Were you considered a bad boy?" and "Do you feel that nobody quite understands you?" Unfortunately (at least for Woodworth), the war ended before he had the opportunity to try it within the military and ascertain its usefulness. Psychologists continued to use it after the war, however, and it was considered one of the earliest self-report measures of neuroticism.

Although Woodworth's test was one of the first objective tests of personality, another kind of personality test was being developed even before the war. One of the earliest projective tests of personality, with open-ended response formats that were thought to reveal the respondent's unconscious desires, needs, feelings, and thought processes, was the familiar word association test originated by Galton and then studied by Cattell but most influentially developed for use in personality assessment by Carl Jung (1875–1961) in Switzerland and then Grace Kent (1875–1973) in the United States. Jung conceptualized word associations as revealing information about the personality types of introversion and extroversion, as well as revealing unconscious processes that could be related to normal and pathological phenomena, such as complexes. According to Jung, complexes were strongly or emotionally valenced sets of related attitudes requiring active repression. He carried out empirical work on word associations, starting with a list of 400 words administered to 38 people of different educational levels and under different conditions of attention. Respondents would be read a set of

words and were then asked to respond as quickly as possible with the first word that came to mind; words were chosen to sample common or frequent complexes, such as the mother complex. Latency or reaction time would also be recorded, along with the response, with the assumption that longer reaction times would be indicative of a complex. Other deviations from normal responding, such as repetition of a word, the inability to make a response, and a senseless response, were all considered indicative of complexes.

Jung published some of this empirical work in the *Journal of Abnormal Psychology* in 1907 and then published a series of lectures he had given on the topic at Clark University in the *American Journal of Psychology* in 1910. Grace Kent, in collaboration with a psychiatrist A. J. Rosanoff, used Jung's word association method to develop the Kent-Rosanoff Word Association Test in 1909–1910, as we mentioned in Chapter 5. In her research, she administered 100 words, selected to be fairly neutral, to 1,000 individuals and tabulated the responses so as to record the number of times any word (such as "nail") had occurred as a response to each word in the series (such as "hammer"). Any response in further experiments was then assigned a value according to the number of times it was listed in the frequency table. For example, the association hammer–nail was recorded 185 times, so the response "nail" would get a value of 185. For the purposes of calculation, the researchers divided this number by 10 to get 18.5. Responses that did not appear in the table were classified as "individual reactions" and assigned a value of 0. In normal people, the average number of individual reactions was 7, with that number increasing as education increased. She then compared the normal responses with those from resident patients at the Danvers State Hospital in New York. What the test produced was a precise measurement of the tendency of a person to respond along the same lines as the peer group. It was regarded as a measure of the conformity of thought processes and was used as well to detect complexes or response abnormalities indicating thought disturbances.

FIGURE 6.10 Carl Jung

FIGURE 6.11 Grace Kent
Courtesy of the Archives of the History of American Psychology, University of Akron, Akron, OH.

Although the development of projective tests accelerated in the post–World War I period, especially after the publication of Hermann Rorschach's (1884–1922) famous inkblot test in 1921, projective tests have never been used in mass testing the same way objective tests have been. By their nature, projectives are more suited for the individual, clinical situation and have remained largely the purview of psychologists working with clients in private, hospital, or clinic settings or for research (for more on projective tests, see Chapter 7).

WORLD WAR I AND ITS IMPACT ON AMERICAN PSYCHOLOGY

The postwar period saw some immediate aftereffects of psychologists' war work, some of which we have already mentioned. Despite some dubious results from the mass intelligence testing, psychologists received major funding to develop tests that could be used in schools and for college placement. By 1922, 3 million children a year were being tested with various forms of the intelligence test. Thanks to the work of Scott's committee, industrial psychologists emerged from the war with increased professional prestige that

translated directly into more work from the business community. Psychological consulting firms were established to provide vocational testing, among other services. Thus, overall, their experiences in the war provided psychologists with a strong platform from which they were able to solidify their professional authority and create significant niches for their expertise.

To summarize, the World War I testing programs provided psychologists with an unprecedented opportunity to introduce the tools of their trade to a large segment of the American public. The progressivism of the pre- and postwar periods, with its emphasis on reforming American society to meet the challenges of industrialism, urbanism, and renewed statism, provided a supportive and facilitative backdrop for psychologists' work. This reformist attitude was felt quite keenly in education, where reformers like John Dewey (1859–1952) were advocating more practical, experiential education based on an understanding of both the students' past experiences and current abilities. Although Dewey's educational philosophy did not directly involve testing, by advocating an individualized system of instruction whereby teaching would be matched to each student's unique abilities, he indirectly justified the use of intelligence testing to determine a student's potential and match this with appropriate instruction. By 1910, almost all states required that children stay in school until the age of 16. This resulted in more children in schools and more practical challenges for teachers and school administrators. Increased immigration meant that students had more diverse backgrounds. Concerns about juvenile delinquency also ran high in this period. It was hoped that psychologists might be able to identify what we would now call "at-risk" youth and help them stay out of trouble. In short, there was a lot of testing, and a lot of sorting, to be done.

Finally, as we mentioned in Chapter 4, the popularity of scientific management in this period contributed to the ease with which psychologists could introduce testing into

American society. As we have already discussed, in the 1890s, Frederick Winslow Taylor (1856–1915) began to promote a school of thought about how to run industry more efficiently. He argued that the production process should be functionally analyzed and standardized and the best way to perform a job was to break it into the smallest units of time and motion and recombine them to produce the most efficient system. In the workplace, psychologists were demonstrating that vocational testing allowed employers to have employees "functionally analyzed" and sorted into the jobs for which they were best suited, which in turn would increase productivity. The sorting of students by IQ was seen as improving the efficiency of the educational system by breaking the masses into smaller, more uniform, units that could all be taught in the same way within their stream. Terman had alluded to psychologists as educational engineers, and indeed, it appeared that by the 1920s these engineers had begun their own system of scientific management in the schools. As historian Paula Fass has noted of the significance of the intelligence test in the American context, "It crystallized the needs of a whole culture. It provided Americans with a powerful organizing principle, a way of ordering perceptions, and a means for solving pressing institutional and social problems" (1980, p. 434).

INTELLIGENCE TESTING AROUND THE WORLD: CENTER OR PERIPHERY?

So far, we have shown how central intelligence testing was to the science and practice of American psychology in its first several decades, as well as how central it was to a society looking for ways to deal with several emerging social problems. But was intelligence testing as central, to both psychology and society, in other parts of the world? If not, why not? What contextual factors may have relegated

testing to the periphery of psychological research and practice, and the concerns of society, in other parts of the world? Were other forms of testing, such as personnel, vocational, or ability testing, more central than intelligence? If so, what practical needs were they responding to? In this section, we examine these questions by looking at the reception and evolution of testing in four other countries: France, Britain, the Netherlands, and Germany.

The French Twist

We have discussed the seminal role that Binet played in the development of intelligence testing. We have also outlined his concerns and caveats about the nature and use of the tests and noted that these were largely overlooked by American psychologists in their zeal to quantify, classify, and sort. This begets important questions: What happened to intelligence testing in France? What happened to Binet's test in its homeland? More generally, did testing and its applications gain as strong a foothold in France and elsewhere as they did in the United States?

Although Binet died prematurely in 1911, well before the outbreak of World War I, he had begun a study with Simon developing an intelligence test to be used in the French military. However, his pilot results were misinterpreted and publicized by a French military official, and the research never got off the ground. Moreover, they reflected Binet's belief that detailed, individualized assessment was necessary as the basis for test formulation.

After Binet's death, the directorship of his laboratory was given to Henri Piéron (1881–1964), an experimental psychologist of diverse interests. At this point, with the transition in the laboratory and the advent of war, work on intelligence testing was put on hold. When Piéron resumed this line of work, assisted heavily by his wife Marguerite Piéron, he adhered closely to Binet's view of intelligence as multifaceted and complex and to his view of tests as tools for creating individual, diagnostic formulations rather than as technologies of mass classification. Collaboratively, the Piérons developed an intelligence test for vocational guidance that they used extensively at L'Institut National d'Orientation Professionelle, cofounded by Henri Piéron in 1929 to help French students make career decisions. The test, reflecting the Piérons' belief in the multifaceted nature of intelligence, contained seven parts. The end product of the test was a graphical profile, not a number for ranking, that clearly indicated the individual respondent's relative strengths and weaknesses to be used for individualized recommendations. The test was intended to fill a fairly specialized need in a system that already had a structure for selecting students for either higher education or vocational training. It was intended to help students in the vocational stream make more specific decisions about career options. The intent was not mass testing and policy recommendations but individualized assessment (for more on Piéron and his work, see Chapter 8).

The Binet-Simon test was also used by French child psychiatrist Georges Heuyer (1884–1977) in the 1920s. He developed a medicopsychological examination procedure for assessing juvenile offenders that was adopted by the French Society of Legal Medicine in 1927 as compulsory for all minors appearing in French courts. Heuyer's use of the tests to give a quick gauge of the child's mental level came under attack by some, who were displeased with what they perceived as a cavalier, American-type attitude to using the tests for screening. Heuyer was careful to point out, however, that the test was but one of many in a comprehensive examination with six components.

Thus, despite lively interest in the tests and their use for specific purposes, by the 1920s and 1930s, unlike the United States, France had no tradition of mass testing. One of the primary reasons for the absence of mass intelligence testing in France was that, as one historian has noted, the French simply "did not need them" (Schneider, 1992, p. 128). As we have already mentioned, the structure of the French educational system was quite different from the American system. Although both countries supported universal education, France had a centralized, national system, unlike in the United States, where each state controlled its own colleges and universities. Thus, France already had in place an elaborate system of national examinations that automatically funneled students into university placements or vocational training. The educational system itself functioned as a gatekeeper for identifying the intellectual elite who would proceed to higher and more specialized training, and intelligence tests were largely reserved for the problem of identifying the mentally deficient. The United States, although no less meritocratic, did not develop such a state-supported system, partly because of an underlying belief, as one historian of psychology has put it, in the "free play of talents among self-determining individuals" that would allow the most talented to rise to the top (Carson, 2007, p. 3).

Finally, the development of intelligence testing also reflected differences in the way psychology, more generally, developed in each of the two countries. As we have already discussed, American psychology came to rely quite heavily on quantification and measurement as indicators of its scientific status and technological potential in the early years of the 20th century. Employed on a large scale, the intelligence test provided both scientific legitimacy and practical efficiency. While no less scientific in orientation, French psychologists relied more heavily on a tradition of clinical observation and thus were more comfortable with the individualized use of tests to achieve circumscribed practical aims, such as individual vocational counseling.

The British Context

Yet a different picture of the development of intelligence testing emerged in Britain. As we have previously discussed, Galton's formulation of intelligence as hereditary and biologically based was highly influential. He believed that intelligence could be assessed by measuring the strength of the nervous system through sensory, motor, and perceptual tasks and that performance on these tasks was indicative of a unitary, biologically based, heritable trait. Charles Spearman's (1863–1945) development of his two-factor theory of intelligence, first published in a 1904 paper titled "General Intelligence: Objectively Determined and Measured" postulated that a general factor—g—or **general intelligence**, worked through specific intelligences to produce abilities on specific tasks. Spearman's work was motivated, in part, by the desire to elaborate on the theoretical underpinnings the Galtonian conception of intelligence. The practical goal, in this tradition, was to collect thousands of responses to these simple tests to chart the distribution of individual variation in the population, which would be used to support and propel the eugenicist agenda. Tests of higher, more complex mental functions, such as Binet and Simon were developing, were not Galton's, or Spearman's, concern. First, this kind of assessment would take too long. Second, they were convinced that their relatively simple tests were tied to a unitary factor of general intelligence that was heritable. Third, they could use individual deviation from statistical norms to diagnose *social* pathology without the need for extensive individual assessment. Their system was designed to serve an administrative, not a clinical, function. Interestingly, however, it was for just such an administrative function that the Binet test usurped (in fact, preempted) the Galtonian-type tests of sensory functions. As sociologist Nikolas Rose has written of this kind of test,

> Yet despite the link it forged between the social requirements and psychological assessments, despite its certainty of the possibility of assessing intelligence through the measurement of sensory functions, and despite the corollary that psychologists possessed the rights and capacities to adjudicate in cases of suspected pathology of the intellect, these claims fell on deaf ears as far as

administrative procedures for diagnosing the feeble-minded were concerned. (1985, p. 123)

The Binet-Simon test was introduced in Britain not by psychologists but through the medical profession. It was through this conduit, and for the practical task of identifying the mentally deficient, that the Binet test succeeded and was adopted whereas tests of sensory and motor ability failed to be taken up. According to Rose, the Binet-Simon test provided the crucial link between the measurement of internal, individual mental capacities and the measurement of behaviors that could be linked to social norms. By forging this link, despite their repeated acknowledgment of the inherent limitations of the test, Binet and Simon had produced a measure of adaptation to social norms and requirements that was well suited to the administrative demands of identifying the feebleminded. Combined with this was the professional monopoly of this task by physicians, who kept both educators and psychologists well out of what they saw as their exclusive clinical domain. Intelligence was just one factor among many others in formulating a specific case and making recommendations. Thus, in Britain, medicine displaced psychology in the individual diagnosis of intellectual pathology, and eugenic psychologists were extremely critical of the Binet test, citing lack of theoretical sophistication and the assessment of acquired (i.e., language) rather than innate characteristics, for example. Such critique was unsurprising, given Binet's divergent viewpoint on the very nature of intelligence as malleable and heavily influenced by environment and learning.

Although British psychoeugenicists (to use Rose's term) objected to the Binet test, they nonetheless conceded that it was here to stay, and by 1920 they had succeeded in statistically revising and restandardizing the test so that it was in line with their conceptualization of intelligence as a "normally distributed, innate, heritable, general cognitive capacity" (Rose, 1985, p. 140). Instrumental in this work was Cyril Burt (1883–1971), who was later found to have fabricated much of the data on which he based his claims of the heritability of IQ.

Through the 1920s, several developments in Britain contributed to the waning of the centrality of the problem of mental deficiency as a social concern and the use of tests to detect it. Primary among these were legislative equivocations over enforced institutionalization and sterilization of mental defectives and increased emphasis on noninterventionist practices, such as mental and moral hygiene enacted within the private sphere of the family. With the rise of the Nazi Party in Germany, eugenicists lost their last vestiges of credibility. Although intelligence tests could be used for many other purposes, their utility for the psychoeugenicists was curtailed, and any public receptivity to their aims was significantly foreclosed.

Dutch Society

In the Netherlands, unlike in England and to some extent the United States, intelligence testing was not tied to a tradition of viewing intelligence as a unitary, heritable faculty, and eugenics occupied a comparatively marginal position in Dutch society. Although as late as the 1920s some researchers were still publishing studies of skull size as an indication of intellectual ability, a Dutch variation of the Binet-Simon test, called the Binet-Herderschêe test after the psychologist who revised it, was in use starting with its publication in 1919 through the 1960s (although it was never actually fully restandardized on a sample of Dutch children). It too was originally devised to identify subnormal children for educational purposes. The Netherlands legislated mandatory education in 1901. Herderschêe was a eugenicist, but he believed not in a unitary theory but in the multifaceted nature of intelligence. The Netherlands never passed eugenic legislation. Although there were certainly proponents, eugenics was never a major preoccupation and those social scientists who adhered to a eugenicist agenda were, apparently, professionally

marginal. As two historians of Dutch psychology have written, "Altogether then, the debate over the introduction of intelligence testing in the Netherlands ... lacked the sharp edges that it has in the United States and in Britain" (Mulder & Heyting, 1998, p. 356). They argue that the cultural and ethnic homogeneity of the Netherlands failed to provide eugenicists with a fertile ground for their techniques.

Another inhibitor of the mass use of intelligence tests to address eugenic concerns was the structure of Dutch society itself. In 1917, to settle a long-standing political dispute among religious groups over the control of primary education, the Dutch constitution was changed to sanction an educational system divided into autonomous and separate religious spheres. Thus, Protestant, Catholic, and Neutral pillars were created. This **pillarization** of Dutch society extended well beyond the educational system into almost all aspects of social, cultural, political, and economic life, from the arts, to the workplace, health provision, sports and leisure, and even media. Two consequences of this pillarization for academic psychology were a resistance toward technoscientific incursions into the private realm of the family and a lingering distrust of a purely materialistic, reductionistic, and deterministic science. Protestants, Catholics, and other denominational groups were generally opposed to a completely mechanistic and economical approach to daily life and were critical of purely empirical, as opposed to more interpretive and holistic, approaches. Science, in this context, could be useful, but only as it accorded with religious beliefs and Christian conduct. Intelligence testing and eugenics, inasmuch as they exemplified this technoscientific trend, were never embraced.

Germany and Psychotechnics

The situation in Germany provides our last point of comparison. Although German psychologist William Stern (1871–1938) was responsible for suggesting the calculation of mental age

FIGURE 6.12 William Stern
Courtesy of the Archives of the History of American Psychology, University of Akron, Akron, OH.

divided by chronological age from Binet's test to produce the IQ, Stern's program of **differential psychology** encompassed more than intelligence testing. His approach stressed the understanding of the total personality in its individuality, what he later termed "personalistic psychology." Stern was also committed to the thoroughgoing *application* of psychology in all domains of public life, from education to the courtroom to the workplace. It was this latter attitude (i.e., the importance of practical application rather than mass intelligence testing per se) that seems to have characterized the testing movement in German psychology, at least through the First World War.

In 1900, Stern coined the term **psychotechnik** (*psychotechnics*, sometimes regarded as an extension of Taylor's scientific management system) to refer to the practice of studying

individual differences for "human management" purposes. Stern did early work on the psychology of eyewitness testimony for which he devised picture tests to test subjects' visual memory, such as the Farm Kitchen Test and the Bunny Birthday Party Test. In 1908 he cofounded the *Journal of Applied Psychology* with Otto Lipmann. His German colleague, Hugo Münsterberg (1863–1916), who came to the United States to replace William James (1842–1910) as the head of the psychological laboratory at Harvard University, also did testimony research but is even better known for systematizing the field of psychotechnics in his 1913 book *Psychology and Industrial Efficiency* (for more on Münsterberg, see Chapter 4).

In the German context, World War I provided ample opportunity for the development of psychotechnics (although the development of psychotechnics was certainly not limited to Germany; it spread rapidly throughout Europe and North America). For example, under the direction of Max Rubner at the Kaiser Wilhelm Institute for Labor Physiology in Berlin, pilots and transport personnel in the German military were tested for the effects of fatigue on performance. Various manual and physical dexterity tests, as well as tests of concentration, attention, and reasoning, were devised as well for personnel selection purposes, and these practices proliferated after the war, spreading rapidly into business and industry. Although paper-and-pencil tests were sometimes used, psychotechnics gradually became associated primarily with apparatus tests, often constructed by the researchers. The apparatus was often designed to emulate as closely as possible the actual work tasks or skills that would be required of a particular occupation. For example, during World War I, German psychologists Walther Moede (1888–1958) and Curt Piotrowski (1873–1944) were asked to screen potential drivers of costly army motorcars to reduce the high accident rates. In the laboratory, they built a simulated driving situation and measured subjects' abilities to react to different challenges and dilemmas. As a result of the success of this program, Moede and Piotrowski were contacted by the head of the Royal Saxon Railroads and were asked to extend their methods to testing railroad personnel. The railroads had become an important means of transportation during the war, and safety problems associated with conductor error were a constant concern. In 1917, they installed a testing laboratory in Dresden and thus began an important and enduring liaison between psychotechnicians and the railroads, not just in Germany but throughout Europe and the United States as well (for more on German psychotechnics between the world wars, see Chapter 8).

WHAT DID THE TESTS TEST?

In the case of psychotechnics and other personnel selection procedures, the nature and form of the tests were often directly related to the readily identified demands of specific occupations. In the case of intelligence, however, considerable diversity and lack of clarity were found in how the construct was both conceptualized and operationalized. Given this state of affairs, as the popularity of intelligence testing increased and versions of the test proliferated, it occurred to some psychologists that they were not certain of what the intelligence tests were testing. What did psychologists variously understand intelligence to be?

In answering this question, the historical record tells us two things for certain. First, a complete lack of agreement occurred among psychologists on a precise definition of intelligence, and second, a remarkable consensus existed that this disagreement was of no practical importance. No one could agree on how to define intelligence. Was it reasoning ability, judgment, abstract thinking? Was it a unitary entity, or were there multiple facets in each individual? Was it hardwired or acquired? From the practical standpoint of constructing and administering tests, did it matter?

In a 1921 issue of the *Journal of Educational Psychology*, leading investigators of personality were asked to describe "What I conceive intelligence to be." The experts' answers ran the gamut from the ability to adapt to the environment to the capacity for abstract and symbolic thinking. Despite no conclusive replies to, or even agreement on, an answer to this question, the development of tests to measure intelligence and the use of these tests to make important decisions about people's lives continued apace. Intelligence testing was proving to be both practically useful and immensely profitable. This led to an almost embarrassing state of conceptual affairs around psychology's most vaunted construct; namely, most proponents of IQ testing agreed on a single working hypothesis: Intelligence is what intelligence tests tested.

SUMMARY

One of the first ways that early psychologists proved their usefulness to the public, and emphasized their scientific standing, was through the development and administration of mental tests. Although mental tests were first developed in the laboratory to produce a body of data about basic processes such as attention, sensation, and perception, they quickly provided a successful point of contact between the new psychologists and consumers of everyday psychology who were eager to hear what the new scientists of the mind could tell them about their own abilities. Educators were interested in the potential of the tests to provide information about learning and, eventually, to help make decisions about student training and placement.

The technology of mental testing advanced considerably with the work of Binet, who extended the tests beyond basic mental processes to assess higher functions, like language and reasoning. When imported to the United States by Goddard, the Binet test encountered a receptive audience. With American psychologists' involvement in World War I, intelligence testing, as well as vocational aptitude testing and tests of emotional fitness, defined the work of psychologists and brought the tests to an even larger audience. After World War I, due to ever-increasing urbanization and immigration, the American educational system was in need of an efficient method for sorting students of highly varying levels of ability. The intelligence test proved to be just such a technology. Interestingly, in France, Britain, the Netherlands, and Germany, the intelligence test fared differently than it did in the United States, due to the variations in social policy, values, and needs that uniquely characterized each country. Since Psychology and its products arise out of and return to the society of which they form a part, different societies produce different psychologies, that is, psychology is socially constructed.

In the background of these practical developments was remarkably little consensus as to the very nature of the concept that had garnered American psychologists, at least, so much cultural currency. Whether believed to be hardwired or acquired, unitary or multifaceted, intelligence was, nonetheless, measurable. Debates about the nature of intelligence continue, heatedly, to this day.

BIBLIOGRAPHIC ESSAY

There is no paucity of sources on the history of intelligence testing. A few of the sources that have significantly informed our thinking are Ray Fancher's *The Intelligence Men* (1985), which provides an extremely useful and sensitive account of the development of intelligence testing told through the lives of its major protagonists, as well as the controversies that have beset the enterprise. We drew upon it for various aspects of this chapter but especially the sections on Galton and Binet. We also consulted Michael Sokal's indispensable edited volume, *Psychological Testing and American Society, 1890–1930* (1987), especially his chapter on Cattell and mental anthropometry. JoAnne Brown's *The Definition of a Profession* (1992) was useful for its analysis of the role of intelligence testing in the professionalization of psychology.

Leila Zenderland has written the definitive biography of Goddard, *Measuring Minds* (1998), effectively demonstrating how he recanted his extreme hereditarian views by the end of his career. Terman's life and career is ably chronicled by Henry Minton (1988), who has argued that Terman held to a committed liberalism and the progressive belief that science was an instrument of social progress throughout his lifetime. In his book *Schools as Sorters*, Paul David Chapman (1988) also covers Terman's work on intelligence testing, further embedding it in the social problems and progressive ideals of the early 20th century. Paul McReynolds (1997) has written a useful biography of Witmer.

For our coverage of the rise of intelligence testing in the American context, along with the aforementioned books, we drew upon several journal articles among a large literature. We drew heavily on Paula Fass's excellent article "The IQ" (1980) to contextualize the rise of IQ testing in the school system, where it was seen as a scientific method for regulating and organizing an increasingly unruly and heterogeneous democracy. Her discussion of Dewey's educational philosophy and how it fit into these goals was also helpful. For our coverage of the impact of World War I on American psychology we used Daniel Kevles's article "Testing the Army's Intelligence" (1968) and Franz Samelson's article "World War I Intelligence Testing and the Development of Psychology" (1977). For the different paths and experiences of Yerkes and Scott during the First World War, we drew upon Richard von Mayrhauser's chapter "The Manager, the Medic, and the Mediator" (1987), in which he argues that Scott met with more success because of his comparative lack of ambivalence about applied psychology generally and because of the perception by the military that Yerkes was more interested in collecting data than in being of practical service. For information on early personality tests, we consulted Ludy Benjamin Jr. and David Baker's comprehensive work, *From Séance to Science* (2004). For more information on Woodworth's Personal Data Sheet and subsequent personality measures used in industry, see Robert Gibby and Michael Zickar's article "A History of the Early Days of Personality Testing in American Industry" (2008). Jung's 1910 publication, "The Association Method," presents the lectures he gave on the topic while visiting the United States with Freud in 1909 and is available online at the Classics in the History of Psychology website (http://psychclassics.yorku.ca/).

In the section titled Sorting the Sexes, we drew upon Katherine Milar's article "The First Generation of Women Psychologists and the Psychology of Women" (2000), as well as Henry Minton's article concerning the same period, "Psychology and Gender at the Turn of the Century" (2000). Rosalind Rosenberg's book *Beyond Separate Spheres* (1982) has an extremely useful account of Woolley's work and an informative discussion of the "new woman." For more details about Woolley, consult Jane Fowler Morse's article "Ignored but not Forgotten"

(2002). The author is Woolley's granddaughter. For information on Hollingworth's work, we used Stephanie Shields's article "Ms. Pilgrim's Progress" (1975b). There are two book-length biographies of Hollingworth, one written by her husband, Harry Hollingworth (1943), and one written by an educational psychologist that focuses on her later work with gifted children (Klein, 2002). For information on the professional patterns of women psychologists after World War I, we used Laurel Furumoto's chapter "On the Margins" (1987). Margaret Rossiter's canonical two-volume work *Women Scientists in America* (1982, 1995) has much useful information about women psychologists, as well as important contextual information about women in science more generally.

For the development of intelligence testing in the French context, we relied heavily on two sources: William Schneider's article "After Binet" (1992) and John Carson's masterful comparative volume on the evolution of intelligence testing in the American and French contexts, *The Measure of Merit* (2007).

You can also find a highly informative autobiographical statement by Henri Piéron in the fourth volume of the series *A History of Psychology in Autobiography* (1952). It sheds light not only on his career but also on the character of the French higher educational system and French experimental psychology in the early decades of the 20th century.

Intelligence testing and its discontents in the British context are discussed by Nikolas Rose in his book *The Psychological Complex* (1985), and we have drawn heavily on this work for this short section. For our brief discussion of intelligence testing and eugenics in the Netherlands, we consulted Ernst Mulder and Frieda Heyting's article "The Dutch Curve" (1998). For more information on pillarization and its effects on Dutch academic psychology, see Peter van Strien's "Transforming Psychology in the Netherlands" (1991).

For the development of psychotechnics in Germany, we drew upon Andreas Killen's article "Weimar Psychotechnics between Americanism and Fascism" (2007), as well as the short illustrated chapter on psychotechnics by Peter van Drunen (1997) in the extremely useful volume *A Pictorial History of Psychology*. In this same volume, Horst Gundlach (1997) has a useful chapter on the application of psychology to the railroads, and Wilfrid Schmidt (1997) has an informative chapter on Stern. Münsterberg's career and contributions to applied psychology are chronicled and analyzed in Matthew Hale's book *Human Science and Social Order* (1980).

Chapter 7
TIMELINE 1830–1940
(In 25-year increments)

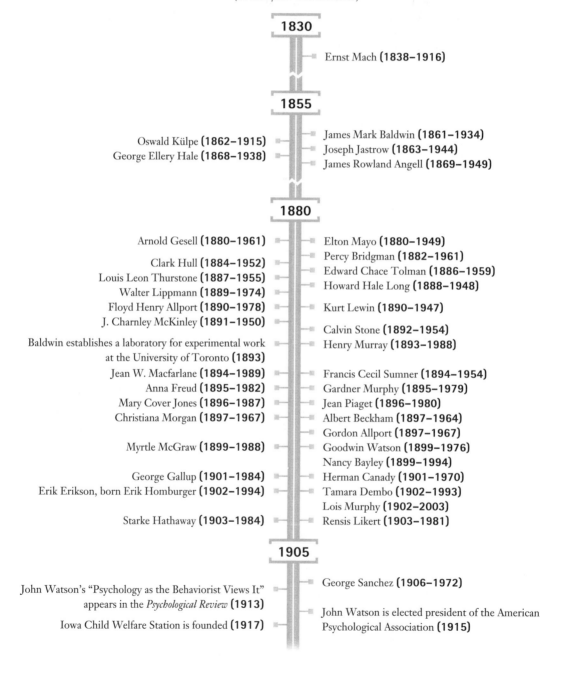

1830

Ernst Mach (**1838–1916**)

1855

Oswald Külpe (**1862–1915**)
George Ellery Hale (**1868–1938**)

James Mark Baldwin (**1861–1934**)
Joseph Jastrow (**1863–1944**)
James Rowland Angell (**1869–1949**)

1880

Arnold Gesell (**1880–1961**)

Clark Hull (**1884–1952**)
Louis Leon Thurstone (**1887–1955**)
Walter Lippmann (**1889–1974**)
Floyd Henry Allport (**1890–1978**)
J. Charnley McKinley (**1891–1950**)

Baldwin establishes a laboratory for experimental work
at the University of Toronto (**1893**)
Jean W. Macfarlane (**1894–1989**)
Anna Freud (**1895–1982**)
Mary Cover Jones (**1896–1987**)
Christiana Morgan (**1897–1967**)

Myrtle McGraw (**1899–1988**)

George Gallup (**1901–1984**)
Erik Erikson, born Erik Homburger (**1902–1994**)

Starke Hathaway (**1903–1984**)

Elton Mayo (**1880–1949**)
Percy Bridgman (**1882–1961**)
Edward Chace Tolman (**1886–1959**)
Howard Hale Long (**1888–1948**)

Kurt Lewin (**1890–1947**)

Calvin Stone (**1892–1954**)
Henry Murray (**1893–1988**)

Francis Cecil Sumner (**1894–1954**)
Gardner Murphy (**1895–1979**)
Jean Piaget (**1896–1980**)
Albert Beckham (**1897–1964**)
Gordon Allport (**1897–1967**)
Goodwin Watson (**1899–1976**)
Nancy Bayley (**1899–1994**)
Herman Canady (**1901–1970**)
Tamara Dembo (**1902–1993**)
Lois Murphy (**1902–2003**)
Rensis Likert (**1903–1981**)

1905

John Watson's "Psychology as the Behaviorist Views It"
appears in the *Psychological Review* (**1913**)
Iowa Child Welfare Station is founded (**1917**)

George Sanchez (**1906–1972**)

John Watson is elected president of the American
Psychological Association (**1915**)

Russian Revolution **(1917)**

Laura Spelman Rockefeller Memorial is founded **(1918)**

Journal of Abnormal Psychology becomes *Journal of Abnormal Psychology and Social Psychology* **(1921)**

APA forms an associate membership class **(1926)**

Research at Western Electric results in the Hawthorne effect **(1927)**

Gordon Allport publishes his Test of Ascendance—Submission **(1928)**

Great Depression **(1929–1941)**

Woodworth publishes his Psychoneurotic Test, later renamed the Woodworth Personal Data Sheet **(1917)**

Sumner becomes the first African American to earn a PhD in psychology **(1920)**

Yerkes's *Psychological Examining in the U.S. Army* **(1921)**

Committee for Research in Problems of Sex forms **(1921)**

Floyd Allport's *Social Psychology* **(1924)**

Bridgman's *The Logic of Modern Physics* **(1927)**

Harvard Psychological Clinic is founded **(1927)**

Ernst Mach Society is founded **(1928)**

Institute of Human Relations is founded at Yale **(1929)**

1930

Murphy's *Experimental Social Psychology* **(1931)**

Robert V. Guthrie **(1932–2005)**

Society for Research in Child Development is founded **(1933)**

Gallup founds the American Institute of Public Opinion **(1935)**

Lewin's *Principles of Topological Psychology* is published in English **(1936)**

Gordon Allport's *Personality: A Psychological Interpretation* **(1937)**

Dollard et al.'s *Frustration and Aggression* **(1939)**

Association of Consulting Psychologists forms **(1930)**

Oakland Growth Study begins **(1931)**

Tolman's *Purposive Behavior in Animals and Men* **(1932)**

African American Long receives his EdD in psychology from Harvard **(1933)**

SRCD begins its journal *Child Development* **(1935)**

Murray and Morgan develop the Thematic Apperception Test **(1935)**

Goodwin Watson is elected first president of the Society for the Psychological Study of Social Issues **(1936)**

Spanish Civil War **(1936–1939)**

Out of the ACP, the American Association for Applied Psychology forms **(1937)**

Murray's *Explorations in Personality* **(1938)**

Psychologists' League is disbanded **(1939)**

Second World War **(1939–1945)**

United States enters World War II **(1941)**

Hathaway and McKinley publish the Minnesota Multiphasic Personality Inventory **(1942)**

7

AMERICAN PSYCHOLOGICAL SCIENCE AND PRACTICE BETWEEN THE WORLD WARS

A science that can endure the ravages of two such distempers as behaviorism and psychoanalysis and recover without permanent disfigurement must have a lusty constitution.

—Joseph Jastrow, *Has Psychology Failed?*, 1935

INTRODUCTION

In the period between the two world wars, Psychology became fully indigenized in the United States. That is, what began as a borrowing or importing of a science that originated in a German context with the purpose of providing support for the foundations of rational knowledge, became localized to the American context. Behaviorism, as we discussed in Chapter 3, was one form of this indigenized American psychology. Both psychoanalysis, which grew in popularity among the American public in this period, and behaviorism, which had its own brand of popular appeal, were incorporated into the everyday psychology that many Americans began using in their lives. Americans also witnessed the rise of the testing industry, and many were exposed firsthand to psychologists' handiwork, if not to psychologists themselves.

After World War I ended, American psychologists were able to generate a great deal of publicity from their army testing program. Leaders of American psychology, like Robert Yerkes (1876–1956), wrote articles for popular magazines extolling psychologists' skills in discovering important abilities and differences among Americans. Due to the efforts of psychologists like Yerkes and many others, the period from the end of the First World War until the entry of the United States into the Second World War was when many Americans discovered Psychology and found it useful in their everyday lives. Yet the Psychology on view was certainly not one that emanated from a unified science or profession; rather, it was marked by a range of competing and sometimes contradictory approaches. In this chapter, we explore this diversity, examining the science that could be characterized as the

mainstream approach or the center, neobehaviorism, and the psychologies of the periphery: developmental, sexuality, personality, and social.

We begin this chapter by offering a brief counterstory to the standard historical account. We offer a narrative about the spread of psychological ideas among the American public. In doing so, we demonstrate the link between the psychological sensibility expressed in an earlier era in phrenology, mesmerism, and New Thought and the vernacular psychology of the interwar period, which, we argue, was important for the acceptance of disciplinary Psychology.

Then, before delving into the mainstream of American psychological science, we highlight two of the structural frames that facilitated the growth of diversity within psychology: organizations and philanthropical support. We then provide an account of the dominant outlook in academic psychology in the period between the wars, that is, neobehaviorism.

In the United States, programs of research developed on many topics outside the mainstream. This was when social and personality psychology emerged as distinct fields of study. Extensive research focused on emotions, sexuality, and child development, much of it well funded by philanthropies; we offer a brief account of this work, as it indicates the extent to which psychological ideas and practices spread in American social and professional life.

WHO OWNS PSYCHOLOGY?

The period between the two world wars was crucial for the development of psychology in North America. Psychologists were initially able to argue that their army testing program had been a great success, thus validating the utility of psychology (and specifically, testing) for addressing and solving social problems. Many of their claims were disputed by American public intellectuals such as Walter Lippmann (1889–1974). Lippmann, in a series of articles published in the liberal magazine *The New Republic* in 1922, took the psychological profession, and individual psychologists, to task for several issues. He pointed out psychologists' inability to define intelligence, criticized the hereditarian assumptions upon which many of their pronouncements were based (he felt they were scientifically unfounded), and lambasted them for their arrogance in brandishing a tool of enormous social import so carelessly. As he wrote, "How easily the intelligence test can be turned into an engine of cruelty, how easily in the hands of blundering or prejudiced men it could turn into a method of stamping a permanent sense of inferiority upon the soul of a child" (Lippmann, 1922, p. 297).

But whatever the outcome of these debates, what could not be challenged was the impact of testing on the public's imagination. The notion

that an understanding of human character and ability could be gained through some type of psychological test captured the public imagination. At the same time, interest in popularized notions of Sigmund Freud's psychoanalysis grew tremendously. Since the public did not make fine distinctions between psychology and psychoanalysis, the net result was a fascination with psychology. As Canadian humorist Stephen Leacock famously stated in a *Harpers* magazine article in 1924, Americans were experiencing an "outbreak of psychology" (Leacock, 1924, p. 471). In this section, we offer a brief interpretation of why psychology was so fascinating to the American public.

Who *owns* psychology? How can we understand the psychological imagination of the North American public in this interwar period? After the war, American psychologists like Yerkes, John B. Watson (1878–1958), Grace Adams, Joseph Jastrow, and many others used the popular media—newspapers, magazines, radio broadcasts—in attempts to shape the public's perception of psychological science and practice. Yet, at the end of the interwar period it was not clear that psychologists *owned* their subject any more than they had at the beginning. The public was more psychologically minded, yet its understanding was not due to the public's embrace of disciplinary Psychology; rather, there appeared to be just as much reliance on the psychology of nonprofessionals as that of psychological scientists. As Benjamin and Bryant (1997) have pointed out in their history of popular psychology magazines in this period, much of the most widely read material was authored by nonpsychologists. Why was this so?

The reciprocal relationship between disciplinary psychologists and the public has been marked by misconnections and misunderstandings in the social and behavioral sciences, especially for psychology. From the beginning of the *discipline* of Psychology in North America, psychologists often turned to popular media both as authors and as willing subjects of popular expositions. By the mid-1920s, hundreds, possibly thousands, of popular presentations of psychology by both psychologists and nonpsychologists had been published. Often in these popular articles, psychologists sought to *own* psychology by discrediting nondisciplinary "psychologies." They failed. One reason that psychologists failed to own their subject matter was that an everyday psychology, an epistemology of everyday experience, already existed. As we have seen in previous chapters, and will see in the development of psychology in Britain in the next chapter, there had been a growing sense of the interior life, a sense of a private self, since the early modern period of the 17th century. The technologies of the self that we discussed in earlier chapters (the mirror, conduct books, and diaries) and the subsequent use of readings of the human body (physiognomy and phrenology) to reveal inner characteristics and determine external behavior came together in the United States in the 19th century with mesmerism, spiritualism, and New Thought to create an everyday psychology, a psychological sensibility it might be called, in the American public. It was this as much as any scientific findings that prepared the context for the successful indigenization of disciplinary Psychology.

In America, particularly, the existence of an everyday psychology created an audience for the popular expressions of academic Psychology. So, in the 1920s, a rapid expansion of both disciplinary Psychology and popular psychologies was promoted by nonprofessionals. While this chapter focuses mainly on the expansion of disciplinary Psychology, we should keep in mind that this occurred in the context of a public that was receptive to its expertise but not willing give up its own everyday psychology.

The everyday understanding of self and others that is gained from experience often appears as more veridical than the testimony of experts. After all, as Adams wrote, "The domain which the psychologist explores is accessible to everyone who realizes that he has a mind" (1931, p. 16). In the United States, the growth of both everyday psychology and disciplinary Psychology occurred in the context of the rise of a therapeutic ethos, that is, a focus on feeling good and placing high value on positive self-esteem; perhaps this self-focus was even stimulated by the growth of psychology. The other context that was crucial was the emergence of a mass culture of consumerism, which transformed American identity into that of the consumer. A practical result of these processes was the psychologization of every aspect of life. As we explain in this chapter, business, industry, and work were primary sites for psychology, ranging from advertising, with its model of the person as a target for persuasion and manipulation, to industry, with its need to have a manageable worker. The 20th-century sense of the self as an individual defined by internal psychological processes resulted. Everyone became his or her own psychologist, as historian Roger Smith has so elegantly stated (1997).

ORGANIZATION AND COOPERATION

In this context of avid public interest in all matters psychological, the growth of disciplinary Psychology was facilitated by new organizations and by the emergence of a new player in science, the philanthropic foundation. Such foundations promoted an ethic of scientific cooperation that affected several fields of psychology and helped create borderlands of scientific work that provided new opportunities for psychologists.

Organization

The American Psychological Association (APA) was the only truly national organization of psychologists in the United States as World War I ended. Membership growth of the APA was modest over the first 50 years of its existence. From 31 members in 1892, there were 125 members in 1899, 308 in 1916, 530 in 1930, and 664 in 1940. In 1926, the associate class of membership was formed and it was in this class that most growth occurred, so that there were 2,079 associate members in 1940. The growth in full members, available only to those who met rather stringent criteria, was respectable in these years. However, the growth of the new associate member category better represents the growth of the field and the great interest shown in psychology by the public. The APA's leaders had rather cynically created the class of associates in the mid-1920s as a way to raise money to buy several of the leading journals in the field. Associates paid dues but held no voting privileges. The only real benefit was being able to say that they were associates of the APA. Many of these associates were women and Jews, thus not readily acceptable to the mostly male, university scientists of Anglo-Saxon or northern European descent who ran the APA, as historian Andrew Winston has shown (1998).

The other mark against many of these associates was that they were primarily engaged in applied work. In the period between the wars, the applied work of psychologists fell into four semidistinct areas of practice: clinical, consulting, educational, and industrial–business. The range of employment settings for applied psychologists was impressive. Applied psychologists were located in schools, many kinds of clinics, homes for the mentally retarded, courts, prisons, police departments, psychiatric hospitals, guidance offices in educational settings, psychotherapy offices, social agencies, state and federal agencies, film and radio studios, personnel offices, advertising and marketing firms, life insurance companies, and private consulting firms. Applied psychology in the interwar period was, to use a business metaphor, a bull market.

Because the APA did not support applied work, new organizations emerged that were intended to provide such support. Out of a New York State organization for consulting psychologists, a new quasi-national organization was formed in 1930, the Association of Consulting Psychologists. It evolved into the American Association for Applied Psychology (AAAP) in

1937. These new applied organizations addressed the practical issues that applied psychologists faced: education and training standards, internships, licensure or certification by state boards, standards of practice, and employment of its members. By the time the Second World War began, the AAAP was beginning to make substantive progress on behalf of its members. As we discuss in Chapter 9, during that war, a new initiative to reform the APA to make it more inclusive and more responsive to both scientific and professional concerns led to the incorporation of the AAAP into a reorganized APA.

The dominance of APA was challenged on other fronts as well. The impact on Psychology of the Great Depression that began in fall 1929 was great. Unemployment and underemployment were two of the major consequences of the Depression. Many younger psychologists, whether they did applied work or were academic scientists, were unable to find work at all or unable to find work as psychologists. However, the leaders of the APA, who were already well established and not affected as severely by the Depression, refused to become involved in the employment crisis. The Depression had also revealed major fault lines in American capitalism in terms of social justice and social equality in American life.

These two factors came together for several of the younger psychologists. Many of them were active in politically leftist or socialist groups, such as New America. Out of their frustration with the APA and in an effort to do something to address social problems, two new organizations of psychologists were formed: the Psychologists' League and the Society for the Psychological Study of Social Issues (SPSSI). The Psychologists' League was based in New York City and was organized to work for full employment of psychologists, especially in such government programs as the Works Progress Administration. They had some success in finding jobs for psychologists and certainly provided support for one another.

By 1940, however, the initial enthusiasm and energy had waned and the league eventually dissolved.

The other major group that was formed during this period, the SPSSI, is discussed later in the section on social psychology.

Cooperative Research and Philanthropy

In the period just before and after World War I, many scientists advocated the benefits of cooperative research. Cooperation in science in this era was a joint project by prominent scientists and philanthropy officers to minimize the importance of disciplinary boundaries and to facilitate the application of science to issues of human importance. This was a new phenomenon that reflected the reorientation of American society toward cooperation, as part of the search for a modern order. Contemporary scholars have characterized this long-range project as one involving social control, social engineering, and human engineering.

Cooperation among scientists during World War I had been valuable to the war effort, and the scientists involved saw the power of organized, collaborative scientific research. After the war, prominent scientists, such as the astronomer George Ellery Hale (1868–1938) and his colleagues at the National Research Council (NRC), which had been organized to help with the war effort, were able to use the successes of scientific cooperation during the war to argue that scientists needed to develop an ethos of collaboration. Many scientists feared that organization would lead to control by outside bodies, but Hale and other leaders of the movement were able to persuade enough scientists and university leaders to become involved in cooperative research. Psychologist James Rowland Angell (1869–1949) promoted the value of cooperative research as a method of increasing productivity and efficiency of scientific work. "Organization is the clue," Angell wrote, "to ensuring that full use is made of the 'intellectual capital' of the nation's scientists" (1920, p. 252).

Concomitant with the push for cooperation was the encouragement of interdisciplinary research, for scientists from disparate but related fields to collaborate in the investigation of scientific issues that lay on the border between them. Philanthropic foundations also encouraged such cooperative interdisciplinary research through offering financial support, believing that the best ideas of scientists could help ameliorate social problems. In the interwar period, foundation officers and scientists worked out a new relationship with the shared goal of making a better society through the general advancement of knowledge. Research fellowships and cooperative research projects were two of the methods used to facilitate the mutual goals of the scientists and the foundations.

For psychology, the new era of cooperative research and the availability of funding helped the field grow and diversify. We briefly discuss two new areas that benefited from these factors: developmental psychology and sex research. But first, we turn to an account of the primary outlook in mainstream academic psychology, neobehaviorism. As we demonstrate, philanthropy played a role here, too.

THE KINGDOM OF BEHAVIOR: MAINSTREAM PSYCHOLOGY, 1920–1940

Mainstream psychological scientists in this period worked primarily in the neobehaviorist mode, attempting to show that lawful relations between stimuli and responses indicated how organisms adapt to varying conditions, that is, how organisms learn. Some neobehaviorists attempted to derive formal systems that would describe the laws of behavior.

The study of a small albino rodent, *Rattus norvegicus* var *albinus*, in an enclosed space became the predominant activity in North American psychology laboratories for nearly 60 years. The behavior of the rat under controlled conditions of stimulation was taken as a stand-in for the likely behavior of humans. Psychologists who embraced this approach argued that the learning demonstrated by these rats was analogous to the adaptation of other organisms. Several variants of this approach came to the fore, sometimes termed behaviorism, **neobehaviorism**, or in the work of Burrhus Frederic Skinner (1904–1990), radical behaviorism. Behavioral psychology became the mainstream of North American experimental psychology. As we show in this section, this had implications for the philosophy of science, for methodology, for technology, and for the organization of scientists.

Watson declared in 1913 that "psychology as the behaviorist views it is a purely experimental branch of natural science. Its theoretical goal is the prediction and control of behavior. Introspection forms no essential part of its methods" (p. 158). You may recall that in Chapter 3 we discussed Watson's development of behaviorism within the context of the Progressive Era and showed how the kind of psychology he advocated fit well with that era's search for order and rationality in society. We also indicated that Watson was not the only person at the time to argue for a focus on observable behavior rather than unseen conscious states as the appropriate data source for a scientific psychology. Watson was powerfully positioned, however, to make the case. He was the editor of *Psychological Review*, chair of the Psychology Department at the Johns Hopkins University, and elected president of the APA for 1915. Still, as historian Franz Samelson (1981) has pointed out, the field of psychology did not immediately move lock, stock, and barrel to behaviorist psychology.

In this era, most academic psychologists who were actually doing experimental work (that has always been only a relatively small proportion of those who were trained as scientists) were still using introspection and reaction-time methods to study phenomena such as attentional processes; a few psychologists were using recently developed psychological tests. The theoretical framework was predominantly functionalist (processes of conscious states), although many worked

within the structuralist (mental contents) model developed by Cornell University psychologist Edward Bradford Titchener (1867–1927). By the early 1920s, however, the terms "behavior" and "behaviorist" were being widely used without necessarily indicating Watson's behaviorism. By the late 1920s, enough psychologists were doing behavioral research to indicate that the mainstream of American psychological science was becoming behaviorist.

What might have facilitated this change? One factor was that those psychologists who were graduate students and early career psychologists when Watson called for a focus on behavior were by the mid- to late 1920s moving into leadership positions, and they had certainly been more receptive to Watson's emphasis on observable behavior. Second, this generation of psychologists seemed to experience "physics envy" more keenly than their predecessors. That is, as the natural sciences like physics were making such huge strides and garnering great public acclaim (e.g., the work of Albert Einstein and Niels Bohr on relativity theory and quantum theory), the datum of an unseen consciousness carried little weight among their scientific colleagues. The annual meeting of psychologists was held in conjunction with other scientists, including physicists, making this state of affairs perhaps painfully obvious. Behavior, however, was observable, thus potentially predictable and subject to control in a scientific milieu that placed a high value on prediction and control. As noted, behaviorism fit better with the political culture of the time. It was easier for those in power to grasp how a behaviorist psychology could improve society than it was for them to understand how a psychology of conscious mental states could do so.

Scientific contributions and developments also propelled the move toward behaviorism. One was the eruption of an argument in Germany about psychology's status as a science. This seems obscure, perhaps, but it proved important for reshaping the methodology of scientific psychology. The genesis of this debate was the split between Wilhelm Wundt (1832–1920) and his former student, Oswald Külpe (1862–1915), over the appropriate philosophy of science for Psychology. At the time the controversy began, Külpe was Wundt's chief assistant in the Psychology Laboratory at the University of Leipzig. As we noted in Chapter 3, Wundt argued that many psychological phenomena could not be studied experimentally. Those that could be so studied—simpler cognitive processes—obeyed laws of psychic causality rather than physical causality. For Wundt, psychology was not and could not be a strictly natural science. Külpe came to disagree, and when he left Leipzig for a position at Würzburg, he made his disagreement open and engendered a controversy that continued for many years. At the heart of the disagreement with Wundt was a different conceptualization of science. Külpe embraced the **positivism** of the physicist Ernst Mach (1838–1916) and philosopher Richard Avenarius (1843–1896). This positivism asserted the primacy of experience as the basis of knowledge; that is, that the experience of the observable world is foundational to science. Experience is experience; thus, there are not two kinds of experience, mental and physical. In this approach to psychology, mentalistic explanations are not acceptable. Wundt, of course, had argued that psychological or "psychic," as he termed it, events have psychological causes. His experimental psychology was constructed on mentalistic explanations.

Külpe and his colleagues and students at Würzburg proceeded to develop an experimental psychology on a positivist basis and to include in it complex mental processes, such as thought, that Wundt had declared off-limits. Theirs was to be a scientific psychology of experience. The redefinition of psychology in this way, based on the experienced, observable physical world, proved crucial for the future of Psychology. It meant that Psychology would focus on what could be observed rather than internal mental states. In the American context, which as we have seen, was (and is) practically or pragmatically oriented, this provided another justification for

what came to be labeled behaviorism. As Watson had argued, if psychology were to be a natural science, it had to give up its focus on the unseen mental states and turn its focus to what could be observed, the behavior of organisms. By the late 1920s and into the 1930s, American psychology became even more deeply infused with positivism through such constructs as operationism and logical positivism, both direct descendants of Machian thought. In particular, these constructs were embraced by several psychologists who came to be labeled neobehaviorists.

Neobehaviorism

During the 1920s, the mainstream of psychological science embraced the study of behavior. Implicit in this approach was the Darwinian notion of evolution by natural selection. Humans are part of nature; thus, adapting to their surroundings is key to survival. Metaphors employed for this adaptation included adjustment and learning, which could be observed in behavior. Conditions of learning could be experimentally manipulated; thus, the scientific laboratory was the appropriate site for the discovery of its laws. Given the continuity of species demonstrated in Darwinian theory, the behaviorists argued that nonhuman animals could be used as stand-ins for humans in studies of learning. As noted earlier, the animal that came to be preferred for this analogous role was the white rat.

By the 1930s, two new important influences had been introduced into behaviorism, giving it its name, neobehaviorism. **Operationism** was taken from the work of physicist Percy Bridgman (1882–1961). In his book, *The Logic of Modern Physics* (1927), Bridgman argued that each construct introduced by scientists should be specified in terms of how it is measured. An **operational definition** is the set of methods or techniques used to measure the construct. No references to mental processes or internal feeling states were allowed. So, in the psychology of the time, a scientist might operationally define hunger by giving the exact weight of the rat and exactly how long the rat had been without food. **Logical positivism** was the influential philosophy of science based on the positivism of Mach that decreed that all scientific constructs had to be linked to observable events. In the United States, to which several of these philosophers immigrated, this group of philosophers was called the Vienna Circle. In Vienna, they were known as the Ernst Mach Society.

Both operationism and logical positivism were incorporated into the new behaviorism by the 1930s. Both were powerful influences that many new leaders of experimental psychology hoped would give their science greater legitimacy and would help confirm that psychology was, indeed, a natural science.

Watson's theoretical approach had been the conditioned reflex model developed most completely at the time in the laboratory of Russian physiologist Ivan Pavlov (1849–1936). Clark Hull (1884–1952), one of the most prominent neobehaviorists, also adopted a conditioned reflex model for his ambitious program of research.

Hull had hoped earlier in his life to be an engineer, but a bout with polio left him slightly disabled and his application to engineering programs was rejected. He taught school for a period before returning to college, where he eventually earned his doctorate in psychology at the University of Wisconsin. He conducted applied research in the first decade or so of his career and was recruited to Yale University in 1929 to fill a need for someone with a strong interest in applied work.

Yale, at this time, had established the Institute of Human Relations with a large grant from the Rockefeller Foundation. The institute was interdisciplinary, and research there was intended to shed light on the social problems of the day. As we noted at the beginning of the chapter, philanthropical foundations were heavily committed to supporting interdisciplinary and cooperative scientific research programs. For the Rockefeller Foundation, this was an effort to see whether large-scale philanthropical support could facilitate social engineering through

FIGURE 7.1   Clark Hull
Courtesy of the Archives of the History of American Psychology, University of Akron, Akron, OH.

scientific research. Hull proved one of the most adept of the Yale scientists in using this support to further his own research aims, if not those of the institute or the Rockefeller Foundation.

Even as Hull began his systematization of learning principles at Yale, he kept his interest in the applicability of his research to human problems. With colleagues, for example, he studied alcohol consumption. He also had ambitions to understand even more serious disruptions of normal human functioning, the psychoses. He proposed using a modified form of Pavlovian conditioning to study these problems. One Rockefeller administrator described Hull in 1934 as the American Pavlov, who "uses Yale sophomores instead of dogs" (Weaver, 1934). In fall 1935, Hull decided to initiate a program to correlate the tenets of psychoanalysis with conditioned reflex theory. He drew upon work being done in

Chicago that suggested several possible links between psychoanalysis and Pavlov's conditioned reflex theory. Based upon this work, Hull sought to establish a research program that integrated conditioned reflexes and psychoanalytic therapy techniques to address such serious problems as psychoses, juvenile delinquency, bullying, and frustration. Hull's efforts were pointed toward bringing the irrational (exemplified by psychoanalysis) under the control of orderly, systematic science and were part of his larger project for a unified science.

As Hull, his graduate students, and his postdoctoral fellows worked on these projects, the theoretical apparatus they developed grew ever larger. Hull was convinced that the principles of learning, of an organism's adjustment to the environment, could be captured as a set of mathematical theorems and corollaries. Learning was mathematically described in terms that specified linkages among drive (e.g., hunger drive, operationally defined as hours without food), habit strength, reinforcement, and several other variables. It was a complex theory that required constant adjustments, with new findings added in mathematical formulas to already complex formulations. Eventually, this system grew too elaborate to test, and many adherents withdrew from trying to do so. Nevertheless, during the heyday of Hull's system (1935–1952), it was the most cited body of work in American experimental psychology.

Edward Chace Tolman (1886–1959) is the other major neobehaviorist we discuss. Tolman brought to his work a more broad-minded view of experimental psychology than did Hull. Nevertheless, Tolman argued that all we need to know about human behavior could be learned from experiments with rats.

Tolman grew up in a devout Quaker home. His brother, Richard, became a physicist and was one of the scientists who helped develop the first atomic bomb. Like his brother, Edward graduated from the Massachusetts Institute of Technology with a degree in theoretical chemistry. However, he was drawn to philosophy and

enrolled in graduate study at Harvard University to pursue his interest. He became interested in psychology through his professors at Harvard and a summer spent in Germany, where he met the young Gestalt psychologist Kurt Koffka (1886–1941). Course work in comparative psychology introduced him to Watson's recent work in behaviorism, and Tolman eventually came to see the behaviorist approach as the route he wanted to follow. He lost his first job at Northwestern University during World War I because of his pacifism. Tolman then took a position at the University of California, Berkeley, in 1918, where he spent the rest of his career. The psychology building at Berkeley is named for him.

Tolman dedicated his most influential book, *Purposive Behavior in Animals and Men* (1932), to the white rat. As the title indicates, Tolman's approach assumed that behavior was goal directed. Unlike Hull and many other neobehaviorists, Tolman did not accept that learning consisted of chains of conditioned reflexes. Rather, the rat, and by extension, the human, was constantly learning about the environment, but much of this learning was latent; that is, it would not be demonstrated until the occasion called for it.

Tolman and one of his graduate students, Charles Honzik, conducted a study that they argued was a convincing demonstration of latent learning (Tolman & Honzik, 1930). The study had three conditions: (1) a control group of rats allowed simply to wander through the maze with no reward; (2) a learning group, where rats were rewarded from the beginning for finding their way through the maze; and (3) the latent learning condition, where the rats were not rewarded until the 11th day of the experiment. As would be predicted by Hull and other neobehaviorists who saw learning as a matter of reward or reinforcement, the rats in the learning condition quickly reduced the number of errors (false directions in the maze) and the number of errors dropped daily. However, latent learning, that is, Tolman's theory that learning occurs constantly and only needs the right conditions for it to be demonstrated, was supported by the behavior of the rats in the latent learning condition. For these rats, the number of errors matched that of the control group for the first 10 days. However, on the 11th day, when reward was introduced, the number of errors of these rats was dramatically reduced and quickly became fewer in number than those of the learning group. Tolman interpreted this as supportive of his theory that learning is purposive, or goal directed.

This work, and more like it, became the center of experimental psychology in the period between the wars. While the number of experimental psychologists was not large, it is accurate to state that work on conditions of learning or adaptation was central. If we look beyond the center, as we do next, we see that other significant bodies of psychological research and application emerged in this period.

DEVELOPING DEVELOPMENTAL PSYCHOLOGY

Developmental psychology in the United States was not institutionalized until the period between the world wars. Of course, psychological theories about development had arisen before this period. Freud (1856–1939), William Stern (1871–1938), and Alfred Binet (1857–1911) in Europe, as well as G. Stanley Hall (1844–1924) and James Mark Baldwin (1861–1934) in North America, all contributed theories and experimental work to understanding the psychological development of children. As we saw in an earlier chapter, Hall was involved in the child study movement from early in his career and even began a journal devoted to developmental issues and education. Baldwin wrote two books devoted to what we would now call the cognitive development of children in the 1890s, based on Darwinian evolutionary theory. He established a laboratory for experimental work at the University of Toronto in 1893. His ideas on children's cognitive development were influential in

shaping the developmental theories of French Swiss psychologist Jean Piaget (1896–1980), whose work is discussed later in this book.

Despite this work, no consistent body of experimental research was devoted to explicating children's development until after World War I. One of the precedents for establishing such research was the nursery school movement, which began in England in the early 1900s. The idea of a preschool, prekindergarten setting to nurture young children gained a place in America after the war. Many of these nursery schools were established in university centers, often in association with home economics programs, and were occasionally linked to psychology or education programs. These university-based nursery schools often became laboratories for the scientific study of children. Teachers College at Columbia University in New York became one of the early settings for this work, as did the University of Iowa, where the Iowa Child Welfare Station was funded by the state legislature with psychologist Bird Baldwin as director. Other important sites were the Merrill-Palmer School in Detroit, where the psychologist Helen Bradford Thompson Woolley (1874–1947; see Chapter 6) was head of research, and the Psycho-Clinic at Yale, directed by psychologist–physician Arnold Gesell (1880–1961). At most of these locations, the research was interdisciplinary in nature, often investigating both physical and psychological growth factors, as well as nutrition and home care.

This was the foundation for the launch of major research programs that began by the late 1920s, once major financial support was offered by private philanthropies. Over the next 15–20 years, philanthropies like the Commonwealth Fund, the various funds of the Rockefeller Foundation, and the Josiah Macy Jr. Foundation all provided what was then large-scale funding for developmental research, often with an applied angle (e.g., parent education). Fellowships for graduate study, funds to establish laboratories and support workers, and subventions for publications were all crucial for the emergence and growth of developmental psychology, especially studies of children's development.

The Laura Spelman Rockefeller Memorial (LSRM) fund (one of the Rockefeller Foundation funds) played the key role in these efforts in the 1920s. In 1923, the director of the memorial, psychologist Beardsley Ruml assigned social scientist Lawrence Frank the task of articulating a plan to spend $1 million a year to benefit children. Frank came up with a plan to do so through encouraging research and education related to children's development. Out of this plan, research institutes were established as independent centers at several universities across North America. The list is impressive.

Teachers College at Columbia began the Child Development Institute, which was able to lure Woolley, then the nation's most prominent woman psychologist, from the Merrill-Palmer School in Detroit; the Iowa Child Welfare Research Station was also endowed with funds to add to the support they received from the state of Iowa. Over the next few years, the LSRM gave money to begin child research institutes at the University of Toronto, University of Minnesota, and the University of California, Berkeley. In each case, the memorial insisted that the institutes be set up as separate from the established academic departments, partly because the research was intended to be interdisciplinary and partly to keep academic department heads from diverting funds away from child research. This last point sounds harsh, but many departments of psychology did not perceive research on children as serious experimental science, seeing it instead as a place for women who were not wanted in academic departments of psychology. In addition, many researchers did not want children around their laboratories.

University-based institutes were the major focus of foundation support, but not the only focus. The LSRM also provided the money to establish a Committee on Child Development at the prestigious NRC. Led by well-known experimental psychologist, Robert Sessions Woodworth (1869–1962) of Columbia, the committee administered an important fellowship program that made it possible for many graduate students to earn their doctorates while doing developmental research. Most recipients were women; the list of NRC fellows in this program is impressive even today and includes several women who went on to make major scientific contributions, including Myrtle McGraw (1899–1988) and Mary Cover Jones (1896–1987).

Knowledge dissemination was also a critical role played by the Committee on Child Development and funded by the LSRM. Several key conferences were held under the committee's auspices, where leading researchers from various relevant fields were brought together to share research results and identify key issues for future research. Perhaps even more importantly, Woodworth was able to overcome many obstacles to help found the interdisciplinary scientific organization, the Society for Research in Child Development, in 1933. Two years later, the society began its journal, *Child Development*, with funds from the General Education Board, another of the Rockefeller philanthropies. The organization and *Child Development* became the preeminent society and scientific journal for developmental research.

Out of this initiative, several longitudinal studies were inaugurated and continued for many years. Here, we give just a brief overview of these studies. Lewis Terman (1877–1956; for more on Terman, see Chapter 6) was funded by the Commonwealth Fund to conduct a longitudinal study of gifted children. More than 1,500 children were identified as gifted and enrolled in the research program in 1923. While the IQ was the basic predictor used in this study, personality and social variables were also included. The goal was to determine how well the IQ predicted life outcomes. The study has continued until the present day, although almost all of the original participants have died.

The major group of longitudinal studies was conducted at the Institute for Human Development at the University of California, Berkeley, beginning in the late 1920s. Each study had its own personnel, with little overlap. These studies were interdisciplinary, with psychologists and physicians typically providing the leadership. The Guidance Study was led by psychologist Jean W. Macfarlane (1894–1989). The study was meant to examine the impact of parental guidance on child outcomes, such as performance in school. The experimental group consisted of intense interaction between child and parent around issues related to school and relationships, with the control group not receiving any particular emphasis on parental guidance. In January 1939, a young child psychoanalyst joined the staff of the Guidance Study. Erik Homburger, a Danish artist who had been personally trained in child analysis by Anna Freud (1895–1982), had fled the Nazis with his American wife in the early 1930s. After a few years at Harvard's Psychological Clinic and Yale's Institute of Human Relations, he accepted the offer to come to Berkeley. Homburger had never known who his real father was, especially since his mother had misled him more than once about his father. With the move to California, Homburger saw an opportunity to do what so many Americans do: reinvent himself. He legally changed his last name to Erikson, declaring that since he did not know his real father he would become his own father. Erik Erikson (1902–1994),

became one of the 20th century's best-known psychologists and public intellectuals. His theory of identify formation and development became standard fare in most undergraduate courses.

The Berkeley Growth Study at the Institute for Human Development was led by psychologist Nancy Bayley (1899–1994). The study followed 74 infants for 40 years and covered mental and physical development. Bayley, who later in her career worked at the National Institute of Mental Health in suburban Washington, DC, is probably best known for the assessment instrument that grew out of this study, the *Bayley Scales of Infant Development*. Most graduate students in North American clinical and counseling programs become familiar with this scale in their training.

The Oakland Growth Study (originally the Adolescent Growth Study) was led by Harold and Mary Cover Jones. The study began in 1931 and followed adolescent boys and girls well into adulthood to assess their physical and psychological development. For example, Mary Cover Jones reported that boys who were slow to develop physically often also showed evidence of slower psychological maturity, although they typically were able to "catch up" psychologically in their 20s.

Sidebar 7.1 Focus on *Mary Cover Jones*

Mary Cover Jones was an important developmental psychologist, but many students may recognize her name not because of her association with the Oakland Growth Study but because she conducted the classic follow-up to John B. Watson's famous Little Albert study. In her last year of undergraduate studies at Vassar College, Mary Cover attended a weekend lecture given by Watson in New York City, in which he described his work on the conditioning of fear in the infant known as Little Albert. In this study, conducted with Cover's friend and Vassar graduate Rosalie Rayner, Watson presented Albert with several white furry objects, including a white rat, paired with a loud noise. Although he was not initially afraid of any of the objects, including the rat, the loud noise did startle Albert. With enough pairings, he began to exhibit a fear response in the presence of the objects even when the loud noise was absent. Watson's description of this study cemented Cover's desire to pursue psychology as a career and convinced her that, if fear

(Continued)

could be established where none existed before, she might be able to reduce or eliminate an already-established fear.

Cover began her graduate work at Columbia University in fall 1919 and completed her master's degree by summer 1920. That same summer, she married fellow graduate student Harold Jones. In 1923, she was appointed associate in psychological research at the Institute of Educational Research, Teachers College, Columbia University. During this time, she conducted her study of Peter. Briefly, as part of her position as a research associate for the Institute of Educational Research, Mary and her family were living in Hecksher House, an organization that housed children who had been abandoned by, or temporarily separated from, their parents. Here she ran across an appropriate subject for her study, a boy who had developed a strong fear of white rabbits.

She decided to treat Peter's fear with various fear-reducing procedures to see which would be most effective. The most successful procedure, she discovered, was that of direct conditioning, in which a pleasant stimulus (food) was presented simultaneously with the rabbit on several successive occasions. At first the rabbit was placed far enough away from Peter that he was not nervous. As the rabbit was gradually brought closer to him in the presence of his favorite food, Peter grew more tolerant, and he was finally able to touch it without fear.

After publishing these results (1924), Mary completed her dissertation work, writing a thesis on the development of early behavior patterns in young children.

In summer 1927, the Jones family (they now had two young daughters) packed their bags and headed West. Harold had been offered a position at the recently established Institute for Child Welfare at the University of California, Berkeley, and was given an academic position in the Department of Psychology at the university. Mary took a position as research associate at the institute, since antinepotism rules prevented her from being offered a position in psychology. She soon became involved in the Oakland Growth Study, and her involvement would color the rest of her career. She would eventually publish more than 100 studies using data from the study.

In 1952, Mary and her husband produced the first educational television course in child psychology. In 1960, she served as president of the Division of Developmental Psychology of the APA, and in 1968 she received the organization's G. Stanley Hall Award. In a keynote address delivered at a 1974 conference, she offered this assessment of her career and her personal and theoretical outlook:

FIGURE 7.2 Mary Cover Jones
Courtesy of the Archives of the History of American Psychology, University of Akron, Akron, OH.

My last 45 years have been spent in longitudinal research in which I have watched the psychobiological development of our study members as they grew from children to adults now in their fifties.... My association with this study has broadened my conception of the human experience. Now I would be less satisfied to treat the fears of a 3-year-old, or of anyone else, without a later follow-up and in isolation from an appreciation of him as a tantalizingly complex person with unique potentials for stability and change. (Jones, 1975, p. 186)

Developmental research in psychology as a scientific endeavor dates from this era. Certain universities came to be known as the best places to go if one wanted to be trained as a developmental psychologist. The University of California, Berkeley, was one of those sites, as were the programs at University of Minnesota, led for many years by John Anderson (1893–1966), and the University of Iowa. The number of scientists engaged in developmental research did not approach the number engaged in behaviorist research; still, this became one of the streams that ran parallel to the mainstream of experimental psychology in these years and represents the diversity of psychology that only grew after World War II.

RACE, ETHNICITY, INTELLIGENCE, AND RESISTANCE

In the interwar period, resistance to the uses of intelligence tests to denigrate racial and ethnic minorities in the United States grew. The tradition of such uses grew out of a movement called **social Darwinism**. Briefly, theories of human evolution—those of both Charles Darwin (1809–1882) and Herbert Spencer (1820–1903)—were employed to explain differences among humans as grounded in the laws of nature, with some races having evolved further than other races (Darwin, 1859; Spencer, 1855; see Chapter 1). Alternatively, evolutionary theories were used to argue that some races had failed to evolve or even showed evidence of degeneration.

Social Darwinism, although not a coherent body of theory or practice, took many forms and generally was composed of arguments that "survival of the fittest" (Spencer's phrase) operated at the level of society, as well as in biological processes (Spencer, 1864, p. 444). In everyday terms, this was taken to mean that competition, among individuals or corporations or among nations, was the way the real world worked and that those who won were those who were best adapted to the conditions of the day. Thus, the status quo was the order of nature and reflected the operation of the laws of nature. Those who were wealthy or successful were so because they were the most fit. Their success and wealth was "natural."

When applied to those who were poor, disabled, ill, or occupied a lower rung of the social ladder, social Darwinism dictated that these individuals also owed their position to the natural order of things. Thus, it would be unnatural, or rather, against nature, to intervene, to offer better education or better health care, or to make laws ending discrimination. Manipulating the environment to reduce disparities or level the playing field would not, in the long run, work because these individuals were the way they were—naturally. If helped artificially, it was argued, such undesirables would dilute the vigor of the nation.

These ideas were also applied to racial groups. In Europe, race generally referred to what today we would call ethnicity, that is, Celts, Slavs, British, and so on. In the United States, especially after the Civil War, scientific racism and social Darwinism were most often employed to validate the superiority of Whites and the "natural" inferiority of African Americans, American

Indians, Mexicans, and increasingly, Asian immigrants. These "races" were, as indicated earlier, seen as inferior because of either failure to evolve or degeneration. It was at this historical juncture that the new Psychology entered the picture to offer a scientific view of the psychological qualities of different races.

Psychologists and Scientific Racism

We have already discussed the work of Yerkes and his colleagues in the massive army intelligence testing program (see Chapter 6). Here, we extend this discussion briefly to give a flavor of the mainstream attitude of experimental psychologists to racial hierarchy research in the first decade or so after the end of World War I. The interpretation of the data from the testing program reflected the racial attitudes and concerns in the United States at that time.

Yerkes and his colleagues interpreted the test results as indicating that certain "racial" groups were, indeed, less intelligent than others. Among enlisted men or draftees, those of northern European or Anglo-Saxon descent scored highest, with eastern and southern Europeans scoring lower. African Americans scored lower than those of European descent. Yerkes took his analysis even further, comparing scores among African Americans based on lightness or darkness of skin color. Those who were "yellow," that is, who had more "White" blood, scored highest, with those who were blacker scoring the lowest. Here is an excerpt from his report:

An interesting attempt was made at [Camp] Lee to further distinguish within the negro group on the basis of skin color. Two battalions were classified as lighter or darker on the basis of offhand inspection. Two other battalions were classified as black, brown, and yellow on the basis of skin color. The median score of the "black" negroes in *a* was 39, that of the "yellow" was 59; while that of the "brown" negroes fell between these values. (Yerkes, 1921, p. 531)

The interpretation of Yerkes and his colleagues reflected the beliefs and the concerns of the dominant majority group at that time, that is, Whites of northern European descent. Their interpretations fit with the eugenics movement (see Chapter 6). Eugenics ("good birth"), a word coined by Francis Galton, supposedly was a science of improving the human race through better breeding. In Great Britain, positive eugenics focused on encouraging the talented classes to have more children. In the United States, a negative eugenics emerged that focused more on lowering the number of children born to the poor, alcoholics, the "feebleminded," African Americans, and other undesirable groups. In Nazi Germany, a little later in the 20th century, the same principles were applied with disastrous effects to Jews, Gypsies, and the physically and mentally disabled.

Challenges to Psychometric Racism

The interpretation of the army testing results was not unique to psychologists, nor was it new in the field of psychology. By the time of World War I, the development of paper-and-pencil testing technology to assess intelligence (see Chapter 6) had already begun its long and continuing usage as a sorting methodology, most often employed to validate the superiority or inferiority of one group or another.

When the Binet-Simon test (1905) was brought to the United States by the eugenicist and Quaker psychologist Henry Herbart Goddard (1866–1957) in 1908, one of its first uses was to assess racial differences in intelligence. This inaugurated a period that has been called the era of psychometric racism by African American historian of psychology Robert V. Guthrie (1998). Several intelligence tests were developed: the Binet, the Stanford-Binet, the Yerkes-Bridges Point Scale, and so on. In the hands of primarily White psychologists, members of visible minorities, as well as eastern and southern Europeans, were "proven" to be intellectually inferior to Whites of northern European and Anglo-Saxon descent.

This situation began to change in the 1920s, first in a negative reaction to the excessive eugenicist claims of psychologists and other scientists who overemphasized the role of heredity in psychological abilities and moral character. A second reason was the development of convincing arguments that emphasized the role of environment and opportunities in shaping intellectual abilities. Some of this work was done by minority psychologists.

For example, George Sanchez (1906–1972), a psychologist of Mexican descent (Chicano), investigated the psychological testing of Mexican American children in the 1930s. He argued that his results showed that the use of intelligence tests standardized on White children were inappropriate for use with Chicano children who did not have the same language proficiency or cultural experiences as White middle-class children (Sanchez, 1932, 1934; Padilla, 2009).

In addition, a Rockefeller philanthropy connection to the work of African American psychologists arose in this era. The LSRM developed a program of grants and fellowships for which minority scholars were eligible. When the LSRM was ended, the Rockefeller General Education Board provided scholarships. In addition, the Rosenwald Fund specifically targeted improving African American education as one of its goals. Many African American psychologists received fellowships from one or more of these funds and used them to further their education, typically using them to complete their doctoral degrees at predominantly White institutions, as few opportunities existed for doctoral work at historically Black colleges and universities.

The question of intelligence and intelligence testing was one focus of the research conducted by several African American psychologists in the interwar period. The *Journal of Negro Education* published many articles on the subject of "Negro" intelligence, by both Black and White psychologists. In 1934, the journal devoted a special issue to "The Physical and Mental Abilities of the American Negro."

Howard Hale Long (1888–1948), an African American educational psychologist, published on various topics addressing problems in education. Long was the fifth African American male to earn a doctoral degree in psychology. He received his EdD from Harvard in 1933. He spent much of his career as associate superintendent of public schools in Washington, DC, where he saw the problems of inequality in educational resources firsthand. It was these inequalities, such as lower funding for "Negro" schools than for White schools, that led Long to argue that any differences in academic achievement were due not to inferior intellectual ability among Black schoolchildren but to lack of environmental resources (Long, 1935).

Numerous other minority psychologists were working at this time. Other African American psychologists in this period included Herman Canady, Herman Long (1912–1976), Albert Beckham, Oran Eagleson (1910–1997), Alberta Turner (1941–1988), and John Brodhead (1898–1951). Many of them published research on issues of race, intelligence, and achievement (see Guthrie, 1998).

Beckham (1897–1964) earned his master's degree at New York University (NYU) and then taught for several years at Howard University before returning to NYU to earn his doctorate. At Howard, he began a clinic for working with African American children. His dissertation topic was "A Study of the Intelligence of Colored Adolescents of Different Economic and Social Status in Typical Metropolitan Areas" (1929). He recruited 1,100 participants from New York City; Washington, DC; and Baltimore. The focus of the research was to analyze the intelligence test results in relation to socioeconomic status. The results indicated that environment played a critical role in determining test results. Beckham then spent much of his career with the Chicago Board of Education Bureau of Child Study. He married Ruth Howard (1900–1997), who was the first African American woman to earn a PhD in a psychology department, at the University of Minnesota in 1934 (see Chapter 11). The two of them established guidance counseling clinics at many Chicago schools that served large minority populations. They also established and were codirectors of the Chicago-based Center for Psychological Services. In Chicago, they were able to put their theories about nurturing the intellectual capacities of minority children into practice.

Canady (1901–1970) succeeded Francis Cecil Sumner (1895–1954), the first African American to earn a doctorate in psychology (at Clark University, 1920), at West Virginia State College in 1928. According to Guthrie (1998), Canady made West Virginia State into the most productive psychology department at a historically Black college or university of its time. It was Canady who first questioned the role that racial differences between the examiner and the examinee may play in obtaining accurate results on intelligence tests. He showed the importance of establishing rapport to gain the most accurate assessment of intelligence (Canady, 1936). This was particularly true for minority children. Canady also contributed research that highlighted the difficulty in obtaining the same testing environment for Black and White participants. This necessitated, Canady argued (1943), great care in making any comparisons among races on test results. By the time America entered World War II, then, psychologists of color were successfully challenging the results of scientific and psychometric racism.

SEXUALITY RESEARCH

In the early 1920s, the Rockefeller Foundation provided funds to the NRC to support a wide-ranging program of sexuality research. Many elites felt that the mores of society were being undermined by an overemphasis on sexuality in American popular society. Social problems, such as prostitution, White slavery, masturbation, and the spread of sexually transmitted diseases needed to be addressed. Medicine had been the traditional authority in sexual matters, but now it was argued that a scientific understanding of human sexuality was needed. To meet this perceived need, philanthropies such as the Rockefeller Foundation moved to provide resources to develop an organized effort to understand sexuality and ameliorate any negative social effects it might have. The result was the creation of an interdisciplinary and cooperative approach that involved scientists from many disciplines, including psychology. As we saw in the example of developmental psychology, this was part of the postwar effort to rationalize and reorder American life through science. One scholar has characterized this work as "human engineering" (Haraway, 1989).

The Committee for Research in Problems of Sex (CRPS) was formed in 1921 to direct this work through a review and funding of proposed research projects. Psychologist Earl Zinn had originally suggested the need for this approach, and another psychologist, Yerkes, whom you met in earlier chapters, became the powerful chairman of the CRPS.

The scope of the research supported by the CRPS between 1921 and the beginning of World War II was broad: hormonal, nutritional, climatic, psychological, and racial contributions to sexuality. Scientific fields included all the biomedical sciences, including psychology, as well as anthropology and other social sciences. Several areas within psychology were funded, but comparative psychology was especially well funded, perhaps because Yerkes was a comparative psychologist. He justified animal research as the best way to understand human sexual behavior.

One of the best-funded psychologists in the interwar period was comparative psychologist Calvin Stone (1892–1954). Stone was a diligent researcher who produced a steady stream of research publications and supported several talented graduate students in their research. His research investigated the role of instincts, maturation, and development in animal sexual behavior. He and his students addressed both the neural and the hormonal control of this behavior. Stone's comparative work not only was pursued for its intrinsic interest and value, but also was justified as having value for the understanding of human sexual behavior.

Yerkes and his students at Yale studied primate sexual behavior in a program that greatly expanded after Yerkes received a Rockefeller Foundation grant of $500,000 in 1929 to establish a primate research station in Florida. Yerkes and his students developed a program that was founded on the belief that comparative research was the best way to understand human sexual behavior and so offered the possibility of controlling sexuality.

Both Stone and Yerkes embraced the goals of addressing social problems through scientific research. This was, as we saw in the case of developmental psychology, the intent of the philanthropies that funded their work. Sexuality research was science in the service of social order.

PERSONALITY PSYCHOLOGY

"Personality" in the contemporary sense of the word is a 20th-century term. Much of what it came to refer to in Psychology had been covered by the term "character" in earlier times. One of the earliest usages of "personality" as a scientific term in the United States was by Frederic Lyman Wells (1884–1964), whom you met in Chapter 5. Wells was influenced in his use of the word by the theoretical and clinical work of Sigmund Freud. As historian of psychology Ian Nicholson (1998) has shown, in the 1920s and 1930s "personality" as a term came to signify something new: an American identity appropriate for a new era dominated by urban concerns.

It was Gordon Allport (1897–1967) who brought the term personality into regular use by academic psychologists. Allport was also instrumental in the development of social psychology

as an organized research field within American psychology, along with his older brother, Floyd Henry Allport (1890–1978). The Allports grew up in a devoutly religious Midwestern home, with some expectation that they might become missionaries. However, both Floyd and Gordon ended up earning their graduate degrees in psychology. Gordon completed his undergraduate degree at Harvard in 1919, the year Floyd earned his doctorate there. After teaching in Istanbul for a year, Gordon returned to graduate work in psychology at Harvard, where he studied personality traits for his doctoral dissertation. His literature reviews of research and writing on personality in the 1920s remain among the most important documents for understanding the field at the time he entered it.

The important personality theories in academic circulation at the time of Gordon Allport's entry into psychology included the type theories of Carl Jung (1875–1961), the body–personality typologies of German psychiatrist Ernst Kretschmer (1888–1964) and American William H. Sheldon (1898–1977), and of course, the approach of Freud. Allport brought personality, however, into the research domain of academic psychology and made it an important area of research and application. Methods for assessing personality became the domain of the academic psychologist.

Assessing Personality

The popularization of the results of the army intelligence tests created a craze for psychological tests of all kinds in the 1920s. Some tests were legitimate, and many were the work of charlatans. Personality in its new usage as an indicator of a new kind of American self was one of the most popular applications of the testing craze. Magazines in the 1920s carried many advertisements urging the reader to take the latest personality test. The term became so popular that it became nearly synonymous with the word "psychology" during this era. Academic psychologists were among those who developed these tests.

Woodworth, whom we mentioned in Chapter 6, developed what is probably the first personality test by an American psychologist. His Psychoneurotic Test (1917), later renamed the Woodworth Personal Data Sheet, was an early attempt to capture problems of personality. Many personality tests followed. Gordon Allport published his Test of Ascendance–Submission in 1928, and Robert G. Bernreuter's Personality Inventory (1933) incorporated some of Woodworth's Personal Data Sheet and was used for assessment of normal and neurotic personality functioning.

Most of these early personality tests were derived rationally. That is, the test developer began with logical categories that were intended to capture either normal psychological functioning or disordered psychological functioning as it was understood at the time. Attitudes, emotions, and psychopathology were all part of the mix. It is not surprising, then, that difficulties often arose in standardizing such instruments and that many came to view these devices skeptically.

In the 1930s, at the University of Minnesota, work began on another approach to assessing the disordered personality, or at least discriminating between normal and abnormal personality functioning. Psychologist Starke Hathaway (1903–1984), assisted by psychology student and later American psychology leader Paul Meehl (1920–2003) and neuropsychiatrist J. Charnley McKinley (1891–1950), gathered data from observations of mental patients in the psychiatric unit at the University of Minnesota Hospital to construct the Minnesota Multiphasic Personality Inventory (MMPI). The test was constructed as a series of true-or-false statements, such as, "I like to play drop the handkerchief." No single item indicated pathology or its absence; rather, it was a pattern of responding that held meaning. The items were grouped into scales, known only to the assessor, which indicated depression, psychosis, or even whether people were masculine or feminine in their responses. The MMPI proved

to be of professional value for both psychiatrists and psychologists. For the former, it was thought to remove the vagueness that was characteristic of psychodynamic tests, such as the Rorschach Projective Technique, and reduce the time demands on the psychiatrist. For the psychologist, it meant an expanded professional role as a part of a medical team, since the psychologists were expected to have expertise in assessment work. In the hierarchy of American medicine, this meant that the psychiatrist always held the superior position.

The Rorschach Projective Technique was developed by the psychoanalytically oriented psychiatrist Hermann Rorschach (1884–1922) shortly before his untimely death. Rorschach had been deeply influenced by the ideas of both Freud and Jung and developed the test as a way to elicit unconscious material by providing ambiguous stimuli on which the person would "project" responses that reflected underlying issues. The test was brought to the United States in the 1920s, and its usage by psychologists in medical and other clinical settings became widespread. By the late 1930s, as psychologists were establishing their usefulness as test specialists in such settings, their understanding and skill with the Rorschach often greatly enhanced their status with other medical personnel, especially since it appeared to offer psychologists some unique insight into the patient that was inaccessible to other professionals.

Henry Murray, the Harvard Psychological Clinic, and the TAT

The Thematic Apperception Test (TAT) was developed in the Harvard Psychological Clinic in the mid-1930s. It was a **projective test** produced as a result of efforts to find a psychometric approach to eliciting unconscious motivation. Christiana Morgan (1897–1967) developed the test from an idea generated by one of the graduate students, Cecilia Roberts, who was working with her. Roberts had taken time off to be with her ill son. Out of boredom, she asked him one day to tell her a story based on a picture in a magazine. He generated a rich fantasy and was able to continue doing so with new pictures. Morgan took this idea and, using both original art and copies of pictures and photographs from popular periodicals and literature, created the TAT. The clinic staff began using the test in the mid-1930s, and it formed an important part of their major book from this period, *Explorations in Personality*. The book was an indicator of the creative matrix of ideas and innovation that was happening at this time in the clinic, inspired and nurtured by Henry Murray (1893–1988).

Murray was born in New York City to an English father and an American mother. He earned his undergraduate degree at Harvard in 1915. As he reported in his autobiography, his undergraduate interests were rowing and social life. He walked out of the only course in psychology he ever took, after one class. After marriage in 1916, he earned his medical degree from the College of Physicians and Surgeons and later earned his PhD in biochemistry from Harvard.

During this period, Murray met Morgan, a woman who was to become his spiritual partner, collaborator in psychology, and paramour for the next 40 years. In 1925 he traveled to Switzerland and met with Jung, who encouraged him to pursue his interests with Morgan, and that summer they became lovers. In 1926 he returned to Harvard, where he was assistant director of the new Psychological Clinic. In 1928 he succeeded Morton Prince (1854–1929) as the director and soon developed the clinic into the major center for the study of personality in America. He gave Homburger (later Erikson) his first job (1933) and was B. F. Skinner's first psychology professor.

Murray attracted a remarkable group of students and colleagues over the next two decades; many of them went on to become leaders in the development of personality psychology. This group included Robert White (1904–2001), Donald McKinnon (1903–1987), Isabelle Kendig (b. 1889), Sam Beck (1896–1980), Nevitt Sanford

FIGURE 7.3   Henry Murray
Courtesy of Harvard University Archives, call # HUP Murray, Henry A. (3).

(1909–1996), Saul Rosenzweig (1907–2004), and Homburger (Erikson). Why did Murray have such success with his work at the clinic in these years? Those whom he had worked with later recalled that Murray provided a creative environment, that he was interested in great recurrent problems of human life, that he gave his students and colleagues great latitude to work on problems of interest to them, that he was generous with his time, and that he encouraged an interdisciplinary approach. Murray was also an outsider to academic psychology and often took an approach meant to shake up his academic colleagues. For example, he once remarked, "Academic psychology is a mountain of ritual bringing forth a mouse of a fact"(Murray, 1967, p. 305).

Murray built up the clinic as a center for Freudian and Jungian analysis. In doing so, he created numerous professional opportunities for women and, as noted, collaborated with Morgan in the development of the TAT. In 1938 he published the first volume of research from the clinic, *Explorations in Personality*. In the book, Murray and his team explored only a handful of cases with a series of remarkable assessments, using multiple measures from the TAT to Homburger's Dramatic Productions Test. Their in-depth analyses offered a rich and thick description of the strengths and problems of the people studied. The book remains a landmark in personality assessment. However, it is likely never to be repeated, partly because the sheer cost of bringing together so many people with such varied expertise would be prohibitive.

Murray was never interested in being part of the mainstream of American psychology or even of American life; he remained the outsider who nevertheless changed the direction of the main currents of psychological thought. One of Murray's mantras may be the best way to end this account. Murray was fond of saying, "Every man knows something about himself which he is willing to tell; he knows something about himself that he is not willing to tell; and there is something about himself that he doesn't know and can't tell" (as cited in Robinson, 1992, p. 176).

Personality, Personnel, and the Management of the Worker

A major concern of business, industrial, and political leaders during the interwar period was industrial unrest and worker dissatisfaction. After the successful Bolshevik revolution in Russia and its depiction of the worker as social hero, industrial leaders were fearful of the spread of Communist ideas in the United States. The struggle to establish effective unions in some of the country's largest industries had been marked by conflict, at times violent, but by the 1920s and 1930s such unions were in place in many industries. The Great Depression of the 1930s did lead to labor unrest, as millions of workers lost their jobs.

Psychologists had already established their science as a potential aid to social management (see Chapter 6). The growth of applied psychology in business and industry was further opportunity to demonstrate the usefulness of the field. The use of personality tests and the development of personnel management were examples of this utility. Industrial problems were almost always linked by management to the maladjustment of the individual worker. What psychology offered was a way to identify this maladjustment and to ameliorate the problem or remove the worker.

One method of doing so was through the use of personality tests. Most early personality tests were oriented toward identifying negative or neurotic characteristics. Specialized language was drawn from test results to describe the person (e.g., hysteroid and epileptoid). The focus on neurotic tendencies, of course, made it appear that the source of workplace problems lay within the worker, not in the structure of the work, much of which had become highly repetitive and was closely supervised in accordance with the scientific management principles of Frederick Winslow Taylor (1856–1915). Nevertheless, personality assessment of workers was widespread, with tests like the Bernreuter Personality Inventory and the Humm-Wadsworth Temperament Scale each administered to more than 2 million workers in the first few years after their development.

Personnel counseling and management was another facet of psychology's application in this era. While it had diverse roots, the most salient example is the research and application that derived from what was called the Hawthorne effect and the theorizing of psychologist Elton Mayo (1880–1949). Mayo was an Australian psychologist who came to the United States in 1923. For a few years, he was associated with the University of Pennsylvania and then in 1926 was invited to join the Harvard Business School faculty, where he remained until his retirement in 1947. His early research and consultation focused on reducing worker fatigue through the use of rest schedules, in the hope of reducing worker dissatisfaction.

In 1927, Mayo was asked by the personnel director of the Western Electric Company to review some recent research that had been conducted at the company's plant in Hawthorne, Illinois. It was this research that came to be labeled the **Hawthorne effect**. Briefly, research on improved lighting, as part of a series of studies on improving worker productivity, revealed that while improved lighting itself had little effect, the increased attention paid to the workers did result in higher worker morale and productivity, the so-called Hawthorne effect. Mayo's review of this research provided an entrée for him into consulting work with Western Electric, where he could test his theories of interviewing, counseling, and worker adjustment. The next phase of the research was an examination of the impact of a series of workplace improvements (rest periods, shorter hours, etc.) on six women workers in the relay assembly test room. Interviews with the women revealed that it was the increased attention they received, not the workplace improvements alone, that led to increased satisfaction and productivity. The interview program was extended to workplace supervisors, which provided such favorable results that Western Electric decided to expand it to the entire plant. Under Mayo's direction, the interviews were modified to move away from a survey of attitudes to an in-depth exploration of personality and psychological awareness. His method of interviewing was based on the approach used by Piaget to conduct his child interviews. Mayo did not believe that the workers' complaints about wages or working conditions reflected real problems; rather, the problem was internal maladjustment within the workers. Mayo believed that the benefit of the interviewing lay in the reduction of worker dissatisfaction through workers' verbalization of discontent.

The expanded interview program was led by Mayo's student Fritz Roethlisberger (1898–1974). Over the next few years, it was recalibrated several times due to financial pressure but was considered a success nonetheless. Mayo argued that it improved productivity by 30 to 40 percent. By the late 1930s, the Western Electric program was being emulated in several other industries and corporations. It gave rise to a new profession, the personnel consultant. Psychologists became the leaders of this new profession, often serving as the supervisors of the workplace counselors. Out of this trend grew the modern field of human relations.

THE DISCIPLINARY EMERGENCE OF SOCIAL PSYCHOLOGY IN AMERICA

The history of social psychology is ... more a history of the contingent boundaries between disciplines and the

contingent divisions of intellectual labour than of the construction of a specialty in its own right.

—Roger Smith, *Norton History of the Human Sciences,* 1997

Questions concerning the appropriate subject matter of social psychology, who should study it, and with what methods have been as contentious as any in the history of psychology. Questions about whether social psychology should take the individual in social context, or social life itself, as its unit of analysis; the nature of the relationship between the individual and the social; and whether social psychology belongs more properly to the domain of the sociologist, the psychologist, or for that matter, the historian, political scientist, or economist, reflect only a few of these complexities. As a result of this state of affairs, and the desire to establish some boundaries (contingent though they were, and remain), social psychology as a subdiscipline of scientific psychology in the United States began to take on a distinctly recognizable form in the first decades of the 20th century to set itself apart from sociology, which was also engaging in boundary work at this time. That is not to say that the history of social psychology has thus sidestepped these thorny matters or that everyone is in agreement. Indeed, these questions continue to preoccupy the field. In this section, however, we limit ourselves to tracking a few important developments that defined social psychology as a subdiscipline of Psychology during the interwar years in the United States.

One of the ways in which psychologists in the 1920s attempted to differentiate themselves from other scholars studying social life was to define social psychology in terms of the study of the behavior of the individual—who was presumed to have an *a priori* nonsocial dimension of existence (perception, emotion, memory)—when this individual was placed in social or interpersonal situations such as friendships, groups of various kinds, and organizations. Floyd Allport is often cited as the major figure in the crystallization of this distinction. Although he was by no means the first American psychologist to write on matters "social psychological"—Baldwin, William James (1842–1910), John Dewey (1859–1952), George Herbert Mead (1863–1931), and others had all contributed before this—it was his insistence on the primacy of the study of the *individual* in social psychology that stands as his legacy. He referred to the idea that social behavior was not reducible to the sum of its individual parts as the **group fallacy**. In 1924, Allport published a textbook on social psychology in which he laid out his view of the proper boundaries for the field, stating that social psychology should be "the science which studies the behavior of the individual in so far as his behavior stimulates other individuals, or is itself a reaction to their behavior" (p. 12). Despite this distinction, interdisciplinary collaborations between psychologists and sociologists continued.

Social psychology grew in size and scope during the 1920s and 1930s and had close relationships with other subdisciplines of psychology, such as industrial, personnel, and developmental psychology. In 1921, the *Journal of Abnormal Psychology* became the *Journal of Abnormal Psychology and Social Psychology*, with Prince (the physician who founded the Harvard Psychological Clinic in 1927) and Allport as coeditors. The new social psychology, with its emphasis on the individual, adopted much of the behavioristic ethos that characterized American psychology as a whole during this period, as well as reflecting the adjustment ethos of the concurrent mental hygiene movement. One of the major topics of study was attitudes, which replaced instincts as a primary explanatory construct. Social psychologists devised methods for measuring attitudes, assessed attitudes toward political concerns, and recorded how attitudes changed in the presence of other people. This was also the period in which public opinion polling began as a major scientific enterprise. George Gallup (1901–1984) founded the American Institute of Public Opinion in 1935. As historian Sarah Igo has convincingly shown (2007), although psychologists did not contribute to the founding of this field, scientific survey

methods became an important part of social psychology's arsenal during and after World War II.

In the 1930s, two major books appeared to chronicle developments in the new experimental social psychology, Gardner (1895–1979) and Lois (1902–2003) Murphy's *Experimental Social Psychology* in 1931 and Carl Murchison's *Handbook of Social Psychology* in 1935. In the former, the authors focused a large part of their text on the social aspects of child development, an approach that gained momentum throughout the next decade. In the latter, Murchison provided a comparative perspective, soliciting chapters on social behavior in different species, and in different "races of mankind." John Dashiell (1888–1975), Allport's colleague at the University of North Carolina, wrote a chapter titled "Experimental Studies of the Influence of Social Situations on the Behavior of Individual Human Adults," which summed up nicely the approach that Allport had espoused for the new field. Gordon Allport, Floyd Allport's younger brother, wrote the chapter on attitudes. Like his older brother, Gordon fully endorsed social psychology's emphasis on the individual. Unlike Floyd, who was essentially a behaviorist, Gordon's theoretical stance on the nature of the individual was more holistic. Gordon became well known as a personality theorist, as we mentioned earlier, publishing *Personality: A Psychological Interpretation* in 1937, although his interests were often at the intersections of social and personality psychology.

The field of attitude research was a good exemplar of how social psychology was solidifying its scientific credentials. As historians of psychology Jill Morawski and Betty Bayer have noted, "It is through controlled, quantitative attitude studies that social psychologists significantly refined their experimental techniques of control and numeric exactitude" (2003, p. 230). Louis Leon Thurstone (1887–1955), who had worked in the Committee on the Classification of Personnel led by Walter Dill Scott (1869–1955) in World War I, devised a method for scaling attitudes, which he published in 1928. This was replaced a few years later by a method devised by Rensis Likert (1903–1981). You may recognize the widely used Likert scale format. It should be noted that, although social psychologists were certainly using experimental techniques in this period, several historians have pointed out that experimentation did not become normative in social psychology until the post–World War II period (Cherry & Borshuk, 1998). That is, although social psychology was *becoming* experimental, experimentation was not necessarily the *paradigmatic* method at this time.

Another prominent topic of interest in the 1930s was research on aggression, especially investigations of the frustration–aggression hypothesis by the interdisciplinary group at Yale's Institute of Human Relations, founded in 1929 by a grant from the Rockefeller Foundation to facilitate interdisciplinary teaching and research among all disciplines concerned with the study of mankind (see the previous section on Hull). In 1939, a group of psychologists led by John Dollard (1900–1980), who was actually trained as a sociologist, published *Frustration and Aggression*, which drew on psychology (e.g., behavioristic learning theory) and psychoanalysis to theorize the relationship between frustration and aggression, stating that aggression can always be traced to some form of frustration and frustration leads to several responses, including aggression (Dollard, Miller, Doob, Mowrer, & Sears, 1939). The social relevance of this work was fairly clear. Growing anti-Semitism in Germany, the Spanish Civil War, the Great Depression, and racism in the American Deep South (and elsewhere) were examples of the hypothesis at work.

The 1930s also saw the arrival in America of several important German émigré psychologists in the Gestalt tradition, namely, Max Wertheimer (1880–1943), Wolfgang Köhler (1887–1967), and Koffka. The most important for social psychology was Kurt Lewin (1890–1947). In the next chapter, we discuss his career in Germany before his arrival in the United States.

FIGURE 7.4   Kurt Lewin
Courtesy of the Archives of the History of American Psychology, University of Akron, Akron, OH.

Arriving at Cornell in 1933, where he spent two years before moving to the Iowa Child Welfare Research Station, Lewin was responsible for reintroducing the importance of the group in American social psychology. Through his development of **field theory**, he stipulated that, although the effects of specific stimuli on individual behavior could still be recorded, they had little meaning unless they were considered in the context of the total situation, or "field," of which they were a part. While at Cornell, where a position was created for him in the Department of Home Economics, he was joined by his former student from Berlin, Tamara Dembo (1902–1993), and an American, Jerome Frank (1909–2005), who had studied with him in Berlin after starting his graduate work at Harvard. They worked in the nursery school on the problem of how to train teachers to influence the eating behavior of children. His friends and colleagues, the psychologists Fritz and Grace

FIGURE 7.5 Meeting of the Topological Group at Smith College in 1940. Kurt Lewin is seated with his legs crossed in the front row on the right. Tamara Dembo is in the very top row, fourth from the right.
Courtesy of the Society for the Psychological Study of Social Issues.

Heider, worked with Lewin to translate his book, *Principles of Topological Psychology*, which was published in English in 1936. A few years earlier, in 1933, a group of Lewin's students and colleagues first met, on an informal basis, to discuss theory and exchange ideas. The group continued to meet fairly regularly until well after Lewin's death. They became known as the Topology Group and included, at various times, some of the most well-known psychologists in the history of the discipline.

In 1935, upon the expiration of his 2-year contract at Cornell, Lewin moved to the Iowa Child Welfare Research Station, where he was able to secure research positions for Dembo and Roger Barker (1903–1990). Together they conducted studies on frustration and regression in children. While at Iowa, Lewin developed several

experiments on group behavior that brought him significant attention. One of these was a study published with Ronald Lippitt (1914–1986) and Ralph White (1907–2007) and titled "Patterns of Aggressive Behavior in Experimentally Created Social Climates," in which the researchers artificially created groups in the laboratory under different styles of leadership (authoritarian, democratic, and laissez-faire) to see how behavior and performance were affected. He was also interested in the differences between German and American culture. In 1944, Lewin moved from Iowa to the Massachusetts Institute of Technology to set up the Research Center for Group Dynamics. When he died prematurely at age 56 in 1947, the research center moved to the University of Michigan and later became part of the influential Institute for Social Research there.

FIGURE 7.6 David Krech
Courtesy of the American Psychological Association Archives.

In 1936, a group of concerned psychologists decided that, in fact, their discipline was not taking an active enough stance toward several important social issues. One issue of immediate concern was the rising unemployment of psychologists, as we mentioned earlier. Some felt that their national organization, the APA, was not doing enough to deal with the problem of placing new PhDs and felt they could pressure the national organization on this issue. More broadly, however, a feeling arose that a professional group should be formed that would promote the conduct of research on social issues and the use of scientific psychological knowledge in understanding matters of social relevance. The organization was championed by David Krech (previously Isadore Krechevsky, 1909–1977), who sent a circular to members of the APA to assess support for the new group. In September 1936, at Dartmouth College, the SPSSI was officially born. Krech had received more than 200 expressions of interest and collected $63 in advance dues and donations (no small feat during the Depression years).

Goodwin Watson (1899–1976) was elected SPSSI's first president. The organization quickly set up a publishing program, producing yearbooks dealing with industrial conflict, civilian morale, and human nature and peace, all during World War II. SPSSI was also actively engaged in academic freedom cases, providing funds for legal proceedings and writing letters of support, often on behalf of professors who would not sign the Loyalty Oath of the McCarthy era.

Although Lewin's research was rigorous, experimental, and even at times mathematical, he was always concerned with the real-life implications and uses of research, as well as the need for research to arise out of life problems. During World War II, he developed an approach known as **action research**, the purpose of which was to work with participants in the research to generate data and use the results for social change. As a result of this attitude, he attracted a bevy of students who were interested in applying science to social problems.

SUMMARY

It was in the period between the two world wars that American psychology began to grow into a full-fledged science. Just as importantly, psychologists began to make many applications to social problems during this period, thus gaining stature, or at least prominence, in the public eye

as well. We hope we have conveyed the richness and diversity that came to characterize psychological research and practice in this period, as well as some practical concerns and controversies with which psychologists were faced. We have shown how neobehaviorism became the center of

American psychology. Even so, other emergent areas of psychological research developed in the peripheries of the field, including personality, developmental, and social psychology. The growth of Psychology as a science and, increasingly, as a professional practice was predicated on the increasing psychologization of American life. As we pointed out, in the period between the two world wars, the American public became fascinated with psychology but did not readily discriminate between its everyday and disciplinary expressions. These events laid the foundation for the rapid growth of Psychology in the United States after World War II.

BIBLIOGRAPHIC ESSAY

A rich literature focuses on the history of psychology in the interwar period. In this chapter we mention relatively few sources, but the careful reader can then use these sources to further explore any of our topics.

The great statesman of 20th-century American psychology, E. R. (Jack) Hilgard, wrote perhaps the finest descriptive history of American psychology, *Psychology in America: A Historical Survey*. We consulted it frequently as a resource, especially because Hilgard personally knew many of the protagonists in our story.

The reciprocal and nonlinear relationship between the discipline of Psychology and the everyday psychological sensibility is one of the most interesting and relatively underexplored topics in the history of psychology. We drew upon our own work (e.g., Pickren, 2000), as well as the work of Richard Brown (1992), John Burnham (1987, 1988), Ludy Benjamin Jr. (1986, 1997), and Paul Dennis (2002).

The organization and expansion of American psychology in the interwar period has been well documented. Psychologists of the era noted the proliferation of areas of expertise, as can be found in the two articles by Frank Finch and Maurice Odoroff (1939, 1941). Ingrid Farreras (2005) provides an excellent historical background to the issues relevant to the development of clinical psychology in the period. Donald Napoli, in his *Architects of Adjustment* (1981), a book that is lamentably out of print, offers both excellent description and thoughtful, clear-eyed analysis of this growth. Michael Sokal offers a rich account of many aspects of psychology's development in the 1920s in his aptly titled chapter, "James McKeen Cattell and American Psychology in the 1920s" (1984).

A large scholarly literature focuses on the role of philanthropic foundations and their support for the sciences in our period. Robert Kohler's *Partners in Science* (1991) offers a broad perspective and points to many other useful sources. For the social sciences, including psychology, Martin and Joan Bulmer's work (1981) was useful. For a different interpretation of the same material, see Donald Fisher, *Fundamental Development of the Social Sciences* (1993). Foundations were important in fostering research on children and their psychological development. Dennis Bryson's *Socializing the Young* (2002) was extremely helpful as a resource for understanding philanthropy and developmental psychology, as was Hans Pols chapter in *The Development of the Social Sciences in the United States and Canada* (1999). Elizabeth Lomax's account (1977) remains a critical resource for understanding the role of one foundation, the LSRM, in funding child development research. Alice Smuts (2006) offers a thoroughly researched account of the development of developmental science.

Standard histories of psychology have placed neobehaviorism at the center of the history of American psychology. Thus, a substantial literature surrounds this topic. For its background, we drew on the work of Kurt Danziger (1979, 1999), John O'Donnell (1985), Martin Kusch (1995, 1999), Ruth Leys and Rand Evans (1990),

Brian Mackenzie (1972), and Franz Samelson (1981). Ernest R. Hilgard (1987) offered clear descriptions of the scientific contributions of Hull and Tolman, as well as fascinating reminisces about his interactions with them. Cheryl Logan's award-winning article (1999) skillfully delineated the emergence of the white rat as the experimental animal of choice for American behavioral research. Jill Morawski's article (1986) astutely contextualizes the work of Hull and other neobehaviorists at Yale's Institute of Human Relations.

The topic of race and psychology in this era holds some of the best-known historical research alongside some of the least-known research from the era. Robert Yerkes's account of the World War I testing effort for the National Academy of Sciences (1921) is an indispensable firsthand document of psychological testing. In it you can find the implicit and explicit attitudes toward race and intelligence (also see Brigham, 1923). This has been well documented by historians. Carl Degler's 1991 study of social Darwinism helped clarify its history. We also found Graham Richards's *Race, Racism, and Psychology* (1997) to be helpful. Otto Klineberg's 1935 volume on race helped give the field a different direction. What most historians have overlooked, however, was the response to the race and intelligence issue from those who most often suffered from the racist misuse of intelligence tests, African American and other ethnic minority psychologists of the time. The notable exception is the account offered by Robert Guthrie in *Even the Rat Was White* (1998). Readers can find a small sample of relevant scholarship by African American and Latino scholars in the References section (e.g., Canaday, 1936, 1943; Sanchez, 1932, 1934). The journal *Cultural Diversity and Ethnic Minority Psychology* published a special issue devoted to the history of ethnic minority psychology in the United States in fall 2009.

Comparative approaches to sexuality research hold a fascinating literature. We consulted Don Dewsbury's excellent work on Yerkes. Dewsbury has published many articles on the subject; we found his recent book *Monkey Farm* (2005)

useful, as it is a thorough guide to much of the literature. The contributions of Stone have been documented as well (Pickren, 2006). The best guide to the history of comparative sex research, however, remains that of Sophie Aberle and George Corner (1953).

Several excellent accounts describe the development of the history of personality psychology as a field within scientific psychology. We found the work of Ian Nicholson on Gordon Allport especially helpful (1998, 2003). Erik (Homburger) Erikson shows up in several sections of this chapter. Larry Friedman's fascinating biography of him (1999) makes him even more interesting than we indicate. The uses of personality tests in industry comprise a fascinating and controversial topic. The standard work is Richard Gillespie (1991), but you may also wish to consult the recent work of Robert Gibby and Michael Zickar (2008), Stephen Highhouse (1999), Yeh Hsueh (2002), or Kevin Mahoney and David Baker (2002). Rod Buchanan's 1994 article on the development of the MMPI remains authoritative, although the topic needs more scholarship before we fully understand its importance.

Social psychology, much like personality psychology, emerged as a specialty field within American psychology in the interwar period. Indeed, many of the same figures were involved in both fields (Nicholson, 2003). Histories of its development are not as rich as we might wish, but the work of Robert Farr (1996) is helpful. Particular studies that were helpful to us included Alfred Marrow's biography of Lewin, *The Practical Theorist* (1969); Jill Morawski's and Betty Bayer's brief history (2003); and Sarah Igo's excellent history of the development of the opinion survey (2007). Larry Finison's work (1976, 1978, 1979) on the Psychologists' League and the founding of SPSSI was also invaluable. Finally, Kurt Danziger's article "Making Social Psychology Experimental" (2000) and many others in a special issue of the *Journal of the History of the Behavioral Sciences*, edited by Ian Lubek (2000), informed our account of the history of social psychology.

Chapter 8
TIMELINE 1740–1950
(In 25-year increments)

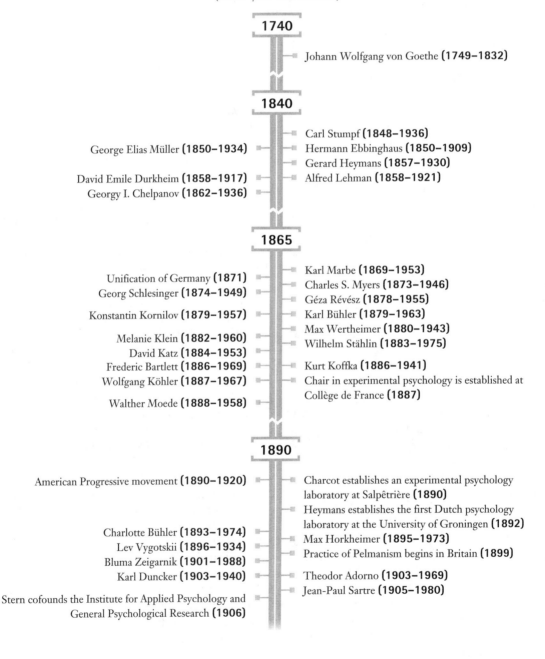

1740

Johann Wolfgang von Goethe **(1749–1832)**

1840

Carl Stumpf **(1848–1936)**

George Elias Müller **(1850–1934)**
Hermann Ebbinghaus **(1850–1909)**
Gerard Heymans **(1857–1930)**

David Emile Durkheim **(1858–1917)**
Alfred Lehman **(1858–1921)**
Georgy I. Chelpanov **(1862–1936)**

1865

Unification of Germany **(1871)**
Karl Marbe **(1869–1953)**
Georg Schlesinger **(1874–1949)**
Charles S. Myers **(1873–1946)**
Géza Révész **(1878–1955)**
Konstantin Kornilov **(1879–1957)**
Karl Bühler **(1879–1963)**
Max Wertheimer **(1880–1943)**
Melanie Klein **(1882–1960)**
Wilhelm Stählin **(1883–1975)**
David Katz **(1884–1953)**
Frederic Bartlett **(1886–1969)**
Kurt Koffka **(1886–1941)**
Wolfgang Köhler **(1887–1967)**
Chair in experimental psychology is established at
Collège de France **(1887)**
Walther Moede **(1888–1958)**

1890

American Progressive movement **(1890–1920)**
Charcot establishes an experimental psychology
laboratory at Salpêtrière **(1890)**
Heymans establishes the first Dutch psychology
laboratory at the University of Groningen **(1892)**
Charlotte Bühler **(1893–1974)**
Max Horkheimer **(1895–1973)**
Lev Vygotskii **(1896–1934)**
Practice of Pelmanism begins in Britain **(1899)**
Bluma Zeigarnik **(1901–1988)**
Karl Duncker **(1903–1940)**
Theodor Adorno **(1903–1969)**
Jean-Paul Sartre **(1905–1980)**
Stern cofounds the Institute for Applied Psychology and
General Psychological Research **(1906)**

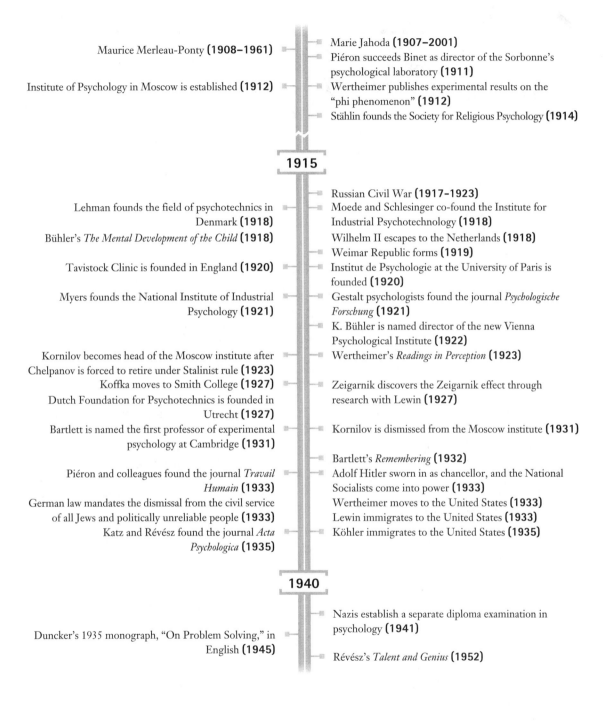

Maurice Merleau-Ponty **(1908–1961)**

Marie Jahoda **(1907–2001)**
Piéron succeeds Binet as director of the Sorbonne's psychological laboratory **(1911)**

Institute of Psychology in Moscow is established **(1912)**

Wertheimer publishes experimental results on the "phi phenomenon" **(1912)**
Stählin founds the Society for Religious Psychology **(1914)**

1915

Russian Civil War **(1917–1923)**

Lehman founds the field of psychotechnics in Denmark **(1918)**
Bühler's *The Mental Development of the Child* **(1918)**

Moede and Schlesinger co-found the Institute for Industrial Psychotechnology **(1918)**
Wilhelm II escapes to the Netherlands **(1918)**
Weimar Republic forms **(1919)**

Tavistock Clinic is founded in England **(1920)**

Institut de Psychologie at the University of Paris is founded **(1920)**

Myers founds the National Institute of Industrial Psychology **(1921)**

Gestalt psychologists found the journal *Psychologische Forschung* **(1921)**
K. Bühler is named director of the new Vienna Psychological Institute **(1922)**

Kornilov becomes head of the Moscow institute after Chelpanov is forced to retire under Stalinist rule **(1923)**
Koffka moves to Smith College **(1927)**
Dutch Foundation for Psychotechnics is founded in Utrecht **(1927)**
Bartlett is named the first professor of experimental psychology at Cambridge **(1931)**

Wertheimer's *Readings in Perception* **(1923)**

Zeigarnik discovers the Zeigarnik effect through research with Lewin **(1927)**

Kornilov is dismissed from the Moscow institute **(1931)**

Piéron and colleagues found the journal *Travail Humain* **(1933)**
German law mandates the dismissal from the civil service of all Jews and politically unreliable people **(1933)**
Katz and Révész found the journal *Acta Psychologica* **(1935)**

Bartlett's *Remembering* **(1932)**
Adolf Hitler sworn in as chancellor, and the National Socialists come into power **(1933)**
Wertheimer moves to the United States **(1933)**
Lewin immigrates to the United States **(1933)**
Köhler immigrates to the United States **(1935)**

1940

Nazis establish a separate diploma examination in psychology **(1941)**

Duncker's 1935 monograph, "On Problem Solving," in English **(1945)**

Révész's *Talent and Genius* **(1952)**

HOLOGY IN EUROPE BETWEEN THE WORLD WARS

> Psychologists, like other scientists, are creatures of their political and cultural times and places.
> —Mitchell Ash and William Woodward, *Psychology in Twentieth-Century Thought and Society*, 1987

INTRODUCTION

In Chapter 4, we examined the indigenization of disciplinary Psychology in the national context and culture of the United States. We continued our discussion of those developments in Chapter 7. Here, we return to the European context to examine psychology in Germany and other European countries, with our primary focus on developments in the period between the two world wars. Multiple centers of scientific practice and application developed across Europe in this period, each with its own rich history. Although many of these centers are worthy of extensive discussion, we have chosen to start this chapter with the development of Gestalt psychology as our primary example. Gestalt psychology has a complex history, with nuances that are beyond the scope of a textbook, but in our efforts we hope to demonstrate how important it is to understand the cultural context of a science when reconstructing its history and intellectual legacy.

Beyond the story of Gestalt psychology, we give a brief overview of some developments in psychology in various European countries between the world wars. Although similarities appeared among countries in how Psychology developed as a science and set of professional practices, many differences occurred as well. As for differences, philosophy and philosophical concerns continued to inform much of European psychology in this period, more so than in either America or Britain. In terms of similar trends, in most European countries during this period, some form of the application of Psychology to work, law, and education became a major preoccupation of psychologists. The term used for this was **Psychotechnik** (psychotechnics). We introduced this term in Chapter 6 with a discussion about its use before World War I. In this chapter, we give examples of psychotechnics in Germany, France, the Netherlands, and Russia. Britain, similarly, had many such applications of

psychology in the 1920s and 1930s, although the British did not use the word "psychotechnics" to describe what they did.

As you read, please keep in mind that each country has its own history and traditions that shaped the kind of psychology that developed, just as we saw in Chapter 4 on the indigenization of Psychology in the United States. One way to analyze these traditions is to examine the formation of national organizations of psychologists. As we noted in an earlier chapter, the first national psychological organization was the American Psychological Association, established in 1892. The development of national organizations outside the United States occurred first in Europe (see Table 8.1). Many of these organizations underwent changes in name, mission, or scope of inclusion, often due to war or political upheaval. For many of the earliest national organizations, their mission was to promote scientific research. However, over the course of the 20th

Table 8.1 Establishment of National Psychological Organizations

Country	Year Psychological Organization Founded
Britain	1901
France	1901
Germany	1904
Italy	1910
Hungary	1928
Netherlands	1938
Georgia	1941
Switzerland	1943
Denmark	1947
Poland	1948
Finland	1952
Spain	1952
Austria	1953
Iceland	1954
Sweden	1955
Turkey	1956
Russia	1957
Czechoslovakia	1958
Greece	1963
Portugal	1965
Romania	1965
Ireland	1970

century, several organizations came to place greater emphasis on the practice of psychology.

At the risk of making our account too simplistic, we can broadly state that the development of psychology in the countries of continental Europe (e.g., Germany, France, and the Netherlands) remained closely tied to philosophy for much of the period before World War II. That is, the research programs of experimental psychologists were often linked to questions raised by philosophical concerns over how knowledge is gained (epistemology) or even the status of truth claims (ontology). However, it is also clear that beginning in the early 20th century and well into the 1920s, emphasis on practical applications of psychology was growing. British psychology in the interwar period had a practical, applied focus, although philosophical issues were also present.

PSYCHOLOGY, NATURAL SCIENCE, AND PHILOSOPHY IN GERMANY AND AUSTRIA

We begin this section using German psychology between the world wars as our example. We have chosen to highlight the work of Gestalt psychologists but hasten to point out that German psychology was represented by many schools of thought and increasing emphasis on the application of Psychology, which we discuss in a separate section. After discussing the Gestalt psychologists, we give a brief account of the work of Karl and Charlotte Bühler and their colleagues at the Vienna Psychological Institute and then turn to the fate of Psychology under the Nazis in the period between 1933 and 1941. Finally, in this section, we offer a brief account of the psychology of religion in Germany and its links to similar studies elsewhere in Europe and the United States.

Gestalt Psychology in Germany

As we noted in Chapter 3, Wilhelm Wundt (1832–1920) was not the only psychologist to establish a laboratory and train graduate students in Germany. George Elias Müller (1850–1934), Hermann Ebbinghaus (1850–1909), and others were important pioneers in the development of Psychology as a discipline. German experimental psychology largely remained focused on the normal adult mind, employing a limited variety of methods and techniques, from experimental introspection to memory for nonsense syllables.

German experimental psychology remained a subspecialty of philosophy well into the 20th century, only gaining its professional independence under the Nazis. As a subspecialty of philosophy, the overall cultural function of psychology, like other fields within the artistic–philosophy faculties (see Chapter 3) was training the sons and daughters of elites in German *Kultur*. While the field certainly experienced growth in the number of professorial chairs and the associated assistants and "dozents" who were trained in the specialty, Psychology in Germany and Austria (to include the two main German-speaking societies) experienced steady growth rather than the explosive growth that occurred in the United States over a similar period. By 1914, there were 14 psychological laboratories in Germany, most often located within the philosophy faculty. Still, enough growth occurred that two thirds of the entire philosophy faculty in German-speaking universities signed a joint protest to the German government in 1912, insisting that no more psychologists be appointed to chairs of philosophy.

Beginning around 1910, a group of young psychologists, led by Max Wertheimer, created a major alternative to the Wundtian tradition. They called their approach "Gestalt theory," although it is more often referred to as **Gestalt psychology**. Their insistence on studying the relationship between the part and the whole in terms of perception and cognition led them away from the analysis of the constituents, or individual elements, of mental structures and psychic processes.

Broadly viewed, Gestalt theory or psychology was part of a resistance movement within German science and society to the mechanistic science of Hermann von Helmholtz (1821–1894) and his colleagues (see Chapter 1). The term "Gestalt" has no exact equivalent in English but roughly corresponds to "form" or "configuration." Wertheimer and his colleagues did not invent the term; rather, they extended its use in new directions. The great German philosopher, dramatist, and scientist Johann Wolfgang von Goethe (1749–1832) had imbued the term "Gestalt" with notions of wholeness that fit within German beliefs in the unity of the people, the community, and the nation. By the last part of the 19th century, Goethean uses of *Gestalt* or *Gestalten* had become part of a growing resistance to the mechanistic view of a universe atomized into its physical and chemical constituents. This reductionism was the view propounded by the German scientists we discussed in Chapter 1,

such as Helmholtz, Emil du Bois-Reymond (1818–1896), and their colleagues in German physiology and medicine. Their critical insights into the working of the physical universe, predicated upon their willingness to accept only physicalist explanations of cause and effect, not only had led to key scientific insights but also had contributed to the rapid industrialization of Germany and had helped make it a world leader by the end of the 19th century. The success of their mechanistic scientific worldview and the rapid industrialization of Germany evoked contradictory responses from many Germans. On the one hand, science and industrialization were evidence of German leadership in the rise of modernity; after unification in 1871, they helped make Germany a respectable modern nation-state. On the other hand, by the last third of the 19th century, the same developments left many Germans with a sense of human life as no more than mechanical and devoid of the richness of meaning that was part of the German philosophical heritage.

Many thoughtful Germans resisted or even rejected the underlying worldview as antithetical to the German soul and German *Kultur*. Gestalt became a path to renewal of German social and intellectual life, with contributions from many areas of the arts and sciences. The sciences of life and the mind became central to arguments for this renewal. Philosophers like Alexius Meinong (1853–1920) at the University of Graz and Christian von Ehrenfels (1859–1932) at the University of Prague introduced ideas about Gestalt qualities into their work. Meinong attracted students, including Vittorio Benussi from Italy, and their theorizing and experimental work became known as the Graz School. The Austrian philosopher Ehrenfels embraced this vision of Gestalt as a unifying principle of order in a struggle against chaos and the decline of German *Kultur*. In 1890, Ehrenfels argued in his paper "On Gestalt Qualities" that human perception is relational and not primarily built out of association of individual elements. That is, we perceive in terms of wholes (Gestalt). The standard example is music perception, where the perceived melody is not in the individual notes but in the whole relationship of those notes to one another. Ehrenfels later extended his idea of Gestalt to address larger questions of social order, aesthetic appreciation, and human purpose. While a professor at the University of Prague between 1896 and 1929, Ehrenfels had as a student a young local man whose passion was music. This student, Wertheimer, became the founder and leader of Gestalt theory in Psychology.

Wertheimer (1880–1943) was originally a law student at Prague but, drawn by his love of music and his acceptance of Ehrenfels's ideas about Gestalt and perception, switched to become a student in the philosophy faculty in 1900. After earning his degree, Wertheimer and a friend began work on psychological aspects of lie detection and testimony, work that Wertheimer took up again for his doctoral dissertation at the University of Würzburg. Before enrolling for his doctoral work, however, Wertheimer spent time in Berlin where, among other things, he worked in the laboratory of prominent psychologist Carl Stumpf (1848–1936). In Stumpf's laboratory, Wertheimer was supervised by the physicist-turned-psychologist, Friedrich Schumann (1863–1940), on studies of visual perception. Schumann was engaged at the time in experimental demonstrations of the inadequacy of reductionist theories of space perception. Wertheimer later incorporated many of these findings into his formulation of Gestalt theory. He then went on to earn his doctorate at the University of Würzburg, where his mentors were Oswald Külpe (1862–1915) and Karl Marbe (1869–1953). From 1905 to 1912, Wertheimer worked in several places, including a long stint with Stumpf in Berlin.

Wertheimer and his colleagues, Kurt Koffka (1886–1941) and Wolfgang Köhler (1887–1967), began to develop Gestalt theory in Psychology in an era in which wholeness in personal and national life became an important part of the fabric of German experience. The Gestaltists sought to develop an approach that would articulate the psychological richness of life. In research that at times owed more to an aesthetic sense of wholeness than to a technological imperative of deterministic cause and effect, Wertheimer, his peers, and their students brought their relational research to studies of perception (e.g., figure–ground relationships), language, symbolic thought, and insight in ways that yielded new understandings. As historian Mitchell Ash has argued, it is important to note that they saw their psychological theorizing and experimenting as a specialization that fit within the traditional boundaries of philosophy (Ash, 1995). Like their teachers, and indeed, like the founder of the German experimental psychology movement, Wundt, Wertheimer and his colleagues conducted their work in the service of helping solve philosophical problems, especially questions of epistemology and cognition.

The particular knowledge claims of the Gestalt theorists were threefold: First, the constituents of consciousness are not elements but structures whose relations are not simple stimulus–sensation connections; second, behavior is structured, as well, in interaction with particular environments that provide contexts for action; and third, the phenomenal structures of consciousness are supported by underlying brain processes that themselves are not necessarily associative in nature but may also follow the relational nature of Gestalt. These basic knowledge claims were extended into numerous domains in the post–World War I period, as the leaders, Wertheimer, Koffka, and Köhler, settled into the institutionalization of their approach.

Each of the three Gestalt Psychology leaders spent the years of World War I refining their thinking and research. In the case of Wertheimer and Koffka, they also spent a significant portion of the war doing research that contributed to the German war effort. Wertheimer left his military research position in 1916 to return to the University of Berlin, where he became a friend of Albert Einstein and taught as part of the philosophy faculty. Köhler, however, was stranded on the island of Tenerife for

FIGURE 8.1   Max Wertheimer
Courtesy of the Archives of the History of American Psychology,
University of Akron, Akron, OH.

the duration of the war, where he conducted important research on animal insight.

At the end of the First World War, Germany experienced a brief revolutionary period, during which the monarch, Kaiser Wilhelm, abdicated. In August 1919, the Weimar Republic was formed and lasted until the National Socialists came to power in 1933. This was a time of economic and political instability and social flux, as Germany experienced hyperinflation of its currency and more than 20 changes in government. The long-standing German norm of the role of education in creating cultivated people who would lead and safeguard German *Kultur* was challenged. Many of the cultural elite blamed technology and what they called mechanistic science for Germany's problems and embraced calls for wholeness in science and life. Within the life and mind sciences there arose various responses:

"holistic," "organismic," and "Gestalt" were terms used to describe approaches in several fields, including Psychology. Gestalt theory in psychology is perhaps best contextualized and best understood as part of this cultural framework.

After the end of the war and the establishment of the Weimar Republic, Wertheimer, Koffka, and Köhler found positions in respectable institutional settings. Of the three, Köhler held the most prestigious appointment, successor to Stumpf as the director of the Psychological Institute at the University of Berlin; Köhler remained as director until he resigned in protest of Nazi policies in 1935 and immigrated to the United States. Wertheimer was a member of the Berlin institute from 1918 to 1929, when he moved to Frankfurt University; he moved to the United States in 1933 after the Nazis came to power.

FIGURE 8.2   Wolfgang Köhler
Courtesy of the Archives of the History of American Psychology,
University of Akron, Akron, OH.

FIGURE 8.3   Kurt Koffka
Courtesy of the Archives of the History of American Psychology,
University of Akron, Akron, OH.

Koffka returned to the University of Geissen after the war and remained there until he left in 1927 for a position at Smith College in Massachusetts, where he was offered advantageous conditions for research. It is worth noting that all three of these men taught a mix of philosophy and psychology courses in the philosophy faculty. The Gestalt theory research program blossomed during the period of the Weimar Republic.

Wertheimer had published his experimental results on apparent movement, the **phi phenomenon**, in 1912. The perceived motion, he argued, was a Gestalt, was not reducible to individual elements, and thus was not explicable in terms of associations. Wertheimer, by all accounts, was a deep thinker who sought to determine the range of the Gestalt phenomena he had found experimentally. To do so, he worked on a further formulation of Gestalt principles before publishing them in 1921 in a new journal, *Psychologische Forschung*, founded by the

Gestalt psychologists and the neurologist Kurt Goldstein (1878–1965). Wertheimer called for investigating consciousness—cognition, perceptual organization, and so on—as people actually experience it rather than in an analytical, bit-by-bit, associative manner. Rather than enforcing a demand for rigorous objectivity in the methodologies used, as was the norm in North American psychology, Wertheimer insisted that objectivity resided in the phenomena themselves, as given. Wertheimer and his colleagues sought a way to describe the invariant principles of order that inhered in the phenomena under study.

Perceptual organization remains the most frequently cited example of Gestalt theory. In Wertheimer's most complete and complex description of laws of perceptual organization, *Readings in Perception* (1923/1958), he called the most general principle the **law of Prägnanz**. This law states that human perception has a tendency toward the organization of any whole or Gestalt into as good or as simple a structure as conditions permit. Wertheimer had presented this basic concept as early as 1914 at a meeting of the Society for Experimental Psychology. There he called it the law of simple formation, "according to which visible connection of the position, size, brightness, and other qualities of components appears as a result of Gestalt apprehension" (Wertheimer, 1914, cited in King & Wertheimer, 2005, p. 156). Specific examples of the law of Prägnanz include the laws of proximity, similarity, continuation, and closure (see Figure 8.4).

The laws and related concepts that emerged in this period formed the core of the research program at Berlin, Geissen, and Frankfurt. The Gestalt theorists attracted talented students who, working in collaboration or independently, tested Gestalt concepts in laboratory settings, often in creative ways. By the time the theorists left or were forced out of Germany, a substantial body of experimental work supported Gestalt principles of cognition and perception.

Köhler and Wertheimer in Berlin supervised graduate students' work on brightness contrasts,

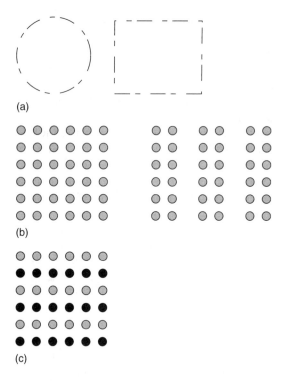

(a)

(b)

(c)

FIGURE 8.4 Laws of Prägnanz a) Closure b) Proximity c) Similarity

demonstrations of Prägnanz and depth effects in motion perception, comparative research on pattern discrimination, escape learning, figural perception in several species, and priority of organization over habit in perceptual memory, among many other topics. Karl Duncker (1903–1940), perhaps one of the most able of Wertheimer's and Köhler's students in Berlin, conducted groundbreaking work on productive thinking and problem solving. Duncker won a fellowship to study in the United States and completed his master's thesis at Clark University in 1926 with an experimental study that articulated productive thinking as occurring in stages that are closely connected and may or may not result in sudden insight into the solution. Duncker returned to complete his doctorate at Berlin in 1929. In his dissertation he argued that the perceiver is a part of the perceptual field, not outside it, and that this changes the dynamics of

perception. Most people have experienced this, for example, when sitting in traffic at a signal and the vehicle next to yours begins moving; you usually have a momentary sense that you are moving as well. Duncker's 1935 monograph, "On Problem-Solving," was published in English in 1945. In the monograph he reported on the phenomenon of "functional fixedness," the tendency to see a problem and its solution in only one way (e.g., a hammer can only be used to drive a nail into wood). This usually results in an inability to find new solutions to problems. The monograph became one of the most influential documents in the shaping of cognitive psychology in the second half of the 20th century.

This intensely productive period of Gestalt research led by Wertheimer, Koffka, and Köhler came to an end in 1935, when Köhler stepped down as director of the Psychological Institute at the University of Berlin. Koffka had already left, as mentioned, in 1927, for Smith College, where he had a productive career until his death in 1941. Wertheimer left, as mentioned, in 1933, and spent several years at the New School for Social Research in New York City until his death in 1942. Gestalt research did continue under the National Socialists, but never again in Germany was there a period as rich in ideas and research results from the Gestalt perspective as from 1922 to 1935. Before turning from Gestalt psychology research, however, we discuss the contributions of a younger member of the Gestalt group, Kurt Lewin.

Kurt Lewin (1890–1947)

Lewin was also a student of Stumpf at the University of Berlin, earning his doctorate under him in 1916. Like the other Gestalt theorists, Lewin worked in the tradition of conducting natural science research under the umbrella of philosophy. Perhaps more than the other theorists, however, Lewin was strongly committed to practical issues. He is well known for his statement that "there is nothing so practical as a good theory" (Lewin, 1944, p. 27).

Lewin's appointment at the Psychological Institute at the University of Berlin was in the applied psychology program, which was reflected in the research he and his students conducted. It is important to point out that Lewin's work was different from that of his colleagues who were engaged in what was termed psychotechnics, which we discuss later. Beginning early in his career, Lewin sought to make the industrial workplace oriented toward workers' needs rather than just increased profits. In this he was similar to American psychologist Lillian Moller Gilbreth (1878–1972), whom we discussed in Chapter 4. Until he left for the United States in 1933 (because of the Nazis), Lewin and his students completed a body of research that was impressive and influential in its own time and that has continued to be influential in social psychology, the study of group dynamics, the field of organizational behavior, and social justice research and action. In all of his work we can see an attempt to humanize psychological science and use it to make a more humane world.

Lewin's research program may be best characterized as a psychology of action and emotion. He was concerned with motivation, for example, how the instructions of experimenters influence participant's actions. For Lewin, actions were structured wholes, not reducible to individual elements. The person acted within a physical and social space that was part of the **action whole**.

Lewin extended this work to personality theories. Stimuli in the environment activate psychological processes within the person, which then results in action or emotion. The impact of the stimulus varies according to its psychological force for the person. Thus, not only is action a result of external stimuli, but dynamic internal factors are also part of the action whole. Lewin used the term **life space** to indicate that personality is a totality that includes the organism and its psychological environment at a given moment.

The growth of Lewin's thought and practices over the years was due, in part, to the dynamic relationships he had with a series of gifted graduate students. Lewin was committed to democratic processes, including within his research group. Rather than being a stuffy formal professor, Lewin sought to fully engage his students and develop meaningful research in collaboration with them. Many women found places as graduate students with Lewin. This may have reflected his stated desire from early in his career, when he wrote that he wanted to liberate "women from the conventional restrictions on their freedom" (cited in Ash, 1995, p. 265). Here we discuss the research of two of the remarkable women who were Lewin's students.

Bluma Zeigarnik (1901–1988) was born in Lithuania but moved to Berlin with her husband in 1922 to pursue doctoral work with Lewin, earning her degree in 1927. She is best known for the **Zeigarnik effect**, discovered in the course of her research with Lewin. It was customary for Lewin and his students to carry their discussions to a local café at the end of a working day. Lewin noticed that their waiter had a remarkable ability to remember everyone's order without writing it down. But when asked after everyone had paid what had been ordered, the waiter could not remember. Zeigarnik took this on as a dissertation topic, to investigate memory for completed and uncompleted tasks.

Zeigarnik recruited 164 participants for her study, in which they were instructed to complete as many of the manual tasks presented as rapidly as possible. They were interrupted on half of the tasks and left alone for the other half. When asked afterward to recall the tasks, the participants had better recall for uncompleted tasks. This lack of completion, Zeigarnik argued, fostered tension in the participants, and this tension facilitated memory for the task until it was released by completing it.

While this standard account is adequate, a fuller explanation places the Zeigarnik effect within the larger picture of Lewin's notion of action wholes. Lewin and Zeigarnik believed that in any experiment the experimenter and participant share a life space; thus, the experimental situation is interactive and potentially collaborative. Rather than focus solely on participant performance (i.e., whether participants performed the tasks correctly), Lewin and Zeigarnik interacted with participants to encourage them in the tasks, varying their interaction with each participant to bring about the best possible results from each one.

Tamara Dembo (1902–1993) also emphasized experimenter–participant interaction in her doctoral study. Dembo was born in Russia and came to the University of Berlin in 1921, completing her dissertation in 1931. Her dissertation research examined the dynamics of anger. The theoretical rationale behind her study was related to Sigmund Freud's (1856–1939) idea that frustration would lead to aggression. But rather than extrapolate from recall of childhood traumas or frustrations, as a psychoanalyst would, Dembo created an experimental situation that was designed to elicit anger directly. In the study, the experimenter set out to frustrate the participant's completion of the assigned tasks, which all appeared within reach to the participant. These tasks included tossing a ring to land on a bottle and grasping an object outside the assigned area. The situation always began as fun but grew tense as the experimenter frustrated the participant while continuing to insist that each of the tasks or problems had a solution. With increasing levels of frustration, some participants tried to escape the tension through daydreaming or pretending they were no longer there, but almost all of them finally resorted to demonstrations of anger, or even rage.

Dembo interpreted the results as indicating the importance of the total situation that included the participant, the experimenter, and the actions that occurred in the experimental space. The anger was not, Dembo argued, reducible to a stimulus–response analysis, where stimulus *a* (frustrating the participant) evoked response *b* (angry outbursts). Rather, the frustrations were cumulative and involved the total situation—the participant, the researcher, their actions, their interactions, and the physical space

they inhabited. Dembo described these results using Lewin's topological model of fields and vectors in dynamic interplay to produce the experimental results.

Before Lewin left for the United States, he had many remarkable students. As we noted, many of them were women. In addition to Zeigarnik and Dembo, Maria Rickers-Ovsiankina (1898–1993) and Gita Birenbaum (1903–1952) were students with Lewin. Zeigarnik returned to Russia, where she and her husband suffered greatly under Stalinist rule. Zeigarnik's husband was imprisoned, accused of being a spy for the Germans, and she experienced many obstacles in her career, perhaps because she had earned her doctorate outside the Soviet Union and was considered tainted by Western non-Communist influences. Dembo and Rickers-Ovsiankina immigrated to the United States, where both had notable careers.

Before leaving this account of psychology in Germany and turning to developments in Austria, it is worth mentioning another example of a philosophically oriented subfield of psychology that grew up in this period: the interface between psychology and religion.

The Dorpat School of Religious Psychology

The intertwined fields of psychology and religion received some attention in Germany in this period, similar to work in the Netherlands and the United States. Grand theorists such as Oswald Spengler and Eduard Spranger incorporated religious language into their psychological theories. Within religious circles, theologians such as Wilhelm Stählin (1883–1975) promoted the connection of psychology and religion; Stählin founded the Society for Religious Psychology in 1914, which began publishing its journal later that same year. Around the end of the First World War, a different approach, characterized by empirical methods, emerged at the University of Dorpat, now called Tartu University. As a young theologian, Karl Girgensohn (1875–1925) came to Berlin in 1900 for advanced study. While there, he also attended lectures by Stumpf on experimental psychology, thus connecting with people who became key figures in the later development of Gestalt psychology. During this period, Girgensohn wrote his first book on psychology and religion. In 1909, he took a leave of absence from Dorpat to spend a year with Külpe, only recently moved from Würzburg to Bonn. There, Girgensohn became immersed in learning about Külpe's systematic experimental introspection and determined that he had found a method for investigating religious experience.

As an example of this approach, Girgensohn recruited 14 participants for his study using systematic experimental introspection, which was an attempt to study the process of thought. After extensive practice, the participants were exposed to brief presentations of religiously oriented stimuli and asked to report on their thoughts and feelings about them. Apparently, the participants were incredibly open about their religious experiences. On the basis of this research, Girgensohn published his major text on the psychological structure of religious experience. As we saw in our discussion of Gestalt psychology and its use to explain philosophical issues, Girgensohn's book was meant to address an ongoing debate in the philosophy of religion. Girgensohn drew a conclusion based in Gestalt theory, that religious experience is a whole configuration (a gestalten) of thought, feeling, and will and cannot be understood as a series of experiences added together.

Girgensohn died at the relatively young age of 50 in 1925, leaving the field of the empirical study of psychology of religion in the hands of his student, Werner Gruehn (1887–1961). Over the next decade, Gruehn and his students extended the research program to the study of the religious experience of children and youth. The other major extension was the study of individual differences in religious experience. This work, led by Carl Schneider (1891–1946), resulted in the construction of a typology of people in terms of their religious experience, with two major types emerging, the mystical and the rational.

Just as the trend in German psychology during the 1920s and 1930s was toward the practical, so too was the study of religion and psychology. The finding of a range of individual differences led many religious professionals to ask for guidelines and other materials to help them guide their charges' religious experiences.

German Psychology After 1933

The National Socialists came to power in Germany in spring 1933. Within a few months, the impact of their policies was felt in German educational and professional institutions. On April 7, 1933, the law for the reconstitution of the state civil service mandated the dismissal from the civil service of all Jews and politically unreliable people. In Psychology, several full professors were dismissed outright because they were Jewish. Numerous psychologists at more junior levels also lost their positions. Many of the psychologists immigrated to England and the United States.

The only psychologist to publicly protest the Nazi policies was the non-Jew, Köhler, at the University of Berlin in 1933. By 1935, his position at the institute had been made untenable by the authorities. He resigned from his position as the head of the Psychological Institute and immigrated to the United States.

However, Psychology as a discipline eventually prospered under the Nazis. Under their rule, psychologists continued to press their case with the civil service for more appointments. What turned the tide for the field was the decision by the military that psychologists might be able to offer practical assistance in meeting military needs, as they had done during World War I. In particular, the military turned to psychology for personnel selection, especially for officers but also for other specialists. The number of psychologists employed in military service also increased dramatically in this period. In 1930, only about

30 psychologists were in the military; by 1942, there were at least 450 military psychologists (Geuter, 1992). Their work resembled the work that psychologists were doing for the American military in this period. German psychologists provided tests relevant for military applications, such as tests of spatial orientation and sensorimotor coordination. What is now called personality assessment was also a major emphasis but was labeled characterology and expression analysis in the German context. The specifics of this work went beyond simple racial typologies to encompass the study of handwriting, facial expression, meaning of body movements, and so forth. It was rooted in an older German tradition of the body as a carrier of psychological and emotional meaning.

The success of psychologists in Germany under the Nazis is indicated by the establishment in 1941, for the first time, of the diploma examination in psychology, apart from philosophy or pedagogy. This meant that a person could be trained as a psychologist alone without the caveat of also qualifying as a philosopher or educational specialist.

Psychology in Vienna

Karl Bühler (1879–1963) became the director of the newly created Vienna Psychological Institute in 1922. The institute, like the Berlin Psychological Institute in the same era, became a center for innovative psychological research and its applications. Bühler and his wife, Charlotte (1893–1974), attracted good students and staff, many of whom made important contributions to psychology. Staff members included Egon Brunswik, Marie Jahoda (1907–2001), and Paul Lazarsfeld (1901–1976).

Karl Bühler earned a medical degree in 1903 and then a PhD in psychology the next year. He served as Külpe's research assistant for several years. He married Charlotte in 1915, and together they began research on children's cognitive development, work that was published as *The Mental Development of the Child* (1918; English translation, 1930). The Bühlers proposed that children's development followed an evolutionary progression from controlling instincts to the mastery of sensorimotor skills and then to true intelligence through language. Applied to school education, their theoretical approach was supportive of active learning in the classroom. The book quickly gained wide acceptance in the field. Thus, when the Vienna city government wanted to start a psychological institute that they hoped would contribute to educational reform, first in Vienna and then throughout Austria, Karl Bühler was hired as the first director.

The work of the institute was divided into three nearly autonomous sections. One was devoted to experimental research, especially various aspects of visual perception. It was led by Karl Bühler, who held a view of the conscious mind as an active, directed process. Like the work of his mentor, Külpe, and that of the Gestalt theorists, the work in this section of the institute was relevant to philosophical questions. The most outstanding of the section's researchers was undoubtedly Brunswik (1903–1955), who had earned his doctorate under Bühler in 1927 and then stayed on as a researcher at the institute until 1937. His work on perception begun in Vienna was developed into a major body of psychological theory after he moved to the University of California, Berkeley, in 1937 at the invitation of the noted neobehaviorist Edward Chace Tolman (1886–1959).

Charlotte Bühler led the section on child and youth psychology. While city education officials hoped that her work would prove immediately applicable to school reform, Bühler and her staff argued that their first priority was research that would establish the psychological and parallel biological parameters of child and youth development. Bühler's research focused on the cognitive and personality development characteristic of each stage of growth. The work was generously supported by the Laura Spelman Rockefeller Memorial, which, as we saw in the previous chapter, was instrumental in creating the field of developmental psychology. The Vienna Psychological Institute was the only non–North American center to receive these funds.

Finally, the section on economic and social psychology pioneered the use of the social sciences in social justice research, among other endeavors. The section's director, Lazarsfeld, became one of the most prominent sociologists in the United States after he immigrated. His wife at the time, Marie Jahoda, also had a remarkable career in social psychology, both in the United States and in Britain. Their most visible project while based in the institute was a study of unemployed workers in the town of Marienthal, in which they used innovative methods to study the impact of unemployment. The members of the research team all had strong socialist leanings, and they expected to find that unemployment would have created revolutionary attitudes. Instead, they found that the strongest attitudes and emotions were ones of resignation and withdrawal. Nevertheless, the workers maintained a strong sense of community among themselves and strong support for one another.

Sidebar 8.1 Focus on *Marie Jahoda*

Marie Jahoda was born in Vienna, Austria, in 1907 to an upper-middle-class, secular Jewish family. Jahoda's parents were active Social Democrats, and Jahoda became a leader in the Austrian socialist youth movement. She later described her parents as free thinkers and remarked that the socialist movement was their substitute for religion. Her parents also held progressive attitudes toward women's education, and Jahoda was encouraged to pursue an advanced degree. She studied at the University of Vienna with the Bühlers in their recently established Psychological Institute and during this time married Lazarsfeld and gave birth to a daughter, Lotte.

In 1926, Lazarsfeld established a research unit for social psychology and marketing research as a branch of the Psychological Institute. Jahoda worked in the research unit during the years of her doctoral studies. During this time, she helped carry out the monumental study of the psychological effects of unemployment in Marienthal, a small Austrian village, which was published in 1933 in German and reprinted in 1972 in English. As a result of this research, Jahoda and her colleagues concluded that unemployment did not create social unrest and revolutionary tendencies; rather, it led to resignation, passivity, and lowering of expectations to avoid frustration.

Jahoda and Lazarsfeld separated in the early 1930s, and in 1933 they divorced and Lazarsfeld moved to the United States. In November 1936, Jahoda was arrested for her underground political activities on behalf of the Austrian socialists. After a period of imprisonment, she was released on the condition that she leave the country—meaning her daughter, family, and work—immediately. She heartwrenchingly agreed and left for England. There, she continued her research on unemployment, undertaking a study of a relief project implemented in a small mining town in South Wales. To study the

FIGURE 8.5 Marie Jahoda
Courtesy of Lotte Bailyn.

(Continued)

impact of the program, she spent four months living in the community. She also did applied work on civilian and enemy morale for the British Foreign Office.

In 1945, with the close of the war, Jahoda moved to the United States to be reunited with her daughter, who had spent the war years there with Lazarsfeld. Jahoda's first position was with the research department of the American Jewish Committee, where she studied several topics, including the reduction of prejudice, the authoritarian personality, and the relationship between emotional disorders and anti-Semitism. In 1949, Jahoda moved to a position at New York University, where she later became associate director of the Research Center for Human Relations.

Jahoda's research reflected her timely concern with social issues. In the 1950s she conducted a series of investigations of the impact of McCarthyism (the suppression of political opinions and the blacklisting of suspected Communist sympathizers) that was prominent in this period of the mounting cold war. She did research on interracial housing, which we discuss briefly in Chapter 9. She also undertook important work on the concept of positive mental health, resulting in her 1958 monograph *Current Concepts of Positive Mental Health*. That year, she moved again, this time back to Britain. She had married British Labour Party member Austen Albu. In England, she took up an academic post at Brunel University and then moved to the University of Sussex. In this period, she turned her attention to psychoanalysis and its impact on American psychology and continued her commitment to the study of unemployment, publishing a book on the topic in 1982. Jahoda's long and socially engaged career ended with her death in 2001.

PSYCHOLOGY, NATURAL SCIENCE, AND PHILOSOPHY ACROSS CONTINENTAL EUROPE

Generally, the pattern of development of psychology across continental Europe was similar to what we have seen in German-speaking countries. That is, experimental psychology remained closely linked to broad philosophical concerns. Still, the social, political, and educational traditions of each country were important determinants of the growth of Psychology and opportunities afforded psychologists.

Laboratories for conducting psychological experiments were established in many European countries by the early 20th century. For example, Gerard Heymans (1857–1930) established the first Dutch psychology laboratory in 1892 at the University of Groningen. In Italy, the early psychology laboratories were most often located in psychiatric or industrial settings, although the laboratory instrumentation and rationale were

often oriented to philosophical questions of cognition or perception. The institutionalization of Psychology in France occurred as part of philosophy, with concurrent links to clinical settings and the use of patients suffering from mental disorder to understand normal mental functioning. An academic professorial chair in experimental psychology was established at the country's most prestigious institution, the Collège de France, in 1887, with a laboratory of physiological psychology established two years later across the street at the Sorbonne and a small laboratory for experimental psychology by Jean-Martin Charcot (1825–1893) at the Salpêtrière Hospital in 1890. During the interwar period, psychology in these countries remained tied to philosophical roots while taking on new expressions as the number of psychologists grew.

Psychologists in the period between the world wars both drew upon older established traditions and generated new approaches. Their work was a mixture of empirical, experimental, and philosophical methods. For example, in social psychology little experimental work was conducted; rather, scholarship was more often devoted to thoughtful reflections on topics of social psychology. Mass or crowd psychology had its origins in Italy and France and found new expression in the interwar period in studies of leadership. Beginning in 1923, the Institute for Social Research at the University of Frankfurt am Main, usually referred to as the Frankfurt School, developed a critique of the impact of capitalism on families and interpersonal relations. Led by Max Horkheimer (1895–1973) and Theodor Adorno (1903–1969), the Frankfurt School members argued for theory and practices that would overcome the alienation and separation of individuals and the social world and would result in social justice. The members of the Frankfurt School left Germany after the Nazis came to power and spent the war years in New York City, affiliated with Columbia University. These are a few examples of the rich intellectual traditions that sprang from psychological perspectives, although they may not have been empirical or experimental in nature.

Developments in France

In France, academic psychology still struggled for its institutional identity during the interwar period, caught between philosophy and physiology. Thanks to the leadership of Henri Piéron (1881–1964), however, Psychology in France greatly expanded its influence in French academic life.

Piéron became the most prominent French psychologist of this period. He was trained in philosophy and took a degree in physiology, with a thesis on sleep. Piéron succeeded Alfred Binet (1857–1911) as the director of the psychological laboratory at the Sorbonne in 1911, as we discussed in Chapter 6. By the 1920s, he was the chief proponent of experimental psychology in France. Piéron's main scientific interest was the psychophysiology of the senses; thus, the core of his work was laboratory-based experimentation.

However, his work was multifaceted and he did not restrict himself to psychophysiological studies.

Piéron's leadership stimulated the growth of French psychology in several ways. In 1920, he and distinguished colleagues, including Pierre Janet (1859–1947), founded the first French program for graduate study in psychology, the Institut de Psychologie at the University of Paris. Piéron and his wife Marguerite were also major figures in the development of French applied psychology, specifically as they continued Binet's work in the development of intelligence testing after World War I, as we detailed in Chapter 6.

While the work of Piéron and his colleagues played an important role in expanding French experimental and applied psychology and legitimating it in the eyes of the public, there remained other approaches to psychological phenomena. Of enduring interest was the tradition of psychopathological studies, which were seen as forming a continuum with normal psychological functioning. Led by Janet and George Dumas (1866–1946), such studies indicated that psychopathology offers a "natural" experiment and from its expressions we can adduce the richness of normal mental life. Henri Wallon (1879–1962) and Jean Piaget (1896–1980) conducted studies of the psychological development of the child. Wallon employed a dialectical model to describe the successive stages of development. Rather than smooth, distinctive transitions between stages, Wallon suggested that development is often discontinuous due to competing or conflicting demands. Piaget, who was French Swiss, initially studied his own three children to discover how thinking develops. He noticed that his children often made similar mistakes in their reasoning when at a similar stage of development. This led him to focus on the development of reason and morality, and he suggested that continuity between stages was more characteristic than noncontinuity.

Finally, strong connections existed between philosophers and psychologists, as French philosophers in this period often theorized on psychological processes. Among such psychologically minded philosophers were Jean-Paul Sartre (1905–1980) and Maurice Merleau-Ponty (1908–1961). The latter wrote extensively about the psychological processes of language and perception. While he held the chair of Child Psychology and Pedagogy at the Sorbonne, Merleau-Ponty intensively studied children's acquisition of language. Merleau-Ponty also critiqued and extended the work of the Gestalt psychologists. His interest in the descriptive psychology of his time influenced the development of his theories of intersubjectivity, which argues that reality and experience only occur in human interactions and shared spaces.

Developments in the Netherlands

During the interwar period, psychology took a somewhat different direction in the Netherlands. The country is geographically situated close to Germany, France, and Britain and has historically been influenced by each of these larger countries. As noted earlier, Heymans developed an empirical psychology closely linked to philosophy. His methodology resembled that of psychologists in Britain; that is, he employed questionnaires and used statistical correlations in his data analysis, while his philosophical orientation remained German. He popularized psychology by developing a typology of character, which articulated eight personality types and illustrated them with material from the lives of well-known people. By the 1920s, however, his approach lost favor among other psychologists.

The uniqueness of Dutch psychology in this period was due to an unusual social arrangement in the country. As we discussed in Chapter 6, to avoid religious strife, each broad religious group, i.e., Protestants, Roman Catholics, developed their own schools, political parties, community groups, sports, and so on. Those who were not religious also had their own social, educational, and political groups. Psychologists were part of this

pillarization, so Protestant psychologists studied psychological phenomena and problems from a Protestant perspective, Catholic psychologists from a Catholic perspective, Neutrals from a nonreligious perspective, and so on. In this compartmentalized atmosphere, which reached its peak in the interwar years, the empirical approach of Heymans was discounted in favor of a more holistic view drawn primarily from German sources. In this instance, it was not Gestalt psychology. Rather, it was a psychology predicated on the German historical–philosophical tradition of *Geisteswissenschaftliche* that emphasized the wholeness of the soul and was intended to lead to *Verstehen*, or self-understanding. This approach suited the pillarized Dutch society. The psychology that resulted was applied in education, business, vocational guidance, and pastoral work.

It would be misleading to say that no empirical psychology existed in the Netherlands in this period. Heymans's successor at Groningen, H. J. F. W. Brugmans (1884–1961), and the Hungarian émigré psychologist Géza Révész (1878–1955) at the University of Amsterdam both continued doing experimental work and training graduate students. Révész earned his doctorate under Müller at Gottingen in Germany (1905). After several years at the University of Budapest, he was recruited to the University of Amsterdam. In Hungary, Révész's research focused on music and musical talent. After moving to Amsterdam, his work on identifying talented and gifted children resulted in one of the key books in the area, *Talent and Genius* (1952). With the German psychologist, David Katz (1884–1953), he founded *Acta Psychologica* (1935), one of the world's foremost psychological journals.

The University of Groningen in this period was also the academic home of Frederik J. J. Buytendijk (1887–1974). Buytendijk was a polymath, contributing in the fields of biology, physiology, anthropology, and Psychology. Within Psychology, he pioneered comparative studies in habit formation and form perception in animals. He was well connected with scientists and philosophers across Europe, including the Gestalt theorists. Lewin's student, Dembo, spent nearly two years with him conducting comparative psychological research. Buytendijk moved to Utrecht University in 1946 as chair of General and Theoretical Psychology. With colleagues, he fostered the development of existential phenomenology, which was an important alternative center of Dutch psychology and a source of applied theory in education.

Psychology in Russia and the Early Years of the Soviet Union

In the 19th century, an "objective" psychology developed in Russia that was primarily an effort to investigate and explain psychological phenomena in physiological terms. It was strongly antimentalist. Ivan Sechenov (1829–1905) and Ivan Pavlov (1849–1936; see Chapter 3) were the primary representatives of this approach. By the late 19th century, the experimental psychology then being developed in German universities had also found a place in Russia. The philosopher Nikolai Grot, for example, incorporated German psychology into his coursework, thus exposing students to developments elsewhere. One of those students, Georgy I. Chelpanov (1862–1936), pursued training in the new experimental psychology after he began his career at Kiev University in the 1890s. On trips to Germany in that decade, he studied with some of the leading experimentalists, including Wundt. Wundt became his model for how to organize Psychology as a scientific discipline.

Chelpanov earned his PhD in 1906 from Moscow University and accepted a faculty position there in the same year. Determined to firmly establish the new Psychology in Russia, Chelpanov lectured and trained select students in the then-standard German experimental topics of perception, memory, reaction time, attention, and various psychophysical studies. As a result of his activity in the new Psychology, in 1910

a wealthy merchant family gave money to establish the Institute of Psychology in Moscow. While construction was under way, Chelpanov made summer trips to reestablish professional connections with experimental psychologists in Germany and the United States. In doing so, he not only made sure he was up to date on the latest developments in Western psychology but also succeeded in making Russian psychology visible in the scientific community.

The new facilities were completed in 1912 and soon earned a reputation of being among the best-staffed and best-equipped experimental psychology laboratories in Europe. Chelpanov drew talented younger scientists to work with him and attracted bright students for graduate study. His personal orientation was pluralistic; that is, he did not dictate the theoretical orientation of his assistants. Thus, there was considerable diversity in theory, method, and topic, from behaviorism to studies of memory to phenomenology. By the time of the Russian Revolution in 1917, the Moscow institute was well known and accepted among literate Russians and was known in European and American scientific circles.

After the revolution and the ensuing civil war, events were not so kind to Chelpanov. Among his assistants were younger men who were thoroughly committed to the ideals of the Bolshevik revolution. As the new government became stabilized and bureaucratic attention was turned to science and scientists, Chelpanov became suspect because he refused to accept ideological supervision to bring his research into line with the state. In 1923, he was forced to retire, and for a period in the 1930s and 1940s, his contributions to Russian psychology were either ignored or denigrated. In the 1930s, Soviet authorities even removed his name from the plaque honoring the founders of the Institute of Psychology.

Konstantin Kornilov (1879–1957) became the head of the institute when Chelpanov was forced to retire. Kornilov actively sought Chelpanov's dismissal and charged that his former professor and boss failed to live up to Marxism's demands. Kornilov had been a political radical before the revolution; now it was his turn to lead psychology in directions that fit with Marxist theory. The psychology of language was his specialty. He was dismissive of the Völkerpsychologie approach to language. Although uses of the term "Völkerpsychologie" varied, Chelpanov had favored Wundt's approach, which made the study of language a subject of Psychology. Kornilov moved the study of language more toward a sociological approach so that social interaction became the focus of study. More broadly, Kornilov moved the institute toward a Marxist psychology, which incorporated elements of American behaviorism, Pavlovian reflexive psychology, and Gestalt theory. Kornilov himself eventually fell out of favor with the Soviet bureaucracy and was dismissed from the institute in 1931.

During the brief period of Kornilov's leadership, Lev Vygotskii came to Moscow, where he developed a multifaceted research program, including an innovative approach to studying children's development. His collaborations with Alexander Luria (1902–1977) and Alexei N. Leontiev (1903–1979) created a continuing research tradition, now often referred to as cultural–historical psychology. Vygotskii first came to public attention with his literary criticism, around the time of the Bolshevik revolution. He completed his studies in Moscow in 1917 and returned to his hometown of Gomol until 1924. At first he was preoccupied with his mother's illness (tuberculosis) but then took positions teaching in public schools. He taught philosophy and literature, along with psychology. In a local teacher's college, he established a small psychology laboratory.

Vygotskii returned to Moscow in January 1924, where he gave a talk at the Psychoneurological Congress in which he defended psychology as the study of the conscious mind. This was the period when all sciences had to be brought into line with Marxist principles and the favored

psychology was behaviorism imbued with Pavlovian conditioning approaches. Vygotskii wrote and defended his doctoral dissertation that same year and remained in Moscow as a faculty member of the newly renamed Moscow State Institute of Experimental Psychology, where Kornilov was the head.

Vygotskii attempted to understand human consciousness and chose the study of children's development as the route to this understanding. In his work, he came to show that the social and historical context of a child's life is critical for the development of psychological functions. He and his colleagues and students developed an ambitious program of research that encompassed the study of memory and attention, the effects of brain damage on cognitive development, verbal thinking, practical intelligence, and cross-cultural studies of ethnic minorities. In much of their work, attention was given to the practical application of their results to children's education. This was demanded of them by government authorities.

Vygotskii died of tuberculosis in 1934 at the young age of 38. His work and ambitious research program was continued, however, by an ardent group of former students and colleagues. Five members of Vygotskii's research group moved in 1931 to Kharkov, then the capital of the Ukraine, where they attracted other young scholars to join them. Although many of the group members held positions at other locations, they came to be called the Kharkov School. Members of this group, led by Leontiev, expanded the range of Vygotskii's work, including emphases on activity theory and the cultural–historical approach. Research topics included development of aesthetic perception, concept formation, tool-mediated play, and studies of memory. Much of this work remained unknown outside Russia until the 1980s. However, by the end of the century, activity theory and cultural–historical psychology had found new adherents around the globe.

FIGURE 8.6 Lev Vygotskii
Courtesy of the Archives of the History of American Psychology, University of Akron, Akron, OH.

PSYCHOTECHNICS

The applications of psychology to problems of industry, business, and vocational choice expanded remarkably from the end of the First World War until the Second World War. The German psychologist and, later, Harvard University professor Hugo Münsterberg (1863–1916) popularized the term "psychotechnics" in the United States in his book *Psychology and Industrial Efficiency* (1913), but his work drew upon the foundation laid by German psychologist William Stern (1871–1938), as we pointed out in Chapter 6.

The European study of work had begun in the mid-19th century to address problems related to rapid industrialization. Much of the work had been conducted by physiologists, such as Angelo Mosso (1846–1910) in Italy, and other medical specialists, like the psychiatrist Emil Kraepelin (1856–1926), and addressed problems of fatigue and related worker issues that reduced productivity. After the war, the earlier emphasis on fatigue and work performance was merged with the differential psychology of Stern to form the field of psychotechnics (see also Chapter 6). Much of this work was initially conducted using standard or slightly modified laboratory apparatus, although by the 1930s some work had shifted to the increasingly popular paper-and-pencil test approach.

By the end of World War I, psychologists in several countries had demonstrated the usefulness of psychology in many settings. This earlier work provided the foundation for the rapid growth of psychotechnics between the world wars. The Bolshevik revolution in Russia created fear in other European countries that they, too, might be vulnerable to social and political unrest caused by problems between labor and industry. An additional factor in the growth of psychotechnics included labor shortages due to the incredibly high casualty rate on both sides of the Great War and the need to reintegrate returning war veterans into the workforce. Almost all European countries had also suffered major damage to their industrial infrastructure, resulting in a need and opportunity to rebuild their industrial and business base. Although the system of scientific management created by Frederick Winslow Taylor (1856–1915) was influential in Europe, as it had been in the United States earlier, in each case it had to be modified to avoid labor conflicts.

It was perhaps in Germany that psychotechnics had its most extensive and rapid growth. As we have seen, precedent for this had been set by the early work of Stern in Breslau and Hamburg. In 1906, Stern cofounded the Institute for Applied Psychology and General Psychological Research. In 1918, psychologist Walther Moede (1888–1958) and engineer Georg Schlesinger (1874–1949) cofounded the Institute for Industrial Psychotechnology as part of the Technical Academy in Berlin-Charlottenburg. This linkage between psychotechnics and technical colleges in Germany became the norm in the interwar period. While psychologists struggled to gain new chairs of psychology in regular academic settings, psychotechnical professorships were established at six technical colleges between 1918 and 1927. In addition, a Division of Applied Psychology was added to the Psychological Institute of the University of Berlin, which, as noted earlier, was Lewin's academic location. In addition to the professorships (remember there could be only one professor at a time in each location within the German higher education system), numerous positions were added in lectureships, assistant professors, and assistants. This was the growth area for psychology in Germany during this period, as the successive German governments and German society sought to use scientific and technical interventions to bring greater stability to what became an unstable period. In 1919, a law was passed that required the consultation of psychologists for all occupational and employment agencies. In the early 1920s, the German Ministry of Labor created a special branch to address psychotechnical work. Members of the agency included state officials, labor and industry representatives, and psychotechnicians. The goal was to use psychotechnics as part of the reconstruction and stabilization of the country. The hope was to place German work on a rationalized basis and thus reduce labor conflict. This effort bore striking resemblance to the aspirations of the American Progressive movement (1890–1920) and, indeed, reflects a craze for all things American among many

Germans in the 1920s. By 1922, 170 psychotechnical testing sites could be found throughout Germany.

Psychotechnics was employed to facilitate positive labor relations, as well as to improve working conditions through workplace analyses, ergonomic planning, and aptitude tests. For example, in the German postal service, in the division that regulated female telephone operators, psychologists sought to reduce the stress that the women were thought to experience by making the work process as routine as possible. Personnel selection strategies were implemented for hiring, and time and motion studies were used to improve worker efficiency. At first, this strategy worked, but by the late 1920s, distrust had grown both between the engineers and the psychologists involved and between the workers and the psychotechnical staff. The workers, quite rightly, perceived that psychotechnics favored employers and grew deeply suspicious of their efforts, fearing that results would be used to extract more work from them or otherwise exploit them. This reflected a growing sense in German labor of the overregulation and control of life so intensely depicted in the classic film of Fritz Lang from this era, *Metropolis*. By the 1930s, psychotechnics in Germany had lost much of its appeal, especially among workers, although it retained its sponsorship from industry.

In France, Psychology and other sciences were applied extensively to the study and improvement of work. As we noted in Chapter 6, in 1928, Piéron was a co-founder of the first French institute for the training of vocational guidance counselors, Institut National d'Orientation Professionelle (National Institute of Vocational Guidance), which was expanded to become the National Institute of Labor Studies and Vocational Guidance in 1942. Piéron and his colleagues, especially the psychiatrist Eduoard Toulouse (1865–1947) and the physiologists Jean-Marie Lahy (b. 1875) and Henri Laguier

(b. 1888), created an influential science of work in France, which they labeled *psychotechnique.* What set their work apart was their use of methods developed from the experimental laboratory and the development of psychological and physiological tests that could be used to improve personnel selection and labor processes, including ergonomics.

Piéron and his colleagues were well connected in the business and political world. These connections helped them gain openings for their ideas and methods to improve many aspects of work. Although influenced by Taylor's ideas of scientific management and the need to improve industrial efficiency, their psychotechnics focused on matching the worker with the work, thus leading to happier workers, as well as increased productivity. Piéron brought to these numerous interlocking projects his training and expertise in psychophysiology and the measurement of intelligence.

As we mentioned in Chapter 6, Piéron and his wife Marguerite formulated their tests of intelligence on the basis of their belief that intelligence was multifaceted. Thus, their test was composed of sections that measured comprehension, creativity, verbal ability, numerical ability, and critical thought. In the hands of the Piérons, the test "score" was not one number, such as an IQ. Rather, the scores on each section were used to generate a profile that indicated strengths and weaknesses in different domains.

Piéron's colleagues, Lahy and Laguier, later extended this multifaceted approach to careers and work to include tests of psychophysiological functions (e.g., reaction time, fatigability, and ambidexterity). The result of their efforts was an extensive range of applications to industries and work sites across France and into several other European countries. Clients of this group of psychotechnicians included the Paris public transport system, two of the French railroads, and the national education system. For the Paris public transport system, the group devised tests for screening driver applicants, with the goal of reducing accidents and improving efficiency. Thousands of applicants were screened each year. When the results were published, it was reported that the reduction in accidents and improved efficiency had resulted in an average saving of more than 1 million francs a year. In 1933, the group founded a journal devoted to psychotechnics, *Travail Humain.* While we have given an example of one group of scientists working in the field of psychotechnics, numerous others existed across France.

As in many other European countries, the application of psychology to business, industry, and careers was a growth industry in the Netherlands between the wars. Vocational guidance for individuals and personnel selection for businesses were among the key applications of psychologists. At the beginning of the 1920s, psychologists such as Brugmans and Jacob Prak (b. 1898) used a linear assessment model that was premised on the cumulative or additive nature of results from sensorimotor, cognitive, and intellectual tests to determine how to best fit a person to a particular position. For private firms and industries, they developed selection tests for several occupations, including engineers and telephone operators. Other psychologists followed suit, including Rebecca Biegel, who set up a laboratory for psychotechnical work in the Dutch postal service.

However, the growing influence of the German holistic movement *(Geisteswissenschaftliche)* during the 1920s led away from this associative model to an insistence on the uniqueness of each person. In the holistic mode, each person was assessed in terms of their total character, and interpretive methods prevailed. Movements, expressions, drawing, and handwriting were all used to gain a sense of the total person. An example of this approach was the Dutch Foundation for Psychotechnics, founded in Utrecht in 1927 by a theologian who later became a psychologist,

David J. van Lennep (1896–1982). Because of the pillarization of Dutch society, these interpretive or characterological approaches were fitted to the desired characteristics of members of each of the pillars: Catholics, Protestants, or Neutrals. One professional result was the increased workload; that is, psychotechnicians were needed for work in each of the pillars (see also Chapter 6).

The development of psychotechnics in Germany, France, and the Netherlands was broadly exemplary of psychotechnics across much of Europe, especially where industrialization and labor were issues. For example, in Italy, Sante de Sanctis (1862–1935), a psychiatrist who spent most of his professional life working as a psychologist, turned his prodigious abilities to psychotechnics after World War I. He published his research on vocational choice, the laws of work, and particular studies on fatigue and the "psychoergographic" work curve. The Catholic priest Agostino Gemelli (1878–1959), after de Sanctis the most influential psychologist in Italy between the wars, contributed to the development of applied psychology, in addition to his better-known work on theory and experimental psychology.

Similar developments occurred in Spain. Despite the long tradition of philosophical psychology and the heavy hand of the Catholic Church, the few psychologists in Spain began applying their skills to problems of an industrializing and modernizing society: traffic problems, personnel selection, vocational guidance, and so on. The civil war that erupted in the mid-1930s had a profound and regressive effect on psychology. The field did not fully recover until after the death of dictator Francisco Franco (1892–1975). In Denmark, psychologist Alfred Lehman (1858–1921) founded the field of psychotechnics in 1918. His work for the military was influential, and the field grew rapidly. Independent psychotechnical institutes were founded, and principles were applied to career guidance, personnel selection, and work efficiency. Clearly, the demand for applied psychology was present in many post–World War I societies. The improvement of work efficiency and the increase in labor productivity were central to much of the demand, but it should not be overlooked that social management of the labor force was also part of psychotechnics' appeal to management.

PSYCHOLOGY IN BRITAIN

The United Kingdom has a different history. Psychology as an experimental or even applied science was regarded with skepticism by universities and other scientists until well after the First World War. After the war, Psychology began making inroads as both an academic subject and an applied science. By 1920, the British Psychological Society counted more than 600 members, ahead even of its American counterpart.

Before we provide more details about organized or disciplinary Psychology in Britain, we should highlight the great public interest in psychology as it applied to improving everyday life and satisfaction that dated from the end of the 19th century. This everyday psychology owed little to the discipline of Psychology, until at least after World War II. In this sense, it indicates a continuation of the trends toward self-understanding and self-direction that we chronicled in Chapter 2. It is perhaps best understood as the continuation and expansion of "the psychological" represented at an earlier time by physiognomy, phrenology, and mesmerism.

British historian Mathew Thomson has documented the rapid growth of this everyday psychology, often called practical psychology, across Britain in the first four decades of the 20th century. Hundreds of thousands of Britons were engaged in one or more aspects of everyday psychologies. One example was Pelmanism, which was begun in 1899 and remained popular until well into the interwar period. The aim of Pelmanism was mental training to help Britons regain their brain power by improving the efficiency of their cognitive processes, especially memory. As it grew in popularity, it came to be seen as an aid to self-improvement generally.

Pelmanism was just one of the everyday psychological approaches that attracted followers. Others included the practices of the Psycho-Therapeutic Society and the Federation of British Practical Psychologists. By the early 1920s, a movement was taking place toward forming local clubs, and many of them came to be organized as practical psychology clubs, federated into the Practical Psychology Clubs of Great Britain. Journals, such as the *Practical Psychologist, Emblem, You*, and others, as well as books for the everyday reader, were quite popular in the interwar period, as they were in the United States. These societies, clubs, and publications were all developed apart from disciplinary or professional Psychology. This is an indication that the sense of interiority and psychological self-awareness that we documented as originating in the 17th century had continued to grow among the population and needed little help or encouragement from professionals or disciplinary scientists. This raises the question in regard to Britain, just as it did in America, "Who owns psychology?"

Psychology at Cambridge

Turning to disciplinary Psychology, the center of British psychological science in the interwar period was, without a doubt, Cambridge University. Like its older counterpart, Oxford University, Cambridge was reluctant to accept Psychology as a distinctive academic discipline. Philosopher James Ward (1843–1925) laid the groundwork for the eventual acceptance of Psychology at Cambridge in the late 19th century. His article on the new experimental psychology and psychophysics in the 1876 edition of *Encyclopedia Britannica* was a clear exposition of the new scientific psychology. In 1897, the physician–psychologist–anthropologist William H. R. Rivers (1864–1922), was appointed Lecturer in Experimental Psychology and the Physiology of the Senses. Rivers proved to be a key figure in several disciplines and is primarily known for his anthropological work before World War I and his effective psychotherapies during the war. However, he was a rigorous experimentalist in his psychological work, using the psychophysiological study of the senses as a training tool to instill the need for careful observation and attention to methods in his psychology students. One of those students was Charles S. Myers (1873–1946).

At Cambridge, the establishment of psychology as a scientific discipline and an acceptable academic unit was primarily due to the work of Myers. Myers became the director of the newly built Cambridge Psychological Laboratory in 1913. Myers had raised the money and contributed a great deal of his personal wealth to finance the building. During his military service in the First World War, he coined the term **shell shock** to describe men whose behavior was disoriented and who appeared to be hysterical. He first supposed that their behavior was due to brain concussion from shells exploding near them. Although that proved not to be the case, it was a useful first attempt to draw attention to their need for care.

Myers returned to Cambridge after the war, where he was able to secure the institutional place of experimental psychology, arranging for it to be linked to physiology. His horizons had expanded so that he saw many needs and opportunities for psychology in addressing social problems. He became disgusted with the narrowness of academic politics at Cambridge and resigned in 1922, after making sure that his former student, Frederic Bartlett, was appointed Reader in Experimental Psychology.

Myers's interest in applying psychology to the social problems of Britain was manifested in the founding of the National Institute of Industrial Psychology (NIIP) in 1921. The NIIP grew out of the work of the Industrial Health Relations Board, which had been established by the British government to investigate industrial labor and production problems associated with the war. The work of the NIIP was similar to that being done in the field of psychotechnics that was sweeping across Europe. The NIIP addressed problems of low productivity, human factors in industrial accidents, and malingering at work, as well as problems of productivity. As in psychotechnics, vocational guidance and occupational selection were important applications. The central emphasis in all its work was the psychology of the worker and the work situation. Attention was paid to the "human factors" of motivation, personality, temperament, and intellectual abilities, not just to improving the financial bottom line. The NIIP quickly grew to be the largest organization of psychologists in Britain, numbering 50 staff and 1,600 members by 1930. It attracted many of Britain's finest psychologists, either as staff members or as consultants who served on its research committees. For example, Cyril Burt (1883–1971) was director of the program in vocational guidance. He used his position to promote the use of intelligence testing for industrial and work purposes. Other psychologists included Britain's first woman psychologist, Beatrice Edgell (1871–1948); Eric Farmer (b. 1888); Susan Isaacs (1885–1948); and C. W. Valentine (1879–1964), to name only a few.

The NIIP was a commercial operation, providing its consulting services and research for a fee. Its clients included both private firms and governmental agencies. Through its staff and the researchers it was able to retain on its committees, the NIIP was able to offer a range of services, such as personnel management, personnel selection, and staff training. One of the NIIP committees revised the Stanford-Binet Intelligence Scales for use in Britain.

The NIIP was successful on several levels. Not only did it provide expert advice and consulting on various worker and industry issues, it also helped individual workers discover careers for which they were best suited. Perhaps most importantly, the NIIP reconfigured the British understanding of the psychology of work. It made the adjustment of the worker central to efficient and productive work. Human relations

FIGURE 8.7   Frederic Bartlett
Copyright UK Medical Research Council, 2009. Used by kind permission.

and its concomitant, human resources, became the focus and, through these influences, work was psychologized in Britain.

Academic psychological research in this period is best characterized by the research of Bartlett (1886–1969). Bartlett is best known today for his pioneering research on memory, or forgetting, as he might say. His work has been reinterpreted and misinterpreted many times and in many ways since his seminal volume, *Remembering* (1932), appeared. He had been a student with Myers before the war and was named Myers's assistant just before World War I. After the war, as noted earlier, he became Reader in Experimental Psychology; then, when the university created a professorial chair in experimental psychology, Bartlett was the first to be named professor of experimental psychology at Cambridge University, a position he held from 1931 to 1951. Today, his work is thought of as an early cognitive psychology, but Bartlett considered it social psychology, as he regarded the context in which we learn to be crucial to our memory of what we have learned.

Bartlett's study of serial reproduction of memory was the core of the first half of *Remembering.* He used an old story, "The War of the Ghosts," as his memory text. Participants were to read it and then tell it to another person, who in turn told it to another person, and so on. Many readers of this text have played this as a game, sometimes called "Telephone." What struck Bartlett about this as a study of memory was how the participants changed the story to make it more conventional. In a second variant of the study, Bartlett used pictures as the stimulus and observed what happens when participants recall the content of the pictures in social contexts. Throughout, Bartlett emphasized the social nature of memory and insisted on understanding memory as a reconstruction (for more on Bartlett and his legacy for cognitive psychology, see Chapter 13).

Disciplinary Psychology in Britain was more extensive than we have depicted here. We mention three diverse examples to give a sense of the range of disciplinary Psychology in the interwar era. Beatrice Edgell, the first British woman to hold a doctorate in psychology, did important work on memory and comparative psychology, as historian of psychology Elizabeth Valentine (2001) has documented. Cyril Burt had an extensive program of research during the interwar years on heredity and intelligence, in addition to the applications he conducted through the NIIP. Some of his results were called into question years later, when it was found that he had falsified some of his data. Finally, an unusual approach to social psychology emerged in the 1930s, the mass observation movement, that sought the input of everyday people about their lives as well as observations of social behavior in connection with numerous mundane activities.

FIGURE 8.8 W. H. R. Rivers

War and Psychology in Britain

British psychologists were active in both world wars, but their experiences in each were somewhat different, as might be expected. The British suffered many more casualties than their American counterparts in the Great War and saw 80,000 cases of shell shock by the end of it.

As mentioned, it was the versatile psychologist–anthropologist–physician Rivers who formulated a treatment for shell-shocked soldiers based on Freudian talk therapy. The success of Rivers's approach was such that it created a space for the growth of psychoanalysis in Britain after World War I. Psychoanalysis thrived in Britain between the wars. Analysts like Melanie Klein (1882–1960) and, later, Freud and his daughter Anna (1895–1982) were there. Perhaps the most influential site for psychoanalysis in England was the Tavistock Clinic. The clinic was founded in 1920 to help soldiers who suffered from shell shock, furthering the work begun by Rivers. Over the next two decades, the Tavistock Clinic became a leading center for psychoanalytic approaches to treatment. The noted attachment theorist, John Bowlby (1907–1990), was associated with the clinic both before and after World War II.

As Freud's works were translated into English, and British psychoanalytic thinking developed, a heightened sensitivity to the important role of emotion in warfare had created an opening for both psychiatrists and psychologists by the Second World War. In addition to screening men for mental defects that would make them more likely to succumb to the stress of combat, service provision was required to keep men fighting. Detecting malingering was another major task for which psychologists were deemed uniquely suited, although reports of their methods might appear somewhat unsophisticated to modern readers. Overall, psychoanalytic ideas and their application to understanding war and treating its casualties were somewhat more prominent in Britain than in the United States.

Another interesting application of psychological expertise to the problems of war in the British context was child analyst Susan Isaacs's research on the effects of children's separation from their families as a result of the evacuation of London. She collaborated on this project with attachment theorist Bowlby and others and made recommendations to government agencies about the need to direct increased attention to the psychological impact of separation.

The expertise of academic psychologists was also enlisted in the war effort. Bartlett was appointed to the Royal Air Force's Flying Personnel Research Committee. Under these auspices he collaborated with his colleague, Kenneth Craik (1914–1945), on research on skill acquisition and how to apply these principles in the training of bomber and fighter pilots. They also studied the effects of fatigue on performance. In 1944, in acknowledgment of the importance of their work, the British Medical Research Council established the Applied Psychology Research Unit and named Craik as director. Although Craik died tragically in a car accident two days before the end of the war in 1945, Bartlett remained affiliated with the unit for many years.

SUMMARY

The period between the world wars was marked by the growth and expansion of disciplinary Psychology in Germany, Britain, and many other European countries. As we have pointed out, psychology found diverse expressions that reflected local, regional, and national contexts. In the case of Gestalt psychology in Germany, we showed how the notion of Gestalt was a reaction against the reductionism and mechanism that had come to characterize German science by the end of the 19th century. It was also a reaction against the industrialization that had changed German society and threatened to diminish the tradition of social and intellectual life known as German *Kultur*. Gestalt psychology was an expression of this reaction, with its return to holism and emphasis on understanding in context. The political conditions of the interwar period supported the institutionalization of this school of thought, but with the rise of National Socialism, the major Gestalt theorists emigrated from Germany to the United States and continued their careers far from their homeland. Under the Nazis, psychology continued in a somewhat different form. It became formally separate from philosophy and acquired a distinctly applied function. We also looked at the development of psychology in Austria, specifically through the activities of the Vienna Psychological Institute, whose multidisciplinary staff and theoretical eclecticism led to the incorporation of a range of research topics and problems.

We then turned to the development of psychology in continental Europe, focusing on France and the Netherlands. Although noting the continuing close relationship between psychology and philosophy, we also saw the expanding use of empirical approaches and the edge toward application. We highlighted the institutional, social, and political traditions that were important determinants of the growth of psychology and the opportunities afforded psychologists in each country. Before turning to application, we took the opportunity to outline the emergence and development of psychology in Russia, where the political conditions radically affected the discipline both institutionally and intellectually. We reviewed the pioneering contributions of Chelpanov, including the founding of the Institute of Psychology in Moscow, and the influence of his successor, Kornilov. Vygotskii's cultural–historical psychology and the work of the Kharkov school were also outlined.

Psychotechnics was the name given to the application of psychology to work and industry that proliferated in the interwar period. We traced the evolution of psychotechnics in Germany, France, and the Netherlands. Although a tradition of psychotechnics developed in each country, the specific form psychotechnical work took was determined by the practical and institutional exigencies of its contexts. We concluded this chapter by offering a glimpse of psychology in Britain, contrasting its development with that of its continental counterparts. In Britain, a well-established and influential tradition of everyday psychology, including psychologies of self-improvement such as Pelmanism, existed in tandem with institutional Psychology. Psychology, both experimental and applied, was somewhat less well entrenched in the British university system until after World War I, when its reputation improved. The psychology department at Cambridge was one of the most important in the country, and we discussed the work of members of this department, such as Myers and Bartlett.

In offering these sketches of psychology during and between the world wars in these specific locations, we hope to create an overall sense of how psychology, and Psychology, are truly part and parcel of the societies of which they form a part. While psychological methods, theories, and practices are developed in highly specific loci, they also transcend these points of origin to color how individuals, organizations, and even nations think about themselves. This process is an example of the reflexivity we talked about in the introduction to the text. In exploring how extraintellectual and extrascientific factors like politics, revolution, war, practical problems, and even interpersonal and institutional rivalries affect the production of knowledge and the development of practice, we are also invoking a social constructionist analysis.

BIBLIOGRAPHIC ESSAY

We were fortunate to be able to draw on a rich literature concerning the development and growth of psychology in Germany. The work of Mitchell Ash (1980, 1991, 1995), as well as the chapters in the volume co-edited by Ash and William Woodward, *Psychology in Twentieth-Century Thought and Society* (1987), were instrumental in helping us craft the first half of this chapter. The fine volume by Wertheimer's son, Michael, and his colleague, Brett King (2005), was illuminating for both scientific and personal details about Max Wertheimer. Ulfried Geuter's (1992) volume on psychology in Nazi Germany was helpful for far more than its coverage of the Third Reich. We know of no other English language source that gives so much detail about the development of applied psychology in Germany between the world wars. In addition, the excellent scholarship of Anne Harrington (1996) and the earlier volume by Donna Haraway (1976) placed the Gestalt psychologists in a larger context of German life. We are also grateful for the scholarship on other figures from this era, particularly that of René van der Veer (2000) and the moving tribute to Zeigarnik by A. V. Zeigarnik (2007). Our two main sources on psychology and religion in Germany came from Jacob Belzen (2001) and American psychologist of religion David Wulff (1985). For the material on the Vienna Psychological Institute, we relied again on the scholarship of Ash (1987) and on that of David Leary (1987); both chapters are in the excellent Ash and Woodward (1987) noted earlier. For material on Jahoda's life and career, we consulted a chapter by Stuart Cook (1990) in Agnes O'Connell and Nancy Russo's useful volume *Women in Psychology*.

The work of Peter van Strien (1991, 1997) and Trudy Dehue (1995) and a recent article by René van Hezewijk and Hendrikus Stam (2008) were excellent sources for the history of psychology in the Netherlands. We know more about the history of psychology in Italy due to the excellent group of scholars gathered around Guido Cimino in Rome and other key cities. We relied on recent scholarship (Cimino, 2006; Degni, Foschi, & Lombardo, 2007; Colombo, 2003; Lombardo & Foschi, 2008), as well as the classic chapter by Sante de Sanctis in volume 2 of *A History of Psychology in Autobiography* (1936).

The history of psychology in France is extremely complex. For our account we drew on the work of Jacqueline Carroy and Régine Plas (1996), Plas (1997), Cristina Chimisso (2000), and Jaap van Ginneken (1992). William Schneider's excellent articles from 1991 and 1992 were helpful for their clearly articulated view of Piéron and the study of work in France. Martin Jay's older but still useful volume (1973) on the Frankfurt School found its way

into our hands and its information onto our pages.

Only in recent years has growth occurred in English-language literature on the history of psychology in Russia or Soviet Union. As happened so often while writing this text, we found Roger Smith's *Norton History of the Human Sciences* (1997) useful. The recent article by Irina Sirotkina (2006) in the special issue of *Physis* helped orient us to the development of psychology in Russia. The work of Alex Kozulin (1985) on one of the key figures in the founding of experimental Russian psychology, Chelpanov, was helpful. David Joravsky's *Russian Psychology* (1989) is idiosyncratic in style but was extremely valuable as an aid. For events after the Bolshevik revolution, including the contributions of Vygotskii, we relied on work by Craig Brandist (2006), Smith (1997), and recent scholarship by Anton Yasnitsky and Michel Ferrari (2008).

Psychotechnics and its spread throughout Europe is one of the most fascinating aspects of the history of psychology. For an overview of the history of the scientific study of work, we relied on the excellent volume by Anson Rabinbach, *The Human Motor* (1990). Van Strien (1997) offered an excellent synopsis of the field. Geuter (1992) and Lothar and Helga Sprung (2001) helped us understand the spread of psychotechnics in Germany, while Andreas Killen (2007) demonstrated so clearly the problems that emerged with its continued use. Our too-limited coverage of psychotechnics in Spain and Denmark was informed by Helio Carpintero (2001) for the former and Peter Triantafillou and Afonso Moreira (2005) for the latter.

Mathew Thomson's *Psychological Subjects* (2006) is arguably one of the best-written and most important volumes on the history of psychology in recent years, yet it remains relatively unknown in North America. It was invaluable as our guide to understanding the development of an everyday psychological sensibility in England in the first half of the 20th century. L. S. Hearnshaw's *Shaping of Modern Psychology* (1987) was useful for its coverage of British psychology. Martin Roiser (2001) was our source for the social psychology technique of the Mass-Observation project. Psychology at Cambridge in this period has a fascinating history. We relied on the work of Alan Collins (2006), Alan Costall (1992), Elizabeth Johnston (2001), and Adrian Wooldridge (1994) and the indispensable work of Nikolas Rose (1989) for our text. The profile of psychology at Cambridge provided by Frederic Bartlett himself in 1937 was extremely helpful, as was the description of the Industrial Health Research Board in the work of R. S. F. Schilling (1944). Elizabeth Valentine's biography of Edgell (2001) was inspiring and gave us another view of psychology in this period.

Chapter 9
TIMELINE 1880–1970
(In 25-year increments)

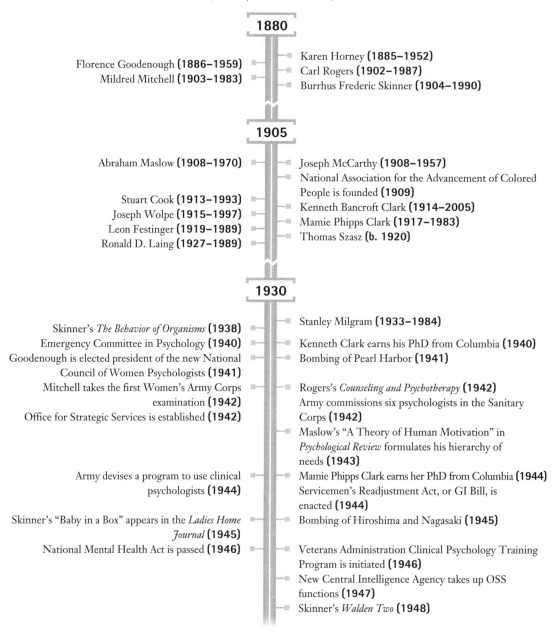

1880

Florence Goodenough **(1886–1959)**
Mildred Mitchell **(1903–1983)**

Karen Horney **(1885–1952)**
Carl Rogers **(1902–1987)**
Burrhus Frederic Skinner **(1904–1990)**

1905

Abraham Maslow **(1908–1970)**

Stuart Cook **(1913–1993)**
Joseph Wolpe **(1915–1997)**
Leon Festinger **(1919–1989)**
Ronald D. Laing **(1927–1989)**

Joseph McCarthy **(1908–1957)**
National Association for the Advancement of Colored People is founded **(1909)**
Kenneth Bancroft Clark **(1914–2005)**
Mamie Phipps Clark **(1917–1983)**
Thomas Szasz **(b. 1920)**

1930

Skinner's *The Behavior of Organisms* **(1938)**
Emergency Committee in Psychology **(1940)**
Goodenough is elected president of the new National Council of Women Psychologists **(1941)**
Mitchell takes the first Women's Army Corps examination **(1942)**
Office for Strategic Services is established **(1942)**

Army devises a program to use clinical psychologists **(1944)**

Skinner's "Baby in a Box" appears in the *Ladies Home Journal* **(1945)**
National Mental Health Act is passed **(1946)**

Stanley Milgram **(1933–1984)**

Kenneth Clark earns his PhD from Columbia **(1940)**
Bombing of Pearl Harbor **(1941)**

Rogers's *Counseling and Psychotherapy* **(1942)**
Army commissions six psychologists in the Sanitary Corps **(1942)**
Maslow's "A Theory of Human Motivation" in *Psychological Review* formulates his hierarchy of needs **(1943)**
Mamie Phipps Clark earns her PhD from Columbia **(1944)**
Servicemen's Readjustment Act, or GI Bill, is enacted **(1944)**
Bombing of Hiroshima and Nagasaki **(1945)**

Veterans Administration Clinical Psychology Training Program is initiated **(1946)**
New Central Intelligence Agency takes up OSS functions **(1947)**
Skinner's *Walden Two* **(1948)**

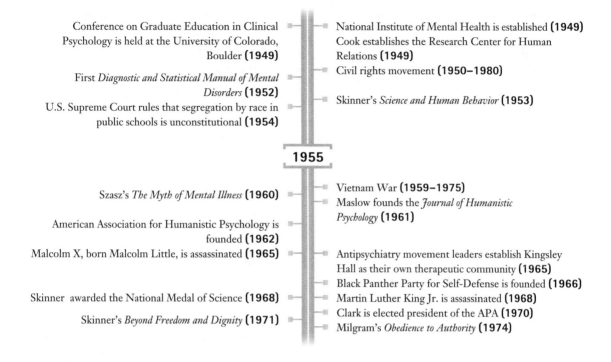

Conference on Graduate Education in Clinical Psychology is held at the University of Colorado, Boulder **(1949)**

First *Diagnostic and Statistical Manual of Mental Disorders* **(1952)**

U.S. Supreme Court rules that segregation by race in public schools is unconstitutional **(1954)**

National Institute of Mental Health is established **(1949)**

Cook establishes the Research Center for Human Relations **(1949)**

Civil rights movement **(1950–1980)**

Skinner's *Science and Human Behavior* **(1953)**

1955

Szasz's *The Myth of Mental Illness* **(1960)**

American Association for Humanistic Psychology is founded **(1962)**

Malcolm X, born Malcolm Little, is assassinated **(1965)**

Skinner awarded the National Medal of Science **(1968)**

Skinner's *Beyond Freedom and Dignity* **(1971)**

Vietnam War **(1959–1975)**

Maslow founds the *Journal of Humanistic Psychology* **(1961)**

Antipsychiatry movement leaders establish Kingsley Hall as their own therapeutic community **(1965)**

Black Panther Party for Self-Defense is founded **(1966)**

Martin Luther King Jr. is assassinated **(1968)**

Clark is elected president of the APA **(1970)**

Milgram's *Obedience to Authority* **(1974)**

THE GOLDEN AGE OF AMERICAN PSYCHOLOGY

In a posture of scientific detachment and indifference, a truly relevant and serious social science cannot ask to be taken seriously by a society desperately in need of moral and empirical guidance in human affairs.

—Kenneth B. Clark, *Dark Ghetto*, 1965

INTRODUCTION

We begin this chapter with a discussion of the impact of World War II on the field of American psychology. Psychologists' involvement in World War II not only provided abundant professional opportunities but also changed the character of postwar psychology, its relationship to the state, and its relationship to society in deep and far-reaching ways.

Sociologist–historian Nikolas Rose has argued that the experience of war transformed how psychologists subsequently conceptualized and intervened in individual and social life, thus changing how subjectivity itself was both governed and experienced (1985). From human engineering to human factors research, to advanced systems for selection and classification, to interventions for the trauma of combat, psychologists built on their war experiences to shape postwar American life in innumerable ways. The United States's involvement in World War II had a transformative impact on American psychology, which in turn shaped psychology's relationship to post–World War II society. Through the connections made with government agencies, funding for psychological science applied to wartime needs created enduring bonds between psychologists and federal agencies. These connections laid the foundation for psychologists to participate in the immense growth in federal funding of science and practice in the postwar period and then to offer unprecedented levels and types of services to eager consumers.

The leading psychological organization in the United States, the American Psychological Association (APA), was reorganized during the war to incorporate more applied psychologists. Military service needs pulled many psychologists into clinical work with combat-stressed soldiers, work that had long been the province of medicine and competing professional groups such as psychiatrists. This demand helped facilitate the development of clinical psychology, which became the leading field in psychology after the war at the impetus of federal mental health policy makers. The first part of this chapter examines the experiences of psychologists leading up to and during World War II. We then turn to the war's impact on the field in the immediate postwar years and explore what has been termed the "golden age" of Psychology.

PREPARING FOR WAR

As historian James Capshew has noted, "The war launched American psychologists on a highly visible trajectory as cultural authorities on the human psyche" (1999, p. 6). If World War I caught American psychology unprepared, the same cannot be said of its readiness for World War II.

Partly because of their previous experiences, and partly because of the more developed state of the field and the more immediate involvement of the United States in the Second World War, American psychologists mobilized efficiently and were ready to offer a range of services to contribute to the war effort. With a record of war experience, they also had less trouble convincing the military of their potential usefulness. The APA and the American Association for Applied Psychology (AAAP) each struck emergency committees soon after Adolf Hitler invaded Poland in September 1939, when Britain and France declared war on Germany. A few months later, the committees were combined into one joint committee. The chairman of this committee, Walter Miles (1885–1978), suggested that the National Research Council (NRC) sponsor a conference on psychology and government service to help unify Psychology's war efforts, and in August 1940, this meeting was held in Washington, DC. Representatives from six of Psychology's largest national organizations were invited to attend: the aforementioned APA and AAAP, the Psychometric Society, the Society for the Psychological Study of Social Issues, the Society of Experimental Psychologists, and Section I (Psychology) of the American Association for the Advancement of Science. One important outcome of this meeting was that an interorganizational advisory group, christened the Emergency Committee in Psychology (ECP), was formed to provide national level coordination and oversight of psychology's involvement in the war. Committee members included 10 prominent psychologists representing each of the national groups, as well as several members at large. Karl Dallenbach (1887–1971) of Cornell University chaired the committee. Notably, all were men.

THE NATIONAL COUNCIL OF WOMEN PSYCHOLOGISTS

This all-male committee did not go unnoticed by several prominent women psychologists who, like their male colleagues, were interested in contributing their services to the war effort. When it became clear that the all-male ECP was unprepared and unwilling to involve women psychologists in their activities, about 30 women members of the AAAP confronted Robert Brotemarkle (b. 1892), the AAAP representative to ECP, with their concerns. Although sympathetic, Brotemarkle told the group to be patient and reassured them that eventually plans would be made to include them in the subcommittees and activities of the ECP. In the meantime, they were reminded that they could volunteer their services to the war effort and "keep the home fires burning." Although patronized, the women waited in good faith.

When, almost two years later, nothing had been done to include them in Psychology's mobilization, a group of about 50 New York female psychologists began meeting to discuss how they could use their professional skills in the national emergency. In November, a subgroup of these women met in Columbia University psychologist Alice Bryan's (1902–1992) Manhattan apartment to draw up a charter for a national organization of women psychologists. Although the ECP then formed a subcommittee to investigate women's roles in the war, it was too little, too late. On December 8, 1941, one day after news of the bombing of Pearl Harbor, the National Council of Women Psychologists (NCWP) was formed. Florence Goodenough (1886–1959), a highly respected research psychologist, was selected as president. Although not particularly sympathetic to the group's gender-based agenda, Goodenough was willing to lend her name to an organization that would apply its members' expertise to relevant problems. By the middle of 1942, 234 doctoral-level women psychologists had joined the NCWP.

From its inception, some tension occurred within the group over its objectives. Although fully aware that they were being edged out of military positions because of their sex and that they were not being invited to fill the academic positions that their male colleagues were leaving

FIGURE 9.1   Florence Goodenough
Courtesy of the Archives of the History of American Psychology, University of Akron, Akron, OH.

vacant, women were still reluctant to organize the NCWP around issues of professional discrimination. They were sensitive to being perceived as a special interest group at a time of national emergency. Male psychologists and members of the ECP amplified this sensitivity by denying that sex discrimination existed in psychology and suggesting that, in drawing attention to gender issues in a time of war, women either were being self-indulgent or were undermining their status as scientists by highlighting their special status as women. For scientists, many argued, pure merit should determine professional success. Nonetheless, despite this ambivalence over their proper aims, the formation of the NCWP marked the first time women had come together as a professional group to work toward professional advancement. Whether they actually achieved this advancement is debatable.

The members of the NCWP decided to focus their efforts on civilian work at the community level. In cooperation with local agencies, they provided psychological testing for local selective service boards, coordinated

childcare for working parents, trained nursery school workers, and assisted in the selection of women officer candidates, to name a few activities. Members also gave public lectures and compiled educational materials to help solve community problems engendered by the war. Thus, although effective and busy on the home front, the NCWP gave up its attempts to lobby for more women in the War Department and was unable to place women in academic and clinical positions vacated by their male colleagues. Their efforts left largely untouched the division between the separate spheres of psychological work for women and men that emerged before the war.

A notable exception to this trend of women's exclusion from the masculine sphere of war work was the experience of Mildred Mitchell (1903–1983). Before the war, Mitchell worked for the Minnesota State Bureau of Psychological Services. In 1942, she took the first Women's Army Corps examination offered in the state. When she learned she would have to wait before being called up by the army, she approached the navy and was allowed to enlist as a lieutenant, even though her male peers were commissioned as lieutenant commanders. Undeterred, Mitchell practiced clinical and personnel psychology during the war and was subsequently able to leverage her war experience into several senior psychologist positions in the Veterans Administration (now the Department of Veterans Affairs; VA). Her accomplishments indicate both the importance of war work for subsequent professional advancement and the relative rarity of her experience. By the end of the war, fewer than 40 women psychologists had served in the American armed forces, and only 20 were employed as psychologists. By comparison, more than 1,000 of their male counterparts had served.

WAR SERVICE

Psychology was deployed in the service of World War II in literally hundreds of ways. These were watershed years for psychology in many parts of the world, and several historians have written about the impact of war work on the character of psychology and its relationship to the state, both during and after wartime. In the United States, personnel selection and classification issues were again central to psychology's functions. Industrial and consulting psychologist Walter Van Dyke Bingham (1880–1952), who had served on the Committee on the Classification of Personnel in World War I, quickly emerged as a leader in this area. Appointed head of the World War II Committee on the Classification of Military Personnel, Bingham and his committee developed the Army General Classification Test (AGCT), which became the primary personnel selection tool throughout the war. In an attempt to sidestep the controversies surrounding intelligence testing in World War I, the AGCT was presented as a test of general learning ability, which would be influenced by *both* inborn ability and educational experience. It was constructed to be as sensible, practical, and nonthreatening as possible, consisting of 50 items assessing vocabulary, arithmetic, and block counting. It was deemed a valid tool for selecting men for specialized training and was administered in unprecedented numbers. By the end of the war, about 9 million men had taken the AGCT.

A somewhat more specialized, and certainly more covert, personnel selection procedure was developed by psychologists working for the Office for Strategic Services (OSS). The OSS, a precursor to the Central Intelligence Agency (CIA), had employed a small number of psychologists, such as Robert Tryon (1901–1967) of the University of California, since 1942. In 1943, staff became interested in using assessment techniques to select men suitable for intelligence work and formed a planning group, which included Tryon, to establish a special assessment unit for this purpose. The unit was formed in late 1943 and featured six psychologists, including the dynamic Henry Murray (1893–1988). In the 1930s, Murray had developed the well-known projective personality test,

the Thematic Apperception Test, with Christiana Morgan (1897–1967), and was the director of the Harvard University Psychological Clinic (see Chapter 7). The assessment procedures developed by the OSS assessors reflected Murray's commitment to understanding the whole person and diverged significantly from a strict reliance on objective paper-and-pencil tests. Although men did fill out lengthy personal history and demographical questionnaires and completed other objective and projective personality tests, the majority of the assessment consisted of situational challenges conducted over a 3-day period. Potential secret agents were put through a simulated enemy interrogation, were asked to build a structure with the help of two troublesome confederates, and took part in various other stress- and frustration-inducing tasks. Some of these methods were imported and adapted from the methods employed by the German military.

Psychologists were also involved in a lucrative project to help train aircraft pilots. Funded by the Civil Aeronautics Authority and coordinated by the NRC, this project focused on selecting the most capable men to receive pilot training but also addressed the issues of performance under stress, measurement of successful learning, and instruments for selection and classification. A novel arrangement was forged between scientists and the military: Whereas, in the past, the government had always provided its own laboratories and scientists, in this project the work was meted out to various university laboratories across the country in a loosely coordinated network that received little direct oversight from military authorities.

Human factors psychology also developed during the war. The design of increasingly complicated weapon systems, tanks, and aircraft brought with it a higher probability of human error, the costs of which were both deadly and expensive. The Army Air Forces (now the U.S. Air Force), after experiencing several accidents in which pilots crash-landed their planes because they mistook the landing gear instrumentation for the wing flap adjustments, approached psychologists to conduct research on how best to design instruments and consoles so as to reduce the possibility of human error. Psychologist William Jenkins was assigned to this task and, in a series of experiments, identified eight knob shapes that proved to be error free. Psychologists designed altimeters that were easier to read and bombsights that produced fewer errors in visual judgment. After the war, human factors psychologists continued to work for the military and on military contracts administered by the Human Resources Research Organization, as well as for private industry.

As historians Ellen Herman and Donald Napoli have discussed, most psychologists involved in designing and executing these programs felt that they were both making a patriotic contribution and advancing science and psychology (Herman, 1995; Napoli, 1981). Few called into question the aims of the military or the ethics of the work. However, after the bombing of Hiroshima and Nagasaki in 1945, Murray, for one, became an ardent pacifist; recommended the immediate dissolution of the OSS; and strenuously criticized the establishment of the CIA. Well before this, Gordon Allport (1897–1967) reminded his colleagues that although psychology might benefit from the war, the nation would not necessarily benefit from the kind of psychology practiced in the service of the war. Inevitably, relationships among individual researchers, private universities, and government agencies were being transformed as psychologists (and many other social scientists) received large-scale funding from government bodies for the first time. This created a maelstrom of conflicting agendas that permanently changed the face of social science research in the ensuing decades.

PSYCHIATRIC CASUALTIES AND THE CONSOLIDATION OF CLINICAL PSYCHOLOGY

The area in which psychologists perhaps achieved their most influential professional advancement, however, was in the clinical treatment of soldiers suffering from battle fatigue or combat neurosis. As the war progressed and ever more men entered combat, the number of psychiatric casualties increased. Psychological difficulties were initially attributed to personality defects or personal weakness, and many men were simply diagnosed as unfit to serve and were discharged. Soon, army psychiatrists could not keep up with the demand for their services, and psychiatric wards filled to overflowing. In 1942, the surgeon general of the army commissioned six psychologists in the Sanitary Corps and assigned them to army hospitals. It was not until 1944, however, that the army devised a systematic program to use clinical psychologists, many of whom were trained only in assessment and not in treatment or psychotherapy. In part, this change was necessitated by the increasing realization that the traditional method of dealing with combat soldiers' psychiatric problems, that is, diagnosis and discharge, was allowing too much manpower to slip away. The army reoriented its strategy to consist of treatment and redeployment and thus required many more mental health professionals to provide services. Psychologists were already working in the military and, despite their limited training in psychotherapy, were called in without much resistance by psychiatrists, who quickly began referring clients to ease their inflated caseloads. By 1945, 450 clinical psychologists were serving in the army, and they were spending an average of 25 percent of their time treating patients.

The postwar demand for mental health services on the domestic front, as returning veterans flooded VA hospitals, ensured that federal funding would continue to flow to training programs for clinical psychologists. It was in this context that training programs in clinical psychology were formalized, established, and proliferated. The context of this development, given clinical psychology's close alliance with the VA system, was important in shaping the nature of clinical psychology training and influenced the careers of hundreds of psychologists, many of whom were returning veterans themselves taking advantage of the education benefits conferred by the GI Bill.

GOLDEN AGE OF PSYCHOLOGY

The North American public became increasingly psychologically minded as the 20th century progressed. The appeal of psychology and the rise of the psychological expert in the 1950s and 1960s were grounded in the culture of post–World War II America. Especially for White middle-class Americans, links among the superficial normalcy of the 1950s, the reversion to traditional gender roles, the escalation of cold war fears, and a host of other factors facilitated a striking rise in the popularity of psychotherapy and dramatic increases in federal support for research and training in psychology by the VA and the National Institute of Mental Health (NIMH). These events were ultimately connected to the emergence of the human potential movement in the mental health professions and the rise of a counterculture in the 1960s.

We begin this section with a brief overview of American cultural and social life in the 15 or so years after the end of World War II. This sets the stage for the discussion of the role of federal policy makers and the impact of their decision to greatly increase funding for mental health research and training. The chapter then moves to brief accounts of the work of Burrhus Frederic Skinner, the humanistic psychology movement, and postwar social psychology. We show in each of these accounts how the impressive growth of Psychology was intimately linked to developments in postwar North American culture.

The critical context for the development of Psychology after the war was the emergence of mental health as a purchasable commodity in the eyes of the public. American consumerism rapidly expanded after the end of World War II.

An economic resurgence occurred, and the population growth now called the baby boom began. The growth of the population and the market economy profoundly affected American life. The growth of the suburbs was phenomenal as couples, many of them military veterans' families, pursued the American dream of homeownership. The new prosperity after the war made life seem glamorous again after years of economic depression and the rationing of consumer goods during the war. In many ways, this is when the role of consumer became the critical component of American identity.

The new postwar prosperity and its baby boom led to an increased demand for housing. Many Americans began to speak of the **good life**, measured by the purchase of an individual home in a neighborhood, often far from the cramped urban spaces of the previous generation. "Cookie-cutter" suburbs, such as Levittown on Long Island, New York, sprang up around many American cities. Better living through consumption became the norm for middle-class Americans. Their new suburban homes were filled with gadgets of every kind: toasters, vacuum cleaners, electric irons, electric mixers, electric shoe shine kits, and preeminently, the television set. The home was reorganized around television; its possession and use created a new discourse about family togetherness and domestic values. This was modernity for postwar Americans. The power to purchase household aids gave the American family a sense of technological mastery and everyday convenience greater than any it had experienced before.

Despite the creature comforts of the good life, anxiety was a reality for many Americans in this era. The sources of this anxiety were many, from the cold war and its threat of nuclear annihilation, to the pervasive threat of Communism and its sympathizers hyped by Senator Joseph McCarthy of Wisconsin, to the fear of juvenile delinquency among their own children. Racial oppression and the growing struggle to end it were the concern of African Americans and many of their White allies. Many women, after experiencing a greater freedom during the war as they served the war effort on the home front through defense work and other useful occupations, were again expected to conform to White middle-class norms regarding the authority of the male in the household. Millions experienced this regression as numbing and demeaning but found it difficult to challenge. For men, a widespread fear was that White American middle-class men were becoming too conformist and losing their masculinity, as historian Elizabeth Watkins has shown (2008).

In this era, too, new drugs, such as Miltown and Valium, were developed and initially marketed as "minor" tranquilizers to anxious men in gray flannel suits, to use novelist Sloan Wilson's title of a popular novel of the era. When criticism of such use arose, pharmaceutical companies redirected their marketing strategy to target women. Such drugs became "mother's little helpers." Given these anxieties, perhaps it is not surprising that many middle-class Americans got what one scholar called the "suburban jitters" (Spigel, 1992). In addition to the use of tranquilizers, psychological help became, in this context, an attractive option to help deal with the jitters. At precisely this cultural moment, psychological ideas came to the forefront of popular culture.

In the first 20 years after World War II, psychoanalysis reached its peak of popularity and cultural influence in America. Psychoanalytic ideas seemed to be everywhere in popular culture—in movies, books, magazines, even comic books. However, psychoanalysis ultimately did not prove to be a good fit with middle-class culture. Its bleak view of human nature, and its rather limited promise that the patient might be able to move from misery only to common unhappiness as a result of treatment, was not attractive to many who tried it. Nevertheless, psychoanalysis created the cultural opening for psychological therapies.

Everyday Americans did not make fine distinctions among psychological ideas. Talking about one's problems to a professional became

desirable as a way to deal with the problems of everyday living. The new clinical psychologists that we discuss later were in a position to take advantage of the public's eagerness for psychological expertise. In a cultural moment marked by a strong consumer ethic, mental health became another commodity, purchasable through paid sessions with a mental health professional. These professionals were increasingly clinical psychologists, not psychoanalysts.

These cultural and social processes reflected the continuing psychologization of North American culture. But it was not the emergence of a psychologically minded consumer culture alone that created the **commoditization of mental health**. Other large-scale forces were also at work.

POSTWAR INITIATIVES FOR TRAINING MENTAL HEALTH PROFESSIONALS

Policy makers in the postwar period became concerned about the nation's mental health and the perceived need to keep the United States competitive in the world. Their concern translated into funds for training mental health professionals and conducting psychological research. The amount of such funding increased exponentially between 1948 and 1968. This had two important consequences. First, it led to the dramatic expansion of research topics far beyond the prewar emphasis on learning theory. While many of the funds came through the NIMH, ostensibly to produce knowledge about mental health and illness, almost any project that related to human behavior and social functioning received support. This resulted in a golden age of psychological research, an era when available funds increased significantly each year and the field was characterized by a rich eclecticism of research topics and theoretical developments. Second, the programs and funding for training more mental health professionals remade the field of clinical psychology, as we detail later. In this part

FIGURE 9.2   Cover of one issue of *Psychoanalysis*, the comic book
Collection of the authors.

of the chapter, we discuss the expansion of research, training, and practice and the rise in the cultural authority of the psychologist in the postwar era.

During World War II, the number of psychiatric casualties among American soldiers alone was high: 2 million men were rejected for military service, and during the fighting 500,000 psychiatric casualties occurred, most of whom suffered from what was then called war neurosis or combat fatigue. Even before the war was over, policy makers in Washington were concerned about what the high rate of psychiatric casualties might mean for the public. Did the high rate indicate that the mental health of Americans was fragile? Was America as a country on the verge of an epidemic of mental disorder?

The use of atomic weaponry against Japan, while it brought the war to a quicker end, also raised fears at home. What if America's enemies had such a weapon and decided to use it against the United States? A great deal of anxiety arose among Americans in the immediate postwar years, mixed with relief that the war was over. In this potentially volatile mix, policy makers sought programs that would prevent or ameliorate mental problems among both the military veterans of the war and the public. In 1946, the federal government began programs to meet these goals through funding mental health research, providing funds to train more mental health providers, and creating a mix of direct mental health services. We give brief accounts of two of those programs: the VA Clinical Psychology Training Program and the funding initiatives of the NIMH.

The success of these programs owed a great deal to the Servicemen's Readjustment Act (1944), better known as the GI Bill. The bill provided funding for the education of the nation's veterans. Such funding created the conditions for the rapid growth and expansion of higher education in the postwar period. Over the next few years, more than 6 million veterans enrolled in America's colleges and universities. This was the beginning of the democratization of higher education in the United States. The field of psychology was one of the most attractive of all university and graduate programs. When policy makers made funding available through the GI Bill and the VA and the NIMH, they created the conditions for the accelerated growth of psychology as a science and profession in the United States. As we show in the next chapter, the rapid growth of psychology also had important implications for psychology around the world.

CLINICAL PSYCHOLOGY AND THE VA

Approximately 16 million American veterans were discharged back into civilian life in the first three years after the war. Many of these veterans needed medical care, as well as help reestablishing their lives. Numerous veterans also needed help dealing with mental problems. These responsibilities belonged to the VA.

In 1946, within a year of the war's end and amid the general discharge of soldiers from active military service, the VA reported that nearly 60 percent of its hospital beds were occupied by veterans, mostly from the just-concluded conflict, suffering from mental illness, thus crowding out patients with other medical problems. The VA medical and psychiatric services were also grossly understaffed, often due to low pay, poor working conditions, and low morale.

The VA made two responses to the crisis. One, it established a large network of mental hygiene clinics across the country where veterans could go to get help with various complaints on an outpatient basis. However, these clinics simply did not have enough trained personnel—psychiatrists, clinical psychologists, or clinical social workers—to meet the demand for services. One partial solution was group psychotherapy. Two, the VA reorganized its medical services to include a Neuropsychiatry Division responsible for the coordination of psychiatry, neurology, and psychology to handle the enormous demand for mental health services. To increase its supply of trained mental health professionals, the VA implemented training programs to increase the number of psychiatrists, clinical psychologists, psychiatric nurses, and clinical social workers.

It was in this context that the VA Clinical Psychology Training Program was initiated in 1946. James Grier Miller (1916–2002), a Harvard-trained physician and psychologist, was put in charge of the Clinical Psychology Training Program. Miller worked with the leadership of the APA to establish training standards for this new kind of clinical psychologist. Recall that before World War II the number of clinical psychologists was small and the bulk of their work was linked to assessment of school-related problems; few were actively engaged in psychotherapeutic work. As we noted in an earlier chapter, the APA had historically been uninterested in dealing with issues like training standards or ethics for clinical and other applied psychologists. With the reorganization of the APA during the war, in which the AAAP had been incorporated into the APA, the number of applied psychologists, including clinical, was growing and the need to address practical issues of training and education was recognized. As historian of psychology Ingrid Farreras (2005) has shown, the APA committed to establishing training and education standards for accrediting clinical psychology programs reluctantly and under a great deal of pressure. As much as any other factor, the scientists who led the APA were worried that unless high training standards were established, this new type of psychologist might end up bringing discredit to the entire field of Psychology. This led to the agreement between the APA and the VA to make the doctoral degree the entry-level criterion for clinical psychology. To have accreditation criteria for clinical psychology training programs in place in time to accept students, the suggestions for training clinical psychologists promulgated by David Shakow (1942) were used as a guide. We discuss the formal development of the scientist–practitioner model and the contributions of Shakow later.

In autumn 1946, the first group of 225 students began their training within the VA program at 22 universities. From the beginning, the students received a mix of classroom instruction and hands-on clinical training. The training was a mixture of standard academic work in experimental psychology and on-site exposure to clinical work under the supervision of (mostly) master's level psychologists who had made their careers in the VA. Each year, the number of psychologists in the VA program increased so that by the early 1950s, when the first students began to graduate with PhDs in clinical psychology, the field of American psychology was beginning to change. The VA clinical psychology program was one of the key factors in remaking American psychology into a science-based profession. Approximately 36,000 clinical psychologists were trained in the program from 1946 to 2005.

NATIONAL INSTITUTE OF MENTAL HEALTH

The National Mental Health Act of 1946 created the NIMH as one of the National Institutes of Health (NIH), located in the Washington, DC, suburb of Bethesda, Maryland. Psychiatrist Robert Felix (1904–1990) was the first institute director. By 1960, the NIMH was the dominant force in mental health in the United States. Along with the VA program, the NIMH combination of financial support for research and massive funding for training mental health professionals helped fuel the growth of psychology to such an extent that one wag quipped in the early 1960s that if psychology continued to grow at the pace it was then on, by 2010 every person in the world would be a psychologist. The NIMH effort not only spurred the growth of psychology but also greatly increased the role of the federal government in the daily lives of its citizens. We noted in earlier chapters that one reason for the success of the discipline of Psychology was its usefulness in social management; in postwar America, this role was magnified. As Psychology became identified with the field of mental health, it sacrificed much of its liberatory potential in the service of the maintenance of social order.

The NIMH as a government agency played several roles. One of the mandates, as we mentioned, was to increase the number of mental health professionals. Taking its cue from the VA, the NIMH targeted psychiatry, clinical psychology, psychiatric nursing, and clinical social work as the chosen fields. The proportion of funds was divided so that psychiatry received 40 percent and the other three professions received 20 percent each of the allocated funds (after all, the NIMH was run by psychiatrists). Money for training was provided in several ways; fellowships for individual students were central, but the NIMH also provided money to departments to hire faculty in areas most relevant to training. Over the first 20 years of funding (1948–1967), the NIMH provided $58.89 million for clinical psychology training; several million more went into stipends for counseling and a few other fields of psychology. In this period, 9,803 students received training stipends in clinical psychology alone (Schneider, 2005). Along with the VA training program, the NIMH training funds helped create the dramatic growth of clinical psychology. The net effect was to make the field of Psychology, especially clinical psychology, particularly appealing to potential graduate students.

The other major impact of the NIMH on training was its financial support of the Conference on Graduate Education in Clinical Psychology held at the University of Colorado, Boulder, in late summer 1949. What emerged from this conference was a model that emphasized the importance of training clinical psychologists to be scientists first, practitioners second, thus the famous **scientist–practitioner model** of clinical psychology. The model was developed from the earlier template laid out by Shakow in 1942 and then expanded by the Committee on Training in Clinical Psychology, led by Shakow. By the time of the Boulder conference, Shakow was the major psychology consultant to the NIMH, which gave his ideas enormous influence both with that institute and with the APA, the conference sponsor. At the conference, 73 psychologists participated,

FIGURE 9.3 David Shakow
Courtesy of the Archives of the History of American Psychology, University of Akron, Akron, OH.

with representatives from all APA-accredited training programs, plus representatives from the NIMH and the APA (Raimy, 1950). As noted, the APA leadership was intensely concerned to see that the emphasis on clinical training did not diminish the status of experimental psychology or impair psychology's standing with the public. Thus, the emphasis was placed on the scientist side of the model.

CHALLENGES TO THE NEW CLINICAL PSYCHOLOGY

The scientist–practitioner model or, "Boulder model," as it is typically called, smoothed the way for more universities to establish clinical psychology training programs. However, the model was not without controversy or criticism. Nor was it always honored by the psychology departments at American universities. By the mid-1950s, reports began to circulate of clinical psychology graduate programs that, in fact, offered little by way of clinical training and even sought to diminish the appearance of doing so. Some psychologists complained that the model was overly medicalized; by that they meant that symptoms were all seen as within the person, ignoring the role of such social–structural elements as socioeconomic class, poverty, and systematic bias against women and racial and ethnic minorities. Thus, a person trained as a clinical psychologist would potentially only see the problems as individual or intrapsychic and might ignore the structural problems. In this sense, then, some saw psychologists as servants of the status quo, helping maintain unequal and discriminatory social systems. Alternatives began to be developed almost before the ink was dry on the proceedings of the Boulder conference. In Chapter 12, we discuss some of the changes.

Psychology versus Psychiatry

The practitioners also engaged in a long-running battle with psychiatrists over recognition as an independent mental health profession. The battle was primarily about cultural authority, that is, which profession was entitled to the privileged position of mental health expert and who was best qualified to deliver the services that would facilitate a return to mental health. The conflict was intense at times, as psychiatrists sought to have psychotherapy restricted to those holding a medical degree and to prevent psychologists from gaining status as a regulated profession through licensure. The struggle over who owned psychotherapy was particularly intense because psychotherapy itself defied easy definition. It was difficult for psychologists and psychiatrists alike to claim that they were the superior provider of a service no one could define and even

fewer knew how to train for. Ultimately, the psychotherapy pie proved big enough for both professions to claim a healthy wedge. The battle over these issues was fought nationally through the professional organizations, as well as state by state, for more than three decades. Eventually, psychologists gained licensure in every state by the 1980s.

Antipsychiatry and the Treatment of Mental Disorders

A challenge to both psychiatry and clinical psychology came from a somewhat unexpected source beginning in the late 1950s, a movement that came to be called antipsychiatry. Although we focus on the North American scene, antipsychiatry was a movement that developed in many European countries, perhaps having its most effective expression in Italy.

If the 1960s are to be viewed as a reaction against the oppressive conformity and restrictive values of the 1950s, nowhere is this reaction more pronounced than in the antipsychiatry movement that also emerged in this period. In 1960, libertarian psychiatrist Thomas Szasz (b. 1920) published *The Myth of Mental Illness* in which he forcefully railed against the concept of mental illness as analogous to physical disease. He argued that attributing deviant behaviors to some malfunctioning inner mind only stigmatizes the sufferer, gives power to the psychiatrist, and deprives those labeled mentally ill of individual freedom and dignity of responsibility for their own actions. He believed that there could be diseases of the brain that would give rise to bizarre thoughts and behaviors but that these should be regarded as physical diseases, not mental illness. He believed that most bizarre behavior arose from real problems in living and that psychotherapy could be effective not in treating mental illness but in helping people explore these problems in living. He viewed medical psychiatry as pseudoscience based on the unproved and unprovable myth of mental illness. One

FIGURE 9.4 R. D. Laing

of Szasz's contemporaries in the antipsychiatry movement was Scottish psychiatrist Ronald D. Laing (1927–1989). Laing believed that to be sane in an insane world was itself a sign of pathology and that many people who received the label "schizophrenia" were reacting quite justifiably and understandably, perhaps even creatively, to maddening circumstances. Consistent with other theorists of the time, Laing suggested that psychotic breakdown was the result of constant exposure to confusing, often irreconcilable messages from important figures about how one should be or was versus how one actually was. He characterized this as a constant state of "mystification." Like Szasz, he viewed medical models of mental illness as shams, whose only function was to impart power to the psychiatrist and to control people who acted in ways that were considered troublesome or deviant. In 1965, after studying for several years at the Tavistock Clinic in London, he joined with colleagues to set up a therapeutic community called Kingsley Hall in which patients and therapists lived together. Sexual experimentation and hallucinogenic drugs featured prominently in the community, and Laing argued against the use of psychopharmaceutical agents to control psychosis. Like Szasz, he did not argue against the need for intervention, but he viewed biological intervention as inappropriate for essentially psychological and behavioral

problems. Although most contemporary mental health professionals reject the claims of Szasz and Laing regarding the nature of mental illness, it is important to consider how psychiatric labels continue to confer power on the medical establishment and stigmatize those who receive them.

DIVERSIFYING PSYCHOLOGICAL RESEARCH IN THE GOLDEN AGE

The impact of the large-scale funding initiatives of the VA and the NIMH was not restricted to clinical psychology and its practice. Psychological research greatly expanded with the monies provided by government agencies. Although we focus on the VA and the NIMH, other federal funding sources included the Office of Naval Research and the Department of Defense, while private philanthropies, especially the Ford Foundation, also made major contributions to research initiatives in psychology. The net result of this enormous investment in psychological science was a major expansion of the discipline in the number of psychologists and in the range of topics that psychologists investigated. We begin with research within the VA and then move to the broader results fostered by NIMH funding.

VA Clinical Research

The large numbers of soldiers who experienced psychiatric problems during the war and occupied 60 percent of the VA hospital beds after the war prompted the VA to incorporate research into its postwar plans in hopes of preventing mental breakdowns or at least reducing their severity. By the end of fiscal year 1948, four psychological research laboratories had been established in the VA. The neuropsychiatric (as it was called then) research emphasis began with evaluating the effects of lobotomies and other mental health treatments and was then extended into research on possible psychological factors in various disease states, including tuberculosis, cardiovascular disease, and other relevant areas, such as suicide. In the 1950s and 1960s, a critical focus for the VA was research on the new psychotropic medications.

One innovation of the VA was the use of a cooperative research paradigm. Since the many VA hospitals and clinics were all under one command, it became possible to plan and coordinate multisite investigations on one problem and then compare findings in the hope that this would result in better clinical treatment. Among the mental health personnel in VA settings, the psychologists were clearly the superior researchers, and they took the lead in the design, conduct, and analysis of the cooperative research programs.

A prominent example of the VA cooperative research programs is the research of psychologists in the then-new area of psychopharmacology during the 1950s and 1960s. This research helped establish the validity of the new drug treatments for various serious mental illnesses. The VA committed major financial and human resources to compare treatment effects of the new psychotropic drugs then coming on the market. Such comparisons were vital for improving clinical care. However, one unforeseen impact of the research was on the diagnostic and classification scheme of mental disorder. The behavioral outcomes focus of the research psychologists at the VA led to a revision of the older, more psychoanalytic scheme put forward in the first two editions of the American Psychiatric Association's *Diagnostic and Statistical Manual of Mental Disorders (DSM)*. By the third edition of the *DSM*, the disorders were increasingly described in terms of behaviors rather than unseen psychodynamics. This resulted in a lasting change in the way mental disorders were classified and diagnosed.

The NIMH and the Expansion of Research

The first NIMH director, Robert Felix, was guided by his belief that there should be no directives or constraints placed on the researchers who received NIMH funding. Felix argued that since we did not know the cause of most mental disorders or the most effective treatments, investigators should be free to pursue a topic wherever it led them. The product of Felix and the NIMH's philosophy was the golden age of psychological science, as the NIMH became the largest single funder of psychological research. This approach fit with the other programs of government funding of scientific research and helped create what scholars have called the beginning of big science; large-scale funding changed forever the scale and scope of scientific research in the United States. As we show, the resulting growth of American science, including psychology, had implications for the influence of American-style science around the world.

The U.S. Congress granted increasingly larger appropriations for the NIH for more than two decades after the end of the war, making it possible for an increasing number of grant applications, on a range of topics, to be funded. Evidently, so much money was available that even applications for studying ethnomusicology were funded. This was the funding atmosphere both for the clinical training programs discussed earlier and for the vast expansion of psychological research. Psychology, if it did not become big science, certainly became medium-sized science.

The expansion of research topics in psychology in these years was remarkable (see Table 9.1). As the United States came out of the war, the mainstream of academic psychology was still neobehavioristic. But an examination of the first 15 years of NIMH funding (1948–1963) of psychological research in the United States shows a steady expansion of research areas. While behavioral topics remained important and were well funded, now research programs on cognition, memory, computing, social psychology, psychotherapy research, and a range of nonlearning theory work on animal behavior garnered major funds and grew substantially in the number of investigators and influence in the field.

Table 9.1   Top Recipients of NIMH Research Funding, 1948–1963

Institution	Researcher	Project	Amount (in dollars)
Harvard University	Henry Murray	Competitive and cooperative social interaction	287,601
University of Michigan	Ronald Lippitt	Intercenter program on families, youth, and children	176,608
Clark University	Tamara Dembo	Mental development in palsy	238,616
University of Wisconsin	Harry Harlow	Social behavior of primates	524,350
Johns Hopkins University	Jerome Frank	Evaluation of group and individual psychotherapy	141,137
New York University	Isidor Chein	Drug addiction among minors	246,412
University of California	Richard Lazarus	Antecedents and consequences of psychological stress	191,779
Yale University	Neal Miller	Behavioral laws of motivation and conflict	532,200
University of Chicago	Carl Rogers	Process and facilitation of personality change	118,360
University of Illinois	Charles Osgood	Communication of information on mental health	219,329
Stanford University	Leonard Horowitz	Studies in verbal learning	230,239
Columbia University	James Bieri	Individual, social, and informational effects on judgment	122,693

We examine the growth of cognitive psychology and cognitive neuroscience in a later chapter. Here, we focus on the work of Skinner and show how his science, and increasingly his technology, of behavior fit with the cultural context of post–World War II America. We then discuss the growth of humanistic psychology and its corollary, humanistic psychotherapy. Finally, we focus on developments in social psychology, beginning with Kurt Lewin (1890–1947) and social action research and moving to a consideration of experimental social psychology.

B. F. Skinner, Culture, and Controversy

B. F. Skinner (1904–1990) remains one of the icons of 20th-century psychology. His name continues to be recognized around the world, and for a period during his lifetime, he was considered one of America's foremost scientists. He was awarded the National Medal of Science in 1968, only the second psychologist to receive this

distinction (Neal Miller, 1909–2002), received it in 1964). In the April 1970 issue of *Esquire* magazine, Skinner was named one of the "100 most important people in the world today," along with such diverse luminaries as Fidel Castro, Pablo Picasso, and Richard Nixon. In 1971, he received a Kennedy International Award for his role in founding the field of behavior modification, which was used to improve the lives of people with developmental disabilities. That same year he published his controversial book *Beyond Freedom and Dignity*, which appeared on the *New York Times* best-seller list for 26 weeks (Rutherford, 2000, 2003).

Skinner grew up in a small town in the state of Pennsylvania, where even as a child he was fascinated with ways to make everyday life easier by devising gadgets. During his undergraduate years, which he spent at Hamilton College in New York, he began to envision himself as a writer. After spending a postgraduate year attempting to write from his parents' attic, including a brief foray to Greenwich Village and then a tour of Europe, Skinner concluded that, at least as a writer, he had nothing important to say. In the course of his reading during that year, however, he encountered a review of John B. Watson's (1878–1958) *Behaviorism* by philosopher Bertrand Russell. Upon reading Watson and the newly translated works on conditioned reflexes by Russian physiologist Ivan Pavlov (1849–1936), Skinner decided to pursue graduate training in psychology at Harvard, where he enrolled in 1928. He earned his doctorate in 1931. Because of the Great Depression and the absence of jobs, after graduation Skinner remained at Harvard until 1936, first on a fellowship from the NRC and then as a member of the Harvard Society of Fellows. During this time, he refined his ideas on learning and eventually, in 1938, published *The Behavior of Organisms*, where he elaborated the distinction between respondent, or Pavlovian, classical conditioning and **operant conditioning**.

Operant psychology subsequently formed the core of his scientific and philosophical systems. The term "operant" referred to organisms operating on their environments to produce consequences. Skinner demonstrated that these consequences exerted powerful effects on behavior. Out of this work, he gave specialized meanings to everyday words, such as reinforcement and punishment. Much of his experimental work was conducted in specially designed operant chambers (popularly called "Skinner boxes") in which he precisely controlled and manipulated various aspects of an organism's environment to determine the effect on behavior. Although he worked with several species, including rats, he soon came to favor pigeons as a laboratory animal.

Skinner took a position at the University of Minnesota in 1936 and remained there until the end of World War II, in 1945. During the latter part of the war, Skinner became interested in making his own contribution to the war effort. Convinced that he could design a missile guidance system using the skills of his favorite laboratory animal and the principles of operant

psychology, he pitched his idea to government officials and received a $25,000 contract from the National Defense Research Committee in 1943. The money was administered through the General Mills Company in Minneapolis, and aided by the technical skills of General Mills engineers, Skinner and his coworkers undertook Project Pigeon. Although Skinner's group was able to train pigeons to guide missile devices reliably and accurately toward a target, his funds ran out before the project could be field tested. Unfortunately, the interest of government officials also ran out, and then the war ended. Although promising, the pigeon missile guidance system never came to fruition, but Skinner had had his first taste of the challenges of application.

Skinner left the University of Minnesota for the University of Indiana in 1945 and remained there until 1948. In 1945 he published a popular article titled "Baby in a Box: Introducing the Mechanical Baby Tender" in the *Ladies Home Journal*. Presented with a challenge by his wife, Yvonne, to make childcare easier as they anticipated the birth of their second daughter, Skinner designed and built a better crib. Christened the baby tender and then the **air crib**, it was an enclosed, temperature- and humidity-controlled space that allowed the baby to sleep unencumbered by clothes and blankets. The tender had a Plexiglas front that allowed the baby an unobstructed view of the surrounding environment. Among the many favorable features of the new crib was less laundry for the parents, as well as less exposure to noise and germs and more mobility for the baby. When Deborah Skinner was born, she acclimated easily to her ultramodern environment, and Burrhus Frederic Skinner decided to "go public" with his invention.

Reactions to the baby tender were mixed. Many readers expressed their concerns about the safety of the device and the potential for neglect inherent in the spectacle of a conveniently boxed baby. Tellingly, however, many readers praised the device as an improvement on the traditional crib and seemed more comfortable with the idea that advances in household technology that allowed for more control of the domestic sphere could extend to the nursery. As Skinner's biographer Daniel Bjork has written:

> It is ... important to underscore that Skinner's America, from graduate school at Harvard in the 1920s through the 1950s, not only accepted the automobile, the airplane, and the electrification of cities as progressive modernization; it assumed as a matter of course that humans could control their environment through the efforts of inventors and industrial scientists. (Bjork, 1996, p. 146)

With his article on the baby tender, Skinner was introduced to the American public (or at least readers of the *Ladies Home Journal*), for better or for worse, as a social inventor as well as a behavioral scientist.

In 1948, Skinner left Indiana for a position at Harvard, where he remained for the rest of his career. Upon his arrival at Harvard, he set up the Harvard Pigeon Laboratory where, under his directorship, dozens of students and colleagues conducted controlled laboratory experiments with various animals on schedules of reinforcement, discrimination, stimulus control, and many other topics. The research program he built at Harvard, coined "the experimental analysis of behavior," became an almost independent movement, parallel to psychology but not quite integrated into it. Nevertheless, Skinner was a major recipient of large federal grants, which enabled him to expand his laboratory and investigate a range of behavioral phenomena. They also allowed him to explore the applied potential of some of his ideas.

As we have shown, Skinner had long been fascinated by the technological possibilities of his work. Many scholars have analyzed his orientation in relation to the technological ideal of science espoused by one of his influences, early modern English philosopher–scientist Sir Francis Bacon (1561–1626). For Bacon, the essence of understanding nature was the ability

FIGURE 9.5 B. F. Skinner at Harvard around 1950

to control it. Skinner felt that he had conclusively demonstrated how behavior was completely controlled by environmental contingencies. It was therefore imperative, for Skinner, that we arrange these contingencies in ways that would best ensure the survival of the culture and the species. Early in his career, he played with some of these ideas in a fictional utopian novel, *Walden Two*, published in 1948 on the heels of his work with the baby tender. In creatively envisioning a sustainable society where human behavior was engineered through complex systems of positive reinforcement, Skinner tipped his hand as to the cause that would energize much of the latter half of his career: building a better world through behaviorism.

In the 1960s, Skinner devoted much of his time to educational issues. Convinced that he could use operant principles to improve on the practices of traditional teaching, he formulated an approach known as programmed instruction. At the heart of programmed instruction was the method of breaking large units of material into small incremental steps to be presented sequentially via a device know as a teaching machine. In this way, students would be reinforced immediately for the provision of correct answers by being able to progress through the program and could do so at their own pace. With such individualized instruction, Skinner believed that students could learn more in shorter amounts of time and experience less frustration and that teachers would be freed from the rote aspects of their job to work more intensely with individual students. As with the baby tender, the reception of the teaching machine was mixed. Embedded in the educational technology movement and Cold War fears of the late 1950s and 1960s, teaching by machine came either to be regarded as a necessary and welcome antidote to the perceived decline of the American education system or as another example of the mass conformity and social anomie of an increasingly technocratic and dehumanized world order. Again, Skinner appeared at the center of a heated cultural debate not entirely of his making.

In 1971, Skinner turned up the heat on this debate even further, reaching the pinnacle of his public acclaim (or notoriety) with the publication of *Beyond Freedom and Dignity*. In this book, he laid out some of his most pressing social concerns, along with a plea for the systematic adoption of the science and technology of behavior to address them. How can we have good government and a society in which war, poverty, environmental degradation, and other threats to human welfare are reduced or even eliminated? The answer, Skinner suggested, was to give up our antiquated, sentimental, belief in free will. Personal freedom, he argued, was an illusion. What mattered was to more effectively manage the contingencies present in the environment that each of us live in and that control everyday actions on individual and global scales all the time. He exhorted his readers to give up their unscientific, outdated belief in "autonomous man" and to embrace that all of our behavior is shaped not by an interior sense of freedom or dignity but by the contingencies in our environment that reward and punish us. His position generated intense controversy and vehement ad hominem attacks. He received many heated and angry letters comparing him to Adolf Hitler and Joseph Stalin, questioning his sanity, and accusing him of totalitarianism, among other evils. Since media loves controversy, Skinner was asked to appear on radio and television talk shows and was featured prominently in the popular press. Despite all of this attention, Skinner often felt that he was unable to convey his arguments effectively in the public arena. Whether he was effective or not, the content of his message was a difficult one for

most Americans to receive dispassionately. His arguments struck at the heart of what it meant to be not only an American but also a human.

After the furor over the book died down, Skinner gradually withdrew from public life and returned to his scholarly and professional pursuits. However, those who followed him took his principles and began to apply them to a range of human behavior problems in settings as diverse as classrooms, hospitals, prisons, and the workplace. **Behavior modification** programs were developed to improve classroom behavior and learning, to restore schizophrenic patients to functioning, and to rehabilitate juvenile delinquents and incarcerated criminals (Rutherford, 2009). Many of these programs were controversial themselves and catalyzed social and political debates about civil liberties, research ethics, and other policy issues, eventually affecting federal legislation concerning the treatment of human subjects in biomedical and behavioral research, which we discuss in Chapter 12. More positively, children with serious developmental disorders like autism, it was discovered, could be treated effectively with applied behavioral principles. Within a few years, applied behavior analysis was (and remains) the treatment of choice for autism. In the realm of clinical disorders, behavioral therapies, many of them operant based, proved successful in treating many disorders, such as attention deficit disorder and anxiety. Finally, applied behavior analysis for training animals for entertainment in settings like Disneyland, Sea World, and many other amusement parks became a lucrative occupation. Today, many pet owners are familiar with operant principles, whether Skinner himself has ever been mentioned or not.

Skinner's career, and his ongoing legacy, illustrate how psychology came to be perceived as useful by Americans. Skinner stands as an almost paradigmatic example of an *American* scientist, despite his "assault on some of the Western world's most prized ideals," as one journalist characterized his 1971 book (Stevens, 1971, p. 29). Inasmuch as Skinner was guided by an unerring faith in science and technology to solve the world's problems, and a profound (although perhaps idiosyncratic) spirit of meliorism and social progress, he was truly a product—and provocateur—of American values.

THE THIRD FORCE: HUMANISTIC PSYCHOLOGY CHALLENGES THE STATUS QUO

To understand how and why the **third force** of humanistic psychology emerged in the 1960s, we need to take a step back to the previous decade. As we noted earlier, in the 1950s American popular culture was infused with psychoanalysis. As increasing numbers of psychologists were trained to provide mental health services, many of them learned and practiced forms of psychodynamic therapy, the dominant theoretical orientation of psychiatry. They administered projective personality tests based on Freudian concepts and diagnosed their patients with the heavily psychoanalytically inflected *DSM*, first published in 1952.

Although dominant, psychoanalysis was not the only theoretical outlook and approach. During the 1950s, behavioral learning theorist Joseph Wolpe (1915–1997) proposed systematic desensitization, a technique based on classical conditioning, to treat fears and phobias. As the decade unfolded, Skinner's brand of behaviorism and the set of behavior change techniques based on his work—behavior modification—were also growing in use and influence, as we alluded to earlier. In 1953, Skinner published *Science and Human Behavior*, in which he made explicit his desire to extend the principles of behavior control discovered in the laboratory to human behavior, the design of cultures, and the remediation of social problems.

Both behaviorism and psychoanalysis, some psychologists argued, were based on a rigidly deterministic model of human nature. In psychoanalysis, patients were viewed as beholden to sexual and aggressive instincts, which unconsciously drove their behavior against their will. The best outcome of psychoanalytic therapy, so Sigmund Freud (1856–1939) wrote, was to convert misery to common unhappiness—not a particularly optimistic view of the human condition. Skinner's radical behaviorism refuted the existence of all internal agency and rejected free will and self-determination as causes of behavior, relegating all control of behavior to the environment. In his view, our current behavioral repertoires are governed by our past reinforcement histories. He suggested that the way to achieve a better world was to further manipulate the consequences that are already controlling our behavior to achieve prosocial ends. Although Skinner had utopian visions for a society built on principles of positive reinforcement, many of his readers regarded his mantra of prediction and control as decidedly dystopian.

Culturally, the 1950s have been cast, and were experienced by many, as an era of enforced conformity, fueled by McCarthyism and cold war fears. To be a patriotic American, one was advised to embrace traditional gender roles, consume an appropriate number of American-made products, and (especially in the case of many White, suburban housewives) quietly bury anxiety with tranquillizers, lunch hour martinis, and sometimes time on the Freudian couch. Adaptation, not challenge, was the order of the day, and both psychoanalysis and behaviorism appeared to fit hand in glove with this ethos.

Beginning in the 1950s, several psychologists reacted to the pessimism and determinism of psychoanalysis and behaviorism, and the social anomie of the era, by formulating an alternative theory of human nature that gained popularity as the decade progressed. Called the *third force* because it was an alternative to psychoanalysis and behaviorism, humanistic psychology posited that adaptation and adjustment to "normalcy" (rigidly defined) had obscured our ability to know our true needs and live authentically as humans. Humanistic psychologists suggested turning our attention back to those qualities that make us most human: creativity, agency, free will, intentionality, self-determination, imagination, and values. They rejected the determinism and pessimism of psychoanalytic and behaviorist theories and posited an essentially optimistic view of human nature in which all humans possessed innate capacities for growth.

Two of the most well-known developers of humanistic psychology in the United States were Carl Rogers (1902–1987), best known for formulating client-centered psychotherapy, and Abraham Maslow (1908–1970), who developed a hierarchy of needs and stressed self-actualization as the highest form of human development. Rogers actually began developing his ideas in the 1930s. He had had a fairly religious upbringing and was trained in both theology (at the Union Theological Seminary) and psychology (at Columbia's Teachers College). In the 1930s he began working with children in a child guidance clinic in Rochester, New York, and came to regard a nurturing and positive environment as the key element in fostering healthy development. Although not a striking insight in and of itself, Rogers extended this idea to the counseling situation, publishing *Counseling and Psychotherapy* in 1942. In this book, he recommended that counselors, instead of offering advice, be active listeners but in a nondirective way. Rogers believed that the best way to help people discern what their needs were, and to reorient them to the "organismic valuing process" from which they had become derailed, was to offer certain conditions consistently and thoroughly in the therapeutic relationship. He isolated the therapist conditions most likely to lead to growth in psychotherapy by meticulously recording and coding transcripts of unedited psychotherapy sessions. He was the first psychotherapy researcher to adopt this empirical approach, for which he received more than $118,000 in grant support from the NIMH in the mid-1950s. His work and that of psychiatrist–psychologist Jerome Frank (1910–2005) spawned the burgeoning field of psychotherapy process research that builds on his pioneering methods.

FIGURE 9.6   Photo of Carl Rogers
Courtesy of the Carl R. Rogers Collection, Department of Special Collections, Davidson Library, University of California, Santa Barbara.

Rogers's research revealed that therapists who provided empathy, congruence, genuineness, and unconditional positive regard were most likely to help clients grow in therapy. To explain this, he suggested that each person has an innate capacity to discern what is positive and growth enhancing personally but that the ability to discern and make decisions based on this process becomes obscured when that person encounters conditions of worth. **Conditions of worth** are implicit and explicit messages that people will only be acceptable and accepted *if* they are this way or that way. The job of the therapist is to provide a relationship in which conditions of worth are eliminated or minimized so that the client can recover this innate capacity toward growth.

Although Rogers's **nondirective** (which later became **client-centered**) **therapy** is perhaps rarely practiced in its pure form today, its influence has been considerable. The most consistent finding in the psychotherapy outcome literature is the power of what have been termed "common factors" or relationship variables that are necessary for any form of therapy to be successful. These common factors are similar to the conditions that Rogers isolated in his research. Most therapists today are trained to provide active listening, appropriate mirroring, and empathy as the foundation for delivering all types of therapy modalities, whatever other specific techniques may be involved.

In 1956, Rogers and Skinner met for a public debate on their respective philosophies of human nature. Clearly, the Rogerian notion of an innate, internal capacity for self-direction and self-determination was at odds with the Skinnerian renunciation of internal agency. Most of all, they differed on the role of social control. On the one hand, Skinner argued that control was inevitable and ubiquitous and that our only option was to use a science of behavior to better harness that control. A logical extension of his argument was that democratic political philosophy, which was based on the individual's ability to self-determine and organize, was an outmoded and obsolete ideology. Rogers, on the other hand, with his belief in personhood and the individual's innate ability to self-regulate, was a proponent of (and his philosophy was an outgrowth of) these democratic ideals. As the 1960s counterculture unfolded, Rogerian beliefs in personhood and self-determination proved more symbiotic with the tenor of the times than Skinner's message of increased social control.

Another, somewhat unwilling, counterculture icon, Maslow, concurred with Rogers on the importance of personal growth but came to his position via a different career trajectory. As a graduate student, Maslow studied primate behavior with Harry Harlow (1905–1981) at the University of Wisconsin and then returned to New York, where he was a faculty member at Brooklyn College for many years. Although trained as an experimental, laboratory psychologist, and well regarded by his scientific

peers, Maslow was critical of the laboratory ethos and what he regarded as its antitheoretical, anti-intellectual stance. In New York, he was a junior member of an intellectually rich group that focused on culture and personality studies. This group included some of the seminal thinkers of the time: Kurt Goldstein (1878–1965), Margaret Mead (1901–1978), Karen Horney (1885–1952), and others from whom Maslow learned to think deeply and broadly about the intersections of psychology, culture, and personality development. From Goldstein, Maslow learned the concept of self-actualization as a strategy of growth and adaptation in life. Subsequent exposure to Adlerian psychology and cultural anthropology convinced him that a broader, more all-encompassing perspective was required in psychology. He thus set about breaking down what he saw as the rigid distinctions between subjectivity and objectivity, science and religion, and psychology and everyday life. He also set himself the task of creating an institutional presence for humanistic psychology by founding the *Journal of Humanistic Psychology* in 1961 and the American Association for Humanistic Psychology in 1962.

Maslow is best known for his formulation of the hierarchy of needs, first expressed in a 1943 article in which he suggested that all humans must first meet their basic needs for food, shelter, and safety before moving up the hierarchy to the needs for belongingness and love and then esteem, achievement, and respect. At the top of the hierarchy was the need for self-actualization, which Maslow characterized as the progress toward becoming all one could become, a key component of his alternative B-psychology (*B* for "becoming"). To self-actualize, all other needs had to be satisfied, at least most of the time. Maslow identified the characteristics of individuals he deemed to be self-actualized, including William James (1842–1910), Albert Einstein, and Eleanor Roosevelt. All of these people, he argued, were perceptive, self-accepting, spontaneous, autonomous, empathic, and creative. They also experienced what Maslow called "peak experiences," mystical states in which awareness and

FIGURE 9.7 Abraham Maslow
Courtesy of the Archives of the History of American Psychology,
University of Akron, Akron, OH.

self-consciousness were heightened, one felt simultaneously powerful and powerless, and one was filled with awe and ecstasy. Maslow's articulation of self-actualization and peak experiences resonated strongly with the counterculture, but Maslow himself was disparaging of the movement. He was a supporter of the Vietnam War and viewed hippies and flower children as overindulged and underdisciplined. One of his major proponents who then became a counterculture icon himself was the student radical Abbie Hoffman. Hoffman had been a student of Maslow's at Brandeis University and embraced Maslow's work as foundational for the counterculture revolution. Maslow attempted to distance himself from Hoffman and other "fringe elements" but was never able to block the appropriation of his ideas by this group and the human potential movement more generally.

Maslow was elected president of the APA for 1968 and was developing a new extension of his work into what he called transpersonal psychology when he began to experience serious health problems. He died of a heart attack in California in 1970.

COMPLICATING SOCIAL PSYCHOLOGY

As we saw in Chapter 7 on American psychology between the world wars, the field of social psychology had begun to coalesce in the 1920s. From its beginning, tension existed between those who advocated a more experimental approach and those who wanted to use various methods in the service of understanding and ameliorating social problems. This tension continued after the war. In this section, we discuss the work of Kenneth Bancroft and Mamie Phipps Clark on racial identity and the problem of discrimination, as well as the social action research inspired by the émigré psychologist Lewin.

Psychologists, Racial Identity, and Civil Rights

Numerous Black and White psychologists and intellectuals in the postwar period made the compelling argument that social institutions as they then existed, whether educational, housing, or vocational, were structured in ways that damaged members of minorities, in particular, children. The research of social psychologists Kenneth and Mamie Clark revealed just how damaging these structural barriers were for American children, both Black and White. We begin the account of their work by tracing the development of their research agenda from its beginnings in the late 1930s.

Kenneth (1914–2005) and Mamie (1917–1983) Clark were both graduates of Howard University in Washington, DC, and both earned their doctorates from Columbia, Kenneth in 1940 and Mamie in 1944. Mamie's master's thesis at Howard, "The Development of Consciousness of Self in Negro Pre-school Children," was on racial identity in children. Working from a method suggested by the earlier research of Ruth Horowitz (Hartley, 1910–1998), Mamie sought to understand how racial identity formed in Black preschool children: When did it form? What were the parameters? Was the valence positive or negative?

Kenneth joined Mamie in the research, and they jointly published a series of articles in the 1940s based on their work (Clark & Clark, 1939a, 1939b, 1940, 1950). With Black and White children in Northern and Southern schools, the Clarks expanded on the experimental methods of Horowitz to include line drawings, doll preferences by color, and preferences in coloring with crayons of various objects. They found that many African American children equated attractiveness and positive qualities with White dolls and attributed negative characteristics with the darker-colored dolls, yet accurately perceived themselves as being African American.

Kenneth Clark later recounted that this work was so disturbing to him and Mamie that they did not want to pursue it for several years. However, the National Association for the Advancement of Colored People (NAACP) Legal Defense Fund was at that time pursuing several court cases to end segregation by race in public schools and asked the Clarks to work with the team to bring evidence to the cases of the psychological damage done by racial segregation.

In 1952, the U.S. Supreme Court agreed to hear the NAACP cases, combining them all under the case of **Brown v. Board of Education of Topeka, Kansas**. Kenneth Clark, along with social psychologists Isidor Chein (1912–1981) and Stuart Cook (1913–1993), wrote a brief in support of the NAACP position titled "The Effects of Segregation and the Consequences of Desegregation: A (September 1952) Social Science Statement in the *Brown v. Board* Supreme Court Case" (1952/2004). On May 17, 1954, the Court handed down a unanimous decision, ruling that segregation by race in public schools was unconstitutional. In footnote 11 of the decision, the justices cited social science research, including material in the Social Science Statement, the first time that psychological research had been cited in a Supreme Court decision. The decision was monumental in bringing change to the United States, with some legal scholars citing it as the most significant legal decision for social policy of the 20th century. As part of the growing civil rights movement in the United States, it was a landmark decision (Jackson, 2001). The Clarks went on to develop effective community interventions with children and families through their Northside Center for Child Development. Their work is an example of how to use social psychology to address social problems.

Sidebar 9.1 Focus on *Kenneth and Mamie Phipps Clark*

The biographies of Kenneth and Mamie Clark are bound up with some of the most crucial events of 20th-century U.S. history. As we recounted in the text, their studies on racial identification among African American children were crucial evidence that U.S. Supreme Court justices used to overturn segregation by race in public schools. But their lives and contributions did not end with their "doll studies."

Mamie Phipps came to Howard in 1934 from her home in Hot Springs, Arkansas, where her father was a physician, and the only African American physician for miles around. She switched from her early intent to major in mathematics at Howard to a major in psychology. This was due, in part, to having met a student a couple of years ahead of her, Kenneth Clark. Clark had been born in the Panama Canal Zone but had grown up in New

York City after his mother divorced his father and returned there. Clark later remarked that he learned his activism from his mother, who taught him, "the excitement of people doing things together to help themselves" (as cited in Pettigrew & Jones, 2005, p. 650). At Howard, Clark had studied political science, but he came under the mentorship of Francis Cecil Sumner, the first African American to earn a doctorate in psychology. After earning his master's at Howard, Clark enrolled at Columbia for doctoral work, where his mentor was Otto Klineberg.

Phipps, meanwhile, earned her BA at Howard and then, after she and Kenneth were secretly married, conducted research on racial self-identification among young Black children for her master's thesis. It was this work of Mamie's—Kenneth later joined her in it, and they published several joint studies—that eventually lent powerful support to the U.S. Supreme Court decision in *Brown v. Board* (1954).

Kenneth earned his doctorate in 1940 and in 1942 became a faculty member at the City College of New York. Mamie came to Columbia in 1940 and earned her doctorate in 1944. She soon realized that having a doctorate did not provide immediate benefits in finding appropriate employment. After working at various social service agencies, she decided to follow her inspiration about improving the lives of children and in 1946, with a loan from her father, opened the Northside Testing and Consultation Center in the basement of the Paul Dunbar Apartments in Harlem. She changed the name in 1947 to the Northside Center for Child Development. Mamie was the center's director, while Kenneth was the director of research. For Mamie, the center was a way for her to use her training, intelligence, and sense of social justice to make a difference in the lives of children and families, to give children security is how she put it. For Kenneth, the center represented the convergence of academic life and social policy.

The Clarks's commitment to use social science for social justice occupied the remainder of their lives. Mamie remained the center's director until her retirement in 1979. Under her leadership, the center grew to provide a full range of family and educational services. She built a network of support, ranging from auctions to the philanthropy of the Rockefeller family. Mamie was active in the initiation of the national Head Start program. She was involved in her community in Harlem and beyond, serving on the boards of directors of numerous educational and philanthropic institutions.

Kenneth was actively involved in the U.S. civil rights movement. The fame he garnered from the *Brown v. Board* decision led him into personal friendships with Martin Luther King, Jr. and Malcolm X. In 1962, Kenneth became the director of the President's Committee on Juvenile Delinquency program in Harlem, the Harlem

(Continued)

FIGURE 9.8   Kenneth and Mamie Phipps Clark
Courtesy of the Library of Congress.

Youth Opportunities Unlimited. Although initially a success, the program faltered due to conflict over control of its funding. Kenneth went on to do several important systemwide education studies and in the 1970s founded Metropolitan Applied Research Center, which was dedicated to bringing social science research to urban problems.

This kind of social psychology had its American origins in the 1930s, but its European origins date to the work of Lewin at the Psychological Institute of the University of Berlin in the 1920s, discussed in Chapter 8. We turn to examples of the social action research inspired by Lewin and give an example of his influence in applying social psychology to social problems of racial discrimination and interracial housing in New York in the postwar period.

Broadly, Lewin conceptualized a social psychology that was engaged with communities and addressed real-life problems. In this sense, it was different from the emerging experimental social psychology that began in the interwar period and became dominant after the war and that focused increasingly on variables (e.g., attitudes and cognition) that could be studied in laboratory settings. Lewin's social action research was the prime example in its period of how social scientists could bring their expertise to bear on real social problems while remaining true to their scientific training. The place where the research occurred was the community, rather than a laboratory. Or, one could say, the community was the laboratory.

In 1944, Lewin moved to the Massachusetts Institute of Technology, where he and a talented group of young faculty and graduate students embarked on expanding social psychology into new domains, especially through the study of what they called group dynamics. He also became a consultant to the New York City–based Commission on Community Interrelations (CCI). Lewin helped the commission plan a program that would use social psychological research methods to both understand and intervene in problems of intergroup relations, specifically to reduce anti-Semitism and discrimination against members of all minority groups. Lewin brought social

psychologist Stuart Cook in as the commission's first director, and an innovative series of studies and interventions was planned. Unfortunately, Lewin died suddenly in 1947.

Cook carried on the work of the CCI after Lewin's death, aided by a talented staff of psychologists, including Chein (second director) and Harold Proshansky (1920–1990). The CCI also engaged the services of notable consultants and advisers including African American social scientist from Fisk University, Charles S. Johnson (1893–1956), Marie Jahoda, Gordon Allport, and Kenneth Clark. Two of the research actions programs were community self-surveys of race relations (developed at Fisk), which helped citizens identify racial prejudice in community settings as a means to increase awareness of discriminatory practices, and the **incident control project**, which was designed to teach people "how to stop the bigot"; that is, how to intervene in a public display of racist remarks and behavior. These projects and others showed that a place still existed for a nonreductive approach to social psychology, with the research done in the community rather than a laboratory. The commitment was to science, but to science in the service of social problems rather than strict methodological purity.

Interracial Housing

In 1949, Cook moved to New York University (NYU) to establish the Research Center for Human Relations, where he stimulated research on intergroup relations. Cook attracted a bright and promising group of psychologists to the Center, including Milton Schwebel (b. 1914), Jahoda, and Morton Deutsch (b. 1920); they were joined by Chein from CCI in 1953.

Jahoda, Deutsch, and Cook were each involved, separately, in studies on interracial housing.

Interracial housing research was an investigation of the **contact hypothesis**. A simplified definition of this hypothesis is that intergroup contact (where groups are different on some important dimension such as skin color, ethnicity, or social class) under certain conditions can reduce prejudice and produce more positive intergroup attitudes (since the 1950s, researchers have added several caveats and constraints to this definition).

The context for the research on the contact hypothesis was the large in-migration of African Americans to the northern United States, which increased after World War II, and the continued immigration to the United States from Europe and elsewhere. The amount of intergroup contact had risen dramatically in the postwar period and had important implications for labor and housing policies. In New York, the sheer size of the population made such contact unavoidable. Because of the Great Depression of the 1930s, housing stock had not kept up with the rise in population, and New York City and nearby cities saw a rise in the number of housing developments with mixed housing; at this time, mixed housing referred to Black and White residents. Some developments or apartment buildings were fully integrated. Some were area segregated; that is, Whites lived in certain buildings, Blacks in others. This created a natural laboratory for the kind of action research then stimulating so many young social psychologists. It raised questions such as, "What was the impact of these new housing patterns?" "What were the implications for the contact hypothesis?" "Was prejudice reduced when different races lived together?"

The general conclusion from three separate research projects was supportive of the contact hypothesis. Marie Jahoda (1907–2001), who had come to the United States after fleeing Nazi-occupied Vienna (see Chapter 8) along with a colleague from Columbia, found that in those buildings where both races lived, tenants reported a higher number of friendships

with members of the other race and Whites had more favorable attitudes toward integrated housing. Deutsch and Mary Evans Collins (b. 1918) compared biracially segregated housing in Newark and integrated housing in New York City, using qualitative methods—interviews and participant observations—to study interracial contacts in the housing projects. The two New York City projects were fully integrated, while the ones in Newark were area segregated, with Blacks and Whites in separate buildings. The African American population was at least 40 percent in each of the projects. Tenants differed significantly in their attitudes. Whites in the integrated housing reported favorable attitudes, held Blacks in high esteem, and recommended interracial housing to others. Their research led the Newark Housing Authority to change its policies to encourage integrated housing.

To follow up on the Deutsch and Collins study, Cook and staff members at the Research Center of Human Relations undertook a larger project on interracial housing outside New York City. In the four housing projects studied, all were building segregated, but the buildings were interspersed so that while a building may have been all White, it would have been next to an all Black residence. Their data suggested that the intergroup contact found in interracial housing was an effective means of reducing racial tension and prejudice (Wilner, Walkley, & Cook, 1955). Oddly, apparently in none of these studies were the attitudes of African Americans about intergroup contact assessed.

What happened to this community-oriented, social-action psychology in the Lewinian tradition? As historian Fran Cherry has pointed out and social psychologist Deutsch has echoed, the kind of social psychology that was practiced in New York City at CCI and the NYU Research Center for Human Relations gave way to an experimental social psychology at times more concerned with methodological rigor and acceptance by the psychological mainstream than with immediate, pressing social problems. By the mid-1960s, experimental social psychology had become institutionalized as the Society for Experimental Social Psychology. The emphasis was increasingly on manipulating intrapersonal variables in laboratory settings to understand social cognition, social behavior, or both. This yielded some striking results, such as Leon Festinger's (1919–1989) studies of cognitive dissonance and

Stanley Milgram's (1933–1984) obedience experiments. This split between laboratory methods and real-life settings eventually led to what historians have called the crisis of social psychology in the 1970s, when many social psychologists began to wonder about the social relevance of their research.

SUMMARY

American psychology expanded rapidly after World War II. In this chapter, we examined this expansion in the context of the growth of consumer culture and the large-scale funding by policy makers worried about the nation's mental health. The impact of federal funding not only increased the number of psychologists but also changed the discipline, pushing it beyond its rather narrow focus on learning and behavior by providing the money to make a wider range of topics open for investigation. This has been referred to as the golden age of psychology in the United States.

However golden it was, there were still problems. The APA had to deal with a range of thorny professional issues involving training, ethics, and practice after decades of studiously

avoiding these areas. The initial training model of the scientist–practitioner mollified the hardcore experimentalists within psychology but was soon criticized for its failure to consider the larger social and institutional contexts in which people live. These differences have remained a thorn in the side of the discipline.

The consequences of psychology's growth reached far beyond North America. As the United States became the world's most powerful country, its influence reached into almost every part of the world. Students came to study in America, often sent by their governments, so that the society back home could benefit from America's expertise and leadership. This had profound implications for the growth of psychology elsewhere, as we discuss in our next chapter.

BIBLIOGRAPHIC ESSAY

Historical research on the post–World War II era in American life has rapidly increased over the last few years. We were fortunate to be able to draw on this good scholarship. The work of Paul Boyer (1994), Kenneth Jackson (1985), Michael Johns (2003), Karal Marling (1994), Margaret Marsh (1990), Elaine May (1988), Robert Samuelson (1995), and Lynn Spigel (1992) gave us a rich, multifaceted overview of American thought and culture in the first two postwar decades. For an overview of developments in American psychology in

the postwar era, we relied on the excellent volumes of James Capshew (1999), Ellen Herman (1995), and again, Donald Napoli (1981). Nathan Hale's volume on American psychoanalysis in the postwar era provided indispensable guidance (1995). Both of us have published articles and books examining various aspects of American psychology in this era, and we drew liberally upon our previously published work (Pickren, 2005).

For organizational issues, we relied on Ernest Hilgard and Capshew (1992) for information about the reorganization of the APA during the war. On the development of the NCWP, we drew on the work of Capshew and Alejandra Laszlo (1986) and the reminiscences of two participants, Alice Bryan (1983, 1986) and Mildred Mitchell (1983). Our material for American psychology's golden age was drawn from many sources, including some of our own work. Here we relied on the authors we cited earlier for the cultural context and used the fine recent scholarship of Andrea Tone (2009), David Herzberg (2009), Elizabeth Siegel Watkins (2008), and William Bird's *Better Living* (1999). Two fine volumes by Loren Baritz were also helpful, his *Servants of Power* (1960) and *The Good Life* (1989).

The rapid growth of Psychology, especially clinical psychology, in the postwar era was due to several factors, which we hope we have conveyed. We found the work of Capshew (1999), Herman (1995), and Rod Buchanan (2003) crucial for our account. Rod Baker and Wade Pickren's article (2006) and volume on the VA and psychology (2007), and the chapters in the edited volume by Pickren and Stan Schneider (2005) were helpful, especially the chapters by Don Dewsbury (2005), Ingrid Farreras, (2005) Schneider (2005), and Charles Rice (2005). Seymour Sarason's 1981 article, "An Asocial Psychology and a Misdirected Clinical Psychology" remains an insightful and trenchant critique of the failure of American clinical training programs to incorporate contextual and structural factors into the work of psychologists. Another side of the discontent with the then-standard training model is found in the chapter by Karl Pottharst and Arthur Kovacs (1964).

The all-important role of the NIMH in postwar mental health developments has still not attracted as much serious scholarship as it warrants. The overall picture of the growth of postwar funding of science was drawn from Derek Price (1963). Gerald Grob's examination of mental health policy in this era (1991) was an excellent source for us. The history of the NIH by Stephen Strickland (1972) remains a vital resource, although it needs to be updated. Rachael Rosner's chapter in Pickren and Schneider (2005) is an excellent examination of the history of

NIMH efforts to fund psychotherapy research. Although unpublished, Jeanne Brand and Philip Sapir's (1964) history of the first 15 years of the NIMH was indispensable.

Skinner was a central figure in postwar American psychology. Serious historical scholarship has only recently begun to examine his work and legacy. Alexandra Rutherford's research (2000, 2003, 2006, 2009) has been an important contributor to improving our understanding of Skinner's influence. James Capshew described Skinner's Project Pigeon (1996). Daniel Bjork has authored a good biography of Skinner (1993) and examined Skinner's contributions as a social inventor (1996). Historian of psychology Laurence Smith (1992, 1996) has placed Skinner's work in a larger historical and philosophical context. Ludy Benjamin, Jr. has helped us understand Skinner as an inventor, with his history of teaching machines (1988) and his history of Skinner's work on the air crib (Benjamin & Nielsen-Gammon, 1999).

For our section on humanistic psychology, we relied on Ian Nicholson (2001), Herman (1995), and Capshew (1999). Various chapters in Don Freedheim's edited volume, *History of Psychotherapy* (1992), were also helpful. The recent volume by Susan Myers-Shirk (2009) provided an insightful analysis of the ongoing relationship among religion, pastoral counseling, and the work of Carl Rogers and other humanistic psychologists.

Finally, we drew on the historical scholarship of Frances Cherry and Catherine Borshuk (1998) to help us understand the tensions in postwar social psychology. We also relied on contemporary scholarship from the postwar era for our account on interracial housing research (e.g., Deutsch & Collins, 1951; Jahoda & West, 1951; Wilner et al., 1955). The history of psychologists and civil rights work has received careful attention from several scholars. We drew on the work of John Jackson (2001), Shafali Lal (2002), Gerald Markowitz and David Rosner (1996), Pickren and Henry Tomes (2002), as well as Gwen Bergner (2009). We are grateful to our friend, Larry Nyman (1976), for his willingness to share his lengthy interview with Kenneth Clark.

Chapter 10
TIMELINE 1850–1990
(In 25-year increments)

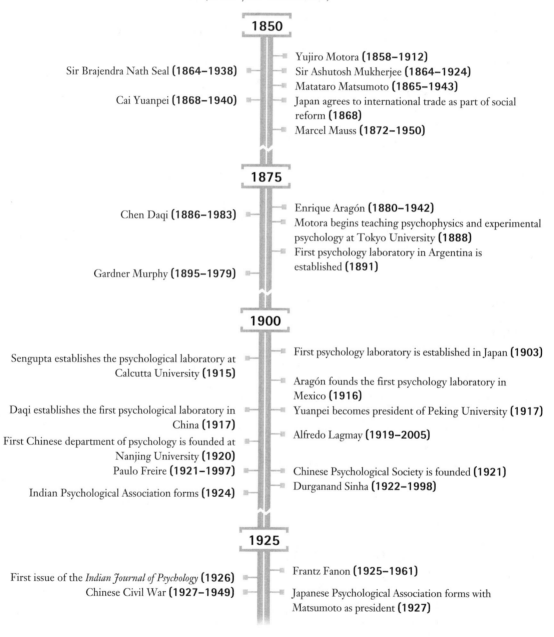

1850

Yujiro Motora **(1858–1912)**

Sir Brajendra Nath Seal **(1864–1938)**

Sir Ashutosh Mukherjee **(1864–1924)**

Matataro Matsumoto **(1865–1943)**

Cai Yuanpei **(1868–1940)**

Japan agrees to international trade as part of social reform **(1868)**

Marcel Mauss **(1872–1950)**

1875

Chen Daqi **(1886–1983)**

Enrique Aragón **(1880–1942)**

Motora begins teaching psychophysics and experimental psychology at Tokyo University **(1888)**

First psychology laboratory in Argentina is established **(1891)**

Gardner Murphy **(1895–1979)**

1900

Sengupta establishes the psychological laboratory at Calcutta University **(1915)**

First psychology laboratory is established in Japan **(1903)**

Aragón founds the first psychology laboratory in Mexico **(1916)**

Daqi establishes the first psychological laboratory in China **(1917)**

Yuanpei becomes president of Peking University **(1917)**

First Chinese department of psychology is founded at Nanjing University **(1920)**

Alfredo Lagmay **(1919–2005)**

Paulo Freire **(1921–1997)**

Chinese Psychological Society is founded **(1921)**

Durganand Sinha **(1922–1998)**

Indian Psychological Association forms **(1924)**

1925

First issue of the *Indian Journal of Psychology* **(1926)**

Frantz Fanon **(1925–1961)**

Chinese Civil War **(1927–1949)**

Japanese Psychological Association forms with Matsumoto as president **(1927)**

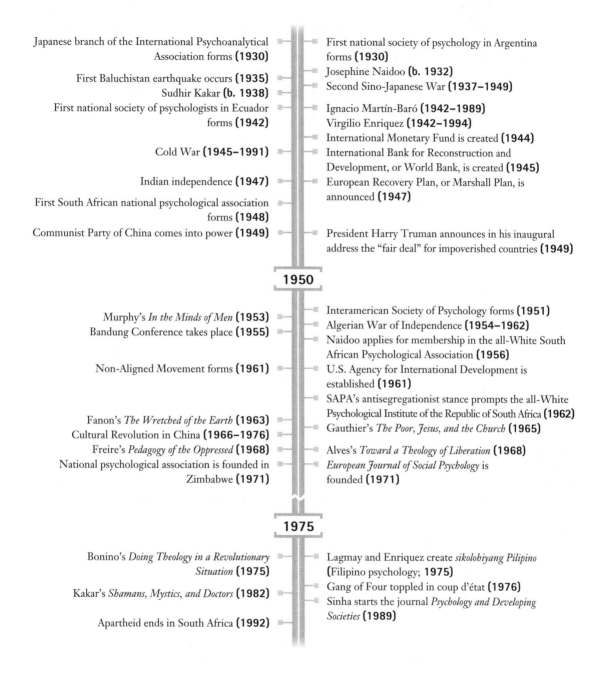

Japanese branch of the International Psychoanalytical Association forms **(1930)**

First Baluchistan earthquake occurs **(1935)**

Sudhir Kakar **(b. 1938)**

First national society of psychologists in Ecuador forms **(1942)**

Cold War **(1945–1991)**

Indian independence **(1947)**

First South African national psychological association forms **(1948)**

Communist Party of China comes into power **(1949)**

First national society of psychology in Argentina forms **(1930)**

Josephine Naidoo **(b. 1932)**

Second Sino-Japanese War **(1937–1949)**

Ignacio Martín-Baró **(1942–1989)**

Virgilio Enriquez **(1942–1994)**

International Monetary Fund is created **(1944)**

International Bank for Reconstruction and Development, or World Bank, is created **(1945)**

European Recovery Plan, or Marshall Plan, is announced **(1947)**

President Harry Truman announces in his inaugural address the "fair deal" for impoverished countries **(1949)**

1950

Murphy's *In the Minds of Men* **(1953)**

Bandung Conference takes place **(1955)**

Non-Aligned Movement forms **(1961)**

Fanon's *The Wretched of the Earth* **(1963)**

Cultural Revolution in China **(1966–1976)**

Freire's *Pedagogy of the Oppressed* **(1968)**

National psychological association is founded in Zimbabwe **(1971)**

Interamerican Society of Psychology forms **(1951)**

Algerian War of Independence **(1954–1962)**

Naidoo applies for membership in the all-White South African Psychological Association **(1956)**

U.S. Agency for International Development is established **(1961)**

SAPA's antisegregationist stance prompts the all-White Psychological Institute of the Republic of South Africa **(1962)**

Gauthier's *The Poor, Jesus, and the Church* **(1965)**

Alves's *Toward a Theology of Liberation* **(1968)**

European Journal of Social Psychology is founded **(1971)**

1975

Bonino's *Doing Theology in a Revolutionary Situation* **(1975)**

Kakar's *Shamans, Mystics, and Doctors* **(1982)**

Apartheid ends in South Africa **(1992)**

Lagmay and Enriquez create *sikolohiyang Pilipino* (Filipino psychology; **1975**)

Gang of Four toppled in coup d'état **(1976)**

Sinha starts the journal *Psychology and Developing Societies* **(1989)**

INTERNATIONALIZATION AND INDIGENIZATION OF PSYCHOLOGY AFTER WORLD WAR II

The turn away from a unifocal linear history to a socially contextualized polycentric history is not a matter of merely antiquarian interest.

—Kurt Danziger, "Universalism and Indigenization in the History of Modern Psychology," 2006

INTRODUCTION

In this chapter, we enlarge our discussion to consider the postwar developments in psychology in many places around the world. We do so under the rubrics of internationalization and indigenization of psychology. You will notice immediately that our standpoint, the place from which we begin, both here and throughout the book is North America. In that sense, things that happen elsewhere are international, just as events here are to those who live in other countries. We attempt to keep our standpoint obvious and refrain from privileging North American psychology or treating it as the norm or the metric against which all others are measured. We may not succeed in every instance.

We frame the chapter with the concept of **intellectual geography of center and periphery**, which we borrow from historian Kurt Danziger (2006). Danziger argues that before World War II several centers of psychology existed, places with intellectual, institutional, and economic resources that provided a distinct character to the psychology produced there. In this model, these centers included Leipzig, Berlin, London, Paris, and several major universities in the United States. We have noted this in earlier chapters, for example, in our characterization of German psychology as historically linked to the empirical exploration of epistemological questions, meant to produce and maintain German *Kultur*. American psychology in the interwar period, we noted, was characterized by behaviorism, which had little appeal elsewhere in the world. Each of these pre–World War II centers also had peripheries, with communication between each center

and its peripheral outposts. What characterized psychology, then, was the existence of multiple psychologies, as the psychology produced in each center was typically incommensurate in epistemology, methods, and practices with psychology produced elsewhere. This is one reason the Gestalt psychologists who immigrated to the United States found it so difficult to find a home for their approach to psychology. Yet each psychology claimed universality, that is, that its model of psychological reality was applicable to all human mentality, behavior, and emotions, everywhere. This incommensurability has been masked in most historical accounts, especially textbook histories, under the banner of schools.

Danziger suggests that a shift took place after World War II so that the resources available in the United States to train psychologists and fund research far outstripped those available elsewhere, thus making the United States the primary center for postwar psychology (2006). This was true, Danziger points out, even when we account for the Soviet Union as an alternative center during the Cold War. This is another way of stating what we discussed at length in the previous chapter: The indigenization process in the United States produced a distinctly Americanized psychology. Yet what happened with the ascendancy of the United States after World War II, with its rise to superpower status in military, economic, and political aspects, was that its sciences gained ascendancy as well. In psychology, this came to mean that the adjective "American" no longer was used to describe the psychology produced there. Rather, American psychology became the norm, so when the term "psychology" was deployed, it meant, by default, American psychology. We should point out, that in any field when a word or phrase becomes normative it passes out of conscious reflection so that people no longer examine it critically. It becomes, to use the favorite term of the theorist Raymond Williams (1921–1988), a **keyword**.

With American psychology as the primary center, there still remained much communication with other countries, which became the periphery. Now, however, most communication was one way, with psychologists in the United States sending information and receiving little. American trends, methods, and models increasingly became the norm. American journals became the most sought after sites of publication. It was (and is) difficult for a psychologist in a Third World country to publish in a First World journal. This created a huge imbalance in the communication of scientific results. As Danziger argues, if American psychologists are not aware of recent research published in India, they suffer no penalty. If, however, Indian psychologists do not keep abreast of recent developments in American psychology, then it only confirms that Indian psychology has little to offer.

This model of center and periphery can help us understand the developments described in this chapter. In the first two to three decades

after 1945, American psychology was exported to other countries that simply did not have the resources to compete with American scientists. In Europe, this was primarily due to the devastation inflicted by war. In non-European countries, it was due to a complex array of factors having to do with postcolonialism, poverty, and local politics and social customs. Yet, by the 1960s in some countries, and only a few years later in other locations, resistance to the American hegemony in psychology began to grow and continues to this day. Paradoxically, even in the resistance, people still often embrace some of the basic assumptions of Western or American psychology. It has been difficult to reenvision psychology on bases different than the American norm. In this chapter, we offer a historical account of these events with the intent of contributing to a **polycentric history** of psychology.

INTERNATIONALIZATION AND INDIGENIZATION

The United States became one of two dominant world powers in the three decades after the end of World War II. Its military, political, and economic power brought it great influence around the world. Psychology, as we saw in the previous chapter, had dramatically grown in the two decades after World War II ended, fueled by the reciprocal interaction between large-scale funding programs for research and training practitioners and increasing psychologization of North American society. Psychology became a (relatively) resource-rich discipline and profession. Its resources, tied to the rise in American influence in other domains, gave it great influence in the rest of the world. We begin in Europe, where American psychologists helped rebuild European psychology and in the course of doing so changed much of the direction and content of psychology there.

In July 1947, the United States announced the European Recovery Plan, more commonly known as the Marshall Plan after then–Secretary of State George Marshall. In 1949, President Harry Truman announced in his inaugural address a "fair deal" for the impoverished countries of the world, whereby the United States would send aid and expertise to countries to help them develop. Here are his words:

> More than half the people of the world are living in conditions approaching misery. Their food is inadequate, they are victims of disease. Their economic life is primitive and stagnant. Their poverty is a handicap and a threat both to them and to more prosperous areas. For the first time in history humanity possesses the knowledge and the skill to relieve the suffering of these people.... I believe that we should make available to peace-loving peoples the benefits of our store of technical knowledge in order to help them realize their aspirations for a better life.... What we envisage is a program of development based on the concepts of democratic fair dealing.... Greater production is the key to prosperity and peace. And the key to greater production is a wider and more vigorous application of modern scientific and technical knowledge. (Truman, 1949/1964, cited in Escobar, 1995, p. 3)

At least in part, these plans or deals can be understood as part of a larger strategy to gain influence for the United States. In the 20 years after the end of World War II, the United States became the preeminent Western power. The only major challenge to its hegemony was the Soviet Union. The two nations became entangled in what was then called the Cold War. The rise of the United States to dominance and the ideological struggle of the Cold War had implications for American psychology, as it became one of America's exports to Europe and elsewhere.

As part of its growing influence and strength—political, military, economic, and intellectual—in this postwar era, the United States embarked on a long-term strategy to increase its influence in many parts of the world, using various means to do so. Economic influence, educational programs, and covert use of intelligence agencies

to undermine and overthrow governments perceived as hostile were all aspects of these strategies. One well-known example was the Marshall Plan, as mentioned. The U.S. Agency for International Development (USAID) was a later expression of this impulse.

In this era, the United States began large-scale programs in many parts of the world to foster economic development. The concept of "underdeveloped" countries emerged, along with its concomitant concept, the developing world or what came to be called the Third World (Escobar, 1995). These offers of aid had complex results that do not easily reduce to statements that they were good or bad. No doubt, the offer to help was attractive to many struggling countries, but the downside was the undue influence from more powerful nations that the help brought with it.

In the postwar era, most European countries were in shambles, with significant losses of population, damaged infrastructure, and in some cases, nonfunctional governments. The various sciences suffered as universities, laboratory space, and national organizations had been damaged.

Within Europe, the structures of science were rebuilt, often with massive amounts of American aid and with the accompanying American influence. In Britain, despite the strictures brought on by the war and diminished faculty, by the mid-1950s significant activity was taking place in cognitive psychology with the legacy of Kenneth Craik (1914–1945) and Frederic Bartlett (1886–1969) and the contemporary work of Donald Broadbent (1926–1993; see Chapter 13). One biographer of Broadbent noted that immediately after the war intellectual excitement was high but books were in short supply. The Cambridge University Psychology Department had but one copy of the standard experimental text by Robert Sessions Woodworth (1869–1962), *Experimental Psychology*, for which students waited their turn. Collegial networks, including personal interactions, tutorials, and lectures, provided the main vehicles for knowledge transmission until recovery began. Psychology in Britain was never dominated by behaviorist approaches; rather, it

FIGURE 10.1 Postwar visit to the Cambridge Psychological Laboratory by Professor A. Michotte and colleagues from the University of Louvain, Belgium, 1948
Courtesy of the University of Cambridge Archives.

retained its emphasis on mental processes and the applications of psychology to problems of industry and schooling.

In social psychology, a strong European tradition existed of intellectual inquiry into social psychological topics, if not a significant amount of empirical or experimental work in the field. For example, Karl (1879–1963) and Charlotte (1893–1974) Bühler and their students at the Vienna Psychological Institute studied social relationships among Viennese schoolgirls in the 1920s, and social psychologist Marie Jahoda (1907–2001) led a study of the effects of unemployment on social networks in the early 1930s, as we discussed in Chapter 8.

After World War II, many areas of psychology—clinical, industrial, social, experimental—came under the strong influence of American methodologies. American research

emphases began to take precedence over local research traditions. This was pointedly true as new generations of psychologists were trained. Increasingly, the literature cited and the methods employed were based on the American model of how psychological science is done: strongly empirical, data driven, with little reference to context or culture, and deliberately nontheoretical.

As European psychologists followed the American style, it seemed the proper route to rebuild psychology. American aid, whether in the form of the Marshall Plan or Fulbright fellowships, provided a conduit for the spread of American ideas and values in science, as well as in daily life. As the French sociologist Marcel Mauss (1872–1950) had written many years before in his now-classic text, *The Gift* (1923–1924/1954), all such aid or gifts bring with them obligations;

they bind the recipient to the giver. So it was in European psychology.

By the late 1950s, European social psychologists were beginning to assert themselves in wanting to fashion a European social psychology. The Romanian-born French social psychologist Serge Moscovici has described the struggle to establish a transnational social psychology in which European cultural concerns and intellectual traditions would be included along with the American emphases (Moscovici & Markova, 2006). Ironically, the work he describes depended greatly on the financial contributions of American funding sources, primarily the U.S. government. By the mid-1960s, a small group of social psychologists organized themselves into the European Association of Experimental Social Psychologists and began publishing their journal, *European Journal of Social Psychology*, in 1971 (Tajfel, 1972).

The case of social psychology in Europe is one of continuing American influence, with the formation of a European identity strengthening communication networks across the continent. This has refocused some topics that social psychologists investigate and has led to original theorization about social phenomena. However, it does not indicate a return to the theoretical and analytical roots of European social psychology.

In Germany, to take another example, psychology was reconstituted after the war with, at first, much the same complexion as before the war. Applied psychology experienced rapid growth in education, industry, and counseling centers. The theoretical underpinnings and methodology were typically carried over from earlier approaches. However, by the mid-1950s, the American influence became much stronger, as a general turn occurred in West German society toward America. The introduction of American approaches to testing—intellectual, aptitude, personality—for vocational and academic purposes was met with some resistance by older members of the discipline, who preferred characterological and intuitive approaches, including graphology (handwriting analysis).

The conflict that ensued was won by those who favored the American approaches.

After 1960, the West German university system was greatly expanded and the presence of psychology grew immensely in terms of its representation in universities, academic majors, and its range of applications. The field of clinical psychology grew more rapidly than any other field, just as it had in the United States in the 1950s. By the 1970s, this led to conflict between academic scientists and clinical practitioners, again echoing American conflicts. Historically, it would not be accurate to say that German psychology has been completely Americanized. Rather, there has been an ongoing influence on German scientific and professional psychology, moderated since the 1980s by the development of strong institutional centers of excellence, such as the Max Planck Institutes.

BACK STORY: WESTERN PSYCHOLOGY IN NON-WESTERN SETTINGS

Before we discuss the history of the post–World War II development of indigenous psychologies, we provide brief historical overviews of psychology in a small sample of non-Western locales. In some of these settings, Western psychology was imported as part of the process of helping make the host country "modern." In other places, psychology was imported as part of the colonization process.

China

China has a long tradition of philosophical thought that includes insight into human personality and relationships. However, for many reasons, no indigenous psychology developed from this intellectual and spiritual tradition, as happened in Western societies. Western psychology was first introduced into China in the late 19th century through translations of psychology textbooks, such as *Mental Philosophy* (translated from the Japanese in 1889) by the American mental philosopher Joseph Haven and the *Outlines of Psychology* (translated 1907) by the Danish philosophical psychologist Harald Høffding. The latter volume introduced Wundtian psychology to China. Japanese scholars also introduced Western psychological ideas into China during a period of Chinese educational reform around the beginning of the 20th century.

The Chinese educational reformer Cai Yuanpei (1868–1940) studied in Wilhelm Wundt's (1832–1920) laboratory in Leipzig in 1908. He became president of Peking University in 1917, and during his presidency the first psychological laboratory was established in China by Chen Daqi (1886–1983), who had studied psychology in Japan. The founding of the laboratory was indicative of psychological activity, so by 1920 the first department of psychology was founded, at Nanjing University, and in 1921 enough psychologists were practicing to found the Chinese Psychological Society.

In the period between the world wars, most Chinese psychologists were trained in the United States, primarily at the University of Chicago and Columbia University. The functionalist approach to studying consciousness and a behavioral orientation characterized the positions of most of these psychologists. One Chinese psychologist, Zing-yang Kuo (1898–1970), became involved in the intense debate in the United States over the role of instincts versus environment, coming down strongly on the side of environment. Several Chinese psychologists, in reflecting on this period, indicated that most of the research was an imitation of what was being done in Europe and the United States, with little original research. However, recent scholarship has indicated that even though many of the methods employed were drawn from Western psychology, the content and topics of a significant number of articles published in the 1920s and 1930s reflected indigenous Chinese beliefs and practices (Blowers, Cheung, & Ru, 2009).

Due to the war with Japan that began in 1937, and through the civil war between the nationalists and the Communists that ended in Communist victory in 1949, Psychology as a discipline was shut down. The first 10 or so years after 1949 saw a strong Soviet influence, but Chinese psychologists were able to reopen the Institute of Psychology at Peking University and restart the Chinese Psychological Society. After a split between China and the Soviet Union, efforts were made to develop a Marxist–Maoist Chinese approach to science, including psychology. The major focus of psychological research in the 1960s was on child development and educational psychology.

In 1966, the Cultural Revolution began in China and lasted 10 years. It was an ultraleftist critique of all things that could be considered bourgeois, including Psychology. Many psychologists were sent to the countryside for reeducation and departments of psychology were closed. Finally, when the leaders of the Cultural Revolution, the so-called Gang of Four, fell from favor, sciences were reestablished in the country.

Since the 1980s, Psychology has grown, although the number of psychologists is small compared to the size of the population. The Institute of Psychology, part of the Chinese Academy of Sciences, has great prestige around the world, and many universities have departments of psychology, primarily playing an educational role rather than training graduate students. Chinese psychologists have taken up many of the research topics that are popular in the United States, leading several prominent Chinese psychologists to point out that Chinese psychology is still too imitative of the West. Perhaps this is so because Chinese psychology did not emerge out of its own cultural and intellectual traditions but was imported from the West. In recent years, a small movement has begun to develop an indigenous Chinese psychology, both on the mainland and in Hong Kong.

Japan

In 1868, Japan made a decision to open the country to trade and exchange with the outside world as part of the social reform and modernization of the country. The desire to learn Western science and technology was a major part of the decision to open up. In 1877, Tokyo University was founded as the first Western-style university. Psychology was taught as part of the general education curriculum but not as a science. In 1888, Yujiro Motora (1858–1912) began teaching psychophysics and experimental psychology at the university. Motora had recently returned from the United States, where he had earned his doctorate in psychology under G. Stanley Hall (1844–1924) at Johns Hopkins University. Motora specialized in psychophysics, publishing both research articles and monographs on the subject, and in 1903 he established the first psychology laboratory in Japan.

His student, Matataro Matsumoto (1865–1943), proved to be the key figure in expanding the field in Japan. Matsumoto went to Yale University in 1896 and earned his doctorate there under the psychologist Edward W. Scripture (1864–1945) in 1899. Before he returned to Japan, he spent a year in Leipzig with Wundt. He established the second Japanese psychology laboratory in Kyoto (1906) and then returned to take up the professorial chair at Tokyo University upon Motora's death in 1912. Through his research, publications, and many graduate students, Matsumoto shaped the early history of Japanese psychology. While he focused mostly on experimental work, he encouraged his students to engage in a range of applications: education, industry, forensics, and vocational guidance, for example.

In the 1920s, eight psychology laboratories were established at Japanese universities; five of the founders had been students with Matsumoto. Most of them earned their graduate degrees at Western universities. In 1927, the Japanese Psychological Association was formed, with Matsumoto as president, a position he held until his death in 1943. In this interwar era, many Western approaches and methodologies were imported into Japan, including psychological tests, such as the Binet-Simon scale and the Rorschach Projective Technique; behaviorism; and Gestalt studies of perception. Several psychological tests were developed in Japan during this period as well. Psychoanalysis was introduced in the early part of the 20th century by two Japanese scholars who attended Sigmund Freud's (1856–1939) lectures at Clark University in 1909. The Japanese branch of the International Psychoanalytical Association was formed in 1930. By the time World War II began, then, Western psychology, in several of its incarnations, was strongly represented in Japan. After the war, not surprisingly, given the American occupation, American psychology came to have a strong influence on the content of Japanese psychology. The topics of research pursued by the mainstream of American psychology became the mainstream of Japanese psychology. Clinical psychology also developed rapidly from the 1950s.

India

Psychology began to be institutionalized in India early in the 20th century. In 1905, Sir Ashutosh Mukherjee (1864–1924), vice chancellor of Calcutta University, included psychology as an independent subject in the postgraduate course. Sir Brajendra Nath Seal (1864–1938) drew up a syllabus for the subject based on courses of study in Europe and America. N. N. Sengupta went to Harvard University where he worked under Hugo Münsterberg (1863–1916), a student of Wundt. Upon his return, he set up the first psychological laboratory in 1915 at Calcutta University. The Indian Psychological Association was formed in 1924; the *Indian Journal of Psychology* began in 1926.

If we look at the period before independence, a period during which most early teachers were trained abroad, we can discern a heavy British influence in the nature of work done in the field of Indian psychology, as seen in studies on reaction time, problems of illusion, and perceptual errors. In many ways, this was a realization of Lord Thomas Macaulay's (1800–1859) dream for India, where the goal in establishing the Indian Civil Service was to put "interpreters between us and the millions whom we govern, a class of persons, Indian in blood and colour but *English in tastes, in opinions, in morals and intellect*" [italics added].

There were notable exceptions. Jamuna Prasad, trained at Cambridge with Bartlett in the 1930s and returned to India, where he engaged in social psychological research. A massive earthquake shook India in the mid-1930s. The public and popular reaction to the quake was one of fear and uncertainty. Thousands of people died. Rumors began to circulate about how many had perished and that another major earthquake would soon occur. Prasad collected many of these rumors. His analysis of the rumors emphasized group or social influences such as affiliation, shared representations of reality, and group norms. A comparison of rumors from other times led Prasad to explain the power of rumors as occurring on four dimensions: anxiety, cognitive uncertainty, search for cultural meaning, and feeling of group identity or affiliation. Prasad first published this in 1935 and followed up in subsequent years with additional publications. His work preceded similar studies by Gordon Allport (1897–1967) and Leon Festinger (1919–1989) by more than a decade. Unlike Allport and Festinger, however, Prasad emphasized the social aspect of rumor rather than the individualistic response to rumor. Festinger later credited Prasad with anticipating his work on cognitive dissonance.

After Indian independence in 1947, many students left India to study in the United States or the Soviet Union, a country with which India had close ties. Some of those students began to question whether the psychology they had learned abroad was right for India and began to develop an indigenous psychology. The story of the development of indigenous psychology in India is central to a later section.

Africa

In sub-Saharan Africa, the discipline of Psychology has not flourished in the sense it has in other parts of the world. However, some psychological principles were exported to Africa in the colonial era as part of educational systems, health services, and the arena of work. For example, the Western concept of private space and personal privacy—so important, as you have seen, to the development of psychology—was exported to Africa under the banner of colonial health services, including psychiatry. Scholars have amply documented the application of social Darwinist views of the psychological inferiority of Black Africans and how such attributions were used to legitimate punitive psychiatric practices.

Still, disciplinary Psychology had only a small place in African life until the middle of the 20th century, with the exception of South Africa. The first departments of psychology were not founded until the 1960s, and only about 20 universities had a department of psychology by the late 1980s. In many countries, if psychology was taught, it was a minor subject. One measure of the growth of a discipline is whether it has a national association of members. By that measure, South Africa was first, with the formation of a national association in 1948. It was not until 1971 that the second national association was founded, in Zimbabwe. Later, associations were formed in Namibia (1990), Uganda (1992), and Nigeria (1990). One of the leading African psychologists in the late 20th century, Bame Nsamenang (b. 1951), suggested that it was the exclusionary practices of Western psychologies to keep out the worldviews of Africans that stymied the growth of psychology there (2004). Africans in the postcolonial phase, in turn, often rejected the formal disciplinary structure of Psychology, as well as its epistemologies. The question of the relevance of Western psychology to African societies was often raised, as it was in almost the entire non-Western world.

In South Africa, psychology has a different history due to its settlement by Europeans and their subsequent domination and oppression of the overwhelmingly larger Black population. Mental testing played an important role early in the development of South African psychology, when questions of mental hygiene and race relations raised fears of a diminution of national intelligence and class wars. Tests were used to sort and bring order to social relations and educational settings. By the 1920s, disciplinary Psychology had a presence in South Africa. As in other settings during the 1920s and 1930s, the applications of psychology to industry, business, and education facilitated greater acceptance of psychology, even though the uses of psychological knowledge were in support of a racist state. Test results were used to justify emergent racist policies that contributed to the segregation of work and social life and the minimizing of opportunities for Blacks. After World War II, psychologists played important roles in designing and implementing the apartheid laws and rules.

The first national psychological association was formed in 1948, in response to the demands of the medical profession for regulation of psychologists, who were increasingly involved in mental health issues. As psychology grew in the 1950s and 1960s, it expanded into new applications for South African psychologists, beyond the usual testing role. Clinical psychology and counseling psychology were the fastest growing subfields, as they were in other countries after the war. The national association, the South African Psychological Association (SAPA) became the regulatory body for psychologists and facilitated the expansion of psychology into the private practice arena.

Until 1956, SAPA, an all-White professional association, had not had to face issues of race within the association. That year, Josephine Naidoo (b. 1932), a Colored psychologist, applied for membership in SAPA. This created a crisis, and she was asked to withdraw her application, which she did. Still, the association had to decide whether to admit non-Whites. This eventually split the association when the vote was in favor of admitting non-Whites. A significant number of psychologists left to form their own, all-White association, the Psychological Institute of the Republic of South Africa (PIRSA). For several years, the membership of PIRSA was larger than that of SAPA, indicating where the majority of psychologists stood on race.

In the early 1980s, these two organizations merged into the Psychological Association of South Africa (PASA). Although the new organization did not formally bar Blacks from membership, it was clear that Whites would dominate the agenda and the policies. Alternative organizations were formed to counter PASA and to work on behalf of ending apartheid. When apartheid finally ended, with the repeal of apartheid laws in 1992, psychologists from the various organizations came together to form a new association, Psychological Society of South Africa. However, by the end of the 20th century, it was not clear that opportunities in psychology were fully available to members of all races.

INDIGENOUS PSYCHOLOGIES

In this same period, the form of psychology that had become mainstream in the United States also became the model for psychology in many developing societies. The model of the intellectual geography of center and periphery that we introduced at the beginning of the chapter fits well for this section. Even more of a one-way conduit of expertise, methods, and normative practices could be seen between the United States and much of the developing world. Students came to be trained in American graduate programs from all parts of the globe, and many returned home to practice their new skills in their cultures, in many cases having to seriously modify what they learned abroad to make a workable science. Such "fitting" work has often been termed indigenous psychology. Here, we describe the context for the emergence of indigenous psychologies and then turn to some examples.

Indigenization in Context

Indigenization is best understood as a historical process occurring in the context of the bipolarized Cold War and emergent postcolonial nation building. As we noted in the Introduction, after the end of World War II, America became a superpower as measured by its military might and in its capitalist, free-market, consumerist economy that became the engine that drove the world's markets. But it was also a bipolar world, with the Soviet Union poised as the alternative superpower whose military and scientific prowess was impressive. In the Cold War that dominated the world for more than four decades, the two sides engaged in constant efforts to influence smaller countries or to pull them into their respective spheres of influence.

In this context, the concept of the developing world was framed by Western social scientists. "Third World," a term coined by French social scientists in the early 1950s, became the phrase that was widely used for these developing nations. "Third World" was originally meant to signify the majority world, whose people had been downtrodden due to First World colonialism and the ill effects of manufactory capitalism. "Third World" also meant to signify, as well, a third way, between capitalism and Communism. The term was meant to honor oppressed people and nations' struggles for self-definition in a postcolonial world.

In the Cold War, a major challenge for the West, especially for American social scientists, was how to understand development and how to win the allegiance of these nations. How did social scientists theorize about how to bring Third World or developing nations into modernity? Beginning in the 1950s, a body of work emerged that came to be called **modernization theory**. "Modernization" was an elastic term used to describe models of development on a historical arc. For simplicity, we use Latham's depiction of modernization theory (2003). First, "traditional" societies and "modern" societies are at either end of the developmental course. Second, social changes are inextricably linked with political and economic changes. Third, development is progressive, moving toward modernity linearly (not dialectically—this was the Cold War). Fourth, traditional societies can transition to protomodern or even modern societies through the influence and impact of the resources of modern ones. The end point for all developing societies was modernity, the developmental point the West, especially the United States, was at already. It was the inexorable process of development. The underlying view of this theoretical approach was that, in the end, the world would be homogenized. The solutions that followed from the theory were intended to help others be like the West, particularly the United States.

Thus, what social scientists, including psychologists, envisioned was an interventionist model. Agencies and institutions were developed to implement this model and extend Western influence. These included the Marshall Plan, the International Monetary Fund and the International Bank for Reconstruction and Development (now the World Bank). In 1961, American President John F. Kennedy instituted USAID. These agencies and institutions and others like them operated at several levels, including a desire to offer assistance where it was clearly needed. At their core, however, they were, and remain, attempts to manage, if not control, a world full of changes and to direct that change toward

Western or American ends. To the degree that social scientists were involved, and they were deeply involved, these agencies were an extension of Enlightenment ideals of progress and reflected the historical truth that the modern social sciences have been, above all else, sciences of social management, however much they may have promised liberation or economic and social growth.

Liberation and Nonalignment in Postcolonial Nations

In about a 70-year period, between roughly 1850 and 1920, more than 450 million people in Asia and Africa came under colonial rule by both European and American powers. It bears remembering that an active goal of colonizing powers was to destroy established worldviews among the colonized people.

Active resistance to this imperialism began after World War I, with the resistance accelerating during World War II and greatly increasing in the postwar era. The first 15 years of the postwar decolonization era saw 40 nations fight for, and in most cases win, independence from their colonizers. Over the next decade, many more "new" countries emerged. Both superpowers sought to win these countries to their side. In the West, modernization theory offered strategies to regain control over these former colonies through economic and political means, using aid, loans, and other less savory forms of persuasion.

However, for many Third World countries, the Soviet Union was an inviting model for development. In little more than a generation, the Soviet Union had transformed itself from a mostly peasant, agricultural, backward nation into an industrial and military power. The Soviet Union was a viable model for many nations aspiring to transform themselves into modern countries, thus fulfilling Vladimir Lenin's prediction that the revolutionary ideal of Communism would find its most perfect expression in the formerly downtrodden and oppressed nations.

FIGURE 10.2   Nehru and Gandhi in 1942

It was these nations, Lenin argued, that would become the leaders of the revolution and lead the way past capitalism. To many leaders in the Third World, the Soviet Union demonstrated what could be done in a relatively short time to become a powerful nation.

What also emerged early in this period, at least by the mid-1950s, among some postcolonial nations was a desire to find a neutral ground between the two superpowers. The Bandung conference held in Indonesia and organized by five Asian countries—Indonesia, India, Burma, Sri Lanka, and Pakistan—that together represented more than 1.5 billion people, was a step in this direction. The participating countries called for cooperation among themselves and a reliance on their own internal resources; the conference led to the formation of the Non-Aligned Movement (NAM) in 1961. NAM was part of the effort to reestablish an identity separate from that given by the imperial powers. Its members' calls for drawing on their own resources had implications for the development of psychology in many places.

Most of the new nations that emerged perceived that science and education were critical if they were to become modern and developed. However, in many cases domestic educational systems were underdeveloped, resulting in the need to send students elsewhere to receive training. Even poor countries sent thousands of students abroad to gain expertise in Western sciences and educational models, including in Psychology. Psychology graduate programs in the United States and in the United Kingdom and Europe trained many students from Third World countries, many of whom returned to their homelands.

Examples of Indigenous Psychologies

Indigenous psychologies have arisen in many places around the world in the postwar period. Psychologists working in other countries discovered the limitations of Euro-American psychology. First-person accounts by psychologists in diverse countries and regions of the world usually retell scientific training in the American or Euro-American tradition; a return to the home country, the discovery that European or American psychology does not provide a close correspondence with their cultural reality, the growing disenchantment with their training, and then the determination to explore and establish a psychology that does fit with their culture. In the Philippines, India, South Africa, Mexico, Korea, China, and many other places, psychologists began to develop psychologies that reflected local knowledge and remained true to their particular cultural settings. In the next section, we give an example of two approaches to indigenization.

Refashioning Psychology for a Cultural Match in India

One impetus for the development of indigenous approaches was the lack of success of imported Western technologies and approaches. In the postwar period, many developing nations imported scientific and technological expertise to help find solutions to a range of problems. India, for example, received a huge grant from the United Nations Educational, Scientific and Cultural Organization to fund Gardner Murphy's (1895–1979) social psychology research on how to increase social harmony, which resulted in his 1953 book, *In the Minds of Men*. Well-known American personality psychologist David McClelland (1917–1998) and later his student, David Winter (b. 1939), were brought in by the Indian government and supported by the Ford Foundation, the USAID, Carnegie Corporation, and others to study and then to improve achievement motivation among Indian businessmen. Certainly McClelland's work was based on modernization theory, that is, that the way to be a modern country was to adopt Western methods and attitudes (McClelland & Winter, 1969). Their work had little long-term effect in India.

Psychological research in the first two decades after Indian independence in 1947 was mostly a series of efforts to replicate Western studies, as would be expected in the center and periphery model. However, the failure of this imitation of Western research to produce desirable results helped open the minds of local psychologists to consider drawing on their own cultural resources to develop psychology. This came at a time when Indian Prime Minister Jawaharlal Nehru, a leader of the NAM, began to ask social scientists in India to address problems in Indian society, such as problems related to caste, rural poverty, and the impact of westernization. This corresponded with the realization by leaders of countries in the NAM that solutions to local and national problems would need more than just expertise from the West or from the Soviet Union.

These efforts to find Indian solutions to Indian problems helped the psychologists who worked on the identified social problems to see that strict adherence to Western methods and topics would not suffice. Two Western-trained psychologists, Durganand Sinha (1922–1998) and Jai B. P. Sinha (b. 1936) (not related), became leaders in the development of Indian psychology. Out of their frustration with the failure of Western psychology in India, and out of their own knowledge of the richness of Indian culture, the Sinhas and a few other psychologists began developing a Psychology that could be applied to a range of Indian issues. By the mid-1960s, a small movement focused on developing a theoretical framework more consonant with Indian culture to better address the needs of the country.

Sidebar 10.1 Focus on *Jai B. P. Sinha*

The growth of psychology in Asia since the end of World War II has been remarkable. We noted in the text the historical pattern of students coming to Western countries, receiving excellent training in psychological science, and then returning to their natal cultures. There, they often found that the psychology they had learned was poorly suited to their homeland. Here we give a more detailed account of this pattern by focusing on a well-known Indian psychologist.

Jai Sinha was raised in a strict Hindu family. His father was a freedom fighter in the Indian independence movement. He developed an interest in psychological topics and was drawn into the study of psychology for his BA and MA. Sinha then received a Fulbright travel grant for study at the Ohio State University. There he was trained in the best American tradition of social psychology. Even before he left the United States, however, he was beginning to wonder about how easily the ideas and practices he had learned would translate to his home country. He has recounted the story of how he shared the results of his research on achievement motivation with the noted psychologist David McClelland. Sinha's results showed that when high-achieving individuals are placed in a low-resource condition they developed strong dislike for their fellow participants. This was counter to the work that McClelland had done on achievement motivation. Recall that McClelland was generously funded to try to raise the achievement motivation of Indian businessmen.

Once back in India, Sinha immediately established himself as an important figure in Indian psychology. However, he found that the route to success that he was following seemed to be taking him ever further from the realities of Indian life. In addition, while he was publishing extensively in Indian journals, he found it increasingly difficult to have his papers accepted in American journals of psychology.

By the mid-1970s and into the 1980s, Sinha focused on the study of leadership and its role in Indian business life. He and his collaborators found that the successful leadership model in India was neither the participative nor the authoritarian model that Western psychologists were reporting. Rather, Sinha and his research group showed that Indians responded best to what they called the nurturant–task model of leadership, which is a blend of task orientation and nurturance. This, Sinha argued, was due to the dependency patterns of Indian culture, the tendency to personalize relationships, and status consciousness. Because the model also incorporated Western notions of reward, Sinha argued that it was a blend of East and West.

The success of Sinha led to many honors and placed him in the leadership of international psychology. He has served on the executive board of the International Association of Applied Psychology and has been in demand as a conference speaker around the world. He was instrumental in founding the Association for Social Engineering, Research, and Training in Patna, India. He is now retired from its faculty, although he continues to write and contribute to psychology in India and around the world.

The practical impact of this movement was the development of a problem-oriented psychology. In this approach, Durganand Sinha and others began to address macrolevel issues of Indian society. To give one example, in a landmark study, Sinha led research on why villagers were having such difficulty with transitioning to more modern ways of life. The conclusion was that the illiterate villagers had not had much exposure to new influences and thus were resistant to government efforts to introduce new systems of agriculture, education, and communication. Sinha argued that psychologists had to understand this aspect of the villagers' mindset to help them. The extension of psychology to these larger-level problems, such as population control, health practices, and poverty, reflected the effort to make psychology socially relevant. To encourage dialogue on these matters and to further the development of Indian psychology, Durganand Sinha started the journal, *Psychology and Developing Societies*, which published its first volume in 1989.

Durganand Sinha later characterized Indian psychology as emerging from dual processes: indigenization from within and indigenization from without. **Indigenization from without** meant that principles and methods learned in American, British, or European graduate programs were not just discarded wholesale; rather, they were reevaluated and modified to fit the Indian context. In a parallel process of **indigenization from within**, some Indian psychologists began to look to more ancient traditions, the Vedas and Upanishads, which are the texts that gave rise to Hinduism, Buddhism, and Jainism, for insights into human nature. These psychologists then sought to fashion an Indian psychology that relied, in part, on these texts as a source for contemporary research and application.

Durganand Sinha argued that the cultural traditions of India provided a firm foundation for a nuanced and subtle psychology more suitable for understanding Indian life than the imported Western psychology. He argued for several years, in numerous publications, that in

FIGURE 10.3 Photo of Durganand Sinha and Muzafer Sherif
Courtesy of the Archives of the History of American Psychology, University of Akron, Akron, OH.

India meaningfulness is inextricably linked to relationships with others and that the goal of life is to find harmony with both nature and society. For psychology to have relevance in India, he pointed out, it must take into account this fundamental fact of Indian existence. The question of identity, for instance, is different in India than in most Western cultures. A person's identity does not lie primarily in that person's individual qualities or characteristics or abilities. Indian identity is primarily relational, that is, defined by family, caste, community, nation, and so forth. There is richness in Indian life, as Durganand Sinha and many others pointed out, that is not readily apparent to outsiders. To be effective, psychology must originate from this basic, taken-for-granted truth of Indian life. To do so, Sinha and others argued, is what makes psychology Indian, not just an imported set of methods, principles, and practices.

Returning briefly to the center and periphery metaphor, it is the center that has the material and institutional resources to support expansion of the field, to extend the center's influence even further. The periphery typically has far fewer resources, making it almost impossible for the psychology of the periphery to come up to the standards of the center. Thus, the hegemony of the methods and theories of the center are maintained. By the end of the 20th century, several Indian psychologists were advocating for an abandonment of the Western ideal, as we showed in the work of the Sinhas. It was suggested that the way forward was to "outgrow the alien framework" by rethinking the basic assumptions of psychology. Doing so, it was argued, would put Indian psychology on new footing by removing the sense of deficiency that arose from the absence of the latest books, journals, or computer equipment.

Psychologists' involvement in mental health work was a late development in India. The country has a long tradition of multiple approaches to health, including mental health. Practitioners come from many orientations, from fakirs and faith healers to psychiatrists. As we pointed out in Chapter 5, psychoanalysis in India began around 1920 and maintained a small but vocal presence in the mental health community. Indigenous approaches to mental health and attempts to integrate those approaches with psychoanalysis were documented by Sudhir Kakar (b. 1938). His book *Shamans, Mystics, and Doctors* (1982) discussed traditional mental health practices in the context of Indian culture. Kakar pointed out that healing practices, including mental health, involved the whole family. As we noted earlier, this reflects the relational nature of identity and the necessity of belongingness to a group. Counseling psychology emerged in India late in the 20th century under the influence of Western educational practices. It has struggled to define its role in Indian life. By the end of the 20th century, counseling psychologists were increasingly called upon to help families and communities deal with the rapid transitions of urban Indian life, as the influence of outsourced jobs from the West drew thousands of young Indians from their families to major cities across India. This meant that these young adults were often living independently of their families and were thrown into new social settings for which they had no guidance. Counseling psychologists sought insights from both Indian cultural traditions and social norms and Western theories of therapy to

meet these challenges. Even though the applications of psychology to mental health work in India have grown, at the beginning of the 21st century the gurus and swamis dominate the field of mental health advice and counseling, most typically through the avenue of cable television channels. In some ways, what they are offering is a truly indigenous approach to mental health.

Fashioning an Indigenous Psychology in the Philippines

In each national setting, psychologists sought cultural resources to help create a psychology that made sense in their particular context. In doing so, some psychologists developed more radical psychologies that rejected much of Western psychology. The Philippines and the work of Alfredo Lagmay (1919–2005) and Virgilio Enriquez (1942–1994) are examples.

The Philippines was a colony of Spain from the 16th century until 1898, and then a colony of the United States from 1898 to 1946. Despite American histories that portray the relationship in a positive light, many Filipinos resented the second-class status accorded their country and the utter dominance of the United States in their politics, economy, and education. Not surprisingly, the first disciplinary psychologists in the Philippines were educated at American universities. Many of them brought the psychology they had learned with them when they returned. There remained a significant Spanish philosophical influence in the country, as well as a German influence centered at the country's oldest university, the University of San Carlos in Cebu City.

In the 1950s, a movement began toward establishing a Filipino psychology that did not owe its epistemology and methods to American psychology. Lagmay earned his PhD at Harvard in 1955 with Burrhus Frederic Skinner (1904–1990). Not long after he returned to the Philippines, he became the chair of the Psychology Department. As chair, he had the department transferred to

FIGURE 10.4 American colonialism in the Philippines

the College of Liberal Arts from the College of Education. He did this to bring a more scientific orientation to the department. He remained department chair for two decades. Under his leadership, new approaches were encouraged. One of the psychologists in the department who became a leader in the new approaches was Enriquez. Together, Lagmay and Enriquez created **sikolohiyang Pilipino** (Filipino psychology). It became a major force and an innovative conceptualization of the power of an indigenous approach to psychology, especially in a colonial and postcolonial context.

Taking a cue from Durganand Sinha in India, Lagmay encouraged the development of methods and topics more suited to the diverse cultures of the Philippines. Enriquez was the point person on this indigenization. He earned his doctorate in social psychology at Northwestern University in Illinois. After his return to the Philippines, he became a force of nature, if you will, within the Philippines until his death in the 1990s. He argued that psychology, to be relevant, has to understand each group of people within its own culture and with their own cultural norms.

To that end, Enriquez and his colleagues at the institute they established, the Philippine Psychology Research and Training House, trained hundreds of students in the emerging methods and practices of *sikolohiyang Pilipino*. This approach was rooted in Filipino culture and history. The principal emphases were on identity and national awareness, social awareness and involvement, and language and culture. It was anticolonial. Research methods included participatory observation, participant action, and qualitative interviews where both parties interviewed each other. Enriquez argued that psychological knowledge in this approach grows out of the collaborative demands of relationships, rather than knowledge that is extracted by an expert from a naive subject. Lagmay and Enriquez argued that this would provide tools toward liberating Filipinos from the constricted worldview imposed by colonialism.

Indigenous psychologies, as we see in India and the Philippines, have historically developed in reaction to, and often in resistance to, the perceived scientific imperialism of Western psychologies. There has usually been a practical dimension as well. Social problems, such as poverty, education, and class or caste issues that have not yielded to the methods or insight of Western psychologies have often been important foci of indigenous approaches.

Toward a Liberation Psychology in Latin America

Central and South America are diverse regions, with multiple language groups, different histories, and different forms of government. Psychology has, as well, different histories across the regions. After Europeans invaded and conquered the indigenous populations, a strong Catholic influence developed. With the establishment of schools and universities, philosophical speculations about human nature characterized the earliest psychologies. By the beginning of the 20th century, Psychology as a science and as a facet of medicine was established.

The institutionalization of psychology in these regions was followed by the gradual growth of psychology associations. The first national society of psychologists in South America was formed in Argentina (1930). Ecuador (1942) followed, and by 1981 national organizations had formed in several South and Central American countries, including Brazil (1949), Mexico (1953), Uruguay (1953), Peru (1954), Venezuela (1957), Cuba (1964), Panama (1965), Colombia (1978), and Nicaragua (1981). Chile and the Dominican Republic also have national psychological organizations.

Psychologists across Central and South America formed the Interamerican Society of Psychology (usually known by its Spanish-language acronym, SIP) in December 1951 during the Congress of the World Federation of Mental Health. The founding members intended for the society to be a small group of prominent psychologists who would work together to foster psychological science in the Americas and the Caribbean. It had only 50 members in 1953, most from the United States, Mexico, and a few Caribbean islands. However, membership grew to more than 900 by 1964 and the society was restructured to accommodate growth. The number of countries represented grew to include many more Latin American countries. By the end of the 20th century, the society had approximately 1,000 individual members from 26 countries.

Scientific psychology began to be taught in Argentina by the early 1890s, with the first laboratory established in 1891. Over the next decade, several laboratories, primarily for teaching demonstrations, were set up in Argentina. Enrique Aragón (1880–1942) founded the first psychology laboratory in Mexico (1916), and the earliest laboratory in Brazil was established by the Polish expatriate Waclaw Radecki (1887–1953) in 1923. Teaching laboratories at normal schools (teacher's colleges) were set up intermittently over the next few decades, but in most countries no experimental psychology laboratories appeared until the 1960s or later.

From the beginning, Europe strongly influenced the development of psychological thought and practice across the region. French influences predominated in Argentina for much of the first half of the 20th century, in both clinical and experimental work. French and Italian influences

were notable in Brazil; for example, the laboratory of the normal school in São Paulo in 1914 was founded and led by an Italian psychologist, Ugo Pizzoli (1863–1934), and the research of the Italian experimentalist, Gabriele Buccola (1875–1885), was influential in the medical school of Rio de Janeiro.

One reason for the European influence was the significant number of European psychologists and psychoanalysts who immigrated to various South American countries. For example, German émigrés included the psychometrician Walter Blumenfeld (Peru; 1882–1967), Betti Katzenstein (Brazil; 1906–1981), and Herbert Brugger (Argentina). Spanish psychologist Emilio Mira y López (1896–1964) worked in both Argentina and Brazil, while Mercedes Rodrigo (1891–1982) worked in Colombia and Puerto Rico. The Polish psychologist Radecki played important roles in establishing psychology in Brazil, Argentina, and Uruguay. Helena Antipoff (1892–1974) was born in Russia, was educated in Paris, and trained with Édouard Claparède (1873–1940) at the University of Geneva. She returned to Russia and worked with associates of Lev Vygotskii (1896–1934), and then had a long and influential career in Brazil. The Hungarian psychologist Oliver Brachfeld (1908–1967) worked in Brazil. The Hungarian psychoanalyst Béla Székely (1892–1955), a student of Freud's, was a key figure in the development of psychoanalysis in Argentina (Geuter & León, 1997). In addition, European psychologists often visited South American countries as guest lecturers or as visiting professors, which added to their influence.

In general, by the 1920s and after, psychology became valued as it was applied to the problems and needs of each country. So, for example, Antipoff, at the teachers' training college in Belo Horizonte, Brazil, brought the "new school" ideas of Claparède and the Vygotskiian cultural–historical model of active learning to the reform and expansion of Brazilian primary and secondary education, as historian of psychology Regina Campos has documented (2001). This same principle applies to other fields.

Psychologists were expected to contribute to the development of industry through personnel selection, vocational guidance, and improvement of worker relations. After World War II, educational and training programs in psychology were developed, the first in 1946, and by the late 1960s, several countries had instituted programs that led to professional degrees that permitted the graduate to work in any of several fields. In these countries, psychology flourished so that by the end of the 20th century Brazil was second only to the United States in the number of psychologists.

A basic historical overview of the institutionalization of psychology, such as the one here, does not indicate the complexity of the development of psychology across Central and South America. To give a better sense of that complexity, we turn to a brief account of efforts to create psychologies that would serve as mechanisms of liberation for the working classes that numerically dominate the population of South America.

Toward a Psychology of Liberation

Liberation psychology in South and Central America is related to the articulation of liberation theology by members of the Roman Catholic Church. In the 1950s and 1960s, popular movements arose in protest against the increasing poverty and marginalization of the poor in much of South and Central America. This provoked a backlash from the wealthy and middle classes to enlist the military and police forces to suppress these movements. In several countries, priests began to preach and write about the calling of Christians to work for social justice as a way of combating economic and political oppression, the visible expressions of sin. One of the first volumes to formally express a liberation theology was *The Poor, Jesus, and the Church* by Paul Gauthier (1965). The Brazilian theologian and psychoanalyst Rubem Alves published *Toward a Theology of Liberation* (1968) and *Religion: Opium of the People or Instrument of Liberation* (1969). Another important work was José Míguez Bonino's *Doing Theology in a Revolutionary Situation* (1975).

Parallel to the theological developments, a movement toward the use of social science for social action and justice began among social scientists. An array of social scientists rediscovered that humans are active agents, not just passive subjects. Among these social scientists, a few psychologists began to argue for a psychology that would address the needs of the peasants and serve as a liberatory force in their lives. Interest developed in work in the community, with and on behalf of the community members. Community psychology as a new field within Psychology began to develop, marked by undergraduate and graduate programs and departments at colleges and universities across Central and South America.

Two contributors to liberation psychology are highlighted here. Ignacio Martín-Baró (1942–1989), was a Jesuit priest and University of Chicago–trained social psychologist in El Salvador. He became a major figure in Central and South America before his assassination by a Salvadoran right-wing death squad in 1989. He was an advocate for a psychology that was developed from the perspective of everyday people and that would serve their needs, rather than a psychology developed in laboratories or in middle-class private therapy offices. The power of his words and his actions are witnessed by his assassination. In one of his essays translated into English after his death, he expressed his view of what psychology must be to be a force for liberation:

> If, as psychologists we wish to make a contribution to the social development of Latin America, we have to redesign our theoretical and practical tools from the standpoint of the lives of our own people, from their sufferings, aspirations, and struggles. We must affirm that any effort at developing a psychology that will contribute to the liberation of our peoples has to mean the creation of a liberation psychology. (1994, p. 25)

His work initiated a movement among psychologists in Latin America, *la psicología social de la liberación* (PSL, roughly translated as "liberation social psychology"), that works in educational

FIGURE 10.5 Paolo Freire
Courtesy of Slobodan Dimitrov.

and community settings to further the goal of using psychology as a positive force in the lives of the poor (Burton & Kagan, 2005). One of the methods is conscientization, an approach developed by the Brazilian educator and psychologist Paolo Freire.

Freire (1921–1997) developed conscientization as part of the popular-education movement. He insisted that education and knowledge do not belong only to the elite and developed education and literacy programs to facilitate critical awareness among the poor. At the time he began his work, literacy was required to vote. His success in teaching literacy and raising critical awareness made him a threat when a military dictatorship came to power in 1964. Exiled, Freire worked in Bolivia and Chile and wrote his highly influential book, *Pedagogy of the Oppressed* (1968 [English translation, 1970]). At the heart of the book is **conscientization**. The goal of conscientization is to engage poor citizens through teaching them to read so that these people recognize themselves as fully human, understand themselves as historical beings, and are able to think for themselves. This process, unique in each setting, Freire claimed, holds the possibility of breaking the yoke of political, social, and economic oppression.

Freire's influence grew in Brazil, even while he was in exile, and his ideas spread across much of Central and South America, where they influenced many of the new generation of community liberation psychologists, such as Maritza Montero and Martín-Baró.

The development of a liberation psychology in South America took place as part of the worldwide movement by colonized and oppressed people around the world to decolonize their consciousness, as well as free them from political and social oppression. The Black and White psychologists in South Africa who worked against apartheid were also important voices that transformed the psychology exported to them into psychologies that were a better fit with their own populations. In North Africa, the principles of liberation psychology were explicated by Martinique-born psychiatrist Frantz Fanon (1925–1961). Fanon trained in France as a psychiatrist and then spent his life working in Algeria. He initially was employed by the French colonial government but went over to the side of the rebels as he witnessed the horrible oppression and brutalizing methods of the French colonial administration and military. Fanon wrote critically about the oppressiveness of colonialism on the psyche of Africans. In his landmark book, *The Wretched of the Earth* (1963), he argued for a psychology grounded in changing consciousness to help oppressed people challenge and change oppressive social structures. In some cases, methods and theories developed in these contexts were reexported back to the West.

SUMMARY

In this chapter, we articulated examples of the intellectual center and periphery model in the history of psychology. We argued that, over the last 50 or more years in psychology, we have been living through a slow change toward a polycentric psychology. That is, rather than a psychology dominated or controlled by Western, especially American, methods and practices, in this period multiple centers have begun to emerge. This has not happened without resistance from the dominant models, but it has been happening. In several countries, psychology has become an important part of intellectual and practical life. Just as we saw happening in earlier chapters in regard to this process in the United States, so in multiple other countries psychology has been and is being indigenized to fit local cultural and national contexts.

One conclusion that can be drawn from an examination of indigenous psychologies is this: Although colonialist oppression was crushing and demeaning to all it touched, people did not relinquish their agency. Nor did they simply embrace ideologies or practices brought by the imperial power. As we show in Chapter 12, many parallels can be found between anticolonial movements throughout the world and the African community's struggle in America in how they transformed their oppressed and marginalized positions. In India and elsewhere, Western principles and practices were sometimes adapted to the local situation, sometimes abandoned, and sometimes countered.

A historical analysis of indigenous psychologies indicates that the process of indigenization in formerly colonized countries will move slowly.

In part, this is because of the intrinsic disciplinary structure of Psychology as a Western construction. Part of the halting development of indigenous psychologies is the continuing influence of the West, which often exerts overt pressure to adopt methods, tests, and clinical practices that bear the approval of the psychological establishment. This often results in the desire among psychologists in non-Western countries to make the indigenous psychology part, as one often reads, of a universal psychology. Historian of psychology Irmingard Staeuble has written convincingly about how difficult this indigenization process is and will continue to be (2004). She has pointed out that the colonial legacy cannot simply be discarded. As she wrote, "In the aftermath of colonial domination and disqualification of ways of life ... the scope of alternatives remains defined by previous transformations" (Staeuble, 2004, p. 198).

This chapter is a contribution toward a new history of psychology, one that we believe will match the trend toward a polycentric psychology. That is, we argue that we need a polycentric *history* of psychology.

Our examination of the work of Martín-Baró, Freire, and others demonstrates that for a psychology to be liberatory it has to be a psychology grounded in real-life human experience that draws on the suffering, strengths, hopes, and aspirations of the people it is intended to serve. In the United States, the closest parallels to the work of Freire, Fanon, Martín-Baró, and Enriquez were in the work of feminists and psychologists of color. We turn to a historical account of this work in the next two chapters.

BIBLIOGRAPHIC ESSAY

The rich literature about psychology in countries outside North America and Europe does not seem particularly well known among scholars and scientists in North America. For our chapter, we drew on only a portion of available material, although we have read widely in the non-Western literature. We began by citing historian of psychology Kurt Danziger (2006) from his work on the indigenization of psychology and the need for a polycentric history.

Peter van Strienen provoked our thinking about the influence of American psychology in the postwar era on the development of psychology in the Netherlands and elsewhere (1997). An important history of European social psychology by one of the important participants in that history, Serge Moscovici, *The Making of Modern Social Psychology* (Moscovici & Markova, 2006), was useful to us. Mitchell Ash (1990), among his many other contributions, has written informatively about the development of psychology as a science and profession in Germany, specifically West Germany, in the postwar era.

An article that moved us to begin the process of understanding psychology in a cultural context and that remains helpful is Anthony Marsella's 1998 *American Psychologist* article. A very helpful perspective was gained from "Psychological science in cultural context" (Gergen, Gulerce, Lock, & Misra, 1996). The development of disciplinary Psychology in Asia has a long history, although we lack an extensive English-language corpus of that history. The older account, *Psychology moving East: The status of Western psychology in Asia and Oceania* (Blowers, & Turtle [Eds.], 1987) remains useful. We found recent work by Geoff Blowers and his colleagues (Blowers, Cheung, & Ru, 2009) and work by Qicheng Jing and Xiaolan Fu (2001) and Matthias Petzold (1987) useful. A well-developed group of historians of psychology in Japan has contributed up-to-date scholarship

on psychology in that country that is far more extensive than we cite here (Oyama, Sato, & Suzuki, 2001; Takasuna, 2006).

Durganand Sinha, one of the subjects of our chapter, has written more about the history of psychology in India than anyone else we know. We relied on several of his accounts (1986, 1994, 1998). The account of the work of Prasad on the psychology of rumor (Bordia & DiFonzo, 2002) gave us a good background on prewar psychology. We found Jai Sinha's autobiographical account (1997) both enlightening and informative about postwar Indian psychology. An additional source of contemporary thought about the development of an indigenous psychology in India was Jai B. P. Sinha's 1995 article. Information about Jai Sinha was drawn from his chapter "In Search of my *Brahman*" from the volume *Working at the Interface of Cultures*, edited by Michael H. Bond (1997). Girishwar Misra's excellent and provocative book from 2007 was very helpful.

Bame Nsamenang (1995, 2004) and Roger Serpell (1984) have both written fascinating and thoughtful critiques of psychology in sub-Saharan Africa. Sally Swartz (1996) has written eloquently about the use of psychiatry as a colonial discipline in Africa. The story of psychology in South Africa has a different cast than in the rest of Africa. Much of that story has been recently documented in a fine history edited by Clifford van Ommen and Desmond Painter (2008). Many chapters in that book informed our work, especially the one by Mohamed Seedat and Sarah MacKenzie (2008). The history of the development of a professional psychology associations in South Africa has been written by Kitty DuMont and Johann Louw (2001).

Our understanding of the history of the concept of the "developing" world was greatly informed by the scholarship of Arturo Escobar

(1995). Michael Latham (2003), among others, has written informatively about the history of modernization theory. We found the work of Odd Westad (2007) on the impact of the Cold War on postcolonial nations both interesting and convincing in its analyses.

Autobiographical accounts of psychologists who are working to develop indigenous psychologies were useful. The various chapters in Bond (1997) and Uichol Kim and John Berry (1993) repeatedly proved helpful. We especially are grateful for Virgilio Enriquez's chapter on Filipino Psychology in the volume. The contemporary writing of the sociologist Mysore N. Srinivas (1966) helped us grasp how modernization was understood and subverted by postcolonial people. The history of counseling in India has been thoughtfully discussed by the Bangalore-based psychologist Gideon Arulmani (2007). Both in his written account and in personal communication he has been most helpful.

The work of Alfredo Lagmay and Virgilio Enriquez in the Philippines is one of the best examples of the indigenization process at work. It has been well documented both by Enriquez (1987) and by his former students, Rogelia Pe-Pua and Elizabeth Protacio-Marcelino (2000).

Historian of psychology and science Hugo Klappenbach has enriched our understanding of the history of psychology in Argentina (2004). Psychoanalysis has a long history in Argentina, and part of that history has been documented by Klappenbach (2004). Cecilia Taiana (2006) has discussed the enduring influence of the transatlantic exchanges between European psychologists and their Argentinean colleagues. The history of psychology in Brazil is part of an active research program being led in Brazil by Regina Campos (e.g., Campos, 2001; Hutz, McCarthy, & Gomes, 2004). A good overview of psychology in Latin America is "Psychology in Latin America today" (Ardila, 1982). Mark Burton and Carolyn Kagan (2005) have written about the legacy of Freire and its current instantiation as liberation social psychology. One of the key participants in that history and one of the leading social psychologists in Latin America, Maritza Montero (1996), has also written about the history of the field.

Finally, our understanding of the challenges of developing psychologies that are indigenous, especially in the face of the pressure from Western psychology, has been greatly enriched by the work of our friend and colleague Irmingard Staeuble (2004).

Chapter 11
TIMELINE 1810–1990
(In 25-year increments)

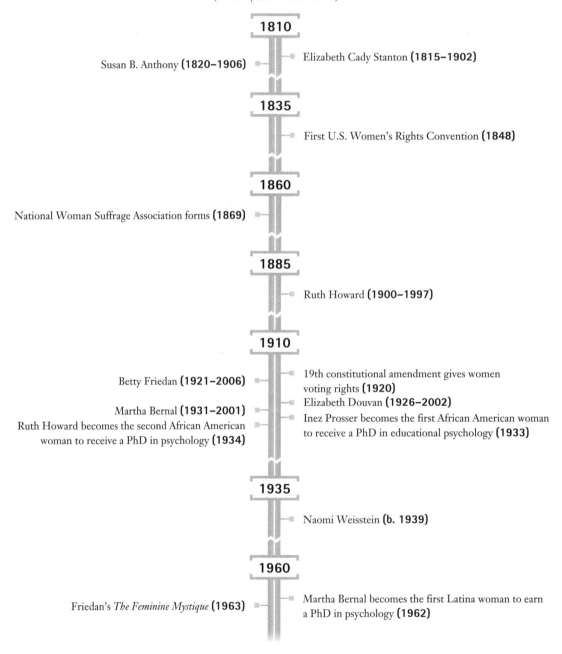

1810

Susan B. Anthony **(1820–1906)**

Elizabeth Cady Stanton **(1815–1902)**

1835

First U.S. Women's Rights Convention **(1848)**

1860

National Woman Suffrage Association forms **(1869)**

1885

Ruth Howard **(1900–1997)**

1910

Betty Friedan **(1921–2006)**

Martha Bernal **(1931–2001)**

Ruth Howard becomes the second African American woman to receive a PhD in psychology **(1934)**

19th constitutional amendment gives women voting rights **(1920)**

Elizabeth Douvan **(1926–2002)**

Inez Prosser becomes the first African American woman to receive a PhD in educational psychology **(1933)**

1935

Naomi Weisstein **(b. 1939)**

1960

Friedan's *The Feminine Mystique* **(1963)**

Martha Bernal becomes the first Latina woman to earn a PhD in psychology **(1962)**

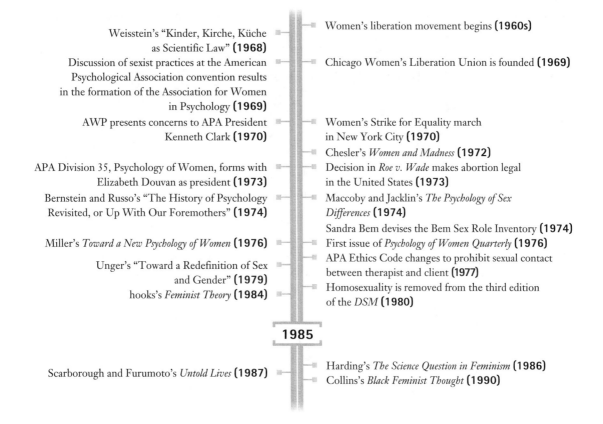

Weisstein's "Kinder, Kirche, Küche as Scientific Law" **(1968)**

Women's liberation movement begins **(1960s)**

Discussion of sexist practices at the American Psychological Association convention results in the formation of the Association for Women in Psychology **(1969)**

Chicago Women's Liberation Union is founded **(1969)**

AWP presents concerns to APA President Kenneth Clark **(1970)**

Women's Strike for Equality march in New York City **(1970)**

Chesler's *Women and Madness* **(1972)**

APA Division 35, Psychology of Women, forms with Elizabeth Douvan as president **(1973)**

Decision in *Roe v. Wade* makes abortion legal in the United States **(1973)**

Bernstein and Russo's "The History of Psychology Revisited, or Up With Our Foremothers" **(1974)**

Maccoby and Jacklin's *The Psychology of Sex Differences* **(1974)**

Sandra Bem devises the Bem Sex Role Inventory **(1974)**

Miller's *Toward a New Psychology of Women* **(1976)**

First issue of *Psychology of Women Quarterly* **(1976)**

Unger's "Toward a Redefinition of Sex and Gender" **(1979)**

APA Ethics Code changes to prohibit sexual contact between therapist and client **(1977)**

hooks's *Feminist Theory* **(1984)**

Homosexuality is removed from the third edition of the *DSM* **(1980)**

1985

Scarborough and Furumoto's *Untold Lives* **(1987)**

Harding's *The Science Question in Feminism* **(1986)**

Collins's *Black Feminist Thought* **(1990)**

FEMINISM AND AMERICAN PSYCHOLOGY: THE SCIENCE AND POLITICS OF GENDER

To be in the margin is to be part of the whole but outside the main body.

—bell hooks, *Feminist Theory: From Margin to Center*, 1984

INTRODUCTION

In the last chapter, we explored how the anticolonial movements and liberation struggles of the 1960s disrupted global power relations and began to challenge the hegemony that American psychology had assumed internationally after World War II. The central position of American, or more broadly, Western, approaches began to be questioned by psychologists from countries or groups previously thought of as at the peripheries, or margins, of institutional Psychology in this period. This challenge to the dominant approach was also being enacted from *within* American psychology by groups that were, as feminist theorist bell hooks has put it, "part of the whole, but outside the main body" (1984, p. ix). Although hooks was specifically describing the marginalization of Black women in the development of feminist theory, theory that at the time largely reflected the experiences of "privileged women who live at the center" (p. x), her characterization aptly describes the position of women and psychologists of color in the discipline of Psychology in America in the early 1960s. They were in the minority and on the margins. We explore the catalytic challenge of psychologists of color to American psychology in the next chapter.

In this chapter, we outline how American psychology, and Psychology, has been challenged and changed by feminism and the politics of gender. The most profound change undoubtedly occurred in tandem with the second wave of the women's movement, which provided the political and intellectual momentum for overarching changes in many areas of personal and public life. Academic Psychology and its institutions were no exception. In this period, feminists who were also psychologists, and psychologists who became feminists used this momentum to move their concerns from the periphery of the discipline to its center, effectively staking out a new field and a new disciplinary presence.

Although the field of feminist psychology was not officially established until the late 1960s and early 1970s, efforts by women to break down sexist barriers and undermine sexist assumptions in Psychology had certainly been undertaken earlier, indeed, since the beginning of the discipline itself. When Psychology was established in the late 1800s, the long trajectory of first-wave feminism was close to its midpoint. In the United States, the beginning of first-wave feminism is often marked by the historic Seneca Falls Convention of 1848, the first women's rights convention in America. At this meeting, Elizabeth Cady Stanton (1815–1902) drafted and read the Declaration of Sentiments in which she

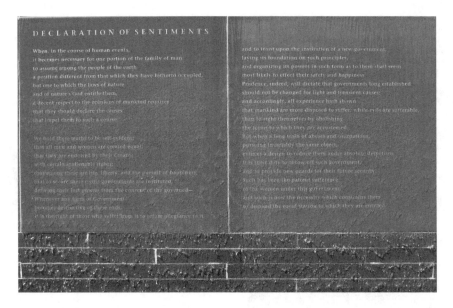

FIGURE 11.1   The Declaration of Sentiments reproduced on a monument at the Women's Rights National Historical Park in Seneca Falls, New York
Courtesy of the authors.

demanded equal rights for women, including the right to vote.

With Susan B. Anthony (1820–1906), she founded the National Woman Suffrage Association. Women's suffrage became a defining goal of first-wave feminism. In 1851, at a women's rights convention in Akron, Ohio, Sojourner Truth (1797–1883), a former slave, gave her famous speech "Ain't I a Woman," in which she demanded that her experience as an enslaved Black woman be recognized in both the suffrage and the abolitionist movements.

In the United States, women finally won the right to vote in 1920 with the ratification of the 19th constitutional amendment, or suffrage bill. Many late 19th- and early 20th-century American women psychologists, such as Christine Ladd-Franklin (1847–1930) and Helen Thompson Woolley (1874–1947), were women's rights supporters and activists. As we show later in the chapter, it was not until the 1970s that their contributions to psychology, let alone their feminist convictions, were rediscovered and written into historical accounts. The emergence of

a women's history of psychology was part of the feminist challenge to the larger discipline and continues to this day.

After women won the right to vote in the United States, feminism as an organized political movement largely dissolved. The Great Depression of the 1930s and the onset of World War II left feminists little time or energy for mass, gender-based activism, with some exceptions. The post–World War II period was characterized by a particularly marked retrenchment to traditional gender stereotypes and roles, despite continued increases in women's participation in the workforce throughout the 1950s. In 1963, Betty Friedan (1921–2006) published *The Feminine Mystique* (1963/1997), which heralded the beginning of second-wave feminism in the United States. In her book, Friedan articulated the despair of many White, middle-class women, herself among them, who were trapped by rigid social expectations in the role of perfect housewife and mother, with no opportunities for personal fulfillment outside the strictures of these highly circumscribed

FIGURE 11.2 Statue of Sojourner Truth at the National Women's Hall of Fame in Seneca Falls, NY.
Courtesy of the authors.

FIGURE 11.3 Betty Friedan

roles. Her assessment of the "problem that has no name" as she characterized the yearning for fulfillment beyond domesticity (Friedan, 1963/1997, p. 15), resonated powerfully with a select group of women, many of whom had witnessed or experienced the opening of employment and public life during wartime and then promptly saw women transformed back into divas of domesticity in the 1950s. This despair, combined with the powerful model of the civil rights movement and the New Left, mobilized many women into political action by the end of the 1960s.

On August 26, 1970, on the 50th anniversary of the constitutional amendment that gave American women the right to vote, American feminists Betty Friedan, Gloria Steinem (b. 1934), and Bella Abzug (1920–1998) convened the Women's Strike for Equality march on Fifth Avenue in New York City. Their mandate was clear: to continue the work left undone by their first-wave predecessors by demanding equal opportunities in education and the workplace; access to safe, legal abortion; affordable childcare; and an equal share of political power. As Friedan wrote in the epilogue to the 10th anniversary edition of *The Feminine Mystique*, "By 1970 it was beginning to be clear that the women's movement was ... the fastest-growing movement for basic social and political change of the decade" (1963/1997, p. 389).

Many of the women who marched down Fifth Avenue on August 26 would have been familiar with Friedan's book, which drew heavily on psychological themes and theories, including psychoanalysis, which she (and many other feminists) criticized, and humanistic–existential psychology, which she drew upon to make the case for women's self-actualization and liberation. Friedan had been a psychology major as an undergraduate at Smith College and had considered pursuing graduate studies in the field. Although she did not become a psychologist, her thinking and her writing were heavily influenced by the psychological theories that she had learned about and that infused popular culture in this period. Psychology both shaped popular views about women and spawned feminist critiques of these views. By the late 1960s, many feminists, both within and external to the discipline, were becoming increasingly dissatisfied with the way academic Psychology had theorized and treated women. Many female psychologists were becoming increasingly aware of, and angered by, the way they themselves were being treated within the institutions of their chosen field. The women's liberation movement proved a tipping point to bring feminist politics to psychology.

BRINGING FEMINISM TO PSYCHOLOGY

In the wake of the burgeoning women's movement, feminist women psychologists (and a few feminist men) waged their own battles within their chosen discipline, demanding that androcentric theories be acknowledged and reformed and that sexist institutional practices be eliminated. One of these psychologists was Naomi Weisstein (b. 1939), an ardent socialist feminist and one of the founders of the Chicago Women's Liberation Union. In her graduate training at Harvard University in the early 1960s, Weisstein had experienced firsthand the sexism that was a common feature of women's experiences in postsecondary education in the 1950s and 1960s. At Harvard, for example, Weisstein has reported that women were banned from one of the libraries because, as she was told, they were thought to distract men from serious scholarship. Weisstein was not allowed access to the equipment she needed to conduct her doctoral research; she was told that, as a woman, she would surely break it. Luckily, she was given access to the equipment at nearby Yale University and was able to complete her work. These and other experiences like them, combined with her fierce intelligence and awareness of critical theory, fueled Weisstein's feminist fire. In fall 1968, she delivered a paper that was destined to become one of the founding documents of feminist psychology.

Originally published by the New England Free Press in 1968 as "Kinder, Kirche, Küche as Scientific Law: Psychology Constructs the Female," a revised and expanded version was published in 1971 and has since been reprinted dozens of times in a range of publications (Weisstein, 1971).

In this article, Weisstein argued that psychology had nothing to say about what women were really like because, essentially, psychology did not know. This failure, she proposed, was due to psychologists' focus on inner traits and consequent ignorance of social context, as well as their failure to consider evidence, favoring instead unscientific theories and beliefs. Ever the scientist, Weisstein carefully reported a growing body of research from social psychology that demonstrated the incredibly powerful influence of situational and interpersonal factors in determining human behavior, and drew out the implications of these findings for understanding *women's* behavior. Without a consideration of social expectations about women and the social conditions under which women lived, she argued, psychologists could have nothing of value to say about women's experiences.

In 1969, emboldened by the women's movement and the pioneering efforts of psychologists like Weisstein, feminist psychologists met at the annual convention of the American Psychological Association (APA) to discuss sexist practices within the field. These practices included job advertisements indicating that "men only" need apply, lack of childcare at the annual convention, and overt sexual harassment. The result of these often angry and heated discussions was the formation, in 1969, of the first organization for women in psychology since the National Council of Women Psychologists in the 1940s: the Association for Women in Psychology (AWP).

Members of the newly established AWP rallied again at the 1970 convention, presenting their concerns to the first (and to date only) African American APA president, Kenneth B. Clark (1914–2005), at an explosive town hall meeting. Here, AWP psychologists Phyllis Chesler and Nancy Henley prepared a statement

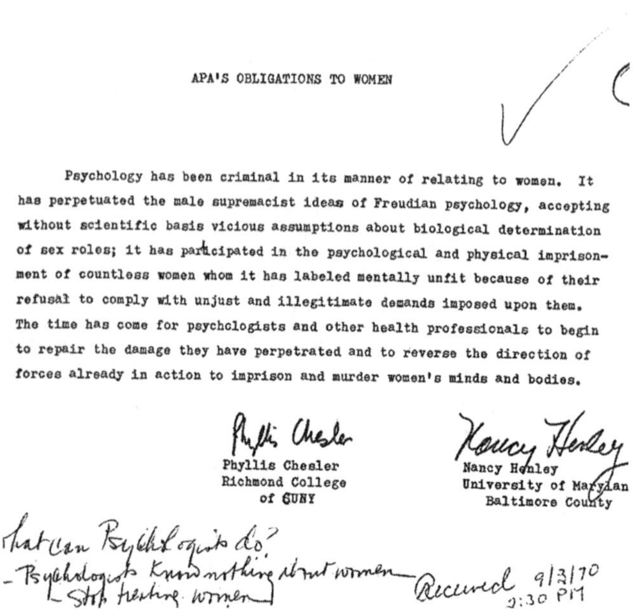

APA'S OBLIGATIONS TO WOMEN

Psychology has been criminal in its manner of relating to women. It has perpetuated the male supremacist ideas of Freudian psychology, accepting without scientific basis vicious assumptions about biological determination of sex roles; it has participated in the psychological and physical imprisonment of countless women whom it has labeled mentally unfit because of their refusal to comply with unjust and illegitimate demands imposed upon them. The time has come for psychologists and other health professionals to begin to repair the damage they have perpetrated and to reverse the direction of forces already in action to imprison and murder women's minds and bodies.

Phyllis Chesler
Richmond College
of CUNY

Nancy Henley
University of Maryland
Baltimore County

What can Psychologists do?
- Psychologists know nothing about women
- Stop treating women

Received 9/3/70
2:30 PM

FIGURE 11.4 Statement of APA's Obligations to Women prepared by Phyllis Chesler and Nancy Henley

Courtesy of American Psychological Association Archives.

on APA's obligations to women and demanded $1 million in reparation for the damage psychology had perpetrated against women's minds and bodies.

Although no money was forthcoming, APA did establish the Task Force on the Status of Women. The task force, chaired by Helen Astin, undertook a two-year study and published a detailed report of its findings and recommendations in 1973. The study uncovered several practices in the field of Psychology that were unfavorable to women and made several recommendations for action. For example, they recommended a formal mechanism for individuals to report sexist and discriminatory treatment in psychotherapy, they demanded accessible and open job recruitment, and they requested an affirmative action plan to mandate equity in remuneration and promotional opportunities for women.

One of their findings, not surprisingly, was that psychological research on, and knowledge about, women was deficient. Most psychological research being published in the field was conducted with White, college-aged men, with the assumption that these results could be generalized to the universal human experience. Research on women's experiences, such as pregnancy and child rearing, menstruation, sexual harassment, and rape, was simply absent. Accordingly, the task force recommended that a division devoted to the psychology of women be established to promote research in this area. In 1973, Division 35, Psychology of Women, was formed. Elizabeth Douvan (1926–2002), a social psychologist at the University of Michigan, was the division's first president. In 1976, the first issue of a new journal, *Psychology of Women Quarterly*, appeared, with Georgia Babladelis (1931–2009) named its first editor. By 1995, Division 35 had grown to become the fourth largest of the 54 divisions in the APA.

FEMINIST CRITIQUES OF CLINICAL PSYCHOLOGY AND PSYCHIATRY, AND ALTERNATIVES

Although many women psychologists had been directed into the applied branches of American psychology since World War I, and had made many important theoretical and practical contributions to this field, by the end of World War II even their professional gains were significantly affected by several forces. Concomitant with the increased formalization of training and practice in clinical psychology and an influx of men into PhD training programs came a rise in clinical psychology's prestige and status. This, combined with the hegemony of psychoanalytic theories that reinforced traditional sex-role stereotypes and the repressive and oppressive cultural values of the 1950s, resulted in heavy exclusion of women from the role of PhD clinical psychologist in the 1950s and 1960s. As a result, most female therapy clients were treated by male therapists, and the theories and practices of the field clearly betrayed an "expert" male vantage point on the submissive, and relatively powerless, female client.

In 1972, Phyllis Chesler published a widely read feminist critique of psychiatry and clinical psychology. In *Women and Madness*, Chesler argued that women in contemporary American society faced an impossible situation. Traditional gender stereotypes, she argued, were often used as the basis for diagnostic categories that pathologized women who conformed to them; at the same time, women who did *not* conform to these gender stereotypes were seen as deviant and disorderly. In sum, both being too feminine and not being feminine enough were interpreted as indications of psychopathology. Chesler was drawing, in part, on the work of other psychologists such as Inge Broverman and her colleagues, who in 1970 had shown that experts' descriptions of mentally healthy men and women paralleled stereotypic conceptions of masculinity and femininity. Mentally healthy men were described as having stereotypically masculine traits, and mentally healthy women were described as having stereotypically feminine traits. However, when asked to describe a healthy adult (sex unspecified), experts' descriptions were closer to their descriptions of a healthy man than a healthy woman (Broverman, Broverman, Clarkson, Rosenkrantz, & Vogel, 1970).

As for (middle class) women in psychotherapy and women in state psychiatric hospitals, Chesler characterized their experience as "just one more instance of an unequal relationship, just one more opportunity to be rewarded for expressing distress and to be 'helped' by being (expertly) [parentheses in original] dominated" (1972, p. 108). She described the psychotherapeutic encounter as the reenactment of a young girl's relationship to her father in a patriarchal society, with its attendant potential for oppression and control, yet its simultaneous promise of safe haven and protection in an otherwise hostile world. Chesler reminded readers, however, that the therapy encounter was rarely safe for women patients, who, more commonly than most would have liked to believe, were being coerced to sleep with their male therapists in the name of treatment. The sexual abuse of female clients by male therapists was occurring with alarming regularity. Even more disturbingly, it was considered a beneficial and acceptable therapeutic practice by many perpetrators and was overlooked by the profession. The ethics of sexual contact in therapy had been ignored in a profession dominated, both numerically and ideologically, by men. In 1977, feminist psychologists were successful in having the Ethics Code of the APA changed to prohibit sexual contact between therapist and client.

During the 1970s, feminist psychologists joined with other groups who protested the inclusion of homosexuality as an official diagnosis in the *Diagnostic and Statistical Manual of Mental Disorders*. It was removed from the third edition in 1980, although egodystonic homosexuality remained. Thus, people who were unhappy with their sexual orientation, regardless of the cause of their unhappiness (e.g., social intolerance, harassment, etc.), could still be diagnosed. In addition to critiquing the ever-proliferating pathologization and medicalization of human experience, feminist psychologists also protested the inclusion of diagnoses that specifically pathologized women's behavior and experiences, such as self-defeating personality disorder and late luteal phase dysphoric disorder (also known as premenstrual dysphoric disorder). Consistent with a feminist analysis, and with some aspects of the antipsychiatry critique, they argued that the social and political contexts in which seemingly deviant behaviors occurred were essential for understanding and ultimately remedying these behaviors. Feminists have consistently argued that women's experiences of gender inequality, sexual harassment and discrimination, poverty, racism, and role stress must all be taken into account to understand their lives. Feminists have also protested the overprescription of psychotropic medication to women and the lack of research on women's response to medication.

In addition to protesting the pathologization of women's experiences and identifying unethical and sexist practices in psychotherapy, feminist psychologists began to formulate their own distinctly feminist approaches. Early in the 1970s, freestanding **feminist therapy** collectives sprang up across the United States. With little or no theory upon which to develop precise therapeutic practices other than the feminist maxim "the personal is political," feminist therapists drew heavily upon the consciousness-raising movement for a model of how to empower and work with women. Gradually, some common principles emerged: an ethical commitment to social justice, greater power sharing and collaboration in the therapist–client relationship, an emphasis on structural rather than intrapsychic explanations for women's problems, a valuing of women's ways of being, and respect for all forms of diversity.

Today, many principles of feminist therapy infuse other forms of therapy, and ethical guidelines reflect many feminist values. It is easy to forget how important and pioneering these early developments were and how necessary feminist principles continue to be for understanding, and hopefully eliminating, many difficulties with which women continue to struggle. Eating disorders and the culture of thinness that fuels them, body image disturbances, violence against women (including rape and domestic assault),

sexual harassment, ageism, poverty, racism, and homophobia are all forces that oppress women and are just a few of the areas where feminist analysis is ongoing and imperative.

SEX DIFFERENCES REVISITED

Earlier in the book we presented some efforts by women psychologists to debunk commonly held beliefs about women's natures that had been imported wholesale into the science of Psychology. Most of these beliefs centered on the ways that women and men differed from each other or ways in which women were hindered because of their biology. In using objective, scientific methods to challenge the validity of these assumptions that often supported widespread beliefs in women's inferiority to men or functioned to keep women in a separate sphere, these early psychologists were practicing a form of feminist empiricism. That is, they were acting on the conviction that if scientific research were done carefully and objectively enough, the results would dismantle and undermine the unscientific and biased assumptions that formed the basis of these commonly held beliefs. The scientific method, used properly, they believed, would expose the truth about sex differences and support the fairer and more just treatment of both women and men.

In 1974, Eleanor Maccoby and Carol Jacklin published a monumental book called *The Psychology of Sex Differences.* Their aims were to review the available scientific evidence to determine which purported sex differences were real and which were not and to review the theoretical positions on how sex differences came about. They identified three primary positions used to explain the development of sex differences: genetic–biological factors, shaping and reinforcement of sex-typed behaviors, and imitation of the same-sex parent through identification or social learning. As they noted in the introduction to this now-classic volume, "We believe there is a great deal of myth in the popular views about sex differences. There is also some substance.... Our primary method will be a detailed examination of the findings of research in which the social behavior, intellectual abilities, or motivations of the two sexes have been systematically studied" (p. 3).

Maccoby and Jacklin undertook a comprehensive review of hundreds of studies on sex differences in six areas (intellectual abilities, temperament, achievement motivation, etc.) covering more than 80 separate traits or skills. They summarized the findings from these studies in more than 85 tables, where they categorized each study as finding no sex difference, a difference favoring boys, or a difference favoring girls. They concluded with a summary that listed the unfounded beliefs about sex differences, the sex differences that were fairly well established, and areas with too little evidence or ambiguous findings. With the data available to them in 1974, Maccoby and Jacklin concluded that four empirically supported sex differences were well established: (1) girls have better verbal ability than boys, (2) boys excel in visual–spatial ability, (3) boys have better mathematical ability starting in adolescence, and (4) males are more aggressive than females, both verbally and physically. Importantly, Maccoby and Jacklin devoted considerable attention to the potential problems with their method, noting that they were reliant on the quality of the studies available and that it was difficult at times to interpret and compare results across studies. Objective measures often yielded different results than self-report measures, and the situational specificity of many findings often went unanalyzed or unnoted in the studies themselves.

As for theories about the origins of sex differences, they concluded that genetic–biological factors had been most clearly implicated in sex differences in aggression and visual–spatial ability, that socialization (shaping and reinforcement of sex-typed behaviors, usually by parents) played a role in some known sex differences but not in others, and that the role of imitation or identification with same-sex parents had

met with the least direct support. They summarized by stating that the learning of sex-typed behaviors was most likely a process built upon biological foundations but that learning a social stereotype based on this biological reality also played a role. Finally, they considered some emerging cognitive–developmental research and concluded, based on this work, that children gradually developed the concepts of masculinity and femininity and that when they became aware of their own sex they worked to match their behaviors to these concepts.

Although Maccoby and Jacklin did not identify their work as feminist (neither feminist nor feminism appears in the index), they were careful to state their conviction that biology was not destiny. Using leadership as an example, they noted that while male aggression may have at one time helped men attain positions of leadership and power, more recent studies were showing that successful leadership required a range of abilities across domains with no sex differences and that women could therefore expect to be able to compete with men for these positions despite being less innately aggressive. As another example, they suggested that although childbearing and child rearing had, at one time, taken up much of women's adult lives and made them ineligible for certain occupational roles, smaller families and longer life spans made this exclusion unnecessary. Finally, they suggested that societies have the option of minimizing rather than maximizing sex differences and that it is up to humans to develop the social institutions that foster the lifestyles they most value.

Some feminist psychologists have interpreted Maccoby and Jacklin's work as fairly conservative and have criticized their emphasis on the biological origins of male–female differences. Others have used their book to highlight the relative paucity of actual sex differences and thus argue for more equitable treatment of men and women.

Regardless, as a monumental example of (potentially) feminist empiricism, Maccoby and Jacklin's book inspired continued research on sex differences, as well as continued attempts to show empirically which differences are real and which are not. Today, feminist empiricists use statistical techniques such as meta-analysis to sort through the morass of available data. Currently, at least two main camps exist. Some feminists argue that a small body of true sex differences exists but that these result largely from socialization and could be minimized with corresponding societal changes. Others argue that women and men are more the same than different and that too much attention has focused on relatively inconsequential differences, to the detriment of women. The differences debate continues.

FROM SEX TO GENDER

Maccoby and Jacklin's classic book did not use the term "gender differences," and we avoided using the phrase in the previous section because the term "gender" itself had not yet been forcefully introduced into psychology. By the late 1970s, this changed. In 1979, feminist social psychologist Rhoda Unger published a widely read article titled "Towards a Redefinition of Sex and Gender" in which she made the distinction between "sex," defined as biological maleness and femaleness, and **gender**, the socially constructed sets of characteristics and traits that are considered appropriate to males and females. With the distinction between sex and gender brought into clearer conceptual relief, the empirical test of sex differences, the mainstay of feminist empiricism, became only one approach among an array of alternatives. It became possible to talk about how people and processes became gendered, rather than seeing masculinity and femininity as some essential, unchangeable quality of being biologically male or female. Although it is often cited for its role in drawing this distinction, the bulk of Unger's article was devoted to a critique of sex differences research in which she concluded that the question of how males and females differed was not inherently a feminist question. As she pointed out, questions about sex differences, invariably cast in terms of how women deviated

FIGURE 11.5   Rhoda Unger
Courtesy of the authors.

from a male-defined norm, were really someone else's questions. They diverted attention from research on ways men and women were similar, the situational constraints on behavior and development, and the unique aspects of women's lives.

With the concept of gender, it also became possible to conceptualize and measure masculinity and femininity in different ways. Even before Unger's 1979 article, Sandra Bem had suggested that each person has both feminine and masculine traits and, furthermore, that an equal representation of each was characteristic of an androgynous—and psychologically healthy—personality. She devised the Bem Sex Role Inventory to measure **androgyny**, and this spawned a copious amount of research in the ensuing years. Although the androgyny construct has been heavily critiqued, it did bring about

FIGURE 11.6   Sandra Bem
Courtesy of Sandra Bem.

a significant body of subsequent research on gender identity.

Viewing gender as an enacted meaning system that structures our experiences in and of the world (i.e., in terms of power relations, access to power, language, the law, self- and other perception, social institutions, etc.) has allowed feminist researchers to ask different questions. If gender is not a binary of inner traits that we express, we can ask questions that go far beyond how women and men differ. We can ask how gender takes on different meanings; how it is expressed in different contexts; how it functions to regulate access to power and status; how it interacts with other social formations, such as class, ethnicity, and sexual orientation to affect people's lives; and how gender narratives have been used to effect or inhibit social change throughout history. Although sex differences research continues, feminist researchers now cut a wider swath of conceptual territory than was possible before gender was taken up in this way.

A THEORY OF THEIR OWN: THE RELATIONAL APPROACH

When Maccoby and Jacklin's book appeared in 1974, several other feminist scholars in the United States were developing approaches that also addressed the notion of difference but in a different way. In 1976, psychiatrist Jean Baker

Miller (1927–2006) published *Toward a New Psychology of Women* (1976/1986). In this slim, classic volume, she suggested that those characteristics typically ascribed to women (by men) and devalued, such as vulnerability, emotional weakness, helplessness, relationality, and connectedness, could actually be redescribed and reevaluated as strengths. This reassessment should take place, she suggested, on women's terms: "The overall attempt of this book is to look toward a more accurate understanding of women's psychology as it arises out of women's life experience rather than as it has been perceived by those who do not have that experience" (Miller, 1976/1986, p. 49). Miller's ideas developed into a **relational–cultural theory** of psychological development that places the ability to sustain relationships as central to human growth and sees disconnectedness as a threat to psychological well-being. According to this theory and the therapy that has been developed from it, disconnectedness can arise out of power imbalances that impel one member in a relationship to hide or distort authentic feelings for fear of being ridiculed or invalidated. Although the power imbalances between women and men are one example, relational disruptions can also occur as a result of racism, classism, heterosexism, and other discriminatory societal practices that affect power relations. These ideas have been developed by many other scholars at the Stone Center at Wellesley College in Massachusetts, where Miller worked until her death in 2006.

At the same time that Miller was developing her ideas, Harvard psychologist Carol Gilligan (b. 1936) was conducting the interviews on self–other relationships and moral decision making that led her to formulate the importance of the "relational voice," the voice that "insists on staying in connection, and most centrally, in staying in connection with women" (1982/1993, p. xiii). In 1973, the landmark decision in *Roe v. Wade* made abortion legal in the United States. Women were given the right to have a voice and make a choice in an area in which they had previously been publicly denied these opportunities.

Intrigued by how individual women might approach the question of whether or not to have an abortion, Gilligan set out to listen to their voices. What she discovered was that women's moral decision-making processes did not map particularly well onto prevailing psychological theories constructed within a completely androcentric framework. Women often valued remaining in a relationship, not inflicting pain, and using both thinking and feeling as the basis for moral decision making in a framework that she came to call "an ethic of care." Consequently, many of their proposals for resolving moral dilemmas were judged, by masculine standards, to reflect a lower level of moral development than men.

Gilligan's and Miller's work and those of their colleagues has sometimes been critiqued for essentializing women and presenting women's supposedly unique qualities as characteristic of all women, regardless of their position in the social hierarchy. It has been argued that other vantage points may be equally or more important to many women, such as those afforded by social class, ethnicity, and sexual orientation. Critics also argue that making the claim for women's uniqueness, and positioning them as in many ways superior to men, simply contributes to the reification of the differences debate. Others dispute Gilligan's basic finding that women's moral reasoning exemplifies an ethic of care, stating that this cannot be generalized to all women and that many women exhibit justice-oriented reasoning just as often on standard scales. Gilligan defends her position, stating, "When I hear my work being cast in terms of whether women and men are really (essentially) [parentheses in original] different or who is better than whom, I know that I have lost my voice, because these are not my questions" (1982/1993, p. xiii). Rather, she is interested in the question of how men *and* women come to speak of themselves in certain characteristic ways, of how girls and women learn to silence themselves, and how to make an ethic of care a more prominent part of human development, not just women's development.

OWNING THE PAST: ORIGINS OF WOMEN'S HISTORY IN PSYCHOLOGY

In addition to institutional changes and the growth of feminist theory and therapy in the 1970s, another important development was the beginning of a movement to replace women in psychology's history. As we have shown, the activism of the second wave produced changes in society *and* in academia. Within the discipline of history, for example, scholars were demanding that the neglect of women, as both subjects of and agents in history, be redressed. Historians were beginning to produce what is now an extensive body of scholarship that recovered and retheorized women and gender in history, sometimes changing the vantage point from which history had traditionally been told. For example, Gerda Lerner, a prominent women's historian, argued that history not only had to include women's contributions but actually should be rewritten from women's points of view. Women, she argued, had always been at the center of history, despite the body of historical scholarship that ignored their centrality. Lerner also emphasized the importance of race and class in differentiating women's experiences and of writing histories that reflected this differentiation.

Within psychology, the process of uncovering and discovering women also unfolded. In 1974, Maxine Bernstein and Nancy Russo wrote an article titled "The History of Psychology Revisited, or Up With Our Foremothers," one of the first publications to point out the complete invisibility of women in accounts of psychology's history. In their article, they argued that Psychology's documenting practices and androcentric biases had led many psychologists to assume that no women had made important contributions to psychology. If we started looking more closely, they suggested, we would indeed find many women who had made important contributions despite multiple barriers to their participation. Reflecting the excitement of the early 1970s, they wrote: "In a time when women are searching for role models and new identities, it is exciting to discover that Taylor of the Taylor Manifest Anxiety Scale is named Janet, that Bender of the Bender-Gestalt test is known as Lauretta, and that the Kent of the Kent-Rosanoff Word Association Test was called Grace" (p. 131).

In 1975, Stephanie Shields published two important articles that documented the early incursion of sexist assumptions, or what she called "social myths," masquerading as science in late 19th- and early 20th-century psychology (Shields, 1975a, 1975b). We have mentioned Shields's work earlier in the book in our discussion of how brain size estimates were used by scientists to argue that women had, on average, smaller brains than men and must therefore be intellectually inferior. We also mentioned her work in our earlier discussion of the **variability hypothesis**, a commonly held scientific belief at the turn of the last century that since males exhibited greater variability in physical and psychological traits, the male species was responsible for fueling evolutionary progress and most women were doomed to mediocrity. Shields also pointed out how early beliefs in the maternal instinct were used to keep women tied to the private, domestic sphere. In another article published that same year, she presented Leta Stetter Hollingworth's (1886–1939) efforts to debunk the variability hypothesis as an early example of the psychology of women.

Articles like these, published in the mid-1970s, reflected the unprecedented interest of women psychologists in reclaiming their history and exploring psychology's past through the lens of gender. This literature has proliferated and continues to grow in the United States. One of the most formative historical studies of early American women in psychology is Elizabeth Scarborough and Laurel Furumoto's 1987 book, *Untold Lives: The First Generation of American Women Psychologists*. In this classic work, Scarborough and Furumoto undertook a systematic study of the first generation of American women psychologists, defined, in part, as those women who had obtained membership in the APA by 1906, to discover what personal characteristics they shared. Somewhat unsurprisingly, they discovered that all were White, middle class, Protestant, and from the Northeast or Midwest. They then devoted most of their analysis to the common experiences shared by these women as they undertook careers as psychologists. As a group, Scarborough and Furumoto discovered, these women experienced several obstacles to their professional training, career development, and advancement that reflected many sexist assumptions about women that pervaded late 19th- and early 20th-century American life. The first obstacle was gaining admittance to higher education. Common wisdom at the end of the 19th century was that higher education for women was undesirable, as it would make them less marriageable; furthermore, it would be harmful to their physical health and reproductive capabilities. G. Stanley Hall (1844–1924) actually claimed that educated women became "functionally castrated."

In addition, many schools, especially the prestigious ones, simply did not accept women. Harvard did not grant PhDs to women until 1963. Women who studied at Harvard before this time received their PhDs from Radcliffe College, its all-female counterpart. Many first-generation women psychologists, such as Mary Whiton Calkins (1863–1930), Margaret Floy Washburn (1871–1939), and Christine Ladd-Franklin (1847–1930), were special students or guests at their graduate institutions because women were not admitted as regular students. Ladd-Franklin and Calkins completed all of the work for their PhDs but were denied doctorates; Washburn was awarded hers only because she moved from Columbia University in New York City, which did not award PhDs to women at that time, to Cornell University, which did. Ladd-Franklin earned her doctorate as a special student at Johns Hopkins University in Baltimore, Maryland, in 1882 but was not actually granted her degree until 1926, almost 44 years after she earned it. Calkins was offered but refused a Radcliffe PhD and has not, to this day, been granted a posthumous Harvard PhD.

These women also encountered obstacles during their training. Often, even when women were allowed into graduate programs, they were denied access to laboratories, equipment, libraries, and special societies. Ladd-Franklin noted that although she wanted to pursue postgraduate studies in physics, she chose mathematics instead because she was not allowed access to the laboratories. She also waged a vigorous campaign to have women admitted to her colleague Edward Bradford Titchener's (1867–1927) all-male Society of Experimentalists, but was ultimately unsuccessful. Women's presence, Titchener argued, would inhibit the men from expressing their views most forcefully and freely; besides, they all liked to smoke. In a later example, Mildred Mitchell (1903–1983), a mid-20th-century woman psychologist, was denied a key to the Harvard Psychology Department so that she could work after hours even though her male peers had 24-hour access to the building. She was thus made dependent on a male escort.

Once graduated, first-generation women faced limited employment opportunities. They were often hired at women's colleges that had no or limited graduate programs. They took on heavy teaching and administrative roles, curtailing their productivity as researchers. Even those who were productive researchers had no graduate student support and thus no students to carry on their legacy. Scarborough and Furumoto also noted the marriage versus career dilemma. Marriage was often a serious impediment to a woman's career. Conversely, if she had a career, she was perceived as unmarriageable. First-generation psychologist Milicent Shinn (1858–1940) wrote an article in *The Century* magazine in 1895 in which she explored the possible reasons for the lower rates of marriage among women with college degrees or advanced education. She concluded that the lower rates of marriage among these women were not because they were less interested in marriage or had personality or physical attributes that made them unmarriageable; rather, educated women, because they could support themselves, could be more discriminating in their choice of mates.

In addition, she concluded that some men were less likely to choose educated women as partners because of their negative perceptions of these women as "too intellectual."

Women who did marry faced the possibility that they could be fired—and many were. It was widely assumed that they would be wives first and professionals only second. By contrast, men who married gained considerable assistance at home and at work, as many educated wives became their unpaid secretaries and research assistants. In their analysis of second-generation American women psychologists, Elizabeth Johnston and Ann Johnson (2008) have shown that antinepotism rules often worked against career advancement. Women married to male psychologists were often offered, and took, subordinate positions so that the couple could remain together, thus advancing the man's career but decelerating that of the woman.

Scarborough and Furumoto restricted their analysis to the fairly small and homogeneous

FIGURE 11.7 Inez Beverly Prosser
Courtesy of the Archives of the History of American Psychology, University of Akron, Akron, OH.

group comprising the first generation of women psychologists in the United States. Because all of these women were White and were navigating an exclusively all-White professional world, *Untold Lives* does not discuss race as a barrier to women's participation in psychology. Given that more than 50 years would pass after Psychology's formal inception before the first African American woman was awarded a doctorate in 1933, race was clearly a powerful barrier to women's—and men's—ability to enter the field (Guthrie, 1976/1993). Indeed, it was only 13 years earlier, in 1920, that the first African American man, Francis Cecil Sumner (1895–1954), received his doctorate.

Johnston and Johnson (2008) have also shown that women in Psychology's second generation were more racially and religiously diverse than their first-generation counterparts. Thus, many experienced the double jeopardy of racism and sexism or anti-Semitism and sexism. Inez Beverly Prosser (1897–1934) was the first African American woman to receive a PhD in educational psychology, from the Department of Education at the University of Cincinnati in 1933. Tragically, she died a year later in a car accident.

In 1934, another African American woman, Ruth Howard (1900–1997), was awarded her PhD in psychology, in the Department of Psychology at the University of Minnesota.

Sidebar 11.1 Focus on *Ruth Howard*

Before she became a psychologist, Ruth Winifred Howard (1900–1997), the daughter of a clergyman, first pursued a career in social work. She was impressed by the constant flux of people who came in and out of her large family's home (she was the eighth child) seeking help for different problems. She decided she wanted to learn how to alleviate these problems. She earned her social work degree at Simmons College in Boston, and after several years as a practicing social worker, Howard decided to return to graduate school. She had been influenced by a chief psychologist at the Board of Education, who seemed particularly adept at seeing people and their problems in their whole cultural and environmental contexts: "Talks with this woman crystallized for me a growing realization that I wanted to learn the dynamics of how a person thinks, feels, and behaves. That meant the study of psychology" (Howard, 1983, p. 58).

With the help of a Laura Spelman Rockefeller Fellowship, Howard enrolled at Columbia in New York City and took up residence at International House, where her relationships with fellow residents from all over the world became part of her "educational portfolio," as she described it. While at Columbia, she participated in formal and informal social psychology seminars with Goodwin Watson, the first

(Continued)

FIGURE 11.8 Ruth Howard
Courtesy of the Archives of the History of American Psychology, University of Akron, Akron, OH.

president of the Society for the Psychological Study of Social Issues, and was mentored by developmental psychologist Lois Meek Stolz. Even though Columbia was stimulating, her fellowship allowed her to attend two universities, so Howard took advantage of this opportunity to transfer to the University of Minnesota. There she enrolled at the prestigious Institute of Child Development. Her primary supervisor was Florence Goodenough. Howard chose as her dissertation topic an examination of nature versus nurture in the physical and psychological development of a sample of 229 sets of triplets, and she received her PhD in 1934.

Soon after her graduation, Howard married fellow psychologist Albert Sidney Beckham and the couple moved to Chicago. There she undertook an internship at the Illinois Institute of Juvenile Research and honed her clinical skills. With the Great Depression still limiting employment in the private sector, she then accepted a job with the National Youth Administration as director of their mental health and training program. Subsequently, she and her husband established a part-time private practice, and she took a position as psychologist with the Provident School of Nursing. She also attended graduate courses at the University of Chicago as a form of continuing education. There she studied client-centered therapy with Carl Rogers and play therapy with Virginia Axline. Volunteering and community service were also prominent aspects of Howard's life. She was a member of the Women's International League for Peace and Freedom and a volunteer for the Young Women's Christian Association. After a long life devoted to psychology and community service, Howard died in 1997, in Washington, DC.

One of the most well-known African American women psychologists, Mamie Phipps Clark (1917–1983), was awarded her PhD in 1944 from Columbia. Quickly perceiving the absence of opportunities available to her as a Black woman in Psychology (or indeed in any profession), Clark set about creating her own career path. She established the Northside Center for Child Development in 1946 and served as its director until her retirement in 1979.

It was not until 1962 that the first Latina, Martha Bernal (1931–2001), received a doctorate in psychology. Bernal earned her clinical degree at Indiana University and spent much of her career working, organizationally and through research, to improve the status of ethnic minorities in psychology. She ended her career at Arizona State University, where she conducted research on the identity development of Mexican American children and worked to improve the training of clinical psychologists in minority mental health.

To date, there has been one African American (male) president of the APA. Of the 13 women elected to this office in the APA's 117-year history, one has (to date) been a woman of color. Latina psychologist Melba Vasquez will serve as president in 2011.

CREATING AN INCLUSIVE FEMINIST PSYCHOLOGY

Diversity, inclusion, and representativeness have been important issues in the psychology of women and feminist psychology. Second-wave feminism has been justifiably criticized as exclusively representing the concerns and outlooks of women at the center—generally heterosexual, White, middle-class women—and ignoring the complex intersections of gender with race, ethnicity, sexual orientation, socioeconomic status, and other important identity categories. Psychology of women and feminist psychology have also been critiqued for failing to consider and

FIGURE 11.9 Mamie Phipps Clark
Courtesy of the Archives of the History of American Psychology,
University of Akron, Akron, OH.

theorize **intersectionality**—the interdependent relations among categories such as gender, race, and class—adequately and for representing the experiences and concerns of middle-class heterosexual White women exclusively. Although feminist psychologists are responding to these critiques, changes to mainstream psychological theory and method are slow in coming. This is partly due to the persistence, at least in the American context, of the gender-differences paradigm, which often excludes consideration of other dimensions of difference and the ways they may come together in unique constellations to affect women's experiences. It is also due to the continued methodological conservatism

of scientific Psychology. Intersectionality is a complex phenomenon demanding a range of methodological approaches. Psychology, as a discipline, has been reluctant to deviate from its natural science persona for fear of being cast as a soft science or relegated to the humanities. As a result, some phenomena that resist simple operationalization or reductionism have received less attention. As feminist psychologist Stephanie Shields (whose historical scholarship we mentioned earlier) has written, "Despite recognition of the significance of intersectionality, empirical application of this perspective has lagged behind, particularly in psychology" (2008, p. 301).

Starting in the 1990s, feminist psychologists, many of them women of color, began both to highlight psychology's lack of attention to the multiple identities that influence women's lives and to theorize intersectionality. Many have been influenced by critical sociologist Patricia Hill Collins's powerful book *Black Feminist Thought* (1990), written to empower Black women by placing their experiences and ideas at the center of analysis and by analyzing these experiences within a paradigm of intersecting oppressions. Gradually, these ideas have been making their way more forcefully into psychology. Early in the decade, Pamela Trotman Reid (1993; see also Reid, 2000) pointed out the absence of poor women in psychological research and subsequently called on multicultural psychologists to bring together gender and ethnicity. In 1995, Latina feminist psychologist Oliva Espin called attention to the liminal position of women of color in psychology, characterizing it as "knowing you are the unknown." (p. 127).

FEMINIST PSYCHOLOGIES IN INTERNATIONAL CONTEXT

American feminist psychology has been heavily imbued with the values of **liberal feminism**, whose major goal has been to ensure equality between women and men under the law. Liberal feminists tend to deemphasize the differences among women along ethnic, religious, and class lines in order to prioritize gender and create a "global sisterhood." Liberal feminism has been critiqued by feminists of color for adopting a false essentialism and universalism. They have responded by developing other theoretical frames such as **multiracial feminism** and U.S. Third World feminism, positioning feminists of color as "outsiders within" and practicing a form of "oppositional consciousness." However, despite these important developments, much of American feminist psychology to date has focused on the barriers to achieving equality for women, and the putative differences between men and women, and comparatively less on the differences among women or the interaction of gender with other social and political formations, as we just noted.

As we have discussed throughout this book, the social and political contexts in which psychology is developed heavily influence what kind of psychology is produced and what goals it serves. The same is true for feminist psychology. Thus, we would expect that variations in dominant feminist ideologies and political trajectories for women, and diversity in the issues facing them, would influence the contours and content of feminist psychology as it is developed around the world. Although the dominant historical narrative in this chapter has been the evolution of American feminist psychology, other countries have had decidedly different narratives.

In Britain, for example, socialist feminism has been a dominant strain of both feminist theory and practice. In **socialist feminism**, to simplify considerably, women's oppression and struggles are tied to the class oppression inherent in capitalism. Just as capitalism operates by keeping the working class subjugated to the ruling class, so too does it operate to keep women subjugated. Class struggles and women's struggles are thus seen as interconnected: Building class consciousness and building women's collective consciousness are linked. Thus, in Britain, feminists were often allied with leftist movements, and this has colored the writings and concerns of many feminist psychologists.

In the Nordic countries, socialist feminism and radical feminism have coexisted. In **radical feminism**, women's oppression by men is seen as the root of all oppression; that is, men's domination of women is viewed as the primary and most universal form of oppression. Working to dismantle patriarchy, male violence against women, and traditional gender roles are all important goals. In the Nordic countries, feminist groups established in the late 19th century have remained continuously active and have typically worked in partnership with the state, rather than in opposition to it. At the end of World War II, the Nordic countries were overseen by Labour parties that worked to transform the daily lives of workers. Included in this set of initiatives was an effort to increase the public participation of women by offering them greater access to education and paid work. Several feminist social scientists were actively involved in the Labour Party and participated in the planning of social and political reforms that would affect women's lives. Much feminist research in psychology and sociology thus concerned women's roles in the workplace and their roles in the family, and conceptualized sex differentiation as based largely on cultural expectations and socialization processes. Policies resulting from this research supported the transformation of social and economic structures to allow both women and men access to the processes of both economic and social production.

The contours of feminist research in Nordic psychology today reflect these roots. For example, studies of childcare and child rearing have focused on what the changing roles of women and men could mean for how children are brought up, not whether day care is good or bad for children. Other lines of research examine how women's identities and relationship to mothering have developed and changed in this context and how heterosexual couples negotiate gender meanings in relationships. As the Nordic countries experience increasing levels of immigration and multiculturalism, feminist researchers are also addressing how meanings of gender and ethnicity are negotiated and how "othering" and hybridization operate in a society in which the majority position is often unmarked and invisible.

By way of contrast, and to further demonstrate the importance of context in understanding the development of psychology, feminist psychologists in India concentrate on several issues arising out of persistent problems in Indian society. As feminist psychologist Vindhya Undurti has noted, social science researchers in postindependence India identified "poverty and deprivation, discrimination and inequalities based on caste, religion, region and gender, and the periodic eruption of conflict between the communal groups based on fundamentalist ideologies" (Undurti, 2007, p. 337) as some of the persistent problems of Indian society that social scientists must address. The development of feminist psychology was affected by the colonial legacy that has colored mainstream Indian psychology until challenges to this Western model began to emerge in the 1970s. This challenge to the dominant model and the call for indigenous psychologies did not immediately include sensitivity to gender, and to this day the more critical, activist work concerning women is performed not in academic Psychology but in women's studies. Nonetheless, Undurti has identified three major themes in psychological research on gender in India: work–family linkages, women's mental health, and violence against women. In the latter

category, although violence against women can take many forms, much Indian research has focused on domestic violence and its relationship to a culture of male entitlement, wherein violence in the marital relationship is largely tacitly accepted. Precipitating factors appear to be economic (e.g., demands for dowry and extended dowry), as well as cultural (e.g., perceived deficiencies in carrying out the responsibilities and obligations of the "good wife," sexual control of wives, and stresses resulting from joint-family situations).

FEMINIST AND POSTCOLONIAL CRITIQUES OF SCIENCE AND PSYCHOLOGY IN THE 1980s

As we discussed in the previous chapter, starting after the end of World War II and accelerating throughout the 1950s and 1960s was a worldwide decolonization movement that, in addition to realigning power axes and shifting the economic landscape, was tied to a significant shift in worldview that has been characterized as the transition from modernity to postmodernity. The values of Western **modernity** had included an epistemological allegiance to objectivity, universality, and the possibility of absolute truth. In this framework, science was a value-neutral "mirror" of a knowable and well-ordered external reality, or as some critics characterized it, modernist science captured the view from nowhere (Harding, 1991, p. 311). Language, in this view, was simply the means by which products of the individual human mind (knowledge) were conveyed to others. Historically, modernity is often traced to the shift from the Middle Ages to the Enlightenment, a time when individual rationality was used to displace the authority of the church and to replace religious belief, superstition, and other forms of dogma as the basis of knowledge.

By the second half of the 20th century, the epistemology and ontological values of modernity were beginning to be questioned. Offered in their place was a revised view of the nature of knowledge and how we come to know what we know. In **postmodernism**, the authority of individual rationality was replaced with a view of self as relationally, as well as socially and communally, forged; the emphasis on universality was replaced by locality; and the search for (or even possibility of) truth with a capital "T" was rejected. Language was seen as the product of a cultural process that carried both power and meaning and was thus a primary site for analysis.

In the postmodern view, all knowledge is contingent and reflexive, depending on the standpoint of the knower and the values brought by that person to the knowledge process. The postmodern framework centers on the understanding and constitution of otherness, the acceptance or tolerance of plurality, the local, the specific, difference, perspective, and the contingent.

Postmodernity developed hand in glove with the decolonization movement, and its tenets undergird much postcolonial scholarship. By deconstructing the discourse of "otherness" promulgated unreflexively by North American and western European scholars, postcolonial researchers have created spaces for new forms of theory and practice across many traditional disciplines and have generated entirely new interdisciplines, such as African American studies, subaltern studies, and gender studies. The feminist critique of science was part of this postcolonial and postmodern challenge. This critique gradually found its way into psychology during the 1980s, when feminist psychologists began to read this literature and apply it to their own field.

In 1986, feminist philosopher Sandra Harding wrote *The Science Question in Feminism* in which she pointed out that women have traditionally been excluded from, or seen as incapable of practicing, objective, rigorous science because science itself has been constituted in exclusively masculine terms. Science as defined by men, she argued, has been aligned with one side of a set of dualisms that are themselves intensely gendered: nature versus culture, rational mind versus prerational body and irrational emotions and values, objectivity versus subjectivity, and public versus private. In this way, science is defined as a masculine pursuit that is incompatible with other ways of being in the world. Harding asked whether there could be an alternative mode of knowledge seeking not structured by this set of dualisms, and she concluded that traditionally marginalized and oppressed groups might provide a source for new modes of knowledge seeking. She formulated **feminist standpoint theory**, in which she proposed that the socially oppressed (in this case, women) can access knowledge unavailable to the socially privileged, particularly knowledge of social relations. Furthermore, the knowledge generated is less distorted because it does not take what is given as natural or true but reveals the socially contingent nature of these "truths" and offers potential for emancipation from currently oppressive practices.

In psychology, several feminist approaches have been articulated in response to the feminist critiques of science. We have mentioned **feminist empiricism**, which takes as its aim the production of gender-fair science in the belief that if all sources of bias or irrationality in the research process are identified and eliminated, the result will be an increasingly accurate reflection of reality that can be used to formulate more equitable social policy. In effect, feminist empiricists believe that better science will be more gender-fair science. In the feminist standpoint position, which is sometimes used to characterize Gilligan and Miller's theories, women's standpoints are brought to the center and psychology is conducted and constructed from their distinctive vantage point. Criticisms and strengths of this approach were outlined earlier.

Finally, some feminist psychologists ally themselves with transformative or **postmodern feminism**. In this view, all knowledge in psychology is constructed, rather than discovered; thus, the central task is not to discover the truth about human nature (since there is no one truth to be found) but rather to critically examine why certain questions have been asked to the exclusion of others—for what purposes, to serve whose interests, and how the methods used to investigate these questions produce certain kinds of data but not others—and to disrupt dominant, oppressive knowledge structures to articulate alternate conceptions of reality. A major goal of this pursuit is to reveal the social consequences of certain kinds of knowledge or representations of the "way things are" to unveil the power interests that they serve so that those subjugated by them can introduce oppositional accounts. Postmodern feminist psychologists examine how psychological discourses—such as the discourses of male–female differences, race and ethnicity, mental health and illness, and sexuality—maintain oppressive power hierarchies such as White privilege and patriarchy.

Two central questions of postmodern feminism thus become, "Why that question?" and "Why that answer?"

One of the main criticisms of feminist postmodernism is that, in its embrace of constructionism, it creates a series of hopelessly relativistic accounts that cannot be evaluated. Which account is better than any other, or closer to the truth? Social constructionists have responded to this criticism by suggesting a set of criteria by which knowledge claims can be adjudicated. As feminist psychologist Stephanie Riger has noted, "Theory and research can be assessed in terms of their pragmatic utility in achieving certain social and political goals, rather than the allegedly neutral rules of science" (1992, p. 736).

More problematic for feminist postmodernists than the charge of relativism, perhaps, is the postmodern rejection of individual autonomy and agency as signifiers of an outdated liberal humanism. This rejection appears to deny women the very identity category of "woman" and the ability to speak with authority about their realities in ways that are taken as essentially valid. Feminist postmodernists, like their feminist empiricist and feminist standpoint colleagues, must constantly be vigilant to ensure that their epistemological positions serve feminist aims.

SUMMARY

In this chapter, we focused on how social, political, intellectual, and disciplinary factors all contributed to the emergence of a distinct field called psychology of women, or feminist psychology, in the 1970s. We featured developments in the United States because of our vantage point as historians of American psychology, but we also drew attention to the ways in which the contextually specific concerns of women and forms of political feminism have influenced the development of feminist psychology in other countries and regions. We outlined the diversity of feminist approaches that characterize the field, including feminist empiricism, standpoint theories, and feminist postmodernism. We also documented the tensions within feminist psychology, especially as they relate to whose voices remain at the center and whose remain at the periphery.

The initial emergence and ongoing practice of feminist psychology are the products of a reflexive process. Early in Psychology's history, as women encountered psychological theories and findings that appeared to mirror sexist assumptions about women but did not accord with their own experiences, they self-consciously used the tools of their science to dismantle these theories and the assumptions on which they were based. As women professionals in an age of rapid cultural and economic change and shifting gender norms, they were encountering both new freedom and, frustratingly, the limits of this freedom. Noting this reflexive process, historian Rosalind Rosenberg has remarked that the writings of women social scientists at the beginning of the 20th century "revealed ... how the very basis of women's understanding of themselves was changing" (1982, p. xiv).

Although these early women psychologists began the process of bringing a feminist consciousness to psychology, it was not until the late 1960s that women's understanding of themselves changed so radically, and was experienced so widely that they were able to successfully challenge the androcentrism and sexism that pervaded the field. As women, as feminists, and

as psychologists, they could no longer collude in the enterprise of conducting research that, at best, did not adequately represent women's experiences and that, at worst, diminished or pathologized it. As both agents and subjects of psychological research, women demanded better treatment.

Feminist psychology was born in the wake of intense feminist activism and critique of the status quo. Although our current period is marked more by feminist backlash than by feminist activism, a new generation of feminist scholars continues to steadily develop and reinvent feminist psychology. In their recent reflection on the "state of the field" of feminist psychology, psychologists Abigail Stewart and Andrea Dottolo highlighted the work of emerging feminist scholars, noting that many young feminist psychologists were aiming explicitly to address race, class, gender, and sexuality as social identities and constructions; were using interdisciplinary perspectives to guide their investigations; were seriously engaged in the theorization of intersectionality; and were drawing on a range of methods to confirm, challenge, or develop feminist theories in new ways. Stewart and Dottolo (2006) concluded, albeit tentatively, that this generation of feminist scholars may be less preoccupied with "staking out claims" about the nature of their enterprise than previous generations, suggesting that feminist psychology has finally come of age.

BIBLIOGRAPHIC ESSAY

For a selective overview of the relationship between psychology of women and second-wave feminism in the American context, consult Ellen Herman's chapter "The Curious Courtship of Psychology and Women's Liberation" in her

book *The Romance of American Psychology* (1995). For general histories of the development of the psychology of women in North America, two good outlines are Alexandra Rutherford and Leeat Granek's chapter (in press) "Emergence and Development of the Psychology of Women" in the *Handbook of Gender Research in Psychology* and "Psychology of Women and Gender" (2003) by Jeanne Marecek, Ellen Kimmel, Mary Crawford, and Rachel Hare-Mustin in the Wiley *Handbook of Psychology* (vol. 1). Organizational histories of the AWP and Division 35 of the APA can be found in Leonore Tiefer (1991) and Nancy Russo and Angela Dumont (1997), respectively.

Betty Friedan's *The Feminine Mystique* (1963/1997), first published in 1963, is a classic that influenced a generation of American feminists and can be read as an important document of 1960s and 1970s liberal feminism in the United States. Naomi Weisstein's critique of mainstream psychological science, including its lack of understanding of women, deserves to be read today. It was reprinted many times and is available on the Internet, but one print source is the version titled "Psychology Constructs the Female; or, The Fantasy Life of the Male Psychologist (with Some Attention to the Fantasies of His Friends, the Male Biologist and the Male Anthropologist)" in the *Journal of Social Education* (1971). Phyllis Chesler's *Women and Madness* (1972) deserves rereading as well, both as a primary historical document of early 1970s feminist psychology and for her prescience in discussing the differential effects of race, class, and sexual orientation on women's lives and experiences of the psychiatric and psychological professions. For a general history of feminist clinical psychology, see Jeanne Marecek and Rachel Hare-Mustin's article "A Short History of the Future" (1991). Also useful for a reconstruction of the original intent and ultimate fate of the consciousness-raising movement and its relationship to psychology and psychotherapy is Naomi Rosenthal's article "Consciousness-Raising" (1984).

A primary source for information on the sex differences debate in the early 1970s is the aforementioned volume by Eleanor Maccoby and Carol Jacklin, *The Psychology of Sex Differences* (1974). Contemporary researchers working on the question of whether significant gender differences exist and what we should make of them include Janet Hyde, who has consistently argued on the side of the gender similarities hypothesis (2005), and Alice Eagly, who has conducted extensive meta-analyses on several areas of the gender differences literature and has concluded that a small number of significant differences do distinguish women from men. She argues that these can be explained via social role theory (Eagly & Wood, 1999).

Rhoda Unger's article "Toward a Redefinition of Sex and Gender" (1979) marked a transition in psychology to thinking about gender as a social construction. You can consult Sandra Bem's article "The Measurement of Psychological Androgyny" (1974) for information on the development of the Bem Sex Role Inventory. Bem has also written a highly readable autobiographical account of her and her spouse's efforts to raise their son and daughter free of gender norms. In *An Unconventional Family* (2001), Bem recounts the failures and successes of the endeavor, and its ultimate outcome is expressed through the words of her children themselves.

Jean Baker Miller's *Toward a New Psychology of Women* (1976) was her original statement of the relational model. Carol Gilligan's *In a Different Voice* (1982/1993) was the first book-length account of her theory of women's development. A somewhat colloquial but quite engrossing look at both of these women's careers and the development of their thinking can be found in journalist Christina Robb's celebratory book, *This Changes Everything* (2007).

Scholarship on the history of women in American psychology is fairly extensive, thanks to efforts by several scholars. One of the earliest calls for raising awareness about the presence of women in psychology's history was Maxine Bernstein and Nancy Russo's 1974 "Up With Our Foremothers" article, which was published in the *American Psychologist*, the flagship journal of the APA. Stephanie Shields's two 1975 articles, "Ms. Pilgrim's Progress" and "Functionalism, Darwinism, and the Psychology of Women," were also published in this widely read American journal. Elizabeth Scarborough and Laurel Furumoto's analysis of first-generation American women in psychology, *Untold Lives* (1987), offers group analysis, as well as individual biographical accounts and shorter cameos on 11 women who received their PhDs in psychology before 1906. There are three volumes in Agnes O'Connell and Nancy Russo's *Models of Achievement* series, which feature autobiographical accounts of dozens of eminent women psychologists, including Howard in volume 1 (Howard, 1983; O'Connell, 2001; O'Connell & Russo, 1983, 1988). In 1976, Robert Guthrie published the first African American history of psychology, *Even the Rat Was White*, which features several biographical sketches of important African American men and women (2nd ed., 1998). Prosser's life and career are profiled and contextualized in a full-length article titled "Inez Beverly Prosser and the Education of African Americans" by Ludy Benjamin Jr., Keisha Henry, and Lance McMahon (2005). Shafali Lal contextualized the work of Mamie Phipps Clark in her article "Giving Children Security" (2002), and Clark's life and career are featured extensively in Gerald Markowitz and David Rosner's book *Children, Race, and Power* (1996). Historians of psychology Elizabeth Johnston and Ann Johnson have published a group portrait of America's second generation of women psychologists (2008).

For basic points about postmodernism and psychology, you can consult Kenneth Gergen's accessible article "Psychological Science in a Postmodern Context" (2001); for social constructionism, see his "The Social Constructionist Movement in Modern Psychology" (1985). Sandra Harding is a feminist philosopher whose explication of three forms of feminist response to the critique of science, feminist empiricism, feminist standpoint epistemology, and feminist postmodernism, were set forth in her book *The Science Question in Feminism* (1986). Her ideas were imported into psychology by feminist psychologist Stephanie Riger in an article titled "Epistemological Debates, Feminist Voices" (1992).

Information on feminist psychology in the Nordic countries was drawn from an article by Hanne Haavind and Eva Magnusson titled "Feminism, Psychology, and Identity Transformation in the Nordic Countries" (2005). The issue of *Feminism and Psychology* in which this article is published is devoted in its entirety to feminist psychology in the Nordic countries. Additional special issues of this journal feature feminist psychology in South Africa (vol. 9, no. 2), New Zealand (vol. 11, no. 3), and Canada (vol. 16, no. 3). Material on feminist psychology and psychology of women in India was taken from Vindhya Undurti's article, also published in *Feminism and Psychology*, "Quality of Women's Lives in India" (2007). A succinct statement of multiracial feminism can be found in Maxine Baca

Zinn and Bonnie Thornton Dill's "Theorizing Difference from Multiracial Feminism" (1996). Chela Sandoval has written about U.S. Third World feminism in her challenging book *Methodology of the Oppressed* (2000).

A contemporary assessment of the status and future of feminist psychology can be found in Abigail Stewart and Andrea Dottolo's 2006 review article "Feminist Psychology" published in the women's studies journal *Signs.*

Chapter 12
TIMELINE 1880–1990
(In 25-year increments)

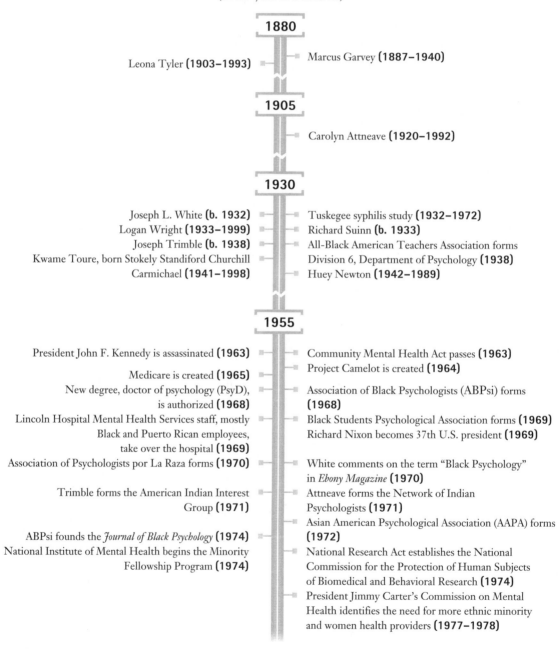

1880

Leona Tyler **(1903–1993)**

Marcus Garvey **(1887–1940)**

1905

Carolyn Attneave **(1920–1992)**

1930

Joseph L. White **(b. 1932)**
Logan Wright **(1933–1999)**
Joseph Trimble **(b. 1938)**
Kwame Toure, born Stokely Standiford Churchill
Carmichael **(1941–1998)**

Tuskegee syphilis study **(1932–1972)**
Richard Suinn **(b. 1933)**
All-Black American Teachers Association forms
Division 6, Department of Psychology **(1938)**
Huey Newton **(1942–1989)**

1955

President John F. Kennedy is assassinated **(1963)**

Medicare is created **(1965)**
New degree, doctor of psychology (PsyD),
is authorized **(1968)**
Lincoln Hospital Mental Health Services staff, mostly
Black and Puerto Rican employees,
take over the hospital **(1969)**
Association of Psychologists por La Raza forms **(1970)**

Trimble forms the American Indian Interest
Group **(1971)**

ABPsi founds the *Journal of Black Psychology* **(1974)**
National Institute of Mental Health begins the Minority
Fellowship Program **(1974)**

Community Mental Health Act passes **(1963)**
Project Camelot is created **(1964)**

Association of Black Psychologists (ABPsi) forms
(1968)
Black Students Psychological Association forms **(1969)**
Richard Nixon becomes 37th U.S. president **(1969)**

White comments on the term "Black Psychology"
in *Ebony Magazine* **(1970)**
Attneave forms the Network of Indian
Psychologists **(1971)**
Asian American Psychological Association (AAPA) forms
(1972)
National Research Act establishes the National
Commission for the Protection of Human Subjects
of Biomedical and Behavioral Research **(1974)**
President Jimmy Carter's Commission on Mental
Health identifies the need for more ethnic minority
and women health providers **(1977–1978)**

National Conference on Expanding the Roles
of Culturally Diverse People in the Profession
of Psychology **(1978)**

National Hispanic Psychological Association
forms **(1979)**

Belmont Report, establishing the use of institutional
review boards, is published **(1979)**

AAPA begins the *Journal of the Asian American
Psychological Association* **(1979)**

First issue of the *Hispanic Journal of Behavioral
Science* **(1979)**

1980

Psychologists for Social Responsibility forms **(1982)**

American Psychological Society, now the Association
for Psychological Science, forms **(1988)**

Ronald Reagan becomes 40th U.S. president **(1981)**

Logan Wright becomes the first person of American
Indian heritage elected president of the American
Psychological Association **(1986)**

Richard Suinn serves as the first Asian American
president of the APA **(1999)**

INCLUSIVENESS, IDENTITY, AND CONFLICT IN LATE 20TH-CENTURY AMERICAN PSYCHOLOGY

The following day we had the big meeting in the Hilton. Then we decided we were going to form the Black Psychologists Association. Our thinking was, APA will not represent us because they have had from 1892 to 1968 to do so, and in fact they unrepresented us.

—Joseph L. White, unpublished interview, 2004

INTRODUCTION

It now seems a cliché to say that the 1960s were a time of social upheaval and dissent in the United States, in much of Europe, and in many other countries. American psychology and psychologists were not immune to this unrest, although organized Psychology, exemplified by the American Psychological Association (APA), had little experience in how to address the causes or impact of the upheaval. In 1965, the APA's governing group debated whether or not psychologists and their organization should become involved in social issues. They deferred action, appointing a Committee on Public Affairs, led by vocational psychologist and future APA President Leona Tyler (1906–1993), to study the problem and issue a report. By the time the committee submitted its report (Tyler, 1969), events had overtaken the APA and the field of Psychology. That year, just as George A. Miller (b. 1920) took the podium to deliver his famous "Giving Psychology Away" speech, 12 African American psychology students took the stage, preempted Miller, and made their own list of demands for greater racial equality and opportunity in Psychology.

So far in this book, we have seen many examples of the embeddedness of science and practice in the social order. In the introduction, we articulated our use of Graham Richards's "little p" and "Big P" psychology concept to indicate the constant reciprocal relationship between science and society. Our account of the development of psychology in Germany highlighted its role as a component of educating the elite and upper classes in German culture. In our account of the interpretation of intelligence testing in World War I we showed how it supported the social hierarchy then in place, and in our discussion of the massive support of the expansion of mental health professions, including clinical psychology, after World War

II we saw psychology used as a means of social management in a time of widespread policy concerns about social stability during the Cold War. Any science or profession can only succeed to the degree that it corresponds to the needs of society. The question remains, "Whose needs are represented?"

In this chapter, we give a historical account of the relationship of psychology and society in the American context, beginning with the 1960s. This is recent history, full of conflicting and competing trends whose meanings have not yet been fully sorted out by the passage of time. To simplify our task, we have chosen to examine the interlocking trends of inclusiveness, identity, and professional conflict through the lens of the largest psychological organization, the APA. In doing so, we necessarily restrict our focus and may miss some events that prove to be more important than those we do include. Still, we think that by using the APA as our lens it will help us understand the social embeddedness of psychology.

We begin with an examination of the social issues of the day: civil rights, race and ethnic identity claims and their impact on psychology, and psychologists' turn toward community work, including community mental health. We then discuss a different sort of identity issue, whether a psychologist is first a scientist or a practitioner. This was an intense conflict within organized Psychology in America, and it was firmly linked to public perceptions about the field of Psychology. Finally, we return to the complex relationship of psychology and government. We first examine the relationship of psychology and government agencies in reference to the use of social science expertise in national security, to indicate that despite APA leaders' public worries about involvement in social issues, many psychologists were already deeply enmeshed in such issues. We then examine the impact of government influence on scientific psychology through funding and the impact of formal review boards on psychological research with humans and animals.

The events we describe in the next section were not unique to psychology or the APA. During the 1960s and into the early 1970s, numerous groups of scientists formed in different disciplines in response to social issues and problems. The trend had begun earlier, as we saw in the 1930s, in the formation of the Psychologists League and the Society for the Psychological Study of Social Issues. The 1960s brought many new groups, some formally organized and some simply informal associations, to bring pressure against war, nuclear power, and energy; to protect the environment; and so on (Agar, 2008). Many of these new movements drew inspiration or methods from older groups, such as the

National Association for the Advancement of Colored People and the civil rights movement. Even before the activism of Black psychologists within the APA, similar groups sought greater inclusion within organized sociology, anthropology, and political science.

TOWARD AN INCLUSIVE PSYCHOLOGY

In historical perspective, the decade of the 1960s was a critical cultural moment for the future of American psychology. This was when questions about identity, the core of psychology's subject matter, began to crystallize as an object of inquiry and action. The liberalizing of American immigration laws in 1964 opened the gates for many people from Central and South America and Asia to enter the United States. This eventually shattered the old racial dichotomy of Black and White; now racial identity in America became a mosaic of red, yellow, brown, black, and white. The influx of racial diversity led to a struggle to make mainstream American Psychology more receptive to people of color; the critical period was from the mid-1960s to approximately 1980, although the struggle continues in different forms today. In hindsight, it was the activism by ethnic minority psychologists that created the conditions of change within American Psychology. The changes ultimately generated from this period of activism extend far beyond the scope of this chapter or this book and continue in the early 21st century.

As we illustrated in Chapter 10, the middle decades of the 20th century were marked by the collective actions of colonized peoples around the world to throw off the yoke of European and American oppression. In French Algeria, the psychiatrist–philosopher Frantz Fanon (1925–1961) articulated the ways that the apparatus of the political establishment could imprison the minds of citizens and demonstrated how psychological disciplines often played a role in facilitating the psychopathology of oppression. In South America, the educator–psychologist Paulo Freire (1921–1997) wrote about the processes of psychological and political liberation that occurred when people experienced conscientization, or the development of awareness that leads to transformation on personal and social levels. Both Fanon and Freire had an enduring influence on the development of postcolonial psychologies around the world, including in the United States.

In the 1960s, a new consciousness arose among younger Black students and intellectuals. Inspired by the writings of Fanon, the legacy of Marcus Garvey (1887–1940), and the contemporary work of Malcolm X (1925–1965), a Black Power movement emerged that focused on the strengths and resiliency of the Black community. "Black Pride" and "Black Is Beautiful" became terms to express what was happening in Black communities across the nation and around the world. In using this language, these leaders facilitated the emergence of an alternative or oppositional psychology, marked by an oppositional consciousness.

In the mid- to late 1960s, psychologists of color in the United States encountered a particularly hostile discipline. American psychological science was firmly committed to the practice of asserting "universal" psychological truths based on research with White, primarily male, undergraduates or white rats. Research and practice in psychopathology were undertaken within a medically inspired framework, with an emphasis on assigning defects or illness to internal states while ignoring social, cultural, and class conditions. A long tradition also existed, as we have seen, of employing psychological tests, especially intelligence tests, to maintain racial oppression and inequality. All of this was cloaked in the mantle of science.

Conditions of inequality in access to education, health care, and wealth creation through homeownership for people of color made access to many professions and fields of work especially

difficult. As documented by Robert V. Guthrie (1932–2005), few Blacks, Latinos, Asians, or American Indians had been admitted to doctoral study in psychology from the beginnings of the field (Guthrie, 1998). Fewer still had earned the doctorate. By the 1960s, however, a small number of Black psychologists, most of whom were still early-career professionals, were influenced by the emergent Black Nationalist movement spurred by the work of Malcolm X and articulated by Kwame Toure (born Stokely Standiford Churchill Carmichael, 1941–1998), H. Rap Brown (b. 1943), Huey Newton (1942–1989), and others. "Black Power," "Black Pride," and "Black Is Beautiful" became not only slogans but also programs implemented in Black communities. In fact, the term "Black," to refer to those who were previously given the label "colored" or "Negro" was appropriated as the preferred racial self-designation in this time. In this atmosphere, then, young Black psychologists like Charles Thomas (1926–1990), Robert Green (b. 1933), Reginald Jones (1931–2005), Ed Barnes (b. 1929; death date unknown), Robert L. Williams (b. 1930), Harold Dent (b. 1928), and Henry Tomes (b. 1932) took it upon themselves to create a psychology predicated upon the strengths and worldview of the African American community.

These young Black psychologists formed the Association of Black Psychologists (ABPsi) in 1968 at the annual convention of the APA. It was not the first organization of African American psychologists. In 1938, psychologist members of the American Teachers Association (ATA), an all-Black educational group, formed Division 6, Department of Psychology, to facilitate communication and strengthen their professional identity. Led by prominent African American psychologists such as Herman Canady (1901–1970), Division 6 sent representatives to the Intersociety Constitutional Convention that led to the reorganization of the APA during World War II. However, the ATA's Division 6 was unable to maintain its momentum after the war.

After its founding, ABPsi grew into a thriving organization with its own agenda, its own mission, and its own identity. It became the professional organization of choice for many African American psychologists. It developed an extensive publication program that includes the quarterly *Journal of Black Psychology*, the monthly newsletter *Psych Discourse*, the *Association of Black Psychologists Publication Manual*, and the *Sourcebook on the Teaching of Black Psychology*.

In part, a Black psychology was a reaction to the mischaracterizations of Black communities and Black individuals by even well-meaning Whites. For example, Black children were typically cast as culturally deprived. Black families were said to be incomplete and the source of Black pathology. ABPsi founder Joseph L. White (b. 1932) commented on this in 1970 for *Ebony* magazine (reprinted in Jones, 1972). This was the first appearance of the term "Black psychology" in print. The following quote gives a sense of the misperception of Black communities by White psychologists and at least one response to these misperceptions by a contemporary Black psychologist:

> Most psychologists take the liberal point of view which in essence states that black people are culturally deprived and psychologically maladjusted because the environment in which they were reared as children lacks the necessary early experiences to prepare them for excellence in school, appropriate sex-role behavior, and, generally speaking, achievement within an Anglo middle-class frame of reference.... Possibly, if social scientists, psychologists, and educators would stop trying to compensate for the so-called weaknesses of the black child and try to develop a theory that capitalizes on his strengths, programs could be designed which from the get-go might be more productive and successful. The black family represents another arena in which the use of traditional white psychological models leads us to an essentially inappropriate and unsound analysis. Maybe people who want to make the Black a case for national action should stop talking about

> making the black family into a white family and instead devote their energies into removing the obvious oppression of the black community which is responsible for us catchin' so much hell. (White, 1972, pp. 43–45)

However, Black psychology was more than a reaction to an oppressive White psychology. As articulated by Thomas, Green, White, Williams, and many others, Black psychology was about the strengths and resilience of Black people and Black communities. In journals such as the *Black Scholar*, the *Journal of Black Psychology*, the *Journal of Social Issues*, and several editions of *Black Psychology* (edited by Jones), it became clear that this was not a protest movement with short-term goals. It was the articulation of a worldview informed by sound scholarship and a commitment to community practice. One of the signatures of Black psychology was the emphasis on community and the strength that the community gives to its members. Communalism is a hallmark of those of African, particularly West African, descent. Black psychology, as it developed, was a psychology of resiliency and strength situated in a sense of community.

Institutional Changes

The formation of ABPsi proved to be a major stimulus to change within American psychology from its inception to the time of this writing. The development of an alternative psychology was part of the movement to build on the strengths of the Black community, but the efforts went further, to the creation of new organizations of psychologists that would serve as a home and a counter to the APA.

After the agreement to form ABPsi at the 1968 convention, its leaders confronted the APA's leadership with an agenda for changes; the agenda included an acknowledgment by the APA that White racism was the major cause of racial unrest in the United States and agreement by the APA that any policy that affected Black communities would include the involvement of

Black psychologists. The long-term agenda was to make psychology more inclusive of minorities. The APA sponsored a follow-up conference at which the main focus was increasing the number of minority faculty and students.

At the 1969 convention, an even more dramatic confrontation of the APA leadership was led by the newly formed Black Students Psychological Association (BSPA). Just as cognitive psychologist George Miller was about to give his presidential address, the oft-cited "Giving Psychology Away" speech, 12 members of BSPA stormed the stage and prevented Miller from speaking until the APA leadership agreed to hear their grievances. The short-term outcome was that ABPsi and BSPA persuaded the APA to address the concerns of Black psychologists about culturally biased testing practices, lack of employment opportunities for African Americans in psychology, and inadequate recruitment and support of Black graduate students (Simpkins & Raphael, 1970).

The events of 1968 and 1969 had effects that reverberated over the next several years. Because the APA was seen as insensitive to the needs and interests of psychologists of color, new organizations oriented to the particular strengths and problems of communities of color were formed to represent psychologists who had been traditionally ignored or underrepresented in mainstream psychological organizations. Hispanic psychologists and Asian American psychologists formed organizations and put pressure on the APA to become more sensitive to and supportive of their issues. As a result, the APA created internal offices and member committees dedicated to increasing the number and role of psychologists of color.

In the early 1970s, two brothers, Derald (b. 1942) and Stanley (b. 1944) Sue, coordinated a series of meetings in the San Francisco area that included various professionals involved in mental health issues in the Asian community.

These meetings eventually led to the founding of the Asian American Psychological Association (AAPA) in 1972. Membership was small at first, and the group struggled to maintain cohesion (Leong, 1995; Leong & Okazaki, 2009). Despite this small beginning, the AAPA had a membership of more than 400 by 2000.

Asian mental health was the original concern of the AAPA; over time, the organization diversified its interests. Advocacy efforts on behalf of Asian Americans led to involvement on U.S. Census issues and to a long engagement against the English-only movement in California. Members of the AAPA developed Asian American psychological theory that was applied to a range of psychological topics, including clinical training and social research. Leaders of the AAPA were among the first to develop theory and practice related to multicultural counseling. The National Institute of Mental Health (NIMH) relied on the AAPA to assist in its efforts to diversify its training population, and members of the AAPA served as key liaisons to the NIMH and other federal agencies for the development of mental health policy. The AAPA began publishing the *Journal of the Asian American Psychological Association* in 1979, followed by a series of monographs beginning in 1995. In 1999, Richard Suinn (b. 1933) served as the first Asian American president of the APA.

In 1971, Carolyn Attneave (1920–1992) formed the Network of Indian Psychologists in the Boston area. About the same time, Joseph Trimble (b. 1938) formed a group in 1971 called the American Indian Interest Group. Trimble's group was formed with support from the Society for the Psychological Study of Social Issues and was affiliated with the society. In 1973, Trimble merged his group with the Network of Indian Psychologists. Attneave changed the name of her group to the Society of Indian Psychologists (SIP) around 1975 (Trimble, 2000). Membership in SIP was always small, numbering around 100 at the end of the 20th century. Members of SIP and other Indian psychologists have worked to increase the number of American Indian psychologists in North America. One notable success was the Indians into Psychology Doctoral Education (INDPSYDE) started by Arthur L. McDonald (b. 1934) in the mid-1980s. By the end of the 20th century, INDPSYDE programs were operating at several colleges and universities in the Far West and there had been a noticeable gain in the number of American Indian psychologists. SIP members also worked with the APA and other ethnic minority psychology groups to support the development of rural minority mental health programs. In 1986, Logan Wright (1933–1999) was the first person of American Indian heritage to be elected APA president.

The National Hispanic Psychological Association grew out of an earlier organization of Hispanic psychologists, the Association of Psychologists por La Raza (APLR), which was founded in Miami in 1970 during the APA convention. The founding group was small, but that number grew to around 40 as a result of an APLR symposium on Hispanic psychology at the 1971 APA convention. Over the next several years, Hispanic psychologists developed a professional network through NIMH-sponsored conferences and involvement with the APA's Board of Ethnic Minority Affairs. In 1979, the National Hispanic Psychological Association was formed and the first issue of the *Hispanic Journal of Behavioral Science* was published. By the end of the 20th century, under a new name, the National Latino/a Psychological Association experienced a new burst of growth and activity.

Training Psychologists to Serve Ethnic Minority Populations

One of the complaints by ethnic minority psychology graduate students from the late 1960s

FIGURE 12.1 Leaders of Black Psychology. From left: Harold Dent, Michael Connor, Joseph White, Thomas Parham, A. J. Franklin
Courtesy of the authors.

on was that much of the extant training had little relevance to the minority experience or to minority communities. Historically, efforts to make graduate training in clinical and counseling psychology more sensitive and more relevant to ethnic minority students were met with resistance by established graduate programs. The resistance and struggle continued into the 21st century in most professional training programs in the United States and Canada.

In the United States, ethnic minorities historically underused mental health services. Some scholars believed that a principal reason for this underuse was the insensitive and inappropriate treatment that was often provided by White, middle-class mental health professionals. Research showed that even when ethnic minorities began psychotherapy the dropout rate was high. This made the issue of appropriate training in ethnic minority issues for all students in professional psychology highly salient.

Sidebar 12.1 Focus on *Joseph L. White*

Joseph L. White, a prominent African American psychologist of the last four decades of the 20th century and an important senior figure of the 21st century, was one of the founders of the Association of Black Psychologists (ABPsi) in 1968. As he recounted in a 2004 oral history, the ABPsi leaders confronted the APA leadership, pointing out the long history of the use of psychological tests and other forms of oppression directed toward the Black community:

> Then we go see the powers that be in APA.... And the eight or nine of us—(Robert) Williams, (Robert) Green, (Charles) Thomas, me, Ed Barnes—we sat on one end, and the power structure of APA sat on the other. We start trying to talk and our perception was that they were the big cheese of psychology so they had the responsibility for all this negative or deficit-deficiency, low IQ business. We asked them to straighten that out. They said they didn't do it. We said, oh no, you did it ... (t)hey said, we're not Yerkes, we're not Terman. We said, no, you are the white folks and you did it, and you need to stop doing it.

Thus began what has proven to be one of the most important series of events in American psychology. The impact of ABPsi on theory, research, and practice in American psychology has been profound and continues today. But White's influence reaches in another direction as well, one more immediate but just as enduring. From his earliest days as a psychologist at Long Beach State University to his current position as professor emeritus at the University of California, Irvine, White has mentored, guided, and influenced hundreds of young men and women of all ethnicities to become psychologists.

FIGURE 12.2   Joseph L. White
Courtesy of the authors.

He then continued to serve as a mentor and guide as their careers developed. This phenomenon he calls "getting on the Freedom Train." Each person he influences and mentors is then expected to do the same for others. From his first graduate student, Michael Connor, to more recent members of the Freedom Train, such as Bedford Palmer, White has helped create a cadre of leaders in American psychology who have been refashioning the ways in which theory, science, and practice are conceptualized. A short list of influential figures who have been members of the Freedom Train includes Thomas and Bill Parham, Jeanne Manese, and Nita Tewari. White has been an authoritative, critical, and positive force for making American psychology inclusive for nearly 50 years. He is still on the Freedom Train, thank goodness!

One way to address this major public health issue was to increase the number of ethnic minority students. The BSPA, ABPsi, and the other ethnic minority psychological organizations stressed this approach from the start of their advocacy with the APA and federal funding agencies. A major step in this direction began in the early 1970s, when several graduate training programs accepted a proposal by ABPsi called the Ten Point Program. The proposal became the foundation for most efforts to increase minority enrollment for the remainder of the 20th century.

Several surveys tracked the impact of the new efforts to recruit, retain, and graduate minority students. It was clear that the efforts had an impact. In 1970, 5 percent of all clinical psychology students were non-Whites; by 1980, the percentage of minority students among all psychology doctoral students was 10.6 percent (Kennedy & Wagner, 1979; Pickren, 2004). So, even though there were real gains in making graduate programs more inclusive, by 1980 plenty of room for improvement clearly remained.

The second major step was the creation of the Minority Fellowship Program. In 1974, NIMH, through its Center for Minority Group Mental Health, began a program of minority fellowships for graduate training in several professional fields. In psychology, it provided more than $1 million a year to fund graduate fellowships for minority students over six years. The Psychology Minority Fellowship Program proved to be a highly successful program for increasing the number of ethnic minority psychologists. In the first three years alone, 56 African American students, 33 Hispanic students, 20 Asian American students, and 6 American Indian students were Fellows.

Parties on all sides agreed that getting more ethnic minority psychologists into the pipeline would provide only a partial solution. What was also needed was to make the training that clinical and counseling students received more reflective of the diversity of the populations that needed to be served. The tipping point for change came in the late 1970s, when the number of ethnic minority psychologists was large enough to make the psychological establishment pay attention to their concerns. In addition, President Jimmy Carter's Commission on Mental Health in 1977–1978 not only identified the need for more ethnic minority and women mental health providers but also strongly urged that mental health training incorporate sensitivity to cultural differences.

By 1977, ethnic minority psychologists were of sufficient number, and sufficiently well organized, to effectively lobby for a greater voice within the psychological establishment on matters relevant to their concerns. Spurred by the activism of Latina psychologist Martha Bernal (1931–2001), federal funding agencies and the APA sponsored the National Conference on Expanding the Roles of Culturally Diverse People in the Profession of Psychology, held at the Marriott Hotel at the Dulles International Airport in Virginia, May 14–17, 1978, better known as the Dulles Conference.

The intent of ethnic minority leaders was to create a unified minority caucus that could work effectively within the APA. In effect, the goal was to create a pressure group within the APA to ensure that organized Psychology's leaders would devote resources to ethnic minority issues, such as training mental health providers to work effectively with ethnic minority individuals. This effort succeeded, so over the next few years, a powerful internal lobbying group was formed within the APA that successfully pressured the APA to become a more inclusive organization.

The Dulles Conference also led to a crucial change in accreditation criteria regarding training for diverse populations. Since the creation of graduate degrees in the fields of clinical, counseling, and school psychology in the late 1940s, the APA had been charged with accrediting programs. In 1979, a revision to the accreditation criteria led to the strongest language yet deployed on behalf of ethnic and racial diversity in psychology:

> Social and personal diversity of faculty and students is an essential goal if the trainees are to function optimally within our pluralistic society. It is the sense of APA Council that APA accreditation reflects our concern that all psychology departments and schools should assure that their students receive preparation to function in a multi-cultural, multi-racial society. This implies having systematic exposure to and contact with a diversity of students, teachers, and patients or clients. (Conger, 1979, p. 489)

This meant that all programs for training in professional psychology, clinical, counseling, and school psychology, had to show they were implementing programs to meet this criterion or risk their accredited status. In practice, many programs quickly found that they could easily circumvent this requirement. This, as we show, helped spur the growth of an alternative training model in the new professional schools of psychology.

We have used examples drawn from the efforts to make psychology inclusive of racial and ethnic minorities to illustrate the challenge of social issues for American psychologists. We want to be clear that psychologists attempted to address many other complex social issues. These included the relationship of psychology to the military, the antiwar movement, abortion rights, and gay, lesbian, and bisexual rights in the 1970s, 1980s, and into the 21st century. These attempts to directly address social problems with principles drawn from the psychological research literature were controversial and, at times, divisive for American psychologists. Many psychologists continued to embrace the older approach that insisted that social concerns were not the appropriate domain for psychological science. As the 20th century closed, an increasing number of private practitioner psychologists insisted on neutrality in regard to potentially divisive public issues, as they worried that taking a stand as a profession might hurt their businesses. But a sizable number of psychologists came to act as though it were possible to be good scientists or practitioners who, informed by psychological science, could also act as concerned citizens. Some of these psychologists joined activist groups, such as Psychologists for Social Responsibility, formed in 1982, whose members were active on several human rights issues. Others developed critiques of psychological science and practice, such as the diverse set of ideas that came to be known as critical psychology, derived from multiple sources,

including Marxism, phenomenology, postmodern, and poststructuralist theories of human agency.

PSYCHOLOGISTS AND THE COMMUNITY

In this section, we examine a particular expression of psychology and social involvement, the development of community approaches. As we noted in the chapter introduction, the 1960s was an era of considerable social upheaval. In this time of social conflict, President Lyndon Johnson invested heavily in social improvement through his Great Society programs, in the hopes of reducing racial conflict and ameliorating the effects of poverty. A small group of psychologists with unusual experiences in community settings seized this moment to gain federal support for initiating a new movement of community-based psychology. These psychologists agreed that addressing structural issues, such as poverty, as well as considering the prosocial development of communities, were critical components of an effective approach to community mental health. Their vision was for community psychologists to play a broad role in encouraging social change, participating in community mental health work, and acting as community development professionals.

The NIMH was an important resource for the development of **community psychology**. Initially, the NIMH was guided by a public health approach oriented to prevention and treatment that entailed community-based services with concern for both mental health and mental illness. The NIMH provided support in the 1950s for community-based mental health services and research in several locations. In St. Louis, Missouri, for example, school-based prevention programs were begun and studied;

in the Boston area, two psychiatrists, Erich Lindemann (1900–1974) and Gerald Caplan (1917–2008), led innovative community mental health programs in the 1950s. Several psychologists were trained in these programs. In Palo Alto, California, social psychologist George Fairweather (b. 1921) developed an innovative program for Veterans Administration (VA) mental patients where they lived in a supportive environment in the nearby community. Fairweather's success with this approach became a model for the use of community approaches among other psychologists.

This body of work helped stimulate the emergence of community psychology as a subfield within mainstream psychology. Alternatives to the individualized private practice treatment approach were already being developed by the early 1960s. Seymour Sarason (b. 1919) at Yale University, and one of the participants at the Boulder Conference, articulated a community-oriented model of clinical training and practice. He was joined by Rochester University psychologist Emory Cowen (1926–2000), who developed a model of prevention of mental disorders through a focus on community intervention. Sarason, Cowen, and other psychologists, such as James G. Kelly (b. 1929) and Forrest Tyler (b. 1925), founded community psychology in the mid-1960s, with an orientation toward research and practice not only in community settings but also with the cooperation and participation of community members. The development of community psychology occurred in tandem with the new federally funded community mental health center movement that began in the 1960s.

Federal support for **community mental health centers** (CMHCs) across the United States was mandated by the community mental health legislation of 1963 and 1965. The CMHCs were the direct result of the successful models of community mental health work mentioned earlier. In 1961, President John F. Kennedy acted on the Final Report of the Joint Commission on Mental Illness and Health to develop a nationwide network of programs that would meet the mental health needs of all Americans. Kennedy asked Congress to pass legislation that would double federal support for clinical, laboratory, and field research and authorize the NIMH to develop plans to treat mental illness in community-based mental health centers. The legislation that was passed reflected public health concepts of prevention and treatment in the community. The legislation generated optimism that the proposed centers could meet the needs of the mentally ill and strengthen the capacities of communities to improve the mental health of citizens. But it was also a potential cost-saving measure for state mental health agencies. Rising costs of care and the success of new psychotropic medications led, by the late 1950s, to massive discharges of mental patients from state mental hospitals.

Once the funding was approved for the network of CMHCs in 1965, a great deal of initial enthusiasm came from mental health professionals and community leaders. However, problems arose within a few years that brought into focus that communities are not homogeneous; issues of race, class, and power could not be ignored in community settings. The CMHC experience also highlighted shortcomings in the professional attitudes of psychiatrists and psychologists.

One of the charges that Black psychologists had made against the APA was that psychologists were exploiting Black communities. That is, researchers would approach Black community leaders with offers of help in exchange for the right to collect data from community members. This, some ABPsi leaders charged, had led to scientific colonialism, where data were collected but the community received no benefit from the research. Combined with the racial tension and outright conflict of the period, this charge created a potentially combustible context for the establishment of CMHCs in Black neighborhoods.

The intent of the CMHCs was to bring mental health services to communities across the socioeconomic spectrum. That this happened in the context of social unrest and the growth of racial and ethnic identity was momentous, because it highlighted the lack of relevance of mental health treatment models predicated on White middle-class assumptions and experiences. In many poor communities (or catchment areas, as they were called), especially poor racial or ethnic minority communities, the placement of CMHCs staffed by White professionals led to increased tension and strife and highlighted the shortage of mental health professionals of color, which had been one of the main points of ABPsi and the BSPA to the APA. The shortage of qualified Black mental health practitioners in Black communities contributed to an increasing sense of distrust between the residents of Black communities and the mainly White mental health professionals. Conflicts had already erupted in some urban Black neighborhoods over White domination of the new mental health centers.

At the time that the ABPsi and the BSPA confronted the APA over the failure to make graduate training inclusive, a vivid example of the need for more racial and ethnic minority psychologists and greater cultural awareness by White psychologists was the takeover by the nonprofessional staff, comprising mostly Black and Puerto Rican employees, of the Lincoln Hospital Mental Health Services in the Bronx in March 1969. The problem was not mental health care but its control by Whites who did not understand Black culture. The takeover lasted for

several months and ended with the effectiveness of the professional mental health staff seriously compromised.

An alternative example from the same era may help us understand the positive potential of paying attention to the characteristics and needs of communities to provide effective services. The Meharry CMHC in Nashville, Tennessee, took a different approach. Its director was Henry Tomes (b. 1932), who had earned his undergraduate degree from Fisk University in Nashville and his doctorate from Penn State in 1963. In 1969, he was appointed the director of the new Meharry CMHC. Tomes recruited a first-rate staff of young psychologists and mental health workers of color, since the catchment area for the center was predominantly African American. Tomes and his staff enlisted members of the community in the development of the center and its services. Paraprofessionals were also recruited and trained from the community, thus providing employment. By the time that Tomes left in 1980 to become commissioner for mental health in the state of Washington, the center had grown to provide services through several satellite centers.

The historical point to be made in contrasting these two centers is that cognizance of actual community needs, and the provision of services to address these needs in a culturally relevant manner, *with the active participation of the community* proved critical in a racially charged era. There could be no community psychology without the involvement of the members of the community.

Training students to be appropriate providers of psychological services in diverse racial and community settings also proved to be a challenge in this era. Few clinical or counseling psychology programs in the United States and Canada fully embraced the challenge. One that did was at the University of Maryland.

In 1970, under the direction of community psychologist Forrest Tyler, the clinical psychology graduate program at Maryland became a pioneer site for a graduate training program focused on community needs. The program incorporated a multicultural perspective, aggressively recruited minority students and faculty, and sought innovative ways to teach students how to work with community members. Tyler and his colleagues self-consciously sought to make the program community oriented and inclusive. Ten students were accepted each year; a minimum of three students had to be members of ethnic minorities. Diversity was also promoted among the training faculty. Various community training sites were chosen so that students were ensured exposure to mental health clients from the full spectrum of social classes and minority groups. Tyler, his faculty, and the students found that an effective program required honesty about difference and learning to respect the uniqueness of each member and the clients they served. However, discontent among the other faculty over the uniqueness of the program and the role of students in program development and recruitment led to pressure on Tyler and the program to change and conform to the mainstream. This eventually resulted in the ousting of Tyler as clinical training director. Even though this program had a short life, it illustrates the challenges that psychologists faced to develop a true community psychology.

A QUESTION OF PROFESSIONAL IDENTITY

Is a psychologist a scientist, a practitioner, or both? In the 1960s, this question emerged in the context of the rapid growth of the number of clinical psychologists who began offering psychological services, primarily diagnostic assessments and psychotherapy, in the private practice of psychology. Answers to this question had implications for American society. By the late 1950s, surveys of the public revealed that when asked what a psychologist does, the great majority of respondents said psychologists help people with their problems.

The Boulder model of training clinical psychologists to be scientist–practitioners (see Chapter 9) came under a great deal of criticism by the early 1960s. Clinical psychologists who identified primarily as practitioners became quite disenchanted with the model. It did not, they argued, adequately prepare clinical psychologists for the actual practice of clinical psychology, which included assessment, diagnosis, and psychotherapy. These early protests indicated the emergence of what became a major fault line in American psychology. Psychologists whose careers centered on academic pursuits such as teaching and research often did not understand the demands of professional service provision that the practitioners faced daily. And the reverse was true as well, in that practitioners were ever further removed from the laboratories where psychological science was done. A common criticism of the Boulder scientist–practitioner model was that it was not very successful at producing scientists; the modal number of research-based publications by scientist–practitioners was zero.

The tension between the academicians and the practitioners grew steadily in the 1960s, with frequent heated exchanges at the annual APA meeting. Groups of private practitioners in California and New York pressed their demands with the APA to improve training. Such groups, although small, were well organized, with a clear focus on professional aims. The APA often seemed to ignore their demands. In 1965, when Medicare was created, for example, the APA was offered the opportunity to have psychological services included in the coverage provisions so that psychologists could be reimbursed for their services to financial need–based populations. The leadership of the APA at the time let the window of opportunity close without action, a move that delayed Medicare coverage for psychological services for several decades. The tension generated by such actions soon turned into outright conflict. By the late 1960s, faced with revolt, the APA sanctioned a new model of training focused on preparing students solely for the practice of professional psychology.

A new degree, the doctor of psychology (PsyD), was authorized. The PsyD degree reflected a practitioner–scholar model of training. The first PsyD program opened at the University of Illinois in 1968. This kind of degree had its proponents over the years, dating back to Leta Hollingworth (1918) and Carl Rogers (1939). The intent of the degree was similar to law and medicine degrees. The knowledge base of student training was research based, while the bulk of the training was designed to be practice oriented. By the end of the 20th century, the PsyD was the fastest-growing degree in psychology. However, rather than resolving the problem of professional identity, it appeared to raise even more concerns about the appropriate roles of psychologists in American society.

While the PsyD degree did not resolve tensions between scientists and practitioners, it did create new opportunities for students of color. The new PsyD programs were more open to innovation than some of the older programs. Perhaps this was because many of them were freestanding proprietary institutions; that is, their financial viability was based on collecting tuition and other fees, so filling seats in a classroom was a necessity. But these developments came just when there was a demand to make graduate training more open to students of color and training programs more oriented toward cultural diversity. By the 1980s, the PsyD programs were successfully recruiting, retaining, and graduating students of color,

resulting in genuine growth in the numbers of professionally trained psychologists of color.

The sequelae of these battles remain in the field even to the present, with an ongoing, although usually submerged, tension between those who see themselves as scientists and those who focus on practice. One major consequence of this tension was the rancorous divide that occurred in the mid-1980s and resulted in the formation of the American Psychological Society, now the Association for Psychological Science. The tension and the conflict built for years before the actual split occurred. The APA members whose main identity was the professional and private practice of psychology grew in numerical strength from the 1960s on and increasingly learned how to assert their voice and gain power within the governance structure of the APA. Thus empowered, they were able to gain control of the APA and direct its resources and aims to achieve their goals. Those who wanted the APA to remain a primarily scientific organization grew increasingly frustrated, forgetting, perhaps, that when they had the numerical and political advantage they had thwarted the goals and hopes of the practitioners. A proposed reorganization plan in the mid-1980s was defeated by a vote of the membership, and almost immediately a large group of dissident psychological scientists, including former APA presidents, left the APA to form what is now the Association for Psychological Science. The question of professional identity remains unresolved.

PSYCHOLOGISTS, GOVERNMENT, AND NATIONAL SECURITY

Since World War II, government agencies and funds have played an important role in the development of American psychology. In Chapter 9, we examined the impact of the VA and the NIMH on the growth and diversification of psychological research and training. In this section, we take another look at the relationship of government and psychology.

In the opening vignette to this chapter, we noted that in the mid-1960s psychologists were debating whether they and their organizations should be involved in social issues. Psychologists had long been deeply involved in the social domain through multiple connections with the federal government, especially its military and security agencies. In 1957, the APA hosted a lavish banquet at which it celebrated 10 years of an intimate relationship with the Office of Naval Research (ONR). A certificate of appreciation was tendered to the ONR representatives present, stating that ONR support of psychology has "aided significantly in the advancement of science, and at the same time, in contributing to the national security" (Darley, 1957, p. 305). In 1956, Darley noted, the ONR had supported more than 140 separate research contracts and grants for psychological research, totaling more than $2 million. Earlier we noted the voluminous NIMH funding for psychological research and training, but it was not until 1961 that the amount of NIMH support exceeded ONR and other Department of Defense (DoD) funding of psychology. What did the ONR and the DoD get for their money, and what did psychology get?

Historian Mark Solovey (2001) has documented how military and security agency funding helped establish psychology as a science useful to the government. Psychologists and other social scientists aided the American effort against the Soviet Union in the Cold War. Between 1961 and 1964, the U.S. DoD support for psychological research rose markedly, from $17.2 million in 1961 to $31.1 million in 1964 (Solovey, 2001). The large amounts of funding for psychological research on personnel selection, ergonomics, and other applications generated an impressive body of research.

Psychologists also contributed to the Cold War goals of counterinsurgency and psychological warfare. This was made explicitly clear by psychologist Charles Bray (1904–1982) in an *American Psychologist* article in 1962. Bray, a Princeton PhD, had been involved in

defense-related work since World War II. In 1957, the DoD's office of Defense Research and Engineering arranged for a large-scale review of social science research results to determine how social scientists, particularly psychologists, could best assist the military's Cold War agenda. The Research Group in Psychology and the Social Sciences was formed and placed under the purview of the Smithsonian Institution for contractual purposes. Members of the research group were well-known psychological scientists at the time and included Arthur Melton (1906–1978), Lyle Lanier (1903–1988), Clifford Morgan (1915–1976), Henry Riecken (b. 1917), and Howard Kendler (b. 1919). All of them had experience working on defense-related topics. Psychologists, Bray argued, were in the best position to help the military deal with the human factors in military hardware (i.e., efficient ergonomic design) and with people in conflict, both hot and cold. As Bray put it, a technology of behavior could offer "proven techniques to deal with people and to get precise information about them" (1962, p. 528). We give an example that illustrates how psychology was used in government service to try to subvert unfriendly governments.

Project Camelot was a DoD-sponsored plan to involve behavioral experts in predicting and controlling Third World revolution and development to gain the upper hand in the Cold War. It was deliberately designed to counter the Soviet Union's war of liberation approach. Project Camelot became an international scandal in mid-1965 when it was inadvertently exposed. The intent was to use psychological expertise to understand guerrilla warfare and to provide guidance for counterinsurgency against Soviet-supported regimes.

With input from such psychologists as Neal Miller (1909–2002), Harry Harlow (1905–1981), and others, the military was persuaded that the behavioral sciences could be used to manipulate individuals and cultures and that they could aid in gathering and interpreting intelligence. In March 1962, the army funded a large gathering of social and behavioral scientists in Washington,

DC. Military leaders let the scientists know what kind of research they were looking for: research that would help them predict human behavior, whether at individual, political, or societal levels. Prediction and population control were at the heart of the military counterinsurgency mission. How, the military wanted to know, could psychologists help them control indigenous peoples, exploit national psychological vulnerabilities, and help them incite and manipulate internal (civil) war to the U.S. advantage? None of the participants publicly opposed the use of psychological knowledge in the service of these aims. They apparently agreed with the military's assertion that the U.S. national interest was synonymous with freedom, prosperity, and social justice all over the world. In 1963, planning for Project Camelot got under way, funded by the Special Operations Research Organization with funds provided by the military. The project's focus was Latin America. The intent was to study the behavioral and social aspects of countries where Communist insurgencies had occurred since World War II and develop a model for how to thwart them, develop counterinsurgencies, or both. However, the project failed when it was exposed in 1965 by a Norwegian sociologist who alerted Chilean behavioral scientists to the real sponsors of a plan being promoted to them for a cultural study of Chilean society. The resulting political backlash both in South America and at home caused the project to be canceled. Thus, even as psychologists were publicly debating involvement in social issues, several psychologists were already engaged in these issues under the banner of national security work.

GOVERNMENT AND THE DIRECTION OF PSYCHOLOGICAL SCIENCE

We turn now to a related question of psychology's relationship with government and to the influence of government funding on psychological research. In Chapter 9, we discussed the impact of NIMH and VA funds on the rapid growth in the numbers of psychologists and the expansion and diversification of psychological research. We noted that in the first 20 years of NIMH funding it was common for the U.S. Congress to appropriate more money for the NIMH than requested in the budget proposed by the president. This began to change in the late 1960s, with a decrease in available funds due to the escalating costs of the Vietnam War and the more conservative administration of Richard Nixon.

By the late 1960s, psychology and government had become thoroughly engaged with each other. The scale of psychological research under the patronage of government grants and contracts had grown immensely, as we have pointed out, until psychology was, if not big science, then at least medium science. Increasingly, this meant that psychologists depended on government for funds to develop and maintain their research programs. Government agencies ultimately owe their allegiance to taxpayers and to their representatives in Congress and the executive branch of the federal government. This created two potential and not mutually exclusive problems for psychology. First, psychological science, like other sciences, became vulnerable to political aims. Second, patronage, especially large-scale patronage, came to influence the direction of research. This was a problem for Galileo Galilei (1564–1642) in the 16th century, and it became a problem for psychological scientists in the 20th century.

During the Nixon administration of the 1970s, the federal budget became constrained with the high cost of the Vietnam War and the increasing costs of entitlement programs, such as Medicare. Too, Nixon and his advisers were socially conservative and deeply suspicious of the "social" sciences. This led to efforts to reduce or stop federal funding for social science projects, including psychology. In the 1980s during the two-term administration of Ronald Reagan, psychology and the social sciences were again targeted. The training program for psychology that had facilitated the remarkable increase in the number of psychologists was ended. Efforts were made to reduce funding for social science research at the National Institutes of Health. There, the CMHC program was reduced to such an extent that it became almost inoperable. Scientific organizations, such as the APA, suddenly realized that they had no effective lobbying mechanism in place to try to stop these changes.

How did these events affect psychology? As we noted earlier, the French anthropologist Marcel Mauss (1872–1950) pointed out in his classic text, *The Gift* (1954), that gifts create obligations. Although the relationship between giver and receiver may be quite subtle, recipients are obliged to accede to the demands of the giver. As long as the federal budget afforded the free flow of funds to psychology, there was little sense of constraint or obligation. By the 1970s, however, and continuing to the present, funds were reduced and obtaining grants became highly competitive.

Federal granting agencies' program and grant officers also began to take a more directive role. Increasingly, federal requests for proposals specified the research that was eligible for funding. The NIMH, for one, also expanded its role in collaborative research with university-based scientists. These new directions often explicitly reflected political priorities. For example, the marked increase in the use of psychotherapy by the American public became a target of a federal research initiative. This was due, in part, to the high cost of insurance coverage and the complaint of both insurers and the public about myriad available psychotherapies. There was a demand by the government to determine the effectiveness of psychotherapies to cut costs. Along with the high cost of psychotherapy services, the increased use of many new psychotropic medications contributed to skyrocketing costs. This led Congress to establish two oversight bodies, the National Center for Health Care Technology and the Office of Technology Assessment, to assess the effectiveness of psychotherapy. The NIMH began a large research program in collaboration with several university researchers to compare several psychotherapies with one another and with psychotropic medication. Manualized treatment and an emphasis on what came to be called evidence-based treatments were among the results of this study. These results pleased insurance companies, which began to refuse payment for treatments that were not evidence based. But they also created major controversies in psychology, as the new rules reduced the income of private practitioners. More importantly, charges were made that the evidence put forward to validate a treatment often did not include any data from racial or ethnic minority patients, thus bringing us back to the issues discussed earlier about the need to truly understand the psychological import of cultural diversity.

Another example of the complexities that arose around federally funded research was the development of guidelines and restrictions on the use of research subjects, both human and nonhuman. As we noted earlier, social activism became a staple of American life by the late 1960s. In the 1970s, some aspects of scientific research became the target of activists. Publicity about the Tuskegee syphilis study, which ran from 1932 to 1972, was the proximal spark for new demands about the protection of human subjects in biomedical and behavioral research. In the Tuskegee (Alabama) study, several hundred mostly poor, mostly illiterate, African American men who had contracted syphilis were left untreated to study the progress and outcome of the disease. When this study came to light, it created a sensation and demands were made on politicians to pass legislation to curb such studies. Once Congress started investigating, other abuses and potential abuses came to light, including the use of psychological behavior modification techniques with prisoners and other vulnerable populations.

What investigators found was little supervision or ethical review of any biomedical or psychological research. And in the case of prisoners, the behavior modification strategies were sometimes abusive. For example, congressional investigators found that psychologists and their assistants were using items that were basic rights—such as acceptable amounts of living space, regular use of clean and working showers, and access to adequate recreation facilities—as rewards dependent on the "acceptable" behavior of the incarcerated individuals.

The results of this investigation and the ensuing congressional debate were not only a public relations problem for psychology but also resulted more positively in the passage of the National Research Act in 1974, which established the National Commission for the Protection of Human Subjects of Biomedical and Behavioral Research to set guidelines for research with human participants. In 1979, the commission published the *Belmont Report: Ethical Principles and Guidelines for the Protection of Human Subjects of Research*. The *Belmont Report* established the use of ethics review boards for all research, including psychological research, with humans at all institutions receiving federal support. Thus,

all university-based psychological scientists who sought federal funding had to make their research protocols acceptable to the institutional review board of their institution. The federal government was then in the position to adjudicate, through the dispensation of guidelines, the ethics of all the research that it funded. A few years later, similar guidelines and review boards were established for research with animals. The instantiation and empowerment of institutional review boards and institutional animal care and use committees provided another potential constraint on scientific research, as the threat of withholding funds proved to be a powerful influence on psychological and other sciences. But because much American psychological research had grown to the scale where it could not proceed without government funding, researchers had to accede to the demands of governmental agencies. One result of these events was the development of lobbying or advocacy offices within American psychological organizations.

By the end of the 20th century, psychological science had become, in some sense, a regulated industry. Professional advancement came to depend on publication of data-based scientific articles and books, and the wherewithal to conduct the research to collect the data, in turn, depended on the ability to win grants and contracts from sources that were now empowered to determine the direction of the research. These research directions were increasingly influenced more by government policy makers than by the scientific curiosity of psychological scientists.

SUMMARY

In this chapter we demonstrated the close relationship between American psychologists and the issues and needs of late 20th-century American

society. The 1960s were indeed a watershed period. Psychologists began the era with questions about their involvement in social issues and problems, but these questions gave way to the realization that their work could not be divorced, and was not divorced, from these issues. The impact of the civil rights movement, racial and ethnic identity movements, and needs and demands of the community all contributed to important changes in psychologists' professional identity and the role of psychological organizations. We described the powerful role of Black psychologists in demanding change within the professional organization that purported to represent them and their establishment of their own organizations. This activism served as an inspiration and template for other ethnic minority psychologists, who in turn organized themselves for change. Clearly, as we have emphasized throughout the book, Psychology does not exist

in a social vacuum, and psychologists are citizens, as well as professionals. The history of the APA's struggles to become more inclusive of diversity is a microcosm of struggles that unfold in the larger society.

We also examined how the government, as the increasingly powerful gatekeeper of funding, played a powerful role in shaping psychological research and practice throughout the end of the 20th century and continuing today. Psychologists also exerted agency in these processes. That is, they were not victims of the larger context but instead participated in creating it. The changes that occurred were a complex interplay between the psychologists and their organizations and the larger community and governmental settings in which they operated.

BIBLIOGRAPHIC ESSAY

The published literature on the topics in this chapter is extensive, although historical synthesis of this literature is somewhat lacking. We relied on oral histories for some of our information. The relevance of the work of Frantz Fanon (1963) and Paolo Freire (1968/1970) for the emergence of postcolonial psychologies, including Black psychology, is now widely known. We are grateful to the social theorist Chela Sandoval for her insightful book on oppositional consciousness (2000). We are thankful for the oral history interview with Black psychiatrist Price Cobbs on a delightful sunny afternoon in San Francisco. He taught us how and what Black Pride and Black Is Beautiful meant and mean (Cobbs, 2005a, 2005b). He should know; he was there.

The late Robert Guthrie's landmark volume, *Even the Rat Was White* (1998), was immensely helpful to us. Wade Pickren still recalls with

great fondness the intense and in-depth conversations with Guthrie—we found we shared a love of good grits. The sad state of affairs surrounding the poor record of training ethnic minority psychologists was well documented by the Lauren Wispe et al. study (1969). Robert Williams was one of the founders of the ABPsi, and he has written three historical accounts that were helpful (1974, 2008a, 2008b; see also the doctoral dissertation of Birdean H. Williams, 1997). The several editions of Reginald Jones's *Black Psychology* were useful, especially the chapter by Wade Nobles on African communalism (1972).

The development of ethnic minority psychological associations is still not well documented, although that is about to change. By the time this volume is published, a special issue of *Cultural Diversity and Ethnic Minority Psychology* will contain detailed histories of each of the associations (Jones, 2009; Leong & Okazaki, 2009; Padilla,

2009; Trimble & Clearing Sky, 2009). Robert Williams has edited a thorough history of the Association of Black Psychologists through biographical and autobiographical accounts (2008b). Thanks to Frederick Leong, we already know a great deal about the formation of the AAPA. Wade Pickren has written about the context of these events, especially the early work by ABPsi and the BSPA (2004). That article covers the efforts to recruit and retain ethnic minority students and owed a great deal to the information provided by Gary Simpkins and Phil Raphael (1970). Pickren has conducted oral histories with both Simpkins and Raphael, which were immensely helpful. The greater rate of mental disorders and the correspondingly low rate of mental health care utilization among ethnic minorities have been well documented for some time (Hollingshead & Redlich, 1958; Sue, 1977). However, these reports are still shocking.

Alternative critiques of North American psychology have grown rapidly in recent years. For our account, we consulted the work of Dennis Fox and Isaac Prilleltensky (1997) and Thomas Teo (2005).

Jim Kelly (2005) has provided a rich account of the beginnings of community psychology. First-person accounts by George Fairweather (1964) were also helpful. Jim Stockdill (2005) has written authoritatively about the problems with the CMHC movement. We are grateful for the careful scholarship of these authors. Gerald Grob (1991) has written a definitive account of the efforts to seriously address mental health problems in America. The volume by Kaplan and Roman (1973) about the takeover of the Lincoln Hospital Mental Health Services revealed more about the attitudes and actions of the center's professional staff than the authors may have intended. Forrest Tyler has written about the innovative program at Maryland (Tyler & Gatz,

1976) and has spoken with us about it in person several times.

The tension between academic psychological scientists and professional practitioners has been a sore spot in American Psychology for many years. An adequate history has still not been written. Still, we can glean a great deal from various publications over the years. We found the chapter by then-young practitioners Karl Pottharst and Arthur Kovacs from 1964 startling in its frank assessment of the failures they perceived in professional training under the Boulder model. Wade Pickren has put this in historical context (2007). Donald Peterson, the founder of the first PsyD program, has written critically about such programs in more recent publications (1992, 2003).

The history of psychologists' involvement with government is long, and given recent controversy over psychologists' involvement in national security interrogations, we trod carefully with our materials here. Historians Ellen Herman (1995) and Mark Solovey (2001) have published solid scholarship showing how enmeshed and how dependent many psychologists have been on government funding over the last 50 years. Much or even most research funded by the government, including the military, has been without blame. This work shows the need to be careful in making sweeping judgments.

Relatedly, psychologists' reliance on federal funds has been crucial for the growth of psychology in America, as we showed in Chapter 9. But it has made psychologists vulnerable to government manipulation, as Stanley Schneider discussed in his account of the efforts of the Nixon administration to stop social science research (2005). Rachael Rosner has documented the mixed experience of federal oversight of psychotherapy research (2005), revealing the roots of the problems inherent in seeking the evidence for "evidence-based" treatment. Finally, Alexandra Rutherford (2006, 2009) has shown how psychological interventions based on behavior modification principles led to abuses, which, in part, stimulated the changes in legislation that led to the current oversight of research with human participants through institutional review boards.

Chapter 13
TIMELINE 1790–1990
(In 25-year increments)

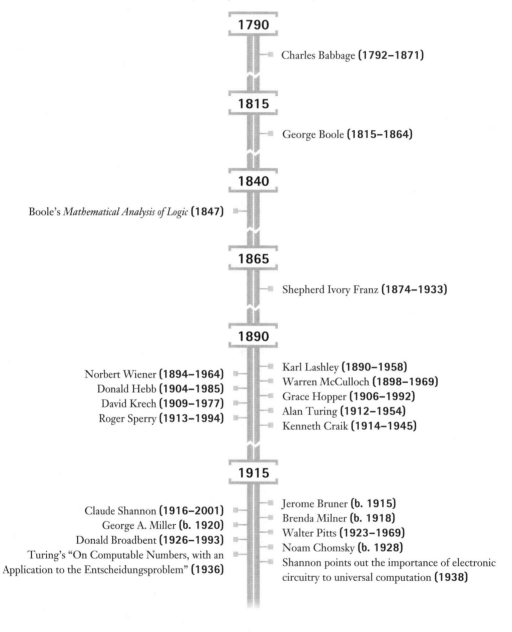

1790

Charles Babbage **(1792–1871)**

1815

George Boole **(1815–1864)**

1840

Boole's *Mathematical Analysis of Logic* **(1847)**

1865

Shepherd Ivory Franz **(1874–1933)**

1890

Norbert Wiener **(1894–1964)**   Karl Lashley **(1890–1958)**
Donald Hebb **(1904–1985)**   Warren McCulloch **(1898–1969)**
David Krech **(1909–1977)**   Grace Hopper **(1906–1992)**
Roger Sperry **(1913–1994)**   Alan Turing **(1912–1954)**
          Kenneth Craik **(1914–1945)**

1915

Claude Shannon **(1916–2001)**   Jerome Bruner **(b. 1915)**
George A. Miller **(b. 1920)**   Brenda Milner **(b. 1918)**
Donald Broadbent **(1926–1993)**   Walter Pitts **(1923–1969)**
Turing's "On Computable Numbers, with an   Noam Chomsky **(b. 1928)**
Application to the Entscheidungsproblem" **(1936)**   Shannon points out the importance of electronic
          circuitry to universal computation **(1938)**

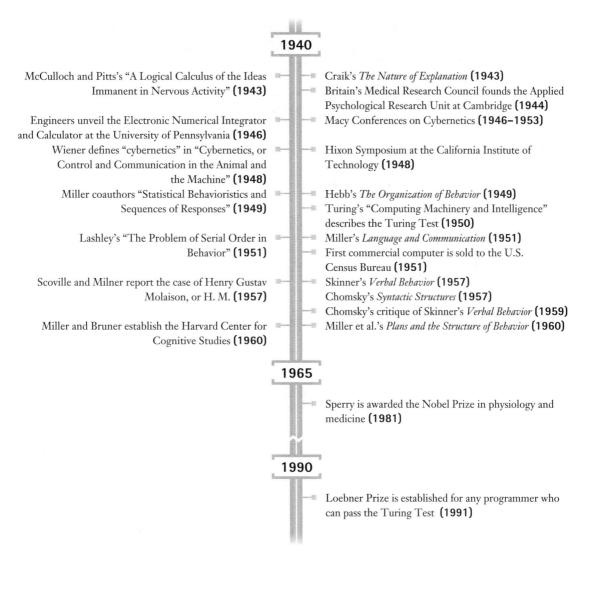

1940

McCulloch and Pitts's "A Logical Calculus of the Ideas Immanent in Nervous Activity" **(1943)**

Engineers unveil the Electronic Numerical Integrator and Calculator at the University of Pennsylvania **(1946)**
Wiener defines "cybernetics" in "Cybernetics, or Control and Communication in the Animal and the Machine" **(1948)**
Miller coauthors "Statistical Behavioristics and Sequences of Responses" **(1949)**

Lashley's "The Problem of Serial Order in Behavior" **(1951)**

Scoville and Milner report the case of Henry Gustav Molaison, or H. M. **(1957)**

Miller and Bruner establish the Harvard Center for Cognitive Studies **(1960)**

Craik's *The Nature of Explanation* **(1943)**
Britain's Medical Research Council founds the Applied Psychological Research Unit at Cambridge **(1944)**
Macy Conferences on Cybernetics **(1946–1953)**

Hixon Symposium at the California Institute of Technology **(1948)**

Hebb's *The Organization of Behavior* **(1949)**
Turing's "Computing Machinery and Intelligence" describes the Turing Test **(1950)**
Miller's *Language and Communication* **(1951)**
First commercial computer is sold to the U.S. Census Bureau **(1951)**
Skinner's *Verbal Behavior* **(1957)**
Chomsky's *Syntactic Structures* **(1957)**
Chomsky's critique of Skinner's *Verbal Behavior* **(1959)**
Miller et al.'s *Plans and the Structure of Behavior* **(1960)**

1965

Sperry is awarded the Nobel Prize in physiology and medicine **(1981)**

1990

Loebner Prize is established for any programmer who can pass the Turing Test **(1991)**

BRAIN, BEHAVIOR, AND COGNITION SINCE 1945

Behaviorism largely ignored mental processes. As a result ... it largely excluded from study some of the most fascinating features of mental life.

—Brenda Milner, Larry Squire, & Eric Kandel, "Cognitive Neuroscience and the Study of Memory," 1998

INTRODUCTION

During the 1950s, in the aftermath of interdisciplinary work during the Second World War, developments in artificial intelligence combined with critiques of behaviorism to produce a renewed interest among psychologists in reinstating complex mental processes as a central topic of study in Psychology. Although behaviorism had never been hegemonic, even in the United States, the behaviorist attitude had certainly colored much of the work undertaken by psychologists for several decades. Hence, many prominent research programs in Psychology during the 1920s, 1930s, and 1940s reflected behaviorism's central tenet—that internal mental processes, or the mind, could not be studied scientifically. During the 1950s and 1960s, this attitude dissipated, and the study of mental processes again became not only acceptable but even cutting edge. As Ulric Neisser wrote in 1967, in his influential text on the new field titled, simply enough, *Cognitive Psychology*, "A generation ago, a book like this one would have needed at least a chapter of self-defense against the behaviorist position" (p. 5).

Rechristened cognitive psychology, this revival of interest in the mind generated a new breed of unapologetic cognitive psychologist who undertook studies of human reasoning, problem solving, memory, cognitive development, and language acquisition, often with reference to the neurological substrates of these processes. Many were influenced by work on computer models of human thinking and **cybernetics**, the study of self-regulating physical and social systems that drew on developments in linguistics, mathematics, philosophy, physiology, and engineering. Cognitive psychologists found themselves embedded in a kaleidoscopic interdisciplinary milieu fueled by the generous funding of wide-ranging interdisciplinary meetings, such as the 1948 Hixon Symposium at the California Institute of Technology, the Macy Conferences on Cybernetics held in New York between 1946 and 1953, and a host of meetings funded by the Social Science Research Council on topics ranging from children's thinking to psycholinguistics.

Continuing our account of psychology in the post–World War II period, this chapter focuses on the emergence and growth of cognitive psychology and cognitive science since 1945, with earlier forays into precursors of these fields where appropriate. We start by presenting some of the research on the neurological substrates of learning and memory that began to reorient psychologists to the possibility of studying the mind and its higher-order functions. We then survey some of the neuropsychological and theoretical research on memory that continued this reorientation and move to developments in computer science, information processing theory, and cybernetics. We highlight how technological developments, such as the computer, both grew out of and made possible conceptualizations of the mind as machine, even if a highly complex one. In addition to the computer, technological advances in ways to see inside the brain contributed to new models of memory and cognition. We then take a brief look at how psychologists and linguists came together to study language, one of the most complex human abilities.

Throughout the chapter, we highlight the role of interdisciplinarity in the evolution of cognitive science, which, by its nature, draws on research and innovations in many fields. Psychologists have played an important role in this evolution, which we highlight here, but their work has been intertwined with the work of many other scientists. It is important to glimpse this wider intellectual context, although we cannot do justice to the diversity of interdisciplinary contributions in one textbook chapter. We end with some thoughts about the rapidly accelerating field of cognitive neuroscience and its distinctly 21st-century version of some familiar 19th-century questions.

THE RETURN OF THE MIND

One of the central tenets of Watsonian behaviorism was that the processes of the human mind were inaccessible to scientific study and were furthermore unnecessary to provide a complete account of behavior, at least in terms of predicting and controlling it (see Chapter 3). Although radical behaviorist Burrhus Frederic Skinner (1904–1990; see Chapter 9) did not object to studies of the nervous system, he felt they were unnecessary and would only support what one could already deduce from the experimental analysis of behavior. As a result, behaviorists and neobehaviorists tended to eschew mentalism and were unlikely to use neurophysiological data as the *basis* for their theories, although some did look to the rat brain for evidence of the effects of learning. For example, John Watson's (1878–1958) doctoral dissertation correlated the growth of central nervous system medullation

with the complexity of behavior in the white rat. Overall, one can safely state that the mind, as a *cause* of behavior and object of study, was out of favor, at least among a vocal majority of behaviorist psychologists. Furthermore, behaviorists and neobehaviorists like Watson, Skinner, Edward Chace Tolman (1886–1959), and Clark Hull (1884–1952) were unlikely to be found in the neurophysiology laboratory.

One of the first serious attacks on this position came from a rebel (more or less) within the ranks: Karl Lashley. Lashley (1890–1958) was a psychophysiologist trained at Johns Hopkins University in Baltimore, Maryland. During his doctoral studies he was influenced by Watson, who educated him in stimulus–response psychology and reflex theory, and by Shepherd Ivory Franz (1874–1933), a neurosurgeon and psychologist who worked on the reeducability of brain-injured patients. Franz taught Lashley the precise surgical techniques he would later use in his cortical localization studies. From the outset, Lashley was interested in the neural bases of behavior and learning. Starting in the 1920s however, Lashley, a self-described "ardent advocate of muscle-twitch psychology" (1931, p. 14), began to doubt the neural reality of the **reflex arc**. The reflex arc was a concept used by physiologists and psychologists to explain learning in terms of three components: a stimulus causing a sensation, the processing of this sensation, and an act or motor response following from the idea. After conducting an extensive series of studies, involving the ability of rats that had had parts of their brains destroyed to relearn maze running, he became convinced that cortical localization was a myth. So too, he reasoned, the reflex arcs that supposedly traversed the cortex to link sensory and effector organs and produce conditioned responses must not exist. If they did, they would have been disrupted by the ablations and rats should have been incapacitated. He used the results of these studies to suggest the concept of **equipotentiality**, the ability of parts of the brain to take over the functions of other parts should they be destroyed, and the

FIGURE 13.1 Karl Lashley
Courtesy of the Archives of the History of American Psychology, University of Akron, Akron, OH.

principle of **mass action**, the idea that the efficiency of performance of a complex function is affected in direct proportion to the degree of brain injury.

Almost 20 years later, in 1948, Lashley gave a paper at an interdisciplinary meeting at the California Institute of Technology called the Hixon Symposium. In his paper, published later as "The Problem of Serial Order in Behavior" (1951), Lashley grappled with how to account for the logical and orderly arrangement of thought and action, especially in the case of complex human behaviors like language or playing a musical instrument or sport. In doing so, he rejected the position that these behaviors can be explained simply as chains of sensory–motor

reactions, one following the next. In providing an alternate account, he critiqued four tenets of the behaviorist position: atomism, associationism, externalism, and the black box. He argued for the top-down structural organization of the nervous system and the idea that inputs into it (i.e., stimuli) always encounter an active and organized system, not a static one.

Lashley received positive feedback on his address from the symposium's participants, with one historian characterizing it as creating a "mini-sensation" (Boden, 2006, p. 266). It was an important critique delivered to an important audience, including many of the architects of artificial intelligence and cybernetics. Moreover, it suggested to psychologists not only that it was permissible to study the brain again but also that it was permissible to study human behavior—thought and action—in all of its complexity. Language, for example, had long been neglected by the behaviorists in their devotion to animal studies. Despite his emphasis on understanding the nervous system, Lashley, however, was not a nascent cognitive scientist. He was not enamored of the developing idea that electronic circuitry and neural circuitry might operate the same way as the brain, writing in 1958, "The brain has been compared to a digital computer because the neuron, like a switch or valve, either does or does not complete a circuit. But at that point the similarity ends" (Lashley, 1958/1960, p. 539). Lashley argued that the brain was far too complex an organ for such a simple analogy and its integrative activities would likely have to be described statistically.

The year after the Hixon Symposium, one of Lashley's former students, Donald Hebb (1904–1985), published *The Organization of Behavior* (1949). In this book, Hebb again drew attention to the contents of the behaviorists' black box, formulating a neurophysiological theory of learning. While perhaps not as directly scornful of behaviorism as Lashley was in his

1948 address, Hebb nonetheless also defied its fundamental precepts by focusing on the neural substrates of the mind. According to Hebb, behavioral patterns are built up gradually over long periods through the connection of particular sets of cells called **cell assemblies**. Cells become connected when they are repeatedly active at the same time. More complex behaviors arise from the connection of cell assemblies into sets he called **phase sequences**. For this reason, his theory is sometimes referred to as a nonbehaviorist form of connectionism. It went beyond earlier work by focusing on groups of cells instead of single-cell circuitry.

One of Hebb's students during a summer course that Hebb taught at Harvard University in 1947, Mark Rosenzweig (1922–2009), was heavily influenced by his teacher's ideas after poring over the prepublication manuscript of *The Organization of Behavior* for the course. Rosenzweig graduated from Harvard and took a job at the University of California, Berkeley, where he began a collaboration with psychologist David Krech (1909–1977) and two other colleagues on the effects of learning on brain tissue growth. Somewhat later, they extended these studies to investigate the effects of enriched environments on neurological development in rats and found that rats exposed to greater variety and challenges in their environments actually developed more cerebral connections. This basic research eventually led to practical applications in the form of the development of programs for early childhood education such as Head Start.

Sidebar 13.1 Focus on *Enriched Environments*

At the University of California, Berkeley, beginning in the 1950s and continuing into the 1960s, an interdisciplinary team led by David Krech, Mark Rosenzweig, and Edward Bennett developed a research program on enriched environments and their potential impact on the brain. The research program had its origins in the work of Donald Hebb. In *The Organization of Behavior* (1949), Hebb reported that he allowed laboratory rats to

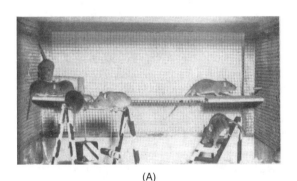
(A)

(B)

FIGURE 13.2   (A) Rats exploring one of Krech and Rosenzweig's enriched environments. (B) Lady Bird Johnson visiting a Headstart "enriched environment" classroom in 1966.

explore his home for several weeks as pets of his children and then put them back in the laboratory. They then showed better problem-solving ability than rats that had remained in the laboratory. They maintained their superiority or even increased it during a series of tests.

Rosenzweig, then a fresh PhD in psychology, heard Hebb talk about this phenomenon in a summer course at Harvard University in 1949. Rosenzweig then took a position at University of California, Berkeley, where Krech soon joined him. Krech had a long-standing interest in the individual differences he saw in animals of the same strain. Krech wanted to know what—biologically or neurologically—could be a basis for the differences in problem-solving ability among animals of an inbred strain. Krech and Rosenzweig were joined by the chemist Bennett and later, in the early 1960s by the neuroanatomist Marion Diamond in an exploration of this research question. Building on Hebb's earlier observation about the "home-schooled" rats, Krech and colleagues devised what they called enriched environments for some of their rats. Upon autopsy, brain sections indicated a much richer network of neural connections than in control rats that had only experienced standard laboratory environments. This work was widely publicized, both in scientific journals and the popular press.

In the late 1950s, psychologists Martin and Cynthia Deutsch were both at the Institute for Developmental Studies, located at New York University. In New York City schools, disparities in educational opportunities and classroom performance between poor Black and White children and those children who were middle class were widely known. The Deutsches received approval from the Board of Education in 1958 to work with schoolchildren in Harlem. The rationale was provided by the work of Krech and Rosenzweig on enriched environments. The Deutsches recruited 4-year-old children from three Harlem school districts. These children attended a special class several mornings a week. These classrooms were enriched environments; that is, they had materials to provide cognitive and social stimulation in several domains. When the children began school the following year, they showed greater gains than similar children who had not had this enriched experience. What followed from this was a change in educational policy and a major contribution to the initiation of a new national program that continues to this day, Head Start.

As psychologists paid increasing attention to internal, cognitive activity during the 1950s, interest in the work of Swiss psychologist Jean Piaget (1896–1980) received a revival in the Anglophone world. In 1960, the Social Science Research Council's Committee on Intellective Processes Research sponsored a conference to consider problems presented in the study of children's thinking. Discussion of Piaget's work permeated the conference. John Flavell's 1963 publication "The Developmental Psychology of Jean Piaget" provided an important point of contact for students entering developmental psychology and was a sign of Piaget's influence.

Piaget investigated, among other topics, how and when children acquire particular perceptual and conceptual abilities. In his studies of individual children, he observed that as they age, children's reasoning progresses not only quantitatively (they can do more problems faster) but also qualitatively. That is, children approach and solve problems differently depending on their developmental stage. He posited a series of fixed stages through which a child will pass, and named them the sensorimotor stage, the to mental structures and representations and cognitive strategies was part of the reorientation of psychology toward cognitivism in this period.

One of the practical questions that arose out of Piaget's work—one that Piaget referred to as the "American question"—especially among educators, was whether or not children's cognitive development could be accelerated by presenting them with tasks from the various stages and training them in higher-level strategies. Could manipulating the child's environment change, or enhance, development? If so, then the environment was an important locus for intervention, both for accelerating normal development and for bringing slow developers up to speed.

NEUROPSYCHOLOGY OF COGNITION AND MEMORY

Another line of research foundational to the later development of cognitive neuroscience was work on the neuropsychology of cognition and memory. In a now-classic 1957 article, William Scoville and Brenda Milner (b. 1918), a student of Hebb, reported the case of a man, H. M. (1926–2008), who suffered from intractable epilepsy. To reduce his seizures, H. M. underwent a procedure known as a bilateral medial temporal resection, in which part of his brain was removed to interrupt the electrical flow of the seizure across his brain. As a direct result of the surgery, he experienced dramatic **anterograde amnesia**, that is, a profound inability to form new memories of events, experiences, or semantic knowledge he gained subsequent to his surgery. Although his working memory was intact, and he could hold new information for short periods, this information would constantly have to be relearned. This made for an extremely interesting case study for two reasons. First, his memory losses could be directly related to the location of the brain

FIGURE 13.3   Jean Piaget
Courtesy of the Archives of the History of American Psychology, University of Akron, Akron, OH.

preoperational stage, the stage of concrete operations, and the stage of formal operations. Each stage is characterized by certain cognitive styles and strategies that the child uses to solve problems. He believed that these changes reflected a biologically evolved pattern or inherited structure but that they emerged not solely according to some inner determinism but in interaction with the child's practical experiences in the world, a process he called **epigenesis**. A synthesized science of evolutionary and developmental psychology, he felt, would be akin to a complete theory of knowledge. Piaget called this large project **genetic epistemology**. The philosophical status and import of Piaget's work notwithstanding, his attention

FIGURE 13.4 Brenda Milner
Courtesy of American Psychological Association Archives.

tissue loss, thus suggesting that the medial area of the temporal lobe was important for particular kinds of memory and not others. For example, in addition to intact working memory, H. M. was able to learn new motor skills without subsequent loss; thus, his procedural memory was unaffected by the surgery. Second, his loss demonstrated that memory could be affected with no other major deficits in perceptual, cognitive, or intellectual functioning. His IQ actually went up after the surgery, probably because he could concentrate better without seizures!

Milner and her students devoted the next 30 years to testing and studying H. M. Their work with him revealed the difference between **declarative** and **procedural memory**—that is, memory for information, facts, or knowledge of which we generally have conscious awareness and memory for skills and procedures that is largely implicit or unconscious. Milner's studies also elaborated the distinction between long- and short-term memory. H. M., or Henry Gustav Molaison (to protect his identity, his real name was not released until after his death in 2008), became known as the man without memories, but he helped us understand memory more

than any other case study in the history of neuropsychology.

Another important neuropsychological contribution was the so-called split-brain studies of Roger Sperry (1913–1994). Sperry, a student of Lashley's, was awarded a Nobel Prize in physiology and medicine in 1981 for his split-brain work. Sperry had access to a small number of severely epileptic patients who had undergone a radical disconnection of the cerebral hemispheres by severing the corpus callosum to contain, reduce, or hopefully eliminate their life-threatening seizures. Interestingly, what Sperry showed was that despite this ostensibly radical procedure, no gross, obviously discernible loss of functioning was observed in these patients. As he put it, "The most remarkable effect of sectioning the neocortical commissures is the apparent lack of effect so far as ordinary behavior is concerned" (1968, p. 724).

However, when more subtle tests involving presentations of stimuli to one hemisphere at a time were employed, Sperry showed that in fact each half of the brain was operating more or less independently of the other half, resulting in what appeared to be two brains, or two minds, in one body. This work contributed to our understanding of the distinctive functions of each hemisphere; however, it also revealed the capacity of each hemisphere to take up the functions of the other, especially in the brains of younger patients. This work revealed a degree of brain plasticity that had not been documented before. It also showed that despite the apparent division of labor between the two hemispheres, in which the left was responsible for language and the right for spatial reasoning, considerable cooperation actually occurred between the two hemispheres in any complex task. For example, as the work of Russian neuropsychologist Alexander Luria (1902–1977) had shown, in the complex task of drawing, the left hemisphere may contribute to the mastery of details while the right hemisphere controls the overall sense of form.

HOW DOES MEMORY WORK?

Concurrent with interest in the neurophysiology of learning and the neuropsychology of memory came attempts to theorize the structure of memory and how it works. An important early work in this area was British psychologist Frederic Bartlett's 1932 book, *Remembering: A Study in Experimental and Social Psychology*. Bartlett (1886–1969) based his book on studies he had conducted during and just after World War I (see Chapter 8). Breaking from earlier writings that stressed psychoanalytic interpretations of remembering and forgetting, Bartlett barely mentioned Sigmund Freud (1856–1939) and took a strictly empirical approach (he was fairly unimpressed by psychoanalytic theories). In one of his studies, he asked people to read a story and then later recall it on numerous successive occasions. He chose as his material a Native American folktale, the "War of the Ghosts," that contained several culturally unfamiliar—to British readers—ideas about the supernatural. Bartlett found that when asked to recall the story readers tended to remember only the gist, being unable to recall the details, let alone the words. Also, in subsequent retellings, they seemed to reconstruct it to bring it closer to culturally familiar ideas about its subject matter. Thus, recall was actually reconstruction, and reconstruction appeared to operate according to some general principles, such as rationalization. In rationalization, subsequent retellings of a story bring it more closely in line with familiar forms, or simplify it.

According to Bartlett, these findings indicated that memory was stored as hierarchically organized, meaningful, schemas (although he disliked this word, preferring "pattern" and "organized setting"). The higher levels encoded the gist of the story, and this gist determined the details recalled at lower levels. Memory was thus active and organized, giving meaning to incoming material in a process Bartlett called effort after meaning. This work suggested that earlier memory experiments that had used meaningless stimuli, such as nonsense syllables, were really assessing a different, and atypical, memory process.

In 1944, Britain's Medical Research Council founded the Applied Psychology Research Unit (APU) at Cambridge University. Bartlett had been campaigning for just such a unit beginning in 1943. His colleague, psychologist Kenneth Craik (1914–1945), was made its first director. Unfortunately, Craik's tenure at the APU was cut short when he was killed in a freak bicycle accident on VE (Victory Europe) Day at the young age of 31. His posterity, however, was assured with the publication, two years before his death, of his book *The Nature of Explanation*. In this book, Craik, who was heavily influenced by both psychology and neurophysiology, suggested that the brain is a system that constructs models representing the world. He proposed that these brain models have some veridical relationship to the thing in the world that they are representing. In his words, "By a model we thus mean any physical or chemical system which has a similar relation structure to that of the process it imitates" (1943, p. 51). He emphasized that this relation structure was an actual "physical working model which works in the same way as the process it parallels" (p. 51). Craik's book did not present new data or discoveries, but it did set a research agenda that was quickly (although independently) catalyzed through similar ideas presented by neurophysiologist Warren McCulloch and his young colleague, mathematician Walter Pitts in America (we elaborate on their contributions later). Several of Craik's papers, published posthumously in 1947–1948, applied systems analysis to human performance and were thus in step with cybernetic developments, to which we return later.

We should not leave the APU without mentioning the work of Donald Broadbent (1926–1993). Broadbent arrived as a graduate student at the APU shortly after Craik died and earned his PhD in 1949. Upon graduation, he was offered a job with the Royal Navy to continue a wartime initiative to study the effects of noise on performance. Arrangements were made for him to undertake the study at the APU, and he ended up working there for the next 25 years.

Broadbent is best known for his information-processing approach to problems of attention and memory. For example, he developed a model of selective attention that involved the famous dichotic listening task in which subjects were asked to respond to different stimuli being presented simultaneously in each ear. When he discovered that information from such multistimulus situations was typically forgotten quite quickly, he was led to the study of short-term memory and developed what is commonly known as the filter model. He suggested that humans have a limited capacity for the intake and storage of information. To regulate this intake, information would enter the system via a temporary, or short-term, store. Some of the information would then be allowed through a selective filter device, thus regulating the flow into short-term memory, while the remaining information would be held for later processing. Broadbent visually represented his model with a flowchart, a strategy that was subsequently adopted widely by information-processing theorists and memory researchers. The author of one biographical sketch of Broadbent suggested that although psychology "has always had its diagram-makers and model-builders ... information flow diagrams were novel, pervasive, and enduring to a degree never reached before" (Weiskrantz, 1994, p. 40).

MINDS AND MACHINES

During the period of the Second World War, three interrelated developments coincided to promote the idea that the mind might actually operate like a machine: computer science, information theory, and cybernetics. As British cognitive scientist Margaret Boden has written, "By 1930, no one had yet argued that mind

and/or mental processes, *conceptualized as somehow distinct from matter*, could be understood in *machine-based* terms [italics in original].... This situation changed in the years around 1940" (2006, p. 168). Psychologists played an important role in enacting this change but in the close company of mathematicians, neurophysiologists, engineers, philosophers, linguists, and anthropologists. Developments in computer science, cybernetics, and information theory set researchers on the path to design a machine that could mimic mental processes—a machine that could reason and problem solve like a human. This became the central goal of the field of artificial intelligence, or AI. We turn first to the history of computer science and then to information theory and cybernetics.

COMPUTATIONS AND COMPUTERS

One of the seminal events in the history of computing, and in the field that came to be known as computational cognition, was the publication of Alan Turing's 1936 paper on computable numbers (see Turing, 1937). Turing (1912–1954) was a British mathematician who, in this paper, proved that a machine (an abstract machine, not a literal one) could compute anything that was computable and thus provided a definition of computation that was used as the basis for developing the digital computer program. Turing's hypothetical machine was christened a Turing machine in 1937. To understand this innovation, we have to take a long stride back in history to the work of another British mathematician, Charles Babbage, whose plan for an analytical engine influenced Turing's conceptualization of a universal computing machine.

Babbage's Engines

Babbage (1792–1871) was the son of a well-to-do English banker and a mathematical whiz. He became an expert cryptologist (code-breaker) and an accomplished engineer who was often consulted on the design of machine tools. He held the Lucasian Chair of Mathematics at Cambridge for 11 years. Despite all of these accomplishments and accolades, however, the one project to which Babbage devoted the last 40 years of his life proved to be a disappointment to him.

Over the course of Babbage's training, which included instruction in Gottfried Wilhelm Leibniz's differential calculus, he observed that the logarithmic tables that were required to perform complex calculations often contained errors, which caused great inconvenience to the "computers," or the people attempting to use them. The mistakes were due not to the difficulty of the calculations themselves but rather to the repetitiveness and monotony of the task of generating them. To correct this state of affairs, Babbage decided to invent a machine that could produce accurate mathematical tables for any polynomial function. He puzzled over the conceptual problem of how to generate these tables and devised a method called the method of differences. He was able to translate this method into a mechanical form and came up with a blueprint for a machine that could perform the method of differences. He called it the difference engine. Unfortunately, although he was able to build a small prototype of the machine, Babbage never built a full-scale difference engine. He basically ran out of money. He had also turned his attention to another problem.

Babbage became interested in one limitation of his new invention. Although it was a sophisticated machine, and definitely ahead of its time, it was still limited to performing a single task, such as calculating polynomial functions. Babbage turned his thoughts to a different kind of machine, one that could, in theory, perform multiple tasks and maybe even any calculational task assigned to it. For a machine to be up to this task (or tasks), Babbage reasoned, you would have to be able to feed data into the machine along with a set of instructions for what to do with the data

and in what order the machine should proceed to carry out these instructions. By changing the data and the instructions from one task to the next, the machine would be able to do almost any kind of computation. Babbage thus conceived of his analytical engine as a "universal machine" or what we would now call a programmable computer.

Again, Babbage was faced with the challenge of how to transform these ideas into mechanical form. He got to work on a blueprint. The machine would need to have several parts: the mill, which we would now call a central processing unit; the store, which we would now call memory; and punch cards, which we would now call programs. Babbage drew up detailed plans from which the analytical engine could be built, but the technical and engineering problems were immense, involving steam-driven gears, cogwheels, and thousands of tiny parts that had to be designed and forged. To be realized, the analytical engine would have to be as big as a steam locomotive. The cost would be enormous, and in fact it proved prohibitive. Unfortunately, Babbage's invention was never fully realized. Nonetheless, the idea of a programmable computer caught the imagination of Turing many decades later.

Before Babbage died, he did see another important development in the march toward conceiving minds as machines. (To be clear, Babbage did not conceive of the analytical engine as equivalent to a human mind; thus, it is not, strictly speaking, an early precursor of artificial intelligence.) In 1847, George Boole (1815–1864) published a revolutionary book called *Mathematical Analysis of Logic* in which he argued that traditional mathematics could be conceptualized as just one form of many possible forms of systematic symbol manipulation. Thus, while mathematical symbols represent specific numbers and the operations (such as addition or subtraction) that they undergo, symbols could also be used to represent logical operators such as "and," "or," and "if." With this idea, he created Boolean algebra and the new discipline of symbolic logic. Later, this led to the question of whether machines could be programmed to deal with symbols, not just numbers, and whether they might therefore be able to perform a host of other logical operations besides purely mathematical calculations.

Turing's Game

Turing, like Babbage, was a mathematical genius and a crackerjack cryptologist. He was employed by the British military during World War II to break German codes. He did so by designing a method whereby, largely through trial and error, a machine would try all letter and number combinations possible until a combination approximating a comprehensible message was generated. Before the war, however, Turing had published the paper we alluded to earlier, in which he offered an explicit definition of computation. Although most people think they intuitively know what it means to *compute* something, most can probably give only specific, limited examples of computations. Turing was able to show, by leading readers through a hypothetical game, how the concept of computation can be expressed in terms of a system of general transformations (moves and rules). The significance of the exercise was to show how "abstract machines could be described in a standard logical form, and how they could be used to do elementary computations out of which all standard arithmetic operations could be constructed" (Boden, 2006, p. 175). By outlining this game in mathematical form, Turing showed that it was possible to design a machine capable of performing any specifiable form of computation.

Toward the Machine-as-Brain Metaphor

In 1938, young Massachusetts Institute of Technology graduate student Claude Shannon (1916–2001) pointed out the importance of electronic circuitry to universal computation. He demonstrated that first, notations in binary code (0s and 1s) could be used to represent not only ordinary arithmetic but also logical propositions—problems of symbolic logic (e.g., true–false and either–or). Furthermore, he pointed out how binary codes could be represented mechanically by sequences of relay circuits capable only of being open or closed. That is, patterns of switches in on-or-off states could be used to represent the 1s and 0s of the binary notation system. This allowed the translation of abstract symbol systems into concrete, mechanical representations. This idea was subsequently applied to the human processing system—or human reason—by the Americans McCulloch (1898–1969) and Pitts (1923–1969) in their 1943 paper titled "A Logical Calculus of the Ideas Immanent in Nervous Activity." In this landmark paper, they conceptualized the brain and nervous system as a network of interconnected neurons, each one capable of being either on or off in the manner of binary switches. As they wrote in the abstract of their paper, "Neural events and the relations among them can be treated by means of propositional logic" (p. 115). Since computers that made use of this idea had already been developed, they therefore implied that the mechanical processes of an electronic computer might serve as a nearly exact model of what goes on inside the human brain. They made explicit the significant, and contentious, conceptual link between machine and brain.

The development of the digital computer proceeded apace during the war. Harvard and International Business Machines (IBM) built the massive Harvard Mark I, which was 55 feet long and 8 feet high. The origin of the phrase "computer bug" can be traced to an actual moth crushed on a relay switch in the Harvard Mark I. The moth was found—and duly recorded in the logbook—by Grace Hopper (1906–1992), a mathematician and renowned computer scientist, who was one of the first programmers of the huge machine. She worked on computer programming languages and was part of the team that later developed the first commercial computer, the UNIVAC I.

At the University of Pennsylvania, engineers built the Electronic Numerical Integrator and Calculator, or ENIAC. Many wartime machines were designed to perform the calculations required to plan trajectories of missiles. There remained one problem, however. Although the new machines could perform complex calculations at amazing speeds, the inputting of programming instructions took comparatively much longer. This inefficiency limited the potential of the machines. This problem, in the case of the ENIAC, attracted the attention of a mathematician from Hungary, John von Neumann (1903–1957), who had been recruited to Princeton University's Institute for Advanced Study in 1933 and was engaged in several highly classified wartime defense projects, including the atom bomb. After a conversation with a member of the ENIAC team, von Neumann became intrigued by the problems of computer design and involved himself in the project. He was able to solve the problem of inefficient programming by coming up with the idea of stored programs (i.e., having the computer internally store many of its operating instructions in its own memory). Recognizing that many complex computations entail the use of some of the same subcomponents implemented in different combinations at different points in the computational process, he was able to stipulate how these subcomponents could be stored in the computer and invoked in different combinations to work on different sets of data. Thus, programs would stipulate various subroutines to be carried out, and complex hierarchies of subroutines could be arranged and executed as a result of simple commands. This arrangement came to be known as von Neumann architecture, and many of the most common programming languages today are based on it.

As a result of von Neumann architecture, attention to computer programming expanded. Advances were made on the hardware side as well, such as the development of transistors and then the silicone chip. In 1950, Turing published a paper titled "Computing Machinery and Intelligence." In this paper, he posed the

FIGURE 13.5 Alan Turing
Courtesy of the Turing Family and King's College Archive Centre, Cambridge.

provocative question, "Can machines think?" Indeed, as computers became ever more powerful and capable of performing increasingly complex functions, it started to become possible to envision a computer that might plausibly mimic the mental processes of a human. The question arose of whether computers were performing tasks that simply *resembled* the act of human thinking or if they were actually performing in a way that was *identical* to it. To play with this question, Turing developed a hypothetical imitation game that became known as the Turing Test. The Turing Test has served as the template for a real challenge to computer scientists and researchers in artificial intelligence.

The imitation game that Turing outlined was actually four games involving different combinations of humans and computers. In the all-human version, a human interrogator exchanges written messages with a man and a woman to figure out which is the man and which is the woman. The actual man is allowed to lie (i.e., pretend he is a woman). One of the human–machine versions has three "players": a human interrogator, a man (played by the computer), and a woman. The man (played by the computer) and the woman can only communicate with the interrogator through typewritten notes. The interrogator's job is to determine which of the two communicators is the woman. As in the all-human version, the computer is instructed to deceive the interrogator (pretend it is a woman). Turing then compared this version to the all-human version of the game, asking, "Will the interrogator decide wrongly as often when the game is played like this as when the game is played between a man and a woman?" (1950, p. 434).

In subsequent real-life versions of this test, computer programmers are challenged to write programs that can respond to questions by a human interrogator on various topics; if the human interrogator cannot tell whether a human or a machine is answering the questions, the program is said to have passed the Turing Test. The Loebner Prize was established in 1991 to be given to any programmer who could pass the test.

The challenge of writing computer programs that, like humans, could solve complex problems was taken up quickly following Turing's paper. Allen Newell (1927–1992) and Herbert Simon (1916–2001) began working together in the mid-1950s to write a program that could simulate proofs for some of the basic theorems in Alfred North Whitehead and Bertrand Russell's *Principia Mathematica*. They named their program the Logical Theorist and it generated a proof of one of the theorems in 1956. Taking this idea further, they sought to develop a master program that could combine the principles inherent in any number of problems, such as making a chess move or composing a piece of music, to more closely simulate human intelligence. They realized that the Logical Theorist, which employed algorithmic strategies, was insufficient for problems that involved large numbers of possibilities, such as which chess move to make or what words and sentences to use in a conversation. A heuristic method of problem solving, which would provide rules guiding the selection of possible moves or choices, was required.

They developed such a master program in 1957, calling it the General Problem Solver. In this program, Newell and Simon employed what they called a **means–end analysis**, in which the current state and end-goal of any particular problem are regularly compared. The option

FIGURE 13.6 Herbert Simon
Courtesy of Carnegie Mellon University archives.

that reduces the distance between the two is determined and chosen at every step until the distance between the current state and the goal is zero (i.e., the problem is solved). With the General Problem Solver, Newell and Simon felt that they had come close to developing a model of how human reasoning and problem solving occur. They did not argue, however, that the mechanics of their model mimicked the "mechanics," or neurophysiological processes, of the human brain itself. This position, that a physical similarity between machine and mind is *not* necessary for a useful theory of artificial intelligence, rose in the early 1960s and became known as **computational functionalism**.

INFORMATION THEORY AND CYBERNETICS

It is difficult to disentangle all of the threads that made up postwar cognitive science. Many of the same people engaged with computational problems also developed cybernetic ideas, and information theory was pervasive. In this section, we start by looking at the concept of information and how it was theorized and then turn to cybernetics, an idea that its proponents extended well beyond the question of how people (and machines) reason and solve problems to how families, communities, and organizations function. Psychologists made important contributions to all of these areas, but their contributions were heavily influenced by the rich exchange of ideas among researchers from various disciplinary backgrounds.

The word "information" is now so commonly and widely used that its meaning seems self-evident. For those who live in the information age in which information management is an ongoing challenge and traveling on the information superhighway is commonplace, it is easy to forget that "information" originally had a precise technical, even mathematical, definition and that this definition and the subsequent idea of information processing formed the core of cognitive psychology as it emerged in the 1950s and 1960s. As historian of psychology Allan Collins (2007) has demonstrated, even contemporary cognitive psychologists may have lost sight of its original meaning and use.

The person who first proposed a precise mathematical definition of information was Claude Shannon, whom we mentioned earlier in the context of binary notation, electronic circuitry, and universal computation. After completing his MA thesis, Shannon spent the war years working on several communication-related projects for the U.S. military, first at the National Defense Research Committee and then at the famous Bell Laboratories. One of his major projects was to figure out how to encipher digital speech systems. He was interested in how a message gets selected from a set of possible messages. Drawing on this work, in 1948 he published a paper in which he defined information as something that reduces uncertainty. That is, anything that allows you to make a choice among alternatives is "informative." Specifically, Shannon proposed a quantitative unit of information as a bit or binary unit. One bit of information was defined as the amount of information conveyed by a signal when only two alternatives are possible. For example, the answer to a yes–no question provides one bit of information. Importantly, Shannon was not interested in the meaning or content of the messages themselves, writing that the "semantic aspects of the communication are irrelevant to the information problem" (Shannon & Weaver, 1949, p. 3). The problem of conveying messages over a telephone line, for example, is essentially one of encoding, transmission, receiving, and decoding. Whatever the content of the message, it has to be encoded as a series of electrical impulses, transmitted, received, and decoded back into speech. The actual content is irrelevant to this process, from the point of view of the information theorist. Thus, Shannon gave information a universal definition, and furthermore, one that was not tied to any particular physical communication system. This technical definition of information formed the basis for information theory, which was taken up by cybernetic theorists, memory and cognition researchers, and even economists and philosophers.

George A. Miller (b. 1920) has been credited with bringing information theory into psychology. After earning an undergraduate and a master's degree from the University of Alabama, Miller went to Harvard in 1940 to pursue further graduate work, earning his PhD in psychology in 1946. From 1944 to 1948, he worked as a research fellow in the Psychoacoustics Laboratory of S. S. (Stanley Smith) Stevens. There, collaborations with the military on problems of speech perception and communication initially guided his work. One of Miller's first projects was a study on jamming radio communications for the U.S. Signal Corps. Since the projects were problem focused, researchers worked in interdisciplinary teams and Miller became used to interacting with mathematicians, physicists, engineers, and linguists. This interdisciplinary, problem-focused approach suited him well, and he became quite proficient in mathematics himself. In 1948, he read Shannon's aforementioned article on information theory and began to think about how it could be applied to problems in psychology.

In 1949, Miller published "Statistical Behavioristics and Sequences of Responses" with coauthor Frederick Frick in which they applied the idea of information as anything which reduces uncertainty to the behavior of organisms. In this article, Miller and Frick introduced two new ideas, the index of behavioral stereotypy and the course of action. The index of behavioral stereotypy was an index of the degree of randomness (unpredictability or uncertainty) in an organism's behavior. This index could be used as a yardstick against which to measure the effects of learning. Presumably, an organism's behavior should become less random (more organized) after conditioning. In essence, Miller and Frick were recommending the use of information theory as a way to analyze and describe sequences

of behavior. Miller used the course-of-action idea in his developing theory of language, which we return to later.

With Miller's paper, information theory was taken up by psychologists. Although Miller's thinking was still behavioristically focused, others quickly brought these ideas to bear on cognitive processes. Moreover, information theory quickly fed into the thinking of cyberneticists, many of whom were psychologists.

In 1948, mathematician Norbert Wiener (1894–1964) defined cybernetics in a seminal article titled "Cybernetics, or Control and Communication in the Animal and the Machine." Although cybernetics had been named and studied well before the article appeared, Wiener made clear the intention of cyberneticists to encompass both machine and man in their theorizing, thus establishing a broad canvas for the new field. Cybernetics was an interdisciplinary research area devoted to the study of self-regulating systems. A central concept was **feedback**, that is, the process whereby information about the results of a system's actions is fed back into the system so as to stop, modulate, or extend the original activity. The focus in cybernetics is on the flow of information in systems; thus, information theory played a central role in its development. The concepts of feedback and systems self-regulation were not new ones. French physiologist Claude Bernard (1813–1878) had discussed self-equilibrating mechanisms in the 1860s. Engineering had many early mechanical examples, such as James Watt's (1736–1819) "governor" device to control the speed of a locomotive. The oft-cited example of a thermostat is an everyday example of a simple, mechanical, self-regulating system. However, the ways in which these ideas were deployed in combination with information theory to encompass both human systems (biological and social) and machine systems was new. Another key concept was purpose or teleology. According to cybernetic theory, to self-regulate systems must have some purpose or goal (e.g., to maintain a constant temperature). Thus, cybernetic systems are not only

FIGURE 13.7 Photo of George Miller
Courtesy of the Archives of the History of American Psychology, University of Akron, Akron, OH.

self-regulating but also purposive, or teleological. With these basic concepts, cybernetic theory ranged far and wide.

One of the key events in the history of cybernetics was a series of conferences held in New York City from 1946 to 1953. The origin of the meetings went back to the early 1940s, when McCulloch met Wiener through their mutual friend, the Harvard neurophysiologist Arturo Rosenblueth. Wiener was working on a military project on the guidance and control of aircraft fire when he came to the conclusion that to solve the self-correcting tracking problem he would need to employ the notion of feedback, both in the plane and in the human gunner as an integrated system. The paper that resulted from this work combined ideas about physiological homeostasis, behavioral processes, and engineering mechanisms to describe a cybernetic organism, an organism that was both man and machine.

Referred to by some as a manifesto for cybernetics, Wiener's paper was presented in 1942 at a meeting in New York sponsored by the Josiah Macy Jr. Foundation. After the meeting, Rosenblueth and McCulloch approached the Macy Foundation's medical director, Frank Fremont-Smith to sponsor a continuing series of interdisciplinary meetings to explore the possibilities of this new cybernetic science. The result was the Macy Foundation conferences on cybernetics launched in 1946, with McCulloch as chair.

Ten meetings of what came be called, simply, the Macy Conferences were held between 1946 and 1953. There were between 20 and 30 participants per meeting: a core group that came to be known as the Cybernetics Group and various invited guests. Included were psychologists, sociologists, anthropologists, physiologists, neurophysiologists, psychiatrists, mathematicians, and engineers. von Neumann gave the opening talk at the first meeting, on the digital computer. Among the social scientists in the original, core, group were Gregory Bateson, Lawrence K. Frank, Molly Harrower, Heinrich Klüver, Paul Lazarsfeld, Kurt Lewin, and Margaret Mead.

The small, invitation-only meetings were the breeding ground for intense discussion and theory building, as well as practical projects. Members often came away from the meetings with new ideas that they tried in their laboratories or fieldwork sites and then returned to talk about results and new directions. To offer a somewhat lighthearted, although nonetheless technically sophisticated, example, Shannon (a guest at several of the meetings), brought a mechanical maze-running rat that he had designed and built to the eighth Macy Conference in 1951. The rat was equipped with an electrical contact "finger" that it used to detect the walls of a 25-square maze. Using feedback from these contacts, and programming that allowed it to avoid blind alleys, the rat could successfully navigate the maze.

Before leaving this section and turning to the problem of language, we should mention the 1960 publication of *Plans and the Structure of Behavior* by Miller, Eugene Galanter, and Karl Pribram. In some ways, this book can be viewed as a synthesis of ideas from computer science, information theory, and cybernetics. The authors state their intellectual debts to many of the figures we have already mentioned—Wiener, von Neumann, Shannon, McCulloch, Newell, Simon, Bartlett, Lashley—and many others, including linguist Noam Chomsky, whom we discuss shortly. Their central contribution was an information-processing model of organized behavior that, although it drew on computer analogies, did not use actual computer programs. If cognitive psychology can be thought of as "the imagination of the computer age applied to knowledge of the mind" (Smith, 1997, p. 837), then this work certainly epitomized the field.

In their book, Miller, Galanter, and Pribram proposed several concepts, including Image, Plan, and TOTE. The Image, much like Bartlett's schema, was a stored representation of all information an organism had accrued about itself and its world. The Plan, like a computer program, was any hierarchical process in the organism that dictated the order in which a sequence of actions or operations was to be performed. Plans were made up of nested feedback loops, or TOTE units. TOTE stood for test–operate–test–exit. With these concepts, Miller and his colleagues drew on the process outlined by Newell and Simon for the operation of the Logical Theorist. In their model, the Image was the source of a desired state or goal, and Plans would guide the execution of subplans designed to test the current state of the organism against the desired end state.

With this publication, Miller revealed his complete conversion to cognitive psychology from his original behaviorist roots. As a demonstration of his commitment to the study of cognition, and his belief in the value of interdisciplinarity to this study, he and his Harvard colleague Jerome Bruner (b. 1915) established the Harvard Center for Cognitive Studies in 1960. Among the luminaries who delivered colloquia at the center during its first year was the young, and already highly influential, linguist Noam Chomsky. His work would challenge behaviorism's remaining adherents by taking on the masterwork of one of its most famous figureheads.

LANGUAGE RETURNS

With the emergence of cognitive psychology came a renewed interest in language, often pursued at the interface of psychology and linguistics in a field appropriately called psycholinguistics. This was not an unprecedented development. In the late 1800s and early 1900s in Germany, the field of *Sprachpsychologie* represented a similar amalgam of ideas, although as one commentator has noted, "What remains today of that earlier psycholinguistics ... is a large body of dust-covered literature" (Blumenthal, 1992, p. 804). One of the early interests of Sprachpsychologie, partly under the influence of the new psychology in Germany, was the study of language through the mechanical analysis of the physical shape of utterances. Wilhelm Wundt (1832–1920) also

made important contributions to linguistics. His approach, however, was more holistic and generative. He viewed the sentence as the fundamental unit of language, with the sentence corresponding to an underlying mental impression it was intended to express.

The rapprochement between psychology and linguistics cooled somewhat in the 1930s through 1950s, partly under the influence of behaviorism and partly under the influence of developments in linguistics that emphasized the study of language systems independent from their relationship to mind and behavior. Despite some attempts to paint the behaviorist period as devoid of work on higher mental functions, behaviorists were not altogether uninterested in language. For example, J. R. (Jacob Robert) Kantor (1888–1984), who called his system interbehaviorism for its attention to the relationship between the organism and its environment, published *An Objective Psychology of Grammar* in 1936. This was a strictly behaviorist account that expunged mentalism and sought to understand language squarely in terms of its function mediating relationships between speakers and between speakers and their environments.

By the late 1940s, interest in language was returning to psychology. In 1947, B. F. Skinner expressed his interest in language in his William James lectures at Harvard and began circulating an "underground" document that eventually appeared as his book *Verbal Behavior* in 1957. In 1951, a small seminar, sponsored by the Social Science Research Council, was held at Cornell University in Ithaca, New York. Eight participants, four psychologists and four linguists, met to exchange ideas. This group formed the National Committee on Linguistics and Psychology, which subsequently organized a larger conference for the summer of 1953 at Indiana University. One product of this meeting was an edited monograph titled *Psycholinguistics*, containing work by both psychologists and linguists. Meetings continued through the early 1960s. The explosion of interest in psycholinguistics was phenomenal. As one historian has noted, "The development of psycholinguistics was so sudden and proliferated so rapidly after 1950 that the field seemed as if it were something totally new" (Hilgard, 1987, p. 248).

In 1951, George Miller published his book *Language and Communication*, one of the founding texts of psycholinguistics. To describe Miller's theory, we need to return to the course-of-action concept we introduced earlier. Although Miller at this time was still behavioristic in his tendencies (this was still almost a decade before *Plans and the Structure of Behavior*), he saw that to measure the randomness or unpredictability of an organism's behavior it was necessary to take into account the whole course of action, not just its smallest component parts. If each component of behavior to some extent depends upon what came before it, then what might appear random is actually ordered to some degree. For example, in the game of Twenty Questions, each subsequent question the player asks is determined by the answer to the question before. In information theory terms, the answers to the questions provide bits of information that allow one to reduce the degree of uncertainty in the realm of possible answers. Thus, Miller reasoned, to analyze any one question without taking into account its relationship to the whole course of action is spurious. The breaking down of language into associations among its smallest component parts had been a mainstay of the associationist, behaviorist position in which Miller had been trained.

Miller attempted to take his ideas, gleaned from information theory, and apply them to language. In his book, he devoted initial chapters to the nuts and bolts of the human communication system and the psychophysical aspects of sound transmission. These sections derived from his original interests in speech and communication and his experience in the psychoacoustics laboratory at Harvard. He then proceeded to elaborate a theory of linguistic behavior that attempted to redress some shortcomings of strict operant approaches to language acquisition and generation. Although operant explanations of how humans acquire individual words seemed fairly straightforward (one is reinforced by the verbal community for saying "ball" in the presence of the appropriate object or in the presence of the letters "b–a–l–l," for example), it was more challenging to explain sentences and larger human speech patterns, which were clearly ordered but not strictly deterministic. Miller reasoned, using the course-of-action idea, that each word in a sentence depends on the word preceding it and following it; thus, a statistical analysis of sentences, conceptualized as linguistic courses of action, might take into account this complexity. Basically, Miller saw information theory as a way to explain how strings of words are combined to form sentences.

As Miller was moving from his thoughts on language to his more general theory of organized behavior, he was influenced not only by Newell and Simon but also by a new orientation in linguistics articulated and championed by Noam Chomsky (b. 1928). Called the transformational generative model, as set forth in Chomsky's 1957 work *Syntactic Structures* and several preceding papers, it suggested (to simplify considerably) that language, or at least syntax (the grammatical structure of language), could be formally described as a generative system; that sentences must be represented at more than one level (later he used the terms "deep structure" and "surface structure"); and that language generation must involve grammatical transformations. Chomsky saw the creation of language as an act arising from the knowledge of a certain set of grammatical rules that are used to combined and recombine elements. Repeated application of these rules produces an endless array of sentences that cannot be accounted for in purely environmentalist terms. As Chomsky's thinking emerged, it became clear that he believed that the complexity of language and linguistic structure (syntax) could only be accounted for in terms of some innate body of linguistic knowledge that allows native speakers of a language to determine whether a given word sequence is grammatical or not. The sentence "Colorless green ideas sleep furiously," despite its apparent nonsensicality, is still intuitively recognizable, Chomsky argued, because it uses certain properties of sentences that speakers of the language inherently know. Although his work had generally been of interest only to mathematicians and linguists, with his 1957 book, the implications of his nativist position soon brought him to the attention of psychologists. Indeed, he could not possibly have made himself any better known than he did when he initiated a battle with behaviorism in the form of a vitriolic critique of Skinner's book *Verbal Behavior*, which appeared in the same year as Chomsky's *Syntactic Structures*.

Although the two books appeared simultaneously, each was mainly received within its own scholarly community. This changed when Chomsky's review of Skinner's *Verbal Behavior* was published in 1959, by which time his views on matters linguistic and his opposition to behaviorism had hardened considerably. As one historian of cognitive science has remarked, "In his pursuit of behaviorism, Chomsky was driven at least as much by political passion as by abstract argument" (Boden, 2006, p. 639). Chomsky held strong political convictions and viewed the role that social scientists had played in military and government agendas as reprehensible. He was, in particular, adamantly opposed to what he saw as behaviorism's vacuity in terms of a moral agenda

and was committed to rationalism (over empiricism) as the appropriate philosophical basis for the pursuit of freedom and justice. Politics aside, Chomsky's critique of behaviorism consisted of three main claims: (1) that behaviorist theories are inadequate to account for the multiple theoretical levels in which grammatical structure is represented; (2) that behaviorists, including Skinner, often used covertly mentalistic terms in their theories without identifying them as such and were therefore violating their own philosophical position; and (3) that only human infants, and no other species, can acquire language because only they have the innate knowledge of its fundamental structure (in the 1960s, Chomsky would come to call this a language-acquisition device). In terms of his direct critique of Skinner's book, Chomsky opined that Skinner's central concepts of stimulus, response, and reinforcement had come to be used so loosely as to be theoretically meaningless and that his specifically linguistic concepts, such as "tact" and "mand," although defined behaviorally, were actually mentalistic concepts. Although Skinner reportedly only ever read the first few pages of Chomsky's attack, others took it up enthusiastically (it was an entertaining read for its vituperativeness, if nothing else), and the behavioristic account of language, if not behaviorism itself, was declared dead.

SUMMARY

We have stressed throughout this chapter the influence of interdisciplinarity on the development of cognitive psychology. Through conferences and meetings that brought together diverse groups of scholars, often to focus on particular topics or problems, psychologists were plunged into the worlds of the mathematician, engineer, philosopher, linguist, and anthropologist. These relationships shaped their thinking about key ideas at the core of cognitive psychology,

such as reasoning, memory, and language. The meetings also provided a model of interdisciplinary engagement that continues to this day, often in institutes devoted to cognitive science or cognitive neuroscience. In part, this original interdisciplinary matrix had been established by the exigencies of war, as the U.S. military sought to bring expertise—of all stripes—to bear on complex problems of defense, communication, strategy, and weapons development. The social sciences, including psychology, did not shy away from these engagements. During the 1950s, Cold War fears continued to stoke the fires of both government and philanthropic agencies that funneled money toward scientists and projects whose work they believed would have some bearing on the success of the emerging military–industrial complex. Many members of the Cybernetics Group, for example, were often pulled from the meetings to attend to government consultancies on "classified topics." As we have noted in earlier chapters, World War II changed the relationship between social science and government in deep and far-reaching ways.

A final note is in order on the contemporary state of many developments we have discussed in this chapter. We stated in the opening paragraphs that, after several years of heavy behaviorist influence, consciousness was allowed back in as a respectable object of study in psychology. We quickly noted, however, that consciousness was rechristened "cognition" and was defined and modeled in ways that reflected the scientific, theoretical, and technical developments in information processing, computer science, and to some degree, cybernetic theory. We also briefly noted some important neuropsychological work on memory, by Milner, Sperry, and others, that examined the relationships among brain, behavior, and cognitive processes. To a large extent, cognitive psychologists have traditionally focused on abstract models of mind as information processor, whereas neuropsychologists have been interested in actual brain anatomy and structure, often in the context of interesting clinical phenomena. As enthusiasm for computer modeling of human intelligence waned in the 1970s and 1980s, even as devoted a cognitivist as Miller admitted that the "human brain–mind system" might be exponentially more complicated than any abstract computational system. The idea that a synthesis of neuroscience and cognitive science might prove incredibly fruitful began to take hold in the 1980s: The field of cognitive neuroscience was born.

Interestingly, the concerns of cognitive neuroscientists inhered around a central topic: the study of consciousness. A primary task of cognitive neuroscience is to connect conscious experiences with cerebral activity in an effort to advance toward a cellular explanation of consciousness. Advances in brain imaging technology have been central to the development of this field. In 1982, it became possible with the invention of positron emission tomography and functional magnetic resonance imaging to observe the brain *in action*. American science administrators declared 1990 the "decade of the brain." Studies purportedly showing the neurological origins of everything from hypnotic states to religious experience poured out of the laboratories. Philosophers came into the fold as well, weighing in on the mind–brain problem, the problem of the embodiment of mind, the nature of consciousness, the limits in our ability to account for it, and many other vexing questions. Although the intricacies of cognitive neuroscience are beyond the scope of this chapter, it seems appropriate to end of this account of the history of psychology quite near where we began: with scientists, psychologists, and philosophers debating the nature of consciousness and how best to account for it. Although their techniques and tools for investigating consciousness are undoubtedly more technically sophisticated than any their late 19th-century forebears could have imagined, the cognitive psychologists of the early 21st century are still faced with many of the same questions, albeit couched in 21st-century terms.

CONCLUDING THOUGHTS

We hope that you have encountered, in the previous pages and chapters, multiple examples of the ways in which Psychology and psychology are intimately embedded in, and constantly involved in shaping, social relations and subjective life. The study of psychology is undertaken by Psychological scientists whose activities are shaped by their own psychologies, forged from a society that Psychology has itself helped create. One of the implications of this reflexivity, as we pointed out at the beginning of our account, is to underscore the importance of historical understanding in psychology. Psychology and history are mutually interdependent and interpenetrative forms of knowledge. The *history* of our efforts to create and use psychological knowledge is itself a form of psychological knowledge, the absence of which renders any contemporary formulation incomplete. As social constructionist psychologists Kenneth Gergen and Carl Graumann have written, "Scientific theory cannot extricate itself from history; rather, psychological understanding is itself servant to historical and cultural processes. Without a reflexive understanding of historical context, the field moves aimlessly into the future" (1996, p. 1).

As Psychology and psychology move into the 21st century, forms of disciplinary practice and psychological knowledge continue to change and arise anew around the world. At the least, historical analysis can impart some meaningfulness to, and perspective on, these changes. At its best, history can open new vistas of psychological inquiry and expose a broader range of possibilities than contemporary discourse appears to allow.

BIBLIOGRAPHIC ESSAY

Foremost among our sources for this chapter was Margaret Boden's masterful, encyclopedic, two-volume work *Mind as Machine* (2006). In a field as incredibly complex and multifaceted as cognitive science, Boden has perhaps come as close as anyone could to providing a complete account, and with a surprising degree of accessibility given the scientific and technical density of the fields described. We drew on many aspects of her work repeatedly for both historical and technical information. We also used the 1985 edition of Howard Gardner's *The Mind's New Science*, which offers a somewhat more concise rendition and is also accessible. Steve Heims's entertaining account of the Macy Conferences on Cybernetics, *The Cybernetics Group* (1991), based on transcripts from the meetings, provides a fascinating glimpse into the social world of science, in addition to much valuable information about the content and significance of the meetings.

Several other chapter-length overviews of the history of cognitive psychology were helpful, both for providing corroborative accounts and for suggesting methods of presentation. These include Frank Kessel and William Bevan's "Notes Toward a History of Cognitive Psychology" (1985), Ernest Hilgard's "Cognitive Psychology and Cognitive Science" (1987), Ray Fancher's "Minds and Machines" (1996), and the concluding chapter of Roger Smith's volume *History of the Human Sciences*, titled "The Past and Present" (1997). Here, Smith covers more ground than cognitive science (including an interesting discussion of sociobiology among other topics), but his ability to synthesize large bodies of research and provide a sensitive and meaningful account is worth careful reading.

Our opening account of Lashley's work drew on the preceding sources, as well as Darryl Bruce's article "Lashley and the Problem of Serial Order" (1994), in which he argues that Lashley's paper was not as pivotal an attack on behaviorism as Gardner's retrospective retelling of the event conveys, and Nadine Weidman's article "Mental Testing and Machine Intelligence" (1994). Although Weidman's focus is different than ours, she presents much useful information on Lashley's training and theoretical evolution.

For information on Bartlett and the work of the APU at Cambridge, we drew heavily on Allan Collins's chapter on the history of memory, "The Psychology of Memory" (2001), and on his article on Bartlett's thinking and career, "The Embodiment of Reconciliation"

(2006). We also found his article on the history of the concept of information, "From H = $\log sn$ to Conceptual Framework" (2007), incredibly useful and recommend it.

For an interesting account of Miller's evolution from behaviorist to cognitivist, including the central role of interdisciplinarity in his scientific identity, we found Hunter Crowther-Heyck's article "George A. Miller, Language, and the Computer Metaphor of Mind" (1996) useful and engaging. Crowther-Heyck has also written an excellent and wide-ranging account of Simon's multifaceted career (2005). Although we do not highlight Simon here, he was a polymathic figure central to the evolution of systems sciences in post–World War II and Cold War America, and Crowther-Heyck's work engages importantly with these contextual factors.

Readers interested in learning more about the intellectual development of McCulloch, who was pivotal in the development of cybernetic science, can consult the excellent articles by Tara Abraham, "(Physio)logical Circuits" (2002), and Lily Kay, "From Logical Neurons to Poetic Embodiments of Mind" (2001).

In our section on psycholinguists, we drew on two chapters in Sigmund Koch and David Leary's *A Century of Psychology as Science*, written by Blumenthal (1992) and Carroll (1992).

Finally, although we have intentionally sidestepped the question of whether a "cognitive revolution" truly occurred in psychology, other scholars have taken up the question enthusiastically. We recommend John Greenwood (1999), Thomas Leahey (1992), and George Mandler (2002) for further reading in this area.

REFERENCES

Aberle, S. D., & Corner, G. W. (1953). *Twenty five years of sex research: History of the National Research Council Committee for Research in Problems of Sex, 1922–1947.* Philadelphia: W. B. Saunders.

Abraham, T. H. (2002). (Physio)logical circuits: The intellectual origins of the McCulloch-Pitts neural networks. *Journal of the History of the Behavioral Sciences, 38,* 3–25.

Adams, G. (1931). *Psychology: Science or superstition?* New York: Covici, Friede.

Agar, J. (2008). What happened in the sixties? *British Journal of the History of Science, 41,* 567–600.

Albanese, C. L. (2007). *A republic of mind and spirit: A cultural history of American metaphysical religion.* New Haven, CT: Yale University Press.

Allport, F. H. (1924). *Social psychology.* Boston: Houghton Mifflin.

Angell, J. R. (1920). Organization in scientific research. *The Review, 2,* 250–253.

Ardila, R. (1982). Psychology in Latin America today. *Annual Review of Psychology, 33,* 103–122.

Arens, K. (1989). *Structures of knowing: Psychologies of the nineteenth century.* Dordrecht, Germany: Kluwer.

Aries, P. (1962). *Centuries of childhood: A social history of family life.* New York: Knopf.

Arulmani, G. (2007). Counselling psychology in India: At the confluence of two traditions. *Applied Psychology: An International Review, 56,* 69–82.

Ash, M. G. (1980). Academic politics in the history of science: Experimental psychology in Germany, 1879–1941. *Central European History, 13,* 255–286.

Ash, M. (1990). Psychology in twentieth-century Germany: Science and profession. In G. Cocks & K. H. Jarausch (Eds.), *German professions, 1800–1950* (pp. 289–307). New York: Oxford University Press.

Ash, M. G. (1991). Gestalt psychology in Weimar culture. *History of the Human Sciences, 4,* 395–415.

Ash, M. G. (1995). *Gestalt psychology in German culture, 1890–1967: Holism and the quest for objectivity.* New York: Cambridge University Press.

Ash, M. G. (2003). Psychology. In T. M. Porter & D. Ross (Eds.), *The Cambridge history of science: Vol. 7. The modern social sciences* (pp. 251–274). Cambridge, England: Cambridge University Press.

Bakan, D. (1966a). Behaviorism and American urbanization. *Journal of the History of the Behavioral Sciences, 2,* 5–28.

Bakan, D. (1966b). The influence of phrenology on American psychology. *Journal of the History of the Behavioral Sciences, 2,* 200–220.

Baker, R. R., & Pickren, W. E. (2006). Veterans Administration psychology: Six decades of public service (1946–2006). *Psychological Services, 3,* 208–213.

Baker, R. R., & Pickren, W. E. (2007). *Psychology and the Department of Veterans Affairs: A historical analysis of training, research, practice, and advocacy.* Washington, DC: American Psychological Association.

Baritz, L. (1960). *Servants of power.* Middletown, CT: Wesleyan University Press.

Baritz, L. (1989). *The good life: The meaning of success for the American middle class.* New York: Knopf.

Bartlett, F. C. (1937). Cambridge, England, 1887–1937. *American Journal of Psychology, 50,* 97–110.

Belzen, J. A. (2001). The introduction of the psychology of religion to the Netherlands: Ambivalent reception, epistemological concerns, and persistent patterns. *Journal of the History of the Behavioral Sciences, 37,* 45–62.

Bem, S. L. (1974). The measurement of psychological androgyny. *Journal of Consulting and Clinical Psychology, 42,* 155–162.

Bem, S. L. (2001). *An unconventional family.* New Haven, CT: Yale University Press.

Benjamin, L. T., Jr. (1986). Why don't they understand us? A history of psychology's public image. *American Psychologist, 41,* 941–946.

Benjamin, L. T., Jr. (1988). A history of teaching machines. *American Psychologist, 43,* 703–712.

Benjamin, L. T., Jr. (1997). Organized industrial psychology before Division 14: The ACP and the AAAP. *Journal of Applied Psychology, 82*, 459–466.

Benjamin L. T., Jr., & Baker, D. B. (2004). *From séance to science: A history of the profession of psychology in America*. Belmont, CA: Wadsworth.

Benjamin, L. T., Jr., & Bryant, W. H. M. (1997). A history of popular magazines in America. In W. G. Bringmann, H. E. Lück, R. Miller, & C. E. Early (Eds.), *A pictorial history of psychology* (pp. 585–593). Chicago: Quintessence.

Benjamin, L. T., Jr., Henry, K. D., & McMahon, L. R. (2005). Inez Beverly Prosser and the education of African Americans. *Journal of the History of the Behavioral Sciences, 41*, 43–62.

Benjamin, L. T., Jr., & Nielsen-Gammon, E. (1999). B. F. Skinner and psychotechnology: The case of the heir conditioner. *Review of General Psychology, 3*, 155–167.

Bergner, G. (2009). Black children, White preference: *Brown v. Board*, the doll tests, and the politics of self-esteem. *American Quarterly, 61*, 299–332.

Bernstein, M., & Russo, N. F. (1974). The history of psychology revisited, or up with our foremothers. *American Psychologist, 29*, 130–134.

Bird, W. L. (1999). *"Better living": Advertising, media, and the new vocabulary of business leadership, 1935–1955*. Evanston, IL: Northwestern University Press.

Bjork, D. W. (1993). *B. F. Skinner: A life*. New York: Basic Books.

Bjork, D. W. (1996). B. F. Skinner and the American tradition: The scientist as social inventor. In L. D. Smith & W. R. Woodward (Eds.), *B. F. Skinner and behaviorism in American culture* (pp. 128–150). Cranbury, NJ: Associated University Presses.

Blowers, G. H., Cheung, B. T., & Ru, H. (2009). Emulation vs. indigenization in the reception of Western psychology in Republican China: An analysis of the content of Chinese psychology journals (1922–1937). *Journal of the History of the Behavioral Sciences, 45*, 21–33.

Blowers, G. H., & Turtle, A. M. (Eds.). (1987). *Psychology moving East: The status of Western psychology in Asia and Oceania*. Boulder, CO: Westview Press.

Blumenthal, A. L. (1992). Psychology and linguistics: The first half-century. In S. Koch & D. E. Leary (Eds.), *A century of psychology as science* (pp. 804–824). Washington, DC: American Psychological Association.

Boakes, R. (1984). *From Darwin to behaviourism: Psychology and the minds of animals*. New York: Cambridge University Press.

Boden, M. A. (2006). *Mind as machine: A history of cognitive science* (Vols. 1 & 2). London: Oxford University Press.

Bond, M. H. (1997). *Working at the interface of cultures: Eighteen lives in social science*. New York: Routledge.

Bordia, P. & DiFonzio, N. (2002). When social psychology became less social: Prasad and the history of rumor research. *Asian Journal of Social Psychology, 5*, 49–61.

Bowler, P. J. (1990). *Charles Darwin: The man and his influence*. New York: Cambridge University Press.

Boyer, P. (1994). *By the bomb's early light: American thought and culture at the dawn of the Atomic Age*. Chapel Hill: University of North Carolina Press.

Brand, J., & Sapir, P. (1964). An historical perspective on the National Institute of Mental Health. In D. E. Woolridge (Ed.), *Biomedical science and its administration*. Unpublished report.

Brandist, C. (2006). Rise of Soviet sociolinguistics from the ashes of *Völkerpsychologie*. *Journal of the History of the Behavioral Sciences, 42*, 261–277.

Bray, C. H. (1962). Toward a technology of human behavior for defense use. *American Psychologist, 17*, 527–541.

Breuer, J., & Freud, S. (1957). *Studies on hysteria*. (Translated by James Strachey). New York: Basic Books.

Brigham, C. C. (1923). *A study of American intelligence*. Princeton, NJ: Princeton University Press.

Broverman, I. K., Broverman, D. M., Clarkson, F. E., Rosenkrantz, P. S., & Vogel, S. R. (1970). Sex role stereotypes and clinical judgments of mental health. *Journal of Consulting and Clinical Psychology, 34*, 1–7.

Brown, J. (1992). *The definition of a profession: The authority of metaphor in the history of intelligence testing, 1890–1930*. Princeton, NJ: Princeton University Press.

Brown, R. H. (1992). Poetics, politics and professionalism in the rise of American psychology. *History of the Human Sciences, 5*, 47–61.

Bruce, D. W. (1994). Lashley and the problem of serial order. *American Psychologist, 49*, 93–103.

Bryan, A. I. (1983). Alice I. Bryan. In A. N. O'Connell & N. F. Russo (Eds.), *Models of achievement: Vol 1. Reflections of eminent women in psychology* (pp. 69–86). New York: Columbia University Press.

Bryan, A. I. (1986). A participant's view of the National Council of Women Psychologists: Comment on Capshew and Laszlo. *Journal of Social Issues, 42*, 181–184.

Bryson, D. R. (2002). *Socializing the young: The role of foundations, 1923–1941*. Westport, CT: Bergin & Garvey.

Buchanan, R. D. (1994). The development of the Minnesota Multiphasic Personality Inventory. *Journal of the History of the Behavioral Sciences, 30*, 148–161.

Buchanan, R. (2003). Legislative warriors: American psychiatrists, psychologists, and competing claims over psychotherapy in the 1950s. *Journal of the History of the Behavioral Sciences, 39*, 225–249.

Buckley, K. W. (1989). *Mechanical man: John Broadus Watson and the beginnings of behaviorism*. New York: Guilford.

Bulmer, M., & Bulmer, J. (1981). Philanthropy and social science in the 1920s: Beardsley Ruml and the Laura Spelman Rockefeller Memorial, 1922–1929. *Minerva, 29*, 347–407.

Burnham, J. C. (1987). *How superstition won and science lost: Popularizing science and health in the United States*. New Brunswick, NJ: Rutgers University Press.

Burnham, J. C. (1988). *Paths into American culture: Psychology, medicine, and morals*. Philadelphia: Temple University Press.

Burr, H. W. (1922, June 24). Christine Ladd-Franklin: A superwoman in the fields of logic and color-perception. *New York Times*, p. 8.

Burton, M., & Kagan, C. (2005). Liberation psychology: Learning from Latin America. *Journal of Community and Applied Social Psychology, 15*, 63–78.

Calkins, M. W. (1930). Mary Whiton Calkins. In C. Murchison (Ed.), *A history of psychology in autobiography* (Vol. 1, pp. 31–62). Worcester, MA: Clark University Press.

Campos, R. H. (2001). Helena Antipoff (1892–1974): A synthesis of Swiss and Soviet psychology in the context of Brazilian education. *History of Psychology, 4*, 133–158.

Canady, H. G. (1936). The effect of rapport on the "IQ." *Journal of Negro Education, 5*, 209–219.

Canady, H. G. (1943). The problem of equating the environment of Negro–White groups for intelligence testing in comparative studies. *Journal of Social Psychology, 17*, 3–15.

Caplan, E. (1998). *Mind games: American culture and the birth of psychotherapy*. Berkeley: University of California Press.

Capshew, J. H. (1996). Engineering behavior: Project pigeon, World War II, and the conditioning of B. F. Skinner. In L. D. Smith & W. R. Woodward (Eds.), *B. F. Skinner and behaviorism in American culture* (pp. 128–150). Cranbury, NJ: Associated University Presses.

Capshew, J. H. (1999). *Psychologists on the march: Science, practice, and professional identity in America, 1929–1969*. New York: Cambridge University Press.

Capshew, J. H., & Laszlo, A. C. (1986). "We would not take no for an answer": Women psychologists and gender politics during World War II. *Journal of Social Issues, 42*, 157–180.

Carpintero, H. (2001). The development of contemporary Spanish psychology. *International Journal of Psychology, 36*, 378–383.

Carroll, J. B. (1992). Psychology and linguistics: Detachment and affiliation in the second half-century. In S. Koch & D. E. Leary (Eds.), *A century of psychology as science* (pp. 825–854). Washington, DC: American Psychological Association.

Carroy, J., & Plas, R. (1996). The origins of French experimental psychology: Experiment and experimentalism. *History of the Human Sciences, 9*, 73–84.

Carroy, J., & Plas, R. (2006). The beginnings of psychology in France: Who was a "scientific" psychologist in the nineteenth century. *Physis, 43*, 157–186.

Carson, J. (2007). *The measure of merit: Talents, intelligence, and inequality in the French and American republics, 1750–1940*. Princeton, NJ: Princeton University Press.

Castel, F., Castel, R., & Lovell, A. (1982). *The psychiatric society* (A. Goldhammer, Trans.). New York: Columbia University Press.

Cattell, J. M. (1890). Mental tests and measurements. *Mind, 15*, 373–381.

Chapman, P. D. (1988). *Schools as sorters: Lewis M. Terman, applied psychology, and the intelligence testing movement, 1890–1930*. New York: New York University Press.

Cherry, F., & Borshuk, C. (1998). Social action research and the Commission on Community Interrelations. *Journal of Social Issues, 54*, 119–142.

Chesler, P. (1972). *Women and madness*. New York: Doubleday.

Chimisso, C. (2000). The mind and the faculties: The controversy over "primitive mentality" and the struggle for disciplinary space at the inter-war Sorbonne. *History of the Human Sciences*, *13*, 47–68.

Cimino, G. (2006). The emergence of "scientific" psychology in Italy between positivist philosophy and psychiatric tradition. *Physis: Rivista Internazionale di Storia Della Scienza*, *43*, 187–219.

Clark, K. B., Chein, I., & Cook, S. W. (2004). The effects of segregation and the consequences of desegregation: A (September 1952) social science statement in the *Brown v. Board of Education of Topeka* Supreme Court case. *American Psychologist*, *59*, 495–501. (Original published in 2004)

Clark, K. B., & Clark, M. P. (1939a). The development of consciousness of self and the emergence of racial identification in Negro pre-school children. *Journal of Social Psychology*, *10*, 591–599.

Clark, K. B., & Clark, M. P. (1939b). Segregation as a factor in the racial identification of Negro preschool children. *Journal of Experimental Education*, *8*, 1961–1965.

Clark, K. B., & Clark, M. P. (1940). Skin color as a factor in racial identification of Negro preschool children. *Journal of Social Psychology*, *11*, 159–169.

Clark, K. B., & Clark, M. P. (1950). Emotional factors in racial identification and preference in Negro children. *Journal of Negro Education*, *19*, 341–350.

Cobbs, P. M. (2005a). *My American life: From rage to entitlement.* New York: Simon & Schuster.

Cobbs, P. M. (2005b). Oral history interview with Wade E. Pickren, San Francisco, CA, March. Washington, DC: American Psychological Association Archives.

Collins, A. (1999). The enduring appeal of physiognomy: Physical appearance as a sign of temperament, character, and intelligence. *History of Psychology*, *2*, 251–276.

Collins, A. (2001). The psychology of memory. In G. C. Bunn, A. D. Lovie, & G. D. Richards (Eds.), *Psychology in Britain: Historical essays and personal reflections* (pp. 150–168). Leicester, England: British Psychological Society.

Collins, A. (2006). The embodiment of reconciliation: Order and change in the work of Frederic Bartlett. *History of Psychology*, *9*, 290–312.

Collins, A. (2007). From H = *log sn* to conceptual framework: A short history of information. *History of Psychology*, *10*, 44–72.

Collins, P. H. (1990). *Black feminist thought: Knowledge, consciousness, and the politics of empowerment.* New York: Routledge.

Colombo, D. (2003). Psychoanalysis and the Catholic Church in Italy: The role of Father Agostino Gemelli, 1925–1953. *Journal of the History of the Behavioral Sciences*, *39*, 333–348.

Conger, J. (1979). Proceedings of the American Psychological Association, Incorporated, for the year 1978: Minutes of the annual meeting of the Council of Representatives. *American Psychologist*, *34*, 468–501.

Cook, S. W. (1990). Marie Jahoda (1907–). In A. N. O'Connell & N. Russo (Eds.), *Women in psychology: A bio-bibliographic sourcebook* (pp. 207–219). New York: Greenwood Press.

Coon, D. J. (1992). Testing the limits of sense and science: American experimental psychologists combat spiritualism, 1880–1920. *American Psychologist*, *47*, 143–151.

Coon, D. J. (1993). Standardizing the subject: Experimental psychologists, introspection, and the quest for a technoscientific ideal. *Technology and Culture*, *34*, 757–783.

Cooter, R. (1984). *The cultural meaning of popular science: Phrenology and the organization of consent in 19th century Britain.* Cambridge, England: Cambridge University Press.

Costall, A. S. (1992). Why British psychology is not social: Frederic Bartlett's promotion of the new academic discipline. *Canadian Psychology*, *33*, 633–639.

Crabtree, A. (1993). *From Mesmer to Freud: Magnetic sleep and the roots of psychological healing.* New Haven, CT: Yale University Press.

Craik, K. J. W. (1943). *The nature of explanation.* Cambridge, England: Cambridge University Press.

Cross, S. J., & Albury, W. R. (1987). Walter B. Cannon, L. J. Henderson, and the organic analogy. *Osiris*, *3*(2nd series), 165–192.

Crowther-Heyck, H. (1996). George A. Miller, language, and the computer metaphor of mind. *History of Psychology*, *2*, 37–64.

Crowther-Heyck, H. (2005). *Herbert A. Simon: The bounds of reason in modern America.* Baltimore: Johns Hopkins University Press.

Danziger, K. (1979). The positivist repudiation of Wundt. *Journal of the History of the Behavioral Sciences*, *15*, 205–230.

Danziger, K. (1980). The history of introspection reconsidered. *Journal of the History of the Behavioral Sciences*, *16*, 241–262.

Danziger, K. (1983). Origins of the schema of stimulated motion: Towards a pre-history of modern psychology. *History of Science, 21*, 183–210.

Danziger, K. (1985). The origins of the psychological experiment as a social institution. *American Psychologist, 40*, 133–140.

Danziger, K. (1990a). *Constructing the subject: Historical origins of psychological research*. New York: Cambridge University Press.

Danziger, K. (1990b). Divergence of investigative practices: The repudiation of Wundt. In K. Danziger, *Constructing the subject: Historical origins of psychological research*. New York: Cambridge University Press.

Danziger, K. (2000). Making social psychology experimental: A conceptual history, 1920–1970. *Journal of the History of the Behavioral Sciences, 36*, 329–347.

Danziger, K. (2006). Universalism and indigenization in the history of modern psychology. In A. Brock (Ed.), *Internationalizing the history of psychology* (pp. 208–225). New York: New York University Press.

Darley, J. G. (1957). Psychology and the Office of Naval Research: A decade of development. *American Psychologist, 12*, 305–323.

Darnton, R. (1968). *Mesmerism and the end of the Enlightenment in France*. Cambridge, MA: Harvard University Press.

Darwin, C. (1859). *On the origin of species by natural selection*. London: John Murray.

Degler, C. N. (1991). *In search of human nature: The decline and revival of Darwinism in American social thought*. New York: Oxford University Press.

Degni, S., Foschi, R., & Lombardo, G. P. (2007). Contexts and experimentalism in the psychology of Gabriele Buccola (1875–1885). *Journal of the History of the Behavioral Sciences, 43*, 177–195.

Dehue, T. (1995). *Changing the rules: Psychology in the Netherlands, 1900–1985*. New York: Cambridge University Press.

Dennis, P. (2002). Psychology's public image in "Topics of the Times": Commentary from the editorial page of the *New York Times* Between 1904 and 1947. *Journal of the History of the Behavioral Sciences, 38*, 371–392.

de Sanctis, S. (1936). Sante de Sanctis. In C. Murchison (Ed.), *A history of psychology in autobiography* (Vol. 2, pp. 83–120). Worcester, MA: Clark University Press.

Deutsch, M., & Collins, M. E. (1951). *Interracial housing: A psychological evaluation of a social experiment*. Minneapolis: University of Minnesota Press.

Dewsbury, D. A. (1984). *Comparative psychology in the twentieth century*. Stroudsburg, PA: Hutchinson Ross.

Dewsbury, D. A. (2005a). Comparative psychology: A case study of development of support for basic research by a federal agency with an applied mission, 1948–1963. In W. E. Pickren & S. F. Schneider (Eds.), *Psychology and the National Institute of Mental Health: A historical analysis of science, practice, and policy* (pp. 31–60). Washington, DC: American Psychological Association Books.

Dewsbury, D. A. (2005b). *Monkey farm: A history of the Yerkes Laboratories of Primate Biology, Orange Park, Florida, 1930–1965*. Lewisburg, PA: Bucknell University Press.

Dierks, K. (2000). The familiar letter and social refinement in America, 1750–1800. In D. Bartin & N. Hall (Eds.), *Letter writing as a social practice* (pp. 31–41). Amsterdam: John Benjamins.

Dobson, V., & Bruce, D. (1972). The German university and the development of experimental psychology. *Journal of the History of the Behavioral Sciences, 8*, 204–207.

Dollard, J., Miller, N. E., Doob, L. W., Mowrer, O. H., & Sears, R. R. (1939). *Frustration and aggression*. New Haven, CT: Yale University Press.

Dresser, H. W. (1919). *A history of the New Thought movement*. New York: Thomas Y. Crowell.

DuMont, K., & Louw, J. (2001). The International Union of Psychological Science and the politics of membership: Psychological associations in South Africa and the German Democratic Republic. *History of Psychology, 4*, 388–404.

Eagly, A. H., & Wood, W. (1999). The origins of sex differences in human behavior: Evolved dispositions versus social roles. *American Psychologist, 54*, 408–423.

Enriquez, V. G. (1987). Decolonizing the Filipino psyche: Impetus for the development of psychology in the Philippines. In G. H. Blowers & A. Turtle (Eds.), *Psychology moving East: The status of Western psychology in Asia and Oceania* (pp. 265–287). Boulder, CO: Westview Press.

Enriquez, V. G. (1993). Developing a Filipino psychology. In U. Kim & J. W. Berry (Eds.), *Indigenous psychologies: Research and experience in cultural context* (pp. 152–169). Thousand Oaks, CA: Sage.

Escobar, A. (1995). *Encountering development: The making and unmaking of the Third World*. Princeton, NJ: Princeton University Press.

Espin, O. M. (1995). On knowing you are the unknown: Women of color constructing psychology. In J. Adelman & G. Enguidanos (Eds.), *Racism in the lives of women* (pp. 127–136). New York: Haworth.

Evans, R. B. (1984). The origins of American academic psychology. In J. Brozek (Ed.), *Explorations in the history of psychology in the United States* (pp. 17–60). Lewisburg, PA: Bucknell University Press.

Fairweather, G. W. (1964). *Social psychology in treating mental illness: An experimental approach.* New York: John Wiley & Sons.

Fancher, R. E. (1985). *The intelligence men: Makers of the IQ controversy.* New York: Norton.

Fancher, R. E. (1990). Freud and psychoanalysis. In R. C. Olby, G. N. Cantor, J. R. R. Christie, & M. J. S. Hodge (Eds.), *Companion to the history of modern science* (pp. 425–441). London: Routledge.

Fancher, R. E. (1996). Minds and machines: Artificial intelligence from the Pascaline to the General Problem Solver. In R. Fancher (Ed.), *Pioneers of psychology* (3rd ed., pp. 437–463). New York: Norton.

Fanon, F. (1963). *The wretched of the earth.* New York: Grove Press.

Farr, R. M. (1996). *The roots of modern social psychology.* Cambridge, MA: Blackwell Publishers.

Farreras, I. G. (2005). The historical context for National Institute of Mental Health support of American Psychological Association training and accreditation efforts. In W. E. Pickren & S. F. Schneider (Eds.), *Psychology and the National Institute of Mental Health: A historical analysis of science, practice, and policy* (pp. 153–179). Washington, DC: American Psychological Association.

Fass, P. S. (1980). The IQ: A cultural and historical framework. *American Journal of Education, 88,* 431–458.

Finch, F. H., & Odoroff, M. E. (1939). Employment trends in applied psychology. *Journal of Consulting Psychology, 3,* 118–122.

Finch, F. H., & Odoroff, M. E. (1941). Employment trends in applied psychology, II. *Journal of Consulting Psychology, 5,* 275–278.

Finger, S. (1994). *Origins of neuroscience.* New York: Oxford University Press.

Finison, L. J. (1976). Unemployment, politics, and the history of organized psychology. *American Psychologist, 31,* 747–755.

Finison, L. J. (1978). Unemployment, politics, and the history of organized psychology: 2. The Psychologists' League, the WPA, and the National Health Program. *American Psychologist, 33,* 471–477.

Finison, L. J. (1979). An aspect of the early history of the Society for the Psychological Study of Social Issues: Psychologists and labor. *Journal of the History of the Behavioral Sciences, 15,* 29–37.

Fisher, D. (1993). *Fundamental development of the social sciences: Rockefeller philanthropy and the Social Science Research Council.* Ann Arbor: University of Michigan Press.

Flavell, J. H. (1963). *The developmental psychology of Jean Piaget.* New York: Van Nostrand.

Fox, D., & Prilleltensky, I. (1997). *Critical psychology: An introduction.* London: Sage.

Freedheim, D. K. (Ed.). (1992). *History of psychotherapy: A century of change.* Washington, DC: American Psychological Association.

Freire, P. (1968/1970). *Pedagogy of the oppressed.* New York: Seabury Press.

Friedan, B. (1997). *The feminine mystique.* New York: Dell. (Original work published 1963)

Friedman, L. (1999). *Identity's architect: A biography of Erik H. Erikson.* New York: Free Association Books.

Fuchs, A. (2000). Contributions of American mental philosophers to psychology in the United States. *History of Psychology, 3,* 3–19.

Fuchs, A. H., & Milar, K. S. (2003). Psychology as a science. In D. K. Freedheim (Ed.), *Handbook of psychology: Vol. 1. History of psychology* (pp. 1–26). New York: Wiley.

Fuller, R. C. (1982). *Mesmerism and the American cure of souls.* Philadelphia: University of Pennsylvania Press.

Furumoto, L. (1979). Mary Whiton Calkins (1863–1930): Fourteenth president of the American Psychological Association. *Journal of the History of the Behavioral Sciences, 15,* 346–356.

Furumoto, L. (1987). On the margins: Women and the professionalization of psychology in the United States, 1890–1940. In M. G. Ash & W. R. Woodward (Eds.), *Psychology in twentieth-century thought and society* (pp. 93–113). Cambridge, England: Cambridge University Press.

Furumoto, L. (1989). The new history of psychology. In I. S. Cohen (Ed.), *The G. Stanley Hall lecture series* (Vol. 9, pp. 9–34). Washington, DC: American Psychological Association.

Furumoto, L. (1992). Joining separate spheres: Christine Ladd-Franklin, woman scientist (1847–1930). *American Psychologist, 47,* 175–182.

Furumoto, L. (1994). Christine Ladd-Franklin's color theory: Strategy for claiming scientific authority? In H. E. Adler & R. W. Rieber (Eds.), *Annals of the New York Academy of Sciences: Vol. 727. Aspects of the history of psychology in America, 1892–1992* (pp. 91–112). Washington, DC: American Psychological Association.

Galton, F. (1869). *Hereditary genius: An inquiry into its laws and consequences*. London: Macmillan.

Gardner, H. (1985). *The mind's new science: A history of the cognitive revolution*. New York: Basic Books.

Gauld, A. (1992). *A history of hypnotism*. New York: Cambridge University Press.

Gay, P. (1988). *Freud: A life for our time*. New York: Norton.

Gergen, K. J. (1973). Social psychology as history. *Journal of Personality and Social Psychology, 26,* 309–320.

Gergen, K. J. (1985). The social constructionist movement in modern psychology. *American Psychologist, 20,* 266–275.

Gergen, K. J. (2001). Psychological science in a postmodern context. *American Psychologist, 56,* 803–813.

Gergen, K. J. & Graumann, C. F. (1996). Psychological discourse in historical context: An introduction. In C. F. Graumann & K. J. Gergen (Eds.), *Historical Dimensions of Psychological Discourse* (pp. 1–13). New York: Cambridge University Press.

Gergen, K. J., Gulerce, A., Lock, A., & Misra, G. (1996). Psychological science in cultural context. *American Psychologist, 51,* 496–503.

Geuter, U. (1992). *The professionalization of psychology in Nazi Germany*. New York: Cambridge University Press.

Geuter, U., & León, R. (1997). The emigration of European psychologists to Latin America. *Cuadernos Argentinos de Historia de la Psicologia, 3,* 67–97.

Gibby, R. E., & Zickar, M. J. (2008). A history of the early days of personality testing in American industry: An obsession with adjustment. *History of Psychology, 11,* 164–184.

Gillespie, R. (1991). *Manufacturing knowledge: A history of the Hawthorne experiments*. New York: Cambridge University Press.

Gilligan, C. (1993). *In a different voice*. Cambridge, MA: Harvard University Press. (Original work published 1982)

Goddard, H. H. (1912). *The Kallikak family: A study in the heredity of feeble-mindedness*. New York: Macmillan.

Goldstein, J. (2003). Bringing the psyche into scientific focus. In T. M. Porter & D. Ross (Eds.), *The Cambridge history of science: Vol. 7. The modern social sciences* (pp. 131–153). Cambridge, England: Cambridge University Press.

Greenwood, J. D. (1999). Understanding the "cognitive revolution" in psychology. *Journal of the History of the Behavioral Sciences, 35,* 1–22.

Grob, G. N. (1983). *Mental illness and American society, 1875–1940*. Princeton, NJ: Princeton University Press.

Grob, G. N. (1991). *From asylum to community: Mental health policy in modern America*. Princeton, NJ: Princeton University Press.

Gundlach, H. U. K. (1997). The mobile psychologist: Psychology and the railroads. In W. G. Bringmann, H. E. Lück, R. Miller, & C. E. Early (Eds.), *A pictorial history of psychology* (pp. 456–459). Carol Stream, IL: Quintessence.

Gundlach, H. (2006). Psychology as science and as discipline: The case of Germany. *Physis, 43,* 61–90.

Guthrie, R. V. (1998). *Even the rat was white: A historical view of psychology* (2nd ed.). Needham Heights, MA: Allyn & Bacon. (First edition published 1976)

Haavind, H., & Magnusson, E. (2005). Feminism, psychology, and identity transformations in the Nordic countries. *Feminism and Psychology, 15,* 236–247.

Hale, M. (1980). *Human science and social order: Hugo Münsterberg and the origins of applied psychology*. Philadelphia: Temple University Press.

Hale, N. G. (1971). *Freud and the Americans*. New York: Oxford University Press.

Hale, N. G. (1995). *The rise and crisis of psychoanalysis in the United States: Freud and the Americans, 1917–1985*. New York: Oxford University Press.

Haraway, D. (1976). *Crystals, fabrics, and fields: Metaphors of organicism in 20th century developmental biology*. New Haven, CT: Yale University Press.

Haraway, D. (1989). *Primate visions: Gender, race, and nature in the world of modern science*. London: Routledge.

Harding, S. (1986). *The science question in feminism*. Ithaca, NY: Cornell University Press.

Harding, S. (1991). *Whose science? Whose knowledge? Thinking from women's lives*. Ithaca, NY: Cornell University Press.

Harrington, A. (1987). *Medicine, mind, and the double brain*. Princeton, NJ: Princeton University Press.

Harrington, A. (1996). *Reenchanted science: Holism in German culture from Wilhelm II to Hitler*. Princeton, NJ: Princeton University Press.

Hartnack, C. (1990). Vishnu on Freud's desk: Psychoanalysis in Colonial India. *Social Research*, *57*, 921–949.

Haskell, T. L. (1985). Capitalism and the origins of the humanitarian sensibility. 2. The *American Historical Review*, *90*, 547–566.

Hatch, N. O. (1989). *The democratization of American Christianity*. New Haven, CT: Yale University Press.

Hearnshaw, L. S. (1964). *A short history of British psychology, 1840–1940*. London: Methuen.

Hebb, D. O. (1949). *The organization of behavior: A neuropsychological theory*. New York: John Wiley & Sons.

Heims, S. J. (1991). *The cybernetics group*. Cambridge, MA: MIT Press.

Helson, H. (1929, July 20). [Review of *Colour and Colour Theories*]. *The Saturday Review of Literature*.

Herman, E. (1995). The curious courtship of psychology and women's liberation. In E. Herman, *The romance of American psychology*. Berkeley: University of California Press. (pp. 276–303).

Herzberg, D. (2009). *Happy pills: From Miltown to Prozac*. Baltimore: Johns Hopkins University Press.

Highhouse, S. (1999). The brief history of personnel counseling in industrial–organizational psychology. *Journal of Vocational Behavior*, *55*, 318–336.

Hilgard, E. R. (1987). Cognitive psychology and cognitive science: Thinking, language, and artificial intelligence. In E. R. Hilgard (Ed.), *Psychology in America: A historical survey* (pp. 221–267). San Diego, CA: Harcourt Brace Jovanovich.

Hilgard, E. R., & Capshew, J. H. (1992). The power of service: World War II and professional reform in the American Psychological Association. In R. B. Evans, V. S. Sexton, & T. C. Cadwallader (Eds.), *The American Psychological Association: A historical perspective* (pp. 149–175). Washington, DC: American Psychological Association.

Hollingshead, A. B., & Redlich, F. C. (1958). *Social class and mental illness*. New York: John Wiley & Sons.

Hollingworth, H. S. (1943). *Leta Stetter Hollingworth: A biography*. Lincoln: University of Nebraska Press.

Hollingworth, L. S. (1914a). *Functional periodicity: An experimental study of the mental and motor abilities of women during menstruation* (Contributions to Education No. 69). New York: Teachers College, Columbia University.

Hollingworth, L. S. (1914b). Variability as related to sex differences in achievement: A critique. *American Journal of Sociology*, *19*, 510–530.

hooks, b. (1984). *Feminist theory from margin to center*. Boston: South End Press.

Hoopes, J. (1989). *Consciousness in New England: From Puritanism and ideas to psychoanalysis and semiotics*. Baltimore: Johns Hopkins University Press.

Hornstein, G. A. (1988). Quantifying psychological phenomena: Debates, dilemmas, and implications. In J. G. Morawski (Ed.), *The rise of experimentation in American psychology* (pp. 1–34). New Haven, CT: Yale University Press.

Hornstein, G. A. (1992). The return of the repressed: Psychology's problematic relations with psychoanalysis, 1909–1960. *American Psychologist*, *47*, 254–263.

Howard, R. W. (1983). Ruth W. Howard. In A. N. O'Connell & N. F. Russo (Eds.), *Models of achievement: Vol. 1. Reflections of eminent women in psychology* (pp. 55–67). New York: Columbia University Press.

Hsueh, Y. (2002). The Hawthorne experiments and the introduction of Jean Piaget in American industrial psychology, 1929–1932. *History of Psychology*, *5*, 163–189.

Hutz, C. S., McCarthy, S., & Gomes, W. (2004). Psychology in Brazil: The road behind and the road ahead. In M. J. Stevens & D. Wedding (Eds.), *Handbook of international psychology* (pp. 151–168). New York: Brunner-Routledge.

Hyde, J. S. (2005). The gender similarities hypothesis. *American Psychologist*, *60*, 581–592.

Igo, S. E. (2007). *The averaged American: Surveys, citizens, and the making of a mass public*. Cambridge, MA: Harvard University Press.

Jackson, J. P., Jr. (2001). *Social scientists for social justice: Making the case against segregation*. New York: New York University Press.

Jackson, K. T. (1985). *Crabgrass frontier: The suburbanization of the United States*. New York: Oxford University Press.

Jahoda, M., & West, P. S. (1951). Race relations in public housing. *Journal of Social Issues, 7*, 132–139.

James, H. (Ed.) (1920). *The Letters of William James*, (2 Vols.) Boston: Atlantic Monthly Press.

James, W. (1890). *The principles of psychology*. New York: Henry Holt.

James, W. (1892). *Psychology: Briefer course*. New York: Henry Holt.

Jastrow, J. (1961). Joseph Jastrow. In C. Murchison (Ed.), *A history of psychology in autobiography: Vol. 1* (pp. 135–162). New York: Russell & Russell. (Original work published 1930)

Jay, M. (1973). *The dialectical imagination: A history of the Frankfurt School and the Institute of Social Research, 1923–1950*. London: Heinemann.

Jing, Q., & Fu, X. (2001). Modern Chinese psychology: Its indigenous roots and international influences. *International Journal of Psychology, 36*, 408–418.

Johns, M. (2003). *Moment of grace: The American city in the 1950s*. Berkeley: University of California Press.

Johnston, E. B. (2001). The repeated reproduction of Bartlett's *Remembering*. *History of Psychology, 4*, 341–366.

Johnston, E., & Johnson, A. (2008). Searching for the second generation of American women psychologists. *History of Psychology, 11*, 40–69.

Jones, J. M. & Austin-Dailey, A. T. (2009). The Minority Fellowship Program: A thirty year legacy of training psychologists of color. *Cultural Diversity and Ethnic Minority Psychology, 15*, 388–399.

Jones, R. L. (Ed.). (1972). *Black psychology*. New York: Harper & Row.

Jones, M.C. (1975). A 1924 pioneer looks at behavior therapy. *Journal of Behavior Therapy and Experimental Psychiatry, 6*, 181–187.

Joravsky, D. (1989). *Russian psychology*. Cambridge, MA: Basil Blackwell.

Jung, C. G. (1910). The association method. *American Journal of Psychology, 31*, 219–269.

Kakar, S. (1982). *Shamans, mystics, and doctors*. New York: Alfred A. Knopf.

Kaplan, S. R., & Roman, M. (1973). *The organization and delivery of mental health services in the ghetto: The Lincoln Hospital experience*. New York: Praeger.

Kant, I. (1998). *Critique of pure reason* (P. Guyer & A. W. Wood, Trans.). Cambridge, England: Cambridge University Press. (Original work published 1781)

Kay, L. E. (2001). From logical neurons to poetic embodiments of mind: Warren S. McCulloch's project in neuroscience. *Science in Context, 14*, 591–614.

Kelly, J. G. (2005). The National Institute of Mental Health and the founding of the field of community psychology. In W. E. Pickren & S. F. Schneider (Eds.), *Psychology and the National Institute of Mental Health: A historical analysis of science, practice, and policy* (pp. 233–259). Washington, DC: American Psychological Association Books.

Kennedy, C. D., & Wagner, N. (1979). Psychology and affirmative action: 1977. *Professional Psychology, 10*, 234–243.

Kessel, F. S., & Bevan, W. (1985). Notes toward a history of cognitive psychology. In C. E. Buxton (Ed.), *Points of view in the modern history of psychology* (pp. 259–294). Orlando, FL: Academic Press.

Kevles, D. J. (1968). Testing the army's intelligence: Psychologists and the military in WWI. *Journal of American History, 55*, 565–581.

Killen, A. (2007). Weimar psychotechnics between Americanism and fascism. *Osiris, 22*, 48–71.

Kim, U., & Berry, J. W. (Eds.). (1993). *Indigenous psychologies: Research and experience in cultural context*. Newbury Park, CA: Sage.

Kimball, M. M. (2000). From Anna O. to Bertha Pappenheim: Transforming private pain into public action. *History of Psychology, 3*, 20–43.

King, D. B., & Wertheimer, M. (2005). *Max Wertheimer and Gestalt theory*. New Brunswick, NJ: Transaction.

Klappenbach, H. (2004). Psychology in Argentina. In M. J. Stevens & D. Wedding (Eds.), *Handbook of international psychology* (pp. 129–150). New York: Brunner-Routledge.

Klein, A. (2002). *A forgotten voice: A biography of Leta Stetter Hollingworth*. Scottsdale, AZ: Great Potential Press.

Klineberg, O. (1935). *Race differences*. New York: Harper and Brothers.

Kohler, R. E. (1991). *Partners in science: Foundations and natural scientists, 1900–1945*. Chicago: University of Chicago Press.

Kozulin, A. (1985). Georgy Chelpanov and the establishment of the Moscow Institute of Psychology. *Journal of the History of the Behavioral Sciences, 21*, 23–32.

Kumar, S. K. K. (2006). Happiness and well-being in the Indian tradition. *Psychological Studies, 51,* 105–112.

Kusch, M. (1995). Recluse, interlocutor, interrogator: Natural and social order in turn-of-the-century psychological research schools. *Isis, 86,* 419–439.

Kusch, M. (1999). *Psychological knowledge: A social history and philosophy.* New York: Routledge.

Lal, S. (2002). Giving children security: Mamie Phipps Clark and the racialization of child psychology. *American Psychologist, 57,* 20–28.

Lashley, K. (1931). Cerebral control versus reflexology: A reply to Professor Hunter, *Journal of General Psychology, 5,* 14.

Lashley, K. S. (1951). The problem of serial order in behavior. In L. A. Jeffress (Ed.), *Cerebral mechanisms in behavior: The Hixon Symposium* (pp. 112–146). New York: Wiley.

Lashley, K. (1960). Cerebral organization and behavior. In F. A. Beach, D. O. Hebb, C. T. Morgan, & H. W. Nissen (Eds.), *The neuropsychology of Lashley* (pp. 529–543). New York: McGraw-Hill. (Reprinted from *Research Publications of the Association for Research in Nervous and Mental Disease, 36,* 1–18, 1958)

Latham, M. E. (2003). Modernization, international history, and the Cold War world. In D. C. Engerman, N. Gilman, M. H. Haefele, & M. E. Latham (Eds.), *Staging growth: Modernization, development, and the global cold war* (pp. 1–22). Amherst: University of Massachusetts Press.

Leahey, T. H. (1992). The mythical revolutions of American psychology. *American Psychologist, 47,* 308–318.

Leahey, T. H. (1997). *A history of psychology: Main currents in psychological thought* (4th ed.). Upper Saddle River, NJ: Prentice Hall.

Lears, T. J. J. (1981). *No place of grace: Antimodernism and the transformation of American culture, 1880–1920.* New York: Pantheon Books.

Leary, D. E. (1978). The philosophical development of the conception of psychology in Germany, 1780–1850. *Journal of the History of the Behavioral Sciences, 14,* 113–121.

Leary, D. E. (1987). From act psychology to probabilistic functionalism: The place of Egon Brunswik in the history of psychology. In M. G. Ash & W. R. Woodward (Eds.), *Psychology in twentieth-century thought and society* (pp. 115–142). New York: Cambridge University Press.

Leong, F. (1995). History of Asian American psychology. *AAPA Monographs, 1,* 1–54.

Leong, F. T. L., & Okazaki, S. (2009). History of Asian American psychology. *Cultural Diversity and Ethnic Minority Psychology, 15,* 352–362.

Lewin, K. (1944). Constructs in psychology and psychological ecology. *University of Iowa Studies in Child Welfare, 20,* 23–27.

Leys, R., & Evans, R. B. (1990). *Defining American psychology: The correspondence between Adolf Meyer and Edward Bradford Titchener.* Baltimore: Johns Hopkins University Press.

Lippmann, W. (1922, November 15). The abuse of the tests. *The New Republic,* pp. 297–298.

Locke, J. (1690). *An essay concerning human understanding.* Penguin Classics Edition. London: Penguin Group.

Logan, C. (1999). The altered rationale for the choice of a standard experimental animal in experimental psychology: Henry H. Donaldson, Adolf Meyer, and the "albino" rat. *History of Psychology, 2,* 3–24.

Lomax, E. (1977). The Laura Spelman Rockefeller Memorial: Some of its contributions to early research in child development. *Journal of the History of the Behavioral Sciences, 13,* 283–293.

Lombardo, G. P., & Foschi, R. (2008). Escape from the dark forest: The experimentalist standpoint of Sante de Sanctis' psychology of dreams. *History of the Human Sciences, 21,* 45–69.

Long, H. H. (1935). Some psychogenic hazards of segregated education of Negroes. *Journal of Negro Education, 4,* 336–350.

Lubek, I. (Ed.). (2000). Re-engaging the history of social psychology. Special issue of the *Journal of the History of the Behavioral Sciences, 36*(4), 317–516.

Maccoby, E. E., & Jacklin, C. N. (1974). *The psychology of sex differences.* Palo Alto, CA: Stanford University Press.

Mackenzie, B. D. (1972). Behaviourism and positivism. *Journal of the History of the Behavioral Sciences, 8,* 222–231.

Mahoney, K., & Baker, D. B. (2002). Elton Mayo and Carl Rogers: A tale of two techniques. *Journal of Vocational Behavior, 60,* 437–450.

Mandler, G. (2002). Origins of the cognitive (r)evolution. *Journal of the History of the Behavioral Sciences, 38,* 339–353.

Marecek, J., & Hare-Mustin, R. T. (1991). A short history of the future: Feminism and clinical psychology. *Psychology of Women Quarterly, 15,* 521–536.

Marecek, J., Kimmel, E. B., Crawford, M., & Hare-Mustin, R. T. (2003). Psychology of women and gender. In D. K. Freedheim (Ed.), *Handbook of psychology: Vol. 1. History of psychology* (pp. 249–268). Hoboken, NJ: Wiley.

Markowitz, G., & Rosner, D. (1996). *Children, race, and power: Kenneth and Mamie Clark's Northside Center.* Charlottesville: University of Virginia Press.

Marling, K. A. (1994). *As seen on TV: The visual culture of everyday life in the 1950s.* Cambridge, MA: Harvard University Press.

Marrow, A. J. (1969). *The practical theorist: The life and work of Kurt Lewin.* New York: Basic Books.

Marsella, A. J. (1998). Toward a "global-community" psychology: Meeting the needs of a changing world. *American Psychologist, 53,* 1–10.

Marsh, M. (1990). *Suburban lives.* New Brunswick, NJ: Rutgers University Press.

Martín-Baró, I. (1994). *Writings for a liberation psychology.* Cambridge, MA: Harvard University Press.

Mauss, M. (1954). *The gift: Forms and functions of exchange in archaic societies.* Glencoe, IL: Free Press. (Original work published 1923–1924)

May, E. T. (1988). *Homeward bound: American families in the Cold War era.* New York: Basic Books.

McClelland, D. C., & Winter, D. G. (1969). *Motivating economic achievement.* New York: Free Press.

McCulloch, W. S., & Pitts, W. (1943). A logical calculus of the ideas immanent in nervous activity. *Bulletin of Mathematical Biophysics, 5,* 115–133.

McReynolds, P. (1997). *Lightner Witmer: His life and times.* Washington, DC: American Psychological Association.

Milar, K. S. (2000). The first generation of women psychologists and the psychology of women. *American Psychologist, 55,* 616–619.

Miller, J. B. (1986). *Toward a new psychology of women.* Boston: Beacon Press. (Original work published 1976)

Mills, W. (1899). The nature of animal intelligence. *Psychological Review, 6,* 262–274.

Minton, H. L. (1988). *Lewis M. Terman: Pioneer in psychological testing.* New York: New York University Press.

Minton, H. L. (2000). Psychology and gender at the turn of the century. *American Psychologist, 55,* 613–615.

Misra, G. (2007). *Psychology and societal development: Paradigmatic and social concerns.* New Delhi: Concept.

Mitchell, M. B. (1983). Mildred B. Mitchell. In A. N. O'Connell & N. F. Russo (Eds.), *Models of achievement: Vol. 1. Reflections of eminent women in psychology* (pp. 121–139). New York: Columbia University Press.

Montero, M. (1996). Parallel lives: Community psychology in Latin America and the United States. *American Journal of Community Psychology, 24,* 589–605.

Morawski, J. G. (1986). Organizing knowledge and behavior at Yale's Institute of Human Relations. *Isis, 77,* 219–242.

Morawski, J. G. (2005). Reflexivity and the psychologist. *History of the Human Sciences, 18,* 77–105.

Morawski, J. G., & Bayer, B. M. (2003). Social psychology. In D. K. Freedheim (Ed.), *Handbook of psychology: Vol. 1. History of psychology* (pp. 223–247). New York: John Wiley & Sons.

Morse, J. F. (2002). Ignored but not forgotten: The work of Helen Bradford Thompson Woolley. *National Women's Studies Association Journal, 14,* 121–147.

Mosvovici, S., & Markova, I. (2006). *The making of modern social psychology.* Cambridge, England: Polity Press.

Mulder, E., & Heyting, F. (1998). The Dutch curve: The introduction and reception of intelligence testing in the Netherlands, 1908–1940. *Journal of the History of the Behavioral Sciences, 34,* 349–366.

Münsterberg, H. (1913). *Psychology and industrial efficiency.* Boston: Houghton Mifflin.

Murray, H. A. (1967). Henry A. Murray. In E. G. Boring & G. Lindzey (Eds.), *A history of psychology in autobiography* (pp. 283–310). New York: Appleton-Century-Crofts.

Myers-Shirk, S. E. (2009). *Helping the good shepherd: Pastoral counselors in a psychotherapeutic culture, 1925–1975.* Baltimore: Johns Hopkins University Press.

Napoli, D. S. (1981). *Architects of adjustment: The history of the psychological profession in the United States.* Port Washington, NY: Kennikat Press.

Neisser, U. (1967). *Cognitive psychology.* New York: Appleton-Century-Crofts.

Nicholson, I. A. M. (1998). Gordon Allport, character, and the "culture of personality." *History of Psychology, 1,* 52–68.

Nicholson, I. A. M. (2003). *Inventing personality: Gordon Allport and the science of selfhood.* Washington, DC: American Psychological Association.

Nobles, W. W. (1972). African philosophy: Foundations for a Black psychology. In R. L. Jones (Ed.), *Black psychology* (pp. 18–32). New York: Harper & Row.

Nsamenang, A. B. (1995). Factors influencing the development of psychology in sub-Saharan Africa. *International Journal of Psychology, 30,* 729–739.

Nsamenang, A. B. (2004). *Cultures of human development and education: Challenge to growing up African.* New York: Nova Science.

Nyman, L. (1976). *Recollections: An oral history of the psychology department of the City College of the City University of New York.* New York: Author.

O'Brien, P. K., & Quinault, R. E. (Eds.). (1993). *The industrial revolution and British society.* Cambridge, England: Cambridge University Press.

O'Connell, A. N. (2001). *Models of achievement: Vol. 3. Reflections of eminent women in psychology.* Mahwah, NJ: Erlbaum.

O'Connell, A. N., & Russo, N. F. (1983). *Models of achievement: Vol. 1. Reflections of eminent women in psychology.* New York: Columbia University Press.

O'Connell, A. N., & Russo, N. F. (1988). *Models of achievement: Vol. 2. Reflections of eminent women in psychology.* Hillsdale, NJ: Erlbaum.

O'Donnell, J. M. (1985). *The origins of behaviorism: American psychology, 1870–1920.* New York: New York University Press.

Ormrod, D. (2003). *The rise of commercial empires: England and the Netherlands in the age of mercantilism, 1650–1770.* Cambridge, England: Cambridge University Press.

Oyama, T., Sato, T., & Suzuki, Y. (2001). Shaping of scientific psychology in Japan. *International Journal of Psychology 36,* 396–406.

Padilla, A. & Olmedo, E. (2009). Synopsis of key persons, events, and associations in the history of Latino psychology.

Padilla, A. M. (2009). A history of Latino psychology. *Cultural Diversity and Ethnic Minority Psychology, 15,* 363–373.

Pe-Pua, R., & Protacio-Marcelino, E. (2000). *Sikolohiyang Pilipino* (Filipino psychology): A legacy of Virgilio G. Enriquez. *Asian Journal of Social Psychology, 3,* 49–71.

Peterson, D. R. (1992). The doctor of psychology degree. In D. K. Freedheim (Ed.), *History of psychotherapy: A century of change* (pp. 829–849). Washington, DC: American Psychological Association.

Peterson, D. R. (2003). Unintended consequences: Ventures and misadventures in the education of professional psychologists. *American Psychologist, 58,* 791–800.

Pettigrew, T., & Jones, J. (2005). Kenneth B. Clark (1914–2005). *American Psychologist, 60,* 649–651.

Petzold, M. (1987). The social history of Chinese psychology. In M. G. Ash & W. R. Woodward (Eds.), *Psychology in twentieth-century thought and society* (pp. 213–231). New York: Cambridge University Press.

The physical and mental abilities of the American Negro [Special issue]. (1934). *Journal of Negro Education, 3,* 317–564.

Pickren, W. E. (2000). A whisper of salvation: American psychologists and religion in the popular press, 1884–1908. *American Psychologist, 55,* 1022–1024.

Pickren, W. E. (2004). Between the cup of principle and the lip of practice: Ethnic minorities and American psychology, 1966–1980. *History of Psychology, 7,* 45–64.

Pickren, W. E. (2005). Science, practice, and policy: An introduction to the history of psychology and the National Institute of Mental Health. In W. E. Pickren & S. F. Schneider (Eds.), *Psychology and the National Institute of Mental Health: A historical analysis of science, practice, and policy.* Washington, DC: American Psychological Association.

Pickren, W. E. (2006). Calvin P. Stone: Solid scientist and citizen. In D. A. Dewsbury, L. T. Benjamin, Jr., & M. Wertheimer (Eds.), *Portraits of pioneers in psychology* (Vol. 6, pp. 119–133). Washington, DC & Mahwah, NJ: American Psychological Association & Lawrence Erlbaum Associates.

Pickren, W. E. (2007). Tension and opportunity in post–World War II American psychology. *History of Psychology, 10,* 279–299.

Pickren, W. E., & Schneider, S. F. (Eds.). (2005). *Psychology and the National Institute of Mental Health: A historical analysis of science, practice, and policy.* Washington, DC: American Psychological Association Books.

Pickren, W. E., & Tomes, H. (2002). The legacy of Kenneth B. Clark to the APA: The Board of Social and Ethical Responsibility for Psychology. *American Psychologist, 57,* 51–59.

Piéron, H. (1952). Henri Piéron. In E. G. Boring, H. Werner, H. S. Langfeld, & R. M. Yerkes (Eds.), *A history of psychology in autobiography* (Vol. 4, pp. 257–278). Worcester, MA: Clark University Press.

Plas, R. (1997). French psychology. In W. G. Bringmann, H. E. Lück, R. Miller, & C. E. Early (Eds.), *A pictorial history of psychology* (pp. 548–552). Chicago: Quintessence.

Pols, H. (1999). The world as laboratory: Strategies of field research developed by mental hygiene psychologists in Toronto, 1920–1940. In T. Richardson & D. Fisher (Eds.), *The development of the social sciences in the United States and Canada: The role of philanthropy* (pp. 115–142). Stamford, CT: Ablex Publishing.

Porter, R. (1989). *Social history of madness*. London: Plume.

Porter, R. (2000). *The creation of the modern world: The untold story of the British Enlightenment*. New York: Norton.

Porter, R. (2003). *Flesh in the age of reason: The modern foundations of body and soul*. New York: Norton.

Porter, T. M., & Ross, D. (Eds.). (2003). *The Cambridge history of science: Vol. 7. The modern social sciences*. Cambridge, England: Cambridge University Press.

Pottharst, K. E., & Kovacs, A. (1964). The crisis in training viewed by clinical alumni. In L. Blank & H. P. David (Eds.), *Sourcebook for training in clinical psychology* (pp. 278–300). New York: Springer.

Price, D. J. (1963). *Little science, big science*. New York: Columbia University Press.

Quinn, S. O. (2007). How southern New England became magnetic north: The acceptance of animal magnetism. *History of Psychology, 10*, 231–248.

Rabinbach, A. (1990). *The human motor: Energy, fatigue, and the origins of modernity*. Berkeley: University of California Press.

Raimy, V. (1950). *Training in clinical psychology*. Englewood Cliffs, NJ: Prentice Hall.

Reid, P. T. (1993). Poor women in psychological research: Shut up and shut out. *Psychology of Women Quarterly, 17*, 133–150.

Reid, P. T. (2000). Multicultural psychology: Bringing together gender and ethnicity. *Cultural Diversity and Ethnic Minority Psychology, 8*, 103–114.

Rice, C. E. (2005). The research grants program of the National Institute of Mental Health and the golden age of American academic psychology. In W. E. Pickren & S. F. Schneider (Eds.),

Psychology and the National Institute of Mental Health: A historical analysis of science, practice, and policy (pp. 61–111). Washington, DC: American Psychological Association.

Richards, G. (1992). *Mental machinery: The origins and consequences of psychological ideas, 1600–1850*. Baltimore: Johns Hopkins University Press.

Richards, G. (1995). "To know our fellow men to do them good": American psychology's enduring moral project. *History of the Human Sciences, 8*, 1–24.

Richards, G. (1997). *Race, racism, and psychology*. London: Routledge.

Richards, G. (2002). *Putting psychology in its place* (2nd ed). London: Routledge

Richards, R. J. (1987). *Darwin and the emergence of evolutionary theories of mind and behavior*. Chicago: University of Chicago Press.

Riger, S. (1992). Epistemological debates, feminist voices: Science, social values, and the study of women. *American Psychologist, 47*, 730–740.

Ringer, F. (1969). *The decline of the German mandarins: The German academic community, 1890–1933*. Cambridge, MA: Harvard University Press.

Robb, C. (2007). *This changes everything: The relational revolution in psychology*. New York: Farrar, Straus, and Giroux.

Robinson, F. G. (1992). *Love's story told: A life of Henry A. Murray*. Cambridge, MA: Harvard University Press.

Roiser, M. (2001). Social psychology and social concern in 1930s Britain. In G. C. Bunn, A. D. Lovie, & G. D. Richards (Eds.), *Psychology in Britain: Historical essays and personal reflections* (pp. 168–187). Leicester, England: British Psychological Society.

Roland, A. (1991). *In search of the self in India and Japan*. Princeton, NJ: Princeton University Press.

Rose, N. (1985). *The psychological complex: Psychology, politics, and society in England, 1869–1939*. London: Routledge & Kegan Paul.

Rose, N. (1989). *Governing the soul: The shaping of the private self*. London: Free Association Books.

Rosenberg, R. (1982). *Beyond separate spheres: The intellectual roots of modern feminism*. New Haven, CT: Yale University Press.

Rosenthal, N. B. (1984). Consciousness-raising: From revolution to re-evaluation. *Psychology of Women Quarterly, 8*, 309–326.

Rosner, R. I. (2005). Psychotherapy research and the National Institute of Mental Health. In W. E. Pickren & S. F. Schneider (Eds.), *Psychology and the*

National Institute of Mental Health: A historical analysis of science, practice, and policy (pp. 111–150). Washington, DC: American Psychological Association.

Ross, D. (1972). *G. Stanley Hall: The psychologist as prophet.* Chicago: University of Chicago Press.

Rossiter, M. W. (1982). *Women scientists in America: Struggles and strategies to 1940.* Baltimore: Johns Hopkins University Press.

Rossiter, M. W. (1995). *Women scientists in America: Before affirmative action, 1940–1972.* Baltimore: Johns Hopkins University Press.

Russo, N. F., & Dumont, A. (1997). A history of division 35 (Psychology of Women): Origins, issues, activities, future. In D. A. Dewsbury (Ed.), *Unification through division: Histories of the divisions of the American Psychological Association* (Vol. 2, pp. 211–238). Washington, DC: American Psychological Association.

Rutherford, A. (2000). Radical behaviorism and psychology's public: B. F. Skinner in the popular press, 1934–1990. *History of Psychology, 3,* 371–395.

Rutherford, A. (2003). B. F. Skinner's technology of behavior in American life: From consumer culture to counterculture. *Journal of the History of the Behavioral Sciences, 39,* 1–23.

Rutherford, A. (2006). The social control of behavior control: Behavior modification, individual rights, and research ethics in America, 1971–1979. *Journal of the History of the Behavioral Sciences, 42,* 203–220.

Rutherford, A. (2009). *Beyond the box: B. F. Skinner's technology of behavior from laboratory to life, 1950s–1970s.* Toronto: University of Toronto Press.

Rutherford, A., & Granek, L. (in press). Emergence and development of the psychology of women. In J. Chrisler & D. McCreary (Eds.), *Handbook of gender research in psychology.* New York: Springer.

Samelson, F. (1977). World War I intelligence testing and the development of psychology. *Journal of the History of the Behavioral Sciences, 13,* 274–282.

Samelson, F. (1981). Struggle for scientific authority: The reception of Watson's behaviorism, 1913–1920. *Journal of the History of the Behavioral Sciences, 17,* 399–425.

Samuelson, R. J. (1995). *The good life and its discontents: The American dream in the age of entitlement, 1945–1995.* New York: Times Books.

Sanchez, G. I. (1932). Scores of Spanish-speaking children on repeated tests. *Journal of Genetic Psychology, 40,* 223–231.

Sanchez, G. I. (1934). Bilingualism and mental measures. *Journal of Applied Psychology, 18,* 765–772.

Sandoval, C. (2000). *Methodology of the oppressed.* Minneapolis: University of Minnesota Press.

Sarason, S. B. (1981). An asocial psychology and a misdirected clinical psychology. *American Psychologist, 36,* 827–836.

Scarborough, E., & Furumoto, L. (1987). *Untold lives: The first generation of American women psychologists.* New York: Columbia University Press.

Schilling, R. S. F. (1944). Industrial health research: The work of the Industrial Health Research Board, 1918–1944. *British Journal of Industrial Medicine, 1,* 145–152.

Schmit, D. (2005). Re-visioning American antebellum psychology: The dissemination of mesmerism, 1836–1854. *History of Psychology, 8,* 403–434.

Schmit, D. (in press). The Mesmerists inquire about "oriental mind powers": West meets East in the search for the universal trance. *Journal of the History of the Behavioral Sciences.*

Schmidt, W. (1997). William Stern. In W. G. Bringmann, H. E. Lück, R. Miller, & C. E. Early (Eds.), *A pictorial history of psychology* (pp. 322–325). Chicago: Quintessence.

Schneider, S. F. (2005). Reflections on psychology and the National Institute of Mental Health. In W. E. Pickren & S. F. Schneider (Eds.), *Psychology and the National Institute of Mental Health: A historical analysis of science, practice, and policy* (pp. 17–28). Washington, DC: American Psychological Association.

Schneider, W. H. (1991). The scientific study of labor in Interwar France. *French Historical Studies, 17,* 410–446.

Schneider, W. H. (1992). After Binet: French intelligence testing, 1900–1950. *Journal of the History of the Behavioral Sciences, 28,* 111–132.

Scoville, W. B. & Milner, B. (1957). Loss of recent memory after bilateral hippocampal lesions. *The Journal of Neurology, Neurosurgery, and Psychiatry, 20,* 11–21.

Seedat, M., & MacKenzie, S. (2008). The triangulated development of South African psychology: Race, scientific racism, and professionalization. In C. van Ommen & D. Painter (Eds.), *Interiors: A history of psychology in South Africa* (pp. 63–91). Cape Town, South Africa: Unisa Press.

Seigel, J. E. (2005). *The idea of the self: Thought and experience in western Europe since the seventeenth century*. Cambridge, England: Cambridge University Press.

Serpell, R. (1984). Commentary: The impact of psychology on Third World development. *International Journal of Psychology*, *19*, 179–192.

Shakow, D. (1942). The training of the clinical psychologist. *Journal of Consulting Psychology*, *6*, 277–288.

Shakow, D. & Rapaport, D. (1964). *The influence of Freud on American psychology*. New York: International Universities Press.

Shannon, C. E., & Weaver, W. (1949). *The mathematical theory of communication*. Urbana: University of Illinois Press.

Shapin, S., & Schaffer, S. (1985). *Leviathan and the air-pump*. Princeton, NJ: Princeton University Press.

Shapin, S. (1994). *A social history of truth*. Chicago: University of Chicago Press.

Shapin, S. (1996). *The scientific revolution*. Chicago: University of Chicago Press.

Sharp, S. E. (1899). Individual psychology: A study in psychological method. *American Journal of Psychology*, *10*, 329–391.

Shields, S. A. (1975a). Functionalism, Darwinism, and the psychology of women. *American Psychologist*, *30*, 739–754.

Shields, S. A. (1975b). Ms. Pilgrim's progress: The contributions of Leta Stetter Hollingworth to the psychology of women. *American Psychologist*, *30*, 852–857.

Shields, S. A. (2008). Gender: An intersectionality perspective. *Sex Roles*, *59*, 301–311.

Shinn, M. W. (1895). The marriage rate of college women. *The Century*, *50*, 946–948.

Shore, M. (2001). Psychology and memory in the midst of change: The social concerns of late-19th-century North American psychologists. In C. D. Green, M. Shore, & T. Teo (Eds.), *The transformation of psychology: Influences of 19th-century philosophy, technology, and natural science* (pp. 63–86). Washington, DC: American Psychological Association.

Simpkins, G., & Raphael, P. (1970). Black students, APA, and the challenge of change. *American Psychologist*, *25* (Suppl. May), xxi–xxvi.

Sinha, D. (1986). *Psychology in a Third World country*. New Delhi: Sage.

Sinha, D. (1994). Origins and development of psychology in India: Outgrowing the alien framework. *International Journal of Psychology*, *29*, 695–705.

Sinha, D. (1998). Changing perspectives in social psychology in India: A journey towards indigenization. *Asian Journal of Social Psychology*, *1*, 17–31.

Sinha, J. B. P. (1995). Factors facilitating and impeding growth of psychology in South Asia, with special reference to India. *International Journal of Psychology*, *30*, 741–753.

Sinha, J. B. P. (1997). In search of my *Brahman*. In M. H. Bond (Ed.), *Working at the interface of cultures: Eighteen lives in social science* (pp. 77–84). New York: Routledge.

Sirotkina, I. (2006). When did "scientific psychology" begin in Russia? *Physis: Rivista Internazionale di Storia Della Scienza*, *43*, 238–271.

Skinner, B. F. (1938). *The behavior of organisms: An experimental analysis*. New York: Appleton-Century.

Skinner, B. F. (1945, October). Baby in a box: Introducing the mechanical baby tender. *Ladies Home Journal*, *62*, 30–31, 135–136, 138.

Skinner, B. F. (1948). *Walden two*. New York: Macmillan.

Skinner, B. F. (1971). *Beyond freedom and dignity*. New York: Knopf.

Smith, L. D. (1992). On prediction and control: B. F. Skinner and the technological ideal of science. *American Psychologist*, *47*, 216–223.

Smith, L. D. (1996). Knowledge as power: The Baconian roots of Skinner's social meliorism. In L. D. Smith & W. R. Woodward (Eds.), *B. F. Skinner and behaviorism in American culture* (pp. 56–82). Cranbury, NJ: Associated University Presses.

Smith, R. (1973). The background of physiological psychology in natural philosophy. *History of Science*, *11*, 75–123.

Smith, R. (1988). Does the history of psychology have a subject? *History of the Human Sciences*, *1*, 147–177.

Smith, R. (1997). *The Norton history of the human sciences*. New York: Norton.

Smith, R. (1997). The individual and the social. In R. Smith, *The Norton history of the human sciences* (pp. 746–798). New York: Norton.

Smith, R. (1998). The big picture: Writing psychology into the history of the human sciences. *Journal of the History of the Behavioral Sciences*, *34*, 1–13.

Smith, R. (2007). *Being human: Historical knowledge and the creation of human nature*. New York: Columbia University Press.

Smuts, A. B. (2006). *Science in the service of children, 1893–1935*. New Haven, CT: Yale University Press.

Sokal, M. M. (Ed.). (1987). *Psychological testing and American society, 1890–1930*. New Brunswick, NJ: Rutgers University Press.

Sokal, M. M. (2001). Practical phrenology as psychological counseling in the 19th-century United States. In C. D. Green, M. Shore, & T. Teo (Eds.), *The transformation of psychology: Influences of 19th-century philosophy, technology, and natural science* (pp. 21–44). Washington, DC: American Psychological Association.

Sokal, M. (2006). The origins of the new psychology in the United States. *Physis, 43*, 273–300.

Solovey, M. (2001). Project Camelot and the 1960s epistemological revolution: Rethinking the politics–patronage–social science nexus. *Social Studies of Science, 31*, 171–206.

Spearman, C. (1904). General intelligence: Objectively determined and measured. *American Journal of Psychology, 15*, 201–293.

Spencer, H. (1855). *Principles of psychology*. London: Longman, Brown, Green, and Longman.

Sperry, R. W. (1968). Hemisphere deconnection and unity in conscious awareness. *American Psychologist, 23*, 723–733.

Spigel, L. (1992). *Make room for TV: Television and the family ideal in postwar America*. Chicago: University of Chicago Press.

Sprung, L., & Sprung, H. (2001). History of modern psychology in Germany in 19th- and 20th-century thought and society. *International Journal of Psychology, 36*, 364–376.

Srinivas, M. N. (1966). *Social change in modern India*. Berkeley: University of California Press.

Staeuble, I. (2004). De-centering Western perspectives: Psychology and the disciplinary order in the First and Third World. In A. Brock, J. Louw, & W. van Hoorn (Eds.), *Rediscovering the history of psychology: Essays inspired by the work of Kurt Danziger*. New York: Kluwer.

Stern, M. B. (1971). *Heads and headlines: The phrenological Fowlers*. Norman: University of Oklahoma Press.

Stevens, W. K. (1971, September 3). In behaviorist's ideal state, control replaces liberty. *New York Times*, 29.

Stewart, A. J., & Dottolo, A. L. (2006). Feminist psychology. *Signs, 31*, 493–509.

Stockdill, J. W. (2005). National mental health policy and the community mental health centers, 1963–1981. In W. E. Pickren & S. F. Schneider (Eds.), *Psychology and the National Institute of Mental Health: A historical analysis of science, practice, and policy* (pp. 261–293). Washington, DC: American Psychological Association Books.

Stone, L. (1977). *The family, sex, and marriage in England, 1500–1800*. New York: Harper & Row.

Strickland, S. P. (1972). *Politics, science, and dread disease: A short history of United States medical research policy*. Cambridge, MA: Harvard University Press.

Sue, S. (1977). Community mental health services to minority groups: Some optimism, some pessimism. *American Psychologist, 32*, 616–624

Swartz, S. (1996). Review: Jock McCulloch, colonial psychiatry and the "African mind." *History of the Human Sciences, 9*, 127–130.

Taiana, C. (2006). Transatlantic migration of the disciplines of the mind: Examination of the reception of Wundt's and Freud's theories in Argentina. In A. Brock (Ed.), *Internationalizing the history of psychology* (pp. 34–55). New York: New York University Press.

Tajfel, H. (1972). Some developments in European psychology. *European Journal of Social Psychology, 2*, 307–322.

Takasuna, M. (2006). The origins of scientific psychology in Japan. *Physis: Rivista Internazionale di Storia Della Scienza, 43*, 319–331.

Taves, A. (1999). *Fits, trances, and visions: Experiencing religion and explaining experience from Wesley to James*. Princeton, NJ: Princeton University Press.

Taylor, C. (1989). *Sources of the self: The making of the modern identity*. Cambridge, MA: Harvard University Press.

Taylor, E. (1999). *Shadow culture: Psychology and spirituality in America*. Washington, DC: Counterpoint.

Taylor, E. (2000). Psychotherapeutics and the problematic origins of clinical psychology in America. *American Psychologist, 55*, 1029–1033.

Teo, T. (2005). *The critique of psychology: From Kant to postcolonial theory*. New York: Springer.

Terman, L. (1916). *The measurement of intelligence*. Boston: Houghton Mifflin.

Thompson (Woolley), H. (1903). *The mental traits of sex: An experimental investigation of the normal mind in men and women*. Chicago: University of Chicago Press.

Thomson, M. (2006). *Psychological subjects: Identity, culture, and health in 20th-century Britain*. Oxford, England: Oxford University Press.

Tiefer, L. (1991). A brief history of the Association for Women in Psychology: 1969–1991. *Psychology of Women Quarterly, 15,* 635–649.

Tolman, E. C., & Honzik, C. H. (1930). Introduction and removal of reward, and maze performance in rats. *University of California Publications in Psychology, 4,* 257–275.

Tomes, N. (1984). *A generous confidence: Thomas Story Kirkbride and the art of asylum-keeping, 1840–1883*. New York: Cambridge University Press.

Tone, A. (2009). *The age of anxiety: A history of America's turbulent affair with tranquilizers*. New York: Basic Books.

Toulmin, S. (1990). *Cosmopolis: The hidden agenda of modernity*. New York: Free Press.

Triantafillou, P., & Moreira, A. (2005). Modern templates of happiness: Performing spiritualism and psychotechnics in Denmark. *History of the Human Sciences, 18,* 87–109.

Trimble, J. E. (2000). American Indian psychology. In A. E. Kazdin (Ed.), *Encyclopedia of Psychology* (Vol. 1, pp. 139–144). Washington, DC: American Psychological Association.

Trimble, J. E., & Clearing Sky, M. (2009). An historical profile of American Indians and Alaska Natives in psychology. *Cultural Diversity and Ethnic Minority Psychology, 15,* 338–351.

Turing, A. M. (1937). On computable numbers, with an application to the *Entscheidungsproblem*. *Proceedings of the London Mathematical Society, 42,* 230–265.

Turing, A. M. (1950). Computing machinery and intelligence. *Mind, 59,* 433–460.

Tyler, F. B., & Gatz, M. (1976). If community psychology is so great, why don't we try it? *Professional Psychology, 7,* 185–194.

Tyler, L. (1969). APA in public affairs: Report of the ad hoc Committee on Public Affairs. *American Psychologist, 24,* 1–4.

Undurti, V. (2007). Quality of women's lives in India: Some findings from two decades of psychological research on gender. *Feminism and Psychology, 17,* 337–356. (erroneously published as Vindhya, U.)

Unger, R. K. (1979). Toward a redefinition of sex and gender. *American Psychologist, 34,* 1085–1094.

Valentine, E. B. (2001). Beatrice Edgell: An appreciation. *British Journal of Psychology, 92,* 23–36.

van der Veer, R. (2000). Tamara Dembo's European years: Working with Lewin and Buytendijk. *Journal of the History of the Behavioral Sciences, 36,* 109–126.

van Drunen, P. (1997). Psychotechnics. In W. G. Bringmann, H. E. Lück, R. Miller, & C. E. Early (Eds.), *A pictorial history of psychology* (pp. 480–484). Chicago: Quintessence.

van Ginneken, J. (1992). *Crowds, psychology, & politics, 1871–1899*. New York: Cambridge University Press.

van Hezewijk, R., & Stam, H. J. (2008). Idols of the psychologist: Johannes Linschoten and the demise of phenomenological psychology in the Netherlands. *History of Psychology, 11,* 185–207.

van Ommen, C., & Painter, D. (Eds.). (2008). *Interiors: A history of psychology in South Africa*. Cape Town: Unisa Press.

van Strien, P. J. (1991). Transforming psychology in the Netherlands: 2. Audiences, alliances, and the dynamics of change. *History of the Human Sciences, 4,* 351–369.

van Strien, P. J. (1997). Psychotechnics. In W. G. Bringmann, H. E. Lück, R. Miller, & C. E. Early (Eds.), *A pictorial history of psychology* (pp. 480–484). Chicago: Quintessence.

van Strien, P. (1997). The American colonization of northwest European social psychology after World War II. *Journal of the History of the Behavioral Sciences, 33,* 349–363.

Van Wyhe, J. (2002). The authority of human nature: The Schädellehre of Franz Joseph Gall. *British Journal of the History of Science, 35,* 17–42.

von Mayrhauser, R. T. (1987). The manager, the medic and the mediator: The clash of professional psychological styles and the wartime origins of group mental testing. In M. M. Sokal (Ed.), *Psychological testing and American society, 1890–1930* (pp. 128–157). New Brunswick, NJ: Rutgers University Press.

Watkins, E. S. (2008). Medicine, masculinity, and the disappearance of male menopause in the 1950s. *Social History of Medicine, 21,* 329–344.

Watkins, O. C. (1972). *The Puritan experience: Studies in spiritual autobiography*. New York: Schocken Books.

Watson, J. B. (1913). Psychology as the behaviorist views it. *Psychological Review, 20,* 158–177.

Watson, J. B. (1924). *Psychology from the standpoint of a behaviorist* (2nd ed.). Philadelphia: J. B. Lippincott. (Original work published 1919)

Watt, I. (1957). *The rise of the novel: Studies in Defoe, Richardson, and Fielding*. Chicago: University of Chicago Press.

Weaver, W. (1934, January 23, 24). Office diaries, Institute of Human Relations, Rockefeller Foundation Archives.

Weber, M. (1930). *The Protestant ethic and the spirit of capitalism* (Talcott Parsons, Trans.). London: George Allen and Unwin.

Weidman, N. (1994). Mental testing and machine intelligence: The Lashley-Hull debate. *Journal of the History of the Behavioral Sciences, 30*, 162–180.

Weiskrantz, L. (1994). Donald Eric Broadbent, 6 May 1926–10 April 1993. *Biographical Memoirs of Fellows of the Royal Society, 40*, 33–42.

Weisstein, N. (1971). Psychology constructs the female; or, the fantasy life of the male psychologist (with some attention to the fantasies of his friends, the male biologist and the male anthropologist). *Journal of Social Education, 35*, 362–373.

Wentworth, P. A. (1999). The moral of her story: Exploring the philosophical and religious commitments in Mary Whiton Calkins' self-psychology. *History of Psychology, 2*, 119–131.

Wertheimer, M. (1921). Untersuchungen zur lehre von der Gestalt, II. *Psychologische Forschung, 4*, 301–302.

Wertheimer, M. (1958). Untersuchungen zur lehre von der Gestalt, II [Xxxx xxxx] (M. Wertheimer, Trans.). In D. C. Beardslee & M. Wertheimer (Eds.), *Readings in perception* (pp. 115–116). Princeton, NJ: Van Nostrand. (Original work published 1923)

Westad, O. A. (2007). *The global cold war: Third World interventions and the making of our times*. New York: Cambridge University Press.

White, C. G. (2009). *Unsettled minds: Psychology and the American search for spiritual assurance*. Berkeley: University of California Press.

White, J. L. (1972). Toward a Black psychology. In R. L. Jones (Ed.), *Black psychology* (pp. 43–50). New York: Harper & Row.

Wiebe, R. H. (1967). *The search for order, 1877–1920*. New York: Hill and Wang.

Williams, B. H. (1997). Coming together: The founding of the Association of Black Psychologists. *Dissertation Abstracts International* (UMI Number: 9822882). Ann Arbor: University of Michigan.

Williams, R. L. (1974). A history of the Association of Black Psychologists: Early formation and development. *Journal of Black Psychology, 1*, 9–24.

Williams, R. L. (2008a). A 40-year history of the Association of Black Psychologists (ABPsi). *Journal of Black Psychology, 34*, 249–260.

Williams, R. L. (2008b). *History of the Association of Black Psychologists*. Bloomington, IN: Author House.

Wilner, D. M., Walkley, R. P., & Cook, S. W. (1955). *Human relations in interracial housing: A study of the contact hypothesis*. Minneapolis: University of Minnesota Press.

Winston, A. S. (1998). "The defects of his race": E. G. Boring and anti-Semitism in American psychology, 1923–1953. *History of Psychology, 1*, 27–51.

Winter, A. (1998). *Mesmerized: Powers of mind in Victorian Britain*. Chicago: University of Chicago Press.

Wispe, L., Ash, P., Awkard, J., Hicks, L., Hoffman, M., & Porter, J. (1969). The Negro psychologist in America. *American Psychologist, 24*, 142–150.

Woodworth, R. S. (1917). Some criticisms of the Freudian psychology. *Journal of Abnormal Psychology, 12*, 174–194.

Woodworth, R. S. (1921). *Psychology: A study of mental life*. New York: Henry Holt.

Wooldridge, A. (1994). *Measuring the mind: Psychological theory and educational controversy in England, c. 1860–c. 1990*. Cambridge, England: Cambridge University Press.

Wulff, D. M. (1985). Experimental introspection and religious experience: The Dorpat school of religious psychology. *Journal of the History of the Behavioral Sciences, 21*, 131–150.

Yasnitsky, A., & Ferrari, M. (2008). From Vygotsky to Vygotskyan psychology: Introduction to the history of the Kharkov School. *Journal of the History of the Behavioral Sciences, 44*, 119–145.

Yerkes, R. M. (1921). *Psychological examining in the U.S. Army* (Memoirs of the National Academy of Sciences, No. 15). Washington, DC: National Academy of Sciences.

Young, R. M. (1991). *Mind, brain, and adaptation in the 19th century: Cerebral localization and its biological context from Gall to Ferrier*. New York: Oxford University Press.

Zeigarnik, A. V. (2007). Bluma Zeigarnik: A memoir. *Gestalt Theory, 29*, 256–268.

Zenderland, L. (1998). *Measuring minds: Henry Herbart Goddard and the origins of American intelligence testing*. Cambridge, England: Cambridge University Press.

Zinn, M. B., & Dill, B. T. (1996). Theorizing difference from multiracial feminism. *Feminist Studies, 22*, 321–331.

Zupan, M. L. (1976). The conceptual development of quantification in experimental psychology. *Journal of the History of the Behavioral Sciences, 12*, 145–158.

GLOSSARY

action research A research approach developed by Kurt Lewin whereby studies are designed both to generate data and to use that data to create social change.

action whole The belief of Kurt Lewin and his students that in any experiment the experimenter and participant share a life space that affects the participant's performance. Lewin chose to interact with participants at varying degrees to create optimal conditions for performance.

air crib A specialized enclosed baby crib invented by Burrhus Frederic Skinner that provides a temperature- and humidity-controlled environment. Constructed with a Plexiglas front, the infant can move freely without blankets or clothing, which reduces laundry and cuts down on the infant's exposure to germs.

androgyny An equal measure of both masculine and feminine traits. The term is usually associated with Sandra Bem's Sex Role Inventory, which measures androgyny.

anecdotal method A method used in early comparative psychology. It refers to collecting descriptions or vignettes of animal behavior from many sources and then sorting them to come up with reliable inferences about the functioning of the animal mind.

anterograde amnesia The inability to form new memories of events, experiences, or knowledge following brain injury or trauma.

argument from design The view that all species were designed by a Divine Creator for their specific place in nature. This view was undermined by the argument that species were mutable and evolved.

associationism The concept that elements derived from sense experience (ideas) combine to form the basis of knowledge, e.g., simple ideas combine to form complex ideas. This philosophy of knowledge posited that the complex contents of consciousness were built from elementary sensations through several laws of association (e.g., contiguity, contrast, and cause and effect).

atomism An approach in science that involved breaking down subject matter to its smallest elements for study.

behaviorism An approach to psychology proposed by John B. Watson that focused on observable behavior and was, thus, at least in Watson's view, more scientific than introspection. Its goal was the prediction and control of behavior. Behaviorism and its descendants dominated American psychology for several decades.

behavior modification The process of deliberately modifying human or animal behavior through the use of behavioral techniques such as positive and negative reinforcement to establish more desirable patterns of behavior.

"big P" Psychology The formal, institutionalized, discipline of Psychology that includes academic departments, journals, organizations, and other trappings of professionalization.

Brown v. Board of Education of Topeka, Kansas A U.S. Supreme Court legal case in 1954 that ruled that racially segregated schools were unconstitutional, leading to the desegregation of public schools in the United States.

cell assembly Donald Hebb's term for a particular group of cells that become connected after being repeatedly activated simultaneously. These cell groupings result in the gradual development of behavioral patterns.

commercial society A new understanding of society, which emerged in the 16th and 17th centuries, principally in England, that people and their relationships were defined by what they bought, sold, or produced, including their labor, capital (financial resources), and land, or even by what they owned or rented.

commoditization of mental health The transformation of mental health services and practices into an everyday commodity for Americans. The process was fueled by changes to American culture's understanding of psychology and the popularity of therapy modalities such as psychoanalysis.

community mental health center A facility created to provide mental health services to communities across the socioeconomic spectrum.

community psychology An area of psychology created to address problems of a social and structural nature, such as poverty, racism, and classism. Psychologists involved in this movement sought to affect individuals by intervening at the level of the community.

complementarity hypothesis The belief, common in late 19th-century Europe and North America, that men and women differed in the very nature of their mental traits, displaying complementary, but not directly comparable, psychological and intellectual strengths. This conviction was generally used to enforce what were then considered appropriate social roles for men and women, with women believed to excel in the realm of the emotional, domestic, and private and men believed to excel in the realm of the rational, professional, and public.

computational functionalism The position, developed in the 1960s, that physical similarity between machine and mind was not necessary for a useful theory of artificial intelligence, as demonstrated by Allen Newell and Herbert Simon's General Problem Solver program.

conditions of worth The implicit and explicit messages that convey to people that they will only be accepted if they are a particular and desirable way. The idea was developed by Carl Rogers as a component of client-centered therapy.

conduct book A popular devotional aid for Christians in the 16th and 17th centuries. Materials in such books were intended to encourage spiritual reflection; self-control (of thoughts, sinful impulses, etc.) was the intended outcome.

conscientization Brazilian educator and psychologist Paolo Freire's approach to *psicología social de la liberación* (liberation social psychology), whereby engaging and educating poor citizens and providing them with reading skills helps them recognize themselves as fully human, thereby creating the possibility that political, social, and economic oppression can be broken.

contact hypothesis The idea, proposed by Gordon Allport, that intergroup contact (when two or more groups differ on some characteristic such as ethnicity or class) can reduce prejudice and foster more positive attitudes toward the other group or groups under certain conditions.

critical history An approach to history that presents psychology as a communal, socially constructed endeavor heavily influenced by time, place, and culture, involving a diversity of constituents, and appreciating the different values and states of knowledge dominant at different times.

cybernetics The interdisciplinary study of self-regulating physical and social systems that draws on developments in linguistics, mathematics, philosophy, physiology, and engineering.

declarative memory Memory for information such as knowledge or facts of which we have a conscious awareness. The term was coined by Brenda Milner through her work with neuropsychological patient H. M.

deism The belief that although God designed the universe and set the clockwork of life in motion, He had no direct influence, and did not intervene, in the day-to-day affairs of humans.

differential psychology The approach of German psychologist William Stern, which stressed the understanding of the total personality in its individuality, what he later termed "personalistic psychology."

division of labor The mechanization of the workplace that created new specific roles where tasks were well defined and performance was closely measured. Adam Smith made much of the division of labor as the necessary arrangement to maximize human productivity and so increase wealth. It was also hierarchically arranged so that different status levels had attendant differences in pay levels. A person could work upward in such a system to become a supervisor or manager of others and thus increase status and pay. This made the workplace a site for competition among workers.

doctrine of specific nerve energies The theory, proposed by German physiologist Johannes Müller, that each sensory modality is specialized to respond in ways that are unique to it. So, visual nerves when stimulated give visual sensations, e.g., pressing on the eye gives a visual sensation, just as looking at an object does.

empiricism The philosophy that all knowledge is gained through experience (i.e., through the senses).

epigenesis A process introduced by Jean Piaget whereby changes and growth in a child's development reflect not only a biologically evolved pattern, or inner determinism, but also the child's practical experiences in the world.

equipotentiality A concept suggested by Karl Lashley that parts of the brain have the ability to take over the function of other parts should those parts be destroyed.

experimental introspection A method of study developed by Wilhelm Wundt and distinguished from existing forms of philosophical introspection by the introduction of laboratory apparatus that would standardize and mechanize presentations of stimuli upon which subjects would report.

feedback A central concept to cybernetics whereby information about a system's actions is fed back into that system so as to regulate future actions.

feminist empiricism The use of empirical, positivist methods to dismantle commonly held unscientific and biased beliefs about women and support fairer treatment of both women and men.

feminist standpoint theory Feminist philosopher Sandra Harding's theory in which the socially oppressed can access knowledge unavailable to the socially privileged. This knowledge is superior, it is argued, because it is not based on dominant assumptions and allows the socially-contingent nature of such knowledge claims to be revealed.

feminist therapy An independent model of therapy created by feminist psychologists in the 1970s that was developed from the maxim "the personal is political." Theoretical background and therapeutic practices were drawn from consciousness-raising movements. Emphasis was placed on a commitment to social justice, greater power sharing and a collaborative relationship during therapy, and structural instead of intrapsychic explanations for women's problems.

field theory A concept developed by Kurt Lewin, which asserts that the effects of specific stimuli are meaningless without reference to the context, or "field," in which those stimuli occurred.

functionalism A proposal by William James that the point of a scientific psychology was to uncover the functions of the mind, not its contents or its structure. It was the position that understanding should be based on an analysis of function rather than structure and that to know what something does is to understand what it is.

gender A socially constructed set of traits and characteristics that are considered appropriate for and are generally ascribed to males and females.

general intelligence (g) Charles Spearman's term for a unitary trait of intelligence presumed to have a hereditary basis, through which more specific intelligences (s) worked to produce abilities on specific tasks. This was part of his two-factor theory of intelligence.

genetic epistemology A synthesized science of evolutionary and developmental psychology that Jean Piaget believed would be important to a complete theory of knowledge.

Gestalt psychology An approach to psychology founded by Max Wertheimer as an alternative to the Wundtian tradition and founded on the Gestalt laws of perception. It is a branch of psychological theory that became influential in the renewal of German life through its emphasis on holism and methods of understanding in context. Gestalt psychologists are interested in studying the relationship between the part and the whole in terms of perception and cognition.

good life A common belief in postwar America that the purchase of an individual house in a suburban neighborhood and the acquisition of modern technology, often in the form of household goods and appliances, were indicative of status and happiness.

group fallacy Floyd Allport's name for the belief that social behavior is not reducible to the sum of its individual parts. He opposed this belief.

Hawthorne effect The term used to describe an increase in worker morale and productivity through increased attention paid to workers. The term was based on a body of research conducted at a plant in Hawthorne, Illinois.

incident control project A project developed by the Commission on Community Interrelations that was designed to teach people "how to stop the bigot" by intervening in a public display of racism.

indigenization The process through which a local culture develops its own form of psychology from within that culture or imports aspects of psychologies developed elsewhere and combines them with local concepts.

indigenization from within A phrase introduced by Indian psychologist Durganand Sinha to refer to the process whereby a culture's own ideas, concepts, and experiences are used to develop psychological theory and practice.

indigenization from without A phrase introduced by Indian psychologist Durganand Sinha to refer to the process whereby principles and methods learned outside of a culture are reevaluated and adjusted to fit the local context.

individual psychology A research program developed by Alfred Binet and Victor Henri in which they sought to develop a set of tests of psychological processes that could provide a complete picture of a person's abilities.

inheritance of acquired characteristics A doctrine, proposed by French theorist and biologist Jean-Baptiste Lamarck, that suggested that changes in the adult organism often created by the use or disuse of body parts or organs, could be passed directly to the offspring. The well-worn example is the neck of a giraffe. According to the doctrine, giraffes stretching their necks to reach higher leaves resulted in an increasingly elongated neck over many generations.

intellectual geography of center and periphery The concept that locations exist whose intellectual, institutional, and economic resources provide a distinct character that becomes influential in shaping the intellectual content and practice in outlying regions.

intersectionality The interdependent relations among categories such as gender, race, and class.

invisible hand A phrase used by Adam Smith to indicate the mutuality of self and other interests, i.e., when every person seeks personal interests, the net result is that the interests of all are served.

just-noticeable difference The threshold of perception, discovered by Ernst Weber and refined by Gustav Fechner. It refers to the smallest increase in physical intensity of a stimulus that can be reliably discriminated as a sensory experience.

keyword Raymond Williams's term for a word or phrase in any discipline that has become normative and is no longer subject to critical examination.

Kultur An aspirational term used to describe German social, political, and intellectual life, thus what it meant to be civilized.

law of conservation of energy In any closed physical system (e.g., frog or human), the law that the sum total of all energies involved remains constant. Hermann von Helmholtz showed how this law applied to all living things, including humans, as well as to the nonhuman physical universe.

law of *Prägnanz* The most general principle of the Gestalt laws of perceptual organization, which states that human perception has a tendency toward the organization of any whole into as good or simple a structure as conditions permit. Specific examples of the law of Prägnanz include the laws of proximity, similarity, and continuation.

Lehrfreiheit The freedom to teach. This principle, developed in the emerging German universities in the 18th century, meant that German professors were free to lecture on any topics they chose, to present them in any way they chose, and to express any views about them, without any interference or direction from university officials or others.

Lernfreiheit The freedom to learn. This principle, developed in the emerging German universities in the 18th century, allowed students to choose their course of study, including what they learned, how often they attended classes, and with whom they studied. Freedom of learning, combined with the prizing of the pure scholar, encouraged most students to study a range of subjects and to sample freely across disciplines.

liberal feminism A branch of feminism that has been prominent in American feminist psychology. Liberal feminists seek to ensure equality between men and women under the law.

liberation psychology A social movement in South and Central America that arose from protests against increasing poverty and marginalization of the poor. It involved liberation theology in the Roman Catholic Church, as well as a move toward the use of social science for social action; humans were seen as active instead of passive agents.

life space A term used by Kurt Lewin to indicate that personality is a totality that includes the organism and its psychological environment at any given moment.

"little p" psychology Psychological subject matter, including both the everyday psychology that has always existed as people make sense of their lives, and the subject matter of disciplinary Psychology.

localization of function The theory that specific mental functions are located in specific places in the brain, e.g., language is primarily a function of Broca's area.

logical positivism The philosophy, based on the work of Ernest Mach and other members of the Vienna Circle, that all scientific constructs must be linked to observable events.

means–end analysis A mathematical analysis whereby the current state of a problem is regularly compared to the end goal. This analysis allows for the option with the greatest reduction in distance between the current state and the end goal to be chosen. This is done during every step of any given problem until the distance between the current state and the end goal is zero.

mechanism A position proposed by Herman von Helmholtz and others that all natural phenomena can be explained in terms of the causal interactions among material particles, without any reference to an external, supernatural force or agency.

mental philosophy In 19th-century American higher education, the system of instruction that dealt with the elements and processes of the mind and how they influenced action.

mesmerism A therapeutic intervention initially developed by Viennese physician Franz Anton Mesmer in the late 18th century, in which a practitioner could induce a trance state.

mind–body dualism The concept, attributed primarily to Descartes, that mind and body are separate entities, each with its own properties.

modernity The epistemological and ontological values commonly associated with Western living including objectivity, universality, and the possibility of an absolute truth. In a modernist view, science is value-neutral and a means to discovering this truth.

modernization theory A body of work that emerged in the 1950s. "Modernization" was a term used to describe models of development on a historical arc, with traditional societies and modern societies at opposite ends of the arc. Modernization theory asserts that traditional societies can become modern societies through the influence and resources of more modern ones and that the end point for all societies is modernity.

moral philosophy In 19th-century American higher education, the system of instruction in the branch of philosophy that dealt with ethics and conduct.

moral sentiment The principle, used by philosopher Adam Smith in the 18th century, that humans need functioning relationships with other people and that this need makes us mindful of the regard and interests of our community and guides us as we act for our own interests.

moral treatment The name given to an early 19th-century treatment approach, initiated by Philippe Pinel in France and William Tuke in England, in which patients with psychological and emotional disturbances would be treated as inherently reasonable to restore them to reason. Patients were provided with more humane and normalized living conditions and were expected to act rationally and contribute their labor by completing institutional tasks.

multicultural feminism A branch of feminism created by women of color in response to liberal feminism's tendency to overlook differences among women in terms of race, class, and religion. Multicultural feminists seek to place greater emphasis on such differences and the oppression that exists among women, not only between women and men.

negative eugenics A method of social and population control that involves restricting the ability of "unfit" individuals to procreate, often through sex segregation or enforced sterilization.

neobehaviorism A theoretical approach to psychology based on behaviorism with the added influence of operationism and logical positivism. It is used to examine observable behavior through the stimulus–response relationship with attention paid to the context in which learning occurs.

New Thought A body of mental science developed in the late 19th century that emphasized the power of the mind to regulate health and well-being. It drew upon diverse systems such as mesmerism and spiritualism.

nondirective (client-centered) therapy An influential therapy modality developed by Carl Rogers whereby therapists provide clients with empathy, congruence, genuineness, and unconditional positive regard to help clients create positive change in their lives and rediscover their innate capacity for growth.

noumenal world One of Immanuel Kant's proposed domains of reality: the external world. It consists of objects in a pure state that exist independent of human experience. This domain of reality can never be known directly because our experience of it is always and inescapably mediated through the activity of our mind and of our senses.

operant conditioning A term used by Burrhus Frederic Skinner as part of his radical behaviorist view that learning occurs when organisms "operate" on their environment to produce consequences.

operational definition A statement of the set of methods or techniques used to measure a construct. In a classic example, hunger would be defined as the number of hours of food deprivation.

operationism The position that scientific constructs should be defined in terms of how each one is measured.

organology Franz Joseph Gall's original term for the method of discerning mental abilities by reading bumps on the head. The term was later changed to phrenology by his followers.

origin myth The retrospective selection of great thinkers and classic experiments that buttresses the legitimacy of present views and imparts a sense of continuity and tradition about the development of psychology.

perception A psychological process that depends on the brain, prior learning, and our experiences.

phase sequence Donald Hebb's term for the connection of cell assemblies into a set.

phenomenal world One of Immanuel Kant's proposed domains of reality: our internal experience of the noumenal world, filtered through our mental and sensory apparatus. Humans never directly experience the pure reality of things in themselves but, rather, experience a series of appearances (phenomena) that are created by an actively perceiving mind as it encounters the noumenal world.

phi phenomenon A visual illusion described by Max Wertheimer, who asserted that the perceived motion of two dots of light flashed in different locations on a screen but seen as a single moving dot was a Gestalt and therefore not reducible to individual elements.

phrenology Franz Joseph Gall's system that related the bumps and protrusions of the skull to underlying mental abilities. Organology was Gall's original term, later changed to phrenology by his followers.

physiognomy An ancient system of understanding human character that was revived and popularized in the late 18th century by Johann Caspar Lavater. Briefly, this system of knowledge about human nature claimed a direct link between the physical, outward appearance of a person and one's inward nature or character.

pillarization A term used to describe the structure of Dutch society in which the educational system and almost all other aspects of social, cultural, political, and economic life are divided into autonomous and separate religious spheres, specifically, Protestant, Catholic, and neutral.

polycentric history The idea that psychology's history cannot be fully understood through a single lens but that many histories of psychology need to be examined to create a complete understanding of psychology's development.

positive eugenics A program developed by Francis Galton. It encourages the interbreeding of eminent individuals to improve the quality of the genetic stock.

positivism Ernst Mach and Richard Avenarius's concept that experience is the basis of all knowledge and that the experience of the observable world is foundational to science.

postmodern feminism A branch of feminism that asserts that all knowledge is constructed rather than discovered, and that the purpose of science is not to discover truths but to critically examine why certain questions have been investigated while others have been excluded. It examines what effects certain forms of knowledge have had on women as a class, and proposes transformative alternatives.

postmodernism A reaction to modernism. It is the philosophy that absolute truths do not exist and knowledge is constructed rather than discovered.

pragmatism The position that scientific ideas and knowledge can never be certain and therefore should be judged according to the work they do in the world, or according to their degree of practical effectiveness.

procedural memory Memory for skills and procedures that is generally implicit or unconscious. This form of memory was described by Brenda Milner through her work with patient H. M.

Project Camelot An American Department of Defense–sponsored initiative created to gain the upper hand in the Cold War through the use of behavioral experts' abilities and techniques, which could be useful in the manipulation of individuals and cultures to gain intelligence information.

projective test A type of psychological test developed to elicit unconscious material from a respondent through responses to ambiguous stimuli, such as inkblots or pictures (e.g., the Rorschach Inkblot Test and the Thematic Apperception Test).

Protestant Reformation A movement led by Martin Luther, Ulrich Zwingli, and John Calvin within the Christian faith that asserted that salvation came by faith alone and that each believer had a direct relationship with God, not dependent on the church. This direct relationship required Christians to pay careful attention to their inner life and devote themselves to spiritual practices.

psychological practice The use of psychological knowledge to make sense of oneself and the world, as well as the practical strategy of self- and social management that arises out of this knowledge.

psychophysics A branch of study involving the physical measurement and quantification of psychological phenomena.

Psychotechnik **(psychotechnics)** A term coined by William Stern in Germany to refer to the practice of studying individual differences for "human management" purposes and applying psychology to work, law, and education. Psychotechnics is sometimes regarded as an extension or variant of Frederick Winslow Taylor's scientific management system.

radical feminism A branch of feminism that views the oppression of women by men as the root of all forms of oppression.

reflex arc A concept used by physiologists and psychologists to explain the transmission of neural signals to produce an immediate motor reaction. Karl Lashley critiqued the concept of the reflex arc, providing evidence through his research with rats that had had sections of their brains destroyed yet were still able to relearn maze running.

reflexivity The fundamental conflation of the agent and the object of study in psychology so that (1) the knowledge produced by agents and the characteristics of these agents themselves influence how objects respond in the very course of their being studied and (2) the knowledge produced by psychology applies as much to the agents of production as to the objects they are attempting to explain.

relational–cultural theory Jean Baker Miller's theory that the ability to sustain relationships is central to human growth and psychological development and that the absence of this ability results in a disconnect that is detrimental to psychological well-being. Disconnectedness often develops from power imbalances (between gender, race, class, sexual orientation, etc.) whereby one member in a relationship hides or distorts authentic feelings for fear of being ridiculed or invalidated.

scientist–practitioner model of clinical psychology A model of training for clinical practitioners that

developed out of a conference held in Boulder, Colorado, in 1949. This model relied on an earlier template created by David Shakow and emphasized that psychologists needed to be scientists trained in research first and practitioners second.

sensation The raw data that comes through our senses.

shell shock A term, coined by psychologist Charles S. Myers, to describe a set of symptoms first observed in combat soldiers in World War I. The symptoms resembled the symptoms of hysteria—paralysis, disorientation, uncontrollable shaking, inability to speak, and many others—all without demonstrable neurological damage.

shout tradition In Methodist revivalism of the 19th century, the openness to deep and profound religious experiences sometimes manifested in marked physical demonstrations, such as shouting, falling down, visions, and trance-like behaviors.

sikolohiyang Pilipino An indigenous psychology created by Virgilio Enriquez and Alfredo Lagmay that became a movement away from the epistemology and methods of American psychology and was more suited to the diverse cultures of the Philippines. Filipino psychology became a major force and an innovative conceptualization of the power of an indigenous approach to psychology.

social constructionism The perspective that a host of extradisciplinary and extrascientific factors indelibly shape how Psychology is defined and practiced, the form and content of the knowledge it creates, and how this knowledge is received.

social Darwinism A commonly held position in the latter half of the 19th century that used the evolutionary theories of Charles Darwin and Herbert Spencer to suggest that differences between humans were grounded in the laws of nature. It was used as an explanation for the differences among races, suggesting that these differences were grounded in one racial group's natural superiority, and for social class differences, which it was believed could be ascribed to a natural process of evolutionary sorting.

socialist feminism A branch of feminism that asserts that the oppression and struggle faced by women can be inextricably tied to the class oppression inherent to capitalism; the struggles of class and women are interconnected.

spiritualism An ancient and diverse system of thought and practices that received renewed interest in mid- to late 19th-century America. It involved communication with the spirit realm and many other psychic phenomena, including telepathy. For many spiritualists, theirs was an experiential religion, based on a belief in the immortality of souls and an afterlife.

therapeutic nihilism The absence of belief in the possibility of developing effective treatment for insanity that characterized psychiatric thinking in the latter half of the 19th century.

third force The emergence of humanistic psychology in the 1960s as the third wave of psychological theory and practice; provided an alternative to psychoanalysis and behaviorism.

uniformitarian hypothesis The theory proposed by geologist Charles Lyell that the physical geology of the earth was formed as a result of long, gradual processes. It contrasted with the notion that geological forms were the result of sudden, catastrophic changes, usually the result of divine intervention or handiwork—as in the biblical flood.

variability hypothesis A commonly held belief in the late 19th century that men displayed greater variability in psychological and physical traits; therefore, they were responsible for evolutionary progress and exclusively capable of eminence. Women, who it was believed did not display the same variability, were thus relegated to mediocrity, or the middle of the distribution of any trait.

Wissenschaft A German concept of science in which science was not determined by its subject matter; it was a way of looking at things. Thus, any topic could be treated scientifically or approached in a scientific manner.

Zeigarnik effect A social phenomenon defined by Bluma Zeigarnik whereby participants have better recall for incomplete tasks than for completed tasks. She believed that tension was created when a task was incomplete and this tension facilitated memory until the task was complete.

INDEX